THE

ZURICH LETTERS.

(SECOND SERIES.)

A. D. 1558 — 1602.

The Parker Society.

Instituted A.D. M.DCCC.XL.

MVNDVS TRANSIT

E R

For the Publication of the Works of the Fathers and Early Writers of the Reformed English Church.

THE

ZURICH LETTERS,

(SECOND SERIES)

COMPRISING THE CORRESPONDENCE OF SEVERAL ENGLISH
BISHOPS AND OTHERS

WITH SOME OF

THE HELVETIAN REFORMERS,

DURING THE REIGN OF QUEEN ELIZABETH.

TRANSLATED FROM AUTHENTICATED COPIES OF THE AUTOGRAPHS,

AND EDITED FOR

The Parker Society,

BY THE

REV. HASTINGS ROBINSON, D.D. F.A.S.

RECTOR OF GREAT WARLEY, ESSEX;
AND FORMERLY FELLOW OF ST JOHN'S COLLEGE, CAMBRIDGE.

CAMBRIDGE:

PRINTED AT

THE UNIVERSITY PRESS.

M.DCCC.XLV.

INTRODUCTION.

SHORTLY after the publication of the volume entitled "Zurich Letters," the attention of the Council of the Parker Society was directed by the late Rev. John Hunter, by whom the copies of those letters were procured and presented to the Society in 1841, to the expediency of instituting a more extended examination into the library and archives at Zurich; as he found reason for believing, upon a subsequent journey thither in 1842, that the contents of those depositories had not been fully explored by him on his former visit. And as several communications had been received, indicating that there were other depositories in Switzerland which would repay examination, it was resolved that a complete investigation should be made, in the hope of procuring some additional documents connected with the history of the English Reformation. For accomplishing this object, the Council availed themselves of the assistance of the Rev. Steuart A. Pears, Fellow of Corpus Christi College, Oxford, who proceeded to Zurich in the summer of 1843, where he was occupied for a considerable time in a full investigation of the contents of the public library and archives in that city: he also made similar researches at Geneva, Strasburg, Basle, Zofingen, Berne, Schaffhausen, and St Gall; necessarily confining his attention to such of the contents of those libraries as referred to the immediate object of his mission. The account of Mr Pears's proceedings cannot be better given than in the substance of his own report to the Council of the Parker Society.

The first object of attention in the town library of Zurich is the Simler collection of the correspondence of the Swiss Reformers. This was made by the late John Jacob Simler, (a descendant of the Josiah Simler so frequently mentioned in the Zurich Letters,) superintendent of schools in the Canton of Zurich, who died August the 5th, 1788. He appears to have examined with great accuracy all the collections of letters, manuscript and printed, public and private, within his reach. He copied fully 18,000 letters with his own hand, arranged them all chronologically, and at the head of each noted the collection, volume, and page in which the original is to be found. The whole work extends to nearly 200 folio volumes, of which 140 are occupied by the period A. D. 1530—1600. This collection, therefore, formed a most accurate guide to the collections of originals in the archives and library at Zurich, Strasburg, and Berne; the libraries at Basle, Zofingen, Geneva, St Gall, and Schaffhausen, besides several private and printed collections of the correspondence of the Reformers.

Mr Pears proceeded to look through these collections of original documents, and to collate the transcripts as they were supplied by the copyists, in the course of which investigation he examined the following repositories.

1. The archives at Zurich, from which the principal part of the letters already printed by the Parker Society had been supplied to the Rev. John Hunter, by M. Meyer von Knonau, the state archiviste.

2. The library at Zurich, in which the collection of original letters is almost as large as that in the archives, though the number of those that refer to England is not so considerable, since nearly all Bullinger's correspondence is preserved in the archives.

3. The library at Strasburgh, in which are four volumes of miscellaneous correspondence, and one volume relating entirely to Fagius and his family.

4. The archives de St Thomas at Strasburgh, to which access was obtained by the assistance of professor Baum. They contain an interesting collection of letters, well arranged.

5. The library at Basle. The collection is very large, but it contains scarcely any thing that bears on the English Reformation.

6. The library at Zofingen. In this is a small collection, with little that is interesting to the Parker Society; but the librarian sent the Council a list of the letters having any relation to the period of the Reformation.

7. The library and archives of Berne. In the latter is contained a large collection of the letters of Calvin and his correspondents.

8. The library of Geneva. Mr Pears found there nearly thirty letters relating to the affairs of the English Church, of which the greater portion refer to a period antecedent to that comprehended in the present volume.

9. Schaffhausen. The ecclesiastical archives in this place chiefly relate to the history of the church in that canton.

10. St Gall. In the city library is a good collection of letters, very few of which, however, have any reference to England.

The members of the Parker Society are indebted for the contents of the present volume to these valuable researches of the Rev. S. A. Pears, kindly assisted as they have been by the local authorities[1] in Switzerland. Many of the letters

[1] Among these may be mentioned the following gentlemen, all of whom manifested a very friendly readiness to assist the operations of the Parker Society; and from many of whom Mr Pears received great personal kindness and attention. At Zurich, M. Meyer von Knonau, the archiviste; and M. Horner, the librarian. At Strasburg, M. Baum, principal of the Protestant seminary; M. Yung, the librarian; M. Roehrich, pastor of St Guillaume. At Basle, M. Gerlach, the librarian; and M. Burckhardt, antistes of the church. At Berne, M. Trechsel, the librarian; and M. Hundeshagen, professor of theology. At Geneva, M. Diodati, the librarian; M. Sordet, state archiviste; and the Rev. W. Hare, the English chaplain. At St Gall, M. Bernet, the librarian. At Schaffhausen, M. Maitsker, the librarian. At Heidelberg, M. Charles Baehr, the librarian.

will be found explanatory of the series already published;
and will supply many chasms in the chronological arrangement of the correspondence, which could not be filled up
till the present investigation had been made.

For the purpose of assisting the reader in the consecutive
perusal of the entire series, a general table of contents has
been compiled for both volumes, in which each letter is
placed in its proper order, and a reference is given in the
margin to the depository in which the original is to be found.

In addition to the letters now published, and which com-
prise the correspondence of the English Reformers during
the reign of Elizabeth, preserved in the collections above
mentioned, there have been obtained upwards of three
hundred others, written during the reigns of Henry VIII.,
Edward VI., and queen Mary, which will form another
volume of the publications of the Parker Society, not less
interesting than the preceding volumes, and from the same
sources.

Nearly the whole of these letters, it will be observed,
have been derived from the original documents at Zurich:
a small portion is from the originals preserved in the other
libraries to which reference has already been made. A very
few letters have been taken from the copies in the Simler
collection, in cases where access to the originals was found
to be unattainable; while the light thrown by some of the
letters of Zanchy and Peter Martyr upon the correspondence
in the present volume, made it desirable that they should be
transcribed, in the absence of the original documents, from
the printed copies of their works.

Many of these letters, it will be seen, refer to the
unhappy disputes respecting the vestments, by which the
church of England was agitated during the earlier portion of
the Elizabethan period. It would be improper to enter into
the question here, and it is also unnecessary; as the reader
who wishes to make himself further acquainted with that

controversy will find in Strype, Collier, Soames, and other writers, such information as he may require upon the subject. It may be well, however, to observe, that the original words rendered by the term *surplice* appear sometimes to have been used by the writers, where, according to the Injunctions, the cope, and perhaps some other habits, may have been included or intended; and indeed considerable uncertainty seems to have prevailed as to the occasions on which these vestments were respectively used, as well as to the precise meaning of some of the terms by which they were designated in the original letters. The various injunctions, with other papers illustrative of the subject, will be found in Cardwell's Documentary Annals, and in other collections of a similar character.

The editor refrains from any remarks upon the various topics treated in these letters; it being his desire, and the object of the Parker Society, that the respective writers should speak for themselves. The notes therefore are only added for the purpose of throwing additional light upon the facts and circumstances mentioned in the correspondence. He avails himself of this opportunity to express his acknowledgments to those friends and correspondents who have directed his attention to some of the annotations of the former volume; and he has noticed at the end of this preface such points as seemed to require correction. The fidelity of the translation may be tested, as in the preceding volume, by reference to the originals, also printed, while the index, it is hoped, will prove a sufficient guide to the persons and circumstances noticed in the body of the work.

H. R.

WARLEY, *June* 28, 1845.

CORRIGENDA ET NOTANDA.

Page 31, note 2, *dele* " Namely at Coventry."

    33, line 22, *for* " the surplice," *read* " those white vestments."

    51,   2, *for* " Oct. 13," *read* " Oct. 5."

    112, note 1, l. 1. *dele* " sir."

    115, line 8, *for* " were," *read* " was."

    146, Date of Letter LVIII. *for* " Aug." *read* " Feb."

    324, note. It will be observed that the date given by Wood, and those of letters CXXXVII. and CXXXVIII. appear to involve the difference of a year.

Page 3, line 34, *for* " contra," *read* " præter."

    The following variations in letter XV. are from a second copy:

    20,   34, *for* " præstandum," *read* " testandum."

    ...   37 *for* " homines desertione afflictos," *read* " [pœnas] hominis desertioni inflictas."

    21,   13, *for* " vulgaris," *read* " vulgari."

    ...   14, *for* " secus," *read* " serum."

    ...   18, *after* " aliter," *insert* " quam dixi."

    ...   35, *for* " amantissime," *read* " ornatissime."

    91, line 5, *for* " certi," *read* " certe."

    207, '   4, *for* " collegisticis," *read* " collegis tuis."

The following emendations are to be made in the First Series.

Page ix. last line, *for* " Norfolk," *read* " Suffolk."

    37, Letter XV*. should be corrected by the copy now supplied on the opposite page.

    63, line 5, *for* " There is, &c." *read* " One other, a native of Wales, is also, &c."

    ...   17, *for* " the word," *read* " Christ ; " and so, page 64, line 14.

Page 63, instead of note 1, insert—[¹ The consecration of these prelates took place in Dec. 1559; that of archbishop Parker on the 17th, and of the others on the 21st. Strype, Ann. I. i. 230—232.]

Instead of note 2, insert—[² Namely, Rowland Merick, consecrated bishop of Bangor, Dec. 21, 1559. Strype, as above.]

Page 164, Art. 2, instead of " In addition to, &c." *read*, " To say nothing of the effeminate and over-refined strains of the music itself, the use of the organ in church is growing more common."

Some variations having been discovered on comparing the transcript of the letter of Foxe, XV*. p. 37 in the First Series, with a facsimile of the original, it is necessary to state that they are not referable either to M. Meyer von Knonau or to the editor.   That letter, the only letter in the volume written originally in English, was not included in the series verified by M. Meyer, but was copied hastily by a transcriber who mistook some few words owing to the peculiarity of the writing; and the variations were not discovered till a facsimile of the original document had been procured by the Rev. John Hunter, on a subsequent visit to Zurich.

JOHN FOXE TO —— FRENSHAM.

Dated at BASLE, *June 27.*

D. Frenshamo et animi et corporis salutem in Christo.

MASTER FRENSHAM. As you in your letters have oft comforted me, so I would I could likewise comfort you: but where my comfort is small, the Lord Jesus, the comforter of all, work in you sure consolation which may comfort both your body and soul! In whom I desire you be strong and valiant, so much as the weakness of your disease can bear. Be nothing discouraged, nor be not out of hope in yourself. I have seen here amongst our countrymen in the like disease greater weakness recover full well.

I desire you, in your contemplation of Christ, let your spirit be so noble and high in him, that ye may tread under your feet all other things, seem they never so strong, mighty, terrible, or great in this world; for he that hath overcome the world, what hath not he overcome in the world? Life or death, sickness or health, things present or to come, height or low, are nothing in Christ. Only, my brother, master Frensham, a hearty faith in Jesus Christ is all together whereby alonely we miserable and corruptible wretches are saved, do stand, do triumph, yea, in death and over death, in sin and over sin, and finally have victory over all evils, sin, death, hell, Satan, and all. For so it hath pleased the Father to save us by this faith only in his Son, to the end that we seeing his justice could not otherwise be satisfied but by his Son, we might the more fear him for his great righteousness, and love him for his great mercy, being saved by this faith in his Son. To this all the scripture beareth witness. The Lord Jesus stir up the quickening and feeling of this faith in our dull senses! To will you this in my prayer as I do not cease, so I do not despair of your recovery altogether: the mighty Lord Jesus, if it be his pleasure, put to his helping hand in restoring your health again! His good will be done. The bottle ye sent is not yet come to me. Basileæ, June 27.

Tuus in Christo,

J. FOXE.

CONTENTS.

APPENDIX.

THE LETTERS

OF THE

ELIZABETHAN PERIOD

ARRANGED IN CHRONOLOGICAL ORDER.

The capitals affixed to the titles in the following list indicate the sources from which the transcripts of the original documents were procured.

A denoting the Archives at Zurich.

L ....the City Library at ditto.

S.C. ....the Simler Collection.

Str. ....the Library at Strasburgh.

Schaff..........the Library at Schaffhausen.

St Gall ......⎫
Berne ......⎬ the respective libraries in those places.
Geneva ...⎪
Zofingen ...⎭

Op. ....the published works of the writers, most of them being also in the Simler Collection.

First Series.	Second Series.			
...	1	Sir A. Cook to Henry Bullinger ....Strasburgh, Dec. 8, 1558.	A
1	...	Thomas Sampson to Peter Martyr ......Strasburgh, Dec. 17, 1558.	L
2	...	Edwin Sandys to H. Bullinger ....Strasburgh, Dec. 20, 1558.	A
...	2	John Haller to H. Bullinger ....Berne, Jan. 11, 1559.	A
...	3	Rodolph Gualter to queen Elizabeth ...Zurich, Jan. 16, 1559.	A
...	4	Rod. Gualter to lord Francis Russel......Zurich, Jan. 16, 1559.	A
...	5	Rod. Gualter to Richard Masters ......Zurich, Jan. 16, 1559.	A
3	...	John Jewel to Peter Martyr ....Strasburgh, Jan. 26, 1559.	L
...	6	Sir A. Cook to Peter Martyr ....London, Feb. 12, 1559.	A
...	7	Richard Hilles to H. Bullinger ....London, Feb. 28, 1559.	A
4	...	John Jewel to Peter Martyr ....London, March 20, 1559.	L
5	...	The same to the same ....London, Apr. 6, 1559	L
6	...	The same to the same ....London, Apr. 14, 1559.	L
7	...	The same to the same ....London, Apr. 28, 1559.	L
8	...	John Foxe to H. Bullinger ....Basle, May 6, 1559.	A
9	...	John Jewel to Peter Martyr...............London, no date.	L
10	...	John Foxe to Henry Bullinger............Basle, May 13, 1559.	A
11	...	Richard Cox to Wolfgang Weidner......London, May 20, 1559.	A
12	...	John Parkhurst to H. Bullinger ....London, May 21, 1559.	A
13	...	John Parkhurst to Conrad Gesner ......London, May 21, 1559.	A
14	...	John Jewel to H. Bullinger ....London, May 22, 1559.	A
...	8	Edmund Grindal to Conrad Hubert ......London, May 23, 1559.	Str.
15	..	John Foxe to Henry Bullinger............Basle, June 17, 1559.	A
15*	...	John Foxe to Henry Frensham ....Basle, June 17, 1559.	A
...	9	Laurence Humphrey to H. Bullinger ...Basle, June 23, 1559.	L
...	10	Edmund Grindal to Conrad Hubert ...London, July 14, 1559.	Str.

b

First Series.	Second Series.		
...	11	Peter Martyr to Thomas Sampson ...Zurich, July 15, 1559.	Op.
16	...	John Jewel to Peter Martyr ....London, Aug. 1, 1559.	L
17	...	John Foxe to H. Bullinger ....Basle, Aug. 2, 1559.	A
...	12	Conrad Hubert to T. Blaurer ....Strasburgh, Aug. 7, 1559.	St Gall
...	13	Thomas Lever to H. Bullinger ....London, Aug. 8, 1559.	L
18	...	John Foxe to H. Bullinger ....Basle, Sept. 26, 1559.	A
19	...	John Jewel to Peter Martyr ....London, Nov. 2, 1559.	L
20	...	John Jewel to Rod. Gualter ....London, Nov. 2, 1559.	L
21	...	John Parkhurst to John Wolfius ......Without date.	L
22	...	John Jewel to Josiah Simler ....London, Nov. 2, 1559.	L
...	14	Peter Martyr to Thomas Sampson......Zurich, Nov. 4, 1559.	Op.
23	...	John Jewel to Peter Martyr ....London, Nov. 5, 1559.	L
24	...	The same to the same....................London, Nov. 16, 1559.	L
25	...	The same to the same....................London, Dec. 1, 1559.	L
26	...	John Parkhurst to Josiah Simler ...Bishop's Cleeve, Dec. 20, 1559.	L
...	15	John Calvin to Sir W. Cecil ....Geneva, after Jan. 29, 1559.	Berne.
27	...	Thomas Sampson to Pet. Martyr.......Jan. 6, 1560.	L
28	...	Bp Cox to Peter Martyr ....London, no date	L
...	16	Earl of Bedford to Rod. Gualter ......London, Jan. 21, 1560.	L
...	17	Peter Martyr to Thomas Sampson......Zurich, Feb. 1, 1560.	Op.
29	...	Bp Jewel to Peter Martyr ....London, Feb. 4, 1560.	L
...	18	Bp Cox to George Cassander ....London, March 4, 1560.	S.C.
30	...	Bp Jewel to Peter Martyr ....London, March 5, 1560.	L
...	19	George Cassander to Bp Cox ....Worms, 1560.	S.C.
...	20	Peter Martyr to Thomas Sampson ...Zurich, March 20, 1560.	A
31	...	Bp Sandys to Peter Martyr ....London, April 1, 1560.	L
32	...	Thomas Sampson to Peter Martyr ...London, May 13, 1560.	L
33	...	Bp Jewel to Peter Martyr....... ....London, May 22, 1560.	L
34	...	The same to the same....................Salisbury, June 1, 1560.	L
...	21	Nicolas Gallasius to John Calvin ......London, June 30, 1560.	Geneva
35	...	Thomas Lever to H. Bullinger ....Coventry, July 10, 1560.	A
36	...	Bp Jewel to Peter Martyr...... ....Salisbury, July 17, 1560.	L
37	...	John Parkhurst to H. Bullinger ......London, Aug. 23, 1560.	A
...	22	Bp Grindal to Conrad Hubert ....London, Oct. 5, 1560.	Str.
38	...	Bp Jewel to Peter Martyr ....Salisbury, Nov. 6, 1560.	L
39	...	Bp Parkhurst to John Wolfius, &c. ...Norwich, March 9, 1561.	L
...	23	Rod. Gualter to the Earl of Bedford ...Zurich, March 16, 1561.	A
40	...	Bp Jewel to Josiah Simler...............London, May 4, 1561.	L
41	...	Bp Parkhurst to H. Bullinger ....Thetford, May 23, 1561.	A
...	24	Earl of Bedford to Rod. Gualter ......London, June 16, 1561.	L
...	25	Richard Masters to Rod. Gualter ......Greenwich, June 16, 1561.	L
...	26	Pet. Martyr to a nobleman in England.Zurich, July 22, 1561.	Op.
...	27	Rod. Gualter to the Earl of Bedford ...Zurich, Aug. 26, 1561.	A
42	...	Bp Parkhurst to H. Bullinger ....Ludham, Sept. 1, 1561.	A
43	...	Bp Jewel to Peter Martyr ....Salisbury, Feb. 7, 1562.	L
44	...	Bp Jewel to H. Bullinger ....Salisbury, Feb. 9, 1562.	A
45	...	Bp Jewel to Josiah Simler ....Salisbury, Feb. 10, 1562.	L
...	28	Richard Masters to Rod. Gualter ......London, Feb. 22, 1562.	L
...	29	Earl of Bedford to H. Bullinger, &c...London, March 16, 1562.	A

First Series.	Second Series.		
...	30	Roger Ascham to John Sturmius ......London, Apr. 11, 1562.	Str.
46	...	Bp Parkhurst to Henry Bullinger......Ludham, April 28, 1562.	L
47	...	Bp Parkhurst to Josiah Simler, &c....Ludham, April 29, 1562.	L
48	...	Bp Parkhurst to Henry Bullinger......Ludham, May 31, 1562.	A
...	31	Bp Grindal to Conrad Hubert.........London, June 6, 1562.	Str.
...	32	Earl of Bedford to Henry Bullinger ...London, June 10, 1562.	A
...	33	Earl of Bedford to Rodolph Gualter ...London, June 10, 1562.	L
...	34	Sir Antony Cook to Henry Bullinger...London, June 14, 1562.	A
...	35	——— to Peter Martyr...................London, June 26, 1562.	L
...	36	Archbp Parker to Matt. Flacius, &c. Croydon, July 18, s. a.	S.C.
...	37	Hierome Zanchius to Bishop Grindal...Strasburgh, no date.	Op.
...	38	Richard Hilles to Henry Bullinger......London, July 31, 1562.	A
49	...	Bp Cox to Peter Martyr.................London, Aug. 5, 1562.	L
...	39	Herman Folkerzheimer to J. Simler ...Salisbury, Aug. 13, 1562.	L
50	...	Bp Jewel to Henry Bullinger............Salisbury, Aug. 14, 1562.	L
51	...	Bp Jewel to Peter Martyr ....Salisbury, Aug. 14, 1562.	L
52	...	Bp Jewel to Josiah Simler ....Salisbury, Aug. 18, 1562.	L
53	...	Bp Parkhurst to Henry Bullinger ......Ludham, Aug. 20, 1562.	A
Ap. i.	...	Peter Martyr to Bishop Jewel ....Zurich, Aug. 24, 1562.	Op.
...	40	Roger Ascham to John Sturmius ......London, Oct. 21, 1562.	Str.
54	...	Bp Jewel to Henry Bullinger............London, March 5, 1563.	L
55	...	Bp Jewel to Josiah Simler ....London, March 7, 1563.	L
...	41	Her. Folkerzheimer to Jos. Simler ......London, March 15, 1563.	L
56	...	Bp Jewel to Josiah Simler ....London, March 23, 1563.	S.C.
57	...	Bp Parkhurst to Henry Bullinger ......Ludham, April 26, 1563.	A
...	42	Bp Grindal to John Calvin...............London, June 19, 1563.	Geneva
58	...	Thomas Sampson to Henry Bullinger Oxford, July 26, 1563.	A
59	...	Bp Parkhurst to Henry Bullinger ......Ludham, Aug. 13, 1563.	A
60	...	Laur. Humphrey to Hen. Bullinger,...Oxford, Aug. 16, 1563.	A
...	43	H. Zanchius to Bishop Grindal, Strasburgh, before Aug. 23, 1563.	Op.
...	44	H. Folkerzheimer to Josiah Simler ...Embden, Aug. 21, 1563.	L
...	45	Bp Grindal to Conrad Hubert ....Fulham, Aug. 33, 1563.	Str.
...	45*	John Abel to Henry Bullinger ....London, Aug. 24, 1563.	A
61	...	Bp Horn to Henry Bullinger............Winchester, Dec. 13, 1563.	A
...	Ap. ii.	Bp Horn's account of the Eng. Liturgy,Without place or date.	A
...	Ap. iii.	H. Bullinger's Remarks on the above, Without place or date.	A
62	...	Bp Parkhurst to Josiah Simler ....Ludham, Feb. 17, 1564.	L
...	46	Hierome Zanchius to Bishop Grindal, near Chiavenna, Aug. 1564.	Op.
...	47	Hierome Zanchius to Henry Knolles, near Chiavenna, Aug. 1564.	Op.
63	...	Bp Jewel to Henry Bullinger............Salisbury, March 1, 1565.	A
...	48	Richard Masters to Rodolph Gualter...London, March 4, 1565.	L
64	...	Bp Horn to Rodolph Gualter......Farnham Castle, July 17, 1565.	A
65	...	Bp Parkhurst to Henry Bullinger ......Ludham, Aug. 18, 1565.	A
...	49	Bp Parkhurst to John Wolfius ....Ludham, Aug. 19, 1565.	L
Ap. ii.	...	Henry Bullinger to Bishop Horn ......Zurich, Nov. 3, 1565.	A
66	...	Bp Sandys to Henry Bullinger ....Worcester, Jan. 3, 1566.	A
67	...	Bp Jewel to Henry Bullinger, &c.......Salisbury, Feb. 8, 1566.	A
68	...	Laurence Humphrey to H. Bullinger, Oxford, Feb. 9, 1566.	A
69	...	Thomas Sampson to Henry Bullinger, London, Feb. 16, 1566.	A

First Series.	Second Series.		
70	...	Bp Jewel to Henry Bullinger............Salisbury, March 10, 1566.	A
Ap. III.	...	H. Bullinger to Laur. Humphrey, &c. Zurich, May 1, 1566.	A
Ap. IV.	...	Henry Bullinger to Bishop Horn, &c. Zurich, May 3, 1566.	S.C.
...	49*	John Abel to Henry Bullinger ....London, June 6, 1566.	A
..	50	Miles Coverdale, &c. to W. Farell, &c., London, July 1566.	S.C.
...	51	William Turner to Henry Bullinger ...July 23, 1566.	L
71	...	L. Humphrey to Henry Bullinger......July, 1566.	A
72	...	Bp Parkhurst to Henry Bullinger ......Ludham, Aug. 21, 1566.	A
...	52	Bp Parkhurst to John Wolfius ....Ludham, Aug. 21, 1566.	L
73	...	Bp Grindal to Henry Bullinger.........London, Aug. 27, 1566.	A
...	53	Theodore Beza to Henry Bullinger......Geneva, Sept. 3, 1566.	A
...	Ap. V.	The church of Scotland to T. Beza ...St Andrew's, Sept. 4, 1566.	A
Ap. V.	...	H. Bullinger, &c. to Bp Grindal, &c., Zurich, Sept. 6, 1566.	A
...	54	Henry Bullinger to Miles Coverdale ...Zurich, Sept. 10, 1566.	A
Ap. VI.	...	H. Bullinger, &c. to L. Humphrey, &c. Zurich, Sept. 10, 1566.	A
...	55	H. Bullinger, &c. to the Earl of Bedford, Zurich, Sept. 11, 1566.	A
...	56	Rodolph Gualter to Bp Parkhurst......Zurich, Sept. 11, 1566.	A
...	57	Rodolph Gualter to Theodore Beza ....Zurich, Sept. 11, 1566.	A
74	...	Richard Hilles to Henry Bullinger......Antwerp, Dec. 20, 1566.	A
...	Ap. IV.	Perceval Wiburn's account of the Church of England. s. a.	A
75	...	Bp Grindal, &c. to H. Bullinger, &c...London, Feb. 6, 1567.	A
...	58	G. Withers, &c. to H. Bullinger, &c. 1567.	A
76	...	Bp Grindal to Henry Bullinger.........London, Feb. 8, 1567.	A
77	...	Bp Jewel to Henry Bullinger............Salisbury, Feb. 24, 1567.	A
78	...	Perceval Wiburn to Henry Bullinger..London, Feb. 25, 1567.	A
...	59	Henry Bullinger to Theodore Beza......Zurich, March 15, 1567.	A
79	...	Bp Grindal to Henry Bullinger.........London, June 21, 1567.	A
...	60	Theodore Beza to Henry Bullinger .....Geneva, July 29, 1567.	A
80	...	Bp Parkhurst to Henry Bullinger......Ludham, July 31, 1567.	A
...	61	H. Bullinger, &c. to Theodore Beza...Zurich, Aug. 3, 1567.	A
...	62	George Withers to the elector Palatine, Without place or date.	A
...	63	Richard Hilles to Henry Bullinger......London, Aug. 23, 1567.	A
...	64	H. Bullinger, &c. to Bp Grindal, &c..Zurich, Aug. 26, 1567.	A
81	...	Bp Grindal to Henry Bullinger.........London, Aug. 29, 1567.	A
...	65	Christopher Mont to Henry Bullinger, Strasburgh, Oct. 2, 1567.	L
...	66	Bp Grindal to Theodore Beza, &c......London, April 17, 1568.	S. C.
82	...	Bp Grindal to Henry Bullinger.........London, June 11, 1568.	A
83	...	Bp Parkhurst to Rod. Gualter, &c .....Ludham, Aug. 4, 1568.	A
84	...	Bp Cox to Henry Bullinger .... 1568.	A
...	67	Christopher Mont to Henry Bullinger, Strasburgh, Dec. 27, 1568.	A
...	68	Queen Elizabeth to John Sturmius ....Westminster, May, 1, 1569.	Str.
85	...	Bp Grindal to Henry Bullinger.........Fulham, Aug. 13, 1569.	A
...	69	John Sturmius to Queen Elizabeth.....Strasburgh, Sept. 6, 1569.	Str.
...	70	John Sturmius to Sir William Cecil...Strasburgh, Sept. 8, 1569.	Str.
86	...	Richard Hilles to Henry Bullinger ....London, Feb. 6, 1570.	A
87	...	Bp Grindal to Henry Bullinger.........London, Feb. 18, 1570.	A
88	...	Bp Cox to Henry Bullinger ....Ely, July 10, 1570.	A
89	...	Bp Pilkington to Henry Bullinger .....July 17, 1570.	A
90	...	Abp Grindal to Henry Bullinger........London, July 31, 1570.	A

First Series.	Second Series.		
91	...	Bp Jewel to H. Bullinger ....Aug. 7, 1570.	A
92	...	James Leith to H. Bullinger............Geneva, Nov. 13, 1570.	A
93	...	Bp Parkhurst to H. Bullinger ....Norwich, Jan. 16, 1571.	A
...	71	Bp Parkhurst to John Wolfius ....Norwich, Jan. 16, 1571.	L
94	...	Bp Cox to Rodolph Gualter ....Ely, Feb. 12, 1571.	A
...	72	H. Bullinger to Abp. Grindal, &c......Zurich, Feb. 1571.	S.C.
95	...	Bp Jewel to H. Bullinger ....Salisbury, March 2, 1571.	A
...	73	R. Hilles to H. Bullinger ....London, March 8, 1571.	A
96	...	The same to the same ....London, July 27, 1571.	A
97	...	Bp Cox to H. Bullinger...................after July 27, 1571.	A
...	74	John Day to H. Bullinger ....London, Aug. 8, 1571.	A
98	...	Bp Horn to H. Bullinger .... London, Aug. 8, 1571.	A
99	...	Bp Parkhurst to H. Bullinger ....Ludham, Aug 10, 1571.	A
...	Ap. i.	Hierome Zanchius to queen Elizabeth, Heidelberg, Sept. 1, 1571.	Op.
...	75	Hierome Zanchius to bishop Jewel ...Heidelberg, Sept. 2, 1571.	Op.
100	...	Abp Grindal to H. Bullinger ....Bishopsthorpe, Jan. 25, 1572.	A
...	76	Rodolph Zuinglius to Bp Sandys ......Cambridge, Jan. 26, 1572.	A
...	77	Henry Butler to Bp Sandys ....Cambridge, Jan. 27, 1572.	A
...	78	Bp Cox to Henry Bullinger ....Ely, Feb. 12, 1572.	L
101	...	Bp Sandys to Henry Bullinger ....London, Feb. 17, 1572.	A
...	79	Richard Hilles to Henry Bullinger...London, Feb. 18, 1572.	A
102	...	Bp Parkhurst to Henry Bullinger......Ludham, March 10, 1572.	A
...	80	Bp Parkhurst to John Wolfius ....Ludham, March 10, 1572.	L
...	81	Malliet to H. Bullinger the younger...Gray's Inn, May 26, 1572.	L
...	82	R. Gualter the younger to R. Gualter, London, June 5, 1572.	A
103	...	Bp Cox to Henry Bullinger...London, Ely House, June 6, 1572.	L
Ap. vii.	...	Rod. Gualter to Bishop Cox ....Zurich, June 9, 1572.	A
...	83	Christopher Mont to Henry Bullinger, Strasburgh, July 8, 1572.	A
104	...	Richard Hilles to Henry Bullinger......London, July 10, 1572.	A
...	84	R. Gualter the younger to Jos. Simler, Cambridge, July 29, 1572.	L
...	85	Lord Burghley to John Sturmius......Woodstock, Sept. 15, 1572.	Str.
105	...	Bp Horn to Henry Bullinger......Farnham Castle, Jan. 10, 1573.	A
106	...	Bp Parkhurst to Henry Bullinger......Ludham, Jan. 20, 1573.	A
107	...	Bp Cox to Rodolph Gualter ....Ely, Feb. 4, 1573.	A
...	86	R. Gualter the younger to Jos. Simler, Cambridge, Feb. 4, 1573.	L
108	...	Bp Cox to Henry Bullinger............Without place or date.	A
109	...	Bp Cox to Rodolph Gualter............Ely, June 12, 1573.	A
...	87	L. Clayson to R. Gualter the younger, Cambridge, June 23, 1573.	L
...	88	Rod. Gualter to the Earl of Bedford...Zurich, July 17, 1573.	A
...	89	Lord Burghley to John Sturmius......London, July 18, 1573.	Str.
110	...	Bp Pilkington to Rodolph Gualter ...July 20, 1573.	L
...	90	Rod. Gualter the younger to Josiah Simler, Oxford, July 20, 1573.	L
...	91	Sir John Wolley to John Sturmius ...Orpington, July 24, 1573.	Str.
...	92	William Cole to Rodolph Gualter......Oxford, July 26, 1573.	L
111	...	Laurence Humphrey to Rod. Gualter, Oxford, July 28, 1573.	L
112	...	Archbp Grindal to Henry Bullinger...York, July 31, 1573.	A
113	...	Archbp Grindal to Rodolph Gualter...York, July 31, 1573.	L
...	93	William Barlow to Josiah Simler......London, Aug. 2, 1573.	L
114	...	Bp Sandys to Henry Bullinger ....London, Aug. 15, 1573.	A

First Series.	Second Series.		
...	94	Rodolph Gualter to Bishop Cox.........Zurich, Aug. 26, 1573.	A
...	95 [1]	Robert Cooch to Rodolph Gualter, Queen's Palace, Aug. 13, 1573.	A
...	96	Rodolph Gualter to Bishop Sandys ...Zurich, Oct. 8, 1573.	A
...	97	John Sturmius to Queen Elizabeth ...Strasburgh, Nov. 16, 1573.	Str.
115	...	Bp Cox to Rodolph Gualter ....Ely, Feb. 3, 1574.	A
116	...	Bp Parkhurst to Henry Bullinger......Ludham, Feb. 6, 1574.	A
117	...	Bp Parkhurst to Josiah Simler ....Ludham, Feb. 7, 1574.	L
...	98	Henry Bullinger to Bishop Sandys ...Zurich, March 10, 1574.	A
...	99	Henry Bullinger to Archbp Grindal...Zurich, March 10, 1574.	A
...	100	Rodolph Gualter to Bishop Cox ......Zurich, March 16, 1574.	A
118	...	Bp Parkhurst to Henry Bullinger......Ludham, June 29, 1574.	A
119	...	Bp Parkhurst to Josiah Simler ....Ludham, June 30, 1574.	L
...	101	Antony Corranus to Henry Bullinger, London, July 7, 1574.	A
120	...	Bp Cox to Rodolph Gualter ....Ely, July 12, 1574.	L
121	...	Bp Cox to Henry Bullinger ....Ely, July 20, 1574.	A
...	102	William Cole to Rodolph Gualter ......Oxford, July 31, 1574.	L
122	...	Laurence Humphrey to Rod. Gualter, Oxford, Aug. 2, 1574.	L
123	...	Bp Sandys to Henry Bullinger ....Fulham, Aug. 9, 1574.	A
124	...	Bp Sandys to Rodolph Gualter ....Fulham, Aug. 9, 1574.	L
...	103	Queen Elizabeth to John Sturmius ...Bath, Aug. 23, 1574.	Zofing.
...	104	Rodolph Gualter to Bishop Cox ......Zurich, Aug. 26, 1574.	A
125	...	Bp Cox to Henry Bullinger ....Ely, Jan. 25, 1575.	A
...	105	William Barlow to Josiah Simler ......Eton, Jan. 25, 1575.	L
126	...	Bp Cox to Rodolph Gualter ....Ely, 1575.	A
127	...	The same to the same.....................Ely, July 31, 1575.	A
...	106	Nicolas Bernius to Bishop Horn ......Guernsey, Dec. 13, 1575.	L
...	107	William Barlow to Josiah Simler ......Eton, March 13, 1576.	L
128	...	Bp Cox to Rodolph Gualter ....Ely, 1576.	L
130 [1]	...	Bp Horn to certain brethren ....Waltham, Jan 15, 1576.	L
...	108	Hierome Zanchius to Archbp Grindal, Heidelberg, July 22, 1576.	L
129	...	Bp Horn to Rodolph Gualter............Waltham, Aug. 10, 1576.	L
...	109	William Barlow to Josiah Simler ......Waltham, Aug. 11, 1576.	L
...	110	Rodolph Gualter to Archbp Grindal...Zurich, Aug. 24, 1576.	A
...	112 [1]	J. Rainolds to R. Gualter the younger, Oxford, Aug. 13, 1576.	L
...	111	Lewin to John Sturmius..................London, Aug. 25, 1576.	Str.
...	113	Lewin to John Sturmius..................London, Sept. 8, 1576.	Str.
...	114	Sir F. Walsingham to J. Sturmius, Hampton Court, Oct. 27, 1576.	Str.
...	115	The same to the same.....................London, April 23, 1577.	Str.
...	116	The same to the same......... ....London, July 22, 1577.	Str.
...	117	Sir Philip Sidney to Hubert Languet, At Court, Oct. 1, 1577.	L
...	118	Rod. Gualter to George Buchanan......Zurich, Dec. 22, 1577.	A
...	119	Sir Philip Sidney to Hubert Languet, At Court, March 1, 1578.	L
...	120	L. Humphrey to Abraham Musculus, Oxford, March 3, 1578.	Zofing.
...	121	Sir Philip Sidney to Hubert Languet, At Court, March 10, 1578.	L
...	122	L. Humphrey to Abraham Musculus, London, June 5, 1578.	Zofing.
131	...	L. Humphrey to Rodolph Gualter......Oxford, Aug. 11, 1578.	L
...	123	George Buchanan to Rodolph Gualter, Without place or date.	Op.
...	124	Sir F. Walsingham to John Sturmius, Antwerp, Sept. 5, 1578.	Str.

[1 These letters are inadvertently misplaced in the printing.]

First Series.	Second Series.		
132	...	L. Humphrey to Rodolph Gualter......Oxford, Dec. 17, 1578.	L
...	125	Richard Hilles to Rodolph Gualter ...London, Jan. 10, 1579.	L
133	...	Bp Cox to Rodolph Gualter ....Feb. 28, 1579.	L
...	126	Earl of Bedford to Rodolph Gualter ...Exeter, Feb. 28, 1579.	L
...	127	William Cole to Rodolph Gualter......Oxford, Feb. 28, 1579.	L
...	128	Hubert Languet to Peter Hubner ......Baden, June 4, 1579.	Zofing.
...	129	George Buchanan to Rodolph Gualter, July 24, 1579.	Op.
134	...	Archbp Sandys to Rodolph Gualter ...London, Dec. 9, 1579.	L
...	130	Rodolph Gualter to George Buchanan, Zurich, March 8, 1580.	A
...	131	Hierome Zanchius to Sir F. Walsingham, Neustadt, Sept. 24, 1581.	Op.
...	132	Queen Elizabeth to the Swiss Cantons, Oatlands, Sept. 1, 1583.	S.C.
...	133	Queen Elizabeth to the four cities, &c. Oatlands, Sept. 1, 1583.	Schaff.
135	...	Queen Elizabeth to the Swiss Cantons, Greenwich, July 18, 1590.	A
...	134	Dutch church in London to the lord Treasurer, Lond., Apr. 16, 1591.	S.C.
...	135	Queen Elizabeth to the king of Poland, Greenwich, April 16, 1591.	S.C.
...	136	Lord Stafford to Wolfgang Meier ......Greenwich, Aug. 6, 1593.	Str.
...	137	State of Zurich to Queen Elizabeth ...Zurich, Aug. 12, 1600.	A
...	138	Caspar Thoman to Caspar Waser......Oxford, Feb. 1601.	S.C.
...	139	John Johnston to Caspar Waser ......St Andrew's, Aug. 1, 1601.	S.C.
...	140	The same to the same.....................St Andrew's, Feb. 8, 1602.	S.C.
...	141	Thomas Savile, &c. to Henry Wolfius, Without place or date.	L

LETTER I.

SIR ANTONY COOK TO[1] [HENRY BULLINGER].

Dated at STRASBURGH, *December* 8, 1558.

MOST excellent and justly honoured prelate, my friend and beloved brother in Christ, Dr Sandys, has brought me your very gratifying letter, in which you not only congratulate us Englishmen, and rejoice on our behalf, that the most merciful God has visited our affliction, and wrought out the redemption of his people, (which feeling of yours is truly most worthy of a good and pious minister;) but also, like a nurse who cherishes her children, you are anxious that no evil beast should hurt us, nor any misfortune interrupt this happiness that is now begun. Your advice indeed is most prudent and affectionate, and you point out to us those very things from which we have most to fear. I wish that those who will now be of the queen's councils may anticipate these evils, and diligently guard against them. There is however great hope, especially if the reports from Antwerp are to be depended upon, that the spirits of the papists are entirely cast down, and that they will not offer to attack us, unless our own discord should afford them an opportunity. The thing now to be deprecated is, lest any dispute and party-feeling should arise about [the queen's] marriage; for if that should take place under favourable auspices, every thing else will go on far more happily and with greater security. As to Philip's paying his addresses to her[2], I am not surprised at it, especially as the precedent is a new one: but if he consults his own interests, he will prefer the friendship of the queen to a marriage with her; and as to herself, she would not now, I think, marry a foreigner if she could; nor do I see how, if she were so inclined, she could do it

---

[1 This letter has no address, but is stated in the Index to the volumes in the Archives to have been written to Bullinger.]

[2 See first series, Letter II. p. 5, note 5.]

without the greatest danger. But in this matter I look very little to human counsels; for it is most true, as you write, that the disposal of kingdoms is in the hand of God. If the queen, mindful of the great mercy she has received, will but place her confidence in God;—if she will daily say unto the Lord, Thou art my fortress, my rock, and my refuge, there will neither be wanting to herself the spirit of a Judith or a Deborah, nor wisdom to her counsellors, nor strength to her army. On the other hand, the counsels of her enemies will be defeated, their swords blunted, and the horse with his rider fall to the ground. God grant that this may be the case, through Christ Jesus our Lord! Amen.

We are expecting another letter[1] from England in two or three days, and will take care that, should there be any news, good or bad, you shall be informed of it, whom we shall evermore reverence and acknowledge as masters and brethren who have so well deserved at our hands. Farewell. Strasburgh, Dec. 8, 1558.

Your excellency's most devoted,

ANTONY COOK.

LETTER II.

JOHN HALLER TO HENRY BULLINGER.

Dated at BERNE, *January* 11, 1559.

I HAVE extricated myself by the Lord's blessing from the legation to Lausanne, lately committed to me; for nothing more troublesome could have befallen me. Other persons are sent, who will manage every thing far better than I could have done. Meanwhile, I know not what will happen. We are expecting the result. Our English [exiles] at Arau have

---

[1 One letter arrived at Strasburgh Dec. 19, and Sandys wrote to Bullinger on the following day. See first series, Letter II. p. 3.]

this day petitioned our senate, through Lever the bearer of this letter, for licence to depart, having returned thanks for the shelter that has been afforded them. They were therefore dismissed with free permission, and with great congratulation from all godly persons. We are afraid, however, that they have returned too soon; but as we consider their presence will be necessary, we cannot blame their resolution. Meanwhile there are given to them letters testimonial of their conduct; and as they employed me as their interpreter with the senate, I proposed also, upon the recommendation of master Consul Negelin, what you lately suggested to me with respect to writing a letter to the queen. This proposition was so agreeable to the senate, that they are sending a letter to be delivered to her majesty by the parties themselves. There is therefore no occasion for your people to write to ours again upon this subject; but let them rather address the queen independently of us, which you will easily manage with your friends. I have not at this time anything else to write. These good people are in haste, wherefore I have been obliged to hasten likewise. All our friends salute you, especially Musculus[2]. Farewell. Berne, Jan. 11, 1559.

Yours,

J. HALLER.

LETTER III.

RODOLPH GUALTER TO QUEEN ELIZABETH.

Dated at ZURICH, [*January* 16], 1559.

GRACE and peace from God the Father through Jesus Christ. All godly persons, most serene queen, congratulate your royal majesty, for that God, who alone is wont to

[2 Wolfgang Musculus was invited by the magistrates of Berne in 1549, to the professorship of divinity there. He died in 1563.]

confer and transfer kingdoms, has raised you to the throne
of your ancestors.   But for my own part, I am of opinion
that we should rather congratulate the church of Christ herself ; upon which, in this last time, wherein antichrist is putting forth all his powers in his last struggle, the Lord has
caused a new star to arise, in that, according to the prediction
of the prophet, he has given you to her as a nursing mother,
who have hitherto been her faithful daughter.   We acknowledge in this the wonderful goodness of God, who, when one
would least expect it, looks upon his church, and relieves it
from the pains of persecution.   But for your majesty we
implore a spirit of fortitude and wisdom, under the guidance
of which you may continue to accomplish what you have
already begun.   For all godly persons are well acquainted
with that pre-eminent faith, whereby, in the reigns of your
father Henry, and your brother Edward, princes of pious and
holy memory, you embraced the light of gospel truth, and
resolved stedfastly to maintain it amidst dangers of every
kind.   And now many good men are every where proclaim-
ing, that your majesty is seriously thinking of purifying
the church and restoring religion ; and I can easily believe
that it is so, as I have been assured by credible witnesses,
that (as Paul writes concerning his son Timothy) you have
from your childhood known the holy scriptures.   Wherefore,
relying upon the clemency and piety of your majesty, I have
not hesitated to send this my letter, both to congratulate
your realm, and deliver the sentiments of my mind respecting
the restoration of religion, with greater freedom perhaps than
becomes an unknown individual.   For this I think is allowable in the ministers of the church, especially in regard to
those to whom God was pleased to entrust his church, when
he foretold that kings should be her nursing fathers, and
queens her nursing mothers.

But here, most serene queen, two things appear to me
especially worthy of regard : first, that every reformation of
the church and of religion be conducted agreeably to the
word of God; and next, that no opportunity be afforded to
any among your counsellors, whose endeavours are tending to
that object, either entirely to hinder this most holy and of all
things most necessary work, or at least to persuade you that
it should still be deferred.   For, with respect to the first, we

know that there are not a few persons, who, though they perceive that popery can neither honestly be defended, nor conveniently retained, are endeavouring by and bye to obtrude upon the churches a form of religion which is an unhappy compound of popery and the gospel, and from which there may at length be an easy passage to the ancient superstition. But since the apostle testifies that the church is born by the word of God, and that we must be born again in Christ, and made new creatures ; whatever is in any measure repugnant to the doctrine of Christ, must be put off and laid aside together with the old Adam : nor can any reformation of the church be really acceptable to God, unless it agree in every respect with his word : and for this reason the scripture commends the faith of David, of Hezekiah, and Josiah, because they reformed the church according to divinely prescribed laws ; while it reprehends in no obscure terms the slothfulness of others, who, though they wished to be regarded as the re- formers and defenders of religion, yet retained the high places in which the people had been accustomed to offer sacrifice, contrary[1] to the commands of God. And your majesty is aware of that saying of Christ, who declares that the *new piece* of evangelical doctrine will not suit the *old garments* of superstitions. And he also solemnly warns us not to put the fermenting and wholesome *new wine* of his gospel into *old leathern bottles,* unless we would have not only these to perish, but that to be spilled at the same time. From the experience of not a few instances in our Germany, we assur- edly know it to be impossible ever to consult the peace of the churches, or the purity of religion, as long as any relics of superstition are retained. For as those who are weak ascribe to them much more than is right, so the ignorant are made to stumble by them ; and at the same time, by their means, the enemies of truth entertain the hope of some time bringing back and restoring superstition.

Nor in a case of this kind is it expedient to listen to any reasonings of the flesh, which, though it has put its hand to the plough, is for the most part accustomed to look back, and seek out on every side occasions of delay. For, as the apostle bears witness, it is the very end and aim of the preaching of the gospel, that by the obedience of faith we should be subject

[1 The Latin has *propter* Dei preceptum, probably for *præter.*]

to the word of God, who alone both suggests the most whole-some counsels of action, and at the same time assists them by his Spirit to attain a favourable result. We have David for an example, who, notwithstanding he experienced many troubles in the beginning of his reign, and had to deal with many enemies, some of whom by open violence, and others by treacherous artifices, aimed at his destruction; yet, being enabled by the blessing of God to overcome them all, he restored both the civil government and religion with great glory and incredible success. I might bring forward many examples of this kind; but there is by no means any occasion to do so before your majesty, who has not long since seen something similar in king Edward, your brother, of most pious memory, who, when scarcely out of his boyhood, was an object of admiration to all kingdoms by reason of his remarkable zeal for godliness and the restoration of religion, and bravely overthrew the tyranny of antichrist throughout his realm. By which example God would shew, that anti-christ has very little, or rather no strength to defend his kingdom, as soon as the light of the divine word has dispersed the darkness in which he is wont to hide himself. But because our ingratitude deserved it, a just God took to himself in peace our most godly king (as he did Josiah of old), that he might not see the dreadful dispersion of religion, which would doubtless have appeared more painful to him than death itself. But the same God, again manifesting his compassion for the kingdom of England and the church at large, has raised you up, that by the activity and zeal of your majesty might be happily completed what the most godly king your brother had piously and successfully begun. Pursue therefore, most serene queen, with unshaken resolution, what no godly person doubts that you have long since conceived in your mind; and with your favour gladden the church, which is eagerly expecting from your majesty the true maintenance of doctrine and religion, and regard all delay as unlawful which is connected with danger to the soul of any individual whatever. This is the desire of all godly persons, and for which they are suppliantly praying to God, who can both bend to your subjection the minds of your people, and protect you from every danger, while labouring for his glory. I touch upon these things very

briefly, because I am well aware that your majesty is not
wanting in either a correct judgment, or faithful and prudent
counsellors.

I may be considered, I confess, as wanting in discretion,
for having offered this advice unsolicited. But I willingly
incur the charge of indiscretion, provided only I may perform
that duty, which both my public ministry in the church requires, and which I acknowledge myself to owe, by reason of
personal benefits, to your England ; in which I was formerly
received[1], when almost a boy, with the greatest kindness, and
from which time I have had among the English not a few
friends, whom I regard as by no means the last in my esteem.
Among these John Parkhurst easily holds the first place ;
a man pre-eminent for his erudition, and the stedfastness of
his faith, and who has firmly retained, even to this day, that
pure faith in Christ, which two and twenty years ago he
began to profess, when I was residing in Oxford ; and has
so confirmed the same, amidst the sore troubles of a lengthened exile, that he has often been a wonder to me, and I have
rejoiced in having such a man for my guest, in whom
I might have constantly before me a lively pattern of christian
faith and doctrine.   Should your majesty think fit to honour
him by any especial favour, you will do a service of which
you will have Christ Jesus as the most faithful recompenser ;
and I dare engage that Parkhurst himself will be a labourer
in the vineyard of the Lord not to be repented of.

I send your majesty my homilies[2] upon the general epistle
of the apostle John, dedicated to king Edward of pious
memory, but never read by him, because it seemed otherwise good to God the Father, who would not permit to an
ungrateful world the longer enjoyment of so great and rare
an intellect. I therefore request your majesty, that, if only for
the most delightful remembrance of your brother, you will
deign to receive and honour them with your patronage, until

[1 Gualter first came to England about the year 1537, in company with Nicolas Partridge.   His diary of that journey is still
preserved at Zurich, and may probably appear in a subsequent
series of these letters.]

[2 The volume is entitled : In Joannis Apostoli et Evangelistæ
Epistolam Canonicam Homiliæ xxxvii. In ejusdem apostoli duas
posteriores epistolas, Homiliarum sylvæ. Authore Rodolpho Gualthero Tigurino. Tiguri, apud Froschoverum, anno M.D.LIII.]

an opportunity be afforded me of more clearly testifying my respectful regard towards your majesty. May God the Father of mercy direct your majesty by his Spirit, protect you with his favour, and preserve you for many years in health and safety to his church and the kingdom of England! Amen. Dated at Zurich, the chief city of Switzerland, in the year of man's salvation 1559.

Your majesty's most devoted,

RODOLPH GUALTER,

Minister of the church of St Peter's, at Zurich.

LETTER IV.

RODOLPH GUALTER TO THE LORD FRANCIS RUSSEL[1].

Dated at ZURICH, *Jan.* 16, 1559.

GRACE and peace from God the Father through Jesus Christ! Though, most illustrious prince, I am well aware of my low estate, yet for many reasons I feel myself moved and impelled to make known to your clemency by letter the affectionate regard that I entertain towards your country. For when all godly persons are congratulating England with all their hearts, upon its having obtained a queen whose piety had been already proclaimed through the whole world, and by whose zeal it is universally hoped that true religion will be restored, which had for some years past been wretchedly on the decline; I should deservedly be deemed ungrateful, if in this general rejoicing I alone were to be silent, who for many reasons acknowledge myself deeply indebted to England. For, to say nothing of the incredible kindness which I formerly[2] experienced in your country, and the personal favours that I there received, the public cause of

[1 This was Francis, second earl of Bedford, to which title he succeeded in 1555. He had gone out of England in queen Mary's time, and staid some time at Zurich. Burnet, III. 411.]

[2 See above, p. 7, note 1.]

the church of Christ most justly demands it of me, that
although I can neither aid you by any counsel or authority
in the restoration of religion, I may at least by some token
or other manifest the affection of my mind. And this has
been my chief reason both for sending a letter to the queen's
majesty, and it also principally induces me to write to
your clemency. I am encouraged also at the same time by
your noble qualities, which many of our friends have frequently declared to us, and of which we were allowed to
behold no obscure evidences, when in your journey into
Italy last year by way of Zurich you made such diligent
inquiry into all things which make for the cause of the church
and of religion, that it was easy to be perceived that this
cause was far more dear to you than all other things whatever. And indeed I was even then rejoicing over you in
silence, inasmuch as I perceived that the grace of God in
you was not vain or inactive: but I now rejoice the more,
both for yourself and England, as I understand that you are
advanced by the queen's majesty to the highest dignity[3], in
which you are enabled both to give public evidence of your
godliness, and to deserve well of your beloved country,
and render that service and worship to God, which is more
acceptable to him than any other. For since he regards his
church (as he testifies by the prophet) as more dear to him
than the apple of his eye, and vouchsafed to redeem the same
by the death of his only-begotten Son; he certainly will have
it held in the highest esteem by all, and especially by kings,
and the counsellors of kings, who he foretold by Isaiah
should be its nursing fathers and guardians, which office appears to me to constitute the chief dignity of all sovereigns.
For to rule over a wide extent of country, to extend their
empire by land and sea, and restrain their subjects by the
force of law, is in the power of impious persons, and those
who are ignorant of God, such as we know to have existed
formerly in almost all kingdoms. But to kiss the Son
of God (as the divine and royal psalmist speaks), and to
cherish and defend his spouse, this truly is that glorious and

[3 The earl of Bedford was created a privy councillor on Elizabeth's accession, and when the care of correcting the liturgy was committed to Parker and others, he was one of the few to whom the
matter was imparted. Camden, Elizabeth, p. 16.]

incomparable honour of princes, which is only conferred upon those whom God, of his special grace, has chosen to be vessels of his glory ; and who, enlightened by his Spirit, have consecrated themselves entirely to him.   And indeed, most illustrious prince, many good men testify that you are of this character, and many too have experienced it up to the present time.   And I entreat of God in my continual prayers, that he may evermore preserve you such, and direct both your counsels and those of others, to whose fidelity is now entrusted the management of affairs, to the glory of his name, and the advancement of the church, and the welfare of the country ; which object you will doubtless be permitted to accomplish, if only in the true fear of the Lord, which the most wise Solomon has declared to be the beginning of wisdom, you will bear in mind that those things which relate to the church and to religion are no where to be sought for but from the fountains of holy scripture.   Nor does it become us here to be affrighted by any dangers, since the Lord, who ordains the counsels of action, directs also with his hand the events of such counsels ; so that though they may sometimes seem to make little progress, yet they will at length terminate in a most happy issue.   And though all things may deceive us, when, by reason of the world's ingratitude, God deprives even the most godly counsels of their effect, it is nevertheless no little satisfaction to know that we have done our duty, so that the blood of those whom their own perverseness has destroyed, cannot be required at our hands.

You must attribute, most illustrious prince, the freedom of my advice, not to temerity, but to my affection for England, and to your own clemency, the consideration of which has emboldened me to write as I have done.   I should very fully commend to your clemency master John Parkhurst, were I not aware that he is much loved and valued by you, as I easily discovered when you so friendly and affectionately came to visit him at my house.   And he is indeed worthy to be loved, as well for the singular godliness which he gave proof of by his exile, as for his sound learning, so opposed to any fondness for contention.   Nor do I doubt but that he will prove of great use, if your clemency should think proper by your influence to promote him.   May the

Lord Jesus direct and defend your clemency to the advancement of his church and of pure religion! Amen. Zurich,
Jan. 16, 1559.

[RODOLPH GUALTER.]

LETTER V.

RODOLPH GUALTER TO RICHARD MASTERS[1].

Dated at ZURICH, *Jan.* 16, 1559.

GREETING. I congratulated myself not a little in the
years gone by, when, in the reign of Edward the sixth of
pious memory, you first began to renew the duty of correspondence which had been interrupted for many years. But
now, most learned sir, and esteemed brother in Christ, I have
far more reason to congratulate both you and myself, as I
understand that such times by the mercy of God are
restored to your England, when, under the protection of a
most godly queen, the liberty of worshipping God in truth
will again be granted to godly men, and the letters of our
friends can be conveyed to and fro without danger. We
acknowledge in these things the wonderful wisdom and goodness of God, who is wont to temper with joyful changes the
afflictions of his church, lest we should be entirely overwhelmed in the waves of temptation. May he also grant
that the hopes of the faithful, which they have universally
begun to entertain respecting the kingdom of England, may
be fully realized! And this I the rather expect will be the
case, if so many of you as are there placed in any degree
of authority, will bear in mind that the charge of the church
and of religion especially belongs to you, and you do not
follow their counsels, who, perceiving that popery can neither
honestly be defended nor entirely retained, adopt those artifices by which they invent a form of religion of a mixed,
uncertain, and doubtful character, and obtrude the same upon

[1 Richard Masters was physician to queen Elizabeth.]

the churches under the pretext of evangelical reformation
from which the return to papistical superstition and idol-
madness is afterwards most easy. I do not write this, as
knowing that there are any such persons among you, but
as fearing lest there may be such. For we have now experienced in Germany for some years, to the great detriment
of the churches, the extent of influence possessed by men of
this character; forasmuch as their counsels appear to the
carnal judgment to be full of moderation, and especially
adapted to the promotion of concord: and it is likely
that the common enemy of our salvation will also find
suitable instruments among yourselves, by the aid of which
he will endeavour to retain the seeds of popery; which
must be firmly resisted with the weapons of holy scripture and of the divine word, lest, while we endeavour to
avoid giving some small offence at the first beginning,
many things be allowed, as if to endure only for a time,
which it will afterwards be scarcely possible by any effort,
and not without the most grievous struggles, altogether to
remove. The churches of Germany have seen many examples of this evil, by the consideration of which we are
taught to regard with suspicion whatever is in any respect
at variance with the sincere doctrine of the word. And you
must not think that I am induced to give you this warning
from any other motive, than because I am so wonderfully
attached to your England by reason of my former intercourse, of which the mere recollection is even at this day
most delightful to me.

Our friend Parkhurst, my brother and most beloved
guest, whom I wish most earnestly to commend to you, will
give you every information respecting our affairs. He has
now endured for five whole years the painful anxieties of exile,
during which however he has united incredible patience with
admirable stedfastness of faith. He is at this time returning
to his country full of joyful hope, that he may aid, according
to his ability, the cause of the reviving church. And I
doubt not but that he will do her good service, as he has a
remarkable knowledge of the scriptures, and is most devoted
to the truth, and has a thorough abhorrence of controversy, the lovers of which are scarcely ever of any use in
the church. You will therefore do well to aid him by your

influence, and bring him forward to the utmost of your power. And no circumstance will ever be more gratifying to myself, than to learn by a letter from you that the recollection of our friendship is still fresh on your part, which certainly can never be effaced from my own mind. Farewell, most excellent sir. Zurich, Jan. 16, 1559.

[RODOLPH GUALTER.]

LETTER VI.

SIR ANTONY COOK TO PETER MARTYR.

Dated at LONDON, *February* 12, 1559.

YOUR letter, most excellent sir, together with that of master Bullinger, I have myself placed in the queen's hands. How exceedingly she was affected by the perusal of them, Cecil bears witness, who saw her tears arise as she was reading them. She[1] inquired whether you were willing to return to England; for she had heard, it seems, something of the kind. I replied, that I had no doubt of your willingness, by reason of your exceeding love and regard towards the late king Edward, herself, and the whole commonwealth of England; but that at that time I had heard nothing certain from you by letter; yet I wished that she would take measures for having one of the universities adorned by your excellence. She will write, I hope, on this subject very shortly both to yourself and the Senate of Zurich.

We are now busy in parliament about expelling the tyranny of the pope, and restoring[2] the royal authority, and re-establishing true religion. But we are moving far too slowly; nor are there wanting[3] at this time Sanballats and Tobiases

[1 See first series, Letter VII. p. 20.]

[2 The Bill for the restitution and annexation of the firstfruits, &c. to the imperial crown of this realm passed the House of Lords on Saturday, Feb. 4th. That for restoring the supremacy passed the upper house on Wednesday, Apr. 26. See D'Ewes, Journals, p. 29.]

[3 Namely, the Romish bishops. See first series, Letter IV. p. 10, note 1.]

to hinder and obstruct the building of our walls. Wherefore we ought the more to think upon that exhortation, " Pray without ceasing." The zeal of the queen is very great, the activity of the nobility and people is also great ; but still the work is hitherto too much at a stand. The advice, *Trust in God, and lean not to your own understanding,* is not sufficiently impressed on the minds of some parties : neither that saying, *He taketh the wise in their own craftiness.* But the result of this meeting of parliament will, as far as I can judge, confirm my hope. Salute much, I pray you, in my name master Bullinger, and the rest of your brethren. Take every care of your health, and that you may be able to bear the journey. Farewell. London, Feb. 12, 1559.

Altogether yours,

ANTONY COOK.

LETTER VII.

RICHARD HILLES TO HENRY BULLINGER.

Dated at LONDON, *February* 28, 1559.

MUCH health. I received, my honoured sir, with a willing mind your letter to me dated on the 22nd December last. There was something, however, in it which I did not read so willingly, namely, that some persons had written to you more than once, that I disdained to receive your letters. For I never disdain to read the letters of any one, and especially yours ; as in my judgment it would be the greatest arrogance to slight the letters of so learned and venerable a man. But as long as our cruel and superstitious queen Mary reigned in this country, I was so afraid for my property, and of getting into danger, yea, even for my life itself, that I scarcely dared to write to persons of your character, or to receive letters from them. Man, you say, is prone to fall, and in many things we all of us offend. It is not therefore to be wondered at, if I also should have stumbled, and begun to stand in awe of and fear men, more than I ought to have done; as well also as to entertain opinions which many years since I held in the greatest abhorrence. To that I was drawn over by reading the volumes of some of the holy fathers, in which, if I am not mistaken, there are some doctrines, handed down too by the consent of almost all of them, but which are in no wise agreeable to the doctrine held by yourself and those like you. I do not choose however to write more upon this subject, because if you think fit to reply to my letter, I have neither time nor inclination to write an answer in return: it is so irksome to me to write Latin, and I am now almost entirely out of practice, as I am no longer in habits of intercourse with those learned men who express their thoughts in the Latin language. I certainly feel much obliged to you for having thought proper to recal to my remembrance, how I once knew that grace and compassion is most abundant with the Lord, who does not cast out, but receives with kindness, those who return to him. I confess therefore my past offence unto the Lord, I give glory to the Lord, and from the Lord I implore mercy, as you recommend me to do, nor have I any doubt but that I shall obtain it. And I will take care to be faithful for the future, and will promote, as you advise me, to the utmost of my power the true religion, of which the chief part is contained in the confession of faith[1] exhibited to the invincible emperor Charles V. at the assembly at Augsburg in 1530. Commend me, I pray you, to master Peter Martyr, and to Julius his attendant, and to your most honourable wife. My wife heartily salutes you and all of them, and wishes you all much health. Farewell. London, Feb. 28, 1559.

Yours,

RICHARD HILLES, *Anglus.*

[1 The Confession of Augsburg was first presented to the emperor Charles V. on June 25, 1530. It was signed and subscribed by John, elector of Saxony; George, marquis of Brandenburg; Ernest, duke of Lunenburg; Philip, landgrave of Hesse; Wolfgang, prince of Anhalt; and the imperial cities of Nuremberg and Reutlingen. The matter was supplied by Luther, and reduced into form by the eloquent pen of Melancthon. See Mosheim, Cent. XVI. chap. iii. 1, 2.]

With respect to religion, silence has been imposed upon the catholic preachers (as they are called) by a royal proclamation[1], and sufficient liberty is allowed to the gospellers, to preach three times a week during this Lent[2] before the

[1 The proclamation is thus given in Strype, Annals, i. ii. 390.

By the quene. The quene's majesty, understanding that there be certain persons, having in times past the office of ministery in the church, which do now purpose to use their former office in preaching and ministery, and partly have attempted the same; assembling, specially in the city of London, in sondry places, great nomber of people; whereupon riseth amonges the common sort not only unfruteful dispute in matters of religion, but also contention, and occasion to break common quiet; hath therefore, according to thauthoritie committed to her highness, for the quiet governaunce of all maner her subjects, thought it necessary to charge and commaund, like as hereby her highness doth charge and commaund all maner of her subjects, as well those that be called to ministery in the church, as all others, that they do forbear to preach or teach, or to gyve audience to any maner of doctrine or preachyng, other than to the gospels and epistels, commonly called the gospel and epistel of the day, and to the ten commaundments in the vulgar tongue, without exposition or addition of any maner, sense, or meaning to be applyed or added; or to use any other maner of publick prayer, rite, or ceremony in the church, but that which is already used, and by law receaved; or the common letany used at this present in her majesty's own chappel, and the Lord's prayer, and the crede in English; until consultation may be had by parlament, by her majesty, and her three estates of this realme, for the better conciliation and accord of such causes as at this present are moved in matters and ceremonies of religion.

The true advauncement whereof, to the due honour of almighty God, the increase of vertue and godlyness, with universal charitie and concord amonges her people, her majestie moost desyreth and meaneth effectually, by all maner of means possible, to procure and to restore to this her realme. Whereunto, as her majestie instantly requireth all her good, faithful, and loving subjects to be assenting and ayding with due obedience; so, if any shall disobediently use themselfes to the breach hereof, her majesty both must and will see the same duely punished, both for the qualite of thoffence, and for example to all others neglecting her majesties so reasonable commaundement. Yeven at her highness palais of Westminster, the xxviith day of December, the first year of her majesties reigne. See first series, Lett. III. p. 7.]

[2 In the queen's first Lent, on the 23rd of February, Mr Grindal preached before her majesty. In which Lent there preached also divers other learned protestant divines, and the first of note in king Edward's time : viz. Dr Cox, Dr Parker, Dr Bill, Dr Sandys, Mr Whitehead : all of whom, excepting the second and third, had but lately come from exile. Strype, Grindal, p. 35.]

queen herself, and to prove their doctrines from the holy scriptures. The public assembly too, or common council of this realm, or Parliament[3], as our people call it, has now been sitting nearly six weeks. Nothing however has yet been publicly determined with respect to the abolishing popish superstition, and the re-establishment of the christian religion. There is however a general expectation, that all rites and ceremonies will shortly be reformed by our faithful citizens, and other godly men, in the afore-mentioned parliament[4], either after the pattern which was lately in use in the time of king Edward the sixth, or which is set forth by the protestant princes of Germany, in the above-named Confession[5] of Augsburg.

LETTER VIII.

EDMUND GRINDAL TO CONRAD HUBERT[6].

Dated at LONDON, *May* 23, 1559.

HEALTH in Christ. I believe that William Salkyns, the servant of Richard Hilles, who lived with us a long time at

[3 That sitting of the Parliament began on Wednesday, Jan. 25, and was dissolved on May 8.]

[4 The Act of Uniformity passed the House of Commons on April 20. The English service-book began to be used Sunday, May 12, in the queen's chapel; and in St Paul's on the Wednesday following. Strype, Grindal, p. 35.]

[5 There were thoughts now of receiving the Augustan Confession, the better to join in league with the German protestants. On this subject Bullinger thus wrote to Utenhovius: "I see," said he, "no small disturbances like to arise in England also, if the Augustan Confession be received, which some would have; a thing very unworthy in many regards. This gives vexation to all the purer churches, and would infect them all with its leaven. I pray God restrain men otherwise pious, but sufficiently troublesome to godly men and the purer religion. And you know what was done in Poland. Beware, and lay to your helping hand, that it be not received. King Edward's reformation satisfieth the godly." Strype, Annals, I. i. 259.]

[6 Conrad Hubert was preacher at St Thomas's, Strasburgh, and the editor of Bucer's *Scripta Anglicana*, which he dedicated to archbishop Grindal in 1577, both because he had been one of Bucer's chief

Strasburgh, is well known to you.   I lately handed over to
him some writings of Bucer, to be delivered to you.   One
was, his public disputation when he took his doctor's degree;
another was concerning the entire controversy[1] between himself and Yong, whom you used to call *fungus*.   Whether this
latter contains any thing else, I know not; for it is written
in such a way as to require a conjuror rather than a reader;
except that to you perhaps, who are conversant with the
writings of this individual, it will not be a matter of so much
difficulty to find out and unravel the meaning.   Dr Parker,
who sent me these manuscripts, wrote word that he had also
some other fragments; but when he had brought them forth
from the hiding-places, in which they had been concealed
during the whole of these incendiary times, he found them
gnawed by the rats and entirely spoiled: so that if you should
derive any pleasure from those you have, you will immediately
lose it again, because you are deprived of all hopes of receiving
any more in future.   You told me that you had a copy of
the answer to the Antididagma[2], turned into Latin by Martin

friends at Cambridge, and also had procured most of the pieces then
published.   See Strype, Grindal, 298.   This letter is preserved in the
archives of St Thomas's at Strasburgh.]

[1 The controversy between Bucer and Yong was thus.   One of
Bucer's questions (in a public disputation at Cambridge) was, that *the
good works which any seem to do before justification have the nature of sin*.
Hereat Yong took great offence, and complained to the senate of the
university against him, saying that Bucer was in a grievous error.
The issue was, that Yong entered the lists of disputation with the
reverend man against his tenet.   Both of them penned their disputations, and Bucer sent a copy of his to Cheke to communicate to
bishop Ridley, and in August 1550 wrote to Mr Grindal, president of
Pembroke Hall, and chaplain to the bishop, desiring him to acquaint
the bishop diligently with the truth of the case.   (The letter is given
in Bucer's *Scripta Anglicana*, and also in Strype's Life of Grindal,
p. 467.)   Bucer said that he confessed and believed what the king's
homilies taught of good works.   Yong and his party could not but acknowledge that they were pressed hard with the king's homilies; and
so, in effect, they confessed they made for Bucer against them.   And
yet these very homilies they had subscribed to.   Abridged from Strype,
Memor. II. i. 327.]

[2 The Antididagma was a work ascribed to John Gropper, one of
the canons of Cologne, and published by the clergy there, in opposition
to the book of Reformation drawn up by Bucer, Pistorius, and Melanc-

Bremius. We have nothing more of Bucer's here that I know of. I doubt not but that Salkyns will faithfully deliver every thing at your Strasburgh Fair.

Receive this brief account of our affairs in England. We found our church miserably torn in pieces, and all but over-thrown. We were indeed urgent from the very first, that a general reformation should take place. But the parliament long delayed the matter, and made no change whatever, until a peace had been concluded[3] between the sovereigns, Philip, the French king, and ourselves. But now at last, by the blessing of God, during the prorogation of parliament, there has been published a proclamation to banish the pope and his jurisdiction altogether, and to restore religion to that form which we had in the time of Edward the sixth. If any bishops or other beneficed persons shall decline to take the oath of abjuration of the authority of the bishop of Rome, they are to be deprived of every ecclesiastical function, and deposed. No one, after the feast of St John the Baptist next ensuing, may celebrate mass without subjecting himself to a most heavy penalty. It is therefore commonly supposed that almost all the bishops, and also many other beneficed persons, will renounce their bishoprics and their functions, as being ashamed, after so much tyranny and cruelty exercised under the banners of the pope, and the obedience so lately sworn to him, to be again brought to a recantation, and convicted of manifest perjury. We are labouring under a great dearth of godly ministers: for many, who have fallen off in this persecution, are now become papists in heart; and those who had been heretofore, so to speak, *moderate* papists, are now the most obstinate. But it is our part to do what we can, and commit the whole to God. In conclusion, I pray you to commend us and our church to God in your prayers; and diligently salute masters Marpach and Sebald in my name. Farewell in the Lord, most courteous sir, and very dear brother in Christ. London, May 23, 1559.

Your most attached in the Lord,

EDMUND GRINDAL, *Anglus.*

thon in 1543, at the request of Herman, archbishop of that diocese. See Sleidan, Hist. Ref. Lib. xv. Vol. II. p. 199.]

[3 Namely at Câteau Cambresis, in April 1559.]

I am in doubt (for I have a very bad memory) whether I or Lakin[1] undertook to send you the whole[2] account of the exhumation of Bucer and Fagius. But lest you should altogether be disappointed of your wish, I have positively determined to write on the subject to Dr Parker, who will, I hope, take care that a true description of the whole affair shall be prepared for me. Should he do this, I will take care that it shall be forwarded to you. If Lakin, who is now absent from London, will do the same, you may collect from each what is most important. Again farewell. I doubt not, but that with your wonted kindness you will see that the inclosed letters are forwarded by the earliest opportunity.

LETTER IX.

LAURENCE HUMPHREY TO HENRY BULLINGER.

Dated [at BASLE,] *June* 23, [1559.]

AN opportunity is now afforded me of doing what my duty has long required from me; which however the sudden arrival and departure of the messenger, and want of time, will not allow me to perform as I ought, and as I could wish. You must therefore, at this time, with your fatherly kindness, take in good part both the shortness of my letter, and my negligence in writing.

There came to me from master[3] Abel a packet of letters

[1 Thomas Lakin was one of the exiles with Grindal at Strasburgh.]

[2 Jan. 26, 1556. Commissioners from cardinal Pole, viz. Watson, bishop elect of Lincoln, Scot, bishop of Chester, and Christopherson, bishop elect of Chichester, came to Cambridge; and after a formal process, caused the body of Martin Bucer, late the king's professor of divinity, buried in St Mary's, to be taken up and burnt; and so also was served the body of Paul Fagius, late the king's professor of Hebrew, buried in St Michael's church; which was looked upon as barbarous. Strype, Memor. Eccl. III. i. 510.]

[3 See first series, Letter XV. p. 35.]

inclosed in mine, and which I send to your reverence by the bearer, a native of Zurich, a trustworthy man, and one not unknown to you. The other packet that you inquired after, I have not yet been able to meet with, though I have made diligent search after it, and do not yet cease my inquiries, as well for my own sake, as for that of yourself and others. They tell me that the waggoner gave it to some one at the sign of the Wild Man of the Cave[4]. What became of it afterwards, I know not. Should the letters fall into my hands, of which indeed I have no hope after so long an interval, I will do my best endeavour, that, God willing, they may reach you. And this, excellent sir, is the first motive which now induces me to write. Another is, either the illness or death of my friend Frensham[5]: if he is alive, that by the consolation, exhortation, and aid, which you so well know how to afford, you may comfort him on his bed of sickness. He has always exceedingly valued your advice, and, if I mistake not, will listen to it even at his latest moments. If he is no longer living, you will cherish his remains with such care as is befitting one who is at rest in the bosom of Abraham, or rather of Christ. Both master Foxe[5] and myself are anxious to know what is his state, that is, whether he has departed, or is yet alive; that if living, we may either personally visit him, should there be occasion for it, or attend him with our absent prayers; and if he be not alive, that we may at least honour the funeral of our very dear friend with a pious tear.

The third reason for my now wishing to write, namely, that I might thank you for all your kindness towards myself and others, when I was living with my friends at Zurich, I will defer till another opportunity. Meanwhile I commend your piety and holy labours to the Lord, whom I pray to guide by his holy Spirit, and to advance unto all honour,

[4 See first series, Letter XV. p. 35.]

[5 See first series, Letter XV*. p. 37. Frensham was now dead. His will is still preserved at Zurich, by which it appears that he left a large portion of his property to charitable purposes, among others, to the poor of Halden, Northam, Woodchurch, Cranbrook, Frittenden and Biddenden. The first words of this document are, "In Dei nomine, Amen. Testamentum meum et voluntatem ad suam gloriam dirigat Deus."]

piety, and holiness, both our own church now reviving, and
yours which has been long established.   Amen. June 23.

Your most devoted,

LAURENCE HUMPHREY.

LETTER X[1].

EDMUND GRINDAL TO CONRAD HUBERT.

Dated at LONDON, *July* 14, 1559.

GREETING.   As I have been formerly accustomed, very
dear brother in Christ, to make the most friendly use of
your kindness, when I was present with you, so I shall not
hesitate, when absent, to entreat your assistance in a matter
which I hope will be of no great difficulty to you.   For I
am in want of some amanuensis to be always at hand in
those important[2] occupations and employments to which I
am daily called.   As we labour under the greatest want
of good ministers, we are obliged to employ our own young
men, who might be qualified for this office, in the ministry of
the churches.   I therefore request your piety, that, if you
can meet with any one of your young men who is willing to
undertake this employment, and to serve me in this matter
upon suitable terms, (of which I leave the arrangement to
yourself,) you will take care that he be sent over to me, and
make use of the services either of John Abel or William
Salkyns in this matter.   I should require in the individual
to be sent, that he should be ready at writing Latin, and

[1 The original of this letter is preserved in the archives of St
Thomas's, Strasburgh.]

[2 Grindal was employed with others to draw up a form of
prayer and public worship to be laid before parliament; and was
also one of the eight protestant divines at the Conference at Westminster, in March.   He was employed too in the summer of this
year as a commissioner for the royal visitation in the north. Strype,
Grindal, p. 35.]

that his hand-writing should be tolerably good. He should, moreover, be somewhat acquainted with Greek, and especially with Hebrew, and should take delight in the study of the holy Scriptures. All these qualifications are generally to be met with in your young men. And I offer these terms on my part. First, I will bear the expenses of his journey hither, and have written to John Abel respecting the advancement of the money; and I could wish, if it were possible, that he should come over in his company. In the next place, I will not employ him in any laborious or servile work, but in reading, writing, and similar occupations; excepting only that he will sometimes be required to wait at table, &c. I will give him, moreover, besides his board and two suits of clothes after the English fashion, a fixed salary of twenty Rhenish dollars, or which is the same thing, twenty English crowns, besides what may be added from my liberality, as occasion shall arise. Lastly, if either on account of ill health, or any other reasonable cause,—for example, if England should not agree with him, or if he should be called away by his parents or friends,—I will also defray the expenses of his return home. And should he wish to learn our language, which does not very much differ from the German, it will not, I hope, be difficult for me to provide for him in a respectable way. If I do not appear to you to propose terms sufficiently liberal, I am quite ready to allow your prudence to assign more liberal ones, and, the Lord willing, I will perform them, if only you will provide me with a respectable and godly youth, whom I will endeavour so to treat, that he shall not repent of having visited England. I request you to salute master doctor Marpach in my name, without whose aid and assistance I am well aware that this business cannot be accomplished; but I hope that with his wonted kindness he will lend a favourable ear to my request. For the person, whoever he may be, will not be the less useful to your churches, if he shall return to you with the collected experience of some years' travel.

The state of our church (to come to that subject) is pretty much the same as when I last wrote to you, except only that what had heretofore been settled by proclamations and laws with respect to the reformation of the churches, is now daily being carried into effect. The popish bishops

are almost all of them deprived; and if any yet remain, they
will be deprived in a few days for refusing to renounce their
obedience to the pope. They are however treated with
sufficient lenity, not to say too much so; for they are allowed
to retire into private life, and devour, as master Bucer used
to say, the spoils of the church. Many persons think that
they begin to repent of their firmness, now they see the
French King[1], Henry II., in whom their chief hope was
placed, taken off not without the manifest declaration of
divine vengeance. Many of our friends, who were in exile
in Germany, are now marked out for bishops. This is all
that I had to write respecting our affairs. I shall be able,
I trust, to send you in a few days the account of the
burning of Bucer's [bones.][2] I pray you to send me all
the German works of Luther, bound by your bookseller
Christopher [Froschover.] Abel or Salkyns will pay the
money. This is one reason why I wish for a German
amanuensis, because I am unwilling entirely to forget your
language. Should you not meet with a suitable person
among your friends at home, write, I pray you, to those
at Basle, that you may procure me some one even from
thence. Write back, I pray you, in three words, what you
have been able to do for me. I leave other matters to be
more fully explained by John Abel or William Salkyns. I
wish you all health in the Lord. London, July 14, 1559.

Yours wholly in the Lord,

EDMUND GRINDAL, Anglus.

[1 Henry II. of France was killed in a tournament, July 10, 1559.]
[2 See Historia vera de vita, obitu, sepultura, &c. D. Martini Buceri
et Pauli Fagii. Argent. 1562.]

LETTER XI[3].

PETER MARTYR TO [THOMAS SAMPSON.]

Dated at [ZURICH,] *July* 15, 1559.

I SEE you, my friend, altogether in your letter. You are afraid on both sides: for if you reject the ministry, you seem to let go an opportunity of directing things in a proper manner; while, if you undertake the offered function, you have just and good cause to fear lest you should appear to assent to those ordinances, which not only impair and weaken the pure worship of God, but also corrupt and marvellously bring it to decay; although they may seem to have but little weight and importance in the eyes of men who are but faintly disposed towards the gospel; for they count all such things as matters of indifference. But will any one who is somewhat better instructed in religion, when he sees you, a messenger of Christ and zealous trumpeter of the gospel, arrayed in these vestments, praying at an altar before the image of the crucifix, repeating holy words, and distributing the sacraments,—will any one, I say, not think that these rites are not only tolerated, but also approved by you? Whereby no credit will be given you hereafter, when you teach otherwise. For he whose teaching is at variance with his actions, builds up the things that he destroys, and in like manner destroys the things that he builds up. Neither can the example of the apostle be alleged in excuse for such conduct, who for a time retained the Jewish ceremonies with a safe conscience; since the Mosaic institutions were brought in of old by the authority and law of God, and neither devised by man's understanding, nor condemned in regard to worship. But the things of which we now speak were both instituted by men without any divine sanction, and have splendidly

[3 This letter is addressed, in the printed volume of Martyr's letters, to a certain friend of his in England; whom Strype considers to have been bishop Grindal. From the internal evidence, however, of this and subsequent letters addressed to the same person, they appear with greater probability to have been written to Thomas Sampson. See below, p. 32.]

subserved that worship which all godly persons do now
abominate.   I would that those who have thought fit that
these things should be preserved, had perceived that, as
long as they remain, the gospel is not sufficiently established.
Truly, if we hated superstitions from the heart, we should endeavour by all means that their very vestiges should be rooted
out.   I would that we had been somewhat better instructed
by the obstinate zeal of our adversaries.   They diligently
avoid every thing that in any measure savours of our religion, and of set purpose, as far as they are able, depart
from the simple worship of Christ and the most ancient
custom of the apostles.   Why do not we take care in like
manner to depart as far as possible from their pernicious
institutions, and aim at apostolic simplicity, not only in doctrine, but also in the administration of the sacraments?

I do not see how the things retained by you can properly be regarded as matters of indifference. . Certainly since
they present to the beholders an express resemblance of the
pernicious mass, wherein ungodly men will exceedingly delight
themselves; (for they will say that the mass was so holy a
thing that the splendid representation thereof could not dis-
please even us; for though we do not retain it, we nevertheless imitate it in many remarkable ways;) who thereupon shall prevent such of the bystanders, in whose hearts
popery still remains, from adoring the image of the crucifix?
Undoubtedly they will do it, nor can the intention of their
mind be prevented.   And will the contrivers of these counsels
say that this is not done through any fault of theirs, but
through the fault of those who are badly taught, and too
much addicted to their own superstitions?   They cannot
however deny that they give the occasion; and woe unto
those by whom the offence cometh! Neither can they bring
any one proof for their opinion either out of the holy scriptures, or the ordinances of the primitive church.   But if the
desire only of making a new covenant drives them to these
things, we must remember that the covenant made of old
between us and God is far more excellent than any covenants
of man; and we must diligently take heed, lest, while we
follow after civil things, we suffer the loss of heavenly things.

Wherefore, my very dear brother in Christ, since things
are in this state, I give you two pieces of advice; first,

that you still retain the function of preaching, and cease not, both in public and private, to defend the truth of doctrine, and to declaim against rites which are full of offence and occasions of falling. The other is, that you abstain from the administration of the sacraments, until these intolerable blemishes be removed. By these means the opportunity of doing good will not be lost, neither will you confirm others in their superstition by your example. And this is not only my advice, but the same is also the opinion of the reverend and most excellent master Bullinger. As to your former question, I remember that I sent you an answer, but my letter has probably been lost or intercepted. And I would have now replied a second time, but that I know not where your letter is, and when I looked for it, was not able to find it. If therefore you wish another answer, you will not think much of writing your questions over again. Salute all our friends. Here master Bullinger, my wife, and Julius with his wife and the rest of our family, salute you. And I especially salute your wife, and Jane. July 15, 1559.

[PETER MARTYR.]

LETTER XII[1].

CONRAD HUBERT TO THOMAS BLAURER.

Dated at STRASBURGH, *Aug.* 7, 1559.

HEALTH in Christ our Saviour. Three days since, most worthy and much honoured sir, I received a letter[2] from my intimate friend, master Edmund Grindal, who, after having been some time in exile in this country, with some other Englishmen, on account of their profession of the gospel, has, under the changed state of religion, by reason of his well known piety and learning, been recalled by the queen, and lately[3] appointed to the bishoprick of London. Your son

[1] The original of this letter is preserved in the library at St Gall.]
[2] See above, Letter X. p. 22.]
[3] Grindal was not consecrated till Dec. 21, 1559.]

Diethelm will make known to you what, among other things, he requested of me in that letter, and acquaint you at the same time with the advice of myself and some of our friends. With your wonted piety and good sense you will, if you approve the plan, add your consent, and will scarcely feel disposed to neglect what seems, in my opinion, no common opportunity of advancing your son, who is very dear to me; and especially as you are blessed with so large a family. Indeed, to confess the truth, your intention of removing Diethelm as it were from his studies to the office of schoolmaster, never met my approbation; and I know not whether it has not hitherto been frustrated by Providence, as he himself will be able to explain to you more fully. In few words, my worthy Blaurer, I wish you to be convinced of this respecting me, that your friend Hubert loves you and yours most exceedingly, and is extremely anxious to promote your welfare.

I am compelled to be brief, partly by reason of the haste of him who is setting out on his journey, and partly by reason of matters connected with the press, with which I am all but overwhelmed. Wherefore, if there be any thing else which it may interest you to know, you have here a living epistle, and that a far more agreeable one. Farewell happily in Christ, with all who belong to you. Strasburgh, Aug. 7, 1559.

Yours,

CONRAD HUBERT.

LETTER XIII.

THOMAS LEVER TO HENRY BULLINGER.

Dated at London, Aug. 8, 1559.

Much health in Christ. As I know that you will receive fuller and better information respecting many of the most important affairs of the state and church of England by the letters of others, I will now write to you, according to my slender ability, about a few things of less consequence. On returning from you towards England, in the course of my journey I saw at Strasburgh a proclamation[1], that is, an edict published by the authority of queen Elizabeth, strictly prohibiting all preaching and exposition of holy scripture, or any change of religion throughout all England, until the great council, which we call the Parliament, hereafter to be called together, shall have come to a decision respecting religion. When then I returned to England, I saw, according to the proclamation above mentioned, or rather, I shrunk from seeing, masses and all the follies and abominations of popery, everywhere sanctioned by the authority of the laws, and the gospel no where to be met with, except among some persons at London, who were either admitted to preach before the queen at court on a few stated days, only in the time of Lent, or else in a congregation that remained in concealment during the whole time of persecution, and then not venturing forth beyond such private houses as were open to them, on the cessation of the persecution, they were permitted by queen Elizabeth in open private houses, but in no public churches. For there had been a congregation[2] of faithful persons concealed in London during the time of Mary, among whom the gospel was always preached, with the pure administration of the sacraments ; but during the rigour of the persecution under that queen they carefully concealed themselves, and on the cessation of it under Elizabeth they openly continued in the same congregation. But as their godly mode of worship was condemned by the laws of the realm, the magistrates, though they connived at their fre-quent assembling in private houses, would not allow them, notwithstanding, to occupy the parish churches. In conse-quence of which, large numbers flocked to them not in the churches, but in private houses. And when the Lord's supper was administered among them, no strangers were admitted, except such as were kept pure from popery and even from the imputation of any evil conduct ; or who, ingenuously acknowledging their backsliding and public offence, humbly sought pardon and reconciliation in presence of the whole assembly. I have frequently been present on such occasions, and have seen many returning with tears, and many too in

[1 See above, p. 16, note 1.]
[2 See first series, Letter III. p. 7, note 7. See also Foxe's Acts and Mon. for some interesting details relative to this congregation.]

like manner with tears receiving such persons into communion; so that nothing could be more delightful than the
mutual tears of all parties, on the one side lamenting their
sins, and on the other congratulating them on their reconciliation and renewed communion in Christ Jesus.

Some of us preachers, who had returned to England from
Germany, being much affected with these things, and considering that the silence imposed for a long and uncertain period
was not agreeable to the command and earnest injunction of
Paul, to preach the word of God in season and out of season,
having been requested to do so, forthwith preached the gospel
in certain parish churches, to which a numerous audience
eagerly flocked together. And when we solemnly treated of
conversion to Christ by true repentance, many tears from many
persons bore witness that the preaching of the gospel is more
effectual to true repentance and wholesome reformation, than
any thing that the whole world can either imagine or approve.
For while these things were taking place among private individuals, without the sanction of any public authority, behold,
at the very same time masses were being celebrated with all
the idolatrous superstition of popery among persons distinguished for their influence, their wealth, and their public
offices, and this with the whole authority of law, proclamation,
and practice. And now popery is at length abolished by
authority of parliament, and the true religion of Christ
restored: this unclean world, both in the one and the other,
seeks after nothing but base lucre and filthy pleasure. Very
many persons are so drawn over from that to this, that they
are neither willing to purify the dross of the one, nor embrace
the purity of the other, but are disposed to frame themselves
after the fashion of this world. For there are many who
love, possess, and ostentatiously glory in the monuments of
superstition, the emoluments of lucre, the liberty, yea, even
the pleasures of the flesh, to the great scandal and disgrace
of the religion they profess. But God will at length give
the victory to the little ones of the weak flock of Christ,
against the powerful tyrants of the world. For all the sanguinary bishops here are deposed; learned, pious, and
discreet persons are sent forth to visit all parts of England[1].
Zealous preachers of the gospel, who used to preach at first

[1 For an account of this visitation, see Strype, Annals, I. i. 245, &c.]

contrary to the queen's proclamation, have now, by means of letters sealed with the queen's seal, free licence to preach throughout all England. And I, who have long been preaching the gospel among the most ignorant persons in the remoter districts[2], have determined, God willing, to return tomorrow from London to them and others like them, who have seldom or never heard any exposition of the gospel of Christ. For such persons seem to me most of all in want of, and most ready to receive, the edification and consolation afforded to them in Christ's gospel.

But I must not write any more of myself, except only that I wish now to promise you by letter, what I will at all times faithfully perform according to the opportunity and ability which God shall give me ; namely, that I will use every endeavour that you and your countrymen, who so kindly provided for us English, when in exile for the sake of religion, may be assured that we are not unmindful of so great kindness, and that we shall ever continue grateful for it.

Commend us to the prayers of all the godly. Salute for me your wife, my excellent hostess, with your children, and all your household, to whom I wish abundant blessings from God in Christ. Salute the ministers of your church, and especially its chief pillars, masters Bernardine, Martyr, and Gualter. May the Lord Jesus long preserve you to the edification of his universal Church in Christ! Amen. London, Aug. 8, 1559.

Yours ever faithfully attached in Christ,

THOMAS LEVER.

[2 Namely, at Coventry. See first series, Letter XXXV. p. 86.]

LETTER XIV.

PETER MARTYR TO[1] [THOMAS SAMPSON.]

Dated at Zurich, *November* 4, 1559.

The letter that you sent me on the 27th of August, I received towards the end of October: wherefore if I am somewhat late in my reply, it is no fault of mine; especially since trustworthy couriers to Strasburgh are not often to be met with. But with respect to the subject of your present inquiry, I know that I have written at length in another letter; so that either my letter must have miscarried, or you had not received it when you last wrote. But that you may not be disappointed of my advice and assistance, I will repeat what I have before written. There seems no reason why you should trouble yourself about impropriations; for you have nothing to do with the question, whence or how the queen may choose to afford a maintenance or stipend either to the bishop or the parochial clergy. But should they seem to be destitute of suitable provision, you may petition and intercede on their behalf; or if you have more than enough yourselves, impart to them somewhat of your own comfortable means of subsistence. With respect also to wearing the round cap or habit at other times besides that of divine service, I think you ought not to contend more than is necessary; for superstition does not properly seem to have any thing to do therein. But in regard to the use of garments as *holy* in the ministry itself, seeing they have a resemblance to the mass, and are mere relics of popery, master Bullinger is of opinion that you should not use them, lest a thing that occasions offence may be sanctioned by your example. But though I have always been opposed to the use of ornaments of this kind, yet as I perceived the present danger of your being deprived of the office of preaching, and that there will perhaps be some hope that, like as altars and images have been removed, so

[1 There is no address to this letter, but it is acknowledged by Sampson in Letter XXVII. of the first series, p. 62.]

this resemblance of the mass may also be taken away, provided you and others who may obtain bishopricks, will direct all your endeavours to that object, (which would make less progress, should another succeed in your place, who not only might be indifferent about putting away those relics, but would rather defend, cherish, and maintain them;) therefore was I the slower in advising you rather to refuse a bishoprick, than to consent to the use of those garments. However, as I saw that offences of that kind must be altogether avoided, I easily fell into his opinion. But where altars and images are retained, I myself of my own accord maintain, as I have also written to you in another letter, that you must by no means officiate.

This is all that I can write upon the present subject. And you must take care on your part not to do any thing against your conscience. But I am afraid lest my letter should arrive too late, which fault however is none of mine, for I have not omitted any opportunity of writing. Lastly, I wish you to understand that questions of this kind are also full of difficulty to us here, and therefore advice cannot be so easily given. As to myself, when I was at Oxford, I would never wear the surplice in the choir, although I was a canon, and I had my own reasons for doing so. Wherefore I recommend you also to take advice upon the spot. I know that my example ought not to be considered sufficient to determine you; but that which then influenced me, influences me still, and perhaps also may influence you, namely, to do nothing which might give any sanction to what my conscience disapproves. You bade me write briefly, and I have briefly written. Take it in good part, pray for me, salute our friends. Master Bullinger salutes you, as doth also my wife, and Julius with his wife. Fare you well, my most loving brother and esteemed master in Christ. Zurich, Nov. 4, 1559.

[PETER MARTYR.]

LETTER XV.

JOHN CALVIN TO SIR WILLIAM CECIL.

Dated at GENEVA, [after *January* 29, 1559[1].]

THE messenger to whom I gave in charge my commentaries upon Isaiah to be presented to the most serene queen, brought me word that my homage was not kindly received by her majesty, because she had been offended with me by reason of some writings[2] published in this place. He also repeated to me, most illustrious sir, the substance of a conversation held by you, in which you seem to me more severe than was consistent with your courtesy, especially when you had been already assured by my letter, how much I promised myself from your regard towards me. But though sufficient reasons prevent me from vindicating myself by a serious discussion, yet lest I should seem by my silence to confess in some measure the consciousness of having done wrong, I have thought it right to state, in few words, how the matter stands. Two years ago John Knox[3] asked of me, in a private conversation, what I thought about the government of women. I candidly replied, that as it was a deviation from the original

[1] This letter seems to have been written after the one dated Jan. 29, 1559, in Calvin's letters, Ep. 275. The original is preserved in the archives of the church at Berne.]

[2] One of these was composed by John Knox, and printed at Geneva, in the reign of queen Mary, about the year 1556 or 1557, and entitled *The first blast against the monstrous regiment and empire of women.* The other was printed by Christopher Goodman in 1558, and bare this title; *How superior powers ought to be obeyed of their subjects, and wherein they may lawfully be disobeyed and resisted. Wherein also is declared the cause of all this present misery in England,* [namely, in queen Mary's time,] *and the only way to remedy the same.* See Strype, Annals, I. i. 177, &c. These books were answered by Aylmer, afterwards bishop of London, in a tract entitled "An Harborowe for faithful and trewe subjectes, against the late blowne blaste concerning the government of women," printed at Strasburgh, April 1559.]

[3] Cecil, writing to Sadler and Croft, says, "Of all others, Knoxees name, if it be not Goodmans, is most odiouse here; and therefore I wish no mention of hym hither." Sadler, I. 532.]

and proper order of nature, it was to be ranked, no less than
slavery, among the punishments consequent upon the fall of
man; but that there were occasionally women so endowed,
that the singular good qualities which shone forth in them,
made it evident that they were raised up by divine authority;
either that God designed by such examples to condemn the
inactivity of men, or for the better setting forth his own
glory. I brought forward Huldah and Deborah; and added,
that God did not vainly promise by the mouth of Isaiah, that
queens should be the nursing mothers of the church; by
which prerogative it is very evident that they are distinguished from females in private life. I came at length to
this conclusion, that since both by custom and public consent
and long practice it has been established, that realms and principalities may descend to females by hereditary right, it did
not appear to me necessary to move the question, not only
because the thing would be invidious, but because in my
opinion it would not be lawful to unsettle governments which
are ordained by the peculiar providence of God. I had no
suspicion of the book, and for a whole year was ignorant of
its publication. When I was informed of it by certain parties,
I sufficiently shewed my displeasure that such paradoxes
should be published; but as the remedy was too late, I
thought that the evil which could not now be corrected, should
rather be buried in oblivion than made a matter of agitation.
Inquire also of your father-in-law[4], what my reply was when
he informed me of the circumstance through Beza. And
Mary was still living, so that I could not be suspected of flattery. What the books contain, I cannot tell; but Knox himself will allow that my conversation with him was no other
than what I have now stated. But although I was moved
by the complaints of some godly men, yet, as I had not been
informed in time, I did not dare to make any decided opposition, lest greater confusion should ensue. If my easiness
has occasioned any offence, I think there would have been
just reason to fear, lest if the subject had been brought under
consideration, by reason of the thoughtless arrogance of one
individual, the wretched crowd of exiles would have been
driven away not only from this city, but even from almost

[4 Sir Antony Cook, whose daughter Mildred was married to Sir
William Cecil in 1546.]

the whole world; especially since the mischief could not now be remedied, otherwise than by applying a mitigation. I am indeed exceedingly and undeservedly grieved, in proportion to my surprise, that the ravings of others, as if on a studied pretext, should be charged upon me, to prevent my book from being accepted. If the offered present were not acceptable to the queen, she might have rejected it by a single word, and it would have been more candid to have done so. This certainly would have been more agreeable to myself, than to be burdened with false accusations, in addition to the ignominy of a repulse. However, I shall always reverence both the most serene queen, and shall not cease, most illustrious sir, to love and respect yourself also, for your most excellent disposition and your other virtues, although I have found you less friendly to me than I had hoped, and though you say nothing about mutual good-will for the time to come. From this however, I am unwilling to draw any unfavourable conclusion. Farewell, most accomplished and esteemed sir. May the Lord evermore be present with you, guide, protect, and enrich you with his gifts. Geneva. As I am in doubt whether my former letter has reached you, I have thought right to send you a copy.

[JOHN CALVIN.]

LETTER XVI.

FRANCIS, EARL OF BEDFORD, TO RODOLPH GUALTER.

Dated at LONDON, *Jan.* 21, 1560.

HEALTH in Christ. I received your[1] letter written to me last January, and choose rather to answer it in this present January than not at all; lest I should not only seem tardy in writing, but altogether unmindful of you, or forgetful of my duty in this respect. That it has not been performed sooner, you will interpret for the best, when you consider that we are separated by a very great distance,

[1 See above, Letter IV. p. 8.]

and cannot often light upon trustworthy persons to convey our letters to you. At length, however, to begin my reply, I would have you know, that the piety of your letter, the importance of your advice, your singular regard and sincere anxiety for our church, and the clear indication of your good-will towards myself, have been very gratifying to me; and I thank you for your commendation and counsel. I wish I could deserve the praises you bestow upon me as my applauder: I wish I were able to follow the counsel of my adviser as much as I desire to do; to act upon it, as well as keep it in my remembrance. I wish it were my happiness to behold our affairs in such a state as I desire, and as you recommend; we should then be in a far more prosperous as well as a more exalted condition. But your prudence is such, that you cannot be ignorant that the first beginning of nascent affairs is attended with the most difficulty, and that the wisest counsels are not immediately followed by a happy result, but that it is accomplished by degrees; and that religion, like every thing else, has crude and weak beginnings, as well as its increase, and progress, and maturity. And in reliance on a good hope, and reposing on the compassion of our most merciful God, I think that I can truly promise that this our religion, wounded and laid low as it were with a whirlwind by the tyranny of the time, and now, by God's blessing, again beginning in some measure to revive, will strike its roots yet deeper and deeper; and that which is now creeping on and advancing by little and little, will grow up with greater fruitfulness and verdure. As far as I can, I am exerting myself in this matter to the utmost of my poor abilities: others too are labouring for the same object, to which especially is directed the godly diligence of certain preachers, and particularly Jewel, now elected a bishop, and your friend Parkhurst; to both of whom, excited by your commendation of them, as well as by the report of their virtues, I am most favourably disposed, as I ought to be, and consider them deserving of the greatest honour and advancement. We have need of these and other artificers and architects to build up the church of God. We have need also of your assistance. We commend ourselves and our England to you, and to your godly prayers. Pray that God may build up this house, already begun, into a holy temple, to the glory of his name and the consolation of his people; and may he bless your pious labours. Farewell, most learned and courteous sir. Salute for me all my brethren in the Lord, to whom I wish every happiness. May Christ prosper your endeavours, that you may daily more and more exert yourselves to subvert and destroy the kingdom of Satan, the pomp of the world, and the power of antichrist, so that the church of Christ may be preserved among you and in all other places safe and unshaken. London, Jan. 21, 1560.

Yours heartily,

F. BEDFORD.

LETTER XVII.

PETER MARTYR TO [THOMAS SAMPSON[1].]

Dated at Zurich, *Feb.* 1, 1560.

GREETING. I have received, my very dear brother in Christ, and most honoured master, two letters from you at the same time, namely on the 24th of January; the one, dated in the month of October, the other in December. Wherefore you perceive how long they are in coming. I have already replied twice to your inquiries; but if my letters are intercepted, or are so long in reaching you, you must not charge me with neglect, but should rather lament the ill fortune of our letters than find fault with me as though I had discontinued my duty of writing. However, setting aside complaint, I come to the subjects upon which you require information. In the first place, I exhort you, by reason of the great want of ministers in your country, not to withdraw yourself from the function offered you: for if you, who are as it were pillars, shall decline taking upon yourselves the performance of ecclesiastical offices, not only will the churches be destitute of pastors, but you will give place to wolves and antichrists. By remaining without any office you will be so far from amending those

[1 See above, Letter XI. p. 25.]

things which you dislike, that you will hardly retain what is now conceded. But if you sit at the helm of the church, there is a hope that many things may be corrected, though not all. You say that they have taken away the church[2] lands; but consider that *you* have not alienated them. These things have been done without your concurrence, so that there is no blame in this respect to be laid upon you. Meanwhile, what income is left for the parochial clergy? They must be maintained by the bishops. In this matter we must put our trust in God, who will open some way, and point out some means for their support. He feedeth the fowls of the air, he clothes the lilies of the field; nor doth he ever forsake any one who is rightly walking in his vocation. But you must take heed lest you be thought by those who seek occasions against you, as though you had an eye to wealth and personal interest.

As to the square cap and external episcopal habit, I do not think there is need of much dispute, seeing it is unattended by superstition, and in that kingdom especially there may be a political reason for its use. Touching the garments which they call holy, I confess the case is somewhat more difficult, and one that troubles me not a little, so that I wonder they are so pertinaciously retained. For I should wish every thing to be done with the greatest possible simplicity. I think however that if peace could obtain between the churches of Saxony and our own with respect to doctrine, this sort of garments would never make a separation; for though we should by no means approve of them, we would nevertheless bear with them, congratulating ourselves upon our having got rid of them. You may therefore use those habits either in preaching, or in the administration of the Lord's supper, provided however you persist in speaking and teaching against the use of them. But I can never recommend any one, either when about to preach or to administer the Lord's supper, to have the image of the crucifix upon the table.

[2 The queen now (chiefly to gratify some of her courtiers) made exchanges with her bishops by the authority of a late act of parliament; taking to herself their ancient good manors and lordships, and making over to them in exchange tithes and impropriations. Strype, Grindal, 42.]

As touching the correction of the papists for things past, you must remember that punishments have been more than once discontinued for the sake of peace; and that an amnesty hath sometimes been granted in the church, and that heretics have been received with their former honours and dignities, provided only they would subscribe unto sound religion. Care however must be taken by you, that in future they do nothing in opposition to the religion now received. But as to those who are presented to you by their patrons to be promoted by reason of advowsons, such persons ought not to be instituted by you without subscribing to the religion which is now established; which if they will not do, I think you are at liberty to reject them.

With regard to the unleavened bread which is used at the holy Supper, none of our churches, as you are well aware, have any contention about it, nay, indeed, they all every where make use of it. And whereas you write that very many persons are offended with the episcopal habits and the holy garments, as they call them, I can easily believe it. But you will avoid all blame in this matter, if you will shew in your sermons that they are also offensive to yourselves, and if you will endeavour by every means in your power that they may sometime be laid aside. But concerning those processions in Rogation-week, which seem to have been derived from the Ambarvalia[1] of the heathen, I scarcely know what I can rightly advise you. This I say, that superstition is altogether to be avoided. But if in these processions only prayer is made to God, that he will graciously supply us with new fruits, and grant us a good use of them, and thanks be given at the same time for the sustenance of the year preceding, superstitions perhaps will seem to have been sufficiently avoided: although both magistrates and people should be instructed against such ceremonies, and every effort must be made to get rid of them as relics of the Amorites.

These were the things, my brother, that I had to write at present. May God either commend these to your judgment, or suggest better! Upon the whole matter I have conferred with Master Bullinger, who both gives his assent,

[1 The Ambarvalia were solemn processions in honour of Ceres. See Virg. Georg. I. 338, &c.]

and sends you his hearty salutations. My wife too, with Julius and Anna, desire their commendations to you and all yours. Zurich, February, 1560.

Yours wholly,

PETER MARTYR.

LETTER XVIII.

BISHOP COX TO GEORGE CASSANDER.

Dated at Ely House, LONDON, *March* 4, 1560.

WERE I to attempt, my very dear friend in Christ, to enumerate all your friendly offices towards me, I should indeed labour to no purpose. Meanwhile, you must know that they are treasured up in the inmost recesses of my heart, as obligations which it will be impossible for me ever to forget. After it seemed good to our Lord, on whose providence we evermore depend, to recall me to my country, I left Worms among the foremost [of the exiles] and went to Cologne, in the hope of meeting both Cassander and Cornelius, and of bidding them farewell; but I could find neither of them. From thence I proceeded straight to England, where, thank God, since the death of Mary, every thing is quiet. Elizabeth, the lover and patron of godliness, is on the throne, and by her the popish superstition is driven away, the gospel of Christ re-established, the popish clergy banished, the shepherds of Christ restored. The Lord grant that we may shew forth our profession of the gospel of Christ by a life worthy of the gospel, lest hereafter a worse thing happen to us! There is no open quarrel, but yet there does not exist an entire agreement among us with respect to setting up the crucifix[2] in churches, as had heretofore been the practice. Some think it allowable, provided only that no worship or veneration be paid to the image itself: others are of opinion,

[2 See first series, Letter XXVIII. p. 66, and Letter XXIX. p. 67.]

that all images are so universally forbidden, that it is altogether sinful for any to remain in churches, by reason of the danger so inseparably annexed to them. But we are in that state, that no crucifix is now-a-days to be seen in any of our churches. As I have always deferred very much to your judgment, I earnestly request you to be so kind as briefly to let me know your opinion upon this subject. I have nothing at this time worth writing to you about, except that our neighbours, the Scots, are under some apprehension from France, those especially who embrace the gospel, and who form a tolerably large proportion of the population. We must pray the Lord to vouchsafe to be on their side. I should be rejoiced to hear, on account of the respect I bear him, that your Duke is promoting the true religion of Christ in spite of all the papists. Farewell in Christ, my very dear Cassander, and salute your most faithful Achates, and my beloved masters Gerard the merchant, John and Gualter Gymnicus and Ambrosius, of Duisburg. From the city of London in England, at my house in Holborn. March 4, 1560.

Your much attached,

RICHARD COX,

Bishop of Ely.

LETTER XIX.

GEORGE CASSANDER TO BISHOP COX.

Dated at [Worms, 1560.]

I HAVE received from you, reverend sir, a letter[1] written at London on the 4th of March; the reason of my tardy and brief reply to which has been a severe illness, which attacked me shortly after the receipt of it, and from which I have hardly yet begun to recover. I was glad to hear of your

[1 See the preceding letter.]

advancement to the dignity, or rather the work and office, of
a bishop; and I pray God to grant you his Spirit, by whose
aid you may fulfil that office to your own salvation and the
edification of the flock committed to your charge. And I
thank you too, that notwithstanding your elevation to so great
a dignity, you have not been unmindful of my inferiority
and lowliness; and I willingly accepted your little present of
two crowns, which were inclosed in the letter, as a token of
our former intimacy.

I understand that you are not altogether agreed among
yourselves with respect to the setting up the image of the
cross or the crucifix in the church; but I do not sufficiently
understand whether the question refers to the mere figure of
a cross, or also to the image of Christ hanging upon it. I
have seen here a certain print, which contained a cross only
in the middle, with some texts of holy scripture in the
English language written on each side; whence I suspect
that your question only refers to the figure of the cross.
But I acknowledge your modesty in requesting my opinion
upon this matter: for when you abound in so many copious
fountains yourselves, why should you drink water from so
insignificant and turbid a streamlet? As however you desire
it, I will briefly declare my sentiments. Your excellence is
aware, in what frequent use and in what great esteem the
figure of the cross was held among the early Christians;
insomuch that it was every where placed and represented in
their buildings, sacred and profane, public and private; and
this too before the practice of setting up other images in the
churches, whether of Christ himself, or of the saints, had
come into use; that on the destruction of all monuments of
idolatry, by which every thing was defiled, the figure of the
cross, which was as it were a sacred symbol of Christianity,
succeeded under better auspices into their place. And like
as the word *cross* in the writings of the evangelists and
apostles mystically signifies the passion, death, and triumph
of Christ, and the afflictions of the saints; so also by the
figure of the cross every where set up, and meeting the eye,
they intended all these things to be set forth, as it were by
a mystic symbol, and infixed in men's minds: wherefore they
made a great distinction between the figure or representation
of the cross, and all other images. Upon which subject you

may see Charlemagne[1], Lib. ii. c. xxviii. against the synod of
the Greeks: "for in the latter there is a simple and bare
signification, while in the former there is a secret and mys-
tical representation." Whence it was not regarded as a bare
sign, but as a kind of mystery; so that it was not only represented substantially and by painting, both in churches
and other buildings, and upon the walls of houses, but was
also frequently signed by the hand upon the forehead and
breast: to which fact the most ancient ecclesiastical writers,
both Greek and Latin, unanimously bear witness. This observance therefore, as it is of the greatest antiquity throughout all churches, I am unwilling should be regarded as
superstitious, though I would have the superstition of the
people, which is commonly discovered even in the most
excellent regulations and institutions, to be repressed and
guarded against; and this seems to have been your object
in that representation which I saw here.

But take it, I pray you, in good part, if I freely state
what I consider wanting in it. First of all, in representing
this figure of the cross, I could wish that regard were had
to the appearance and form of its archetype, that is, of the
true cross on which our Saviour was offered; which also, were
it attended to in other images of illustrious and holy men,
would occasion less inconvenience: namely, that they might
be preserved and looked upon only as memorials, in the same
manner as we see at this day the effigies of the Roman
emperors and other illustrious personages preserved in
medals. Moreover, it is evident what was the form of the
cross, both from some ancient images and statues, some of
which I have seen, and very clearly from that most ancient
writer Irenæus[2], and a more recent one, Gregory of Tours;

[1] The title of this chapter is, " Quanta ratione mysterium dominicæ crucis ab imaginibus distet, quas quidem illi eidem æquiparare
contendunt." One sentence from this chapter may be quoted: Non
ergo per materiales ab opificibus conditas imagines, sed per crucis
mysterium, quæ a Judæis putatur scandalum, a gentibus stultitia, su-
perba sæculi et inflata sapientia corruit. Nec per picturam quandam,
sed per crucem patuit, quod stultum Dei est, quanto sit hominibus
sapientius, et quod infirmum Dei est, quanto sit fortius hominibus.
Caroli M. de impio imaginum cultu. Lib. iv. Hanoveræ, 1731.]

[2] Irenæus was born A.D. 140, and suffered martyrdom A.D. 202.
Gregory of Tours was born A.D. 543, and died A.D. 595.]

and which is also supported by the reason of the thing itself. For how, I ask, could it be possible for a human body, weighed down at the approach of death, and hanging down in a stretched out position, not to tear asunder by its bulk and weight the palms of the hands that were nailed to the cross? And the possibility of this occurrence was so provided for, that about the middle of the standing and upright post there was let in a little board, upon which rested the feet of the person doomed to this punishment; and the nails were fastened in such a way that the appearance was not so much that of a man hanging as one standing. The words of Irenæus are plain. "The form of the cross," he says, "has five ends and extremities, two in the length, two in the breadth, and one in the middle, upon which the person who is fastened with the nails rests his weight." To this entirely agrees Gregory of Tours. "The reason therefore," says he, "that there were four nails in our Lord's cross is this: two were fastened to his hands, and two to the soles of his feet; and the question is, why the feet were nailed, which in the holy cross rather seemed to hang down than to stand. But it is evident that an opening was made in the upright post, and that the end of a small board was let in to this opening, and upon this board were nailed the sacred feet, as it were those of one in a standing posture[3]." I have seen representations of a cross of this kind of a considerable size, not only some pourtrayed many years ago in this country, but also a very remarkable one painted in the remotest part of Armenia, and which an Armenian priest used to carry about with him in his prayer-book, described in the language and characters of his nation; in all which figures a little board of this kind was evidently jutting out, according to the description of Irenæus

[3 Irenæus, cont. Hæres. Lib. ii. c. 24. Ipse habitus crucis fines et summitates habet quinque, duos in longitudine, et duos in latitudine, et unum in medio, ubi requiescit qui clavis affigitur. Greg. Turon. de Glor. Mart. Lib. i. cap. 6. Clavorum ergo Dominicorum gratia, quod quatuor fuerint hæc est ratio: duo sunt affixi in palmis, et duo in plantis, et quæritur cur plantæ affixæ sint, quæ in cruce sancta dependere visa sunt potius quam stare. Sed in stipite erecto foramen factum manifestum est. Pes quoque parvulæ tabulæ in hoc foramen insertus est. Super hanc vero tabulam tanquam stantis hominis sacræ affixæ sunt plantæ.]

and Gregory of Tours : which things, although some persons
may deem them too trifling, I do not think will be displeasing to others who have a regard for what is decent.

Another point that I propose to lay before you, is,
whether it would not be more suitable, if, instead of those
texts of scripture with which you have surrounded and
fenced on all sides that figure of the cross, there were written
such texts as explain the mystery and hidden signification of
it ; which are both sufficiently numerous in the writings of the
new testament, and exceedingly well adapted to the instruction
of the people, and contain the whole mystery both of our
redemption by Christ and of our regeneration in Christ. Of
which kind are those in the second chapter of the Epistle to
the Colossians [vv. 13—15.] *And you, being dead in sins
and the uncircumcision of your flesh, hath he quickened together with him, having forgiven you all trespasses; blotting
out the hand-writing of ordinances that was against us,
which was contrary to us, and took it out of the way, nail-
ing it to his cross ; and having spoiled principalities and
powers, he made a shew of them openly, triumphing over
them in himself.* Also in chap. i. [vv. 18—20.] *And he,*
that is, the Son of God, *is the head of the body, the church;
who is the beginning, the first-born from the dead, that in
all things he might have the pre-eminence : for it pleased
[the Father] that in him should all fulness dwell, and
making peace through the blood of his cross, by him to reconcile all things unto himself, whether they be things in
earth, or things in heaven.* And in Gal. vi. [14.] *But
God forbid that I should glory, save in the cross of our
Lord Jesus Christ, by which the world is crucified unto me,
and I unto the world.* And 1 Cor. i. [17.] *Lest the cross
of Christ should be made of none effect.* Gal. ii. [19.]
*For I through the law am dead to the law, that I might
live unto God. I am crucified with Christ.* And Matt.
x. [38.] *He that taketh not his cross, and followeth
after me, is not worthy of me.* And chap. xvi. [24.] *If
any man will come after me, let him deny himself, and take
up his cross, and follow me.* These and similar texts would
instruct the people in the true use of the mystery of the
cross : but this you will with your wisdom determine better
than I can. I should be very indiscreet in thus pretending

to teach you, did I not think it improper for me not to declare in some way or other my respect for you. You will, I doubt not, receive this my rude and unpolished writing with the same modesty and courtesy with which you have written to me. Farewell.

[GEORGE CASSANDER.]

LETTER XX.

PETER MARTYR TO [THOMAS SAMPSON[1].]

Dated [at ZURICH,] *March* 20, 1560.

GREETING. I have not replied before to the letter that you wrote to me on the sixth of January, because I did not receive it until the first of March, and at Zurich couriers are not easily to be met with. Now you must be persuaded of this, that those things which grieve you and others like you, do also very much grieve both myself and my brethren. But I do not think it worth while to reply to your questions a second time, because I suppose all my letters have reached you, in which I gave such answer as I was able, though perhaps not such as the subject required, or so much as you yourself wished for : nevertheless I said what then seemed to be to the purpose. The things which you fear, we can avert from you no otherwise than by our prayers, which, believe me, we diligently offer and will continue to do. Finally, to come to your last question; to have the image of the crucifix upon the holy table at the administration of the Lord's supper, I do not count among things indifferent, nor would I recommend any man to distribute the sacraments with that rite. But you, who are in the very midst of the contest, must not expect counsel from hence, as we are at so great a distance from you : you must take counsel on the field of contest itself. A calling is not rashly to be thrown

[1 Strype (Life of Grindal, 47) refers to this letter as addressed to Bishop Grindal; but it rather seems to have been written in reply to that of Sampson, printed in the first series, Letter XXVII. p. 62.]

away, nor yet to be undertaken with injury to the truth.
The sum of the matter is, that the worshipping of images
must in no wise be tolerated. Neither master Bullinger
nor myself count such things as matters of indifference,
but we reject them as forbidden. Unless however you are
driven to this strait, do not refuse the ministry that is offered you.

As to writing a letter to the queen upon this matter, you
must understand that I am now so overwhelmed with business, that were I ever so willing, I should not have it in
my power. For I have been the sole lecturer in the school
for nearly two months, the reason of which there is no occasion to commit to writing. Besides this, I do not think that
any letter of mine will have much weight. I have already
written twice, publicly and privately, and have been unable
to discover whether my letters were received. Moreover,
if, as it is reported, it be the determination of your countrymen to embrace the Confession of Augsburgh, and court an
alliance with the [German[1]] protestants, you may judge for
yourself in what esteem my letters, and the letters of those
like me, will be held. The only thing I can do, I will not fail
to do; namely, to pray that your state and church, together
with your most serene queen, may flourish in all happiness.

I have communicated your letter, as you wished me,
to master Bernardine. He is in a weak state of health, both
through old age and the diseases incident to that time of life:
yet he did not decline the office of writing [to the queen[2],]
but promises to do so as soon as he is able. As to Bullinger,
I have no doubt but that he will write, for he is exceedingly
zealous in this matter; but though he has read your letter,
he has not yet pointed out any suggestions that I can inform
you of. But you are indeed wonderful people. You pay no
attention to the *public* letter of the Swiss, nay, you do not
even answer it: how much notice, I pray you, will *private*
letters obtain from you? But keep these things to yourself,
and do not send any answer to them, for fear the letter should
be lost or intercepted. Farewell. Master Bullinger, all our
fellow-ministers, my wife, Julius and his wife, salute you.

[1 The German protestants retained the crucifix in their churches.
Strype, Grindal, 48. See above, p. 17, note 5.]

[2 See first series, Letter XXVII.]

A son was born to me on the second of March, and died on the tenth. Salute all your friends in my name, and cease not to love your Martyr. March 20, 1560.

Yours wholly,

PETER MARTYR.

LETTER XXI. [Extract.]

NICOLAS GALLASIUS[3] TO JOHN CALVIN.

Dated at LONDON, *June* 30, 1560.

I WAITED upon the bishop, by whom I was received very courteously. I presented to him, my father, your letter, which he read in my presence with an open and cheerful countenance, and forthwith briefly related to me its contents; expressing his thanks to you for having written to him in so friendly a manner, and also for reminding him of his duty. He then accosted the elders who had accompanied me to his residence, to some of whom my arrival was by no means agreeable, and exhorted them not to be ungrateful to God and you, since they had obtained more than they had dared to hope for; that they should follow my recommendations, and henceforth act in all circumstances by my advice, and

[3 Nicolas des Gallars was recommended by Calvin to be minister to the French congregation in London, at the desire of Grindal, bishop of London, that he would send over some honest able person for that place. Strype, Cranmer, 594. The following extract, taken verbatim from the original document in the archives of Geneva, refers to this subject: "Apres le deces de la Royne Mariè d'Angleterre, et a l'advenement de Elizabeth sa sœur, les persecutions y cesserent et y eut quelque liberté pour les Chrestiens. L'Eglise de Londres requist a Geneve ung ministre pour redresser l'estat nagueres ruyne, et obtint Nicolas des Gallars. Alors s'en departirent les Angloys de Geneve, ayans pris humble congé de la Seigneurie, le 30 de May 1560, et presenté ung livre de leurs noms et de leurs enfans, pour estre a tousjours retenus au debvoir qu'ils avoient a la ville. Car les ungs avoient acquis le droict de bourgeoysie, et tous ensemble se estoient honnestement portez. Les Ecossois aussi s'en allerent en leur pays, ou l'Evangile commençoit aussi à florir." Chroniques de Roset, Liv. VI. Chap. 58.]

shew themselves friendly towards me, and admonish the whole
church of their duty towards me. Then turning to me apart,
he offered me his good offices, and that I might have familiar
access to him as often as I wished. I requested that all matters in our church might be determined by his authority, by
which means our people would be more effectually kept to
their duty; and that he would be pleased to be present, or
rather to preside, at the reading of your letter to them. He
replied, that in this matter he resigned all his authority to
myself, but that he would willingly attend if he could be of
any use. He afterwards added something about appointing
as my colleague Peter Alexander[1], who was acceptable to the
people, and had begun to gather a church before my arrival;
and who was the more acceptable, because he neither required
any salary, nor was likely to become a burden to what is
now a poor and necessitous church; for he has a valuable
prebend at Canterbury, the revenue of which he could easily
receive during his absence under the plea of this appointment. I replied that I would farther deliberate and confer
with him upon this matter, but that I would take no steps
without consulting him[2].

[1 Peter Alexander of Arles was entertained in the family of archbishop Cranmer from the year 1547, and so forward for some years,
till he became a prebendary of Canterbury, and had also the living of
Allhallows, Lombard Street, conferred upon him by the said archbishop. He was afterwards divorced from his wife by queen Mary's
commissioners, and fled over to Strasburgh, and became minister of
the French church there. See Strype, Mem. II. i. 321.]

[2 The above extract contains all that relates to England. There
are at Zurich several very long letters written by Gallasius, relating,
however, principally to the dissensions caused by Alexander in the
French church in London, and referring repeatedly to the interposition of the bishop on his behalf.]

LETTER XXII[3].

BISHOP GRINDAL TO CONRAD HUBERT.
Dated at LONDON, *Oct.* 13, 1560.

GREETING. I send you at last, most courteous Hubert, the promised account of the exhumation[4] of Bucer and Fagius, which I have caused to be carefully drawn up by a certain learned man, who was a spectator of the whole tragedy. Many reasons have occasioned me to be thus late in performing my promise. They have arisen, partly, from my official engagements, which, in this restoration of evangelical doctrine that, by the goodness of God, we have lately accomplished through the instrumentality of our most illustrious queen, have been numerous and important; and partly, from the opportunity embraced by the university of Cambridge[5] of restoring the reputation, as they call it, of masters Bucer and Fagius by a public and solemn decree. For I was loth that there should go forth any testimony of my country's ingratitude and cruelty towards the remains of Bucer, (although it was oppressed at that time by the tyranny of the Romanists,) before the memorial of its gratitude and affection. You

[3 The original of this letter is preserved in the archives of St Thomas at Strasburgh.]

[4 See above, p. 24.]

[5 Archbishop Parker, Bishop Grindal, and Dr Haddon, by virtue of power committed to them by the queen, wrote letters to the Vice-Chancellor, Dr Andrew Pern, and the rest of the University of Cambridge, to restore Martin Bucer and Paul Fagius, deceased in that university, to their due honour. The said letters being read in the senate, it was asked, *Placetne vobis ut gradus et honoris titulus, quæ olim Martino Bucero et P. Fagio publicis hujus academiæ suffragiis adempta erant, eisdem in integrum restituantur, et omnes actus contra eos aut eorum doctrinam rescindantur?* which they all agreed to. This was done July 22; and on the 30th Dr Acworth, the public orator, made an oration publicly in St Mary's in honour of these learned men; which done, Dr James Pilkington preached from the 112th Psalm. See Pilkington's Works, Parker Society's Edition, p. 651, Strype, Parker, I. 170, and Historia de obitu Buceri, &c. appended to Buceri Scripta Anglicana, Basil. 1577, p. 935, &c.]

4—2

have therefore not only the account of the exhumation of
Bucer, but also that of his restoration and in some.measure
his revival.   I send you likewise, by way of appendix, some
writings of Bucer himself, which had hitherto lain unnoticed
among the papers of the most reverend Archbishop of Canterbury, and which he has given me for this purpose.

Salute, I pray you, in my name your whole college, both
of ministers and professors ; especially masters Marpach, John
Sturmius, Zanchius, Andernach, and Sebald.   Commend to
God in your prayers our churches, now again becoming united
in Christ their head.   Both I myself, and all the rest of us,
who were received there with so much kindness and hospitality during the time of our exile, pray for every blessing
and happiness to the state of Strasburgh, and are prepared
to shew every manifestation of gratitude in our turn, if we
can any way be of use to it.   Salute likewise my very
courteous host, master James Heldelin, the minister at Was-
selheim, together with his most excellent wife.   May the
Lord preserve you all, and guide you by his Spirit!   Amen.
Dated at London, Oct. 13, 1560.

Your much attached in Christ,

EDMUND GRINDAL,

Bishop of London.

I have sent, for the most part, the originals themselves.
Should there be any errors either in the arrangement or
orthography, you will use your own judgment in correcting
them.

LETTER XXIII.

RODOLPH GUALTER TO FRANCIS LORD RUSSEL.

Dated at ZURICH, *March* 16, 1561.

GRACE and peace from God the Father through Jesus
Christ.   The letter, most illustrious prince, which your
clemency wrote to me on the twenty-first of January[1] last

[1 See above, Letter XVI. p. 36.]

year, has been delivered into my hands. It was on many
accounts exceedingly gratifying to me, both as affording a
clear evidence of your truly pious and christian mind, and
also as presenting such an account of the general state of
religion among you, as could not but be most delightful to all
who wish well to England in particular, and generally to the
church at large. But although I have always felt desirous
of replying to your letter, I have deferred doing so even to
this day, because I considered it unbecoming in me to interrupt your clemency, occupied as you are in far more important
engagements, with a letter of so little consequence. But now
the bearer of this[2], John Henry Fabricius, gives me an opportunity of writing. He is of honourable extraction, and a
youth of good disposition and of great promise. His father
is a man of the highest authority in our republic, and the
chief standard-bearer, as they call it. After having first
provided for the care and instruction of his son at my house
for three whole years, he sent him into France to carry on
his literary pursuits in that country. After a short time he
was placed at court by the king of Navarre, where, among
other noble youths, he was at first in the service of the queen,
and afterwards in that of the king himself; and at length,
after the completion of the time that young men of that
rank are usually employed, he was honourably dismissed.
His father however, thinking that on account of his son's
age, it will be to his disadvantage to keep him at home,
and knowing that the courts of the German princes are full
of drunken and debauched characters, by intercourse with
whom youths even of the best disposition are more likely to
be corrupted than benefited, has determined, upon my advice,
and especially upon that of master Bullinger, to send him to
England, if he may by any possibility obtain a situation either
with your clemency, or the queen's most serene majesty, or
with any other godly nobleman. He has a fair knowledge
of Latin, and has made greater progress both in speaking
and writing French, than a native of Germany can easily
expect. He has learned all the duties of a life at court, and
possesses such talent and activity, that we hope his services
will neither be unpleasing nor unprofitable to any one who
may think fit to receive him. We desire however most

[2 See first series, Letter XLVI. p. 108.]

especially to commend him to your clemency, because we have great expectations from you, and are aware that you possess extensive influence with the queen's majesty and the other nobility of the realm.   And if your exceeding kindness will allow us to do so, we entreat you again and again to consider this excellent youth as commended to your good offices.   For thus you will not only do a kindness to that most worthy man, his father, but will also bind to you, by no common obligation, the whole state of Zurich, in which, if he live, he will one day hold an important post.   May God the Father of mercy guide your clemency by his Spirit, and evermore preserve and confirm you in the knowledge of his Son Jesus Christ!   Amen.   Dated at Zurich, March 16, in the year of the incarnation of Christ, 1561.

[RODOLPH GUALTER.]

LETTER XXIV.

FRANCIS, EARL OF BEDFORD, TO RODOLPH GUALTER.

'Dated at LONDON, *June* 16, 1561.

MUCH health.   So great was the kindness of you all towards me when I was in your country, and especially that of yourself and master Bullinger, that I shall not consider myself to have conferred, but to have received a favour, whenever it may be in my power to oblige you in any matter.   The young man[1] whom you recommended to me I have placed in the service of her serene majesty's vice-chamberlain[2], a pious and influential personage.   I hope therefore that he is honourably provided for.   Meanwhile, should any thing occur to him, wherein he may be profited by my assistance, I shall not be wanting; and I desire you to be assured that the same assistance will always be at the service both of yourself and your church at large.

[1 John Henry Fabricius.   See the preceding letter.]
[2 This was Sir Francis Knowles, who had been an exile at Frankfort in queen Mary's time, and was afterwards vice-chamberlain, and captain of the guard, and one of the privy council to queen Elizabeth.]

You will learn from Julius[3] a full and detailed account of the state of our affairs, so that I will not dwell upon them at this present time. Meanwhile, may you, with all pious persons, be well and happy, and make use of me as your friend as often as occasion shall arise. London, June 16, 1561.

Your piety's and learning's most devoted,

F. BEDFORD.

LETTER XXV.

RICHARD MASTERS TO RODOLPH GUALTER.

Dated at the Palace, GREENWICH near London, *June* 16, [1561.]

IMMEDIATELY after the coronation[4] of our most illustrious queen I received your letter[5], most beloved Gualter, by the hands of our friend Parkhurst on his return to us from Zurich. I wrote in reply not long after, but my lettter was sent to Antwerp; and, as I am given to understand after a year's interval, it was lost in the sea, and the bearer of it was drowned likewise. I was not in truth so much grieved at the loss, as apprehensive that from my not having answered your letter after so long a silence between us, you would accuse me of having slighted your friendship; as indeed you might have done with reason, had not this just ground of excuse acquitted me of the charge. Burcher increased my apprehension, and Julius confirmed it, each of them coming over to us from Zurich without bringing me a letter. But do not, I pray you, my Gualter, entertain so unfavourable an opinion of me. For it has always been my nature so much to dread the charge of neglected friendship, that I would rather choose to run into the contrary extreme. Nor do I

[3 Julius Santerentianus, the friend and attendant of Peter Martyr, was now on a visit to England, and about to return to Zurich. See first series, Letters XL. and XLI.]

[4 Queen Elizabeth was crowned Jan. 15, 1559.]

[5 See above, Letter V. p. 11.]

think there is any one who has just reason to complain of me in this particular. For why should I slight that which is acquired in an honourable way? And I would rather embrace, and reverence, and all but superstitiously cultivate such a friendship as literary pursuits and moral integrity (which are the two closest bonds of friendship) produce, increase, and uninterruptedly preserve with persons like yourself, that is, with learned and worthy men. I pray you to consider that I am yours, and that you and every thing belonging to you are most delightful to me, and cherished as they ought to be. And this, should I be able to oblige you in any way, you shall find in fact to be the case. For I am not different from what I used to be, when during my residence at Oxford I enjoyed your most delightful intimacy and agreeable conversation, what time true religion was at its lowest ebb.

With respect to your letter, I most solemnly assure you, that it was shewn to our queen that, taught by the misfortunes of others, she might perceive again and again what advice she might derive from it for the establishment of the true religion, and the avoiding of a mixed one; and I took care that it should be shewn to those of our nobility whom I knew to be ready to promote what you piously recommended. But as I have a living epistle in Julius, there is no occasion to tell you the result. I doubt not but that our gracious God will bring to a happy maturity what has been successfully begun; and this let us entreat in our common prayers. Farewell, and be assured that there is no one who wishes you more abundant and greater blessings, and who, in short, loves and esteems you more heartily than Masters. Once more, and a thousand times, farewell. From the court at Greenwich near London, June 16, [1561.]

Yours heartily as though I were

Your brother,

RICHARD MASTERS.

LETTER XXVI.

PETER MARTYR TO A VERY HONOURABLE NOBLEMAN[1] IN ENGLAND.

Dated at ZURICH, *July* 22, 1561.

FOR very many and great causes, most noble prince, I am exceedingly bound unto your highness. For you bear such regard towards me, a humble and obscure individual, whom you scarcely once saw in England, as that you have now entertained with singular courtesy and benevolence my attendant Julius, and have shewn him no ordinary, but very great kindness in the management of his business; for which cause I am exceedingly thankful to your highness. And besides this, you have written me a letter: a letter, shall I say? yea, rather praises and commendations both of my learning and virtues, which although I do not acknowledge that I possess, yet I could not but rejoice in your good opinion, because I understood it as a most certain testimony of your love and good-will towards me; nor can I consider myself as being loved by you for any other reason, than for the sake of godliness and religion. I forbear to mention the singular desire that you manifest for my return to England, and which you affirm to be shared by pious and learned men in common with yourself. But how great a favour is it, that you have suggested to the queen's majesty the expediency of my recall, and have interested her in my favour! In fine, you have promised to afford me every kindness and comfort in your power, and have expressed the reasons, and those very honourable to you, of this your regard, namely, the love

[1 This nobleman is supposed by Strype to have been Thomas, duke of Norfolk, at the instigation of his tutor, John Foxe. This endeavour, he adds, of getting Martyr into England proceeded, no question, from an order made by the archbishop and bishops at Lambeth, where they sat by commission: which was, to raise a contribution out of their own revenues for learned strangers to be placed readers in the universities, both for their stipends, and for the defraying of their expenses in their journey. Ann. I. i. 381.]

of your country, and exceeding anxiety for the advancement
of God's word. Who can help loving such a prince? Indeed
I should be devoid of godliness, not to say of common courtesy, should I ever forget so much good-will and so many
benefits. I will therefore endeavour, and this by every means
in my power, that they may never escape my memory.

But now as touching my return to England, although I
am unable to answer as I could earnestly desire, do you,
most noble prince, with your usual kindness, take in good
part what I write in reply. First of all, I would not have
you think that I have any thing more at heart, than the
solid and firm well-being of England in the Lord. Wherefore I could desire even now, no less than I did in times
past, to promote the interests and edification thereof, and
to do what would be both acceptable and profitable to your
kingdom and church. But at this present time, such is the
situation in which I am placed, that I am engaged to the
state and church at Zurich, and am not therefore my own
master. I have therefore inquired the opinion and inclination
as well of the magistrates, as of my fellow-ministers upon this
matter. And indeed I found in them a singular zeal and
most ready mind to satisfy your desire. For you must not
think any thing more acceptable to, or desired by them,
than that the truth of the gospel may be spread abroad as
far as possible. But on the other hand, they no less prudently than lovingly take into consideration my constitution,
state, and age; and are somewhat apprehensive lest, burdened as I am and in some measure broken with age, I
should be unable to bear the fatigue of the journey, which
is rather long, variable, and not every where without difficulty. They see moreover that no small danger is to be
apprehended in different places on the route; and they consider too, that I am called forth to much more severe labours
than I undergo in this place. Wherefore they think it very
likely that I shall be unable to serve either them or you;
and are therefore of opinion that it is much better for me to
remain here, where by teaching, writing, and publishing my
commentaries, I may be of use both to them and you, and
others, according to my ability.

But in this double kind of answer, the first part seems
to me to have the nearest approach to the truth; for I am

myself also afraid of being unable to endure the journey and labours. But in the other part I think that they are themselves mistaken, who judge that I can be of so much use by remaining quiet in this country; for they make much more account of my lucubrations than they deserve. Aware as I am of the little pretensions I have to learning, I agree with them to remain here solely on account of the first reason assigned. For I am easily led to believe that I shall be so liable to be weakened and broken up by the labours of the journey, as to be rendered altogether unprofitable. Wherefore I entreat your highness first of all, and next those godly and learned men, to accept of my good-will in a case where, by reason of my infirmity, they cannot obtain the object itself that they desire to be accomplished. For necessity is a hard weapon, the striving against which seems to be nothing less than tempting God. But I would have you, right honourable prince, remember in the mean time, that in whatever part of the world I may be placed, I shall ever be most beholden to your highness. And I entreat you in my turn, not only to retain your love to your country and zeal for the advancement of religion, but to endeavour daily more and more to increase the same in your christian heart; whereby the wings of the gospel of the Son of God, which were formerly cut short, may grow again, and so grow, that it may swiftly and with abundant fruit pervade all your provinces, cities, and towns. Assuredly, if you shall continue to be inflamed with this double care, according as you have begun, both almighty God will approve you, and all discreet and godly men will honour you as a worthy citizen and a profitable prince. May God long preserve you in health and happiness through Christ! Given at Zurich, July 22, 1561.

[PETER MARTYR.]

LETTER XXVII.

RODOLPH GUALTER TO FRANCIS, EARL OF BEDFORD.

Dated at ZURICH, *Aug.* 26, 1561.

I REJOICE greatly that my letter of recommendation of John Henry Fabricius was acceptable to your clemency. He certainly extols, in the highest terms, the kindness of your clemency towards himself, and your favourable inclination towards us all; for which reason he seems worthy of the continuance of your clemency's regard and patronage. I have informed his father, a person of the highest authority among us, of the great regard and favour with which you honour him; and he has requested me in his name to present his best acknowledgements to your clemency. We will all of us take care, should an opportunity arise, that you may not seem to have conferred a benefit upon those who are ungrateful. We have learned from our townsman Julius, that your England is happy and flourishing, both as to religion and in all other respects; and we pray God, the Father of our Lord Jesus Christ, that he may continue to carry on with his favour what is well begun, to the desired end and the glory of his name. The Roman antichrist[1] is urging the continuance of the council of Trent, and has on his side both sovereigns and princes of no small influence. But Christ the Lord, to whom all power is given in heaven and earth, is stronger than they all. He beholds the attempts of those who take counsel against him, and laughs them to scorn from on high, as David witnesseth in the Psalms. I forbear to write more, for fear of longer detaining your clemency, who is occupied in numerous and more important engagements. May God the Father of mercy direct you with his Spirit, and continually preserve and confirm you in the knowledge of his Son Jesus Christ! Amen. Dated at Zurich, Aug. 26, 1561.

[RODOLPH GUALTER.]

[1 Namely, Pius IV., who re-assembled the council of Trent in 1561.]

LETTER XXVIII.

_____

RICHARD MASTERS TO RODOLPH GUALTER.

Dated at LONDON, _Feb._ 22, 1562.

HEALTH in the Lord always. Before I received your letter, most learned Gualter, written in favour of that excellent young man Henry Fabricius, what services I offered him on his first arrival in this country, both for your sake, and that of your friends, I will not now relate, but he will tell you in person on his return: nevertheless, to confess the truth, I did not then understand that you felt any greater interest on his behalf, than you would for any other inhabitant of Zurich. But as soon as I perceived by your letter how dear he was to you, I again called upon him with all diligence, and made every inquiry which I thought might be of use to him; and encouraged him as earnestly as I could to let me know if there were any thing of which he stood in need, and in which I could oblige him: and I promised not to be wanting to him in any respect, so that he might have at his service even my own house, or whatever else I had it in my power to offer. But he declined all my services, being a youth of extreme modesty, and declared that he was not in want of any thing. I then began to inquire into the reason of his not residing with the earl of Bedford. He tells me that his lordship had placed him with master Knowles, the vice-chamberlain, a truly pious man and one of her majesty's privy council, with a view to his becoming better acquainted with the English court, and especially with that part of the country which our queen at that time determined to visit, in a progress[2] of some length, attended by a great retinue

[2 The queen set out on the 14th of July on a progress into Essex and Suffolk, by way of Wanstead, Havering, Pyrgo, New Hall, Colchester, St Osyth's, Harwich, Ipswich, and so back by Smalbridge, Gosfield, Standon, Hertford, and Enfield. She arrived at St James's on the 22nd September. It was in this excursion that the queen took offence at the slovenly manner in which the church service was performed, and shewed a feeling of dislike to the marriage of the clergy,

of the nobility; the earl himself, meanwhile, residing at his country house, that he might take care of his health, and not suffer it to be endangered, by reason of his corpulence, in the heat of summer by so long a journey.

Immediately after this progress was completed, I happily received your letter, from which I took occasion to wait upon the earl respecting the condition of our friend Fabricius. He gave me the same statement as Fabricius had done before; and told me moreover, that he had given him a horse which cost twenty crowns, and also twenty shillings of our money to defray the expenses of that journey. He added too, that he had good reasons for placing Fabricius with master Knowles, as he knew that he had come hither after leaving France, for the especial object of making himself acquainted with the court and the manners of our people, and our cities; and that on the approach of winter he would receive him into his own household till the beginning of spring, at which time, he said, I have determined to send him back to his friends, as there is no hope of placing him in any honourable situation in the queen's service. Abel however, as far as I can gather from Fabricius, has written to his friends at Zurich absolutely and without any limitations, that the earl would receive him into his constant service; whereas the earl, in his conversation with me, had fixed a time for his return to Zurich, at the beginning of spring, and had no intention whatever of retaining him in his family longer than until the end of the winter. Abel has made Fabricius very uneasy, lest his father should imagine from that letter, that some fault was to be found with Fabricius, because the earl would not retain him longer than till the beginning of spring. But believe me, there is no blame whatever to be attached to the young man, but rather to Abel's credulity, who interpreted to you by letter the words of the earl differently to what he really said. Fabricius, like a good and pious son, fearing nothing upon earth more than the anger of his father, who is in other respects most affectionate towards him, has entreated me to explain to you the bare and simple truth, which I solemnly declare I do.

which gave rise to an order against all resort of women to the lodgings of cathedrals and colleges. See Nares' Burghley, II. 240, 241; Wright's Q. Elizabeth, I. 67; Strype, Ann. I. i. 405, and Parker, I. 212.]

Thus much for Fabricius. As to myself, my excellent Gualter, it will be far more easy for you to conceive than for me to express my obligations to you, both for those very learned discourses you sent me, as also for your very friendly letter. I thank you exceedingly for both, as I ought to do. Abel will give you from me in return, as some token of my love to you, a yard and half of our English cloth, well adapted for hose, and which I entreat you again and again to take in good part. Fabricius I know will give you, better than I can, all the news respecting the Scots and French. God grant that all of us, who bear the name of Christ, may embrace salvation in him by constant faith, and live a life consistent with such profession. Again salute from me master Bullinger, who first begat me again unto Christ, and by his assistance made me to relinquish popery. Farewell. London, Feb. 22, 1562.

Your most devoted,

RICHARD MASTERS.

LETTER XXIX.

EARL OF BEDFORD TO HENRY BULLINGER AND RODOLPH GUALTER.

Dated at LONDON, *March* 16, 1562.

GREETING. I received John Henry, whom you so warmly recommended to me in your letter, with great pleasure, both for your sake and his own. He remained about seven months with the vice-chamberlain[1] of her most serene majesty, with whom I placed him for a time, that he might become better acquainted with our court and manners. I could have wished indeed his farther advancement, and endeavoured to accomplish it: but I am sorry that such is the state of our affairs, especially in these times, that this is more to be desired than expected; and as he dis-

[1 Sir Francis Knowles. See above, p. 61.]

covered, by the experience of many persons, that this was too much the case, he left the court, and has remained in London up to this time at his own expense. He has honourably conducted himself here, and with the greatest probity and sobriety. That no better provision has been made for him in this country, is rather to be ascribed to the difficulty of the times, than to the inclination of his friends.

With respect to religion, and the state of the realm, every thing is here, by the blessing of God, quiet and peaceful as heretofore, and we are in constant hopes of improvement. I pray God that the same may ever be the case with yourselves and your churches. Farewell, with the universal church of God. London, March 16, 1562.

Your piety's most devoted,

F. BEDFORD.

LETTER XXX[1].

ROGER ASCHAM TO JOHN STURMIUS.

Dated at LONDON, *April* 11, 1562.

GREETING. What does this mean, my Sturmius? That Michael Toxites our common friend, and so much wished for messenger, should come hither from your parts without a letter from you to me? Is Cook, or Hales, or any other Englishman whatever, either more attached to you, or more greedy of your letters than I am? But I hear you exclaim on the other hand, Alas! my Ascham, can *you* expostulate with me for my not writing, who have not sent me a single syllable these three years? And indeed, my very dear friend, you speak the truth; and all this expostulation of mine is not to find fault with, or to rebuke you, but altogether an artifice, and got up by me on purpose. For I was afraid of your being beforehand with me, as you justly might have been, in complaining of our mutual

[1 The original of this letter is preserved at Strasburgh.]

silence. But let this pass. I will now, my Sturmius, write
to you truly and openly. This long interruption of our
correspondence has not arisen from inclination on my part,
or forgetfulness of you, or neglect of my duty. I have not
remained so long without writing to you either from want
of matter to write about, or of opportunity of sending
a letter; but when you hear from me the true cause of
my silence, I shall not excite your anger and displeasure
against me, but your grief and sorrow for me, whom I
know you love. For these last four years I have been
so attacked by continual fevers, that one scarcely ever
left me without another immediately following in its place.
And thus my whole state of health is so broken up and
destroyed by these fevers linked and connected with each
other, that a hectic has now seized my entire frame. The
physicians promise me relief some time or other, but give
me no hopes of an entire recovery. And now those who
are my true friends, and among them my very assured
friend John Hales, are frequently chirping to me that mournful announcement of Thetis to her son in Homer[2]: "Your
life will indeed be short, and of no long continuance." And
though we read that the most eminent men have died the
soonest, what is that to me, who am a man not of a lofty
but a humble spirit? I entirely repudiate that kind of consolation, whether from the poet or the historian. But when
I betake myself to our teacher of true and complete salvation, who declares, that so much as is taken from the outward man is added to the inward man[3], I do not give
myself up to lamentation, but anticipate the new joys of a
new life. But more of this at another opportunity; for I
desire at this time to begin a long discourse with you,
though indeed I have at present very little leisure to accomplish it, as our most serene queen is at this time so much
employing me and all my time in writing so many letters.

Your last letter to me was dated Jan. 15, 1560. The
two heads of which, one concerning the Scots' business, the
other concerning the queen's marriage, induced me to give
it to the queen herself to read; in both of which she discreetly noticed and graciously acknowledged and commended
your singular respect towards herself. She exceedingly ap-

[2 See Hom. Il. i. 416.]   [3 See 2 Cor. iv. 16.]

proved your judgment respecting the then existing state of
affairs in Scotland, and even now she greatly values you
for your solicitude about us and our affairs.   The passage
concerning her marriage, I well remember, she read over
three times, with an occasional sweet smile, and a very modest
and bashful silence.   Respecting her marriage, my very
dear John Sturmius, I have neither any thing certain to
write myself, nor does any one else among us, I am sure,
know what to think about it.   It was not for nothing,
my Sturmius, but after due consideration, that in that first
long letter of mine to you I stated, that in her whole manner
of life she more resembled Hippolyte than Phædra.   Which
observation I then referred, not to the graces of her person,
but wholly to the chastity of her mind : for of her own
nature, without the advice of any one, she is so entirely
averse and abstinent from marriage.   When I know any
thing for certain, I will write you word by the first opportunity : meanwhile I can give you no hopes as far as
the king[1] of Sweden is concerned.

I wish you would sometimes write to master Cecil : for
he is both most sound in religion, and most discreet in the
government of the state ; and indeed, next to God and the
queen, the most firm support of both.   He is also very fond
of learning and learned men, and is himself well skilled in
both Latin and Greek.   You wish, I know, to hear from
me respecting our affairs.   But I have nothing that I consider better worth writing about than the queen herself.
I will therefore briefly describe what great and important
matters, since she has taken the helm of government,
she has planned with wisdom, and accomplished with success.   First of all, she dedicated her earliest endeavours to
God, by nobly purifying the religion which she found miserably polluted ; in the accomplishment of which object she
exercised such moderation, that the papists themselves have
no complaint to make of having been severely dealt with.
This peace established with God was followed by a peace
with all the neighbouring sovereigns : and yet, on her accession to the throne she found this kingdom involved in a
double war, with the Scots and the French.   Next, she so
firmly and prudently withstood the Guises in Scotland, who

[1 See first series, Letter XIX. p. 46.]

were plotting wonderful things against us, that there now
exists between both kingdoms, and both sovereigns, as secure a peace and firm an alliance, as can possibly take
place between two most quiet neighbourhoods or most united
sisters. After religion, in the first place, and the state next,
had been restored to so desirable a tranquillity, she applied
her mind to the proper settlement of other internal improvements of the realm.

All the coin that had been debased, and entirely alloyed
with copper, she has restored to the pure silver standard[2];
an arduous and royal task, which neither Edward nor even
Henry himself ever ventured to undertake. She has furnished
her armoury with such exquisite materials, that no sovereign
in Europe, I am sure, can shew its equal. Her navy too
she has so embellished and provided with every necessary,
both as regards the abundance of stores and the ability of
the sailors, that the resources of a wealthy kingdom might
seem to have been expended upon this sole object.

These things are of a public nature, and relate to
the whole realm. Let us now inspect her personal character and pursuits. She is readily forgetful of private
injury, but is a severe assertor of public justice. She does
not excuse crime in any one ; she leaves no one the hope
of impunity ; she cuts off from every one the liberty of
offending. She, least of all princes, covets the property and
wealth of her subjects, and requires her own revenues to be
expended sparingly and economically upon every private
pleasure, but royally and liberally either for any object
of public convenience, or for the splendour of domestic magnificence. But the glory she derives from herself, and the
adornments of talent and learning that she possesses, I have
described to you in another letter. I will now only state
in addition, that neither at court, nor in the universities, nor
among our heads in church or state, are there four of our
countrymen who understand Greek better than the queen
herself. When she is reading Demosthenes or Æschines, I
am very often astonished at seeing her so ably understand,
I do not mean, the force of the words, the structure of the
sentences, the propriety of the language, the ornaments of
oratory, and the harmonious and elegant bearing of the

[2 See first series, Letter XXXVIII. p. 93, note 3.]

whole discourse; but also, what is of more importance, the feeling and spirit of the speaker, the struggle of the whole debate, the decrees and inclinations of the people, the manners and institutions of every state, and all other matters of this kind. All her own subjects, and very many foreigners, are witnesses to her proficiency in other languages. I was one day present, when she replied at the same time to three ambassadors, the Imperial, French, and Swedish, in three languages; Italian to the one, French to the other, Latin to the third; easily, without hesitation, clearly, and without being confused, to the various subjects thrown out, as is usual, in their discourse. That you may yourself see how elegantly she writes, I send you inclosed in this letter a slip of paper, in which you have the word "quemadmodum" written in the queen's own hand. The upper one is mine, the lower the queen's. Let me know in your next letter whether the sight is pleasant to you and the present an acceptable one.

And thus much respecting our most noble queen, who is, besides all this, my most munificent mistress, and also very partial to John Sturmius. And should you ever happen to come to England, you will, I think, hear from her own mouth that Roger Ascham has not been a forgetful friend to John Sturmius in the presence of so great a sovereign. This account of our most excellent queen you will, I believe, read, and I assuredly write it, with the greatest satisfaction to us both. If she would only marry, she would leave no room for higher commendation; and I wish, my Sturmius, that you would call forth all that power which you have derived from the best sources both of wisdom and eloquence, whether of reasoning from Demosthenes, or of diction from Cicero, to persuade her to this step. No cause more honourable can be undertaken by you than this, nor can any greater power of persuasion be desired by me, than that which you possess. We desire her to make choice of whomsoever she pleases; we do not wish other persons to point out any individual for her acceptance, and we are all of us in favour of one of our own countrymen in preference to a stranger. I would have you know these things, in case you should ever feel disposed to consider the subject: for should she but add this single benefit to the number of those she has already conferred upon this country, and which I have just now mentioned, no nation can be more happy than ours. And thus much upon this subject. I will write to you about our other affairs at another time; I now come, my Sturmius, to yourself.

I was glad to learn from your letter, written a year ago to John Hales, that your [commentary on] Aristotle's Rhetoric[1] was finished; and I was wonderfully pleased at your adding, "All of you are mentioned in the book, as also [Sir Richard] Morison and [Sir John] Cheke." I was very sorry to hear, from the conversation of our friend Toxites, that the brothers Werter had carried away all those books with them into Thuringia. Those brothers should beware lest they become more notorious by this exploit, than they are already by birth and learning. They do an injury to you, to the study of learning itself, and to the anxious expectation of many worthy persons, and were I not writing of myself, I should say, especially to me; who, though I was not the original promoter, yet advised you to undertake those renowned works worthy of light and immortality, and most unworthy of darkness and some dirty little chest. But if these excellent fruits of your learning should decay and be lost through the meanness and avarice of these young men, I will assuredly try myself—but I must restrain myself, lest I should speak too severely of them before I have ascertained your opinion about this act of theirs. If therefore you love me, my Sturmius, while I am yet alive, (for, as I have told you, this hectic of mine threatens to shorten my days,) do not allow me to be disappointed of the most delightful enjoyment of these books. I have

[1 The following extract from an English letter of Ascham's to two of the Fellows of St John's in Nov. 1551, will throw light upon this passage. "Sturmius goeth forward in *Rhetor. Aristot.* The first book is sent to Mr Cheke, which was purposed to me, but I had rather it should be sent to him. Mr John Hales, my singular friend, sent me a piece of this Rhetoric this week. I never saw any thing more to be compared with antiquity, and so I think Mr Haddon will judge. Vahan is writing it out apace: if he finish it before the post go, ye do receive it; if not now, ye shall have it shortly. Sturmius is in hand with Analysis Ciceron. such a book as I believe was never set out in our time. *Nobilissimi Worteri fratres* do give him, to find him writers, 400 crowns a year for four years." Ascham's English Works, Lond. 1815, p. 375.]

had both the first and second book; but the first, which I
lent to Walter Haddon, the master of the Court of Requests,
I have lost through the carelessness of his servants. I have
often delighted myself with the perusal of these books, and
was expecting all the rest at this last fair. Take care, I
pray you, that this expectation of mine, connected as it is
with so much honour to yourself, and so much advantage
to all students, be not long disappointed.

I am very glad that, as you write word to Hales, you
have written in behalf of Philip against the sycophant Staphylus[1]. I gather from his writings that he is not only a
mountebank Gnatho[2], but also a sort of honorary Thraso[2].
For the folly and insolence of his ostentation is evident from
the subscription of his letter to the bishop of Auerstadt,
where he says: "To your lordship, &c. Frederic Staphylus, councillor of his imperial majesty;" a thing which
the people care to know, no doubt: nor do I think that
this is the fault of the printer, but the premeditated im-
pudence of Staphylus himself; for he writes the same thing
of himself in his Apologetical treatise against Philip. The
book to the bishop of Auerstadt was written by him in
German last year; turned into Latin, I think, by a Car-
melite friar, and printed at Cologne, all venomous and
slanderous throughout. I entreat of you, not by the Sicilian
muses, but by sacred learning itself, to allow your book
against Staphylus to see the light as soon as possible.

I was wonderfully rejoiced at reading in your printed
letter to our friend Cook, that you had written a work on
the controversy respecting the [Lord's] supper, by no means,
you say, violent, but you hope, full of argument. I can
easily believe you, my Sturmius. For I know your disposition is entirely disposed to quietness and peace, not to
quarrelsomeness and contention. I know also your learning,
by which you are wont both easily to prove what you
undertake, and to overcome when you contend, and where

[1 Frederic Staphylus had once been the pupil and disciple of
Melancthon. He apostatized from Lutheranism to the church of
Rome in 1553, and was made a canon of Saltzburg and councillor
to the emperor Ferdinand I. He died in 1564. His works were collected, and printed at Iñgoldstat in 1613.]

[2 Two characters in the *Eunuch* of Terence.]

you think your powers can be exercised with propriety.
I have met with no greater pleasure these many years,
than when my friend Toxites told me that your studies were
so entirely devoted to sacred literature.   The cause of religion has lost a great deal by the death of Philip [Melanc-
thon] and Martin Bucer[3]; but it will indeed gain yet more
by the accession of John Sturmius to its defence.   I pray
God the Father, and our Lord and God Jesus Christ, that
you may wholly give up yourself to the guidance of that
Spirit at whose call you are summoned from the retreats
of Parnassus and Helicon to the joyful pastures of mount
Sion, the mountain of fatness.   And though I would readily
concede you both a lodging at Rome and an inn at
Athens, so that you may occasionally betake yourself to
which city you please, for the sake of diversion, and of
reviving ancient intimacies and friendships; yet I could wish
that your constant habitation, and the abode not only of your
life, but of all your studies, should be ever fixed in Jerusalem
itself, the city of the great God.   And I believe that many
both brighter flashes and grander thunders of speech can
be shewn by you in our David, Isaiah, John and Paul, than
have ever shone forth in all their Pindars, Platos, Demos-
theneses, or Ciceros.   I pray God, if it is right to make
such a request, to grant me such enjoyment of this life, as
that I may some time see the stings of your pen, either put
forth of your own accord, or roused into action by the provo-
cation of others, against the popish drones, who occupy the
more secret cells and almost all the choicest nests in the very
temple of God.   I fear, my Sturmius, lest I should offend
you more by my present prolixity, than by all that long
continued silence of mine, and neglect of writing: though,
if you choose to divide this loquacious letter into sundry
parts, it cannot be said but that I have now written you
many letters.   But you will, I hope, pardon my prolixity,
which if it prove offensive to you, I pray you to punish by
a letter yet more prolix.

I wish, my Sturmius, to know your opinion about Dionysius of Halicarnassus.   I believe him to have been the same
Dionysius who taught in the house of Cicero, and of whom

[3 Melancthon died April 19, 1560, and Bucer in February 1551.]

frequent mention is made in the letters of Cicero[1]. Cicero exceedingly commends his erudition, but not his moral character. When you leave that one city, and that single age of Philip and Alexander, I do not see what Greek author, Plutarch himself not excepted, you can compare with this Dionysius of Halicarnassus. I wish to know from you whether you consider this opinion of mine to have any foundation, or to be altogether erroneous. His treatise addressed to Tubero concerning his judgment of the history of Thucydides pleases me wonderfully. My wife, knowing how you are beloved by me, loves also your wife, and sends her, as a token of her good-will, a gold ring, made in the shape of an arrow, with this inscription, *The gift of a faithful friend.* Toxites has the ring. Excuse this letter; for our friend Toxites is in such a hurry, that I have no time to copy it. Farewell in Christ Jesus. From my house in London, April 11, 1562.

Your most attached,

R. ASCHAM.

LETTER XXXI.

BISHOP GRINDAL TO CONRAD HUBERT.

Dated at LONDON, *June* 6, 1562.

HEALTH in Christ. I greatly commend your regard, my very dear master Conrad, to the memory of our common instructor[2], Bucer. But I cannot help blaming the ingratitude of others, who are endeavouring to traduce the apostle and father of your city, who was its father[3] in Christ, as the

[1 See his Epistolæ ad Diversos, XIII. 77. and other passages: but the Dionysius meant is not the Halicarnassian.]

[2 Sandys, Grindal, and Bradford were intimately acquainted with Bucer, when he was King's Professor of Divinity at Cambridge. Strype, Parker, I. 55.]

[3 Bucer was admitted in 1523, into the number of the reformed preachers at Strasburg, and subscribed a book with them, which they published in 1524, setting forth the reasons that induced them to renounce popery. He assisted in 1529, as deputy of the church of Strasburg, in the conferences of Marpurg, where they endeavoured to pacify the dissensions between the Lutherans and Zuinglians.]

author of unsound doctrines, or a heretic. For what else
are they doing, when they prevent his writings from being
published? I am surprised that your magistrates allow so
much licence to these new orators, and that the memory
of the departed Bucer is not of more avail with them than
the clamours of these men. But I am unwilling to pry into
the affairs of another state. Your Atlases are too late in
their support of the Saxon heaven, which is now every where
falling to the ground. I lately saw a letter from Bremen,
giving an account of the state of that city. After the
banishment of Doctor Albert[4] they enacted most severe laws
against the Zuinglians, or rather the Albertines, threatening
them with prisons, exiles, and proscriptions. They prevented
a very eminent man, master Daniel a Buren, from entering
upon the office of chief magistrate, which had come to him by
rotation in January last, because he was favourable to our sentiments; and they substituted another person in his place. But
he recovered the mayoralty with the entire consent of the
citizens, and afterwards banished those troublesome preachers,
or rather croakers. It is astonishing that they are raising
such commotions about predestination. They should at least
consult their own Luther on "the bondage of the will." For
what else do Bucer, Calvin, and Martyr teach, that Luther
has not maintained in that treatise? Unless perhaps they
wish to take refuge in some recantation of Luther, whom
they all but regard as a god. Luther has indeed deserved
exceeding well of the church, and is worthy of being celebrated by all posterity. But he would have been more
eminent in my eyes, if these Canaans were not always dis-
covering the nakedness of their father, which all godly persons desire to be concealed. But do you, most learned
Conrad, persevere in defending the fame of Bucer, and
in maintaining the truth. The Lord will not suffer this cause,
which is his own, to be always kept under. I doubt not but
that your modesty and firmness will have much influence
with all godly persons. I congratulate you too upon having
as your colleague and assistant in so holy an undertaking

[4 Albert Hardenberg, the intimate friend of Melancthon, was the
first person who attempted to introduce at Bremen the doctrine of
Calvin concerning the eucharist. He was in consequence expelled
from that city in 1556.]

master John Sturmius, whom I pray you earnestly to salute in my name.

I thank you for the copies, but have not yet been able to receive them. They are perhaps loitering some where on the way. You will receive from Abel or Salkyns[1] (if he bring you this letter) two golden coins of our country, stamped after a new fashion, and in a manner resembling print. Give one of these from me to Sturmius, and keep the other for yourself. I pray you also to salute from me master Doctor Sebald, to whom I have sent another coin of the same kind, which I beg you to deliver to him yourself. My [secretary] Dithelm[2], by his father's command, is shortly to go into France. I wish you every blessing in the Lord. From my house in London, June 6, 1562.

Yours in Christ,

EDMUND GRINDAL,

Bishop of London.

These three pieces of gold, more remarkable for their workmanship than their value, I have inclosed in this letter, and with them an engraving of the second funeral of Bucer, recently published by one of our printers.

LETTER XXXII.

FRANCIS, EARL OF BEDFORD, TO HENRY BULLINGER.

Dated at LONDON, June 10, 1562.

GREETING. John Henry[3], whom you commended to me by your letter, is now returning to you. He has conducted himself with the greatest propriety during his residence among us. I could have wished indeed to have done more for him, both for his own sake and yours; but success does not always correspond to our wishes. As far as

[1 Salkyns was the servant of Richard Hilles.]
[2 See above, Letter XII. p. 28.]
[3 See above, Letter XXIII. p. 53.]

I am concerned, no one shall ever come over from your country recommended to me by you, without being most welcome. Wherefore you must never entertain any doubt as to my mind and inclination towards you. I desire and wish all prosperity and happiness to you and your churches. No more at this present. Farewell, with all the company of the godly. London, June 10, 1562.

Your piety's most devoted,

F. BEDFORD.

LETTER XXXIII.

FRANCIS, EARL OF BEDFORD, TO RODOLPH GUALTER.

Dated at LONDON, *June* 10, 1562.

MUCH health. John Henry Fabricius, who is now re-turning to you, has so honourably conducted himself in all his actions towards every one, as to leave behind him a singular and admirable testimony to his integrity. I for my part have not been wanting to him, whenever I could do any thing to promote his interests; and I would willingly have done more, were promotion as easily obtained here as it is elsewhere. I pray you therefore to take in good part my favourable disposition, which always has been, and will ever continue to be, most ready to exert itself in behalf both of yourself and of your church. I have not any thing more to write at present. May you and your whole church be happy and prosperous! London, June 10, 1562.

Your very loving friend,

F. BEDFORD.

LETTER XXXIV.

SIR ANTONY COOK TO HENRY BULLINGER.

Dated at LONDON, *June* 14, 1562.

YOUR request, most worthy master Bullinger, made to master Wroth and myself by letter some time since, that this youth[1] should obtain some honourable situation in the court of our queen, has been carefully attended to by us; if not exactly according to his wishes, yet so at least as circumstances and our times admitted of. As a longing after his country now recalls him home, I have thought fit to write you these few lines, that you may understand and feel assured that neither length of time nor distance of place can ever diminish, much less expunge or efface, my regard, duty, and respect to you. Salute, I pray you, in my name, masters Peter Martyr, Bernardine, and Gualter, all of whom I mention with distinguishing regard. May our Lord Jesus Christ very long preserve you in life and safety to his flock! London, June 14, 1562.

Your piety's most devoted,

ANTONY COOK.

LETTER XXXV.

———[2] TO PETER MARTYR.

Dated at LONDON, *June* 26, 1562.

MOST reverend and very dear father in Christ, I have no other occasion for addressing your reverence, than that which the inclosed letter supplies; which a certain friend of yours charged me faithfully to deliver to you, together with thirty golden French crowns, which I have given in trust to the bearer that he may bring you them together with the in-

[1 John H. Fabricius.]

[2 This letter is without any subscription, and the first sentence is imperfect in the original MS.]

closed letter. As soon therefore as you receive this letter, and the crowns, or the just value of them, your reverence is requested to inform each of the parties as well as myself by letter, and to inclose the letter to your friend in mine. Let these few words suffice for the present occasion, that your godly studies may not be interrupted by a longer letter. All our godly countrymen earnestly entreat your fatherhood constantly to remember our churches in your prayers; begging God not to suffer the irreligious lukewarmness of the English in regard to religion to fall back again into popery, or something worse. And may the Lord preserve your fatherhood for the good of his church, and evermore give you his blessing! Amen. London, June 26, 1562.

An ardent desirer of your prosperity in Christ,

LETTER XXXVI.

ARCHBISHOP PARKER TO MATT. FLACIUS ILLYRICUS[3] AND OTHERS.

Dated at CROYDON, July 18, [sine anno.]

THIS godly courtesy of yours, reverend sirs, is very gratifying to me, that you have lately caused your commentaries to be delivered to me by a confidential messenger[4]; whereby you have rendered it more easy for me to defend you in your own name, in case any persons should hereafter

[3 Matthias Flacius, or Francowitz, was a native of Albona in Illyria. He was the chief author of that ecclesiastical history, known under the name of the Centuriæ Magdeburgenses, the fourth of which was dedicated to queen Elizabeth, in 1560, and was probably the book sent to archbishop Parker. His principal coadjutors were John Wigand, Matt. Judex, Basil Faber, with whom may be reckoned about fifteen others of less note. Matthias Flacius died in 1575. See Melchior Adam.]

[4 This was probably either Bernard Niger, afterwards mentioned, or Mark Wagner, who visited the libraries of England, Denmark and Scotland, in search of materials for the Magdeburgh centuriators. See Sagittarius Introd. ad Hist. Eccl. p. 254.]

falsely calumniate the doctrine that you profess. Which doctrine indeed and belief of yours, however it may in part fail of pleasing every one, yet I openly admit that you have acted ingenuously and sincerely, in having so fully, so entirely, and so clearly and unambiguously declared your mind and sentiments. Yet, upon due consideration of these your opinions, I cannot but lament that there should be some disagreement among us upon the chief controversies of religion, especially as each party is taught by the same rule of scripture, and animated by the same zeal both for the restoration of the truth and the utter extermination of all error and falsehood from the territories of the church of Christ. Oh, how great an occasion of falling is here presented to good men! how greatly on this ground is the very restoration of the gospel loaded with reproaches and revilings by our enemies! I wish indeed, that each party would listen to the other without prejudice, and with greater patience and attention; and that neither should be so wedded to his opinion, as to render this public cause of religion an occasion of glorying, ambition, and dissent.

With regard to the principal object, for which your private messenger came over, namely, that he might bring back to you some ancient commentaries of such kind as you hoped to obtain from us[1]; you must know, that the more diligent I have been fully to satisfy your wishes in this respect, or rather, to assist in that labour which you have undertaken to the great benefit of the universal christian church, the more unfortunate, to my thinking, has hitherto been the result; and where I had rested my chief hopes of attaining what I desired, I am now left without any hope whatever. And yet, after having sent numberless messengers to many persons and places to no effect, I was at length stirred up to recover the books of master Bale[2], which, it was said, there would be some

[1 The archbishop had acquainted Flacius with a promise of the queen's, to send him certain *vetera monumenta*, to assist him as well in the work of his *Catalogue of the witnesses of the Truth*, as in his other works of ecclesiastical history. See Strype, Parker, I. 219, III. 52.]

[2 John Bale, bishop of Ossory. "His rare collection of MSS.", says Strype, "after his decease, came into our archbishop's hands by

prospect of obtaining, if I chose to make the attempt. I ascertained therefore, upon inquiry, into whose hands they fell after his flight[3] from Ireland; and when a great heap of them was brought to me, I discovered clearly that none of them were, in my opinion, either valuable for their antiquity, or written on any subject useful and adapted to your purpose. When however your friend Niger[4] saw them, together with mine and some others, he said that many of them would be of much use. He has them therefore, upon the condition of returning them within a year. But if you are in possession of so rich a collection and apparatus of the writers of our nation, as is mentioned in your catalogue, I think you must have a far greater number than is left in all England, of which I have any certain knowledge and information: whether it be that some parties are unwilling to oblige you in this useful endeavour, and by reason of some private dislike refuse to consider the public benefit of the church; or whether some are unwilling to have it known that such things are in their possession: and thus, like the dog in the manger, they neither enjoy them themselves, nor allow the enjoyment of them to others. Moreover the queen's majesty's library does not possess the means of affording the assistance which you require, as I have been informed by the person who is appointed its

purchase. For he laid out for them immediately upon his death, fearing they might be gotten by somebody else. And perhaps divers of those books, that do now make proud the university library, and that of Bene't, and some other colleges in Cambridge, were Bale's before they were the archbishop's." Strype, Parker, II. 520. If this statement be correct, since Bale died in Nov. 1563, this letter was probably written in the July following.]

[3 Bale became greatly exposed, at the accession of queen Mary, to the outrages of the papists in Ireland. Once, in particular, we are told, that five of his domestics were murdered, while they were making hay near his house; and, having received intimation that the priests were plotting his death, he retired from his see to Dublin. He afterwards made his escape in a small vessel from that port, but was taken by the captain of a Dutch man of war, who stripped him of all his money and effects, and, when he arrived in Holland, obliged him to pay thirty pounds before he could recover his liberty. See the "Vocacyon of Johan Bale to the bishoprick of Ossorie in Irelande, his Persecucions in the same, and finall Delyverance, A. D. 1563." It is reprinted in the Harl. Misc. Vol. VI.]

[4 Bernard Niger was one of the Magdeburgh centuriators.]

curator and keeper.   This then is the state of the case, that I am unable to satisfy your request, as I could wish; although, before I had been taught by experience, I confidently believed that I could assist you to a greater extent. Certainly the colleges and all the religious houses were plundered, before it was considered what great inconvenience would arise to the church of Christ by this clandestine dispersion and loss of books.   The papists however will not produce any thing; for it is said that when they were in possession of monuments of this kind, which undermined the greatest part of their doctrine, they committed some good authors to the flames, as if they envied the world the perusal of them: and this I know to have been the case with the books of Vigilius[1], which they have abused in this way.

I should have written more upon these things, and upon this laborious yet profitable task which you are undertaking in composing this history, only that I am so prevented, partly by ill health, and partly from other causes, that I cannot give such free consideration to these thoughts as I could wish.   There are some persons who desire that in your history should be set forth the very words of those authors of whom you only make a bare mention. And though this may be very troublesome in a history of such extent, and is of no use to men of much reading; yet it will afford some light to beginners, and will also be of great weight against calumniators.   But I leave the consideration of this to your future discretion.

I send you twenty angels, as a testimony of my obligation to you, which I request you to take in good part. Meanwhile I pray that the Holy Spirit of God may be with you, as the continual helper of your endeavours. Farewell in Christ.   July 18.   Croydon.

Your loving friend,
MATTHEW PARKER[2].

[1 Vigilius was bishop of Thapsus, A.D. 484: but the allusion here is most probably to *Virgilius* (Polydore Vergil), who is reported to have burned the books which he had used in compiling his works. See Foxe, Acts and Monuments, Book VIII. Vol. II. p. 378, edit. 1684.]

[2 This letter was published from the original by Jo. Christ. Wolf, at Hamburgh in 1736, who states that the signature alone, with the preceding words, is in the hand-writing of the archbishop.]

LETTER XXXVII.

HIEROME ZANCHIUS TO BISHOP GRINDAL.

Dated at [STRASBURGH, 1563.]

In congratulating me, honoured master, upon that firmness, such as it was, which the Lord bestowed upon me in the defence of a worthy cause[3], I acknowledge your pious feeling; while in your having presented me with a gift, I perceive that your regard and good-will towards me is of no ordinary character.   For the latter, I feel and return you my grateful acknowledgements: for the former, I request you to aid me with your prayers unto the Lord.   For the reputation and fluent loquacity of the ministers[4], both of which things have very great influence in cities, and especially among the unlearned, are at this time making against me in this cause.   For both in private and in public they easily make the ignorant multitude believe any calumnies against me that they please; and the rather, because I am both a stranger, and unable to speak their language, and have no authority whatever with this kind of men.   The

[3 "Hierome Zanchy, an Italian by birth, was now public reader of divinity at Strasburgh: with him Grindal was acquainted ever since himself lived there, and since his departure kept a correspondence with him.   This year [1563] letters happened between them upon this occasion.   The Augustan Confession about this time began to be pressed vigorously, and particularly in the said town of Strasburgh, upon all the reformed there, or no abiding for them.   This was the cause of great contests and debates between the learned Lutherans in the school there, and Zanchy, who in the matter of the sacrament, and predestination, and some other things, could not accord with their confession."   Strype, Grindal, p. 111 (8vo.)   In Letter XLIII below will be found a full account of the dispute.]

[4 John Marbach seems especially to be alluded to.   He was one of Zanchy's fiercest opponents, and so excessively loquacious as to make Luther say of him, *Ori hujus Suevi nunquam araneæ poterunt telas texere;* "No spider will ever weave a cobweb over the mouth of this Suabian."]

consideration that truth is always wont to conquer, gives me especial comfort; as does also the conviction that the senate is just, and will not act in a hasty or tyrannical manner. In the third place, my friend Sturmius and the visitors, and almost all the rest of the professors and members of our chapter are maintaining the cause, as knowing it to be a just one, to the best of their power, and have united with me in defending it. None of your people can imagine how greatly Satan has vexed, disturbed, and weakened this church and school for the last two years: almost all the older members are dead, and even those two who survive cannot be tolerated by these ignorant young men. If it were permitted me, I could make such statements as, though most true and notorious to all here, neither you nor any other of your countrymen could in any wise believe. I am myself astonished at my own patience, but much more at the patience of the senate. May the Lord be present with his church! It is necessary that Satan, who sometimes transforms himself into an angel of light, should at length be discovered and exposed. I congratulate you, however, upon your peace and agreement in pure doctrine; and I pray the Lord to maintain, protect, and enlarge the kingdom of Christ in your country, and to defend and preserve the queen and nobles of the realm. And may God give success to the affairs in France, according to the desire and judgment of the godly! The result, I see, will be the renovation of the whole world. Farewell.

H. ZANCHIUS.

LETTER XXXVIII.

RICHARD HILLES TO HENRY BULLINGER.

Dated at LONDON, *July* 31, 1562.

THIS letter will inform you, my venerable and loving friend, that I have received yours written at Zurich on the 22nd of June last. And I thank you exceedingly, not only because you were disposed to write to me, but because you condescend to inform me, both what news is now stirring amongst you, and also what, as far as you hear, will be the result. But as to the council of Trent[1], I cannot but think of it rather as a sign of some plot or conspiracy formed against the protestants, than of a synod of faithful catholics simply assembling together in the truth, for the purpose of eradicating, according to their power, such abuses as have crept into the church of Christ. And I am grieved not a little, when I hear that you who profess the gospel in Switzerland, are not able, either by your sound doctrine or your examples of godly life, to draw over your confederate fellow-soldiers to the religion of the gospel; and that they are still so opposed to your endeavours for the reformation of religion, as to cause apprehension that the matter will shortly proceed to a quarrel or open hostilities. With respect, however, to the state of things in France, and especially as to what is going on at Paris and Rouen[2], it is certain, as you say, that we can get as early information as those who live at Zurich; but we cannot positively ascertain, till after a long interval, the truth of what is doing in the upper provinces of France, as at Orleans and Lyons. We English, however, (God be thanked!) are still living in much peace and quietness. Nevertheless the queen appears to be considering the evils that may possibly be hanging over us, and is apprehensive lest any misfortune should arise to the realm by reason of negligence and inactivity; that is, lest any foreign prince (in the event of the disorders, which still exist in France, being settled,) should be stirred up by the Roman pontiff or any other foreign papists who adhere to him, to find some occasion of quarrel against her; when the real ground of offence would be, that the authority of her majesty, in the council of parliament, and by the consent of the whole realm, has done away with his usurped power, and the continuance of the superstitions, abuses, and idolatry which heretofore crept into the catholic church. The queen however has a great number both of soldiers and ships already prepared

[1 The council of Trent was resumed Jan. 18, 1562, under Pius IV, who had succeeded Paul IV in 1559.]

[2 Preparations were now making for the investment of Rouen, which city was garrisoned by the Huguenots, and taken by assault under the duke of Guise, on Oct. 26.]

for the defence of her kingdom, should it be necessary. My wife and children, thank God, are well. She thanks you for your remembrance of her in your letter, and heartily salutes you and your wife, whom I beg you also to salute in my name, as also master Lewis Lavater. Farewell, and take care of your health. London, July 31, 1562.

Yours,

RICHARD HILLES.

LETTER XXXIX.

HERMAN FOLKERZHEIMER[1] TO JOSIAH SIMLER.

Dated at SALISBURY, *Aug.* 13, 1562.

TELL me, my Josiah, what has come into your mind, that in your last letter you thought you had nothing worth writing about to one who is so exceedingly inquisitive about all your affairs as I am? What then? Must I remain ignorant what effect my poor letters produce, how my friends are going on, how my garden is flourishing, which, though then in idea and thought only, had however begun to be formed in rows? But yet I will nevertheless admit that you deserve some thanks, in spite of your short and inauspicious letter, because you did not, happily, omit to mention my father's health. As the bishop of Salisbury had given me a most friendly invitation to visit him, and I perceived that France was so disturbed by civil discord[2] that literary pursuits were altogether at a stand; having left Poictiers I proceeded to Rochelle, a port of France of some celebrity, and visited at my leisure, not without danger, the salt-works of Brouage[3],

[1 Moreri mentions one of this name who was of a noble family in East Friesland.]

[2 Namely, by the wars which had broken out some months before between the Roman catholics and protestants.]

[3 Brouage is near a bay of the sea, 17 miles south of Rochelle.]

and other places in the neighbourhood. But having obtained tolerably fine weather, (for although the wind was
by no means favourable, I did not shrink from a second
trial,) I left Rochelle on the 29th of June[4]. Nothing was
more irksome than the want of a companion to converse
with; so that there came into my mind all at once rocks,
tempests, shallows, pirates, a rascal of a captain, and in
short every thing that might have befallen Arion of old.
But I was in no fear that the God of hosts, who rules the
sea, the winds and the tempests, and who had ever been
my most faithful guide through the whole of my past life,
would forsake me then, because he especially promises to
protect those who go down to the sea. When therefore
we were carried into the bay of Biscay, we kept such
a continued course night and day, that although the storms
were raging as usual, we only once cast anchor. When
we had been tossed about in this manner for the space of
eight days, the much wished for land began at last to
appear in sight, and having left the isle of Wight on our
right, we landed at Southampton. Here I heartily thanked God, and recruited myself, having become a good deal
fatigued by my tossing about on the sea. Three days
after, having fortunately procured a good horse, I arrived at
Salisbury. When the bishop saw me, to the great surprise
of his attendants, he hastened towards me as I was entering,
and closely embracing me, Oh! my Herman, said he, you
are welcome; you are come as a guest than whom I have
received no one with greater pleasure of a long time. He
then particularly inquired how Martyr, Julius, Bullinger,
Josiah, Lavater, Zuinglius, and our other common friends
were going on? whether all was well with them? I
replied that I hoped so, but that I did not know for certain,
as from having been resident in France in such uncertain
and turbulent times, I had received no intelligence of your
affairs either by letter or report. The remainder of our
discourse was employed in conversation upon French mat-

[4 The Lat. has *tertio Cal. Sextil.* But this is evidently a mistake,
as it appears by bishop Jewel's letter to Simler, in the first series,
p. 120, that Folkerzheimer reached Salisbury on the 8th of July. And
on the 20th, as appears from a subsequent part of this letter, he
visited Stonehenge.]

ters. He assigned me two very accomplished young men, acquainted with the French language, for my companions, and they were to conduct me wherever I chose. We viewed the city, the churches, the little rivulets, one of which flows most delightfully through every street.

But although the whole of the city belongs to the bishop, his domestic arrangements delighted me more than any thing else. His palace, in the first place, is so spacious and magnificent, that even sovereigns may, and are wont to be suitably entertained there, whenever they come into these parts. Next, there is a most extensive garden, kept up with especial care, so that in the levelling, laying out, and variety, nothing seems to have been overlooked. A most limpid stream runs though the midst of it, which, though agreeable in itself, is rendered much more pleasant and delightful by the swans swimming upon it, and the abundance of fish, which (the bishop) is now causing to be inclosed in an iron lattice-work. After having most courteously saluted me on the following day, he turned to his attendants, and, " Let the horses," he said, " be saddled and bridled, and take this guest of mine a hunting." Accordingly having taken our dogs with us, when we arrived at the place where the game was wont to hide, we pursued two deer which we had discovered; both of which, before they were worn out with running, the dogs with incredible swiftness quickly came up with, and easily caught and brought them to the ground. There was, however, but little occasion for the halloo with which Xenophon sets on his dogs in hunting, *Well, well, well done dogs, well done;* for our dogs did their duty even without being set on. Do you ask whether we often go a hunting? The bishop indeed, I perceive, does not take much delight in this kind of amusement. What pleasure, says he, I pray you, can possibly be derived from pursuing with fierce dogs a timid animal, that attacks no one, and that is put to flight even by a noise? I should, however, tell an untruth, were I to say that I am not delighted with it. But yet, were I frequently to repeat the same thing, I think it would not afford me so much amusement. But although the bishop never goes out a hunting, and I very seldom, the dogs are by no means idle. The young men are required to provide a supply of venison, that the table may always give proof of the activity of the dogs and the labours of the huntsmen.⊃

But as I like to deal with you after our custom, the custom, I mean, of the most intimate companions, I shall allow myself this liberty of prating, and will not abstain even from the most minute details; though indeed you deserve from me nothing of the kind, who are so cautious as not to weary me either with joking or sober sense. See, my excellent Josiah, how my circumstances have changed in so short a time. When I left France in silence and in concealment, and in the greatest loneliness, I had nothing to relieve my weariness but one little book; every thing was so dirty and loathsome and disagreeable, that the ship would make one sick, even were it laid up on shore. The table was laid out, as Cicero[1] says, not with shell or other fish, but with a quantity of stinking meat. The same person was cook and steward. Piso had no baker at home, nor I from home: he got his bread and wine at a huckster's, and from a public house; but I, poor wretch, as soon as I had emptied my flask, could find no huckster from whom I could procure one, nor any public house, where they would draw one even the smallest quantity at the greatest cost; so that as soon as our wine had failed about the fifth day, we mixed vinegar and water, which to most of us, thirsty as we then were, did not seem very different from it. I reached a fortunate island when I arrived at Salisbury. Immortal powers! what a sudden change I experienced, what power of breathing freely after my long imprisonment! I am transplanted into the magnificent abode of a prosperous individual, with whom, as you know, I have long been on the most intimate and friendly terms. He, remembering our ancient intimacy, received me in such a manner, that he could not have received even his own brother more lovingly. He directed his attendants, most elegant young men of rank, and very different from our dirty crew of sailors, to order some wine to be brought. The butler forthwith makes his appearance, bearing a large golden goblet. And also, when dinner or supper time arrived, how can I describe to you the abundance or magnificence of the silver plate? Yet great as they are, they do not seem to afford much pleasure to their possessor,

[1 See Cic. in Pisonem, 27.]

and appear to have been provided rather for his guests' sake
than his own. But, without entering upon any further details,
you will easily guess the nature of them, and judge of the
difference between a ship and a palace. For my part, I
am quite ready to allow those who choose to philosophize
on the subject, to be of Xenophon's opinion, that domestic
economy is nowhere better understood than on board a
ship, and to require all heads of families to imitate their
carefulness; provided only that I am at liberty to keep my
own opinion.

On the 20th of July[1] we rode into the country with
a large retinue, as the bishop said he would shew me some
things that would astonish me. When I saw the cavalcade
in the middle of the plain, Why, said I, is not Josiah a
witness of this? or Bullinger, or indeed any Zuricher? for
as to Peter Martyr, he is well acquainted with all your
circumstances. I wish, he replied, those worthy men were
here. But what do you think they are now doing? Perhaps,
he said, they have finished their dinner, and I fancy that
I see Martyr seated in his elbow chair. When we had
gone on a little farther, he very kindly pointed out to me
the whole character and bearing of the neighbourhood.
There, says he, stretching out his arm, was formerly old
Sarum; there are the mounds which you can distinguish
even now, and there the ramparts. And then, in another
place, Here was a camp of the ancient Romans[2], of which
these are the vestiges that we see. At length we arrived
at the place which Jewel had particularly wished me to visit,
and respecting which I should hesitate to write what I have
seen, unless I could confirm it by most approved witnesses;
because it has generally been my custom, when I had
ascertained anything to be true, which might at first sight
appear incredible, rather to prefer not to mention it, than
to describe it, lest I should be regarded as unworthy of
credit. I beheld, in a very extensive plain, at a great
distance from the sea, in a soil which appeared to have
nothing in common with the nature of stones or rocks, I
beheld, I say, stones of immense size, almost every one of
which, if you should weigh them, would be heavier than

[1 See above p. 85, note 4.]
[2 The present remains are generally supposed to be Saxon.]

even your whole house. The stones are not heaped one upon another, nor even laid together, but are placed upright, in such a way that two of them support a third. Put forth now the powers of your understanding, and guess, if you are able, by what strength, or rather (for what could strength do in such a case?) by what mechanical power these stones have been brought together, set up, and raised on high? And then, for what object has this immense mass been erected? The bishop says, that he cannot see by what means even the united efforts of all the inhabitants could move a single stone out of its place. He is of opinion, however, that the Romans formerly erected them here as trophies, and that the very disposition of the stones bears some resemblance to a yoke.

But you will wish to know, with what studies I am so killing myself, as to make me seek after so many kinds of relaxation, and recreate myself so often. Believe me, hardly any of a serious nature. Since the time I left Paris, I have given a long holiday to my friends Euclid, Archimedes, and also Ptolemy, and have not once disturbed those grave philosophers. I have bestowed all my labour and industry, if I had any, upon jurisprudence. Meanwhile, however, when I now and then interposed a little history, I carefully noted such things as appertain to the geographical description of Arabia Felix; as, for instance, the localities of cities and rivers, promontories, bays, and fountains. But a description of the sea-coast might be looked for in Arrian, who took a survey of the Red sea and Persian gulph, because Arabia is included within these. At this present time, therefore, I am principally paying attention to histories, of which Jewel's excellent library affords me great abundance.

The affairs of France disturb me greatly. I implore the mercy of our good and gracious God, that putting away the remembrance of the grievous sins that we have committed, and pardoning them through his dear and only Son, he may regard his own glory and name. May he deign to be our guide and leader, and encompass our army not with wall, boundary, or ditch, but, as he has promised, with legions of angels! May the golden sceptre, which he has committed to the all-powerful hand of his Son, be at length brought forth, and break in pieces those vessels of pottery and earthen-ware, and disperse them, as they deserve, like the dust, that they may not be able to find a resting place; but yet so that they may not obscure the praise and glory of his Christ, nor spread darkness over the splendor of his light!

Salute very much in my name your wife, my very dear and excellent father Peter Martyr, Julius, the Bullingers, Haller, Lavater, Zuinglius, Pellican, Gualter, Wolfius, Funckius, Gesner, to whom I wish you would say, that I have written to my brother about the seal-skin; and should he pay no attention to it, as he is newly married, you may promise that I will carefully attend to it myself. Farewell, my dearest Josiah. Farewell. August 13, 1562. Salisbury.

[HERMAN FOLKERZHEIMER.]

LETTER XL[1].

ROGER ASCHAM TO JOHN STURMIUS.

Dated at LONDON, *Oct.* 21, 1562.

MUCH health in Christ Jesus. As we are united together in the same zeal, opinion, disposition, and feeling, with respect to learning, religion, the commonwealth, and a mutual friendship, I often wish and desire that those who belong to us should in like manner be connected by some link and motive to cherish a like affection on their part. And therefore, as my wife has made me a father for the third time, about a week since, I have bestowed upon my little son, in perpetual remembrance of my friendship, the name of Sturmius[2] Ascham. I pray God, and shall daily continue to do so, that as he bears some resemblance of you in name, so he may likewise in your learning and virtue. I deliver him therefore to your fidelity as your own, and, as far as possible, commend him to

[1 The original of this letter is preserved at Strasburgh.]

[2 A letter of Sturmius in reply to this is printed in his epistles, wherein he says: Ego Sturmii Aschami propater esse volo, et ille mihi profilius non futurus est, sed est. Mittam ei imaginem meam; ut si moriar, antequam me videat, post me aliquid mei videat. Sturm. Ep. XVI.]

your protection, although he is not connected with you by
relationship or nation, but by his very name and the wishes
of his parents; so that, in case of my death, you may regard him with the same tenderness, benevolence, and affection,
with which you have heretofore been always accustomed to
regard his father. For respecting the probable shortness of
my life I wrote very copiously with tears, and in far too
mournful a strain, in that long letter[3] of mine sent you last
April by our friend Toxites. I am very anxious to know
whether that letter has reached you. I wrote to you also by
Henry Knolles[4], who is at this time envoy of our most serene
queen to the German princes. From him (for he is very
much attached to you) you will very readily understand the
whole state of our affairs in England. Her most serene
majesty is fully determined and in every respect entirely
prepared to destroy the power and tyranny of the Guises,
to take arms for the safety of the youthful king[5], and in
defence of an inoffensive people[6], without any way intending
any wrong to that king or to that kingdom. On this very

[3 See above, Letter XXX.]

[4 "The last moneth (Sep. 1562) Mr Henry Knolles was sent into
Almain with commission to join with Christopher Mount, and to sol-
licit the prince's protestants both to aid the prince of Condé, and to
consider how the common cause of religion might be defended against
any common confederacy of the enemy." Sir W. Cecil to—. MS.
Cotton. Vesp. c. VII. 224.]

[5 Namely, Charles IX. who was at this time about 12 years old.
He ascended the throne Dec. 15, 1560, on the death of his brother
Francis II. In the queen's declaration of the causes that induced her
to take arms, it is expressly stated that her majesty meaneth not "in
any her actions to prejudice the crown of France, nor to do any other
thing but that which shall stand with the honour of God, the preservation of the French king both in his person and his rights, the safe-
guard of the prince [of Condé] and his company, with all other the
king's true subjects, against the manifest cruelty of the Duke of Guise
and his complices." Forbes, II. 73.]

[6 "Nothing is meant here on our part to make any invasion, but
to enter quietly into these pieces (Newhaven and Dieppe) which by
law of arms we may, considering we take none of them by force; and
as long as the French shall give no other cause, it is meant to use no
war towards them, but to allow of mutual traffic betwixt both the
nations." Cecil, as above. The letter was probably addressed to Sir
N. Throgmorton.]

day, I believe, our troops have entered Normandy[1], which you will sooner know by the report itself, than by this letter.

I wish, my Sturmius, that you would write a separate history of this Guisian conspiracy. Not but that I am well aware, as that friend of ours says upon a like occasion, by what a weight of important undertakings you are oppressed from day to day. But I am not less desirous of your reputation than of my own advantage. The subject is a noble one, and worthy of your learning, abilities, zeal for pure religion, love to that nation, affection for the cause itself, and indignation also against those who are the authors of such impious tyranny and atrocious cruelty. I have often read, and shall always remember, that remarkable passage in a letter of yours to Erasmus[2], your bishop of Strasburgh, in which you treat upon the proper method of writing history. When I consider the ability which that passage proves you to possess, I cannot tell you how greatly I despise all other writers, and earnestly pray Almighty God that you may sometime or other undertake such an employment. This desire of mine has been greatly modified by a report brought over here from Germany, that the German princes had assigned you the province of continuing with your pen what had been passed over by your friend John Sleidan. I have positively stated to our queen that this is the case; let me know, I pray you, whether it is so. I long to know about your Aristotle's Rhetoric, and your treatises, both that against

[1 Part of the English army, under Sir Adrian Poynings, arrived at Newhaven in September: the earl of Warwick, who was commander in chief, did not arrive there till towards the end of October. In a letter to Cecil, dated from Dover Oct. 25th, he writes: "Once again upon very small occasion I went to sea on Friday at night, the wind coming then suddenly, after a little shower, to the north. Notwithstanding it continued not two hours before it came to the south again, yet we laboured all that night, and the next day so long, as we were past hope either to get Newhaven or Portsmouth, and therefore forced to return hither again, where I landed late yesternight, and so must tarry until it please Him to give leave, to whom the greatest princes in this case must obey; wherein, I trust, there shall be found no slackness on my behalf." Forbes, II. 142.]

[2 Erasmus, bishop of Strasburgh, had been a pupil of Sturmius, whom he placed at the head of the college in that city. He was one of the bishops assembled at the council of Trent, and died in 1568. Moreri.]

Staphylus, and that upon the Lord's supper, as well as about your other studies and pursuits. Our friend Hales is in the country. I have written to him to-day. Cook is also in the country. Cecil nobly sustains the description given at the beginning of Horace's second epistle[3], by his zeal, ability, prudence, and firmness, with great credit to himself, and advantage to our own countrymen, and, as I hope, for the welfare of other nations.

As to myself, I was never, thank God, in greater favour with our most serene queen, than I am at present. She reads something either in Greek or Latin with me every day. My wife salutes you and yours. Farewell in Christ. London, Oct. 21, 1562.

Your most attached,

R. ASCHAM.

LETTER XLI.

HERMAN FOLKERZHEIMER TO JOSIAH SIMLER.

Dated at LONDON, *March* 15, 1563.

THOUGH your account, my very dear Josiah, of the great productiveness of the grafts that I inserted, is very gratifying of itself, and I rejoice that I am able at least to be of some use in this humble science and art; yet your friendly exhortation that I should marry on this account, is far more agreeable. Influenced indeed by the bland invitation of nature herself, and by the opinion of both my parents, I do not feel a very great aversion to your advice. But men's constant and daily complaints about their wives, in which they accuse them of being the causes of every thing that is disagreeable, troublesome, and wearisome in life, may well be a warning even to the most favourably disposed, and divert him from

[3 Cum tot sustineas et tanta negotia solus,
　　Res Italas armis tuteris, moribus ornes,
　Legibus emendes &c.

Hor. Ep. II. 1. 1.]

his purpose. Like M. Titurio therefore, who, when he had
nothing to do, threw himself on the grass by way of re-
creation, and said, *I wish this were working;* so it comes into
my mind, whenever I sail, or drive, or ride, to wish that this
were managing one's household, and performing the duty of
a good head of a family. Importuned as I have been by so
many letters from my parents and friends, I should have returned home long since, had not the singular regard of the
bishop of Salisbury towards me compelled me to ask for a
longer leave of absence. And I am deriving this advantage
from my being from home, that, seeing our house is fre-
quented by men of the first rank, I am daily hearing their
grave conversation, not, forsooth, about regulations respecting
light[1], or laws about the eaves of houses, but about for-
tifications, tolls, safe conduct, the importation or exportation
of merchandise, and other things of the like kind. But
why, my Josiah, need I tell you any more of these things?
Two most honourable and excellent men, the bishops of
Salisbury and Worcester, are contending with each other in
their regard and love for me. The bishop of Worcester has
lately presented me with a beautiful and valuable horse, and
most lovingly invites me to visit him as soon as I can.

I have resolved not to write any thing about master Peter
Martyr, for this reason, that I am so affected by the loss of
that man, that it seems very difficult to me to make mention
of him either in conversation or even by letter without tears.
Oh! that 5th of February, when, with our horses tired out
as well as ourselves, we hastened up to London to the meeting of parliament! Oh! how sad, how mournful did that
day prove to us, which announced the death, or rather the
removal and departure, but yet too long, of so great a man[2]!
But there are many things which may afford us comfort, and
diminish our grief and lamentation. And among the rest, if
the death of those persons is glorious, and by no means to
be deplored, who, as one[3] says, have either performed actions

[1] *Servitutes luminum.* This means, in the Roman law, the duty of
a man to allow his neighbour to make openings in his premises, as in
a common wall, for instance, to get light. See Cic. de Orat. I. 38.]

[2] Peter Martyr died Nov. 12, 1562.]

[3] Pliny. Quibus deorum munere datum est aut facere scribenda,
aut scribere legenda.]

worthy of being written, or written things worthy of being performed; we certainly do not regard with sufficient gratitude the exertions and studies of master Martyr, by which he attained unto both of these excellencies, if we continue to bewail his death with so much grief and anxiety, as though he had departed before his time. These and the like topics may be better imagined than described by us both, although more fully by yourself.

I am wonderfully taken, as you have before learned from my letter, with the pursuit of history and antiquity, but yet so as by no means to forsake those studies which you know I have followed for some years. During the last months, for the sake of improvement, I have translated into Latin, in as fitting and appropriate language as I could, Flavius Arrian's Periplus of the Red sea and the Euxine. And because it was somewhat obscure, I think I have thrown some light upon it by commentaries, that is, passages taken from the ancient annals and writings of geographers. I have moreover described the Red sea, the Persian gulph, that of Cambay, the bay of Bengal, with the inland parts of Arabia, Persia, and hither India as far as the Ganges. I followed in this, first of all, the measurement of Ptolemy, and then those which are so laid down by other geographers and by history, as to be capable of being reduced to a careful and accurate determination of longitude and latitude. Farewell, my dear friend, and commend with me to our God the affairs of France. Salute, I pray you, your wife, also the Bullingers, father and sons, Lavater, Gesner, Julius, Pellican, Zuinglius, Haller, Funckius, Gualter, Guldebeckius, the Collins's, and all who know me. Farewell. London, March 15, 1563. Pardon this haste, my Josiah, I pray you, and, if you think proper, salute M. M.

LETTER XLII[1].

BISHOP GRINDAL TO JOHN CALVIN.

Dated at LONDON, *June* 19, 1563.

WE are much indebted, most illustrious master Calvin,
to your piety, and also to your whole church, for having so
long afforded us the services of the most learned master
Gallasius[2]; who has not only left to his successor, master
Cousins, in a state of quietness and good order, the church
which he found at his coming in a most disturbed condition,
but has also by his advice and prudence been of great use
both to myself and our churches. I should not indeed have
willingly let him go, had he not had a better reason for
leaving us than we could wish. Our climate, it seems, does
not agree with his constitution, and has greatly injured his
health, besides depriving him of a beloved wife, (to say nothing
of his children;) so that him whom we now send back as an
invalid, there would be reason to fear, if he remained among
us another winter, that we should not send back at all. It
was therefore of the first importance for him to return to his
native air for the recovery of his health: and we desire
nothing more earnestly than that you may, each of you, be
enabled freely to preach the gospel in your common country.
Although, in the present state of things, partly through the
delay or rather tardiness of some parties, and partly through
the over hasty conduct of others, (to use no severer term,)
there seems but little hope of this; yet I doubt not but that
God himself, by means unknown to us, that we may not glory
in men, will bring the whole matter to a happy issue. I grieve
from my heart that at your age, and with so slender a frame,
you have been attacked, as Gallasius informs me, with a fit of
the gout. I have no doubt but that you have contracted

[1 The original of this letter is preserved at Geneva.]

[2 See above, Letter XXI. p. 49. Gallasius became, in 1564, minister of the church at Orleans; and published, in 1570, at Geneva,
an edition of Irenæus.]

this disorder by excessive study and exertion. Henceforth therefore, you must relax somewhat of your former labours and unseasonable lucubrations, lest, by not sparing yourself, you greatly increase your disease, and become of less benefit to the church. Think of Nazianzene, who, because he did not, when advanced in years, relax at all from that austerity which he practised in early life, was almost constantly obliged to keep his bed, and on that account was rendered less useful to the church. As you and Bullinger are almost the only chief pillars remaining, we desire to enjoy you both (if it please God) as long as possible. I purposely omit mention of Brentius[3], who, having undertaken the advocacy of the very worst of causes, seems no longer to acknowledge us as brethren.

Master Gallasius, who brings you this letter, can give you the best information of the state of our kingdom and church; so that I have at this time no occasion to write upon these subjects. Salute, I pray you, in my name, master Beza and your other colleagues; as also master Antony[4] the professor of Hebrew. May the Lord Jesus very long preserve your piety in safety to us and to his church! London, June 19, 1563.

Your most devoted in the Lord,

EDMUND GRINDAL,

Bishop of London.

[3 See first series, p. 108, note 1.]

[4 Antony Rodolph Chevalier was a learned French protestant, and teacher of that language to the princess Elizabeth. On the death of Edward VI. he retired into Germany, and was made Hebrew professor at Strasburgh. He succeeded Tremellius (whose daughter-in-law he married) as Regius Professor of Hebrew at Cambridge in 1569, upon the recommendation of archbishop Parker; and was also appointed to a prebend at Canterbury. He died in Guernsey in 1572.]

LETTER XLIII.

HIEROME ZANCHIUS[1] TO BISHOP GRINDAL.

Dated at [STRASBURGH, before *Aug.* 23, 1563.]

EXCUSE my delay, honoured sir; for I have but lately returned from the borders of Italy, and have found an almost infinite number of letters, to which I must necessarily reply. You desire to know how our dispute is settled. I will tell you in few words. Our senators, as I hear and see, had determined from the very first so to conduct themselves in this controversy of ours, that the honour of each party should remain as far as possible inviolate; and this for the sake of the office, both of the preachers in the church, and mine in the school. Although therefore during those two years in which the cause was being pleaded before the senate, they were well aware, both from the reading of the charges, the writings of each party, and the opinions of many churches and universities respecting my theses[2], that the action brought against me by my adversaries was most unjust, and that my doctrine, which had been charged with and condemned for both novelty and heresy, was neither novel nor heretical; they nevertheless refused to decide upon the case, or at least, to permit it to be decided by a disputation; but having sent for four divines[3] and some canonists, partly from Tubingen, partly from Deux-Ponts, partly from Basle, they resolved that the dispute should be settled by these parties. They, in the presence of four senators, read over the pleadings and

[1 See above, Letter XXXVII. note 1. Grindal's reply to this letter is printed in his Remains, published by the Parker Society, p. 276.]

[2 These theses contained the declaration of Zanchy's faith concerning predestination, final perseverance, and the Lord's supper.]

[3 These divines were, James Andreas from Tubingen; Cuman Flinsbach from Deux-Ponts; Simon Sultzer and Ulric Coccius from Basle. See Henr. Alting, Hist. Eccles. Palatinæ, p. 298. Ed. 1644.]

writings upon each side; they clearly perceived that great injustice had been done both to myself and to the truth; they reported to the senate their opinion both of the writings and pleadings. Here master Peter Sturmius, the head school-master, said before them all, "What now then becomes of the numerous and grievous heresies which were objected to Zanchius?"

They then made proposals separately to each party to come to an agreement. When the referees came to me, they first of all stated in express terms that the opposite party held the same opinion with myself concerning the predestina-tion of the saints; for that they approved the doctrine of Augustine, Luther and Bucer; and by these three, next to the scriptures, I had most copiously confirmed the whole of what I teach in my lectures and expositions. There only now remained some difference of opinion respecting the Lord's supper. Although therefore they had read my confession respecting the supper, yet they were nevertheless anxious to hear more clearly from myself what I thought about the real presence of Christ therein: for in my con-fession I had offered no opinion upon the subject, but had only discussed three principal heads; first, that not only the symbols were received, but also the thing itself, the real body of Christ, and his real blood, that is, Christ himself; secondly, that each was eaten and drunk, not with the mouth of the body but of the spirit, namely, by faith; thirdly, and this only by the faithful. To this I answered, that I was un-willing to dispute upon this question, because I could not find a single positive declaration in the scriptures respecting the presence of Christ in the supper; but nevertheless, that they might not think that I shrunk from the subject, and dared not explain my opinion upon this question, I would tell them my sentiments. First, that I can in no wise admit that the body of Christ in the supper is present with our bodies: for that a thing is said to be present with any one, when in some way or other it communicates itself to that with which it is said to be present, and is perceived by it; but that a thing is said to be absent, which in no wise communicates itself to, or is perceived by, that from which it is said to be absent; whether that object, in regard to local distance or nearness, be at a less or greater interval. Sultzer[1] was walking up and down the room, while James Andreas[2] was sitting down and conversing with me upon the supper. I brought forward therefore an illustration taken from themselves, in these words: "You, master arbitrators, are said to be, and really are, present with me, that is, with my body, because you communicate yourselves to me and to my senses, and are perceived by me, while I see you with my eyes, and hear you with my ears; and master Sultzer, who is walking up and down, is as much present with me as the rest of you who are sitting; although as respects local distance or nearness he is farther from me than you are, and you are nearer than he. But those who are out of doors, beyond this chamber (for there were some of the servants of these gentlemen outside) are said to be absent, because I neither hear nor see them, nor perceive them by any bodily sense. But it is manifest, that the true and substantial body of Christ is not communicated to my body in the supper; for I do not perceive it by any of my bodily senses, as I neither see it with my eyes, nor hear it with my ears, nor smell it with my nostrils, nor touch it with my hands, nor taste it with my palate. I cannot therefore by any means admit that the body of Christ is present with our bodies in the supper. But that the same true and substantial body of Christ is present with my mind in the supper, where it is most efficacious, I cannot deny; since it is beyond dispute, that it is really communicated to the minds of the faithful, and is really perceived by them: for it is seen by the eye of the believing mind, or the inner man, and is taken by the hand, and eaten by the mouth of the same; and is in such wise eaten that we feel its virtue and salutary effects in ourselves. I cannot therefore deny in the abstract the real

[1 Simon Sultzer was a native of Interlaken. He studied under Bucer, Capito, and Grynæus, and became professor of Greek at Berne in 1533.]

[2 James Andreas was professor of divinity at Tubingen, and one of the chief of those divines employed in 1569 by the special command of the dukes of Wirtemberg and Brunswick, in composing a form of doctrine in which might be decided all the controversies that divided the church.]

and substantial presence, that is, the presence of the real
and substantial body of Christ in the supper, but in that
sense in which I have explained it."

Here James Andreas exclaims with astonishment, "Truly
then you hold the same opinion as we do." "You have
heard, Sirs," I said, "my opinion. If it is also yours, I
rejoice for myself, and congratulate you and the church."
"Now," says he, "I see why you have brought so many
arguments (namely in my confession) against our statement
that 'the body of Christ is also eaten with the bodily
mouth,' because you suppose that we hold the body of Christ
to be eaten with the mouth of our body, as if the body of
Christ were in contact with our mouth and body." "Just
so," I replied: "I supposed from your writings that such
was your opinion." "By no means," said he, "by no means
do we entertain this view, but only express ourselves in this
way by reason of the sacramental union." I then said, "If
these are your sentiments, I do not find fault with that expression; for I also admit, that on account of the sacramental
union there is attributed to the body of Christ what is the
property of bread, and on the other hand, to bread, what
belongs to the body of Christ." "But what," says he, "do
you think of the eating of the unworthy?" "If by this
term," I answered, "you mean men who are clearly ungodly, and destitute of true faith, I cannot admit that the
body of Christ is eaten by such persons. But if you mean
such persons as are endued with faith, albeit a weak one,
and of a more relaxed life than is becoming to a Christian,
I do not deny it; for such were those Corinthians who,
because they had eaten the body of the Lord unworthily,
St Paul says, were judged, that is, were 'chastened[3] of the
Lord, that they should not be condemned with the world.'"
We could not therefore agree about this article. "But I
have no doubt," he said, "that if you will more diligently
examine this article, you will come over to our sentiments."
"I have already," I replied, "examined it with sufficient
attention, and am unable to think otherwise than as I do."
"Well," says he, "we have said enough upon the supper.
We thank God that in this article respecting the supper
there is no great difference among you, since you admit on

[3 See 1 Cor. xi. 32.]

both sides a real and substantial presence." And thus we ended.

They then produced some articles about predestination, and gave them to both parties for their inspection. But they gave them me to read over in such haste, that they would not allow them to remain with me even a single night. At last, when they perceived that I would not subscribe to them, unless they were carefully examined by me at home, they let me have them; but upon condition of my neither copying them nor allowing them to be copied. They added to them, that they might at least determine something respecting the Lord's supper in general, the Confession of Augsburgh, and the articles of concord[1] between Luther and Bucer. In the articles upon predestination I discovered nothing openly impious, and which could not be admitted with a good conscience; as master Calvin afterwards wrote both to me and to our pastor. I perceived only that they were so artfully framed, as to make it evident that the arbitrators were more desirous that the controverted articles should be buried in a certain darkness spread over them, than that the truth should be unfolded in open day. This was one reason among others why I for a long time, that is, almost to the last, refused to subscribe. At length when I perceived that it rested with myself alone, whether on the termination of this serious dispute (which was not confined to one or two, but extended to all the ministers on one side, and all the professors on the other) peace and harmony should be restored; and when I saw that I could subscribe with a safe conscience, especially with a protest being premised, I consented. When therefore I came to the place where our senators and the commissioners were, together with all the professors and some others, after returning my thanks to the parties to whom they were due, I said that I would subscribe, but with this protest premised: first, that I would not that any prejudice should arise through this subscription of mine to other churches, colleges, and the truth; next, that I would not allow any thing derogatory to that doctrine which I have taught here at Strasburgh these eight years, and which is contained in my lectures, disputations, and confessions; lastly, that I might be allowed

---

[1 This was called the concord of Wittemberg, and took place in the year 1536.]

to explain the Confession of Augsburgh, the apology[2], and articles of concord, as well as these present articles, according to the rule of God's word, the doctrine of Augustine, Luther, and Bucer.   I then conditionally subscribed in these words : *This form of doctrine I both acknowledge as godly, and receive it as such.*   H. Zanchius.   The next day, all wrongs having been forgiven, were joined the right hands of fellowship and brotherly love.   Thus was our disagreement settled, without any derogation from the truth of doctrine.

Meanwhile, however, there are not wanting those who blame the act : but such persons do not consider what that passage means, " Christ pleased not himself;" nor do they reflect upon the serious evils occasioned by dissensions.   Why, for the sake of peace among so many, both ministers and professors of the same city, should I not subscribe to the Confession of Augsburgh, and its apology, especially in the way I did, both my interpretation and also protest being allowed by the commissioners?   They are offended at those words in the apology, " that the body of Christ is really and substantially present in the Lord's supper."   But I explained upon what understanding they might be admitted, and how that may be said to be really and substantially present, which is really and substantially partaken of.   When the sun is above our hemisphere, and communicates its real and substantial body to be seen by us, and by means of that body its heat and light to be partaken of, may we not say with propriety that the sun is really and substantially present?   So likewise on the other hand, when having removed to the other hemisphere, because he no longer communicates himself to be seen and partaken of by us, we say he is absent : when yet, in regard to local distance or propinquity, he is as far from us when above ours, as when he is above the other hemisphere. What therefore is to prevent our saying, that Christ's body is really and substantially present to those to whom he really and substantially communicates himself?

But, say they, other persons do not so understand and

[2 John Faber, Eckius, and Cochlæus, drew up a confutation of the Augsburgh Confession; upon which Melancthon published, in 1531, the apology for it here mentioned, and which constitutes a part of the symbolical books of the Lutheran church. See Mosheim, Ed. Soames. III. 148.]

interpret as you do. But I did not subscribe to the interpretations of others, but only to the words of the Augsburgh Confession, and that according to the sense which I acknowledge to be a godly one; and my interpretation was allowed. Calvin certainly thinks differently, and I respect his opinion far more than that of many others; for he truly has the Spirit of God, and looks more to the edification of the churches, than to a certain vainglorious pertinacity in our phrases, expressions, and syllables. He writes to our pastor, that he does not approve of persons simply refusing to subscribe; and recommends their subscribing, provided only exceptions be given in and allowed: and he advises me by letter to make an attestation before the magistrate, that I have been induced to subscribe from an earnest desire of peace, but with those exceptions, and that I now profess and confirm the same. If there had been any hope of obtaining a discussion in which the truth would have openly triumphed, or of a definitive decision, as they call it, being pronounced respecting the whole controversy, or of settling the dispute in any other better way, I never would have subscribed. But as I can hope for none of these things, what, I ask, could I have done? I believe that with your piety and prudence you would have acted just as I did. If I am mistaken, pardon this my opinion of your piety, and pardon likewise, I entreat you, I no longer call it my brevity, but my too great prolixity; and farewell, and retain me in the number of your friends. I salute my four noble gossips[1], masters Wroth, Cook, Knolles, and Heton; and I wish you would communicate to them and to other learned men this my compromise, and candidly write me word what both you and they think of it. May the Lord Jesus evermore guide and protect you by his Spirit!

[H. ZANCHIUS.]

[1 *Compatres*, godfathers to his children. The word *gossip* is from the Anglo-Saxon, *God* and *sib* (*affinity*), and is thus defined by Becon (Acts of Christ and Antichrist), Vol. III. p. 532. "Christian gossips, that is to say, those men and women that have been godfathers and godmothers together of one child at baptism."]

LETTER XLIV.

HERMAN FOLKERZHEIMER TO JOSIAH SIMLER.

Dated at EMBDEN, *Aug.* 21, 1563.

It has happened, Josiah, contrary to all my expectation, and, I fear, to your duty likewise, that I have received no letter from you at the last Frankfort fair. And, in truth, I was exceedingly grieved at the loss of the delightful, and indeed the only enjoyment of our great intimacy, which in the privation of personal intercourse was to be derived from our correspondence. Although those noble and excellent persons[2] earnestly desired to retain me longer with them in England, yet induced by the letters of my friends, and the desire of seeing them, I preferred returning to my country. As soon, therefore, as I had received the horse which the bishop of Worcester had presented me with, and had obtained from Robert[3], the master of the horse, a licence for its exportation, I began to think about my voyage. When the vessel was left on shore at the turn of the tide, we hoisted up the horse, fastened with three ropes round his belly, in such a way that he could be lowered and got aboard. We had intended to sail direct for Belgium; but when we had proceeded about five miles, we were thrown, against our will, by a west wind upon the coast of France. After having somewhat recruited my horse, half dead with hunger, as his rider was with seasickness, I immediately betook myself with much satisfaction to the Belgian frontier. The principal towns on our journey were Calais, Gravelines, Dunkirk, Bruges, Ghent; and then in Brabant, Brussels, Louvaine, Mechlin, and Antwerp; lastly, in Guelderland, leaving Holland on the left, Hoogstraet, Nimeguen, Arnheim and Deventer. At Groningen I met my brother Ulric with his wife and little boy, to our great

[2 Namely, Bishops Jewel and Sandys. See above, Letter XLI. p. 94.]

[3 Sir Robert Dudley, afterwards earl of Leicester.]

delight on both sides. Having staid with him a week, I set off for Embden. Many things have happened in the course of my life which have afforded me very great pleasure; but, immortal powers! what can be compared to that greeting and those embraces of my parents, sisters, and brothers? I do not now feel so much surprised at the great longing of Ulysses, whose home, and wife, and children were so dear to him, that if he could but see the smoke[1] of his country, he would despise immortality. I can never be sufficiently and duly thankful to our good and gracious God, for having so abundantly granted those things which I am often wont to pray for.

The kings of Denmark and Sweden[2] are making preparation for a most destructive war. Duke Eric[3] of Brunswick has gone over to the king of Denmark with a large body of troops. The Dane is said to excel in infantry and cavalry, and the Swede in his navy. There has been more than once a most severe engagement by sea. The king of Denmark, it is thought, will not be able to do any thing in Sweden, even with superior forces, by reason of the number of rivers and lakes, by which, as the bridges are everywhere broken down and cut off, all access is shut out; so that they must necessarily wait for the winter to freeze over the rivers and open a passage.

You have a person with you, by the name of Egbert Brassius, the son of a worthy and excellent preacher. If you will aid him with your advice and assistance in the prosecution of his studies, and notice the young man, who is a great lover of piety and learning, you will do nothing inconsistent with that reputation for kindness that Josiah already possesses. You had intended to come to us, together with Froschover, and pass over from hence to England; and my brother and other friends, as well as myself, earnestly beg and pray you to do so. And this, I hope, will take place during my stay at home; for I am thinking of going into Italy. Farewell, my Josiah, and salute warmly and

[1 See Hom. Od. I. 57, &c.]

[2 Namely Frederick II., and Eric XIV. The occasion of this war was the voluntary submission of Esthonia to Sweden in 1561.]

[3 Eric, son of Eric, duke of Hanover, and grandson of William, duke of Brunswick.]

respectfully in my name your wife, together with the lady
your neighbour[4], the Bullingers, Gualter, Zuinglius, Lavater,
John Frisius, Haller, Julius, Pellican, Guldebeckius, the
Collins's, Funckius, Wolfius, Bibliander, and all our other
common friends.   Embden, Aug. 21, 1563.   Salute too my
young countryman Defholdius together with his tutor.

[H. FOLKERZHEIMER.]

LETTER XLV[5].

BISHOP GRINDAL TO CONRAD HUBERT.

Dated at FULHAM, *Aug.* 23, 1563.

GREETING.   Dithelm[6] Blaurer, who at your advice and
persuasion came over to me in England, is now returning
home at the summons of his father.   I could not therefore
allow one who had been recommended to me by a letter from
you, to return to you without a letter from me.   And it is
also just that I should give such testimony as he deserves,
of his pious and sober conduct during his residence in my
family.   His assistance has been of use to me in many
respects, and would have been much more so, had not the
infinite engagements connected with my office distracted me
in various ways.   But that you may know upon what terms
I have dismissed him, I have paid him, upon leaving me, the
whole quarter's salary, which would have been due next
Michaelmas, viz. four French crowns, together with four
pounds of our money for the expenses of his journey, making
thirteen French crowns and a little over.   I have given him
too some little presents in addition.   My only motive in
writing this is that you may know the plain truth of the
case.   I have also paid Abel, for the expenses of Dithelm

[4 This may perhaps serve to explain the last sentence in Letter
XLI.]

[5 The original of this letter is preserved in the archives of
St Thomas, at Strasburgh.]

[6 See above, Letter XII. p. 28.]

when he first came over from Germany, more than fourteen crowns, because, as it was winter, they were forced by contrary winds to wait somewhat longer on the coast of Flanders.

I hear your disputes are now settled. God grant that the peace may be solid, and sincere, and without disguise! I have no doubt of it on your part. I fear lest the other party may some time or other raise a fresh disturbance. But I heartily congratulate you, my very dear master Conrad, on your pious respect for our common instructor, master Bucer of happy memory, whose reputation you have hitherto defended with so much firmness. I wish you every blessing in the Lord. From my country house at Fulham on the banks of the Thames, Aug. 23, 1563.

Yours in Christ,

EDM. GRINDAL,

Bishop of London.

LETTER[1] XLV*.

JOHN ABEL TO HENRY BULLINGER.
Dated at LONDON, *Aug.* 24, 1563.

PRAISE to God. My friendly greeting and willing service to you, dear master and friend. I sent my last letter to Strasburgh fair, in which I wrote you word that I had received your letter, together with some books, and that I had forwarded the same to master Horn, bishop of Winchester, who has sent me word in return that he intends to send you a letter together with some money, which I have not yet received; but as soon as he sends it, I will forward it to you immediately. He has written me word likewise, that he means to send two crowns for the housekeeper at Zurich who waited at the English house[2] there, and was

[1 This letter was originally written in *German,* and is thus numbered to preserve the continuity of the series translated from the Latin originals.]

[2 This house belonged to Froschover. See first series, Letter LXI. p. 136.]

called the English servant.   Master Pilkington too, who is
now bishop of Durham, has given me a crown for the said
housekeeper, which I send you herewith, and pray you to
give it her.   I have done my best for her, and spoken with
other bishops on her behalf; for John Burcher has both
spoken and written to me respecting some relief for her, and
says that she is a pious poor woman, and faithfully waited
upon the English at Zurich.   John Burcher is now become
a clergyman in the country not far from London, where he
preaches the word of God faithfully, and is much beloved,
and does much good.   His wife has been delivered of a little
girl, and is also well and hearty.

   I have not much news to send you.   Our Lord God is
very angry with us for our ingratitude; for his holy word
is daily preached here among us, and we have not loved nor
followed the same, nor commended it by our lives : wherefore he has this last year sent a great dearth among us, and
now he has sent such a plague[3] and pestilence among us, that
in the city which our English took last year in Normandy,
some thousands have died so wonderfully by reason of the
plague, that our people have quitted the said town, and are
returned from thence with all their goods and artillery and
arms, &c., by which means the plague is so rife in London,
that there are dying by the pestilence five or six hundred
a week : and there is reason to fear that if our Lord should
not have compassion upon us, it will become yet more
prevalent, for it has only just begun.   God give us his
grace and holy Spirit that we may amend our lives, that
his holy name may be praised and magnified thereby; and
then will he take away this plague.   His holy will be done
from henceforth and for evermore.   Amen.

   I have nothing else to write to you about at this time; but
I pray you to salute from me your dear wife, together with
both your sons and their wives, as also master Gualter and
his dear wife, with John Henry Smith[4], and all my other
acquaintance.   The grace of God be with you all, and
preserve you from all evil.   Amen.

                    JOHN ABEL.   England.

   [3 See first series, Letter LIX. p. 132.]
   [4 Namely, John Henry Fabricius mentioned above, p. 53, &c.]

LETTER XLVI.

HIEROME ZANCHIUS TO BISHOP GRINDAL.

Dated from the mountains near CHIAVENNA, *August* 1564.

I SEND you, reverend prelate, my judgment respecting the controversy of the churches about the supper of the Lord, which for certain reasons I have dedicated to my friend master Knolles. I did not indeed write it with a view to its being published, as you may yourself conjecture, both from its brevity and style; but since my friends, and Sturmius among the rest, so highly approved it, as to compel me to publish it, I chose rather by my compliance to appear to my friends wanting in talent, than ungrateful to the churches by my refusal. You will therefore receive this copy as a testimony of my respect. I hope to send you better and more copious tidings very soon. As the Lord had heretofore visited you with the pestilence[1], so he has

[1 Zanchius left Strasburgh in November 1563, and entered on his pastoral charge at Chiavenna in the January following; shortly after which the town was visited by a pestilence, which in seven months carried off twelve hundred of the inhabitants. "When the plague," he says, "actually began to make havock, I enforced repentance and faith, while I had a place to preach in, or any congregation to hear. Many being dead, and others having fled the town (like shipwrecked mariners, who, to avoid instant destruction make towards what coast they can), but very few remained; and of these remaining few, some were almost terrified to death, others were solely employed in taking care of the sick, and others in guarding the walls. They concurred in advising me to consult my own safety by withdrawing for a time, till the indignation should be overpast. I betook myself therefore, with all my family, to a high mountain, not a great way from the town, yet remote from human converse, and peculiarly formed for contemplation and unmolested retirement. Here we led a solitary life for three months and a half. I devoted my time chiefly to meditation and writing, to prayer, and reading the scriptures. I never was happier in my own soul, nor enjoyed a better share of health." Zanch. Op.]

this year visited us, that is, my church at Chiavenna. I call it *my* church, that you may know that I am no longer professor at Strasburgh, but am minister at Chiavenna on the borders of Italy, and which is so called, as being the key[2] of the passage from Italy to Germany, and vice versa. You will learn from a book which I will shortly send you, the reason[3] of my at length leaving Strasburgh.

You know why that worthy Martyr[4] of pious memory could no longer remain at Strasburgh; and therefore he removed to Zurich. Besides that being under bondage to man I had also other important reasons. And the French church that was at Strasburgh was dispersed by the same cause that occasioned my departure. Those good people are no longer satisfied that their professors or ministers should subscribe to the Confession[5] of Augsburgh; but they require also that in every particular, both as to the understanding of that confession, and the interpretation of scripture, they should be of the same mind with their preachers without any disagreement whatever. You know the author of this: may the Lord have pity upon that city! I did everything to retain my professorship, and for this sole reason, that I might at least preserve in the schools the ancient doctrine of that church, and which I know is the christian one. But what can you do, when the Lord sees fit to punish any people by reason of their iniquities?

[2 Zanchius considers the Latin name *Clavenna* to be derived from *clavis*.]

[3 The immediate occasion of Zanchy's leaving Strasburgh was the controversy with Heshusius, the publication of whose book, concerning the eucharist and in defence of consubstantiation, Zanchy had endeavoured to prevent.]

[4 The enemies of Peter Martyr affirmed, that in the doctrine of the Lord's supper he was gone from the opinion of the Confession of Augsburgh, and that therefore it was to be feared he would make some troubles in the church. And though the senate was satisfied with his vindication of himself, yet because he saw that this controversy of the sacrament was daily stirred up with more bitterness of mind, he rejoiced that there was an occasion offered (by his being invited by the senate of Zurich to succeed Conrad Pellican) whereby he might rid himself from these troubles. See his life by Simler, at the end of his Common-Places.]

[5 See above, p. 15, note 1.]

I commend to you that affair of my relative Laurence Limacius. Farewell, my excellent father, and singular good friend. In the month of August, 1564. From the mountains near Chiavenna.

H. ZANCHIUS.

LETTER XLVII.

HIEROME ZANCHIUS TO HENRY KNOLLES.

Dated from [the mountains near CHIAVENNA. *August* 1564.]

My judgment respecting the controversy of the churches upon the Lord's supper, which, most honoured gossip[1], I have dedicated to yourself, to the end that it may be a public and at the same time a perpetual testimony of my gratitude towards you, I had given to that most excellent and most careful, and I may add too, most learned printer John Oporinus[2], to be printed in fair type. But since, as I perceive, he was unable to procure from the censors a licence to print this book, the reason of which I leave you to guess, he transferred it to a printer at Mulhausen. This person,

[1 Lat. *Compater*. Sir H. Knolles was sponsor to Zanchy's daughter. The dedication here alluded to is a long one, and chiefly refers to the subject of the treatise. The last sentence is as follows: Te igitur, humanissime ac generose Knolle, sicut cum hic esses apud vos initio hujus anni, post tuam ad conventum electorum nuper Francofurti pro electore regis Romanorum habitum nomine vestræ reginæ susceptam legationem, delegi mihi in filiæ meæ Læliæ Constantiæ compatrem; tuque ita lubenti animo eam e sancto fonte in tuam profiliam suscepisti, ut ei etiam honorificum δέπας ἀργυροῦν tuæ fideī testimonium donaris, ita in protectorem hujus mei quasi novi filioli eligere decrevi, persuasus te illius protectionem nullo modo recusaturum.]

[2 John Oporinus, or Herbst, was a celebrated printer at Basle. Foxe the martyrologist was employed by him as a corrector of the press. Strype, Cranmer, 514. An account of his life is given in Moreri, and by Andrew Lociscus, *Orat. de vita et obitu Oporini*.]

either through carelessness or want of skill, sent it forth full of errors, which displeased me exceedingly; so that I have been obliged to correct with the pen whatever copies I had in my possession. I send you therefore a corrected copy, and entreat you to take in good part these few pages: I should have sent some more copies to my other friends, if I could have met with any one to be the bearer of them.

As to other matters, we are all, by the blessing of God, in good health, and your little god-daughter, who is now weaned, prattles, runs about, and plays the monkey. You have, I suppose, heard ere this from others about my having left Strasburgh; but you are not, perhaps, at all aware of the reason. It was the same, to tell you in one word, on account of which also the excellent Peter Martyr[3] of pious memory long since departed to Zurich; namely, a bondage to men quite unworthy of a Christian, and much more of a divine. When therefore I perceived that it was no longer permitted me to teach with freedom, nor to defend that doctrine which, drawn as it was from the fountain of holy scripture, those most learned men, Bucer, Capito, Martyr, and Calvin, had held forth to their audience in that very school many years before me, yea, and which I also had for nine years taught there in my lectures, and defended in public disputations; I resigned my former situation, and accepted another, namely, the ministry of the church at Chiavenna. But the Lord has wonderfully afflicted my church, yea, the whole town, with a pestilence, which has destroyed two thirds of it, one third only being left, as we read also in Zechariah[4]. But this pestilence is not only raging here, but also in many

[3 Peter Martyr left Strasburgh in 1556, in consequence of the attacks made upon him by his adversaries for supposed heterodoxy concerning the nature of the Lord's supper. "For both by letters, and by their readings and sermons they so gall him, as there wanted nothing to the accusing of Martyr but the naming of him; yea, and one of the students made an oration openly in the school touching the eucharist, made to this end, that he might of set purpose condemn Martyr and his doctrine. Wherefore since he perceived that his adversaries did daily make more open war against him, and that they did by name reprove him in their books, as also Sleidan in his history maketh mention, he began to deliberate with himself of his departure." See his life by Simler, at the end of his Common Places.]

[4 See Zech. xiii. 8.]

other places, both in Germany, as at Basle, and in France, as at Lyons. May the Lord have mercy upon us all! Italy is free from this evil, but is labouring under a dearth of provision. Your gossip[1] sends her best respects. I beg you to salute my friends, and especially [Sir Thomas] Wroth, [Sir Antony] Cook, and also Heton, my gossips. Farewell.

[H. ZANCHIUS.]

LETTER XLVIII.

RICHARD MASTERS TO RODOLPH GUALTER.

Dated at LONDON, *March* 4, 1565.

SINCE I last wrote to you, very reverend sir, I have received from you three letters abounding in the expressions of your regard towards me; for my not having sooner replied to which I will neither plead in excuse the business in which I was then engaged, nor forgetfulness of you, nor any thing else, except the plague, which was so long raging among us, that the court[2] has been a long time, and at a great distance, absent from London; whither having, by the blessing of God, returned in safety, I have determined to send you this letter. I have received your discourses on the minor prophets by the hands of my friend and fellow-citizen, John Abel; and I understand that they are so esteemed by all learned and godly persons, that there is scarce a single individual at this time in all Europe, who in their opinion can equal or excel you in the interpretation of the sacred writings: and they are anxiously expecting the remaining discourses which you have promised on St John. I have also stated to those who are in chief authority among us, with how great

[1 Lat. *Commater.* See before, p. 104.]

[2 See first series, Letter LIX. p. 132. On October 2, 1563, parliament was prorogued in consequence of the plague, unto October 5, 1564. D'Ewes, Journals, p. 91.]

affection you regard us and our government, when you write that you have, for our sake and that of true religion, so anxiously exerted yourself with those parties who were so exceedingly active in bringing about a treaty between you and the French[3].

The Guisian party in France is getting weaker and weaker every day, so much so, that the cardinal of Lorraine[4], together with his nephew the duke of Guise, were very near being killed the other day from an attack at Paris in the public street by Montmorenci the governor of the city, (the marshal, as they call him) and eldest son of Ann, duke of Montmorenci, the grand master of the cavalry of France, or constable, as he is called; in which tumult there fell five of the armed escort of the cardinal of Lorraine, who, with his nephew, escaped with difficulty to the house of a certain tradesman, where they found a temporary refuge. The commissioners[5] of our queen and of the king of Spain are to meet

[3 See first series, Letter LXIV. p. 141.]

[4 The cardinal was on his return from the council of Trent, in January 1565, and invited all his friends to join him, and swell his escort, that he might make a sort of triumphal entry into Paris, where marshal Montmorenci was at that time governor, and was desirous of mortifying the cardinal's vanity. To put a good appearance on his conduct, he went to the parliament, and said that he had information that somebody proposed coming to Paris with armed followers, which, if it occurred, he would resist with open force. The cardinal was informed of the marshal's design, but paid no attention to it, and entered boldly into the city. Montmorenci soon arrived, and ordered him and his followers to put away their pistols. He had sent a messenger to make the same communication before the cardinal had entered; but that person was not well received, and the marshal immediately set out at the head of a body of horsemen. A skirmish ensued, the cardinal jumped from his horse, and ran into a shop, from whence he gained his own hotel in the night. See Browning, Hist. of the Huguenots, chap. 18, and the authorities there quoted.]

[5 There is among the Flanders correspondence, in the state-paper office, a MS. entitled "A memorial of the matters to be entreated at the colloquie to be holden at Bruges betwixt the commissioners of her majestie; that is, the viscount Montague, Mr doctor Wotton, one of her majesties privy council, and Mr Haddon, of Requests, on the one part, and the commissioners of the king of Spaine on the other. Made at Westminster, the xith of March, 1564 [5,] in the viith year of her majesties reign." The English commissioners arrived at Bruges on the 24th of March, and remained there till the conference was sus-in Flanders at the beginning of this spring, for the purpose of re-establishing the commerce at Antwerp between our merchants and theirs upon its former footing. This for two or three years past has been interrupted by disagreements between the merchants of both countries, to the great detriment of each: in other respects however, as far as government is concerned, every thing is settled and quiet among us. In Scotland the monasteries are razed to the ground, and monkery and idolatry are abolished; the queen alone, of the Guise family, (for she is the sister's daughter of the duke[1] that was slain,) still retaining her mass. Our friend the earl of Bedford is absent from court, and has been so for the last half year, as he is appointed governor of Berwick on the borders of Scotland, and which divides us from them. I have however taken care to inform him in his absence, that you had not forgotten him, and I commended you to him in my letter. Farewell. May the Lord God preserve and direct you to the glory of his name, and that you may long live and labour in his vineyard! London, March 4, 1565.

Yours wholly from my heart,

RICHARD MASTERS.

pended by mutual consent in May. It was renewed in the following year, and again suspended, it being agreed upon in the mean time by all parties that all things should remain in their actual position; that the treaty for free intercourse between both countries should be considered as still in force; and that the merchant strangers settled in either country should be considerately and kindly treated by the governments under which they respectively lived. See Burgon's Life and Times of Sir Thomas Gresham, II. pp. 66, 88, seqq.]

[1 Francis, duke of Guise, was assassinated in 1563 by John Poltrot de Meré at the siege of Orleans.]

LETTER XLIX.

BISHOP PARKHURST TO JOHN WOLFIUS.

Dated at LUDHAM, *Aug.* 19, 1565.

You have no need to thank me, my Wolfius, for so trifling an obligation. Accept, I pray you, with kindness this slight present, as a memorial, such as it is, of my regard for you. I received a letter from you two years since, and by reason of my being at that time overwhelmed with numberless engagements, I did not reply to you separately, but was obliged to satisfy both yourself, and Lavater, and Simler, with one short letter. I have written about our own affairs and those of the Scots to other correspondents. You will learn the news from them; for I am unable to repeat the same intelligence to each. On the 19th of May a barn of mine, two hundred and fifteen feet in length, fell to the ground, without injury either to man or beast. I have almost rebuilt it at a very great expense. Farewell. Salute your wife in my name and that of my wife, together with all our other friends. In haste. Ludham, Aug. 19, 1565.

Yours,

JOHN PARKHURST,

[Bishop of] Norwich.

LETTER XLIX*.

JOHN ABEL TO HENRY BULLINGER[2].

[Dated at LONDON, *June* 6, 1566.]

PRAISE to God! My friendly greeting and willing service to you, my kind and dear sir. Your last letter of

[2 This letter is translated from the German original.]

March 20th has come duly to hand; from which I understand that you have received my former letters. I have also
received two copies of your Swiss Confession of Faith; one of
which, written in Latin, I have, according to your request,
given to master Richard Hilles, who expresses his best thanks.
This book pleases me and many believing hearts exceedingly.
But I am still more delighted with your house-book[1], containing fifty of your sermons, and bearing the Latin title
Decades Bullingeri. In this book all the articles of our
christian faith are fully declared and set forth, and it is com-
forting, and agreeable, and instructive to me to read it.

   Your letters to master Horn, bishop of Winchester, and
masters Jewel and Parkhurst, I have duly forwarded; and
master Horn has written me word that he has received
your said letter[2], in which you have declared your judgment
respecting the cap and surplice. And he has promised me a
copy of that letter, which has been of great service to many
godly preachers and others, who faithfully and diligently perform their ecclesiastical functions. Some persons, however,
are not satisfied with it, those namely, who have thought fit
rather to give up the office of a preacher and minister than
wear a surplice in the administration of the holy sacraments,
or put on a clerical cap. So rigid are they in their opinion,
that they have altogether given up their ecclesiastical vocation, and are therefore deposed from their ministry : which
is greatly to be regretted, especially as they need not put
on a surplice when preaching, as indeed nobody is commanded
to do, except in the administration of infant baptism and of
the Lord's supper. Master Thomas Sampson has written
you a letter[3] upon this subject, and desires to receive your
answer; because he is foremost in opposition to this practice,
and has given up his preferment[4]: and several other preachers

   [1 Germ. *Hussbuch.*]
   [2 See first series, Appendix, Letter II. p. 341.]
   [3 See first series, Letter LXIX. p. 153.]
   [4 Sampson was, by a special order from the queen, deprived by
the archbishop and commissioners of the deanery of Christ-church.
See Strype, Parker, I. 368. The archbishop subsequently wrote in
his behalf to the queen and to the chapter. Sampson afterwards
obtained the mastership of the hospital of William de Wigston, at
Leicester, and a prebend in St Paul's, and by leave and favour of the

have joined him, who are resolved rather to resign their
functions than wear the cap and surplice. Five preachers
have lately been deprived, and sent as prisoners, two of them
to master Horn, bishop of Winchester, two to doctor Cox,
bishop of Ely, and one to master Parkhurst, bishop of Norwich.
These five preachers had been interdicted from preaching, but
notwithstanding the prohibition, they again preached in their
respective churches, in consequence of which our queen and
privy council are much displeased. They were summoned
before the queen's council, and when they made their appearance, much was said to them for having preached contrary
to the queen's orders, and for having afforded a bad example
to the common people, so as to render them disobedient.
Whereupon the five preachers fell upon their knees, and asked
for mercy: in reply to which the lords in council answered,
that if the queen were not merciful and gracious, they would
all have had to undergo severe punishment; but, seeing that
they were preachers of God's holy word, they should have
eight days allowed them wherein to visit their friends and con-
nections, after which they were to proceed, two to the bishop
of Winchester, and two to the bishop of Ely, and one to the
bishop of Norwich, as prisoners, as above mentioned, so long
as the queen and her council shall think fit[5]. One of these
preachers has also caused to be printed a book[6] against the
queen's command respecting the cap and surplice : but as
soon as the authorities heard of it, the book was prohibited,

queen was appointed theological lecturer at Whittington College in
London. See Wood, Athenæ, Vol. I. p. 234.]

[5 Archbishop Parker, in a letter to Haddon, says : "With the assistance of the queen's majesties council we have dispersed a few of the
heads of them, some to the bishop of Winchester, some to Ely, and
some to Norwich, to school them, or at least to have them out of
London till we see cause to restore them their liberty." Strype considers that "Gentleness, as appears hence, was used towards these
ministers that stood out and so were deprived." After noticing their
being thus sent to three of the bishops, he adds: "But it was not long
that they remained so, but were restored to their liberties; and had
leave, or at least connivance to preach." Life of Parker, I. 445.]

[6 This work was entitled, *A brief discourse against the outward
apparel and ministering garments of the popish church:* but the running
title was, *The unfolding of the popish attire.* A full account of the
contents is given by Strype, Ann. I. ii. p. 163.]

the printers cast into prison, and the copies destroyed. Another book[1] was afterwards published by order of the commissioners, wherein is declared the judgment of master doctor Peter Martyr and master Bucer, viz. that every preacher and minister ecclesiastical may wear a surplice, cap, and the other habits, without committing any sin, as you and master Gualter have also written. The opposite party are much dissatisfied with this, and, as far as they dare, write secretly against it; so that, unless our gracious God afford us his aid and support, it is to be feared that it will occasion much hinderance to the spread of the gospel. But our Lord God, I trust, is gracious and full of compassion, and will help us to establish unity and peace, so that the cruel fiend may not occasion a schism.

All things are going on pretty well in Scotland, and all the exiled nobles and lords have returned to their country, and are in possession of their lands and property. The gospel (praised be God!) is still preached, and I hope all will be quiet; for the exiled lords are magistrates in that country. The queen of Scotland, I hear, is in the family way, and expects to be confined within a week[2]. I have nothing else to write to you at present. Salute, I pray you, all my good masters and friends. The grace of God be with us all! Amen.

Yours ever,

JOHN ABEL, England.

[1 For an account of this book, supposed to have been published by the archbishop of Canterbury, see Strype, Ann. i. ii. 174.]

[2 The queen of Scots was delivered of a son, afterwards king James I., on June 19, 1566.]

LETTER L.[3]

MILES COVERDALE, LAURENCE HUMPHREY, AND THO-
MAS SAMPSON TO WILLIAM FARELL, PETER VIRET,
THEODORE BEZA AND OTHERS.

Dated at [LONDON,] *July* 1566.

WE must not only, honoured masters and brethren, appear
troublesome to your reverences by so frequently addressing
you by our friends and our letters, but must seem also very
regardless of our duty to the church, by disturbing you, who
are occupied in matters of far greater importance, with the
relation of our trifles. But yet the unhappy condition of
our times, and fresh troubles, compel us to have recourse to
you, not only that you may be informed more fully of the state
of our affairs, and our own opinion respecting them, but that
we also may more fully understand your sentiments. Our
affairs are not altered for the better, but, alas! are sadly
deteriorated. For it is now settled and determined, that
an unleavened cake must be used in place of common
bread;—that the communion must be received by the people
on their bended knees;—that out of doors must be worn
the square cap, bands, a long gown and tippet; while the
white surplice and cope are to be retained in divine service.
And those who refuse to comply with these requirements,
are deprived of their estates, dignities, and every ecclesiastical office; namely, brethren by brethren and bishops, whose
houses are at this time the prisons of some preachers; who
are now raging against their own bowels; who are now
imposing these burdens not only on their own persons, but
also on the shoulders of others; and this too at a time when
in the judgment of all learned men they ought to have been
removed and abolished altogether. Thus you have the image
and representation, such as it is, of our church.

[3 The original of this letter is in the collection of the late professor Miech of Heidelberg, now in the possession of M. Baehr of
Carlsruhe.]

Now then, hear our opinion upon this state of things. We think that it must be assumed in this question, that the Jewish, Turkish, Christian, and Popish religions have each their own peculiar sacraments and signs; and that external profession ought to be the test and badge of any one's doctrine; and that we are to seek our pattern not out of the cisterns and puddles of our enemies, but from the fountain of the scriptures and of the churches of God; so as not to be connected by any similarity of rites with those from whose religion we are altogether abhorrent: which rule, we read, was diligently observed by our forefathers in respect to the sabbath and passover of the Jews, the fastings of the Manichees, and the trine immersion of heretics. Nor indeed can we regard these things as altogether indifferent, when compulsion is made use of, and when too they are branded with the mark of superstition: nor ought any thing to be obtruded [on the church] by the authority of the sovereign, without its having been lawfully discussed in a christian synod: nor ought agreement in ceremonies everywhere to be required of necessity, especially when it is in common with the enemies of the faith: nor is there any occasion in the church of Christ either for the Aaronic priesthood, or Pharisaical ambition, that sacred garments should be worn now-a-days in the christian temple, or that a dress not common, but distinct and peculiar, should be prescribed for ordinary use. But we think with Celestine, that the clergy should be distinguished from the people by their doctrine, not their garments; their conversation, not their dress; their purity of mind, not their adornment of person; lest we begin to hanker after novelties, tread under foot the order received from our forefathers, impose upon the minds and eyes of the simple, and make room for vain and unprofitable superstitions.

Besides, as many of us as have cast out these things from the churches committed to our trust, cannot restore them without grievous offence and abominable impiety: and since a door would also be opened to other mysteries of iniquity, and the love of the godly be offended, and the pride and boldness of the wicked be encouraged, without even any pretence of edification; and since it is not lawful, according to St Paul's rule respecting things indifferent, for every one to rest in his own persuasion, but that that should be regarded as lawful, which is not displeasing to certain men; we considered it more for the good of the church to stand fast in our liberty with an accession of godly men on our side, than to depart from the opinion we have taken up and the custom we have received, to the scandal of many and the downfall of purer doctrine. This is our opinion, and also that of a most excellent personage. We now, most illustrious and very dear masters and brethren, request you by our most intimate communion in Christ, to point out the cynosure to us who are tossed about on the waves; and either to shew us a better way if we are in error, or confirm us, when doubting, in our holy purpose.

The question, we confess, is nice and difficult, whether it is better to yield to circumstances, or to depart; to admit the relics of the Amorites, or to desert our post. Either alternative is harsh, grievous, and productive of mischief both to ourselves and the church. Which is the better, do you with your wonted wisdom declare, because we are lingering in suspense as in the last extremity[1]. We also request of you and your brother ministers to put forth at the earliest opportunity some treatise on the nature of things indifferent, on ceremonies, on the sacerdotal habit; by which both our church and those of Saxony may be instructed, and the zeal of our sovereigns inspirited to the demolition of all the distinctive marks of antichrist. We make it, lastly, our request, that you would admonish our bishops by letter not to persecute Joseph on account of a garment; nor to rend the church with such a schism for so slight a cause; but that even in the dissimilarity of rites they may preserve the sweetest harmony of spirit and brotherly love. For far be it from us to think of them otherwise than as becomes friends and brethren.

The sum is this. We request these three things; your reply to the questions here proposed by us, and some treatise to all the churches generally; a letter to the bishops privately, and, if you please, to such of her majesty's councillors as you may be acquainted with; so that this whole controversy may issue in a christian reconciliation, and not in a cruel separation. Communicate this letter to all your

[1 Inter sacrum et saxum. *Plaut. Capt.* III. 4. 84.]

brethren, that we may hear what the Lord may speak out of the mouth of two or three witnesses. May the Lord Jesus preserve his church pure and inviolate even to the day of his just judgment! July, 1566.

Your most devoted,

MILES COVERDALE, formerly bishop of Exeter.
LAURENCE HUMPHREY,
THOMAS SAMPSON.

LETTER LI.

WILLIAM TURNER[1] TO HENRY BULLINGER.

Dated *July* 23, 1566.

GREETING. As there was a great variety of opinion among the Jews respecting Christ the Son of God, when he came to sojourn with us here on earth; so from the occasion of your reply[2] to our brethren, which our rulers, as we suppose, have published without your sanction, both in Latin and English, many opinions have lately risen up respecting you, his sworn and faithful disciple and minister, among those who in this country profess a purer religion, and different persons entertain different sentiments respecting you. God grant that as you have not given our countrymen any just occasion of suspecting evil of you, so all may understand your answer in the sense in which you wrote it! Whatever others may think concerning you, I am fully persuaded of this, that if, as is natural to man, you have unwittingly fallen into any error, provided only you are told of it in a friendly and courteous manner, you will be ready to acknowledge it without reluctance, and willingly confess the occasion of it. But, in reliance on your accustomed and well-known candour, I will proceed briefly to relate the opinions of our people respecting you, to the end that you

[1 For an account of Dr William Turner see first series, Letter LXXXIII. p. 206.]

[2 For this reply see first series, Appendix, p. 345. See also Bullinger's letter to Bishops Grindal and Horn, p. 357.]

may be able more fully and successfully to defend yourself
from the imputations that are brought against you.

There are not wanting those who think that our Sama-
ritans, limping on both feet, (for we have many more of this
stamp than sincere professors of the gospel,) have suggested
to you many things quite opposite to the truth, and have
therefore influenced, or at least persuaded you, to hurl all
your darts against our poor wretched preachers, conniving at
the faults of our principal ministers and others, who, for the
sake of an ass's appearance[3], have thrown into prison so many
learned and godly pastors, stripped of all their dignities, and
have exposed the flock of Christ unarmed to wolves, papists,
Lutherans, Sadducees and Herodians. Some persons also
boldly affirm, that there are many things in your answer,
which are not only in manifest contradiction to your own
books heretofore published, but also to the writings of all
evangelical pastors. There are found too some among us,
who think much the same respecting you, the most learned
man and best expositor of christian doctrine in all Europe, as
the Saxon preachers thought of their master Philip Melancthon; who, when Charles V. was attempting to obtrude the
Interimistic[4] and Adiaphoristic impieties upon all the reformed
churches in Germany, to the great jeopardy of christian
liberty and no small injury to the truth, as they themselves
testify in their published writings, passed over to the Inter-

[3 *Ob asini prospectum.* This seems to be a contemptuous allusion
to the ministers' habits, to which Dr Turner was so averse, that in the
year 1565, as dean of Wells, he enjoined a common adulterer to do
his open penance in a priest's square cap.]

[4 Charles V. caused a paper to be drawn up by Julius Pflug,
bishop of Naumburgh, Michael Sidonius, and John Agricola, which
should serve as a rule of faith and worship to both papists and protestants till the re-assembling of the council of Trent. This paper,
because it had not the force of a *permanent* law, was called the *Interim.*
Melancthon, partly from fear of the emperor, and partly from con-
descension to Maurice, elector of Saxony, decided that the whole of the
Interim could by no means be admitted, but that it might be received
so far as it concerned things *indifferent,* (*in rebus adiaphoris.*) This
decision gave rise to the *Adiaphoristic* controversy among the Lutherans, which is here referred to. For among things indifferent
Melancthon reckoned many which Luther deemed of great importance.
See Mosheim. ed. Soames, III. 160, 350, and Schmidii Historia Inte-
rimistica, p. 70, &c.]

imists and Adiaphorists; and afterwards, laying aside all fear, returned to a better mind[1].

Those persons who think most favourably of you, defend you in this manner. They say that nothing was farther from your intention than that your answer should be publicly set forth in Latin and English; and that it was sent to our brethren, as men of learning, not with any view of defining or dogmatising, but simply as a literary exercise. But since it is beyond all doubt that many worthy persons are grievously offended by reason of its publication, I would recommend that, —both for the removal of offence, as well as for the assertion, and vindication from any suspicion of falsehood, of that truth which in so many of your printed works you have maintained with so much courage, piety and assiduity,—you should candidly and openly and fearlessly bear witness, in some published tract, whether you are of opinion that princes or ecclesiastical prelates, whom you call principal ministers, have authority to obtrude upon the pastors of churches against their will, under pain of deprivation and imprisonment, certain prescribed habits, and corresponding ceremonies, whether borrowed from the heathen, or transferred from the Levitical law, or invented or approved by the pope, and destined and employed for the furtherance of idolatry, without offence to christian liberty and manifest injury to the church.

I have written these things to you with the greater boldness, that you may the better ascertain my feelings towards you, while I am anxious for the honour and integrity of your character, and for the freedom of your doctrine from any suspicion of error. July 23, 1566. Farewell.

Yours,

WILLIAM TURNER,

A physician, delighting in the

study of sacred literature.

[1 Calvin complained to Melancthon of his want of firmness; but it afterwards appeared, from the testimony of Beza, that his letter was written under misinformation. Beza's words are: *Philippo etiam officii admonito, quem nonnulli ut in eo molliorem accusabant; immerito id quidem, ut accuratius postea Calvinus cognovit.* See Scott's Contin. of Milner, III. 392.]

LETTER LII.

BISHOP PARKHURST TO JOHN WOLFIUS.

Dated at Ludham, *Aug.* 21, 1566.

For the very learned commentaries of yourself and Martyr upon the two books of Kings, I thank you, and will shortly return the obligation. You will do well to publish your discourses upon Deuteronomy, Judges, Ruth, &c.; for I remember having read some of them in your study, and that they pleased me exceedingly. They will please others too, should it please you to publish them. I have written these few lines with some difficulty, as I have hardly yet recovered from illness[2]. Take my brevity in good part. Gualter will tell you all the news. May the Lord preserve all at Zurich! In haste. Ludham. Aug. 21, 1566.

Yours,

JOHN PARKHURST.

LETTER LIII.

THEODORE BEZA TO HENRY BULLINGER.

Dated at Geneva, *Sept.* 3, (1566.)

There have been sent hither, my father, copies of the letters of each of the Landgraves, which give us hopes that the conferences at Erdfurt will not go forward: I wish this may be the case. What, however, they write in addition, and which I was sufficiently aware of, namely, that provision was made at Augsburg against condemning the foreign churches, does not give me much satisfaction, as I perceive it was craftily done by those parties who thought that our interference would be prevented by these means; for they well knew how to effect this by their counsels. For I pray

[2 See first series, Letter LXXII. p. 167.]

you, if the doctrine of our churches is condemned, and that under the names of Zuinglianism and Calvinism, and so the truth is wounded, whether through our side or that of the most illustrious prince, does it not amount to the same thing? But come, let us wait for what the Lord may bestow, who will, I hope, so order matters, that we may perceive him to be watching over us in this matter also.

With regard to our affairs, I have no news whatever to write about. In France the peace of the churches seems to depend upon the result of affairs in Flanders, which is certainly a wretched state of things. For I can nowise approve that way of proceeding; and though the beginning may appear prosperous, yet I seem to myself to look forward to a most sad and fatal issue, unless the Lord should also give his blessing to their imprudence. The statement made to you about the murder of some of the magistrates and the taking of the city, is entirely false, if that be a true account which I received two days since in a letter written on the 12th of this month, namely, that no harm whatever has yet been done to any priest, nor any image overthrown by our party; but only that an innumerable multitude was present at the sermons which are preached in the open air without the city, and that there is an incredible thirst for hearing the word. Let us therefore commend these things also to the Lord's providence.

I now come to the English affair, which, as it was most painful to me to hear, so I could gladly wish it had been possible that you might have no concern in a matter of so much trouble: but what can you do? Our distressed brethren seek the consolation, advice, and prayers of those churches, by whose love they were formerly refreshed, and hope also to be refreshed at the present time. Some of them, I admit, are rather hard to please, but in so much affliction it is difficult to keep within bounds; and as their object is most excellent, I think this their importunity may be excused. From the statement that you will receive in detail from this our brother[1], of which also he has left a copy here with me, you will learn that the papacy was never abolished in that country, but rather transferred to the sovereign; and

[1 This was most probably Percival Wiburn. See first series, Letter LXXVIII. p. 188.]

that nothing else is now aimed at, than the gradual restoration of what had been in any measure altered. I once thought that the matter was only about caps and I know not what other externals, but I afterwards understood that the controversy was of a far different character; and I now plainly perceive it to be so, not without the utmost distress of mind, which I wish were peculiar and confined to myself alone. First, since an outward call (after due examination as to doctrine and moral character,) not by any single individual, but at least by a congregation of the brethren, is as it were the basis and foundation of an ecclesiastical ministry, what can be more abominable, what more extravagant, than that assumed power of the bishops, by which they admit at their pleasure parties not so called, but who enter the ministry of their own accord; and immediately, without assigning them any cure, approve them as qualified either to serve, as they call it, or to teach; and at length, on the vacancy of any preferment, after the delivery of a written form for a certain sum of money, and the administration of an oath respecting two things, (the one that they will acknowledge the royal majesty as, next to Christ, the supreme head of the church of England; and the other, that they will so comply with the laws of the realm, and especially that famous book of reformation and all the ceremonies, as not in any way to impugn any,) they appoint this or that individual to whatever churches they please? If we inquire into church discipline, what can it be in a country, where, just the same as under the papacy, they have in the place of a lawfully appointed presbytery their deans, chancellors, and archdeacons, who at their pleasure, and as is the practice in the civil court, but according to canon law, pronounce excommunication even on account of suits relative to money and the like; which sentence afterwards the lord bishop or his official sends to the minister, like a judge to his apparitor, to be read in church, namely, to be in force so long only as until the matter is made up with the judge? For there is for the most part the same mode of absolution as of excommunication. And how little are they removed from the law of celibacy, who are forbidden to marry wives without the express permission of the queen, and the assent of the lord bishop and some two justices of the peace; and when married, are forbidden to keep their wives

either in colleges, or within the precincts of the cathedrals[1],
to wit, as counting them impure, or for the avoidance of
scandal? What must we say, when not only the papists are
left in possession of the revenues of their benefices, but even of
their ecclesiastical offices, upon merely taking an oath to maintain the reformation; so that godly brethren are for the most
part placed under the authority, and compelled to submit to
the jurisdiction, of those who are in general both unlearned
and in their hearts the most bitter enemies of true religion?
What must we say when there are openly sold in the court of
the metropolitan dispensations for non-residence, for plurality
of benefices, choice of meats, celebration of marriage out of
the appointed seasons, and even for obtaining a benefice
during childhood, and other things of this kind, than which
Rome herself has nothing more disgraceful or abominable?
What must we say when in a case of necessity, as they call
it, women are allowed to baptize? And as if these things,
with some others not a whit better, were not sufficient, behold! of those very few teachers of the pure gospel, some
are turned out of their offices, and others even thrust into
prison, unless they will swear that they will so inviolably
·approve all these things, as not to impugn them by word or
writing; and will resemble also the priests of Baal in their
square caps, bands, surplices, hoods, and other things of the
like kind. Nor is this the end of their miseries; but it is
also expressly provided, that whatever it may please the
queen's majesty, with the sole concurrence of the archbishop
of Canterbury, to establish, alter, or take away, with respect
to the rites of the church, it shall forthwith be considered as
having the force of law.

Such, then, is the state of the Anglican churches, which,
as it appears to me, is very wretched, and altogether
beyond endurance. But those few persons, [of whom I
spake] ask my advice upon two points: one of which is, by
what means the queen and bishops may be admonished of
their duty? the other, how they themselves must with a
good conscience act in the mean time? As to the first question,
this evil seems now to be remediable by God alone: but yet
I think that some effort should be made, rather than that so

[1 Queen Elizabeth's injunction to this effect is given in Strype,
Parker, I. 217.]

noble an edifice should be suffered to fall to the ground in
silence.   And here two methods occur to me, one of which
indeed will be more troublesome to us, but in my judgment
much more advantageous to them; the other is attended
with less difficulty, but not so direct.   Yours, my father, is
the only church by whose authority both the queen and the
bishops seem likely to be influenced; she, to consider with
herself how far and in what sense queens may be called the
nursing mothers of the church; and they, to restore at length
the church oppressed by their predecessors, as Augustus[2] of
old entertained thoughts of restoring the commonwealth.
For as to our own church, I would have you know that it is
so hateful to that queen, that on this account she has never
said a single word in acknowledgement of the gift of my
Annotations [on the New Testament.]   The reason of her
dislike is two-fold : one, because we are accounted too severe
and precise, which is very displeasing to those who fear
reproof; the other is, because formerly, though without our
knowledge, during the life-time of queen Mary[3] two books
were published here in the English language, one by master
Knox against the government of women, the other by master
Goodman on the rights of the magistrate.   As soon as we
learned the contents of each, we were much displeased, and
their sale was forbidden in consequence : but she notwithstanding cherishes the opinion she has taken into her head.
If therefore you think the present cause worthy of being
undertaken by us, it would seem the most suitable plan, and
most useful to the brethren, that some one should be chosen
from your congregation, if not by the express authority, at
least with the permission or connivance of your magistrates,
to proceed to England on this especial business, and openly
solicit from the queen and bishops a remedy for all these evils.
This would indeed be an heroic action, worthy of your city,
and, as I think, very acceptable to God, even though it should
not altogether succeed according to our wish.   The road
through France is direct and short; for one may with the
greatest ease pass over in eleven days from hence to Dieppe,
a sea-port in Normandy, whence with a favourable wind they
cross over to England in ten hours.   Many of the French

[2 See Sueton. Octav. sect. 28.]
[3 See above, Letter XV., p. 34.]

churches might be visited and confirmed on the way. The
admiral[1] and his brother Andelot[2] might be visited, as they
each of them lie in the very route. Nor would it be difficult
to obtain one or two of the brethren from among the most
learned and zealous, to accompany you, if necessary, on your
deputation, and afford their assistance to your representative.
And if you think that we can be of any use in this matter,
(I mean, by a letter from our church,) there will be no demur
on our part. You are aware that this was the practice in
the ancient church, that even parties uninvited nevertheless
offered their services in extinguishing the flames; and that
by this means many rising disturbances were allayed in
many provinces. Nor have I any doubt that this godly
and charitable legation will be very agreeable to the queen
and the godly bishops, whom I understand to be anxiously
looking out for a suitable opportunity, together with the
keeper[3] of the great seal, a sincere and religious man. Many
also of the nobility are in our favour: many of the other
classes desire our success. It is probable that all of them,
when they perceive that their welfare is an object of so much
anxiety even to foreign churches, will take courage, and
urge the queen's majesty with greater firmness, until they
prevail with her. The time is also very favourable, as the
parliament[4] in that country is about to assemble, when it
is certain that all these things will be brought forward
for consideration. With your permission, my father, I will
also add, that if this counsel shall prove agreeable to you,
master Gualter alone appears so well qualified in every way
to undertake the charge and management and completion
of this business, that, should you make choice of him, he
would seem to have been sent as it were by the voice of
God himself for the refreshment of those distressed brethren,
and even for the preservation of that realm.

This is the one most ready way, as far as I can judge,

[1 Gaspard de Coligny, admiral of France. He was murdered in the
massacre of St Bartholomew, in 1572.]

[2 François de Coligny, Sieur d'Andelot. He died of a fever in
1569.]

[3 Sir Nicolas Bacon.]

[4 This parliament met on Monday, Sept. 30, and was dissolved on
Tuesday, Jan. 2, 1567. D'Ewes' Journal, p. 93.]

and not attended with much trouble or expense. But if you do not approve of it, I think that at least a grave and copious statement should be made by letter, both to her majesty and the bishops, to remind them of their office and responsibility; and especially as you perceive they have abused your letter, contrary to your wishes, to the increase of this mischief. I have myself written to the bishop of London[5] on this subject, and this our brother will supply you, if needful, with a copy of my letter. For I had even at that time heard something of these affairs, and therefore preferred rather to address the bishops by whom this mischief is fostered, than to give any advice to the brethren, especially as I doubted not but that this would be done by yourselves. And I am so far from entertaining any doubt but that you will write what is just and proper, that, if you think fit, I will either countersign your letter, or second it with another upon the same subject.

I now come to the other topic of consideration, namely, whether the brethren can with a good conscience remain in the ministry under these conditions? I am not prevented either by all these corruptions, or the regulations about caps and habits, from recommending them to continue in it; since on the contrary it behoves them for this very reason to be diligent in plucking out from the minds of men all things of this kind, and cutting them off by the sword of the divine word. Many considerations, however, incline me to an opposite opinion, although it is most distressing, in so great a desolation as there now exists in that country, to leave the wretched flock to the wolves who will immediately enter into the fold. For it is one thing to endure what you cannot alter, and another thing to resume, to the certain offence of many persons, what has been already laid down. And you know that Peter[6] was openly rebuked by Paul for no other reason than that he so considered those alone that were weak, as in the mean time to subvert [the faith of] others: nor does the case that we are now treating of seem to me very different. Nay, I rather think that these legislators have much less reason to allege by way of excuse, than Peter had; not only because it

[5 A full account of this letter is given in Strype, Life of Grindal, p. 166. See Beza, Epist. 8.]

[6 See Gal. ii. 11, &c.]

is unjust to compare human traditions with institutions divinely appointed, but much more because there was no one who would be offended by the received rites, such for instance as, that common bread should be made use of in the Lord's supper, that the bread should be broken, and not a wafer placed in the mouth; that there should be no genuflexion, or signing with the sign of the cross; that there should be no standing up at the name of Jesus, and lastly that the ministers should wear a decent cap and habit, though one in ordinary use. The offence therefore, for which a remedy is sought, is only a pretended one; while on the other hand the consciences of numberless individuals are offended by this change, to whom however so little regard is paid, that they are even deprived of their excellent pastors on this very account. What then should the pastors do in this case? Again, since of those things which are so strenuously insisted upon, to the neglect of others of more importance, there are many which are rather to be abhorred by reason of some feeling of devotion connected with them, and which yet lingers in the minds of many, than to be counted as among things indifferent, and which will therefore indubitably bring the people back to their old superstitions, can the ministers themselves with a good conscience restore their use?

But there is another point of far greater importance than all the rest. Seeing that the ministers are bound both to excommunicate and give absolution to whomsoever the bishop or his official may choose; seeing that they are obliged to administer all things in their churches at the beck of others; and, which is the most grievous thing of all, that persons are admitted to the office of teaching solely upon condition of their taking an oath that they will neither by writing nor word of mouth oppose any part of that reformation, that is, those intolerable corruptions, and therefore that they will firmly maintain as law whatever it may please the queen and the archbishop of Canterbury to change, take away, or add; who can submit to this condition with a good conscience? What then? They certainly do not desert their churches, who are either ejected, or who, when commanded to ruin themselves and their flocks, refuse to comply.

I could however much wish, my father, that these and all the other points should be first considered by you, and

your opinion made known to us, before we write any thing
to them upon this subject, since there are dangerous abysses
on either side. If however any middle course can be discovered in this case, it is probably of this kind, that the
parties already ejected should demand a hearing at the next
parliament; on obtaining which, they should shew very respectfully that they are not factious, but that for conscience'
sake they have preferred rather to go out for a time than to
excite any disturbance; after which they may reverently and
calmly shew the mischief that will hence ensue. Should this
plan succeed, they will praise the Lord; if not, let them shake
off the dust of their feet. For, as I have already stated,
we do not see how they can bind themselves by that oath
with a safe conscience. As to those who still remain in the
ministry, I would recommend them, after a respectful protest
before the bishop, and diligent admonition of the people not
to pervert these things to superstition, to continue in the
ministry until the matter is decided in parliament. Should
the decision be such as they can comply with, let them
remain in their office as long as they may be permitted to do
so: but if the bishops persist in doing mischief or giving
their sanction to those who do, I would in that case advise
them manfully to reprove those who deserve reproof, and
rather prepare themselves for the cross, than either act contrary to their duty, or desert the ministry.

Thus much have I written upon this most distressing
subject. I wish indeed I could so discharge my private duty,
as that any other person should take charge of these matters.
For I am well aware of the suspicion I have long laboured
under from parties who are but little acquainted with me.
But I will defend myself with the testimony of my own conscience, and will continue, by God's help, to aid my brethren,
if not by my counsel, which I wish that none of them may
ever require, at least by my prayers. I am anxiously
awaiting your reply. Farewell, my father. May the Lord
Jesus preserve you, who, if at any time, are now especially
necessary to many churches, and may he bless you more and
more! I wish you would salute all our brethren and fellow-
ministers both in my name and in that of our whole congregation. Again farewell. Geneva, Sept. 3, 1566.

Yours,

BEZA.

I have this moment received a letter from Leyden, which states that by letters received by carriers from Antwerp, dated on the 23rd and 27th of August, it appears that a tumult raised by some children against a mass-priest had grown to such an excess, that all the images there were overthrown, and the mass demolished; but that no one was slain except that single priest[1]. The city therefore is now occupied by our friends, if indeed they are ours. If I am not a false prophet, these are the beginnings of greater evils than we have yet witnessed. May the Lord have mercy upon his people!

LETTER LIV.

HENRY BULLINGER TO MILES COVERDALE.

Dated at ZURICH, *Sept.* 10, 1566.

GREETING. You may be assured, my reverend master and very dear brother in Christ, that that letter of mine was not written by me with a view to its being published, nor to increase by its means the flame which has been kindled among you respecting the affair of the habits; but, if it were possible, to extinguish it. And this I think is evident to every one from the letter itself, provided it be read with candour and without prejudice. I treated solely of the vestiarian controversy, and did not enter upon any discussion with regard to other matters, which, I understand, are now subjects of inquiry and dispute among you. And my chief object was this, to convince those who think it better to desert the churches of Christ than to adopt those habits, that it would be more adviseable for them to adopt the habits, and at the same time remain with the churches committed to their charge. But I had no wish to obtrude even this advice upon the brethren inconsiderately, but only to state to them what appeared to me most adviseable in this matter, leaving it in the mean time free to themselves to follow what might

[1 See in Brandt's History of the Reformation in the Low Countries, Vol. I. B. vii. a full account of this tumult at Antwerp, which began by destroying an image of the virgin. He does not mention that any priest was slain. The tumults became general: images, &c., were destroyed in many places.]

seem best. But as I now understand that my letter has been so perverted by some parties, as though [I had discussed] all the subjects controverted among you, (though when I wrote that letter, I did not even know what they were,) I am going to write[2] to some godly and prudent persons, whose authority will, I hope, prevail in this matter, to request they will take especial care that no one make an improper use of my published letter, nor that the impurities (as you call them) be established in convocation under the pretext of that letter; but rather that they will faithfully exert themselves that the liberty of the churches remain unimpaired, and that faithful ministers be not persecuted, and that the church of England be again purified from those things which are foreign to the purity of true religion. I will pray the Lord in the mean time to take these things into his own hand, and happily allay these disturbances; and by the removal of these contentions, to restore tranquillity to the churches. May the grace of the Lord Jesus be with you! Master Gualter salutes you. Entreat the Lord for us. Dated at Zurich, Sept. 10, 1566.

HENRY BULLINGER, Senior,
Yours wholly from my heart.

LETTER LV.

HENRY BULLINGER AND RODOLPH GUALTER TO THE EARL OF BEDFORD.

Dated at ZURICH, *Sept.* 11, 1566.

WHEN we heard, illustrious prince, in the course of last year, that a contention had arisen among you respecting the habits of the clergy, we were greatly afraid that it might extend yet farther, and occasion some greater mischief to the church. At the request therefore of certain pious and zealous individuals we gave such counsel as then appeared to us safe and godly. For we advised the ministers of the churches not to desert them for matters of so little importance, and leave them to be harassed by wolves and superstitious deceivers. But the fear of greater danger, which we then anticipated, was too well grounded. For we hear that you are at this

[2 See the next letter.]

time not only contending about the habits, but that many other things besides are obtruded upon godly ministers, which savour of mere popery; yea rather, which were first fabricated in the school of antichrist, and cannot therefore be admitted or connived at with a due regard to godliness. It has also occasioned us no small grief, that the letter which we wrote privately to a few friends upon that subject, is reported to have been printed[1]; and that many persons extend our judgment respecting the matter of the habits to other things which we did not at that time know to be controverted, and which can never be approved by us. And indeed it is a cause of most just grief, that godly brethren, to whom we desired rather to afford counsel and consolation than to occasion any trouble, are weighed down by the authority of our names: but we are still more distressed at the consideration of the scandal which we doubt not has arisen from this source. Our distress is yet farther increased by the unhappy condition of the church of England, which as we have always loved, we cannot but be grieved with all our hearts, to find that, though scarcely delivered from the sanguinary enemies of a purer faith, and having begun in some measure to revive, she is now weakened by these intestine broils. And whereas, most illustrious prince, we are sufficiently persuaded of your virtue, and there exist not a few evidences of your piety, we have thought good to send a letter to your excellency, of whom so many godly persons have conceived no common expectation. And we pray you to persevere in defending the church, according to your wont, both before her most serene majesty, and in parliament (which we hear will shortly meet) before the nobility of the realm; and not to refuse your patronage to those godly brethren, who, notwithstanding they may have erred in some respects, are yet deserving of pardon, as it is plain that they have been actuated by a fervent zeal

[1 "He [archbishop Grindal] set forth now [1566] in print an excellent and right christian letter of Henry Bullinger, the chief minister in Helvetia, sent to him and two other of the bishops, viz. Horn, bishop of Winton, and Parkhurst of Norwich, concerning the lawfulness of wearing the habits; but drawn up for the satisfaction of Sampson and Humfrey, &c." Strype, Life of Grindal, p. 155. It was printed by Seres, 1566, entitled "The iudgement of the godly and learned father, M. Henry Bullinger, &c., declaring it to be lawful for the ministers of the church of Englande to weare the apparel prescribed by the lawes and orders of the same realme."]

for godliness, and that their sole object is to have the church purified from all the dregs of popery. And not only do they seem to us deserving of the protection of godly princes; but this whole cause is of such a nature, that those who employ their labour and industry in promoting it, give evidence by the act itself, that they are most deserving of the name of princes. The Lord has vouchsafed to illustrious persons the honour of being called the nursing fathers of his church, which dignity indeed far exceeds all the glory and honour of this world. And they will be faithful to such a character, when they not only rescue the church out of the hands of her enemies, restore the preaching of the word, and re-establish the legitimate use of the sacraments; but also take care that she, who ought to be brought an undefiled spouse to Christ, be not stained with any false colouring of superstition, nor render her fidelity suspected by any rites inconsistent with christian simplicity. And the text in Hosea[2] is well known, who warned the Jewish church to put away their adulteries not only from between their breasts, but from before their face. Wherefore we entreat your excellency again and again, that you will now especially continue to exert yourself as you have hitherto done, and endeavour to effect, by your influence with the most serene queen and the nobility of the realm, that the reformation of the church of England, begun with the great admiration of the whole world, be not disfigured by new filth and the restored relics of wretched popery. For should that be the case, not only will the mark of inconsistency be branded upon many in your most flourishing kingdom, but the weak will also be offended; and to the neighbouring churches of Scotland, France, and Flanders, who are yet suffering under the cross, will a scandal be afforded, the punishment of which will doubtless redound to the authors of it. And what is more, the neighbouring enemies of evangelical truth will take an example from you, by which they may also in their respective localities circumscribe the more free worship of the true God by new enactments of tyrannical superstition.

We have spoken thus freely, illustrious prince, not because we have any doubt of your piety; but we do so, partly in reliance upon your very great kindness, and partly moved by the necessity of the case. We desire to afford to

[2 Hosea ii. 2.]

your excellency, and to many others, more ample materials and opportunity for consideration of this subject. And we pray Almighty God, in pity to his church, to restore true peace to her, and to guide your excellency and those like you by his Spirit, protect you with his favour, and uphold you by his powerful arm, to the glory of his name and the preservation of his church. Amen. Zurich, Sept. 11, 1566.

Your excellency's most devoted,

HENRY BULLINGER, Senior,
and RODOLPH GUALTER.

LETTER LVI[1].

RODOLPH GUALTER TO BISHOP PARKHURST.

Dated at ZURICH, *Sept.* 11, 1566.

WHEN we first heard, reverend father in Christ, that a controversy had arisen among you respecting the apparel of ministers, that circumstance alarmed us exceedingly, as we were afraid that if it proceeded farther, it would occasion greater mischief: and on this account we endeavoured, as far as lay in our power, to pacify certain parties, lest they should raise any disturbance about a matter of no very great importance. And certainly we are not deceived in our anticipation, if indeed it is true that we hear, namely, that many other things are obtruded on the churches besides those habits; and that ministers are cast out of the churches for refusing to subscribe to the decrees of certain persons, who either abuse the queen's name, or by their acquiescence make her more determined in matters of this kind, so that she orders everything at her pleasure. It also increases our uneasiness, to perceive that that letter of ours, in which we endeavoured to soothe several persons, has been printed, and that godly brethren are distressed by the authority of our names, and that we are suspected by many of having

[1 Of this letter several copies were taken, Parkhurst making it more common than the writer intended he should, so that falling into the hands of the Puritans, they printed it with one of Beza's in the book called the Admonition to the Parliament, in justification of themselves. Strype, Parker, II. 111. For Bishop Cox's reply to this letter see first series, Letter XCIV., p. 234.]

given our sanction to the abominations of popery. We advised, it is true, the ministers not to forsake their churches on account of the cap and surplice, but to feed the Lord's flock, as far as they could without a compromise of their religious principles. At the same time we never approved the superstition or folly of those parties who obtrude such things upon godly ministers, and sweep together from the pope's school, or rather kitchen, such filthiness as both occasions trouble to good pastors, and is a stumbling-block to the weak. But it appears to us particularly hard, that the bishops should allow themselves to be the instruments of this persecution, and that those who refuse compliance should be ejected by them. I wish they would consider what the Lord meant, when he was speaking of the faithless steward, who, when he ought to have been feeding his household, riots and sports with the drunken, and smites his fellow-servants. For I do not see much difference between his conduct and theirs, who so readily give their sanction to the crotchets of superstitious courtiers, and treat godly ministers with so much cruelty. Nor could I ever have imagined that any one could have been found among the bishops, who would allow himself either to participate in this wickedness by his instrumentality, or at least to encourage it by his cowardly connivance. For we thought that all this had proceeded from some individuals, who abuse the authority of the most serene queen; but we hoped that the bishops would defend the cause of the ministers, and devise some means by which a remedy might be applied to the mischief. Some of those brethren are, I grant, somewhat hard to please, but yet their cause is not a bad one, much less a wicked one; nay, it were rather to be desired that their views might prevail. But as this now seemed to us to be impossible, we recommended them to accommodate themselves to existing circumstances, and put their trust in the Lord, who would some time or other afford them an opportunity of restoring everything to a better state.

But since, my father, I hear your piety especially commended among others, as also that of my friend master Pilkington, for having hitherto refused to eject any one; I have thought myself justified by the privilege of our ancient friendship, in exhorting you to persevere with firmness in your godly conduct, and to bear in mind that we have every one of us too much sin in ourselves, to make it needful for us to partake in the sins of others. Christ is the bridegroom and most determined avenger of his church, and will not allow any injury done to his most faithful servants to go unpunished. And it is to him that we must some time render an account of our stewardship, not to the queen, or pope, or those who assume to themselves the pope's tyranny in the church. Do you, with your accustomed amiability, take in good part what I have written, without consideration indeed, but not without the anxiety of a brother's love. I have written more respecting our own affairs in the letter you will receive after the fair. Zurich, Sept. 11, 1566.

N. B. I have written this letter from the statement of the Englishman, Perceval Wiburn[1].

[ROD. GUALTER[2].]

LETTER LVII.

RODOLPH GUALTER TO THEODORE BEZA.

Dated at ZURICH, *Sept.* 11, 1566.

WE have long feared, honoured brother in Christ, that the disputes which have arisen in England about the affair of the habits, would proceed to a farther extent. For we perceived that some parties were more obstinate in a matter of so little consequence than the then existing state of things in that country could bear : and therefore, at the request of some excellent and godly men, who were apprehensive of the desolation of the churches, we gave such advice as then appeared necessary and useful, and not inconsistent with godliness, and what we knew them already to have received from master Peter Martyr of pious memory. For as the dispute solely related to the habit of ministers, whom the queen would have to be distinguished from the laity ; and as it was expressly provided for weak consciences in the royal

[1 See first series, Letter LXXVIII. p. 187.]
[2 Gualter's name is not affixed to this letter, but the postscript is in his handwriting.]

edict, that no one was to suppose that the worthiness either
of the ministry or of the sacraments consisted in the habit;
and there was at the same time no obscure expectation, that
those things would be changed and corrected with the change
of time; we could not assent to their opinion, who thought
it their duty to desert their churches for the sake of a cap
and gown. For we well knew that either avowed papists,
or Lutherans, would succeed into their places, and introduce
greater follies, and corruption of doctrine at the same time.
We therefore recommended them to accommodate themselves
with holy and godly moderation to existing circumstances,
but diligently in their preaching to admonish the people not
thereby to entertain any suspicion either of superstitious worship or abandonment of the truth; and lastly, that they
should discreetly seek occasions of offering suitable remon-
strance to the queen and nobles of the realm, respecting their
duty on this behalf. And we have no doubt but that by
such means those disorders might have been checked on their
first outbreak, when the council was inclined to act with much
greater lenity, than now, when the minds of many persons
are so exasperated by this lengthened dispute, that, no longer
satisfied with those few and unimportant requirements, they
are endeavouring to impose such things as cannot be allowed
with safety to religion. But you see, my brother, to what a
pass matters have come; and we too see it not without sorrow. Nevertheless, as we know that our brethren have
been actuated by godly zeal in what they have done, we do
not blame them, but think them worthy of commiseration,
and wish it were in our power to succour them by our
counsel and assistance.

As to what seems to you the most effectual remedy in
the present juncture, namely, that either I or some one of our
friends should go over into England, and openly plead their
cause, I should, for my own part, by no means think it troublesome or unpleasant: it would indeed rather be pleasant and
agreeable to visit at the same time the French churches,
whom I love and cherish in the Lord, and to see old friends
in England, and lend a helping hand to the very afflicted
state of the church. Nor should I ever repent encountering
any labour or danger in a cause so good, so holy, and so
necessary. But I am well assured that we can never obtain

permission from our own authorities to go thither uninvited. Nor do I see what advantage can be expected from such a journey, or rather embassy. For the queen, who has in many respects too much abused her power up to the present time by her arbitrary conduct, and has refused to be warned by the advice and remonstrances of her councillors, will be much less inclined to receive counsel from a foreigner : and there is danger, lest our godly brethren should be burdened with the suspicion of having invited me, without having consulted her ; so that either new disturbances might be raised by my means, or existing ones be increased. We see, moreover, that the minds of some parties are so excited, that unless I agreed with them in every respect, I must necessarily quarrel with those for whose sake especially I should encounter so much trouble and peril. There are many additional reasons which persuade us that we ought to attempt nothing of the kind. And we hope to receive a letter by the next Frankfort fair, which will give us fuller information respecting this whole business, and which may perhaps also afford materials for better advice.

In the mean time, that we might not be wanting to the occasion, we have thought it as well to write to both parties, that is, to those of each party with whom we are acquainted, and who have hitherto made use of our counsel. We recommend the bishops not to do any thing, for the sake of any man, that is inconsistent with the truth, and may be productive of offence ; and especially, not to act harshly towards their colleagues and fellow-ministers of the word of God ; and to turn their attention rather to the removal than the restoration of the defilements of popery. We protest also that we are grieved not a little, nay, that no slight injustice is done us, if they abuse our letter to the defence of those things which we neither have approved at any time, nor ever shall approve, unless God take from us our sound mind ; and we hope better things from his goodness than that. And there are yet good hopes of some of them. For it appears, that neither my friend Parkhurst, who holds the see of Norwich, nor Pilkington, who is bishop of Durham, have as yet ejected any minister, nor indeed ever intend to do so. The matter therefore will come under a fuller consideration, and I hope that some of them will return into the right way, as they have probably found out by this time the extent of mischief occasioned by their compliance. Next, as the famous earl of Bedford, who is now in command at Berwick, has very great influence in that country, we have written also to him, to undertake this cause, and resolutely to support it in parliament, which we have no doubt that he will do. For he has afforded many proofs of distinguished piety, and is well acquainted with, and a great admirer of our churches. And this we think will suffice for the present, because we have no acquaintance with any others of the nobility; and it would be useless to write to the queen herself, without knowing how she stands affected towards us. Nor indeed can we promise ourselves much from her, as she has never answered any of our letters. We should also be loth to have those suspected by her, of whose favourable disposition we have good hopes, and whom we know to be much attached to us.

With respect to the other subject of your letter, we agree entirely with you, that we ought not so to regard the weak, as to overthrow the faith of many others. Nor do we approve of those who place divine and human laws upon the same level, or who rashly confound them together. We consider, also, those constitutions worthy of our detestation, which have evidently been framed in the school of antichrist; and we feel that we would rather die a hundred times, than sanction them either by our subscription, or by an idle and shameful connivance. But if the question referred solely to the habit of ministers, and all took their stand upon the words of the royal edict published on this behalf, in which it is expressly denied either that these laws possess equal authority with the word of God, or that they ought to be binding on the conscience of any individual; we do not see why the churches should be forsaken, and left to be torn by wolves, solely on account of the habits. But it is not easy for us to decide upon a case not fully understood, and which is carried on by parties who are evidently contending with each other under the greatest possible excitement. We particularly approve, however, of what you write lastly respecting those ministers who still retain their cures, that they should perform their duty under a godly and modest protest, and await the determination of parliament: and should any thing be enacted contrary to the truth and purity of religion, they should suffer any thing rather than subscribe or assent to the ungodly decrees of others.

Thus, my honoured brother, have I replied to your letter, not so much in my own name as in that of my esteemed father, master Bullinger. And though the danger be indeed evident, yet we trust in the Lord, who will preserve his remnant even in that realm, out of which he will some time or other restore a purer and godlier church.

What you write respecting Antwerp[1] makes us also very anxious. God grant that all things may turn out to the glory of his name and the edifying of his church! All our colleagues desire respectfully to salute you, and especially master Bullinger, who is occupied in writing letters to England, and has imposed upon me the duty of replying to yours. Salute in our name the brethren who minister in your church, and may God bless their labours! Farewell. Zurich, Sept. 11, 1566.

[R. GUALTER.]

LETTER LVIII[2].

GEORGE WITHERS AND JOHN BARTHELOT TO HENRY BULLINGER AND RODOLPH GUALTER.

Dated *Aug.* 1567.

REVEREND fathers in Christ, as you thought proper to read before us the letter of the bishops of London and Winchester, in which they so endeavour to clear themselves with you, as that they seem to obscure the truth, and to try to make the cause for which we are contending appear most frivolous and insignificant; we have thought it necessary to reply to the several heads of that letter in this present writing, that to you who have most kindly promised us all your assistance, the truth may become more clear and evident. And if in

[1 See above p. 136.]
[2 For the letter to which this is in answer, see first series, Letter LXXV. p. 177.]

enumerating these heads we should make any omission or mistake, you will pardon us; both because we have not mentioned the subject any where else, and also because we are hardly capable of remembering every particular.

THE LETTER. They say that very few only have been deprived, and that of these, though pious, yet none, save only Sampson, were men of learning.

THE ANSWER. We reply, that many of them were so learned as to be considered by the bishop of London worthy to preach at Paul's cross, before the most famous and learned congregations in all England; as for instance, Lever[3], Penny[4], Gressop[5], Crowley[6], Gough[7], Philpot[8], Wiburn[9]. The rest of them, having been either distinguished by degrees in the universities, or after due probation in the time of persecution appointed to the ministry, have presided over their churches

[3 Thomas Lever had been master of St John's, Cambridge; from which he was ejected on queen Mary's accession, and went abroad to Frankfort, Zurich, and other places. He was afterwards preferred to a prebend at Durham, of which he was deprived for non-conformity, though he was allowed to retain the mastership of Sherborn hospital, which he held to his death in 1577.]

[4 Dr Penny was a prebendary of St Paul's, of which he was afterwards deprived upon becoming a physician. Strype, Whitgift, 445. See below, Letter LXXXII.]

[5 Mr Gressop was of All-Souls, and reader of divinity at Oxford. He preached March 10, 1560, in the shrouds of St Paul's. Strype, Ann. I. i. 369.]

[6 Robert Crowley had been ordained by bishop Ridley, and in queen Mary's days was an exile at Frankfort. He was preacher at Paul's cross Oct. 19, 1559, and March 31, 1561. He subscribed to the Articles of religion in 1562 as archdeacon of Hereford; besides which he was parson of St Peter the poor, and afterwards of St Giles', Cripplegate, from which preferment he was suspended in 1566. He died in 1588. Strype, Parker, I. 433, &c.]

[7 Strype mentions one of this name among the leading puritans who were cited before archbishop Parker in June, 1571. Parker, II. 66. He had a controversy with Frecknam, who attacked him for a sermon he preached in the Tower.]

[8 This was probably John Philpot of London, ordained together with Percival Wiburn and others by bishop Grindal, Jan. 25, 1559. Strype, Grindal, 54.]

[9 Percival Wiburn had been of St John's, Cambridge, and an exile in queen Mary's time. He was deprived for non-conformity in 1564. Strype, Grindal, 54, 145.]

with the greatest credit. And although some of them were not well skilled in Latin, yet by the help and assistance of some books of Calvin, Musculus[1], and others[2], which have been translated into English, they were fully capable of expounding scripture.

THE LETTER. They assert that there is only one subject of controversy, that namely which they quote, concerning the habits.

THE ANSWER. On the 26th of March 1566 all the London ministers[3] were summoned before the archbishop of Canterbury, the bishop of London, the dean of Westminster, and some canonists; and were there asked whether they were willing to acquiesce in the royal proceedings in matters of religion, ordained and to be ordained; nor was the question confined only to the habits. Those who refused compliance were deprived. The archbishop too, when he grants any one a license to preach, binds him in these words, " provided always that in your sermons you shall not persuade the people to procure any alteration or innovation in religion, beyond or contrary to that which the queen's majesty has already effected, or will effect." If the subject of the habits has ever been proposed to any persons by itself, or any disputation has been held, as appears in that treatise published by the bishops in defence of the habits, they have so defended them as if by their means both the

[1 " Musculus's Common Places came out this year (1563) in folio, translated out of Latin into English, for the use of English divines and others, in order to instruct them in a body of sound divinity, purged from the errors of popery. The author was a learned professor of divinity at Berne in Switzerland, and reckoned among the most profound doctors that had writ in the church of God. The translator was Mr Man, head of Merton college in Oxford, who undertook the work by the encouragement and suggestion of archbishop Parker, and dedicated the book to him." Strype, Parker, I. 298, 460.]

[2 Among the other books here referred to, Marlorat upon St John's gospel, Peter Martyr on the book of Judges, Gualter upon the smaller prophets, are specified in Strype, Ann. II. ii. 146.]

[3 For an account of these proceedings against the London clergy, see Strype, Grindal, 154, and Soames, Eliz. Hist. p. 62. The result was, that sixty-one of them promised conformity; nine or ten were absent, thirty-seven denied. Strype, Parker, I. 429.]

sacraments and ministers might recover that ancient dignity
and reputation which they have now almost lost; as appears
from the examination, division the first, section the first.

THE LETTER. They deny that women ever baptize;
they deny too that they approve of the confession of faith
being required from infants, and the signing with the sign
of the cross.

THE ANSWER. How true is this denial of theirs, appears
from the form of baptism which we gave you, and is also
evident from the *Advertisements*[4] of the bishops, article 16,
where they themselves require that no infant be baptized
otherwise than in the manner prescribed. Besides, the
commissaries of the bishops have suffered many brethren to
be punished with imprisonment, and most severely and un-
christianly treated, for having refused to choose godfathers
and godmothers for their infants.

THE LETTER. They deny that the court of faculties
belongs to the archbishop.

THE ANSWER. Every thing goes forth from thence in
the name of the archbishop under the supreme authority of
the queen. And though in one passage of their letter the
bishops call this court of faculties a fiscal court, it can in no
wise be so designated, unless perhaps you admit that to
be a fiscal court, from which also individual bishops grant
license to solemnize marriage in any place soever, and at
prohibited seasons; which seasons too continue just the same
with us, as they were in the time of popery. Besides, if
this was not a fiscal court when held by the legate *de latere*
of the Roman pontiff (who, when the papacy was flourishing
among us, was fond of loitering here in England); it certainly cannot now in any wise be called fiscal. The reason
is this, because when the supremacy was transferred to king
Henry of pious memory, and all things which by the canon
law belonged to the Roman pontiff as head of the church
were made over to him, he then, being both king and pope,

[4 These Advertisements are printed in bishop Sparrow's collection,
121. WILKINS, Concil. IV. 247. An account of them is given in Strype,
Parker, I. 313. See also III. 84. The following is the article referred
to in the text: "That the fonte be not removed, nor that the curate
do baptise in parishe churches in anye basons, nor in any other forme
then is already prescribed."]

appointed another person, namely the archbishop of Canterbury, as his legate, but upon condition of his making him a yearly payment, as the legate *de latere* was wont to do to the pope of Rome. And this archbishop of Canterbury holds that court upon the same terms, and in the like manner.

THE LETTER. They say that they disapprove the chanting of choristers, and the use of organs.

THE ANSWER. Nevertheless they all adopt them in their churches, and the archbishop of Canterbury especially has caused an organ to be erected in his metropolitan church at his own expense.

THE LETTER. They say a great deal about the convocation, where the clergy, as they tell you, are three times more in number than themselves, and have free liberty to discuss and determine upon any matters whatsoever.

THE ANSWER. They may discuss and determine, but in such a way as that nothing is held to be binding and ratified without the consent of the queen and the archbishop. Whence it arose, that many things of the greatest advantage to the church, which had been adopted by the last convocation but one, were suppressed, and never saw the light. Our case was also proposed to the convocation at the last meeting by a certain most learned man connected with the bishop of Norwich; but one of the bishops interrupted him, saying, "What are these things to you? We begun this matter, and we will make an end of it." He made answer, "We thought the queen was the author of this business, but we now perceive that you yourselves are:" and so they would not suffer the matter to be brought forward. Moreover, there is power given by act of parliament to the queen and the archbishop to introduce whatever ceremonies they please into every church in the kingdom.

These things, most reverend and right worshipful masters in Christ, have we written, relying on your accustomed goodness and piety towards the church of England, of which we are witnesses; both because we are loth that you should be ignorant of the true state of the case, and that you may gain a knowledge of the facts from written documents rather than from a verbal statement. For we have written nothing but what we know to be perfectly true, and clearer than noon-day, and are willing to leave them the right of reply. For all that we have above treated of is manifest from the advertisements of the bishops, from certain royal injunctions, from the formularies of baptism, both of adults and infants, all of which we have before sent you in a Latin translation. You may see the first commencement of a church among us, its progress, and various changes, the origin of our controversy, and the church without a true ministry, accurately described in a letter intended for the most illustrious prince of Heidelberg. And now, our fathers, we make this request, and entreat you in Christ again and again, that (as you have most kindly promised of your own accord) you will soften down the exasperated minds of the bishops of London, Winchester, and the archbishop of Canterbury; and that if you are not able to do any thing more, you will at least obtain thus much, that they may be more gentle towards our brethren who still remain in England; and that if they will not assist them in removing the dregs from their churches, they will at least tolerate them and connive at their proceedings; and that you will, in your promised letters to the bishops of Norwich, Worcester, and Durham, give them due thanks for their kind forbearance, and encourage them, together with their brother ministers who are intent upon the purification of the churches, to persevere in their undertaking. Should we obtain this favour, as your great kindness leads us to expect, we shall not only cease from wearying other churches with renewed petitions, but both we ourselves, and all who are really godly, shall owe every thing to you by reason of the peace and concord restored to the church by your exertions: and may Almighty God bestow upon you an everlasting crown through our Lord Jesus Christ!

Your dignity's most devoted,

GEORGE WITHERS,

JOHN BARTHELOT,

Englishmen.

LETTER LIX[1].

HENRY BULLINGER TO THEODORE BEZA.

Dated at [ZURICH,] *March* 15, 1567. [Extract.]

THIS however I freely confess to you, that I have always looked with suspicion upon the statements made by master Sampson. He is not amiss in other respects, but of an exceedingly restless disposition. While he resided amongst us at Zurich, and after he returned to England, he never ceased to be troublesome to master Peter Martyr of blessed memory. He often used to complain to me, that Sampson never wrote a letter without filling it with grievances[2]: the man is never satisfied; he has always some doubt[3] or other to busy himself with. As often as he began, when he was here, to lay his plans before me, I used to get rid of him in a friendly way, as well knowing him to be a man of a captious and unquiet disposition. England has many characters of this sort, who cannot be at rest, who can never be satisfied, and who have always something or other to complain about. I have certainly a natural dislike to men of this stamp.

[H. BULLINGER.]

[1 The original of this letter, of which this extract only relates to English affairs, is preserved at Geneva.]

[2 In another letter of Bullinger, he sends Beza the letters of certain bishops in England, in order that he may hear something "præter Sampsonis clamores."]

[3 The MS is here imperfect.]

LETTER LX.

THEODORE BEZA TO HENRY BULLINGER.

Dated at GENEVA, *July* 29, 1567. [Extract.]

BUT what good can be expected in England, while things remain as they are? I thought the difficulty was only about the matter of the habits; that some blemishes were left behind, which the bishops were perhaps too tardy in removing, or, as is every where wont to be the case in practice, they were unable to obtain what they most desire. But if the case is as I hear it to be, (and indeed these things can scarcely be invented,) where did such a Babylon ever exist? But although God alone can provide a remedy for these otherwise incurable evils, yet when these brethren[4] had determined of themselves to go to you, I was unwilling to deter them from this their purpose. For though they will not bring you any agreeable tidings, yet I hope you will not regret the having been made better acquainted with those matters than you had ever been before; and they also, bringing back from you both advice and consolation, will be relieved in some measure at least from the burden of their misery and grief. I therefore request you, my father, and not you only, but also the rest of the ministers and my much honoured masters, that you will freely listen to them, notwithstanding their statement is most distressing; and that you will compassionate them as standing in need of counsel and consolation, which indeed I doubt not but that you will do with your singular brotherly love. As to myself indeed, I have adopted this plan, that, suspending my judgment even in matters, as it seems to me, most evident, respecting absent brethren, (over whom too I am not appointed a judge,) I would exhort them to meekness, and rather to alleviate these evils by patience than by any querulous accusations; in which respect I think

[4 These were Percival Wiburn, and probably George Withers. See above p. 142, and Strype, Parker, II. 110.]

that I have found them endued with a spirit of gentleness. And when your authority, which they value most highly as they ought to do, shall be exerted in addition, they will return with a mind yet more tranquillised, and the Lord will doubtless at length provide a remedy. Geneva, July 29, 1567.

Yours,

BEZA.

LETTER LXI.

HENRY BULLINGER AND RODOLPH GUALTER TO THEODORE BEZA.

Dated at Zurich, *Aug.* 3, 1567.

We entertained, very dear brother, the Englishmen you commended to us, with the greatest courtesy in our power. They laid before us some writings, which indeed we had seen before, requesting our advice and assistance, as that of persons possessing much influence with the English bishops. We replied that we had long since done every thing in our power, and were unable to do more; besides, that the bishops had made such answer for themselves, as to make it appear that they were not the aggrieved party. We therefore read them our letter[1] to the bishops upon this business, with the bishops' letter to us in reply. But they alleged that it was not fairly stated by the bishops, for that the case was widely different. As we could not withdraw our entire confidence in the bishops, who have acted in all other respects as men of piety and integrity, we were unwilling to fight and contend with these men, so much after the manner of masters of defence, and therefore declined any farther discussion. What need of more words? The fault seems to have arisen at first from too much rigour on their part, and that in course of time the contest increased, and grew warm, as is always the case when people quarrel; and that the feelings have

[1 See first series, Appendix, Letter V. p. 357 and Letter LXXV. p. 175.]

been so exasperated on both sides, that each party is now
to blame, and hardly any remedy can be discovered for this
mischief. It certainly appears from the conversation of these
men that their minds are entirely set against the bishops; for
they scarcely say any thing respecting them but what is
painted in the blackest colours, and savours of the most
perfect hatred[2]. We must therefore entreat the Lord, the
ruler of all hearts, to remedy this miserable state of things.
What you write, among other things, that you think this evil
is to be mitigated rather by patience than by any querulous
accusations, would be exceedingly approved of by us, if they
also would approve of it. And for ourselves indeed, as we
have no power to dictate to the bishops, so we positively refused to take part against them when they were pleading
their own cause, and making a probable defence both of
themselves and their conduct; nor would we appear to take
part with these their accusers, and so be mixed up in this
controversy. Meanwhile we promised these our brethren with
godly commiseration, that we would write to the bishops, and
intercede with them on their behalf; which promise, God
willing, we will faithfully perform at the next Frankfort fair.
And we can do nothing else at present. They shewed us
moreover a petition prepared to be presented to the most
illustrious prince, the elector Palatine[3]. We did not deter
them from their purpose; for possibly the Lord may be
pleased even by these means to quiet those unhappy disputes.
This is the sum of our transactions with them, although we
had determined among ourselves to have nothing more to do
with any one in this controversy, whether in conversation or
by letter; and this is now our decided resolution. And if
any other parties think of coming hither, let them know that
they will come to no purpose.

You will do us a great favour, if you will give us an
accurate account of the French affairs, about which, and the
queen especially, there are spread wonderful reports. We
are in suspense about them, and therefore pray the Lord to
overturn the crafty and cruel counsels of the ungodly, and
not so much to preserve the churches from evil, as to reconcile

[2 *Odium Vatinianum*, so called from Vatinius, noted for his
scurrility and abusiveness. See Cic. in Vatin. and Catull. 14. 3.]

[3 See the following letter.]

them to himself by true faith and amendment of life. For otherwise we fear, and not without reason, that grievous calamities are hanging over us. I will take care that your letter directed to Zanchius shall be faithfully delivered in a few days. That Baldwin[1] of whom you write has found fault with me in a public lecture at Paris, as a student writes me word from that city, upon the subject of human traditions, and quotes a passage from the second chapter of my Apocalypse. He has added also to his censure a bare-faced falsehood, that he had conferred with me upon this matter, and that I had scarcely any thing to urge in reply; whereas he never accosted me but once, and that in a cursory way, and never conversed with me upon any subject at all. But these men shall proceed no farther, as the Apostle says; for their condemnation shall be manifest unto all. Farewell. Master Gualter salutes you. All the rest of the brethren salute you. Do you also salute our brethren who are with you. Zurich, Aug. 3, 1567.

H. BULLINGER the elder, in
GUALTER'S name and his own.

LETTER LXII.

GEORGE WITHERS TO THE PRINCE ELECTOR PALATINE[2].

[Without place or date.]

IT is not through our fault, most noble prince, that we send you this petition; but violence compels us to do

[1 See the first series, p. 118, note 1.]

[2 "Among the German princes, Frederic III. elector Palatine, in the year 1560, substituted the followers of Calvin's doctrines in place of the Lutheran teachers, whom he displaced, and ordered his subjects to receive the rites and opinions of the Genevans. His successor Lewis, in the year 1576, rescinded the acts of his father, and restored the Lutheran doctrine to its former dignity and authority. But this again fell, on the accession of John Casimir to the government of the Palatine countries in 1583: for he, with his deceased father, Frederic III. had gone over to the side of the reformed, and it was necessary

so, religion urges us, our country demands it of us, in fine,
the church of England now lying prostrate, and (unless some
assistance be afforded to her) on the very brink of destruction,
drives us as it were headlong to adopt this measure. Yet if
that affection towards the church and especial regard to all
godly persons, which so greatly distinguish you above all
other princes, were not sufficiently made known to us, we
should never have presumed to seek shelter under your protection. But now since these things are no secret, (for how
can that be a secret which is manifest to every one?) it is no
wonder that we are easily persuaded that you will afford to
the distressed that protection which you have already led
them to hope for at your hands. Wherefore, most excellent
prince, if, humble as we are in station and unknown to you,
overwhelmed as we are by various calamities, we entreat your
succour on behalf of our afflicted church, this is not an act of
presumption on our part; and though indeed we may seem
a little too bold, you will yet allow us so much liberty of complaining, as you may consider to be warranted by our godly
sorrow. For Satan, though he has not been able to do us
mischief in open warfare, is making secret attacks upon the
church of England; and as he is unable to restore popery
altogether, he is endeavouring, but imperceptibly and by degrees, to bring us back to Lutheranism. In which as there
are many things to be regretted, so there is nothing more
grievous than that it is not now by means of his papists, not
by means of men glutted with the blood of the saints, not by
most abandoned individuals, but by means of our own selves,
by means of those who were heretofore accounted the best
of men, he is now endeavouring to bring the best of men into
danger; and those whom he could not destroy by violence,

again to give Calvinism the pre-eminence. From that time onward,
the Palatine church held the second rank among the reformed churches:
and it possessed such influence over the others, that the religious
instructions, composed for its use by Zechariah Ursinus, and denomi-
nated the Heidelberg Catechism, were received nearly throughout the
whole body." Mosheim. ed. Soames, Vol. III. p. 384, where the following authorities are quoted: Henry Alting's Historia Eccles. Palatinæ, in Lud. Christ. Mieg's Monumenta Palatina, Tom. I. p. 223, &c.
Loscher's Historia Motuum, Part II. Lib. IV. cap. IV. p. 125. Salig's
Historie der Augsburg Confession, Vol. III. Book IX. ch. v. p. 433, &c.]

or sword, or fire, he now hopes to overwhelm by the authority of our own people, and by the opinions and superstition of those who profess the gospel.

But that you may more plainly and fully perceive and understand the nature of the case, it is necessary to point out to you the first rise and origin of the church upon its first beginning and appearance among us, and then its progress and various vicissitudes; that you may thereby learn both how far removed we have always been from perfection, and yet how far we have gone back from that liberty to which, by the blessing of Christ, we had at one time attained. Under the auspices of Henry, the eighth of that name, England drove away the Roman Antichrist[1] from all her borders, but yet in such a manner as that his authority seemed not so much suppressed, as transferred to the king. The mass and other relics of popish filthiness retained their former place and estimation. After the pope was cast out, the monasteries were every where destroyed. Monks, friars, nuns were obliged to lay aside and change their designation and habit; pilgrimages were afterwards forbidden, and the images, by means of which such abominable idolatry was committed, were taken down and broken in pieces; and then, towards the very close of his reign, the bible[2] printed in the vulgar tongue was allowed to all, and the priests in every church were ordered to recite in English the Lord's prayer, the creed, the ten commandments, and the epistle and gospel of the day[3]. And these were the foundations laid in the reign of Henry, upon whose decease prince Edward[4] of pious memory succeeded to the throne; who having called together the most noble and learned men throughout the realm, began to reform the church after

[1 For an account of the various legislative provisions by which, in 1534, the power of the papacy in England was wholly destroyed, see Soames, Hist. Ref. I. 429, &c., and Burnet, Ref. I. 236.]

[2 A royal proclamation issued in May 1540, rendered every parish which should not be provided with a bible before the next festival of All-hallows, liable to a penalty of forty shillings per month as long as this omission should continue. See Soames, II. 453, Burnet, I. 486.]

[3 See Soames, Hist. Ref. II. 158.]

[4 Edward VI. began to reign Jan. 28, 1547.]

their advice. He ordered all the statues and images[5] every where to be thrown down and broken in pieces. Next, he every where abolished the mass and prayers in a foreign language. He permitted the laity to receive the cup as well as the bread in the communion of the Lord's supper. He set forth a form of public prayer written in English; which however scarcely differed in any respect from the Latin, except that all the most glaring errors were abolished. The administration of the sacraments altogether savours of Lutheranism. The clergy[6] were allowed to marry, and their children legitimated by an express act of parliament. Altars[7], organs, the theatrical dresses of the papists, and other things of the like kind were retained under the name of ornaments of the church and of the ministers thereof. Afterwards this godly king, perceiving how far he still was from the mark, took in hand the matter afresh, set forth a new form of prayers, removed and prohibited all the monuments of superstition which he had before left, excepting the surplice and kneeling at the Lord's supper, baptizing by women, and demanding of infants a profession of faith. What he retained however was left so free, that no one who objected to them was compelled to observe them. But the king, who truly feared God, not being yet satisfied with these improvements, was about to put the last finish to this work, and appointed a day for the assembling of both houses of parliament. All

[5 On Feb. 11, 1548, Cranmer received an order of council for transmission through his province, enjoining the indiscriminate removal of images from churches. This order was signed by the protector, the earl of Arundel, the lord Russell, Sir Thomas Seymour, Sir Antony Wingfield, and Sir William Paget. See Soames, III. 227, Burnet, II. 95, and IV. 270, where he has given a copy of the original document.]

[6 For an account of the acts of parliament authorising the marriage of the clergy, see Burnet, II. 141, 306.]

[7 On the 24th of November, 1550, a circular letter was addressed from the council to bishop Ridley and other prelates, enjoining them to remove all altars within their respective dioceses, and to set up a table instead thereof. For disobedience to this injunction, Day, bishop of Chichester, was committed to the Fleet. Soames, III. 573, &c. See also bishop Ridley's injunctions at his visitation in the same year, as given in his works, Parker Society's Edition, pp. 319, 321. Also bishop Hooper's Sermons on Jonas, Parker Soc. Ed. p. 488.]

were full of hope and expectation; but in the mean time our most excellent king was taken away by an untimely death[1]. His sister Mary succeeded as heir to the kingdom: would that she had inherited his piety also! Every thing was then suddenly changed, and the papacy entirely re-established.

But why should I make mention of circumstances so notorious? I will now come to those with which you are probably unacquainted. Although the church seemed at first to be entirely overthrown, and the godly were dispersed in every quarter, yet a congregation[2] of some importance collected itself at London, chose its ministers by common consent, appointed deacons, and, in the midst of enemies more sharp-sighted than Argus and more cruel than Nero, the church of God was again restored entire, and, in a word, complete in all its parts. And though it was often dispersed by the attacks of its enemies, and a very great number of its members[3] perished at the stake, it nevertheless grew and increased every day. In the mean time Mary died. Her sister Elizabeth began her reign[4] to the exceeding joy of all. Then those[5] who had been detained in confinement and in chains for the sake of religion, were set at liberty by the queen's command; those who had been driven into exile[6], returned home again. But the church which had survived in the midst of the flames was abolished by some sort of edict[7]. This indeed was a matter of no difficulty, because

[1 Edward VI. died July 6, 1553.]

[2 For an account of this congregation see Foxe, also Strype, Mem. III. ii. 147. Among their ministers were Edmund Scamler, afterwards bishop of Peterborough, and Thomas Bentham, afterwards bishop of Coventry and Lichfield.]

[3 Among these were John Rough, and Cuthbert Simpson, ministers of the abovenamed congregation, and Margaret Mearing, Hugh Foxe, and John Devenish. An account of their martyrdoms is given in Foxe's Acts and Monuments, Vol. VIII. 443, &c. Edit. 1839.]

[4 Queen Elizabeth began her reign, Nov. 17, 1558.]

[5 A list of some of these is given in Strype, Ann. I. i. 55. The various orders for their enlargement were dated in Dec. 1558.]

[6 Of these there were above eight hundred. A list of the chief of them is given in Strype, Cranmer, 449, and Mem. III. i. 231.]

[7 We find that an order was sent to the lord mayor of London to commit one Thomas Parrys to prison, till further order should be taken by the council, for suffering, contrary to the queen's proclama-

there was a general expectation that one not less pure would
be re-established by the authority of the queen and the laws
of the kingdom.   The high parliament of the whole realm
was assembled, popery again cast out, and the second form
of prayers, which Edward left behind him at his death, was
restored to the church.   But the ceremonies, which, as was
above stated, were retained in the church at the first reformation of Edward, are restored under the same name.   Power,
moreover, was given to the queen and the archbishop, to
introduce whatever additional ceremonies they might think
proper; and they immediately afterwards both discontinued
the ordinary bread heretofore used in the administration of
the Lord's supper, and, for the sake of a newer reformation,
adopted the round wafer[8], after the pattern of that used by
the papists.   And at the pronouncing of the name of Jesus
they have ordered all persons to take off their hats and bow
their knees.   Then on the expulsion of the popish bishops
new ones were to be appointed in their room; and most of
these were of the number of those who had been exiles.
These at first began to oppose the ceremonies; but afterwards,
when there was no hope otherwise of obtaining a bishoprick,
they yielded, and, as one of them openly acknowledged,
undertook the office against their conscience.   In the mean
while they comforted their brethren, whom they perceived
to be still struggling against these things, by promising them
free liberty in the government of their churches; and for
some years they kept this promise.   On the obtaining of
which liberty, they diligently purified their churches from all
the blemishes and defilements of popery.   Others, who had
at first yielded, incited by their example, began to reform
their churches in the like manner.   But when the bishops
perceived that the number and influence of these parties
was increasing among the people, they thought their dignity
would come to nought, unless they compelled the inferior
clergy to adopt the same usages as they did themselves.
They took up the matter therefore at the queen's command[9].

tion, which prohibited all preaching, assemblies of people to meet at
Worcester house, whereof he had the keeping. See Strype, Ann. i. i. 59.]

[8 See Soames, Eliz. Rel. Hist. 243, and Strype, Parker, ii. 343.]

[9 The letter of the queen to the archbishop, for redressing disorders in the church, is given in Strype, Parker, iii. 65.]

They deprived Sampson[1], a most learned man, and possessing very great influence in the church, in the hope that the rest would easily be deterred by the fear of like consequences to themselves. But when, contrary to their expectation, they found them all more prepared for resistance, they made a second attempt; and having summoned together all the ministers[2] of the church in London, they required them to promise obedience to all the commands of the queen, either then or hereafter to be issued respecting religion. And when they stated that they could not do this, under existing circumstances, with a safe conscience, more than thirty of them were deprived in one and the selfsame day. But when they found that this plan did not succeed, but that they had excited the hatred of all, and especially of the godly, against them, they devised another mode of attack, by prohibiting any one to expound the scriptures in his parish without an especial license under the bishop's own seal[3]. Besides this, they have recalled all licenses[4] which had been granted before a certain day, and will renew them only to such persons as shall have professed their assent to all their proceedings. If any one should presume to expound the scriptures without their permission, he is brought to trial as being guilty of contempt; and should he not then conform, they punish him by imprisonment or exile.

You perceive therefore, most excellent prince, the wretched aspect of the church of England; you perceive into what an unsightly state it has fallen. For there being three chief parts of the church, wholesome doctrine, the pure administration of the sacraments, and a rightly constituted ministry, which part also includes a vigorous discipline; I will not touch upon the doctrine of our church, which, though sound in most respects, is however lame in others. In what way the sacraments are disfigured by human inventions, will easily

[1 See above, p. 118, and Soames, Eliz. Rel. Hist. 54.]

[2 The London ministers were cited before the ecclesiastical commissioners at Lambeth, towards the end of March, 1564. Strype, Ann. i. ii. 129. See Soames, Eliz. Rel. Hist. 46.]

[3 The form of license for preaching is given by Strype, Parker, iii. 122.]

[4 All licenses granted before March 1, 1564, were to be void and of none effect. Sparrow's Collections, 121.]

appear from the public form of prayer, the royal injunctions, and the admonitions, or (as they call them) the advertisements[5], of the bishops. But the ministry is in fact nothing at all, nor is there any discipline. For those persons cannot be said to be ministers of Christ, but servants of men, who can do nothing according to the prescript of the word, but are obliged to act in every respect at the nod of the queen and the bishops. What must we say, when most of them are popish priests, consecrated to perform mass; and the far greater part of the remainder are most ignorant persons, appointed at the will of the people, not to the ministry of the word, but to repeat the office of the day or festival, which almost any child might do without difficulty? What must we say, when those who preside over the churches are allowed to be absent from them for the sake of study or attendance on other things? What, when there is an innumerable multitude of persons who have neither any church nor fixed appointment? What, when preaching is a privilege confined to the bishops, who are however but seldom at leisure for this office? What, lastly, when the sword of excommunication is taken out of the hands of the clergy and handed over to lawyers? What kind of a church, most illustrious prince, must you think that to be, in which you can neither hear of the pure administration of the sacraments, nor indeed of any ministry whatever, save of this description?

Wherefore if you possess any interest or influence with our most serene queen, we beg and entreat you to make use of it in so godly a cause, to heal these so great maladies of the church, and to condemn for evermore the entire remembrance of popery; but in such a way that, if you cannot, as we desire, obtain a more complete reformation of the whole church, you will nevertheless earnestly entreat and obtain, (and this we hope you will be able to accomplish,) for those who abominate the relics of antichrist, the liberty of not being obliged either to adopt them against their conscience, or to relinquish the ministry.

And if, most excellent prince, you wish well to us and to our church, which we certainly persuade ourselves to be the

[5 For an account of the book of Advertisements, see Soames, Eliz. Rel. Hist. 42, Strype, Ann. I. ii. 130, and Parker, I. 313. It is printed in Bishop Sparrow's Collections, 121.]

case, you must take especial care to transfer all the blame
from the queen unto the bishops, who do not act the part
of her advisers with the freedom that becomes them, and
which it is right they should exercise. For as to their
asserting both at home and to foreigners that they do not
themselves approve these measures, but that they execute
them at the instigation of the queen, they both themselves
command them in books publicly set forth for that very
object, and state that it is done by the queen after good
and pious counsel, and for the benefit of the whole church.
So that it is not to be wondered at, if, deceived by their
blandishments and flatteries, she adopts some severe measures
against us as though we were rebellious and contumacious.
But as we know that you are of your own inclination sufficiently disposed to help us, and as it is not right that you
should any longer be detained by us from the most important
business of your commonwealth, we will not enlarge our statement any farther, but will now bring it to a close.

[GEORGE WITHERS.]

LETTER LXIII.

[RICHARD HILLES] TO HENRY BULLINGER.

Dated at London, *Aug.* 23, 1567.

I pray for you, honoured sir, and very dear friend, much
health. I received, four months since, from John Abel (who
also desires his best respects) a large volume, namely your
Isaiah, as expounded in your homilies, together with your
very gratifying letter, dated on the 25th of last February.
You have presented me with that volume, that I may have
this gift from you as a memorial of our uninterrupted friendship, which, God willing, it shall be. I have also purchased
from my very dear brother, the aforesaid John Abel, the
book of Daniel with the epitome, expounded in your sixty-six
homilies. Both books delight me exceedingly, and I hope
that the homilies in each volume will be productive of no
little benefit to faithful and diligent readers.

As to your desire of certain information respecting the affairs of Brabant, and your request that I should be mindful of you in this matter to the utmost of my power, whether occupied or disengaged; I have now to inform you, my very dear sir, that I have already committed to writing[1] all that I myself know for certain about these matters, or have been able to ascertain from my friends; and that from such information I have written as it were a little history. And if I can get it translated into Latin (which a schoolmaster of my acquaintance has promised to undertake for me), I will send it you, or at least to Frankfort for you, at the next Lent fair, should it please God that I live till that time. I am very glad that your two youngest grown up daughters so prudently and judiciously manage your household concerns, as that you can remain a widower[2] without discomfort.

It is stated here as a fact, that the duke of Alva[3], who has lately come to Louvaine or Ghent with the forces of the king of Spain, which he has stationed there in lower Germany and at Antwerp in the name of that sovereign, intends to take away the liberties and privileges of all the cities of that country which admitted, or freely permitted, the preaching of the protestants during the past year, and to reduce the lower Germany under a regular monarchy. May the will of the Lord be done, without whose permission he can do nothing! Let us heartily pray him to deign to give us peace in our days. This indeed still remains undisturbed, by the blessing of God, in this realm of England; except that some of our preachers (though not among the most learned), kept back by too great scrupulosity, or overcome by vain-glory or some measure of popular applause, are still occasionally disturbing it by impugning or opposing the ordinance of the queen and the whole realm, touching the use or wearing of

[1 See first series, p. 212.]

[2 Bullinger lost his wife in 1564. She died of the plague, as also did three of his daughters, who were married to Hulric Zuinglius, Lewis Lavater, and Josiah Simler, all ministers of Zurich.]

[3 "The king of Spain's army, led by the duke of Alva, hath already passed through Franche Comté and Lorraine, between Metz, Thou, and Verdun; so as it is thought by this they are come to Luxembourg." Sir Henry Norris to queen Elizabeth. July 23, 1567. MS. Sloane 4126.]

the surplice in the church during the singing of the psalms, the reading of the lessons, and the administration of the sacraments. But I am of opinion with holy Jerome (in his first book against the Pelagians), that it is no offence against God, for a bishop, presbyter, and deacon, and all other ecclesiastics to walk in a white garment in the administration of the sacraments[1]. Moreover, religion requires one kind of habit for the ministry, and another for common use and daily life : and the Egyptian priests (who, as you well know, were Christians in the time of Jerome) wore linen garments not only in divine service, but in common use. (Commentary on Ezek. Lib. XIII. c. 44.)[2] And truly the disciples of Christ, as much as lieth in them, must follow peace with all men, and not be a stumbling-block to unbelievers or to the churches of God. We must pray the Lord to make us all of one mind to dwell in the house of God, which is the church, and to remove all unnecessary contentions and causes of offence. May the Lord preserve you. London, Aug. 23, 1567.

Yours from my heart, &c.

[RICHARD HILLES.]

LETTER LXIV.

HENRY BULLINGER AND RODOLPH GUALTER TO BISHOPS GRINDAL, SANDYS AND PARKHURST.

Dated at ZURICH, *Aug.* 26, 1567.

REVEREND sirs, right worshipful masters, and very dear brethren in the Lord. May the Lord Jesus bless you, and preserve you from all evil!

In proportion to our exceeding regard for you, reverend

[1 Unde adjungis, gloriam vestium et ornamentorum Deo esse contrariam. Quæ sunt, rogo, inimicitiæ contra Deum, si tunicam habuero mundiorem ; si episcopus, presbyter, et diaconus, et reliquus ordo ecclesiasticus in administratione sacrificiorum cum candida veste processerint ? Adv. Pelag. Lib. I. cap 9. Tom. II. p. 277. Antv. 1579.]

[2 Vestibus lineis utuntur Ægyptii sacerdotes, non solum intrinsecus, sed et extrinsecus. Porro religio divina alterum habitum habet in ministerio, alterum in usu vitaque communi. Tom. IV. p. 476.]

masters and very dear brethren, is our grief at the sad dissensions between you and some of your brethren, learned men, who have been deprived of their ministerial offices in England.   You must impute it therefore to our sincere affection, that we have repeatedly wearied your ears with the same complaint.   We have seen and received your apology for your conduct in this matter: but some English exiles have come to us in the mean time, who affirm that the doctors of the church in London, and also of other churches in England, men who had been tried in the Marian persecution, and by whose fidelity and diligence the Anglican churches were preserved during those most cruel times, are now turned out; and not merely turned out, but oppressed with grievous persecution, and even cast into loathsome prisons.   They add, that there are many ministers of the churches in Ireland, who in their opinions and conduct are nowise different from those very persons who are suffering persecution in England; but that by the favour of their bishop, and his intercession with the queen's majesty, they are living in the greatest tranquillity.   Whence they conclude that, if the bishops who are in England would also intercede with the queen's majesty, they themselves would be allowed quietly to retain their charge of the churches committed to them.   And they state, what is very important in this question, that the bishops do not deny that those who are persecuted and degraded have the better cause: for they acknowledge that the church would be established on a better footing, and governed when so established, without those ceremonies and rites and institutions than with them; so that if the option were allowed them, they would rather make choice of a church without them, than that one thus burdened should be committed to their charge.   And this is also most evident from this fact, that the bishops have more than once requested of her majesty in parliament that they might be removed, and the church thereby become more purified and beautified, or at least less burdened.

Wherefore, reverend sirs and very dear brethren, your piety will doubtless stir you up to consult by what means convenient and speedy succour may be afforded to these afflicted brethren, and that they may not be oppressed with so cruel a persecution; but rather that by the clemency of the queen's majesty they may be tolerated in the kingdom, and that the gifts which are in them, so useful to the church, may not be quenched by their abdication. But we need not by many arguments or examples incite you, who are most experienced in all that is godly and just: we only entreat you by the Lord, that if it be in your power either to alleviate or altogether remove the distress of these oppressed persons by your influence with the queen's majesty, you will, for the sake of christian love, afford them your assistance with all faithfulness; and take in good part this our brotherly admonition, and continue to regard us, who have the greatest love for you, with your wonted affection. Farewell, honoured masters. Zurich, Aug. 26, 1567.

BULLINGER and GUALTER.

LETTER LXV.

CHRISTOPHER MONT TO HENRY BULLINGER.

Dated at STRASBURGH, *Oct.* 2, 1567.

MASTER Funckius left this place on the morning of the 27th of September, and on the evening of the same day a letter was brought to me from England, from the reverend bishop of London, to be delivered to your excellency, and which I was unwilling to send to your excellency without one from myself. The bishop of London, I suppose, has given you an account[1] of the parricide perpetrated by the queen of Scots, and her justly deserved punishment; namely, that she has been taken prisoner, and compelled to abdicate the kingdom, after having confessed that her husband had been taken off by her counsel and co-operation; and that her most profligate paramour had taken refuge in some maritime fortress built upon a rock. Praiseworthy is the example and activity of this unpolished nation in the punishment of crime, for which refined Italy would have pleaded in excuse the force and rage of lust. You cannot but be aware of the

[1 See first series, Letter LXXIX. p. 192.]

extraordinary butchery in Flanders[2] : I much doubt whether
those to whom the power of the sword has been committed
by the Lord, can be excused for being idle spectators and
dissemblers in such vast profusion of innocent blood. If it
has been allowed and sanctioned in all ages, and by all
popes, cardinals, monks, clergymen, and scholastic writers, to
wage war against the Turks, because they wage war against
the true religion, and if in such war glory and immortal
honour awaits the slain ; is that man to be accounted as
factious and rebellious, who takes up necessary and just arms
in defence of his altars and his home, for the resistance of
unjust aggression, the maintenance of true religion, and the
transmission of it to posterity ? What if a lawful sovereign
should degenerate into a tyrant, can he be said to be the
minister of God ? Peace must be cultivated, and obedience
rendered ; but at the same time the natural rights, laws, and
customs of kingdoms, dominions, and powers, are to be
maintained, and especially the things which are God's are
to be given to God. Noble was the decree of the emperors
Theodosius and Valentinian ; and worthy that voice of the
majesty of a sovereign, when he professed that he, though a
prince, was bound by the laws : so much does our authority
depend on the authority of the law. Nor are princes so
unrestrained by law, as that they may do every thing according to their own will ; but, as Aristotle says, they ought
so far to excel others by pre-eminence in virtue, as that the
virtue of all other persons may not admit of being compared
with theirs ; and they should be as much superior to others
in justice and equity, as the sun is to the shapeless and rude
elements. There is no legislating at all against such a
person ; inasmuch as he is himself a living and animated law.
The Swiss therefore are to be commended, who have vin-
dicated their freedom from a weak and tyrannical despotism.
I would not wish to sound an alarm against lawful and just
sovereigns, but against those tyrants, who, wherever they
turn themselves, corrupt, disturb, confound, contaminate every
thing by their lust, avarice, cruelty, and pride, overturning
and agitating every thing by their sole will. Such persons
are most deserving of being brought to order by Swiss and

[2 See Brandt's Hist. of Reformation in the Low Countries, Vol. I.
B. VIII. IX. &c.]

Scottish censors. Salute, I pray you, from me your son-in-law Rodolph Gualter. I offer you all the services in my power. Strasburgh, Oct. 2, 1567.

[Yours,]

you know who,

[CHRISTOPHER MONT.]

LETTER LXVI.

BISHOP GRINDAL TO THEODORE BEZA AND OTHERS.

Dated at LONDON, *April* 17, 1568.

HEALTH in Christ. Master John Cousins, the most faithful minister of the French church in this country, and my very dear brother in the Lord, has this day shewn me a letter that he has written to you upon the state of the Dutch church in London, and which he sends together with this. In that letter the origin and substance of all the controversies in the said church are set forth with the greatest simplicity and truth. I pray you therefore, very dear brethren, to give full credit to that letter, and aid with your counsel not only the Dutch church in London, but also the other churches of that language ; and earnestly exhort them to be zealous in the promotion of peace and unity. I doubt not but that your exhortations and admonitions will have great influence with them. I would have written somewhat more fully upon this subject, and also upon the state of our own churches, had not a disorder in my eyes[1], which succeeded a tertian ague, prevented me from doing so. But the Lord, I hope, will afford me a better opportunity at some future time. May the Lord preserve you, my very dear brethren, and bless your ministry! London, April 17, 1568.

Yours in Christ,

EDMUND GRINDAL,

Bishop of London.

[1 See first series, Letter LXXXII. p. 201.]

LETTER LXVII.

CHRISTOPHER MONT TO HENRY BULLINGER.

Dated at STRASBURGH, *Dec.* 27, 1568.

I HAVE lately received two letters from you, the one written on the 13th of December, the other on the 16th, brought to me by master Antony Francis, whom both on account of his learning and piety I would willingly have obliged, if I had had it in my power. As I could not forward more speedily your treasurer's letter to his son, I have given it in charge to master Antony, who is going to-morrow from hence to Heidelberg.

I can write your excellency no certain news from France; for all the tidings brought from that country are so vague, that we dare give very little credit to what is told us. We have this one token, that the affairs of the Huguenots are not yet despaired of, namely, that the king's party, who have at other times put forth vain and inflated exaggerations of any new occurrence in their own favour, are now silent, and have become more moderate. I believe that the Italians[2], having met, as they deserved, with a warm reception, will not rashly make an incursion into France. The cruelty and impious domination of the Spaniards will be retaliated by the avenging arms of the Turks.

The bishop of London wrote to me on the 10th of October, which letter I received at length on the 20th of December. For as we are now deprived of the convenience afforded by Flanders in the transmission of letters, and the German Ocean is now closed against us, we are deprived of the facility both of sending letters and receiving them in return. The bishop in his letter desired me to salute your excellency in his name. I have thought it right to communicate to you, as a friend and well wisher to the affairs of England, the tidings that I

[2 A subsidy of 10,000 ducats was paid by Pius V. to the duke of Savoy, to furnish him with necessary equipments, that he might take the field in France against the Huguenots. Smedley's Hist. of Ref. in France, I. 299.]

have received from thence. The duke of Norfolk, who had till now conducted himself loyally and peaceably in England, as a nobleman should do, puffed up by extravagant and ambitious expectations, entertained the idea of contracting a most unhappy marriage with the parricide and blood-sucking Medea[1]; and inflamed with this project withdrew from court to his ancestral domains. On his presumption being discovered, he was summoned to court by a special messenger; to which summons however he paid no attention, but remained on his paternal estate. The queen, perceiving with her wonted discretion the necessity of putting a stop to such proceedings, sent an officer[2] of the royal guards with a troop of soldiers to apprehend him; on hearing of which he voluntarily commenced his journey to court, but he was stopped by the queen's order, and not allowed to come near the court. After a delay of three days he was committed to the tower of London, where he is still detained. Two other earls[3] were ordered to confine themselves to their own houses, as being charged with the suspicion of being privy to his design. Now that the duke is arrested, and the others reduced to order, the whole kingdom is quiet and tranquil. Unless that serpent is removed out of the way, she will occasion much mischief by the arts and wiles peculiar to her race, like her who dreamed that she was delivered of a burning torch. Our most serene queen has hitherto peaceably carried on the government without any bloodshed: may God grant her a continuance of this happiness!

An ambassador was lately sent over from the king of Spain to the most serene queen of England, requesting liberty of passage in his name for three legions or regiments of Flemish infantry, who were on their way to Spain to be em-

[1 Mary, queen of Scots. See first series, Let. LXXXVII. p. 216.]

[2 Edward Fitzgerald, the earl of Kildare's brother, lieutenant of the band of gentlemen pensioners, met and received the duke of Norfolk at Saint Alban's on his return to court, and conveyed him to Burnham, three miles from Windsor, where the queen then lay. Camden, Elizabeth, p. 131.]

[3 The earl of Pembroke was commanded to keep his house, and brought to a private examination. Camden, Eliz. p. 132. The other nobleman was probably the earl of Arundel, who "had earnestly moved [the duke] to marry the Scottish queen," as the earl of Sussex writes to Cecil, Sept. 11, 1569. MS. Cotton. Calig. c. i. 324.]

ployed against the rebel Moors.   The queen is reported to
have replied on the instant, that it might possibly be attended
with danger for such a number of soldiers to sail along the
coasts of England; for as the winds are changeable and uncertain, and many things may happen to persons travelling
by sea, different from what they expected, if these soldiers,
upon some urgent necessity, should be obliged to bring to in
the English ports, the landing of such numbers could not take
place without mischief, and it would therefore be necessary
for the queen to arm and defend her coasts and harbours
with garrison troops : but if the king chose to bear that
expense, and give security that he would not make any other
use of the German soldiery than against the Moors, she would
be ready to oblige him.   But it must be considered that faith
is not to be kept with heretics, and that, if an oath is to be
violated, it may well be violated for the sake of a kingdom[4].
Pope Julius used to say that oaths were binding on merchants, but not on princes.

We hear no news from Saxony.   The prince of Orange
is still lingering with the Saxon.   The elector himself, it is
said, will be present at the marriage of his daughter[5], who
is to be brought to Heidelberg, where the marriage will take
place on the 5th of February.   Nothing is yet determined
about our sending troops into France.   A small force will
not be able to penetrate; a large one will cost too much
money, and, to go to any expense and incur danger for
the sake of religion, is the work of a Sampson.   I offer
my services to your reverence.   Strasburgh, Dec. 27, 1568.
Let us pray that through the divine mercy we may meet
with better success in the year now approaching.   I wish
you would omit my English[6] titles in the address of your
letters.

> The prudent man, of such possessed,
> Enjoys them in his silent breast.

C. M.

[4 See Cicero, de Off. iii. 21.]

[5 Elizabeth, daughter of Augustus, elector of Saxony, was married
in 1569 to John Casimir, count Palatine.]

[6 Christopher Mont was Q. Elizabeth's political agent at Strasburgh.]

LETTER LXVIII[1].

QUEEN ELIZABETH TO JOHN STURMIUS.

Dated at WESTMINSTER, *May* 1, 1569.

ELIZABETH, by the grace of God, of England, France, and Ireland, queen, defender of the faith, &c. to John Sturmius, our right well-beloved friend, greeting.

We have received your letter written to us on the 19th of March, from those parties to whom you gave them to be delivered to us. And to the individuals themselves we have both given the credit that your letter requested, and have accurately considered every thing that they were ordered to acquaint us with. By which recognizing your former good will towards us, and that care and solicitude respecting our state, which you have long since manifested to us by abundant evidence; though we were not greatly surprised at it by reason of your ancient attachment to us, yet we rejoiced greatly, and now also return you much thanks.

But with respect to the things mentioned by them to us, we have thus determined, that, as we have lately sent over thither with dispatches our faithful servant, Henry Killigrew[2], in whom, together with doctor Mont, our faithful servant, who is well known to you, we wish full confidence to be placed in respect to all our affairs, you may freely make known to them all the circumstances, and communicate them without reserve to either one or both. And when we have been made acquainted by them with such your conference, we will come to such a determination, by God's blessing, upon the whole matter, as may be worthy of the cause and of ourselves. Farewell. From our palace at Westminster, May 1, in the year of our Lord, 1569, and in the eleventh year of our reign.

ELIZABETH R.

[1 The original of this letter is preserved at Strasburgh.]
[2 For an account of this embassy see Strype, Ann. i. ii. 268.]

LETTER LXIX.

JOHN STURMIUS TO QUEEN ELIZABETH.

Dated at STRASBURGH, *Sept.* 6, 1569.

THE individual[3], most serene queen, who has translated the holy Bible into Spanish, is one of those, who, oppressed by the calumnies of wicked men, are unable to retain the position in which they seem in a manner to have been placed by God. That serpent, the enemy of all good men, envies England this man and his work, yea, envies the church of Christ; and this excellent man has been compelled by the evil artifices of his enemies to depart from England. But he has neither laid aside his zeal for religion, nor his good will towards the kingdom of England, nor his veneration for your majesty; and he has overcome the power of the devil, and completed a work which he would willingly have published under the protection of your majesty, if he thought the Spaniards would suffer it without resentment, and if he had considered it worthy of your majesty's patronage: not that he is himself undeserving of the support of the most excellent and powerful, by reason of his virtue and learning, but that he thinks too humbly of himself. He is however desirous that this work and his services should meet with the approval of your majesty, and has requested my recommendation of both; that, if he may not come into England himself, his bible may at least obtain a place, in which, after having been so long and greatly tossed about with its author, it may at length repose in peace. I commend therefore to

[3 Cassiodorus de Reyna is the person here mentioned. He was one of the preachers of the Spanish church in England, which he was obliged to leave upon suspicion of some grievous crime. His translation of the Bible was printed at Basle in 1569, and entitled "La Biblia, que es los sacros libros del viejo y nuevo Testamento, transladada en espagnol, 1569." A revised edition of it was published by Cyprian de Valera, at Amsterdam, in 1702. Horne's Introduction, Vol. II. p. 268. He also published "A defence of the divinity of Christ against the Jews."]

your majesty both this man and his labours against the calumnies of the malevolent. They indeed have received their just punishment, and the end of their life sufficiently proved what their course of life had been. But I so intercede for the author, as also to ask pardon for myself, for being so troublesome amidst this vast pressure of business, especially in these disturbances of the world; believing however, and hoping, that as the prayers and supplications of the humble are not unacceptable to God, so they will not be so to great men and the rulers of empires and kingdoms. I pray God to preserve your majesty in health and safety, happiness and prosperity. Strasburgh, Sept. 6, 1569.

> Your most serene majesty's
>
> > faithful servant and subject,
> >
> > > JOHN STURMIUS.

LETTER LXX

JOHN STURMIUS TO SIR WILLIAM CECIL.

Dated at STRASBURGH, *Sept.* 8, 1569.

I HAVE written to the most serene queen about the Spanish bible[1], and have commended it to her majesty's protection. But I have need also in this matter of the support of your authority, that if this my vindication should be at all questioned, you may afford us your assistance; that the calumny of the Spanish papists may not prove of more avail than the desires of the professors of the gospel in those parts. The bible, I hear, is faithfully translated, and I entertain such an opinion of the party who has translated it, that I would not hesitate even to swear to his fidelity and innocence. He is certainly endued with an acute and erudite judgment. We only petition her majesty to allow the work to be exposed for sale in your booksellers' shops, should any copies happen to be brought over. You have

[1 See the preceding letter.]

already dared, and still dare to do greater things than this; and it is surely the duty of religion to provide a habitation for the Holy Spirit.

We hear nothing in these parts about the French affairs, as all the roads are so entirely blocked up. We have, however, great expectations from you, and also from the conference of our princes at Neuberg. The emperor's commissioners have now been fruitlessly expecting for many weeks the arrival in our city of the envoys of the electors of Saxony and Brandeburgh, and know not how to account for their delay. Farewell, illustrious sir. Strasburgh, Sept. 8, 1569.

Your honour's most devoted,

JOHN STURMIUS.

LETTER LXXI.

BISHOP PARKHURST TO JOHN WOLFIUS.

Dated at NORWICH, Jan. 16, 1571.

MAY you be safe in Christ, my kind Wolfius. On the first of July I received your letter, together with your very learned commentaries on Nehemiah, for which I return my best thanks, and will return the obligation as soon as I can meet with another Abel[2]. Every one most highly esteems your Nehemiah, and is eagerly buying it up. You will do well to elucidate Esther likewise with your lucubrations. I remember that I once saw in your study your homilies on Deuteronomy, Joshua, and Judges, which pleased me so much, that I procured some of them to be copied for me. Do not suffer them, my Wolfius, I beseech you, any longer to contend with the moths and bookworms; but let them be published as soon as possible for the glory of God, the good of many, and the no little increase of reputation to yourself. Whatever news I had to communicate you can learn from my letters to Bullinger[2] and Gualter.

[2 See first series, Letter XCIII. p. 232.]

Salute in my name your excellent wife, and your very dear brother, Gaspar Wolfius[1], a physician, as I hear, of great eminence, and a new framer of calendars. I remember him sitting at table when you so kindly invited Gualter and myself to dinner, and I fancy that I see his countenance yet before me.

Salute moreover those excellent men, Simler, Wonlichius, Haller, Lavater, Wickius, Zuinglius, Froschover, Julius, and all the rest whom I love in the Lord. May the Lord preserve Zurich and all its inhabitants! Amen. Farewell. In haste. Norwich, Jan. 16, 1571.

Yours heartily,

JO. PARKHURST.

LETTER LXXII[2].

HENRY BULLINGER TO ARCHBISHOP GRINDAL, BISHOPS COX AND JEWEL.

Dated at ZURICH, *Feb.* 1571.

RIGHT reverend fathers in Christ, honoured masters, and very dear brethren. I confess myself much indebted to your kindness, that, notwithstanding we are mutually separated by so great a distance, (you indeed dwelling in England beyond the sea, and I living in Switzerland not far from the Alps,) your reverences so diligently cherish, preserve, and daily increase more and more by frequent letters, the friendship and brotherhood long since contracted between us. Wherefore I ought with good reason to manifest my

[1 Gaspar Wolfius was created doctor of medicine at Montpelier in 1558. He edited many of the works of Conrad Gesner, to which he made many additions.]

[2 This letter is the preface to Bullinger's refutation of the pope's bull, entitled "Bullæ Papisticæ ante biennium contra sereniss. Angliæ, Franciæ, et Hyberniæ reginam Elisabetham, et contra inclytum Angliæ regnum promulgatæ Refutatio, orthodoxæque Reginæ et universi Regni Angliæ defensio Henrychii Bullingeri." Londini ap. Joh. Dayum typographum, 4⁰. 1571. See Strype, Ann. I. ii. 355, and Day's letter concerning it, infra Letter LXXIV.]

gratitude and respect to your reverences in every possible way. And forasmuch as, by submitting to my perusal not long since the bull[3] of Pius V., bishop of Rome, which I had not previously seen, nor indeed heard any thing about it, you have afforded me an opportunity of doing, or at least attempting, something for the glory of Christ our only Redeemer, and for the preservation of his church, which is with you in England, against the Roman antichrist; behold, I dedicate to your reverences this my refutation in opposition to that bull, and submit it to your most exact judgments, that it may altogether stand or fall according as your reverences may please to determine. But I pray you to receive with kindness this my endeavour, and exceeding devotedness to the good cause and to your reverences. I am free to confess that my own abilities are very small, and that your learning is most profound; wherefore, had it so pleased you, you would have been able to manage this cause far more successfully than myself. But when I understood that I should gratify your reverences by my labours, such as they are, upon this subject, I was unwilling in any measure to disappoint your expectations. May the Lord Christ grant that my discourse may be to the great profit of many! Be pleased, I pray you, to salute my reverend masters and very dear brethren, masters Robert Horn, bishop of Winchester, Edwin Sandys, bishop of London, John Parkhurst, bishop of Norwich, James Pilkington, bishop of Durham; also John Aylmer, Sampson, Humphreys, Lever, Foxe, and the other companions of your past exile in Switzerland and Germany; to the prayers of all of whom I commend myself. All the ministers and brethren here pray for all of you every happiness in Christ Jesus our Lord. May the Lord Jesus bless your ministry, and preserve you from all evil! Zurich. In the month of February, in the year of our salvation, 1571.

[H. BULLINGER.]

[3 This bull was dated April 25, 1570. See a full account of it in Soames' Eliz. Hist. p. 121, &c. and the authorities there quoted.]

LETTER LXXIII.

RICHARD HILLES TO HENRY BULLINGER.

Dated at LONDON, *March* 8, 1571.

MUCH health in the Lord.   As my son Barnabas Hilles,
my much honoured friend and master, has informed our
beloved brother in Christ, Julius Sancterentianus, by letter
dated on the 26th of last November; I have received your
letter, written on the 27th of August last, here in London
from the learned and pious youth Henry Butler, whom, a
fortnight after I had received the letter aforesaid, I sent on
horseback with trusty attendants to a certain Dunstan Fel-
ton, son of master John Butler deceased, to an English
village named Chilton[1], in the county of Suffolk : from
which place I have received a letter from the aforesaid
Henry Butler, written from the house of his aunt, a widow,
and a very godly matron.   I will also most diligently and
heartily undertake the management of all that business
which in your aforesaid letter you desired me to execute.
But I forwarded to the aforesaid Henry Butler on the 26th
of November, by a trusty messenger, some letters which
master Christopher Froschover delivered to my aforesaid
son Barnabas at Frankfort.   My son Barnabas Hilles has
also received from the aforesaid master Froschover, together
with the aforesaid letters, four books in the German language, which he took care should be faithfully delivered to
the parties to whom they were addressed; and I and my
wife are exceedingly obliged to you for having sent us two
of those books as a present.

I am very sorry that, when you wrote me the aforesaid
letter, you had not yet fully recovered from your illness.   I
hope however that before this time you are much better :
God grant it may be so!   I have not lately received any
letters to be forwarded to you from any of our bishops or

[1 There are two places of this name in Suffolk; the one, a hamlet
in the parish of Clare, the other a small village near Sudbury.]

others residing here in England. Should I however receive
any letters for that purpose at any future time, I will take
care that they shall be sent over to you with all diligence.
Master Edmund Grindal, who now, as you may have heard, is
archbishop of York, is constantly resident, as I am told, near
York, or in the city itself. But I think that he will shortly
come hither to London, as will almost all the other bishops;
for by the queen's majesty's command the famous council of
all England, which among us is commonly called a parliament,
is summoned to assemble. With you, if I remember rightly,
such assemblies are called *comitia imperialia* in Latin, and
in German, *Reichstag*. Master Edwin Sandys, who was
lately bishop of Worcester, is now our bishop of London;
but he is not much known to me, except by sight: and
indeed almost all the other bishops, with the exception of
that most learned and amiable, yea rather divine bishop,
master Jewel of Salisbury, are for the most part unknown
to me. For I am afraid, (although I have never experienced
it myself,) that some of them (as the most learned Jerome
wrote concerning some bishops of his time), placed as it
were upon some high beacon, scarce deign to look upon
mankind, or hold any intercourse with their fellow-servants.
Your friend master Cox, bishop of Ely, who married a year
ago the young widow of master Doctor Turner[2], a physician,
is still living, and, by God's blessing, in good health. But
his predecessor master Thirlby[3], who was bishop of Ely in
Mary's reign, and who resided with the most reverend
Matthew Parker, archbishop of Canterbury, (but under restraint there by reason of his profession of popish doctrine,)
lately died, six or seven months since, at Lambeth, in the
palace of the said archbishop of Canterbury. Some of the
other bishops or prelates, who were placed under restraint by
reason of their obstinacy, are still living; but they scarcely

[2 See Strype, Cranmer, I. 394. Parker, I. 93, 301. See also
Letters LI. p. 124, and LXXXII. p. 203, of the present volume.]

[3 Thirlby at first had his liberty, till he began to preach against
the reformation; but being pardoned, afterwards was in custody of
the archbishop, with whom he lived in much ease and credit for ten
years. He died Aug. 26, 1570, and was buried by the archbishop
in the chancel of Lambeth church. See Strype, Ann. I. i. 213. Parker, I. 278.]

suffer any inconvenience, unless perhaps some regret for their want of liberty, and that they are prevented from the power of speaking or doing mischief. Of all these Nicolas Hethe[1], who under queen Mary was archbishop of York, was the least troublesome, on which account perhaps he found more favour with our most serene queen Elizabeth; for he had no other prison but his own house in the country, sufficiently comfortable, and in a healthy situation.

Here, among us, by the favour of God all things are settled both in church and state. May the Lord long grant us this blessing! I hear too, that the king of France is wisely maintaining that peace which you informed me had been concluded; and I am very glad, and heartily thank God, that in the ratification of that peace sufficient regard was had to the security of the faithful, as you wrote me word, and as we now see to be the case. But I grieve very much, that the pestiferous sect of Arians is budding forth again in many other places besides Switzerland. But when the Lord Jesus shall come to judgment, will he find faith on the earth?

I pray you to salute in my name and that of my wife the aforesaid Julius Sancterentianus. Matters are not yet quite settled between our most serene queen and the duke of Alva[2], touching the release of the persons and goods, or merchandise, of both nations which have been arrested or detained these two years. But though there is no agreement at present, there is some hope of it. But there is no prospect or even hope, as far as I can see or conjecture, of any commerce in future, such as has for many years

[1 Hethe, late archbishop of York, having been Lord Chancellor of England, and having in parliament declared the death of queen Mary, and the just title of the lady Elizabeth, her sister, to succeed; for this duty towards his prince, he lived, after a little trouble, quietly and nobly in his own lordship of Chobham in Surrey, four miles from Windsor. He was always honourably esteemed by the queen, and sometimes had the honour to be visited by her majesty. See Strype, Ann. i. i. 212, and Parker, i. 281.]

[2 For an account of this transaction see first series, Letter LXXXV. p. 209. Queen Elizabeth satisfied to the full the damages which the English merchants had sustained out of the Netherlanders' goods that were here stayed; the rest she restored to the duke of Alva. Camden's Elizabeth, p. 191.]

past been continued between the kings of England and the archdukes of Austria and Burgundy.

There died, on the third of this month, another papist, or, as he seemed to himself, a good catholic, of the name of Boxall[3], who was chief secretary to queen Mary abovementioned. He was a man of much moderation (as he used to boast) and of gentle disposition, and lived also some years under restraint in the palace of the most reverend archbishop of Canterbury. May the Lord Jesus evermore preserve you and yours! London, March 8, in the year of our salvation 1570, according to the computation of the church of England.

Yours from my heart,

RICHARD HILLES.

LETTER LXXIV.

JOHN DAY[4] TO HENRY BULLINGER.

Dated at LONDON, [*Aug.* 8, 1571.]

REVEREND father in Christ, I heartily wish you health. Now that I have finished printing your book[5], which I confidently believe has been completed with accuracy and fidelity

[3 See first series, Letter XCIX. p. 255.]

[4 John Day was printer to Edward VI, and in queen Mary's time a prisoner in Newgate for religion, and afterwards an exile. After the accession of Elizabeth he resumed his printing, and to him posterity is largely indebted for editions of the writings of the reformers, and many works relative to the reformation. He was patronised and much encouraged by archbishops Parker and Grindal, and was the printer of the Acts and Monuments of Foxe. See Strype, Mem. III. i. 320; Ann. I. i. 267.]

[5 This book was Bullinger's confutation of the Bull of Pius V. against queen Elizabeth. In the month of September 1571, the archbishop (Parker) caused it to be fairly bound and sent to her, and further procured the printing of it in Latin, not without the advice of the Lord Treasurer; and had it translated, and printed in English too. Strype, Parker, II. 78.]

according to the copy sent me by the reverend father in
Christ, doctor Cox, and which he had previously corrected
with the utmost diligence; it was his wish, most faithful pastor, that I should take care that half a dozen or more of
these books should be sent over to you, if it could be done
without inconvenience; and I have found a suitable opportunity of effecting this. Moreover, the reverend fathers
themselves will return you in their next letters their most
deserved thanks for the pains you have bestowed in the composition of that book, and which is the greatest evidence of
your good-will to England, which is divided from you by so
great a distance. Meanwhile may the Lord of glory so
comfort you and his universal church by his most holy
Spirit, that his truth may be advanced, and the kingdom
of antichrist confounded and overthrown altogether. And
may Christ the Lord grant that more persons from every
part of the world may exert themselves for this object with
their whole heart, and bestow their utmost pains upon it.
Take, I pray you, in good part my labour, such as it is, in
this work. Farewell, most vigilant pastor. London, in the
month of [August 1571[1].]

Your most devoted,

JOHN DAY.

[[1] The date is wanting in the MS.   Simler dates it as above.]

LETTER LXXV.

HIEROME ZANCHIUS TO BISHOP JEWEL.

Dated at HEIDELBERG, *Sept.* 2, 1571.

IT is true, most learned bishop Jewel, that, though I have always esteemed you by reason of your singular piety and virtue ever since we were together at Strasburgh, I have never written to you, nor congratulated you as I ought to have done, upon the dignity to which your virtue has advanced you. All this I acknowledge to be the case. But if any one should infer from hence that I therefore have held and do hold you in small estimation, I should deny the consequence, and say that such a person is guilty of false reasoning, by putting *non causa pro causa.* For there exist other reasons why this duty has been, I will not say neglected by me, but omitted; though, were I to detail and explain them, my excuse would extend to a greater length than your patience could endure. One of them, however, I cannot pass over in silence : and that is, that after your return to your most beloved country, I was wonderfully tossed about both by land and sea, to the great injury of my affairs; being persecuted beyond belief, partly by the enemies of the truth at Strasburgh, partly by the foes to discipline, with whom the followers of Servetus united their forces at Chiavenna[2]. What person, I ask, could bear in mind all and each of his friends, amidst such great storms as these? And when the first opportunities of congratulating or writing upon any subject are once gone by, it seems quite superfluous and unseasonable to write about such things at any later period. But no occasion for my writing, worthy

[2 Zanchius was appointed professor at Strasburgh in 1553, and remained there almost eleven years. He wrote two treatises against the Servetian or Socinian hypothesis, at the solicitation of Frederic III. elector Palatine, by whom he was appointed divinity professor at Heidelberg in 1568. One of these was entitled *De Dei natura;* the other, *De tribus Elohim uno eodemque Jehova.*]

of your virtue and dignity, has been since afforded me, except at the present time. There has not indeed been wanting a very pressing subject, only it was a personal one, which did not so much recommend, as compel me, as it were, to address you as well as others; but, to speak candidly, I dared not take the same liberty with you as I did with some others, with whom, though they were persons of great consequence, I lived upon a more intimate footing when I was at Strasburgh, than with yourself. For you had gone away to Zurich with Peter Martyr, while we remained at Strasburgh. Whence it arose, that my familiar and friendly intercourse with the other noble and learned individuals increased more and more, which could not so easily be the case as regarding you and myself. This then is one reason why you have heretofore received no letters from me. But I could not at this time on any account omit writing to you; for a matter of importance and one most worthy of you now presents itself, which compels me to address you.

When master Mont[1] returned from England in June last, he informed me, together with some others, that the controversy has again been stirred up in your churches, about certain habits, which her most serene majesty requires the bishops and ministers to wear in the administration of the word or sacraments; and that there are not a few men of your order, who are minded rather to resign their office, and even retire from the ministry, than adopt the use of such habits. From hence, he adds, is to be feared the entire downfall of those churches. He has therefore requested me to write, both to her most serene majesty, to admonish her of her duty; and also to those bishops who are known to me, and with whom I am upon a footing of friendship. He mentioned you among the first, for that, by reason of your virtue and the influence arising from it, you possessed much authority. I excused myself, and alleged my want of ability; but no excuse would avail. At last therefore, after the persuasion of many of my friends, I was ordered even by my most illustrious sovereign to take the matter in hand. Being thus compelled, I wrote first of all a letter[2] to her

[1 See first series, p. 173, note.]

[2 A translation of this letter is in the appendix to the present volume. Archbishop Grindal, to whom it was sent to be delivered to

most serene majesty, and, as I trust, not an improper one, in which I exhort and beseech her not to give ear to such counsels as are certainly inconsistent with the duty of a good sovereign. I desire nothing more earnestly than that her most serene majesty would listen, not so much to my advice as to that of all my colleagues and godly friends, and of our most illustrious prince himself. And that she may do this, we do not so much request from herself, as from God. But since we are ignorant as to what she will do, and it may possibly happen that she will persist in her present opinion; and in the mean time, if the bishops themselves are unwilling in any way to alter their determination, the church will be in danger; our brethren have therefore judged it expedient that some of the more eminent and discreet bishops should be written to, and requested to advise the rest, that, should not the queen by any means be induced to revoke her orders, they ought not themselves on this account to choose rather to desert their posts than to obey the royal command; for that there seems no reason why it should be lawful for a pastor to forsake his flock, so long as he is freely permitted to teach, and to administer the sacraments according to the word of God, although he may be forced to do some things of which he cannot altogether approve; provided only that they are not such as are intrinsically and of their own nature sinful: for if such things be commanded, we must say with the apostles, that we ought to obey God rather than men: and in the mean time each person should abide in his own calling, and take care of his own flock. But if things in their own nature indifferent be prescribed by law and the queen's command, since it is the only alternative, either to resign one's post or to yield obedience to such a command, we ought rather to obey, but with a due protest against it; and the people should be instructed why and for what reason obedience has been paid to such a command, rather than that they should be waiting for the time when their pastor should be deprived, and compelled to resign his flock to another. And this opinion is so plain and evident, both from the sacred writings, and the fathers and ecclesiastical histories, that to

the queen, thought it best, upon the advice of some of the council, not to present it. See Strype, Grindal, 157, and Grindal's letter to Zanchy, in the Parker Society's Edition of his works, p. 333.]

adduce any proof of it to those who are even moderately versed in the scriptures would be altogether superfluous. For a lawful and necessary calling is never to be deserted for the sake of things which are in their own nature indifferent.

We doubt not, most learned Jewel, but that these things are well known to you. We therefore request you to interpose your authority, and with your wonted ability and discretion so consult with your other most reverend and right worshipful episcopal brethren, that they may each of them abide in their respective calling and station. For Satan is surely aiming at nothing else, than that by the separation of the true bishops, whether by right or wrong, from their flocks, the whole church may be thrown into confusion. He must therefore be resisted, lest he should succeed in his most impious and ungodly purpose. May the Lord preserve both yourself and all the other pious and holy bishops to his church, guide you by his Spirit, and by your assistance advance his kingdom! And we pray you most earnestly on your part to entreat the Lord for us, and especially for our most illustrious prince. And I especially commend myself to you, most pious and learned prelate, as also Rodolph Gualter, and Rodolph Zuingle, grandson of the great Zuingle : they are both of them studious and godly youths. You will be informed by them respecting the state of our affairs.

Heidelberg, Sept. 2, 1571.

H. ZANCHIUS,

in his own name, and in that of his colleagues.

LETTER LXXVI.

RODOLPH ZUINGLIUS[1] TO BISHOP SANDYS.

Dated at CAMBRIDGE, *Jan.* 26, 1572.

As master Shepherd[2], the most worthy master of our college, has expressed his intention of paying you a visit, I did not think, reverend father in Christ, that I could do otherwise than send a letter to your eminence, to thank your eminence for your especial kindness and extreme liberality towards me and mine ; and at the same time to make known to your eminence, and that very briefly, the state of my affairs. For it is not fit that you, who are occupied with cares and engagements of far greater importance, should waste much of your labour and time in reading what I have to say. Nor indeed does my situation in life, or rather my lowness of condition, justify my detaining your emi- nence by a lengthened statement. To dispatch the mat- ter therefore in few words, I return you, reverend bishop, my warmest thanks for your singular good-will and favour towards me ; and especially for the godly care and exertions you have bestowed upon the advancement of my studies, and by which you have not only provided me a place in the most flourishing university of Cambridge, but have also procured my admission into a most famous college, and among sober students : for which singular care of yours on my behalf I thank your eminence to the utmost of my power, and promise on my part, as it is my duty to do, that I will never be un- grateful or unmindful of such great benefits, and that I will evermore proclaim both to my countrymen, and especially to my parents, your exceeding liberality to me ; and ever so con-

[1 This Rodolph Zuinglius was Bullinger's grandson. See first series, p. 264, note. He died in the June following the date of this letter.]

[2 Nicolas Shepherd, chosen master of St John's College in 1569, whom, alluding to his name, the fellows, in their letters to Cecil their patron, styled their ποιμένα. He was strongly recommended to Cecil by bishop Grindal, (whose letter is printed in Strype, Life of Grindal, p. 225,) but was deprived of the mastership in 1576.]

duct myself towards your eminence as a godly young man, and one who is descended from godly parents, should do.

In the mean time, however, I would have your eminence know, with respect to my affairs, that I have obtained, in the college where I was placed by your eminence, a situation sufficiently suitable and convenient for the furtherance of my studies; for the master has provided me, by his especial kindness, not only with comfortable rooms and sufficient commons, but with a most excellent tutor, of whose advice and assistance I most freely avail myself, both in prosecuting my studies, and procuring other things that are necessary; so that I think very little will be wanting towards the prosecution of my studies. And I rejoice, not so much on my own account, as for the sake of my studies, that I have the means and opportunity afforded me of hearing that most famous and learned man, master Antony Chevalier[1], to whom our Germany can scarce produce an equal in the knowledge of Hebrew, or one who can bear a comparison with him, except Immanuel Tremellius[2], whom I heard lecturing most ably at Heidelberg in the Palatinate, and from whose lectures, I think, I derived no small advantage; nor do I think, the Lord giving his grace, that I shall profit less by those of this professor. But whatever benefit I may derive from these or any other lectures, I ascribe all to your eminence, by whose singular liberality it has been brought to pass and provided, that I have not only the means of subsistence in the most celebrated university of Cambridge, but also the convenience and liberty afforded me of hearing the most learned professors, by whose assistance I hope to make no small progress in my studies. But in the mean time, not to proceed to an unbecoming prolixity, I commend myself to your eminence, and would entreat the continuance of your protection and patronage; and that you

[1 Antony Rodolph Chevalier was a French protestant, recommended by archbishop Parker and bishop Sandys to be Hebrew professor at Cambridge, where he had formerly assisted Tremellius in 1552. Their letter to the heads of the University is given by Strype, Ann. I. ii. 552. He was also a prebendary of Canterbury.]

[2 John Immanuel Tremellius was a converted Jew, and succeeded Fagius as Hebrew professor at Cambridge in 1550. He was afterwards professor at Heidelberg, and published in 1575, in concert with Francis Junius, a Latin version of the Old Testament.]

will take these few lines in good part, as a slight testimony of my respect to your eminence. May our good and gracious God long keep your eminence in health and safety, and deign to preserve you to his church!

Your eminence's most devoted,

RODOLPH ZUINGLIUS, of Zurich.

Cambridge, Jan. 26, 1572.

LETTER LXXVII.

HENRY BUTLER TO BISHOP SANDYS.

Dated at CAMBRIDGE, *Jan.* 27, [1572.]

As soon as I was restored to the muses, right reverend sir, by your liberality and benevolence, it was my first object to inquire by whom I could send a letter to you to express my gratitude. And after long inquiry, the right worshipful master Shepherd, master of St John's college, offered his services as the bearer of my letter. I determined therefore on no account to let him depart, after so seasonable an offer, without the expression of my grateful remembrance of the benefits you have conferred upon me; and though I had intended most fully to express my thankfulness for your most abundant and praiseworthy exertions on my behalf, yet by reason of their greatness they not only exceed and surpass the power of expression, but also all possible thanks. For if your kindness be compared with that of others, both of my friends and kinsfolk, they will, like the morning star with its brightness, overpower and obscure them all; especially as they have only provided support for the body, and that not without the greatest entreaties; whereas by you not only is my body, oppressed by servitude, restored to its former liberty, but a most wholesome remedy is applied to a mind half dead with grief. For by what medicine can a mind, worn out by anxiety, be sooner restored to health, than by the friendly attentions of master Allen, a man of surpassing integrity of conduct and godly zeal, in the offices of a tutor? Wherefore, my most worthily honoured master and patron, since I can nowise thank you as I ought for these your most abundant favours towards me, much less return the obligation; I beg of you again and again, to deign to be satisfied with the gratitude of my mind, which I have determined to retain inviolate and perfect; promising moreover, that I will never desert the post which I have obtained by your assistance, together with the favour of divine providence, but that I will adorn it with every flower of diligence and virtue. And with this I commit your kindness to the divine goodness, heartily wishing the age of Nestor to you, and to all belonging to you. Written in Christ's college, Jan. 27, [1572].

Your dignity's most devoted

HENRY BUTLER,

a native of Zurich, but of English origin.

LETTER LXXVIII.

BISHOP COX TO HENRY BULLINGER.

Dated at ELY, *Febr.* 12, 1572.

YOUR letter, my beloved brother in Christ, written on the 20th of August, 1571, was brought me in the month of January last past, by the three young men of whom you made mention in that letter[1]. A letter was sent you by me last summer with some copies of a book printed in your name against the pope's bull. Your book indeed, dictated with so much ability and truth, and most correctly written, could not but be most acceptable to me and to all godly persons; and I am bound to confess that we are very much obliged to you for the gift. Moreover, the queen[2] herself

[1 These were Rodolph Zuinglius, Rodolph Gualter the younger, and Henry Butler. See first series, Letter CI. p. 264.]

[2 See first series, Letter XCVI. p. 244.]

has also read your book, and is much gratified. I hope you have long since received[3] both a letter from me, and the books, together with some trifling presents; so that you will fully understand what we have done as to the publishing of your book.

And now to come to your letter. With respect to your young men, you may feel quite satisfied; for the parties to whom you have given them a recommendation will carefully provide for them, with every feeling of friendship and kindly interest. And indeed the zeal, and diligence, and infinite labours of masters Zuinglius and Bullinger and Rodolph Gualter, in the propagation of true religion and the over-throw of the subtle machinations of false religion, abundantly deserve this. As to your son, since you have especially com-mended him to the archbishop of York, the bishop of Salis-bury, and myself, we will so undertake the charge of him, as that you need not feel any anxiety about him; although the bishop of Salisbury[4] (which I cannot relate without tears, as he was the treasure of the church of England) de-parted this life while on the visitation of his diocese, and hath gone from hence to heaven, to his gain indeed, but to our exceeding and intolerable loss. In the mean time we will not be unmindful either of Gualter's son, or of Butler, whom you so repeatedly commend to me. But, in compliance with your wishes, your two young men are placed at the univer-sity of Cambridge, though in different colleges, and in a numerous and learned society.

Our affairs, by the great blessing of God, not to say by a miracle, are in a prosperous condition. The duke of Norfolk[5] lately entered into a secret conspiracy with the papists, and indeed with the pope himself, for the destruction of our most serene queen and her kingdom, nay, for the subversion of the holy gospel of God. But our gracious Lord is always present with his people. The duke was for a long time imprisoned upon suspicion of guilt, and his abandoned wickedness was at length detected. He was brought to trial, and, having been

[3 There is written in the margin of the original letter, in Bullin-ger's hand, *Nihil allatum est, nihil accepi, nec quicquam hujus vidi.*]

[4 Bishop Jewel.]

[5 See first series, pp. 261, 267, and below, p. 198.]

duly convicted, is under sentence of death. The filthy sink of the popish conspirators has at length burst forth. Blessed be the Lord God, who has opportunely brought such wickedness to light! Now, we hope, all things are settled, except that Satan does not cease to go about and roar, seeking whom he may devour. We must aid each other by our mutual prayers.

Master Gualter wrote last year (I think) a letter to my brother Parkhurst, bishop of Norwich; which, as it occasioned some excitement among the men of his way of thinking, who are always planning some innovation or other, and refuse to be subject to the ordinances established in our church, I have thought it right to admonish[1] our brother Gualter to be more cautious, lest either in ignorance or without intending it he may seem by his writings to encourage contentions. Should my expostulation appear too severe, let him consider the feeling from which it has proceeded, certainly from one of good-will and affectionate regard to him. May the Lord Jesus very long preserve you in safety to his church! From the isle of Ely, in England, Feb. 12, 1572.

I had almost omitted mention of the treatise you sent me respecting the authority of scripture and of the church. It is a truly precious book, and worthy of being well handled by all godly persons. The papists however do not cease to yelp against it: there are many propositions, they say, which rest upon the authority of the fathers and of the church, but not upon that of the scripture; of which kind are the following.

Many things necessary to be believed, which are not in the scriptures:

The perpetual virginity of Mary.

The Father is uncreate.

The Son is consubstantial.

The Holy Ghost proceeds from the Father and the Son.

Infants are to be baptized.

One who is baptized by a heretic according to the form of the church is truly baptized.

[1 See first series, Letter XCIV. p. 234, the date of which should have been Feb. 12, 1572. Bishop Cox generally adopted the English computation, according to which the year began on the 25th of March.]

God is three Persons.

The apostles were baptized.

We use things strangled, and blood.

Christ descended into hell.

Water is to be mixed with wine in the cup.

Martyrdom supplies the place of baptism.

Prayers, oblations, and alms, benefit the dead.

No one may be admitted to the Lord's supper before he is baptized.

Your brother in Christ,

RICHARD COX,

Bishop of Ely.

LETTER LXXIX.

RICHARD HILLES TO HENRY BULLINGER.

Dated at LONDON, *Feb.* 18, 1572.

MUCH health. Your letter, my much respected friend, written to me on the 23rd of last August, I received two months since by your grandson Rodolph Zuinglius, who, as I understand, is now studying [at Cambridge]. Rodolph Gualter is also pursuing his studies there : they were both of them here in London on the 15th of last December, not long after they had landed in England at Norwich[2] from Embden in East Friesland. The letters you mention they had taken care to deliver in person to some of our very reverend bishops ; that is to say, they first gave master John Parkhurst's letter to himself at Norwich, then the one to the bishop of London, and they afterwards took care that all the rest should be delivered to the bishops to whom you addressed them. But whether your Rodolph has visited the bishop of Ely, and presented your letter to him, I do not know. Moreover on the sixteenth day of December aforesaid your Rodolph and Rodolph Gualter borrowed from me to the amount of eleven florins and eleven batzen, German money, reckoning a florin at fifteen batzen, for their current expenses here in London, to be re-

[2 See first series, Letter CI. p. 264, note.]

paid by your friend master Christopher Froschover at the next Frankfort fair. My son too, Gerson Hilles, who travelled with them from Frankfort as far as Embden, lent them thirty florins and [1] — batzen of German money, which sum they promised should be repaid at the aforesaid Lent fair to my son Barnabas Hilles, or my servant Robert Mascall, by the same master Froschover; of which payment (as also of that of the before-mentioned eleven florins and eleven batzen) I entertain no doubt. But yet, as you might understand from the last letter you received from me in October, (as I learn from the letter of master Rodolph Gualter, written to me from Zurich on the sixteenth of the same month,) I wrote to your piety, that it would be more for your interest, (I mean yours and master Gualter's,) if you would cause to be paid beforehand at Frankfort the money which you wish to be credited to the two young men here in England, that I may afterwards pay them the amount in this country.

I have received that most delightful treatise you sent me on the authority of scripture and of the church, and I thank your kindness for it. Salute, I pray you, in my name master Rodolph Gualter the elder, and tell him that I am obliged to him for having written to me about the appearance in the sun, which was seen by you [at Zurich] on the 29th of September: it may be, as he himself supposes, that no ordinary example of divine vengeance will at length pursue a guilty and unrepenting world. I am sorry to hear that master Rodolph Gualter was attacked last summer by an acute and burning fever, which brought him so low, that he began to doubt of his recovery. But I rejoice that God has so had compassion on him, as to restore him to health and to the church at the same time; so that he can truly say with the holy prophet David after his sickness, *I shall not die, but live, and declare the works of the Lord.* Nor do I at all doubt but that whatever money I have now advanced to his aforesaid son Rodolph, to the aforesaid amount, namely, of eleven florins and as many batzen, he will faithfully cause to be repaid to me at the next Frankfort fair[2]. And I entreat

[1 The word is omitted in the MS.]

[2 Gualter's son acknowledged a subsequent loan from R. Hilles in the following terms: Chirographa acceptæ pecuniæ. Ego Rodolphus Gualterus Tigurinus hoc meo chirographo testor me a D. Ricardo

you, master Bullinger, by the Lord, not to be offended at my thus writing to yourself and master Gualter a joint letter, and not separately to each of you. For it is now-a-days (and I am certainly much ashamed of it) very troublesome to me to write letters in Latin, as I write them so very slowly ; so that I can scarcely now write as many letters in two hours as I could finish, when I was a young man, in half an hour. But blessed be the Lord my God in all things and at all times ; at all times and evermore, whether in prosperity or adversity! Amen.

It would certainly be just that some part at least of their father's property should go to the lawful heirs of John Butler. But as he himself sold all his patrimony in this country, and, according to law and common right of the realm of England, granted and confirmed the same to a native purchaser and his heirs ; or (as our jurisconsults or lawyers are wont barbarously to speak) he assured, and gave seisin, that is, lawful possession ; no hope remains that the heirs of the said John Butler (and especially those born out of England, and of a mother not an Englishwoman) can re-cover, as our lawyers say, or repossess by the English law the inheritance that is sold, or any part of it, at least so far as I can learn or understand. Henry Butler must therefore have patience, and in this matter not hope against hope.

Since I last wrote to you in the month of August, I have not received any letters either for yourself or master Rodolph Gualter from the reverend the bishops, nor, as I remember, from any other learned men. But if they now wish to write to you by my above-named servant Robert, who is about to sail, God willing, in this present month of February, from hence to Hamburgh, I hope that my son Barnabas will be able safely to convey such letters from Hamburgh for you to the aforesaid master Froschover at Frankfort.

I suppose you have heard that our countryman, the duke

Hilles mercatore Londinensi mutuo accepisse summam tredecim flore-norum et quinque batzionum Germanicorum, quam quidem summam polliceor me prædicti Ricardi Hilles filio Barnabæ Hilles aut famulo Simoni redditurum, aut reddi curaturum, in nundinis autumnalibus Francofordianis proxime futuris, per D. Christophorum Froschove-rum typographum Tigurinum ; in cujus rei gratiam hæc propria manu scripsi et subscripsi. Londini 28 Apr. 1573.]

of Norfolk, has lately been accused of treason; and on the 16th of January he was publickly condemned to death by the peers of the realm of England, according to the custom of the same realm in taking cognizance of offences of this kind.   Among other crimes which I hear he was guilty of, this was one of many, that he sent a large sum of money to one of the two earls[1] who, two years since, was a rebel, and took arms against our most serene queen in the north of England.   He will shortly, it is said, be beheaded[2] here in London, as he deserves.   May God give him grace heartily to repent of his ingratitude and great iniquity that he has committed both against Almighty God and against the queen's majesty! Two men[3] were lately executed here for their impious crimes, who, among other atrocities, plotted together for the destruction of the Lord William Cecil, baron of Burghley, her majesty's chief secretary; as one of them confessed at the gallows.   God by his providence brought the whole matter to light, before that abominable wickedness was carried into effect.   Farewell, and may Almighty God very long preserve you to the advancement of his glory and the edifying of his church! London, Feb. 18, 1572.

Yours, you know who,

HILLES, merchant.

[1 The truth of this accusation was proved by the countess of Northumberland's letters, wherein she thanked the duke for the money wherewith he had supplied her husband and her. Camden's Elizabeth, p. 171, 175.]

[2 The duke was beheaded on Tower Hill, on June 2nd. He was attended on the scaffold by Dr Nowell, dean of St Paul's, and Foxe the martyrologist. See first series, Letter C. p. 261.]

[3 The names of these men were Mather and Berners, who were hired by Borgest, the Spanish ambassador's secretary, to murder Cecil, and the queen also. They were apprehended at the instance of one Herle, their associate, who saved his life by becoming informer, and were executed in February. See Strype, Ann. II. i. p. 123. Camden, p. 176.   For an account of the conspiracies against Cecil at this period, see Nares's Memoirs of Lord Burghley, Vol. II. ch. 10, 12.]

LETTER LXXX.

BISHOP PARKHURST TO JOHN WOLFIUS.

Dated at Ludham, *March* 10, 1572.

Hail, my Wolfius! I rejoice that you are going on with your lectures[4] upon Ezra. If you will publish your discourses and commentaries on the book of Esther, it will be an act worthy of your attainments, and of great advantage to godly students. I much approve your intention of dedicating the work to our most serene queen; but I would not have you be too prolix in your dedicatory epistle. I cannot help blaming the obstinate silence of Horn and Jewel[5]. For either they must be ungrateful if they have not answered your letter, or the couriers faithless, if they have not taken care to forward you their reply. I will write another time concerning your son. I am now so much distracted with engagements, that I have no time to write more. Salute in my name your wife, your brother Caspar, and all friends. In haste. Ludham. My wife salutes you all. March 10, 1572.

Yours,

JOHN PARKHURST, Bishop of Norwich.

LETTER LXXXI.

MALLIET TO HENRY BULLINGER THE YOUNGER.

Dated at Gray's Inn, London, *May* 26, 1572.

Four days since, when your relative, master Rodolph, the son of master Gualter, brought me a letter from my cousin master Peter Chevalier of Geneva, the Hebrew Professor at Cambridge, and likewise the son of master Zuinglius, who has now for some days been confined by illness at his

[4 See above, Letter LXXI. p. 177.]
[5 As Bishop Jewel died in Sept. 1571, (see first series, p. 260) there seems to be an error in the date of this letter. It should probably be 1571, new style.]

lodging in London; I made inquiry of him about a messenger who would faithfully deliver this letter to you: and
when he had assured me that my letter would reach you in
safety, I would not neglect the offered opportunity, lest I
should appear ungrateful to him from whom I have received
so many and such great favours; and the rather, as since I
passed from Germany into France, and from thence into
England, no opportunity of writing to you has presented
itself. For since you are so dear to me, and your country so
delightful, I cannot but very frequently pass whole days and
nights in the recollection of you, and am most exceedingly
desirous of visiting you again, if only the Lord will grant my
wish, in case I should either return home, or undertake a
journey into Italy. Master Charles Liffort was created doctor
of law at Bourges, about three months since; for it was for
that object that he came to Paris, where we lived together
for seven months: he proceeded from thence to Orleans and
Bourges, while as to myself, after his departure, I went to
England, where I undertook the office of tutor and governor
to the earl of Lennox[1], the brother of the king of Scots
who was murdered, and uncle of the present one, not without
a great deal of trouble and hinderance to my studies. But
induced by the entreaties and promises of the principal personages of this kingdom, I could not decline to undertake that
burden for a limited time, since I am at full liberty to leave this
place whenever I choose. The youth is just entering upon his
sixteenth year, and gives great promise of hope for the future.
For in case the present king, his nephew, should die without
lawful issue, he is the sole successor by hereditary right to
the crown of Scotland, and is entitled to be placed at the
head of the kingdom and empire. So also no one is more
nearly allied to the royal blood of England, after the death
of the present queen, than his mother[2], to whom her only
son is the heir; although there is now being held an assembly
of all the states of the realm (which in common language is

[1 Charles, fifth earl of Lennox, brother of Henry lord Darnley,
married Elizabeth, daughter of Sir William Cavendish, by whom he
had lady Arabella Stuart. He died in 1576.]

[2 This was lady Margaret Douglas, who was the daughter of
Margaret, sister of Henry the Eighth, and consequently first cousin
to queen Elizabeth. She died at Hackney in 1577.]

called a parliament[3]), to the end that an undisputed heir to the throne may be appointed by the general consent of all parties, lest in case hereafter of the queen's death any disturbance should ensue. What will be the issue, I know not. I shall be able, by God's blessing, to give you some certain intelligence when the parliament is over. I hear, however, that among other matters the capital punishment of the queen of Scots has been debated. The duke of Norfolk[4] is condemned, and still lies in the Tower. The queen's ambassadors[5] are to go into France three days hence, to ratify the peace between the two kingdoms. The king[6] of France is about to send over the duke de Montmorenci for the same purpose, and he is daily expected here with a numerous retinue. I have nothing more to write at present, but only to beg of you that with your wonted kindness you will not fail to write to me respecting the good health of yourself and your friends, and to acquaint me with all that is going on in your parts. For I hear that the people of Geneva[7] are admitted into the number of the confederate Swiss, which they commonly call Cantons; but I do not yet know whether it be true. I would have replied to master Urban Lowenberger, and also to master Schneeberger, if I knew where they reside; and I beg you will excuse me to them, and salute them very much in my name. Farewell. Dated May 26, 1572. London, from the hostel of the Grays, commonly called Gray's Inn.

Salute my lady your wife in my name, together with all your family. I would not forget your father, whom I mention with honour, and whom I know to be inferior to no one in integrity of mind, probity of character, learning, and eru-

---

[3 The succession to the crown was moved in the parliament that began to sit April 2, 1571. For an account of the proceedings, see Strype, Ann. II. i. 90, and II. ii. 425. The parliament, however, referred to in the text was summoned for May 8, 1572. See Strype, Ann. II. i. 196, and D'Ewes' Journal, p. 207.]

[4 See above, p. 198; and first series, Letter C. p. 260.]

[5 Namely, the earl of Lincoln, lord high admiral, with the lords Dacre, Rich, Talbot, Sands, and others. See Camden's Elizabeth, p. 185, 186.]

[6 See first series, Letter CIV. p. 272.]

[7 This treaty, by which Geneva became allied to the Swiss Cantons, was concluded with Zurich and Berne in 1584.]

dition. Give my respects likewise to masters Gualter, Simler, Lavater, those dear sisters, Truth and Dorothy[1], Simler's wife, and all others, whom you know to entertain a regard for me. Farewell again and again.

Ever yours,
MALLIET.

LETTER LXXXII.

RODOLPH GUALTER THE YOUNGER TO HIS FATHER RODOLPH GUALTER.

Dated at LONDON, *June* 5, 1572.

GREETING. Should I omit any thing, honoured father, in this present letter, you must attribute it, not to myself, but to my sorrowful and distressed state of mind. For a most painful event has befallen us, which though it is very distressing to me to relate to you, it is nevertheless necessary for me to do so, as it especially concerns you to be informed of it. But I think that both yourself and master Bullinger, by reason of your great firmness of mind, will bear with composure this occurrence, by which my most amiable cousin Rodolph Zuinglius has been summoned by Almighty God from this mortal state and the miseries of this world to a heavenly life. But as this requires a more lengthened detail than I can now enter upon in so short a time, as Hilles's son is setting off in haste for Hamburgh, and the whole charge of arranging Zuinglius's funeral has devolved upon myself, I will only state a few particulars respecting him, reserving a further account for master Bullinger at the ensuing fair.

When we were at Cambridge on the 12th of May, Henry Butler was desirous of going to London upon business; and our Zuinglius wished to accompany him, to see if he could procure some money there from the bishops, or from any other quarter, by means of Hilles, as he was in great want of money at that time. I had it in my mind to stay at

[1 These were two of Bullinger's daughters.]

Cambridge, partly because I had not any business of consequence, and partly because I could transact by letter all
that I had to do. At last, however, they brought me over to
their purpose, so that I readily undertook a journey which
was neither inconvenient, nor yet very convenient to me.
Our chief inducement was, that we might see the general
assembly of the nobles and bishops of her most serene majesty
in parliament. We set off therefore on the 12th of May,
during an exceedingly high wind, so that we could not go on,
but were obliged so to struggle against it, that in the whole of
that day we scarcely completed twelve English miles, which
are equivalent to two of ours. It was then a fast-day (according to the English custom), so that we could procure
nothing in the inns except salt fish and other provisions of
the like kind. On the following day, which was the 13th,
we completed thirty-two English miles, and arrived in London, which is only forty-four miles distant from Cambridge.
The heat was intolerable. Rodolph never complained during
the journey, until we were about eight miles from London;
and still he went on briskly, so that we reached our wished-
for lodging about eight o'clock. On that and the three
following days he ate scarcely any thing. When therefore we dined at the bishop of Ely's on the 17th, he was
taken ill immediately after dinner, and continued so for nearly
eight days, complaining of internal heat, which however could
neither be discovered from his water nor from the pulse.
Doctors Turner[2] and Penny[3] attended him, the latter of whom
is considered by the English as the most skilful physician
in all England; but they could not discover any symptoms
by which to detect the nature of the disease. They had
some suspicion that melancholic humours had flowed into the
vessels of the diaphragm, and excited thirst and occasioned an
increase of fever. At last there came a disorder and pain of
the left side, which they relieved by blisters &c.; so that
within the ninth or tenth day he began to recover. But on

[2 Doctor Turner was son of the celebrated physician of that
name, of whom see above, Letter LI. p. 124.]

[3 This seems to be the Dr Penny "who was once a preacher,
but then was turned a physician, and still enjoyed a good prebend in
Paul's." Strype, Parker, II. 241.]

the day immediately following he relapsed into his old complaint, namely, an inextinguishable heat, which could not be
abated either by three successive bleedings or by any cooling
draughts.   Noises too, evidently not made by any living
creature, were heard above his chamber; they seemed rather
to resemble the falling down of trees, or of men of large
stature; and these things, when I reflected on others of the
like nature, took away from me all expectation of his recovery.   At last, when there was no hope of his getting
better, the bishop of Ely and his wife[1], Turner's mother,
desired to remove him from the public hostel into his own
house.   But as he was unable either to walk or ride on
horseback, and we could not contrive any means of getting
him there by reason of his weakness, we kept him in the inn
till the 4th of June, on which day, by the advice of Turner
and Penny, and at the particular desire of the bishop of Ely,
he was carried to his house in a litter.   But I had long
before this fancied that I saw the image of death in his
countenance; and therefore with earnest prayers to Almighty
God for his blessing, when he arrived at the bishop's residence, we advised him to try to go to sleep, not dissem-
bling in the mean time (as I should wish also to be done in
my own case) his danger, and that the physicians had almost
given him over, and exhorting him to place his confidence in
God.   As Butler had been sitting up with me on the preceding
nights, he began to fall asleep in the first watch of the night,
which was assigned to myself: but when I perceived our
patient breathing hard, I was afraid lest he should be choked
for want of assistance, and called up the bishop's servant,
who exhorting and praying with him bade him trust in
God.   About the middle of the night, when I was alone with
him, he began twice to draw so long a breath, and turn his
eyes inwards, as that he seemed on the very point of departure: I therefore loudly shouted in his ears that he must
commit his soul to God; and this more than once, though my
sobbings impeded my utterance.   I sprinkled rose-water and
vinegar on his face and lips, for the purpose of making him
come to himself, which he did; and taking up a book of
prayers, I began with a loud voice to call upon God with
him; and the servant being again called in, together with

[1 See above, Letter LXXIII. p. 181.]

Butler, we were expecting his last breath every moment.
Meanwhile he called upon God so heartily, and with so much
earnestness, as to excite our admiration. Five times did he
appear to be giving up his spirit, and five times we revived
him when just expiring. About three o'clock in the morning
he began no longer to recognise us, and in some measure to
be delirious: but at length, from four to five, he became more
composed, and offered up most ardent prayers to God; and
about half-past five he neither heard nor saw us, nor was
aware of our being present, and it was only by his breathing
that we knew him to be alive. This, however, began to be
more confined, and by six o'clock to cease altogether; when
at last stretching out his hands to heaven in token of his
great stedfastness, while we were calling to him in the words
of Christ, *God, receive my spirit*, and reciting in his ear the
Lord's Prayer, he expired, and exchanged this mortal life for
the immortal and unspeakable happiness of a heavenly one.

Respecting other particulars I will write to Bullinger at
the ensuing fair; namely, how he inveighed against the ubi-
quitarians, &c.: for I have no time now, partly because I am
wearied out from having been almost without sleep for four or
five nights together, and partly too because the funeral preparations must be attended to within these two hours. He will
be buried in the church of St Andrew's, in London, opposite
the bishop of Ely's house, in the street called Holborn. Every
thing is conducted in a handsome manner. I received during
his illness from the bishop of Durham (who is prevented by
sickness from attending parliament) twelve angels to be
equally divided between us: the bishop of Winchester too
had given us an angel apiece, and Parkhurst one, for all of
which I will account next fair. Not much less than five
angels are owing to the apothecaries, if indeed that will be
sufficient for injections, decoctions, medicines, blisters, and
numberless other expenses of the like kind. I will take
charge of all his furniture as soon as I return to Cambridge,
and will transmit you an inventory; for I think it will be
most convenient for it to be sent from England together with
my own luggage, if God, as I hope, shall allow me to return
to you. But his will be done. If the money [of Zuinglius]
should not be sufficient for his funeral, I will add some of my
own, and will give you an account of every thing very

shortly : I will too, at the same time, reply to your letter, which I have received here, together with four books, which I have forwarded and delivered. Jewel is dead, as you are doubtless aware. Were I to write more, I should both neglect the funeral and also this letter : you will therefore be content with this, and give an account of every thing to master Bullinger. Farewell, my father, and regard me, who am residing here almost against my will, with paternal love; that I may have some consolation. Again farewell. Dated at London, June 5th, on the day that Zuinglius died, 1572. We shall return to Cambridge in three days.

Your most dutiful son,

RODOLPH GUALTER.

LETTER LXXXIII.

CHRISTOPHER MONT TO HENRY BULLINGER.

Dated at STRASBURGH, *July* 8, 1572.

YOUR letter, illustrious sir, written on the 22d of June, was brought me by the means of Lavater's son, a youth of good hope and promise. Various rumours are noised about here, upon light and doubtful authority, respecting the events of the war; and are far more favourable than I dare give credit to. The Gueux[1] have taken the Portuguese fleet laden with rich merchandise, three ships only having escaped during the battle : many cities of Flanders, oppressed by the pride, insolence, filthy lust, and insatiable desire of

[1 Gueux, a term signifying *beggars*, was applied to the party headed by the prince of Orange, from the time of their presenting a petition to the regent, Margaret, duchess of Parma, in 1566. Many of them had now betaken themselves to the sea, and they numbered in the port of Flushing 150 armed vessels making common cause with the prince. See Strada, v. p. 109. Brandt, p. 167. The Spanish fleet was commanded by the duke of Medina Celi. See first series, Letter CIV. p. 275.]

the Spaniards for plunder and destruction, refuse to receive them within their walls; wherefore Alva has declared them rebels to the king. In Flushing alone, a very small town, there have been hung some Spanish persons of rank, who were taken prisoners at sea. Unless the king of France, the queen of England, and the princes of Germany will complete the web they have begun, a horrible butchery and destruction awaits this wretched people. Alva is ruling at Brussels in his usual way, and issuing his orders, and is mustering four regiments of infantry in Luxemberg and Treves. Two stations for recruits have been attacked by the forces of the prince of Orange. The duke himself is quite obstinate, and is preparing for war with great perseverance; while the captains and generals, the counts Bulwiler, Fronsberg, Schomberg, Eberstein and others, are preparing their impious arms. Otto, count Eberstein, was intending, eight days since, to go down the Rhine into Lower Germany in a vessel laden with arms; but was obliged to land a little below Worms, where he was intercepted by the musketeers of the elector palatine, and carried into Altsheim[2].

A conference of the protestant princes will shortly be held at Naumberg in Saxony. The prince of Orange is reported to have set out from the castle of Dillenberg[3] on the 23rd of June into Lower Germany, attended by six hundred cavalry and a thousand musketeers, to the stations designed for the musters and reviews of the troops. In England every thing is now quiet, and the assembly of all the estates of the realm is now sitting, by the decree and authority of which the duke of Norfolk was beheaded on the 2nd of June. I have not yet heard of the fate of the other conspirators.

I forward you these four letters brought to me from England to Hamburgh at this present fair, addressed to master T., and your excellent son-in-law, master Rodolph Gualter, together with my dutiful respects.

Strasburgh, July 8, 1572.

CHRISTOPHER MONT.

[2 A small town between Worms and Oppenheim.]
[3 This fortress gives title to, and is the usual residence of a branch of the house of Nassau.]

LETTER LXXXIV.

RODOLPH GUALTER THE YOUNGER TO JOSIAH SIMLER.

Dated at CAMBRIDGE, *July* 29, 1572.

HEALTH. That I have seldom written to you, my honoured relative, has not arisen from neglect, or displeasure, or forgetfulness; but because I was out of humour with myself, and could scarcely write to any of my friends in the public inn, either at Frankfort or Embden. Besides, when I wrote that letter I was quite unconcerned as to whether it was lost or delivered; for I gave it to a courier whom I did not know. But that I did not send any remembrance to you in that letter, you must ascribe to my thoughtlessness; for, though I very seldom forget you or any belonging to you, you certainly at that time escaped my memory. But as it was not done with an evil intention, you will grant your forgiveness. For can you suppose that I desire to please any one more than yourself? And although this is my abiding feeling, yet in young men, especially those who are not very considerate, the mind is not always where it ought to be. But I forbear to plead my excuse with you, who have already forgiven me, as your letter testifies, or else none would have been written to me. But I wish I could at this time send you something more agreeable than such tidings as must be equally distressing to us both. For on the 5th of June last my cousin R. Zuinglius, whom I grieve to have been taken from us at a time when almost all things are in a state of decline, departed piously and in the faith. He was honourably buried in the presence of the bishops of Ely and London, the latter of whom preached his funeral sermon. But I am unwilling to write to you more upon this subject: wherefore, if you desire any farther information, you can obtain it from the letter to the illustrious master Bullinger, to whom I have sent a full and particular account. It would therefore be superfluous to burden you with a useless description, and at the same time to renew my grief at almost every moment.

But though I know that I am in the Lord's hand, and that no one can die without his will, this event has nevertheless somewhat alarmed me, especially as I see and feel that this climate is injurious to our health. The death of Zuinglius is a proof of this; Butler, who was likewise nearly taken off by the same disorder, is a proof of it; I myself, lastly, am a proof of it; for though (praised be God!) I am still in good health, yet I am not so stout as I was, and indeed am diminishing in size almost every day, and evidently becoming quite thin. Master Turner, who was the physician of Zuinglius, advised me to remove into another place; but since my father blames me so much when any thing untoward happens, I had rather end my life in this place than leave it at any time, even with his permission. I shall not ask anything from him in future; if he can in any way advance my studies, he must look to it himself: as long as I do not cease everywhere studiously to attend to my books, and do my duty, I think that I stand excused before God. He lately told me to go to the dogs, and seek out some one else to wait upon; and if the slightest thing is omitted or overlooked in my letters, as for instance, the forwarding any letter that he may have sent, (for I testify by my silence that every thing has been done that he wished,) he immediately exclaims, and thunders out, "Do I think him such a fool and simpleton, as that I need not to inform him of necessary affairs?" But I will desist from wearying you also with my complaints: meanwhile do you love me, and though my father is still alive, shew yourself also as a father to me, and aid and comfort me with your counsel. I will take care that you shall have no reason to complain either of want of respect or of neglect of duty.

There is nothing new here, or it is already made known to you by the letters of others. I gave your letter to the bishop of London myself, as also to Parkhurst, bishop of Norwich. Jewel had already departed this life, to the great loss both of his country and myself. I will not write more, but you must be satisfied with these few lines, and excuse me who am overbusied in writing other letters. Salute all my friends, especially my sister your wife, whom you must excite by your authority to an increase of mutual

love for me.   Farewell in Christ, my honoured relative.
Dated at Cambridge, July 29, 1572.

Your most attached relative,

RODOLPH GUALTER.

I was lately at Oxford, for the sake of an excursion,
when I called upon Humphrey, who desired me to salute
you whenever I purposed writing.   I have resolved, by
God's blessing, to leave this university shortly, and migrate
to that.

LETTER LXXXV[1].

LORD BURGHLEY TO JOHN STURMIUS.

Dated at WOODSTOCK[2], *Sept.* 15, 1572.

YOUR letters have been delivered to me, most accomplished Sturmius, both that which you wrote privately to
myself, and that written to the queen's majesty; in which
you inform us of the death of master Mont, a man who by
reason of his extreme diligence and fidelity in watching over
the interests of this kingdom, as attested by the experience
of many years, was most highly esteemed by her majesty
and by every one of us. We are not however more affected
by his loss, than we are comforted by the expression of your
good-will and duty, which is, as it were, a just counter-
balance.   And this indeed falls out very opportunely, by
reason of our opinion of your religion, wisdom, and integrity;
especially in these times, when there is need of great prudence and fidelity in exposing the designs and doings of men,
on account of the recent calamities in France[3], and the dis-

[1 The original of this letter is preserved at Strasburgh.]

[2 Lord Burghley was then attending queen Elizabeth on a progress, in which she visited Havering Bower, Theobalds, Gorhambury,
Dunstable, Woburn, Warwick, Kenilworth, Compton, Berkeley Castle,
and Woodstock, at which latter place she is said to have received
the intelligence of the massacre of Paris.]

[3 Namely, the massacre of St Bartholomew three weeks before.
See first series, p. 276, note, and the authorities there quoted.]

turbed state of almost all Europe. Her majesty therefore accepts, as is fitting, the homage of your duty so diligently and readily offered, and will willingly appoint you in the place of Mont, and with the same salary; which, though it be little in proportion to your accomplishments and abilities, we think you will be disposed to estimate rather by the dignity and good-will of her majesty herself, than by its intrinsic value; and that, whatever deficiency there may be in this respect, you will entirely rely upon her favour and beneficence. I would have sent you this stipend, according to the queen's wish, with a letter from her majesty, if I either thought this messenger sufficiently suitable, or felt disposed to entrust him on this journey (which on account of these new perils both of places and times and circumstances seems likely to be a very difficult one) with any thing besides this letter expressive of her majesty's favourable inclination, and also of my personal good-will towards you. Wherefore you will not in the mean time expect any thing more from us, who are exceedingly busied in keeping from our borders the flame of the fires that are burning so near us. When their fury shall have been extinguished or allayed by the divine goodness, you will then find a more convenient way both of transmitting your letters to us, and of receiving this stipend for yourself. Farewell. Dated at Woodstock, Sept. 15, 1572.

Your exceeding well-wisher,

WILLIAM CECIL,
Baron of Burghley.

LETTER LXXXVI.

RODOLPH GUALTER THE YOUNGER TO JOSIAH SIMLER.

Dated at CAMBRIDGE, Feb. 4, 1573.

GREETING. From my father's letter of the 28th of August, I understood that you were suffering from illness, which, I suppose, is the reason you have not written to me.

14—2

It has much distressed me, my honoured kinsman, as it always will do, to hear that you are never free from that gout[1] of yours, and especially since on this account I hear from you less frequently. For myself however, though I should never receive even a word from you, I consider it as a part of my duty and respect to make you acquainted with my affairs. As to what relates to the state of my studies, they are going on just as usual. I am still resident at Cambridge, but shall shortly remove to Oxford[2]; for I am daily expecting a letter of recommendation from Parkhurst to master Humphrey, and as soon as I receive it, I shall leave this place. I have long since been tired of remaining here, where I perceive all things resounding with controversy. Worthy and pious ministers of the word of God are thrust into prison for preaching against idle gluttons. Some are annoyed in one way, some in another, partly by words, partly by deeds, as opportunity is afforded to these tyrants: and thus we hear, "one with mild words rebuked, another with severe." For my own part however, I consider myself as having nothing to do with these things, however they may distress me, as it is more painful to witness hardships than to hear of them. When I return home, I will tell you more at large about the state of affairs in this place. I request of you meanwhile to regard me with favour, and endeavour, as far as lieth in you, that my studies may turn out well. I will endeavour in my turn, and to the utmost of my ability, that the professors may not seem to have been wanting to me, so much as I to them. Salute, I pray you, all friends. Farewell, my honoured relative, in Christ, whom I pray long to preserve you in safety. Dated at Cambridge, Feb. 4, 1573.

Your most devoted,

RODOLPH GUALTER, the younger.

[1 See first series, Letter LV. p. 125, and CXVII. p. 302.]
[2 See first series, Letter CXI. p. 289.]

LETTER LXXXVII.

LUCAS CLAYSON TO RODOLPH GUALTER THE YOUNGER.

Dated [CAMBRIDGE,] *June* 23, 1573.

THOUGH I have returned to my rooms very late from a sail to Chesterton, yet I cannot, my Gualter, in justice to the friendship and intimacy existing between us, do otherwise than write to you; and as I know you wish to be informed of the result of the dispute between us and our swineherd[3], I will relate this also in few words. Having experienced the bad faith of my companions, I was reduced to the necessity of referring the cause of the college to the decision of arbiters, before any witnesses were produced. It was therefore decreed, that I, and another fellow who had been expelled, should be reinstated, and that the statutes of the college, which had been tampered with, should be corrected and restored. And if this is done with the good faith that I expect, I shall not repent either of my expense or my exertions. If not, it is all over with me, and I must seek a better means of livelihood, in which I shall possibly have occasion for your assistance. Time will not allow me to write more, for

> Down rushes from the skies the dewy night,
> And falling stars to quiet sleep invite.

Farewell, and let me know all about your affairs; I, in my turn, will neglect no opportunity of writing. In haste. James salutes you a thousand times, or, as the French say, *millefois.* June 23, 1573.

Your much attached,

LUCAS CLAYSON.

[3 This seems to have been a contemptuous appellation of the master of St John's, Nicolas *Shepherd*, whom the fellows in a letter to Cecil their patron, in 1569, styled their ποιμένα. Not long after, says Strype, viz. in 1573, they are weary of him; make great complaints against him, and by the sentence of the college eject him from being their master. Strype, Whitgift, I. 87, 140.]

LETTER LXXXVIII.

RODOLPH GUALTER TO THE EARL OF BEDFORD.

Dated at ZURICH, *July* 17, 1573.

HEALTH. Had I not already experienced, most illustrious
prince, your kindness and pious zeal in favour of good men,
I should be afraid that my letters, wherein I now commend
one, and now another individual, would be troublesome to
your clemency.

And yet such, occasionally, are the circumstances of my
most intimate friends, that I cannot refuse them this service,
which is an act of kindness in itself, and may be productive
of some benefit to them. And I would have this especially
understood in reference to the bearer of this letter. He is
the son of a noble and excellent man, the baron of Alt-Sax [1],
a youth [2] of good disposition and the greatest hope, who after
having resided some time at Heidelberg, proceeded from
thence to the most illustrious duke of Magdeburg. But
he is now, by his father's desire, coming to England, to
obtain an appointment at the court of her most serene
majesty, suitable to his birth. I hear that he is recommended to the queen by the most illustrious prince, the
elector palatine, whose recommendation will, I doubt not,
have so much weight, as that this of mine will seem altogether superfluous. But as the father of the young man
wished him also to be introduced to my friends, I could not
refuse his request. For he is a most godly man, a distinguished worshipper of God, and no less persevering than
diligent in advancing the kingdom of Christ. For, a few

[1 Alt-Sax, and Forsteck mentioned below, are in the valley of
the Rhine, near Appenzell.]

[2 There are many letters from this youth at Zurich and Zof-
fingen, some of which are from England, but none concerning English
affairs. All shew that he was, as Gualter states him to have been,
a young man of excellent disposition. He was a friend and fellow-
student of Gualter's son at Oxford.]

years since, he banished all unlawful worship from his territory, which is surrounded by papists on all sides; restored
the purer teaching of the word, and established the right
administration of the sacraments, together with a moral discipline worthy of christian men.   He has by this procedure
excited against him the hatred of many, and has for some
time had powerful enemies, who have left no means untried
for his destruction.   But Almighty God has preserved him,
so that now Christ is preached in his territory, the whole of
which had been before occupied by popish superstition.   He
has many sons, whom he wishes to be brought up and educated in the courts of christian princes, that they may maintain
the dignity of his family, (which is of great antiquity and
rank among us,) and at the same time acquire such knowledge as may be an honour to themselves, and bring some
advantage to their common country.   It is fitting too, that
christian princes should forward the wishes of this excellent
and most godly nobleman ; which I think your clemency will
do the more readily, as having heretofore experienced in your
own person[3], what labours and what dangers must be encountered by those, who, having embraced Christ Jesus with true
faith, endeavour to promote his glory.   You will therefore
do, most illustrious prince, as you have often done already,
and aid this excellent young nobleman in obtaining a situation
worthy of his family and parentage, either with her most
serene majesty, or with some other illustrious prince.   Which
if your clemency will accomplish, you will do an act most
acceptable to God, and will perpetually bind to you a most
godly nobleman, and will especially commend yourself to my
countrymen by this new instance of your beneficence.   May
Almighty God graciously preserve your clemency, and direct you by his Spirit to the glory of his name !   Amen.
Zurich, July 17, 1573.

[R. GUALTER.]

[3 The earl of Bedford, when lord Russel, had been committed to
the Fleet at the accession of queen Mary.   The martyr, Bradford, addressed two letters to him, "being then in trouble for the verity of
God's gospel."   He afterwards went abroad, and stayed some time at
Zurich.   See his character described by Whetstone, in the Mirror, &c.
of Francis Earl of Bedford, printed in Parke's Heliconia.   London,
1815.]

TESTIMONIAL OF THE BARON OF ALT-SAX.

To all the faithful in Christ, to whom these present letters testimonial shall come, Laurence Humfrey, vice-chancellor, or commissary of the most noble the earl of Leicester in the fair university of Oxford, wishes health in the Author of salvation.

Whereas a few months since the noble and illustrious lord John Philip of Alt-Sax, free baron of Saxony and Forsteck, &c. in Switzerland, &c. arrived in this university; and, having had familiar intercourse with the most learned men in this university for four months, has exhibited many proofs of his rare and singular attainments; so that he may be regarded as truly noble, not only on account of his illustrious family, but by reason of his erudition and excellent endowments of understanding; it hath seemed good to our university, in testimony not only of its love towards him but of its judgment respecting him, on this 18th day of May, in the year of our Lord 1574, to distinguish and adorn the same with the title of master in arts, to the end that he may not hereafter forget our good-will towards him, and that we may perpetually enjoy the remembrance of our knowledge of him. And whereas he is at length desirous of visiting his native country, we, out of our affection towards him, have not thought fit that he should depart without our testimony. All and each of these things therefore we duly signify to you by these presents, confirmed under the seal of office of the chancellorship of Oxford, in testimony of all and singular the premises. Dated July 30th, in the year of our Lord 1574.

LETTER LXXXIX[1].

LORD BURGHLEY TO JOHN STURMIUS.

[Dated at LONDON, *July* 18, 1573.]

I RECEIVED the letters, Sturmius, which you gave in charge for the queen's majesty and myself to this servant of Philip Sidney, who will deliver this from me in return. There is no need of my now replying to your letter at

[1 The original of this letter is preserved at Strasburgh.]

greater length. I greatly approve your having followed my advice in writing to her majesty; for I knew it would be gratifying to her, as indeed it was. But there is one thing that I wish to recommend to you in future, that when you again write to her majesty you will take care to be a little more exact both in writing and reading over your letter. For there was such carelessness in both these respects, that it could neither be read by her without difficulty, nor by reason of verbal inaccuracy be sufficiently understood. I attributed this to your haste, and perhaps also to the occupations which so pressed upon you, that you were unable to read over your letter. But I am surprised that it was so brief upon the affairs of Germany. I thank you very much for your kind reception of Philip Sidney, and I know that his most honoured parents will thank you a great deal more. Farewell, Sturmius, and should any thing arise that may concern us, take care to let us know as speedily as possible. London, July 18, 1573.

Your honour's very loving,

WILLIAM BURGHLEY.

LETTER XC.

RODOLPH GUALTER THE YOUNGER TO JOSIAH SIMLER.

Dated at Magdalene College, OXFORD, *July* 20, 1573.

HEALTH. Your letter, my honoured relative, was delivered to me by master William Barlow, with whom I had been long since very intimate at Heidelberg. I understood from it that you had been disturbed, and not without reason, by the calumnies of some sciolists here, who, most illiterate as they are themselves, will give liking unto nothing that is not ornamented, and polished, and perfect in every respect. But since it is impossible to satisfy them all, we ought to consider ourselves as having sufficiently performed our duty by commending our endeavours and anxiety for the advancement of learning to the approbation of those who are most worthy. Among the Oxford men, to whom I joined myself in the month of June, there are fewer of this class; partly because they are more simple, and partly because the university abounds with papists, and but few persons devote themselves to the purer faith; so that they will not even look into the writings of our countrymen, for which reason every ground and handle for this particular way of calumniating is cut off from them.

But I have dwelt too much upon this, and especially with you, my most learned relative, whom I know, both in this place and every where else, to be very dear to all good men. A few days afterwards your other letter was brought me, in which you accuse me of negligence, for neither having bought the cloth, nor sent you any letter. As to the last charge, I know that I am very easily accused of neglect, especially when I am innocent. But I suppose you have by this time received my letter by Chevalier, who was prevented by bad weather from coming over to you sooner. As to the first charge, when I first arrived in England, I could do but little with Hilles, who, as he has always this maxim in his mouth, *that money is to the merchant what the plough is to the farmer*, will do nothing without ready money. And as in your later letters to me you made no mention of the subject, I thought you had changed your mind, and that the cloth was no longer wanted. However, when master William Barlow passed through this place on his way back, he took the whole charge upon himself, and promised that he would manage the matter with some merchants in London of his acquaintance. Had I had an opportunity of going to London myself, I would willingly have executed this commission for you. But as Barlow has undertaken it, I do not consider there is any occasion for my assistance.

With respect to my situation at Magdalene college, of which Humphrey is president, I am living at Oxford very comfortably. For there is both an abundance of learned men, and I acknowledge myself very much indebted to them for their singular regard to me. But the especial kindness of masters Humphrey[1] and Cole, to whom I was recommended by master Parkhurst, outshines all the rest. And because this university is more agreeable to me than Cambridge, with

[1 See first series, Letter CXI. p. 289, note.]

the view of living here more comfortably, and with greater honour, I have solicited the degree of master of arts, which was conferred upon me on the 6th of July, with the unanimous consent of the senate of the university; and for the completion of this degree, I am next week to hold public lectures, both in moral and natural philosophy. May God prosper my undertaking and direct all my endeavours to the glory of his name! But I am now desirous of staying here longer than I had intended, partly on account of my degree, and partly by reason of its great convenience. For master Parkhurst has so recommended me to Humphrey, that he has taken upon himself the charge of all my expenses, which he is to receive from him again; so that I shall be able from henceforth to reside here without any cost to my father, which I have hitherto been unable to do by reason of the uncertainty of my expenses. But I request you, my honoured relative, (for it will be of great use to me in my studies,) always to persuade and advise (my father) against my being recalled home sooner than is expedient. For should I be recalled sooner than I expect, my father might probably complain of my want of obedience in that respect. But I well know that both my father and yourself, and all of you will so manage these things, that I have no need to give myself any trouble about them. I will not, therefore, write more, especially at present; and I beg you will be satisfied with this, and love me, as you do. May Almighty God long preserve you in safety with your wife and children! Dated at Oxford, from Magdalene college, July 20, 1573.

Your most attached relative,

RODOLPH GUALTER, the younger.

TESTIMONIAL OF RODOLPH GUALTER THE YOUNGER.

To all the faithful in Christ, to whom these presents shall come. Laurence Humphrey, vice-chancellor, or commissary of the most illustrious earl of Leicester in the fair university of Oxford, perpetual health in the Lord.

As nothing is more agreeable to justice and equity than to bear testimony to the truth, for the lack of which the innocence of individuals is for the most part attacked and weakened by false accusations through the injuries of calumniators; hence it is that, moved by the request of our beloved brother in Christ, Rodolph Gualter of Zurich, we bring to the knowledge of your university, and desire to make known to you by these presents, that the aforesaid Rodolph Gualter has been a scholar of our university for two entire years last past, and has devoted himself to learning in Magdalene college with no less success than diligence, laudably conducting himself in the mean while.   Whence, in acknowledgement of his merits, this young man, amiable for his candour, and respectable in station, as bearing and representing not only the name, but the virtuous example of his most accomplished and exemplary father, master Rodolph Gualter, professor at Zurich, was created master of arts at our famous commemoration, on the 12th of October, 1573. And forasmuch as he is now desirous of visiting his father and his country, we, in manifestation of our regard for him, would not allow him to leave us without our testimonial.   All and singular which we signify to you faithfully by these presents, under the official seal of the chancellorship of Oxford, in testimony of all and each of the premises.   Dated July 30, A. D. 1574.

LETTER XCI.

SIR JOHN WOLLEY[1] TO JOHN STURMIUS.

Dated at ORPINGTON, *July* 24, 1573.

I HAVE been induced, accomplished Sturmius, to write to you at this present time at the desire of my singular good

---

[1 Sir John Wolley was secretary in the French and Latin tongues to queen Elizabeth, in the latter of which he succeeded Roger Ascham.   The queen was now on a progress through Kent.   She set out from Greenwich, July 14th: thence to Croydon, to the archbishop's house, where she stayed seven days: thence to Orpington, the house of Sir Perceval Hart, from whence this letter was written, the original of which is preserved at Strasburgh.   See Strype, Ann. II. i. 465.]

patron, the earl of Leicester; who, as he himself was writing to you about other matters, wished me also to open the way to your friendship and correspondence by a letter of my own. And this I do with the greatest readiness.

For as I have succeeded your friend Ascham in his office about the queen's majesty, so am I exceedingly anxious to be the inheritor also of his friendships and intimacies, and especially with yourself. Receive me therefore in Ascham's place; for though I am far inferior to him in ability and learning, yet I will endeavour to excel him in his love and respect for you. The noble earl has wished me to write to you at this time (although we are now booted and just setting out on a journey) about a matter of no great importance, but which, however, is exciting great disturbances among us.

A great question has for a long time, as I think you are aware, been moved among us, whether ministers and preachers of the word ought to be bound by public authority to use a certain kind of habit, especially such an one as the mass priests used in the papacy: which dispute is so agitated among us, that many parties have chosen to relinquish the preaching of the gospel, and are relinquishing it every day, rather than be obliged to adopt that kind of habit. This affair has certainly occasioned great disorders among us, and the contest has hitherto increased by debate.

The most noble earl therefore is anxiously desirous that you should propose some method of allaying this dispute, which is now so rife, by procuring the opinions of the most learned divines of Germany, especially Beza, Gualter, and others of great note, upon this matter, to be written to our universities. On this subject I will write more at another time: now the departure of the queen from this place is so full of hurry, as scarcely to have allowed me to write even thus much. You will excuse the haste of this letter, which I have written at the command of the earl, and reckon me among your most loving friends. And this I earnestly and repeatedly request of you. Farewell, most accomplished sir. Dated at Orpington, a village in the county of Kent. July 24, 1573.

Your most devoted,

JOHN WOLLEY.

LETTER XCII.

WILLIAM COLE TO RODOLPH GUALTER.

Dated [at OXFORD,] *July 26*, 1573.

THE kindness, most honoured sir, which I experienced
from you beyond all others at Zurich, can never escape from
my memory; wherefore I wish you to believe, that, although
I am very far removed from you in person, in mind and inclination I shall always be a Zuricher. And if all persons
ought to be had in the highest esteem by me from the very
circumstance of their belonging to Zurich, much more is your
son to be regarded with the greatest affection. For besides
his being a Zuricher, the piety and friendship of his father
makes him more acceptable to me, as the learning of his
father does to all godly persons. For as often as your works
are placed before the eyes of the godly for perusal, so often
is the son of such a father held up to commendation. In the
year now passed, when your son was present at our commemoration, I could not refrain from doing you some little kindness. For as soon as I saw him, there came into my mind,
I know not how, the various favours you bestowed on us
Englishmen now many years ago. Wherefore I now plainly
perceive it impossible that such great obligations can ever be
forgotten by me; so fresh and grateful was the recollection of
them. The bishop of Norwich, a man on all accounts to be
honoured by me, has written to me; and I learn from his
letter how much your son is beloved by him; so that I dare
affirm, that, though you are absent in Switzerland, the bishop
of Norwich will no less give his assistance to your son in
every respect, than if you were at hand to provide for him
yourself. You must understand therefore, in few words, that
your Gualter will always be beloved by me, and that I shall
never be wanting to his interests.

There is scarcely any news stirring among us. I hear
that a city in Holland, called Haerlem[1], has at length, after a

[1 The siege of Haerlem lasted ten months; the townsmen, before
they capitulated, being reduced to eat the vilest animals, and even
leather and grass.]

long blockade, in spite of the opposition of the Spaniards, introduced some reinforcements from England and Scotland, and that by this means ample provision is made for the inhabitants in respect of the necessaries of life. And this took place some days since, not without some slaughter on both sides. Some of our nobility[2] are making preparations for a great expedition into Ireland, and are all now on their journey thither. There is a great union of opinion between us and the Scots; and the protestants of that country, with our assistance, have this summer reduced the well-fortified castle of Edinburgh[3]. Their queen is in this country with a certain nobleman[4], to whose faithful custody she is committed, so as not to be able to go abroad without his permission, and without a sufficient guard. I have nothing to write respecting the French affairs. Everything at Rochelle[5] is as yet in a state

[2 Namely, the earl of Essex, the lords Darcy and Rich, and others. They went on an expedition into Ireland against Brian Mac Phelim, who had raised a rebellion in Ulster. They arrived at Knockfergus towards the end of August. See Camden's Elizabeth, p. 201.]

[3 Edinburgh castle was taken on the 28th of May, after having held out against the English upwards of a month, by Sir W. Drury with fifteen hundred men, and the Scottish auxiliary forces. See Camden's Elizabeth, p. 197.]

[4 The queen of Scots was at this time at Sheffield castle, under the custody of the earl of Shrewsbury, who in a letter to lord Burghley, dated Sept. 24, 1572, says, "This queen remains still within these four walls in sure keeping. She is much offended at my restraint from her walking without this castle; but for all her anger, I will not suffer her to pass one of these gates until I have contrary commandment expressly from the queen's majesty. And though I was fully persuaded that my number of soldiers was sufficient for her safe keeping, yet have I thought good this time to increase the same with thirty soldiers more. See Lodge, i. 550, and first series of the Zurich Letters, p. 260.]

[5 The town of Rochelle was the principal rendezvous of the French Protestants, who established themselves there after the massacres of the preceding year. The duke of Anjou besieged it early in the spring, and after some months investment by the best troops and chief nobility of France, the loss of forty thousand by disease and casualty, and a ruinous expenditure both of stores and money, he was forced to compromise, the announcement of his election to the throne of Poland permitting a negotiation, without the shame of acknowledging a defeat: a treaty was therefore concluded towards

of uncertainty. I pray you, sir, to salute very much in my name the venerable father, master Bullinger, and the rest of your fellow-ministers. May Christ preserve you! July 26, 1573.

Your most devoted,

WILLIAM COLE.

LETTER XCIII.

WILLIAM BARLOW TO JOSIAH SIMLER.

Dated at LONDON, *Aug.* 2, 1573.

MUCH health. I send you, most excellent Simler, the cloth, as you requested; but I request this from you in return, that you will let me know in your next letter how you like both the cloth and its price. I availed myself in this business of the assistance of those who ought at least to have some skill in such matters, and whose promises are magnificent enough; but as all truth has perished from the earth, I must entreat you again and again, that you will employ some one who is a judge of such things, and write me word what you think about it before you send a farthing of money: this you will do without any inconvenience or trouble to me whatever. The merchant, who, with God's blessing, will hand over the cloth to Master Froschover at the fair this autumn, will not receive his money before next spring fair, when I mean to employ either him, or some one else, to purchase some articles with it at Frankfort: in the mean time, if you please, you can let me know what you think about the cloth.

We have no news here, except that colonies are being sent over from England into Ireland, to occupy that part of the island which is nearest to Scotland. The Earl of Essex is their leader, and the preparations are very extensive.

the end of June, which secured to all protestants liberty of conscience, but freedom of worship was confined to Rochelle, Nismes, and Montauban. For an account of the siege see Smedley's Hist. of the Reformation in France, Vol. II. ch. xii. and the authorities there referred to; also Browning's Hist. of the Huguenots, p. 102.]

Our civil state, by the blessing of God, is quiet, but in regard to our churches every thing is full of strife and confusion. As soon as I have any leisure (which indeed I have scarcely enjoyed since my arrival in England at the beginning of June), I will at least find out some intelligence or other to send to my host, Master Wiccius, to whom you will present my respects in the mean time. Salute, I pray you, dutifully in my name the reverend fathers in Christ, masters Bullinger the elder and Gualter; likewise masters Lavater, Stuccius, Bullinger the younger, Lemann, and James Frisius. I met your kinsman[1], Gualter's son (who gave me your letter dated April 27th,) at Oxford. I offered him my services, if they could be of use to him in any way, as in duty I ought to do. He has at length obtained a place in Magdalene college convenient for his studies. London, Aug. 2, 1573.

Yours,

WILLIAM BARLOW.

Salute also, I pray you, my friend Julius in my name, and tell him that I have lately spoken to the bishop of London on his behalf, and that I have faithfully taken care of all his letters.

I send you inclosed in this letter a pattern of your cloth, which you can fit to the piece, and thus ascertain that it has not been changed on the road. The price of the cloth is seven pounds four shillings English money; and each pound English is equivalent to eighty batzen.

LETTER XCIV.

RODOLPH GUALTER TO BISHOP COX.

Dated at ZURICH, *Aug.* 26, 1573.

HEALTH. It is with great pleasure, reverend father in Christ, that I have learned both from your letter[2] and those

---

[1 See above, p. 217.]
[2 See first series, Letter CIX. p. 284.]

of others, that the mark of respect by which I gave public attestation of my regard for yourselves and the Anglican churches in the dedication of my homilies[1] on the first epistle to the Corinthians, was acceptable to you and to your colleagues. I have learned it too, by a letter from my son, who is most earnest in his praises of your liberality towards himself; for which, as also for the remembrance[2] which you write word you have sent me, I return my thanks to your reverence, not such as you deserve, or as I wish, but such as I can ; and at the same time I pray Almighty God to afford me some opportunity of shewing that I am not unmindful of the favours which you have conferred upon me and upon my son. He will remain among you till the spring, and it is necessary that he should do so, since the letter in which I inform him of my wishes, will scarcely reach him before November, after the [autumn] fair [at Frankfort] ; at which season a sea voyage is far from agreeable, and not altogether safe. But at the beginning of spring, should nothing happen to prevent it, he will cross over into Denmark, where I have recommended him to my particular friend, master Erasmus Lætus, a divine of the university of Copenhagen, who lately passed through this place from Venice, and promised me his services in entertaining him and sending him on to Rostock ; from whence, after having also visited the Saxon universities, namely, Wittemberg and Leipsic, he will, if it so please God, return home to me. Meanwhile, I request you will proceed as you have hitherto done, and keep an eye to him and his studies, that he may not idly lose his time, nor be corrupted by evil habits.

But to return to your letter, in which also you mention that of mine[3], in which I gave you the reason of my having written to master Parkhurst, bishop of Norwich, on the subject of your controversies; it distresses me exceedingly to be thus brought as it were upon the stage through your quarrels, by the publication of my letters to both parties. It was certainly very wrong and uncourteous in your opponents, to print that letter, which I had written to an old friend in all

[1 See first series, Letter CVII. p. 279, note.]

[2 Namely, twenty-five gulden, or about three pounds of our money. See first series, p. 286.]

[3 See first series, Appendix, Letter VII. p. 362.]

the freedom of friendship and familiar correspondence. It ought to have been enough for them, after abusing my credulity, to have extorted from me that somewhat sharp admonition. I could more easily bear that master Whitgift[4] should insert, in his reply to your opponents, the other letter that I wrote to you on the same subject, since the necessity of the case required it; but it is painful to me to hear them seeking from it a new occasion of complaint, or even of calumniating, as though I had now recanted in your favour what I had before stated to their satisfaction. I am comforted, however, by conscious integrity, and I hope that all considerate persons will perceive that I am very far from incurring the imputation of inconsistency. For they will see that I did not complain to my most intimate friend, without reason, of those parties who, if they acted as I am told they did, deserved a yet more severe rebuke. But when I hear that I have been imposed upon, why should I not stand up in my own defence? I am certainly unwilling to be alienated from excellent and friendly men by the fickleness and peevishness of others: but as far as I can guess from your letter, they have now begun a new web[5], so that I am less surprised at being dragged on the stage by them. You ask me to reply to those nine articles, by the insisting upon which they give you so much trouble. But if these are the only matters in dispute between you, they are scarcely deserving, in my opinion, that any divine should be occupied in the refutation of them; as they savour of nothing but a longing after innovation, and I wish they were not sprinkled with the bitterness of envy or blind emulation.

I. They require the names of archbishops, bishops, and other officials, to be entirely abolished. But I wish they would act with greater modesty, and that in altering the

[4 Dr Whitgift made an end of his confutation of the Admonition to Parliament in Sept. 1572. In this he inserted the letter here mentioned, stating, that forasmuch as the authors of the admonition, for their better credit, had set down in print the epistles of Master Beza and Master Gualter, so he thought good to set down an epistle of Master Gualter, revoking the same upon better information; also another of Master Bullinger, chief minister of Zurich, concerning the same cause. Strype, Whitgift, I. 86.]

[5 Gualter refers to Saunders's book, "The Monarchy of the Church." See first series, p. 281.]

constitution of state or church they would not assume to
themselves greater piety than they possess. I by no means
deny that in all governments there are many things which
might be more conveniently established according to the rule
of antiquity and apostolic simplicity. But since it is the
misfortune of our age, that not even those princes, who have
opened their doors to the gospel of Christ, will allow all
things to be altered and corrected; and as many hindrances
also arise from other quarters, it appears to me better to
bear with patience the imperfections of the kingdoms of this
world, so long as purity of doctrine and liberty of conscience
remain inviolate, than by disputing about the external
government of the church to bring the whole into danger.
And I wonder that they entertain such an aversion to the
name of bishops, which they cannot but know was in use in
the time of the apostles, and always too retained in the
churches in after times: we know too, that archbishops
existed of old, whom they called by another name *patriarchs*[1].
And if in later times they have occasioned so much offence,
by reason of their tyranny and ambition, that these titles
are, not without reason, become odious to the godly; I do
not yet see what is to hinder, that, on the removal of the
abuse, those persons may be bishops, and called such, who,
placed over a certain number of churches, have the management of such things as appertain to the purity of religion
and doctrine. I cannot however dissemble upon this subject,
that there are found every where out of England pious and
excellent men, yea, even some of the nobility, who blame
many things in the manners and pomp of your bishops. And
those who have lately come over from England (as I understand by the letters of my friends) have complained, that
many harsh proceedings have been adopted there against
godly and learned ministers of the word, who heretofore
preached Christ not without some excellent fruit, but who
now, with the connivance, yea, even with the concurrence of

[1 The name patriarch was first given to a bishop by any public
authority at the council of Chalcedon (A. D. 451), which mentions the
most holy patriarchs of every diocese, ὁσιώτατοι πατριάρχαι διοικήσεως
ἑκάστης. The power itself, it is agreed on all hands, existed much
earlier, and was probably confirmed at the council of Nice, A. D. 325.
See Bingham's Antiquities, B. II. ch. xvii. § 6, 7.]

the bishops, are thrust into prison upon the most trifling grounds, and almost without an indictment, or at least such an one as is recognized by law. Whether there be any truth in this report concerning you, I do not know; we certainly promise ourselves better things of you all. But if any thing of this kind should take place, I would again entreat you to consider how cautious you should be, lest, in opposition to the precept of St Peter[2], you exercise dominion over the clergy, or be of the number of those who cruelly beat their fellow-servants. You will forgive me, reverend father, this freedom of speech, for which I have no other motive but that I love you, yea, revere and respect you, and am most anxious at the same time for the honour of your reputation and for the English churches. I hope also that you will not decline any of those measures which shall seem to make for an improved state of the church. And if I well know the greater part of you, I think that you would rather, if it were possible, lay down that burden which you sustain with so great labour, and so much envy of many parties, than stand in the way of a more perfect reformation. But if the most serene queen and the nobles of the realm will not have the existing form of the church altered, I should wish that those other brethren of ours would bear it with patience, and not occasion you any trouble; and that you should in your turn unite modesty and humility to your episcopal dignity, and not contemptuously look down upon those who are labouring in the same vineyard of Christ with yourselves.

II. They contend that the election of the ministers of the word ought to be restored to the people, and not to be in the hands of the bishops. But in this case also I think there is great need of prudence and moderation, lest, while we are urging an extreme right, many persons may have occasion of complaining that we have done them injustice. I confess, indeed, that in the time of the apostles teachers were elected by the public consent of the whole church, and not without fasting and prayer; as is evident in the election of Matthias, as also in the ordination of Paul and Barnabas to the gentiles. And that this method was still in use in the time of St Augustine, is testified by that letter[3] of his, in which he

[2 1 Pet. v. 3.]

[3 The following is the passage referred to, as given by Bingham,

describes the election of his successor Evodius. But then also
it appears, that the more powerful party was that of those
who were superior to the rest, either in the dignity of the
apostolic name, or by reason of their office and the prerogative of their honours. And what was done by Paul is well
known, who for this cause left Titus in Crete[1], that he might
ordain elders and teachers in every city. The same apostle,
too, commands that all things be done decently and in order;
and I do not see how this can be the case without a certain
distinction of ecclesiastical offices. But the whole order of
the church has in these latter times been disturbed by the
tyranny of antichrist, which the superstition of kings and
princes has confirmed. For when these, not properly instructed in the faith of Christ, imagined that their sins could
be expiated by external ceremonies and the purchased prayers
of others, they presently began to found convents of mass-
priests, monks, and nuns, and to enrich them with the revenues arising from yearly produce and from tithes. By
which means it came to pass, that, together with the tithes
and other revenues of the parishes (as they call them) the
right of election (which they called patronage) devolved upon
the priors of convents, bishops, and abbots, and lastly, even
upon abbesses; not now to speak of others who obtained it by
other means. Among us at least (to bring forward this by
way of example), who by the singular mercy of God have now
for fifty whole years enjoyed the free preaching of the gospel,
the election of ministers in many of the parishes rests with
the bishop of Constance, and the popish abbots, who from the
donation of former sovereigns possess the tithes and largest
revenues in the canton of Zurich. And should we seek to
deprive them of their right and possession, which has now
been established by long prescription, what disturbances
should we occasion! what danger should we bring upon our
churches! It seems to us also more advisable, that they

Antiquities, B. IV. ch. ii. § 6. *A notariis ecclesiæ, sicut cernitis, excipiuntur quæ dicimus, excipiuntur quæ dicitis, et meus sermo et vestræ
acclamationes in terram non cadunt. . . . . Hoc ad ultimum rogo, ut gestis
istis dignemini subscribere qui potestis.* He first ordered the notaries
of the church to take the acclamations of the people in writing, and
then required all that could write to subscribe the instrument themselves. August. Ep. 110. (213.)]

[1 See Tit. i. 5.]

should enjoy their right [of presentation] together with the tithes, and allow us peace and freedom of religion, and suffer themselves to be so far controlled by our most noble senate, as not to appoint any incumbent to the churches, who has not been brought up in our church, and approved by a lawful examination. I may add too, that there is no church in the city and canton of Zurich, which has retained the right of electing their ministers, except only that of St Peter's, of which it has pleased God that I should be the minister, and by which I was chosen thirty-one years since by the unanimous consent of the whole people, when I had not yet completed the twenty-third year of my age. And it is almost miraculous, that under the cruel tyranny of the papacy, when partly the bishop of Constance and the canons of the high church, and partly the abbess of the lower college and the other abbots, had dominion over all the churches, and drew the tithes to themselves from every quarter, yet to this church its liberty has remained entire; in which circumstance I recognize the special care of God, by which I have more than once felt myself exceedingly strengthened. In the mean time there is no one who by this example turbulently arrogates the like liberty to himself; nor do I, for my part, disparage the ministers of other churches, as being unlawfully appointed, because a different mode of election has been adopted in their case, which does not come so near to the practice of apostolic times. For why should they be blamed for the iniquity of former times, and which has brought things to such a pass that they cannot be restored without tumult and public danger? We think it better to bear with such things as may be borne consistently with godliness, and without the loss of eternal salvation, but which cannot be altered without peril and disturbance. And if your people will carefully observe this rule, they will afford less room for contention, and you will shortly, as I hope, enjoy the peace you wish for.

III. When they say that no one ought to be tied down to set forms of prayer, I know not in what sense they make the assertion. If they mean this, that we are not superstitiously to attach any virtue to preconceived words of prayer, or to certain forms of praying, I am also of the same opinion; for this rather belongs to exorcists and conjurors. But if they condemn certain forms of public prayer in the church, I should

say that they are mad with their wits about them, and that,
blinded with an excessive desire of innovation, they look upon
every thing with envious eyes, for the purpose of finding out
some occasion of calumniating. For that such prayers have
been in use in all ages, no one can deny; and it is more than
necessary that they should be retained, forasmuch as most persons are either so unfitted, or even perplexed in their minds,
in dangers and temptations, that they can scarce conceive their
prayers in their thoughts, much less in words. And this is
the reason that the Holy Ghost has caused many prayers of
the servants of God to be written out and embodied in the
sacred volume. And Christ himself has delivered to us a
distinct form of prayer, as John the Baptist had also done
before him. But yet this does not prevent individuals from
offering their prayers in private for themselves, and according to the nature of their afflictions, nor from using such
words as the Spirit may suggest: and ministers also may
subjoin, at the close of their sermons, prayers suitable to the
subject they have been treating of; which, however, I should
wish to be done in such a way, as not to neglect and pass
over such prayers as are, as it were, peculiar to, and established by long use, in particular churches.

IV. No man in his senses will say that the sacraments
may be administered without the word of God; since, unless
the word and element go together, there will be no sacrament,
as Augustine[1] has taught us long since. And I do not think
that the Lord's supper, which is a public act of the whole
church, appointed as a memorial and setting forth of the
death of Christ, can be rightly administered without being
preceded by a godly discourse, in which the congregation are
admonished both of the benefit derived from Christ, and
also of their corresponding obligations. The case of baptism,
however, is different, since by means of it even infants are
received into the communion of the church, and as such, it
is evident, are not yet capable of instruction, although they
are comprehended in God's covenant, and are inheritors of
the kingdom of heaven. The reading of scripture then and
prayers may suffice at that time, by which the sponsors

[1 Accedit verbum ad elementum, et fit sacramentum, etiam ipsum
tanquam visibile verbum. August. Tract. 80. in Joh. Tom. IX. col. 445.
Basil. 1541.]

may be reminded of their duty, and the grace of God obtained. Meanwhile, I by no means find fault with the practice of those churches, in which a certain day in every week is appointed for baptism, and a sermon preached, after which as many infants as have been born during that week are baptized in due order. And in our canton infants are baptized for the most part on those days on which stated sermons are preached. But as this is not suitable or convenient in all places, I would not rashly create any difficulty, whereby each church should be prevented the enjoyment of its own liberty without offence.

V. They desire, moreover, that the father alone should answer for his child in baptism, and that no other sponsors be allowed; in which they again betray a useless and over-busy fondness for innovation. For what religion prevents other persons at the invitation of the parents from undertaking this office for their infants, which in former times, when persecutions were yet raging every where, was no less necessary than useful; and which serves at the present day to conciliate friendship, and lastly, is often of great advantage to them when they are grown up, seeing they are admonished and reproved with greater freedom by those who have pledged their faith for them to the church?

VI. There is no need of reviewing what they add concerning the equality of ministers, as I have above spoken upon that subject. We also ourselves condemn that primacy which is connected with ambition and a desire of domination; but the apostle has also taught us that there is a certain order among the ministers of the church, when he says that *some are appointed apostles; some, prophets; some, pastors and teachers;* and as he makes a distinction of gifts and abilities, so does he also of administrations. And I wonder that these men do not look to the construction of their own body, and the arrangement of their own members, which might instruct them how to think upon this subject, and which similitude the apostle makes use of in this argument. Meanwhile, however, let those bear in mind, to whom a higher station is allotted, that they will only properly have pre-eminence over others, when (as Christ has taught us) they are the servants of all.

VII. With respect to Confirmation, I do not suppose you approve of that theatrical display which the papists have admitted among their sacraments. But if those who are rightly

instructed in the catechism, are admitted to the Lord's supper
with public testimony and imposition of hands (which we know
that Christ also practised to young children), I do not see
what occasion there is for any one to quarrel about it.

VIII.   Funeral sermons are not usual among us; and since
men are naturally inclined to superstitions, and those especially,
which are thought to aid the salvation of the deceased, it is
better either to abstain from them altogether, or so to conduct
them, as that all may understand, that whatever takes place
upon such occasions is done for the sake of the living who are
present as hearers, and not for the sake of the departed; of
the salvation of whom, if indeed they died in the faith, and
calling upon the name of God through Christ, we ought
to be so certainly persuaded, that no occasion should be
afforded to any one to doubt about it.   From sermons of
this kind, which we know to have been religiously instituted
by godly fathers of old time, has arisen in later times, in the
papacy, that most lucrative traffic in the fire of purgatory,
masses, and the pomp of funerals; and it is well known what
is wont to take place in some reformed churches, where
these practices are still retained.   For there are not wanting
those, who, to gratify noble families, or even to obtain gifts
and presents of greater value, take up almost the whole of
their sermons with the commendations of the departed, which
are for the most part false, or at least very doubtful, and
therefore occasions of offence.   But yet, if any person can
preach funeral sermons, without danger of superstition, or
any view to his private emolument, to the edification of the
hearers, I should be loth to deprive them of such a liberty.
But to speak plainly, this matter seems to me to be fraught
with danger, partly on account of the propensity of the
vulgar to superstition, and partly by reason of the desire of
gain inherent in most people, and which I think should be
called forth on the fewest possible occasions; lest, when the
ministers become greedy of gain, they render all their teaching, together with religion itself, liable to suspicion.   And I
am influenced too by this consideration, that as God did not
of old ordain any ceremonies for the dead, so he kept away
the priests from funerals, lest by being occupied about them
they should be defiled.

IX.   What reading of the scriptures is in use among
you, I know not.   But I hear that the lessons were ap-

pointed through lack of ministers at the beginning of the reformation revived by her most serene majesty; and we know too, that in former times all the books of holy scripture were read in order to the christian people. Nor do I see what inconvenience can ensue, if any persons take pleasure in readings of this kind; provided only that the office of preaching be not neglected, which it is fitting that all bishops and ministers of churches should frequently perform, that the word of God be not only read by the bye, but rightly divided, as Paul admonishes, and adapted to the instruction, consolation, and edification of all.

I have thought fit to make these brief remarks upon the articles of your adversaries; not that I imagine you have any need of my animadversions, but because, reverend father in Christ, you require my opinion upon these points. And if through ignorance any thing should have fallen from me incorrectly stated, I desire to be told of it. But I wish that all who profess the christian name would make for peace, and exercise themselves with united efforts for the advancement of the kingdom of God, and bear with patience one another's burdens. They would then see that they would never have so much leisure, as that, intermeddling with things that do not belong to them, they could raise disputes about things either unnecessary, or even injurious, to the great offence of the people. For I am greatly afraid that those very persons who now treat with harshness the ministers of Christ, and cannot bear those bishops who are the patrons of purer doctrine, will find out, some time or other, that there are wolves on both sides, who will harass them with new contests, and horribly oppress the church. For thus does God avenge the dissensions of ministers, and the distractions of his church.

I have not seen the book of Nicolas Saunders about monarchy[1]: should I see it, and think it deserving of an answer, I will do as the Lord shall enable me; whom I pray, reverend father in Christ, to preserve, and bless in your most godly pursuits, yourself and your colleagues, and all among you who are diligently doing the work of Christ. Amen. Zurich, Aug. 26, 1573.

Your dignity's most devoted,
RODOLPH GUALTER.

[1 See above, p. 227.]

LETTER XCV.

ROBERT COOCH[1] TO RODOLPH GUALTER.

Dated at the Queen's Palace, *Aug.* 13, 1573.

I AM compelled by the force of conscience to declare my
sentiments, and that upon a most important matter and singular mystery.　My remarks relate to the last supper of
Christ; in the administration of which a mistake is made
now-a-days, and ever has been made, almost from the time
of St Paul; since he placed before the Corinthians a supper
to be eaten, we only a morsel of bread in mockery of a supper.
They used a variety and abundance of meat and drink, so as
to depart satisfied; we return home hungry.　And as Paul
blames too dainty a table, so also does he a too sparing and
scanty one.　Moderation is best.　Neither did our forefathers,
who lived before the birth of Christ, practise that abstinence,
which is rather a fast than a dinner or a supper; inasmuch
as they partook of the [paschal] lamb.　It is not to be
believed, that Christ would take such pains to have a supper
prepared in the guest-chamber at Jerusalem, and invite so
many guests, and yet place nothing before them but a most
minute morsel of bread and three drops of wine.　It is your
part, who have brought forth into the light and view of mankind so many excellent works, to wipe away, or altogether
remove these blemishes of error and superstition.　And this
you have admirably effected in your explanation of those
epistles in which Paul addressed the Corinthians; in which
you have chastised the arrogance of the popes, and the thunders of the papists, and the extraordinary excommunication
and separation of the Calvinists.

[1 Robert Cooch, or Cooke, had been keeper of the wine-cellar
to Edward VI.　He denied the propriety of infant-baptism, in defence
of which Peter Martyr wrote a long letter to him.　Martyr, Ep. 34.
Dr Turner also wrote a book against him, in which he confuted his
opinion respecting original sin.　He was among the exiles under
queen Mary, when he became acquainted with Rodolph Gualter.　He
was now, 1573, one of the gentlemen of the queen's chapel.　See
Strype, Mem. II. 1. 111.]

As I will stand or fall by your opinion as to the manner and method of the supper and the table, so I very much dissent from Beza and others as to the day when Christ took supper with his disciples. For they assign the supper to the fourteenth day, I to the thirteenth, in which, according to the law, the old passover was not to be sacrificed[2]. Christ therefore instituted a new passover in remembrance of his death, and did not eat any other that night with his disciples. I have written some pages upon these subjects, which I intend to print; but I anxiously desire the interposition of your opinion beforehand. And, indeed, nothing can be printed here in England without the licence of the bishops. Wherefore I request you, if possible, to write in return, and let me know what you think it would be best for me to do. Farewell From the queen's palace. Aug. 13, 1573.

Your very loving

ROBERT COOCH.

LETTER XCVI.

RODOLPH GUALTER TO BISHOP SANDYS.

Dated at [ZURICH,] *Oct.* 8, 1573.

YOUR letter, reverend father in Christ, has been delivered to me, and was on many accounts most gratifying to me; both as coming from yourself, and as informing me that my lucubrations on Paul's epistles to the Corinthians were approved of by you, to whose opinion I have always paid

---

[2 Gualter in his reply says, of the question concerning the day of Easter, *hanc difficultatem curiosam potius quam utilem esse;* "this difficulty is more curious than useful." He disagrees with him also on the other point, and says, *Nimis argutum est, quod ad Hebraismum confugis, et sub panis vocabulo omne genus ciborum intelligi debere dicis:* "Your having recourse to an Hebraism, and saying that under the term *bread* all kinds of food ought to be comprehended, savours of too great nicety." The letter is very long, and entirely occupied in arguing these points. MS. note by Rev. Steuart A. Pears.]

much regard, as to that also of the others your colleagues;
and as they testify that they are of the same judgment with
yourself, I very little care about the opinions of others, who
will, I know, be satisfied with nothing less than my approval
of all their ordinances and customs; which indeed I wish I
could approve, and would do so most willingly, if I knew
them to agree in all respects with scripture.   Many parties
now-a-days are insisting upon, I know not what plan of church
government, under the plausible name of ecclesiastical discipline; and they tell us that no churches can exist without it.
But I am greatly afraid, lest they should give birth to an
aristocracy, which will shortly degenerate into an oligarchy,
and be the beginning of a new papacy.   For they are every
where exerting themselves for the establishment of a simple
presbytery; into which some good and pious men are elected
from the congregation at large, but in such a way, as that
the power of making any law rests almost entirely with the
ministers, by whose decision it becomes valid and must be
ratified, although they may be beaten by a majority of votes.
It was lately enacted at Heidelberg, that no one should be
admitted to the [Lord's] supper without having first presented himself to his pastor; for St Paul's rule, that every
man should examine himself, is not sufficient for them.   The
elders of the church did not agree to this enactment; which,
however, notwithstanding is obtruded upon all in the name
of the entire presbytery, nay, of the whole church.   What,
in fine, is to hinder the chief authority from devolving upon
some individual, who is superior to the others in wealth or
influence, and upon whose favour the rest may be dependent?
And indeed an example of this new tyranny was exhibited
there not long since, which ought, with good reason, to
alarm all who wish well to the liberty of the church.   There
is a certain Swiss there, the principal of the college of St
Denys, than whom, as all do testify, no one ever conducted
himself there (let not this declaration be thought invidious)
in a more innocent and godly manner.   Nevertheless Olevianus[1], who is the pastor there, denounced him in the name
of all the elders, that he should not come to the Lord's

[1 Gasper Olevianus was the son of a baker at Treves.   He studied
theology at Geneva, and afterwards became minister at Heidelberg,
where he died in 1587.]

supper.   He added as a reason, that he could not admit him
without doing violence to his feelings.   The man bore the
insult with indignation, as it was natural he should do; and
desired to know what crime he had committed deserving of
so great a punishment.   But they make no reply, farther
than that they persist in their resolution.   So he presents a
petition to the most illustrious prince elector, that he may
compel them to speak openly, and state his crime, if he has
been guilty of any.   But he has not been able to extort any
thing from them up to this day.   This now is their goodly
order in those parts, this their discipline; so that I perceive
you must be on your guard in good earnest, lest new heads
should break forth from the wounds of the Roman hydra yet
scarcely subdued.   But more upon this subject at another
time.

[The remainder is wanting.]

LETTER XCVII.

JOHN STURMIUS TO QUEEN ELIZABETH.

Dated at STRASBURGH, *Nov.* 16, 1573.

MOST serene queen, and most benign mistress: Christopher Lantschadius is the most illustrious individual in the
whole empire of Germany, and on terms of favour and intimacy with almost all the princes, having been diligently and
actively employed for more than forty years in the councils
of the counts Palatine.   He is moreover a man of discretion
and piety, and most favourable to and zealous for pure religion.

Without any suggestion on my part, but of his own
voluntary motion and affection towards your majesty, he is
anxious to be one of the paid agents of your majesty.   The
duchess of Suffolk[2] is acquainted with his virtues and inte-

[2 This lady was Catharine, baroness Willoughby d'Eresby, fourth
wife of Charles Brandon, duke of Suffolk, and brother-in-law to king
Henry VIII.   She married, secondly, Richard Bertie, Esq. with whom
she went into exile for religion in the time of queen Mary.   See the
narrative of their escape in Foxe's Acts and Monuments.   She died in
1580.]

grity, and especially with his hospitality and temperance and moderation. As I know him to be exceedingly well qualified for the business and service of your majesty, I do not hesitate both to recommend and praise him. By his aid and influence we may easily ascertain what is going on in the empire, both of a public and private character; and, moreover, gain access to all the princes.

If he did not of himself solicit an appointment from your majesty, I should nevertheless think it right to conciliate and gain him over: but he does solicit it, as your majesty will understand by the letter which he has written to me upon this subject. Whatever your majesty may determine respecting this honourable and upright man, I pray God it may be happy and profitable to your majesty and to the kingdom of England. Dated at Strasburgh. Nov. 16, 1573.

Your most serene Majesty's

constant and faithful

servant and subject,

JOHN STURMIUS.

<hr>

LETTER XCVIII.

HENRY BULLINGER TO BISHOP SANDYS.

Dated at ZURICH, *March* 10, 1574.

HEALTH. I return you, my honoured master and very dear brother, the warmest thanks in my power for that letter[1] of yours, written at London on the 15th of August last year, and abounding in all kindness, and love, and especial regard to me. Nor have you any reason to doubt of equal love and affection towards you on my part. Let us continue so to love each other in the Lord, as it is certain that brotherly love, and the especial union of brethren, is particularly pleasing to God; and that nothing is more useful,

[1 See first Series, Letter CXIV. p. 294.]

or necessary to his church.   For we perceive at this present
day that nothing occasions greater disturbance in the churches
of God than the discord of those who teach.   For at this
very time the separation of some morose, haughty, and obstinate Lutherans, by which, having torn themselves from us,
they are maintaining and endeavouring to obtrude upon
every one else some of their own superficial opinions, makes
many of the churches in Germany not to know what they
are following after; and in the mean time the course of
the gospel is impeded in many quarters, and dissensions are
fomented and increased, while our common enemies in the
mean time are laughing in their sleeves.   I wish we may not
be compelled to see some time or other these odious contests
draw along with them many parties to destruction!   Wherefore it grieves me in no common degree to learn from your
letter that contentions of this kind are also prevalent in England.   These things are doubtless owing to the wiles of
Satan, who, when he perceives that he is unable to destroy
the churches by threatenings, violence, and persecutions,
from without, has recourse to other artifices, and meditates
the overthrow of the church by domestic broils and the mutual attacks of brethren upon each other.   May the Lord beat
down Satan under the feet of the saints, and compose these
destructive contests with holy harmony and peace!

The young orators, however, whom you describe to me,
as busying themselves in changing the whole face of your
church, and putting on it a new shape, with the confiscation
too of all ecclesiastical property, seem to me to imitate those
seditious Roman tribunes, who gave away the public posses-
sions by the Agrarian[2] laws, that they might obtain wealth
and honour to themselves as individuals; that is, that when
we are turned out, they may come into our place, &c.   But
these parties are endeavouring to erect a church, which they
will never raise to the height they wish; nor if they should
erect it, will they be able to maintain it.   I have seen the
heads of their fabric as delineated by you, with respect to
which I have long since declared my sentiments.   The first
proposition, that the civil magistrate has no authority in
ecclesiastical matters; and also the second, that the church
admits of no other government than that of presbyters, or

[2 See Cicero's three orations against Rullus.]

the presbytery; these two, I say, they hold in common with the papists, who also displace the magistrate from the government of the church, and substitute themselves alone in his place.   Whose opinion I have confuted in my refutation of the pope's bull, and in my defence of the queen of England and her noble realm, &c., which I sent you two years since. I wish that there were no lust of dominion in the originators of this presbytery! Nay, I think the greatest caution is necessary that the supreme power be not placed in this presbytery, much more that it be not an exclusive government. Perhaps this presbytery may be admitted in one or two churches, but not in all; upon which much might be said. But time will bring to light many things that now are hidden.

Of the names and authority of bishops, and also of the election of ministers, our friend Gualter[1] has fully written to the reverend lord bishop of Ely, master Cox.   You may, if you choose, ask him for the letter.

The abuse of ecclesiastical property I think should be removed, lest it should be made subservient to idolatry and superstition.   But the use of it may be good, if it be applied to schools, the ministry, the edifices of the church, and the support of the poor.   Upon this subject I have treated in my Decades, near the end of the work[2].   The church cannot possibly exist without means; and if they are not at hand, they must certainly be collected from the faithful. What madness is it then, to throw away what is already provided, or to yield it up to others who have no claim upon it, and collect entirely new revenues to the great inconvenience of the faithful! I cannot see what these men are driving at. I fear they have some other object than the ostensible one, &c.   And if no one is allowed to preach in any congregation but the minister alone, what is to be done if he should be taken ill, or by reason of other engagements should be unable to preach? Must the church in the mean time be without its assemblies? I know that Chrysostom sharply reproved Epiphanius for usurping to himself authority in another man's church; but that was a different matter altogether.   With us the gospel would not have been so widely

[1 See above, Letter XCIV. p. 225.]

[2 "Fifty Godly and Licensed Sermons." Lond. 1577. Dec. v. Serm 10. foll. 1118, &c.]

propagated, if ministers had confined themselves to preaching only in their own churches.

I also am unwilling that the infants of papists should be baptized against the wishes of their parents. But those who reject them when presented to the church, seem to resemble the apostles, who forbade little children to be brought to the Lord Christ; for which he severely rebuked them.

Concerning the judicial laws of Moses I have treated in my third Decade, the seventh and eighth discourse. These men indeed seem to be inordinately desirous of novelty. I wish they would look beyond their own partialities. May the Lord grant them the spirit of peace and quietness!

No cloth has been brought hither. Our friend Froschover indeed mentioned that he had heard something about some cloth, but that none had been given to him; nor has any been sent hither by any body. Nevertheless I most exceedingly thank your kindness for this your generous beneficence. It has possibly loitered somewhere on the road. But I must request you not to put yourself to any expense on my account in future. I have seen a letter written by these innovators, in which it is said that the bishops send presents to learned men, to draw them over to their side. Presently too they would say that we are Balaams. I know indeed that good men may accept from their friends honorary and friendly presents; but you know what moved Paul not to receive the wages that were due to him. " All things," he said, " are lawful, but all things are not expedient." I had rather that men who are so ready to speak evil and calumniate, should not have the least occasion of detracting from me and my ministry. Take, I pray you, these my sentiments, such as they are, in good part, and continue to love me in return who have such affection for yourself. May the Lord bless you, and preserve you from all evil! Zurich, March 10, 1574.

Be pleased to salute, I pray you, in my name the reverend master Horn, bishop of Winchester, and wish on my behalf every happiness to him and his wife, and make my excuse for not having written at this time a separate letter to himself. I will write at another time when I have more leisure.

Your reverence's most devoted,

H. BULLINGER.

16—2

LETTER XCIX.

HENRY BULLINGER TO ARCHBISHOP GRINDAL.

Dated at ZURICH, *March* 10, 1574.

GREETING. Reverend and right worshipful master, I received in the month of October your letter[1], dated on the last day of July in the past year. But in proportion as it gratified me, from having been so long and so anxiously expected, the more grievously it distressed me, as I understood by it that the contests among you had been revived by certain disorderly young men, who are endeavouring to do away with the whole ecclesiastical system, arranged with so much labour by most excellent men, and to introduce a new one formed after their own pleasure. Idlers of this stamp are to be met with all over the world, who, notwithstanding they are unable to carry their plans into effect, yet in the mean time by these their endeavours disturb and harass many good men, are a stumbling-block to the more simple, excite the hopes of the papists, and grievously impede the progress of the gospel. The reverend bishop[2] of Ely complained to our friend Gualter upon this very subject last year, as did also the reverend bishop[3] of London to myself. He thereupon made answer to some inquiries of his, as I also have now[4] made some few remarks in reply to those of the bishop of London. We are plagued also throughout all Germany by characters of this kind. Nor can I suggest any more wholesome advice in this matter, than that we should turn to the Lord, and earnestly pray him graciously to confound these disorderly tempers, so ready for innovations, and to preserve the churches in peace. I would advise, in the next place, that they be brought back into the right way by friendly conferences or colloquies; and that those who from arrogance and obstinacy will not endure to retrace their

[1 See the first series, Letter CXII. p. 291.]
[2 See the first series, Letter CVII. p. 279.]
[3 See the first series, Letter CXIV. p. 294.]
[4 See the preceding Letter.]

steps, may be so depicted in their true colours, as that they
may acquire less influence with right-minded persons, and so
be rendered less mischievous. But there is no need for me
to instruct you upon this subject, as you have long since
learned by constant experience, and the hitherto prosperous
government of the churches, what ought to be done in this
case, or left undone.

There are persons in Germany who pride themselves
upon being Lutherans, but who are in reality most shameless
brawlers, railers, and calumniators. They never cease to
attack our churches, ourselves, and our doctrine respecting
the Lord's supper[5], which they invidiously disparage among
themselves by the name of Zuinglianism. And they have
lately sent forth afresh against us and our friends at Heidelberg books, which if we should omit to notice, we should
appear betrayers both of sound doctrine and our holy churches.
My beloved son-in-law, therefore, master Josiah Simler, professor of theology in our college, divided with myself the
labour or trouble of writing an answer; so that he was to
reply in Latin and somewhat more at length to the arguments of our opponents, while I wrote in German briefly,
and in a popular style, suited to the apprehension of the
ordinary reader. I send you copies of each book, and request you to receive them with kindness from your most
loving friend, and to read them at your leisure. You are
aware that Brentius[6] (with whom, while he lived, I had a
long and tedious dispute, as our published books bear witness), from his zeal and anxiety for strife and conquest, inter-
mixed with the controversy respecting the [Lord's] supper
many articles of faith, about which his scholars still continue
to dispute, and obscure them, and to raise doubts concerning

[5 For a statement of the respective opinions of Luther and Zuinglius upon this subject, see Coverdale's translation of Calvin's treatise
on the Sacrament, Parker Soc. Ed. p. 463.]

[6 In 1561, Bullinger published a book, wherein he shewed that
Jesus Christ, as to his human nature, is no where but in heaven, at
the right hand of God. This was answered by Brentius, the advo-
cate of the Ubiquitarian doctrine; and this contest lasted two years.
In 1571, Bullinger wrote against the testament of Brentius, which
he published at Wittemberg to forewarn all states not to allow
the Zuinglians a toleration. See Zurich Letters, first series, pp.
108, 243.]

the greater portion of them; as for instance, the doctrine respecting one person and two natures in Christ, the omnipotence and omnipresence (as they say) of the humanity of Christ, his ascension to the heavens, and [his presence] in heaven, &c. We were obliged therefore to reply to those heads: but it will be the part of yourself and other godly men to form a judgment upon these our answers. I pray God that we may have treated upon these points to the great benefit of the church. We replied principally to things, not persons, abstaining from reproachful language, lest we should be made like unto them. In all other respects, by the blessing of God, every thing is quiet in our churches. Our adversaries perceive that the better part of the people are every where joining themselves to our doctrine (which is Christ's), and to the church; they are therefore raging, &c. May the Lord restrain them! Besides, we are continually harassed, at the instigation of the pope, by our allies and neighbours who adhere to him; for he is greatly annoyed that the doctrine of Christ is preached in the neighbourhood of Italy, and is making greater progress than he wishes. He is therefore trying to set us at war with each other. May the Lord preserve us from evil!

Persons who have come from Italy say, that the Venetians are uncertain as to the peace made with the emperor of Turkey, and that they have therefore sent a naval force to Crete, and ships are being refitted, and troops levied. Meanwhile they have an ambassador with the Turk, whose last tidings were that he did not altogether despair; but that it would be useful for the Venetian republic, if they regard their own interest, to take care that they may not be attacked unprepared, in case the expectation of peace should come to nothing. It is moreover certain that no sovereign of Turkey was ever better prepared both by land and sea than this Selim[1]; and it is certain that at this season of spring he will bring forth all his forces against Spain and her allies. The Maltese therefore are crowding in haste to Melita or Malta from all parts of Germany. They are arming too in Apulia, Calabria, and Sicily, &c. What will be the event, the Lord knows, whom I heartily pray to have compassion upon us. There is also being levied an army both of cavalry and in-

[1 Selim II.]

fantry in Germany, below Mayence and above Cologne, which it is said will be marched into Lorraine, though some think into Flanders, and others say into France, under the command of Christopher Count Palatine and Lewis of Nassau. But this is at present uncertain.

The duke of Anjou[2] has passed through Germany into Poland. The murder of the lord admiral and of the Huguenots was cast in his teeth throughout the whole journey. He was magnificently received by the Poles. We have no farther intelligence on this subject. And a rumour is now prevalent, that the king of France is about to ask for two regiments from his Swiss allies. But I can say nothing certain on this matter. I entreat your excellency to communicate these things, if you please, to master Pilkington, bishop of Durham, and make my excuse for not having written a separate letter to himself. I desire that he may be safe and well in the Lord. Certainly, were I not aware of the great intimacy that exists between you, I should have sent him a letter, notwithstanding my numerous and overwhelming engagements. He will have also, in addition to this, a copy of Josiah Simler's reply " on the presence," &c. For I have ordered my friend Froschover to send you two copies, that you might present one to the bishop of Durham. The German copy I have sent only to yourself, and not to him, because I know that he is not able to read German.

At the end[3] of your letter you make mention of sending me a remembrance. But I must request you not to put

[2 The duke of Anjou, afterwards Henry III., quitted France in November, 1573, on his election to the throne of Poland. During the journey he stopped at Heidelberg, where the elector Palatine omitted nothing which could remind him of the massacre of St Bartholomew. In his picture gallery he shewed him a portrait of Coligny, and pointing to it said, " You know this man ; you have killed in him the greatest captain in all Christendom. And you ought not to have done so, for he has done the king and yourself great services." Henry attempted an excuse upon the ground of the conspiracy, to which the elector answered, "We know the whole history of that," and quitted the room. This was not the only mortification of the kind which Henry experienced on his journey. See Smedley's Hist. of Ref. in France, II. 91; Browning, Hist. of Huguenots, 104, and the authorities there quoted.]

[3 See first series, Letter CXII. p. 294.]

yourself to any expense on my account. Any kindness that I have heretofore conferred, or do confer upon you, is entirely voluntary on my part, and not for the sake of any return. Meanwhile any remembrances of our brethren and friends are not without their gratification, as testimonies of mutual friendship, just as I have hitherto laid before you my own labours, in testimony that I am yours, and that I desire to serve and oblige you by every means in my power, and that I love you sincerely. Your friendship in return is quite sufficient for me, if you will also sometimes write to me when you have leisure, as you are wont to do. I know too that friends are fond of contending with each other in sending presents, and that gifts of this kind may be received by good men without impropriety : but I have seen a letter of your innovators, in which they state that the English bishops send presents to learned men, to draw them back to their party. These men forsooth (such is their virulence) would be able to throw disgrace both upon us and our ministry. So that I say with the apostle, "All things are lawful for me, but all things are not expedient." He might himself have accepted a return for his labours, but would not accept it by reason of his adversaries. Nevertheless I return you the warmest thanks in my power for that your beneficence ; and I thank your kindness also for the verses you sent me upon the deliverance of Scotland from civil war by the means of the most serene queen of England. I was much pleased with them. I pray the Lord to strengthen and preserve the queen. May he likewise bless you and all yours, and preserve you from evil! Zurich, March 10, 1574. I commend to you our friend Julius.

Your reverence's most devoted,

HENRY BULLINGER.

LETTER C.

RODOLPH GUALTER TO BISHOP COX.

Dated at ZURICH, *March* 16, 1574.

THE letter[1] you wrote to me on the 12th of June, reverend father in Christ, I received only at the beginning of October by our townsmen, on their return from the Frankfort fair. And I perceive that you were then anxious about the former letter[2], which you had sent at the beginning of spring, together with some articles maintained by your opponents. But I hope you are now relieved from all that anxiety by a letter[3] of mine written in the month of August, and wherein I declared my judgment respecting those articles, according to the grace given me by the Lord. I should wonder at the unreasonableness of those men, did I not know that it is the condition of the church, either to have open enemies, who endeavour by violence and open warfare to overthrow the doctrine of truth; or to be assailed by the treachery of false brethren; or to be harassed with superfluous or unprofitable questions by those who, though they may entertain right notions as to the chief points of doctrine, stir up unnecessary disturbances about external rites and ceremonies. You have long ago endured the violence of most cruel enemies, who have endeavoured to satiate their rage among you with the innocent blood of numerous martyrs[4]; and the arts also of false brethren were detected at the same time: and since, by the blessing of God, you have overcome all these things with admirable courage and constancy of mind, I hope that in this also God will have pity upon your England; so that you may be able at length to enjoy the wished for peace, and to apply your endeavours

[1 See the first series, Letter CIX. p. 284.]
[2 See the first series, Letter CVII. p. 279.]
[3 See above, Letter XCIV. p. 225.]
[4 It is calculated that two hundred and eighty-eight persons were burned for religion in queen Mary's reign, besides those that died of famine and sickness in sundry prisons. See Strype, Mem. III. ii. 554.]

with unanimous consent to the edifying of the church; which
it appears to me absolutely necessary that we should all
diligently aim at, whom the Lord has chosen to be ministers
of his church. For it is sufficiently evident that the Roman
antichrist is employing all his power and exertions towards
this object, namely, that the carrying into effect the council
of Trent may at length produce its intended result. Your
neighbours make no secret of this ; and though they are restrained by ancient treaties with our nation, and the terms
of a general peace, in which provision is made that no one
shall give any trouble to another on account of diversity of
religion, yet they are making many attempts, by which it
plainly appears that they are seeking an occasion of disturbance.

From the kings of Spain and France nothing of a pa-
cific character can be expected; since the latter is neither
moved by the ruin of his country, nor by so many horrible
slaughters of the most excellent persons, to establish a firm
peace among his subjects ; while the former would rather see
that most flourishing and heretofore most productive province
of Belgium utterly destroyed by intestine war, than give
admission there to Christ and his gospel. The bishops of
Germany too, strengthened by I know not what promises,
are not a little furious ; and those among the popish princes,
who have hitherto been acting with some degree of moderation, are now themselves beginning to foam with hostility,
and to punish with severity the worshippers of Christ who
are dispersed throughout their territories. And it has
happened most agreeably to the wishes of them all, that
the brother[1] of the king of France, who has been from his
childhood accustomed to the blood of the saints, has been
raised to the throne of Poland. Nor do I think that the
Roman pontiff would have supported his cause so actively,
had he not wished to make use of his assistance in oppressing
the churches of the neighbouring nation of Germany, to
the end that they may more easily be overpowered in other
places also. And when such dangers are talked about so

[1 Henry, duke of Anjou, afterwards Henry III. of France, defeated
the Huguenots in the battles of Jarnac and Montcontour, in 1569;
and commanded at the siege of Rochelle, when the news arrived of
his election to the crown of Poland in 1573. See above, p. 247.]

generally, it is fitting that we should be roused by them, and with united energies take up the cause of Christ; and not give encouragement to those promoters of disorder, whom either ambitious emulation or even ignorance has so beguiled, that they are unable to see what makes for the preservation of our common church. They wish to revive, as you tell me, that ancient presbytery which existed in the primitive church: but I wish they would think about reviving that simplicity of faith and purity of morals, which formerly flourished, and not attack the commonwealth, the ancient rights and constitution of which Christ does not change! The church of old had need of a government of its own, when it was subject to heathen sovereigns, who not only made light of, but even persecuted the christian religion, and the moral discipline connected with it. But what is that to those, to whom God (as he promised by Isaiah) has given kings for nursing fathers, and queens for nursing mothers; who, in fine, have magistrates well affected towards religion, who are enabled to establish and maintain moral discipline with far greater authority, and consequently more abundant benefit, than if they appointed ten presbyteries in every church? But sovereigns, say they, do not always do their duty. I admit it; but is it lawful for them on this account to appoint a new magistracy? Saul did not do his duty; but Samuel did not therefore appoint a new senate, nay, nor even David, who, notwithstanding he knew that he was anointed king by God, yet would not make any alteration in the commonwealth, but waited for the time when it pleased God to remove the tyrant, and change the form of the government. The same thing may be said of all the prophets, whom we do not read ever to have attempted any thing of this kind under wicked, or at least most negligent, sovereigns.

I greatly fear there is lying concealed under the presbytery an affectation of oligarchy, which may at length degenerate into monarchy, or even open tyranny. Nor do I fear this without reason. For I know (to give one instance out of many) a city [2] of some importance, in which, after this form of discipline had been introduced, within the space of three years were exhibited such instances of tyranny, as would put the Romanists to shame. For last year they

[2 Heidelberg. See above, Letter XCVI. p. 238.]

warned a most excellent man, and one of approved piety, by the public minister of their presbytery, not to present himself at the Lord's supper, because they could not admit him without grievous offence. Surprised at this unexpected edict, he came before these Areopagites, and asked them what he had been guilty of? Then they began to shrink back, and cause delays, and to weave one excuse after another. But he, conscious of his innocence, presented a petition to the chief magistrate of the place, praying him to compel them by his authority to bring the matter to a trial. But not even the prince could obtain this from these great maintainers of ecclesiastical discipline. And when at length they were pressed on all sides, they had recourse to falsehood, and persuaded the prince that the party had abstained of his own accord from coming to the Lord's supper, and that he now wanted to extort from them the reasons of his voluntary staying away. Many other things of this kind have taken place, which it would be tedious to relate. But if they afford such samples, when they have not yet come into full possession of this new kingdom, what must we expect them to do, if they acquire an absolute dominion? Zuinglius, the apostle of our nation, perceived these things long ago; and when Œcolampadius with a good and holy zeal was desirous of bringing back into the church the power of excommunication, he warmly opposed it. But when Œcolampadius would not listen to his advice, and had obtained at Basle what he wished, he was compelled, not long after, to relinquish the scheme he had scarcely begun; and learned by the result that he had been attempting a work of more trouble than profit. I cannot therefore blame those, who oppose themselves to the designs of those parties who are now-a-days agitating this subject with so much asperity. But that they may not have any plausible ground of calumniating, it will be necessary to establish by the authority of the chief magistrate a truly christian moral discipline, by which may be restrained both the ministers of churches, should they live disorderly, and the too great licentiousness of the nobility and the corrupt morals of the people. For should this be effected, they will have no cause of complaint, unless they mean avowedly to aspire to the sovereign authority.

As to myself, it was indeed very annoying to me to be

dragged upon the stage before those whom I had always loved and reverenced as my intimate friends and honoured masters. But as I hear that this liberty of publishing any thing at their pleasure has been restrained by her most serene majesty's proclamation[1], the temerity of these men does not much trouble me. Yet I perceive that more grievous contests will arise for me in other quarters, unless God shall remove this stumbling-block. For there are parties, both in Germany and in a certain other place, who maintain that, unless that form of discipline which they have framed themselves be every where received, the kingdom of Christ cannot possibly hold together. I refrain myself hitherto, lest I should be said to have begun the contest. But if they sound an attack, I cannot but stand forth for the truth of doctrine and the liberty of the churches; and I hope that there will not be wanting those who will defend this cause together with myself.

Thus, reverend father in Christ, have I thought fit to reply to your eminence, and request you will take all in good part. I desired my son[2] by letter in October, either to visit you more frequently, or address you by letter. But I know not whether he is still in England, or whether he has crossed over into Denmark this spring, as I ordered him to do at the autumn fair. If he is still loitering in England, I know that he will be received with kindness both by yourself and my other friends and ever honoured masters. I wish him, however, to return home to me before next winter, unless some situation fall in his way to detain him; upon which subject I have written to my old friend master Parkhurst, the bishop of Norwich. But I had forgotten to state that the Ubiquitarian divines are grown more furious than ever, and are even surpassing themselves in unbridled abuse and lust of slander. For, not contented with what Luther long since wrote rather intemperately against our teachers, they now exclaim that we are all Arians, and worse than Mahomet. I know what spirit actuates them, but I will not

[1 The queen issued out a proclamation against the Admonition to Parliament, and all other books made for the defence of it or agreeable therewith, on June 11, 1573. Strype, Parker, II. 257.]

[2 Bishop Cox had complained to Gualter of the infrequency of his son's visits. See first series, Letter CIX. p. 285.]

now say what is their final object. God grant that I may be mistaken in my opinion! I pray him heartily, reverend father, to preserve you, and bless both your labours and those of your colleagues. Amen. Zurich, March 16, in the year of Christ's birth, 1574.

Your eminence's most devoted,
RODOLPH GUALTER.

LETTER CI.

ANTONY CORRANUS[1] TO HENRY BULLINGER.

Dated at LONDON, *July* 7, 1574.

I AM one of those, most learned sir, who by the aid of your writings have acquired a purer knowledge of christian doctrine. For there befel me some twenty years ago, by the providence of God, a suitable opportunity of studying your books, supplied too by the Spanish inquisitors themselves; whence as I perceive myself to have derived abundant fruit, I am compelled by the duty of gratitude to thank you, since I cannot return the obligation. The son of Rodolph Gualter, who is the bearer of this letter, will explain to you in person what countryman I am, and where I reside. I have also given him a little treatise[2] which I was desirous at this time to publish; but so many errors have crept in through the carelessness of the printer, who is unacquainted with Latin,

[1 Antony Corranus was a native of Seville, who had fled from his own country for the profession of true religion, and became preacher to a French congregation at Antwerp, which he left in 1568, on being appointed preacher to the Spanish congregation in London. At this time, in 1574, he was divinity reader at the Temple. He afterwards read divinity at Oxford, was *censor theologicus* in Christ Church, and obtained a prebend in St Paul's. He died in 1591. Strype, Parker, I. 539. II. 402. Grindal, 185. Remains of Abp. Grindal, Parker Soc. Ed. pp. 309—313.]

[2 Corranus had written certain tables concerning the works of God, wherein he endeavoured to comprehend, as it were in propositions, the holy doctrine of both the Testaments. This work was charged with Pelagianism, for which therefore he met with much trouble, and was fain afterwards to write articles of his faith, printed by Tho. Purfoot in 1574.]

(as are almost all the printers in this country,) that I am quite ashamed to obtrude upon men of learning this lucubration, too barren in itself, so carelessly printed. But as it is not my intention in this writing to boast of the learning that is in me, (for it is little or nothing,) but to shew to the evangelical churches my sentiments respecting the christian religion, to repel the calumnies of certain parties[3]; I could wish on this account that some other printer would put this dialogue[4] to press, and that three hundred copies at most, which have been most shamefully struck off here, should be suppressed.

The articles of religion, which I have placed at the end of the book, are taken from your confession, to confute the malignity of those parties who, from the personal hatred which they bear towards me, have most impudently condemned these same articles, written out by me, and brought forward in proof of my innocence, as thinking they were my own production. You will see an instance of this malignity in a certain page printed here both in Latin and English, with the criticisms of some Aristarchus or other; so that, as they say, you may know the lion by his claws. The younger Gualter will himself give you the page, and relate many other instances of the preposterous way in which certain parties have acted towards me. Meanwhile, I pray you, most vigilant pastor, to reckon me in the number of those whom by your labours and watchings you have brought to the knowledge of Christ; and should there be any thing in this little book which you disapprove of, correct it at your pleasure and with your well known prudence, and when corrected, order it to be printed. If you will do this, you will yet more exceedingly bind me and my services to you for evermore. Farewell. London, July 7, 1574.

Your most loving and respectful,

ANTONY CORRANUS.

[3 The trouble experienced by Corranus both from the ministers and elders of the strangers' church in London, and also from Mr Alvey, Hooker's predecessor in the mastership of the Temple, arose from his varying from Calvin and Beza in the doctrine of *predestination* and *free-will*.   Strype, Parker, II. 402.]

[4 In 1573, Corranus read upon the epistle to the Romans, and in 1574, contracted his lectures into a theological dialogue, and then printed them.   Strype, ut supra.]

LETTER CII.

WILLIAM COLE TO RODOLPH GUALTER.

Dated at Corpus Christi College, Oxford, *July* 31, 1574.

Your son, I perceive, most learned sir, has made arrangements for his return, having been most fully assured, by Simler's letter, of your pleasure respecting him. Though he was on many accounts very dear to me, as commended to me more than once not only by your letters, but by those of the bishop of Norwich; yet I must candidly confess that he has so conducted himself during the short time he has resided amongst us, that of his own right, even if neither of you had been known to me, or had written a word in his behalf, he is entitled on his departure from us to return to his friends with some token of my love. And I much regret that he is so suddenly summoned away from hence, as that by reason of the shortness of time I am not able to honour him as I could wish. For as I was in hopes that he would make a longer stay with us, I confess that I have not treated him according to his merit. And yet as often as he came to see me, he could not but be a most welcome guest: for whenever he was with me, there immediately came into my mind the numberless benefits with which you loaded us English when we were exiles at Zurich.

If you would know what I myself think of your son, I dare make this affirmation respecting him, that he is a youth excellent in morals, pious in religion, and one who has made no moderate progress in learning. And though I myself were silent, our whole university would bear witness to the truth of what I am writing. For, though he is a Swiss by nation, he will nevertheless, even at Zurich, when separated from us by so long a distance, be an Oxford master of arts, having been raised to this degree of honour among us by unanimous consent.

Master Humphrey has given me Simler's book, which he published against the Brentians. I must therefore return everlasting thanks to you, for having sent me the book; to him, as the protector and champion of the church; and to both of you, because you will not allow the enemy to attack the sheepfold at his pleasure. May the Lord preserve you, and grant you a very long life for the common benefit of all godly persons!

Salute, I pray you, the reverend old man, master Bullinger, besides two, who are for many reasons to be especially honoured by me, Lavater and Simler; likewise the printer Froschover, and his corrector, my friend Julius, who was intimately known to me when with Peter Martyr at Strasburgh. If you think that I can in any way be useful here in England, either to yourself or any of your friends, you will find me most entirely at your service. Oxford, from the college of Corpus Christi, July 30, 1574.

Yours, as long as I live,

WILLIAM COLE.

LETTER CIII[1].

QUEEN ELIZABETH TO JOHN STURMIUS.

Dated at BATH, *Aug.* 23, 1574.

ELIZABETH R.

ELIZABETH, by the grace of God, of England, France and Ireland, queen &c., to John Sturmius, greeting.

Your letter dated at Northeim, on the 3rd of August, we received on the 18th of the same month; from which we understand your anxiety about our affairs, and how exceedingly you desire that peace and tranquillity may be established between christian sovereigns and their dominions. And indeed we cannot but greatly approve their exertions, who, by embassies, or any other suitable means, [endeavour to] unite them, that discords may be composed between neighbouring nations, and especially between those which

[1 The original of this letter is preserved at Zofingen. The queen's name at the head is autograph.]

profess [the gospel of] Christ. For this is the noble office of a neighbouring and christian prince.

As we have received so few letters from you, we think that they have not all reached us. As to other matters, we have commanded our secretary, Thomas Smith, to write you our opinion in detail. Farewell. From our city of Bath[1], Aug. 23, 1574, and in the 16th year of our reign.

T. SMITH.

LETTER CIV.

RODOLPH GUALTER TO BISHOP COX.

Dated at [ZURICH,] *Aug.* 26, 1574.

HEALTH. I hope, reverend father in Christ, that my last letter, written in the month of March[2], has safely reached you. I have received yours, written in the month of February[3], by the hands of our friends on their return from the spring Fair. But I do not think there is any occasion for a tedious and laborious examination of it, since I declared in that letter of mine what I thought of those turbulent innovators, and so anticipated your letter in which you complain of them, and not without reason. And indeed the examples which the like innovators are every day affording us in Germany, powerfully induce me to persist in my opinion. For I perceive that nothing can be imagined more ambitious, more insolent, and more absurd, than these men. For though they are daily acting in many respects most iniquitously, they are nevertheless not ashamed to pretend a zeal for God, in those things which, contrary to the word of God, they impiously and maliciously devise against the servants of Christ. And, as far as I can conjecture, many persons, by whose counsel and assistance the fabric of this discipline was chiefly erected heretofore, are now ashamed of them. And by what spirit

[1 The queen made a progress to Bristol this year, and returned by Salisbury.]

[2 See above, Letter C.]

[3 See first series, Letter CXV. p. 297.]

they are actuated, may be gathered from this, that they are so anxious for the attainment of their object, as to deprive parties who deserve well of the church, of the possession and management of ecclesiastical property, without perceiving in the mean time what will be the consequence, should they effect this; namely, that it will come into the hands of others, from whom what is necessary for the support of religion will by no possibility be extorted in future. They would rather, indeed, have it alienated from the churches altogether, than see it in the power of those whom they have once begun to hate. But this is the nature of mankind, not to be able to bear happiness in possession, and to seek for themselves of their own accord evil and anxiety. Nevertheless, it should be your endeavour to oppose these troublesome parties with meekness and prudence, lest some more grievous danger may at length arise out of these contentions; or lest those, who are still opposed to purer religion, may find an opportunity of effecting what they have long desired[4], &c.

LETTER CV

WILLIAM BARLOW TO JOSIAH SIMLER.

Dated at ETON, *Jan.* 25, 1575.

MUCH health. Your letter of the 10th of March 1574, which was the first that came to hand after the receipt of the cloth[5], and informed me of it, was brought me only on the 28th of August last: mention is made therein of another letter written in December, which (notwithstanding another December has now elapsed) I have not yet seen. You may imagine the rest, how trustworthy and regular are our couriers. But, to speak candidly what I think, I was in some doubt, until that 28th of August, whether you had received the cloth with the letter, or not. One great cause of their longer delay, besides the length of the journey, (for they go round by Hamburgh,) was my not having been so

[4 The remainder of this Letter is wanting. The original fragment is in Gualter's hand.]

[5 See above, Letter XCIII. p. 224.]

frequently either in London or at Oxford, but in the west of England, where your letter at last reached me. Three weeks after the receipt of it, I went to Oxford for the sake of meeting our friend Rodolph Gualter, that I might confer with him about this whole business; but contrary to my expectation, and to my great vexation, he had already embarked with a most excellent and noble youth, the lord Philip[1], baron of Hohensaxe, to whom, if it had pleased God, I would, as a matter of courtesy, most willingly have paid my respects in England. You see therefore, my Simler, that it is not owing to any neglect of mine that I have not hitherto answered your letter; neither have I given a commission to any one to demand the money from Froschover in my name. For I am sure, unless I am greatly mistaken, that I expressly wrote to you, not by any means to send the money, before you had let me know what you thought of the cloth, whether you liked it or not; and that I would then take care to have some one at Frankfort to receive the money, and to make some purchases for me there: which was quite enough to relieve you from all that trouble and anxiety, by which I see from your last letter, of the 28th of August, you were so disturbed. And I have therefore given you this explanation in detail, with the view of driving away that anxiety about money matters altogether from your thoughts. For I am under some apprehension lest your next letter also should bring some complaints upon this subject: but as soon as this shall come to hand, (which I hope will very soon be the case,) I feel quite assured you will be abundantly satisfied.

The misfortune which you describe of the Wittenbergers has greatly affected me; it makes me uncertain what to hope, or what to fear: I allow it is most distressing, and threatens, as it were, the ruin and destruction of that most flourishing university. This indeed I think is to be lamented by me in common with the whole race of students: yet on the other hand, since Wittenberg is a city which formerly possessed the most decided supporters of the truth, and who feared God rather than man; that she is in this respect still going on in the old way, is, I say, a ground on which, together with all godly persons, I ought to congratulate her, and to pray

[1 See above, Letter LXXXVIII. p. 214.]

Almighty God to make those men, who are most renowned in every kind of learning, constant unto the end; to increase and crown in them the gifts which he has bestowed.

I will diligently inform you, God willing, of the state of our church, as soon as I know it myself; which in truth is not yet the case; for there are some mysteries about it which I cannot yet fathom. Two famous divines are now lecturing in London; the one a Frenchman, the other a Spaniard. The Frenchman's name is Villers[2], a man of great learning and piety: the Spaniard's is Corranus[3], learned and eloquent, but some worthy men entertain great doubts whether in respect of piety he is to be compared with Villers. He is wont to disparage the authority of some individuals, who have deserved exceedingly well of the church: he is a great admirer of Castalio[4], of whose version of the Bible he declares this opinion, that he is a very bad interpreter, for he has given any thing rather than a literal translation; but if you speak about a paraphrase, then, says he, Castalio excels all other translators by many leagues. I know also, that he made earnest inquiry of a person of my acquaintance, whether or not he had some dialogues[5] on the Trinity by an anonymous individual, printed at Basle, but Castalio, he said, is thought to have been the author of them; and he added that he was very anxious to procure them. I was present at an excellent lecture of his, in which he inveighed against the men of our age, some of whom wish to be called Lutherans,

[2 This seems to be the same Villers that Camden mentions, Hist. p. 209, as having been a preacher in France, who came to England (I suppose to avoid persecution) in a threadbare cloak, and grew rich here by a common collection for him, for reading a divinity lecture. He was afterwards chaplain to the prince of Orange. Strype, Whitgift, I. 477.]

[3 See above p. 254.]

[4 The Latin version of Sebastian Chatillon, or Castalio, was begun at Geneva in 1542, and finished at Basle in 1550, where it was printed in the following year, with a dedication to Edward VI. The best edition of his version is that at Leipsic, 1738, in 4 vols. 12mo, but the folio edition of 1573 is in most request. Horne's Introduct. II. 225.]

[5 The title of this book is "Bernardini Ochini Senensis Dialogi xxx, in duos libros divisi, quorum primus est de Messia, continetque dialogos xviii. Secundus est cum de rebus variis, tum potissimum de Trinitate. Basil, 1563." Castalio, it appears, was the translator into Latin of this and some other works of Ochinus.]

others Calvinists, &c. though neither Calvin nor Luther died
for us; but we are saved, he said, by the blood of the Lamb
slain "for the sins of the world," whereas in the text it is,
"from the beginning of the world." But that I may not
seem to strain out a gnat[1], and perhaps swallow a camel, I
will here conclude, though indeed I am afraid of being a
gnat to a camel. I wish he had staid at Compostella!

I pray you, tell my friend Julius that I am much concerned not to be able to satisfy his wishes, but that I cannot
yet discover who were master Jewel's executors, or in what
way he left his property[2]. Tell him too, that it is not an
easy matter for an individual so little known as myself, to
gain access to the earl of Bedford, to plead his cause before
him; though I have given the letter that Julius put into
my hands for that purpose, to his secretary, who promised
me that he would recommend it to his master as favourably
as he could.

I earnestly pray you to salute dutifully in my name the
very reverend fathers Bullinger, Gualter, my most courteous
host master Wickius, masters Lavater, Stuckius, Henry Bullinger the younger, Lemann, Haller, James Frisius, Gualter
the younger, Julius, and all the rest.

I had intended to send to you, and to that excellent man
master Lavater and others, some treatises printed in England,
not however of any great consequence, by the hands of our
friend Gualter; and should certainly have loaded him with
commissions, had I known of his going away, which, by reason of my being employed in the west of England, it was
impossible I could do. We have nothing new here, unless it
be a new thing to hold a wolf by the ears, or cherish a
snake in one's bosom; which things have ceased to be novelties in this country: for the queen[3] of the north, the plague
of Britain, the prince of darkness in the form of a she-wolf,
is still kept in custody among us.

With respect to money matters, I have written to Fros-

[1 This is the rendering of most of the versions prior to the
Authorised in 1611, which has *strain at*. Matth. xxiii. 24.]

[2 Bishop Jewel bequeathed his estate chiefly for the maintenance
of students. Strype, Parker, II. 49.]

[3 Viz. Mary queen of Scots, who was at this time, 1575, confined
in Sheffield castle.]

chover. But I am longer than I wish to be, and I fear lest
I should be troublesome to you: which however I will nowise
believe, if you will send me a longer letter in return; for
your letters are very gratifying and delightful to me. I
reside for the most part with my very dear relative, master
William Day[4], provost of the king's college of Eton, near
Windsor, twenty miles from London; where we very often
talk together about you with great delight, as well of your
churches, as of your public affairs: you must suppose however
that we shall do this with greater accuracy, if you will persist
in your intention, and not stand waiting for I know not what
coadjutors, from this or that place, or for some one in your
stead. Our friend Julius has sent me a prospectus of this
expected work, which indeed I have not yet been able to
read, by reason of some troublesome engagements that have
arisen from the death of another relative of mine, the son
of the archbishop of Canterbury; for he also had married
one of my sisters, and has lately died. Salute, I pray you,
all your friends in my name. Again and again farewell.
January 25, 1575.

Yours wholly,

WILLIAM BARLOW.

If at any time you can find leisure to send me a print of
the battle of Sempach[5], somewhat coloured, the military stan-
dards especially, you will do me a very great favour. Once
more farewell.

[4 William Barlow was son of bishop Barlow, one of whose daughters married the William Day here mentioned, and who was afterwards bishop of Winchester. Another married, first, Matthew Parker,
the son of the archbishop of Canterbury, and secondly, Tobias Matthew, archbishop of York. The three remaining daughters became
the wives respectively of bishops Westphaling of Hereford, Overton of
Lichfield and Coventry, and Wickham of Lincoln.]

[5 The battle of Sempach between the Swiss and Austrians was
fought A.D. 1386, and terminated in the defeat and death of Leopold
of Austria.]

LETTER CVI.

NICHOLAS BERNIUS[1] TO BISHOP HORN.

Dated at GUERNSEY, *Dec.* 13, 1575.

To the reverend father in Christ, the lord bishop of Winchester, Nicholas Bernius, minister of the word of God, in the name of the church of Guernsey wishes grace and health from the Lord.

As nothing has been at any time more desired by us, and more agreeable to us, reverend sir, than that an occasion should be offered of making you acquainted with the condition and prosperous beginnings of our churches, and especially of assuring you of our duty, or rather of our respectful attachment, towards you; so indeed nothing has been more grievous and distressing to us, than that a subject should now be forced upon us, whereby we are rather compelled to use the language of complaint to you our father, than to congratulate you upon our prosperous advancement in the work of Christ. We should not indeed do this, were it not that in this matter, which belongs also to your office, we have very great need of your assistance and authority: yet we are, nevertheless, to be pardoned, if we are forced to bring you disagreeable intelligence, respecting which we entreat you, in all christian love, to allow us to treat with you at some length, as with one, of whose sincere zeal towards the church of Christ we cannot entertain a doubt.

There has sprung up among the inhabitants of this place a certain Elias Bonamy, a disorderly character, and one not less notorious for impiety and obstinacy than he is powerful in wealth and friends. God seems to have visited in his generation by his just judgment the iniquity of his father[2],

[1 For the reply to this letter, and which is explained by it, see first series, Letter CXXX. p. 321.]

[2 This person seems to have been the Peter Bonamy mentioned by Foxe, as one of the jurats who condemned three women to be burned in Guernsey, in July 1556. He probably died before 1562, as his name does not appear among those who received the queen's pardon upon their submission and confession of their erroneous judgments. See Foxe's Acts and Monuments, VIII. 228, ed. 1839.]

who formerly everywhere persecuted with extreme hatred the church of Christ with fire and sword, even to the last moment of his existence. This man, having been admitted five years since into the congregation of the church, solemnly promised his minister, according to our practice, that he would faithfully obey the word of God and his church, as it becomes a true member of Christ; and for the first three years he pretended that his mind was not opposed to religion: but for the last two years, to our great grief and sorrow, his hypocrisy has been discovered, and he has so neglected the preaching of God's word, as never to present himself for the hearing of it unless compelled to do so, and then as seldom as possible; and what is far more grievous, he has for these three whole years abstained from the holy supper of the Lord, to the great offence of the weak, and has drawn away by his example many from the sacraments, who would at length have fallen away from the church, had not God in pity to them, according to his mercy, brought them back into the way of salvation through the watchfulness of their pastor. The minister meanwhile, in the faithful discharge of his office, privately and frequently admonishes this man in a friendly manner, and endeavours by every possible means to recal the wanderer into the path; but to no purpose, such is the obstinacy of the man. He does not, however, give up the attempt, but again reminds him of his duty in a temperate and christian manner, in the presence of one or two of the elders of the church; and earnestly entreats him to appear before the presbytery, that he may hear somewhat for the glory of God and the salvation of his soul. But the more leniently he is dealt with, the more obstinate he becomes, and pays no more regard to the authority of the ecclesiastical synod, than he did to the majesty of God and of the sacraments. I pass over his scoffing at the assembly of the church, and omit his gibes upon the ministers of Christ and the elders of the church. So when his obstinacy seemed incapable of being restrained by any laws either human or divine, [his minister] consulted his godly and learned brethren, the servants of Christ, respecting this case, as he considered the matter seemed to call for this proceeding; both that a seasonable remedy might be applied to so great an evil, and also that nothing might be determined upon in the church, except what might tend to profit and edification. These persons think that a matter of such importance should be referred to a synod, in which it should be judged of by the word of God alone. All the ministers, therefore, of the word of God in this island, together with some of the elders of their churches and certain godly magistrates, are summoned to a conference, at which our Elias is ordered to be present, that he may hear the proceedings and accusations brought against him, and if he has any means of justifying, or defending, or excusing himself, have free liberty of replying. After artfully endeavouring to turn aside and ward off some of the charges, he pretends that he knows nothing of any church gathered together in this place, and that he acknowledges no presbytery here: at length, however, convicted both by his public actions and by unexceptionable witnesses, as though conscious of guilt, he acknowledges the offence, contumacy, and scandal that he has occasioned, and voluntarily submits himself to the judgment of the ecclesiastical court, not any one mistrusting him. Therefore, that we might not seem to have shut him out from all hope of his recovery, after we had taken proper cognizance of his delinquency and the scandal thereby occasioned, it was determined by the unanimous consent and opinion of all, that he should not only confess his error before the synod with prayer to God, but that, for the removing of the public scandal, he should make an open acknowledgement of his contumacy before the whole church, on Sunday the 27th of November: and he was to do this after a sermon by the minister of the other church, by whom he was to be reconciled both to his own minister and the church at large. Upon hearing the sentence of the church he began to shuffle, and positively refuses to make any public confession of his wickedness. But these are the artifices of Satan, with which you must be too well acquainted, that, the consciences of the weak being wounded by scandals of this kind, he may either hinder or destroy the Lord's building. At length, however, being influenced by our prayers, or admonitions out of the word of God, or rather alarmed, as it were by a thunderbolt, by the threatenings of his tremendous judgment, and the rod of excommunication, he yields to the censure of the church; and in the presence of our assembly suppliantly entreats forgiveness of God, and acknowledges his delinquency and contumacy; and promises that he will do the same publicly in the church on the day appointed him.

Up to this time, reverend sir, every thing went on happily enough; but it is wonderful and lamentable, that a man so often overcome by the word of God, so often warned by his ministers and friends, and, what is more, by the church herself, should not have seriously repented: for on the appointed day, on which he had solemnly sworn that he would bear public testimony of his true repentance and contrite spirit, and make open confession of his fault to the glory of God, the edification of the church, and his own salvation; regardless both of the divine judgment and of ecclesiastical authority, and also of his solemn promise, he perfidiously made answer, (at whose instigation I know not, except at Satan's,) and not without a contemptuous defiance of both the royal authority and your own, that we should sooner drag the moon from the sky with our teeth, than extort from him a public confession of his crimes; nor (such is the hardness of his heart) can he be brought by any means to change this obstinate resolution of the carnal mind, or rather of the devil, and render due obedience to God and the church. The whole matter therefore was referred to the synod again assembled, to which this contumacious man was summoned, and where he made his appearance; and as his hardened heart could by no means be brought to repentance, it seemed good to the church, acting by the authority of Jesus Christ and of his word, that by reason of his perfidy, contumacy, and impenitence, he should be publicly excommunicated on the next sacrament day in all our churches, as a rotten member, from the communion of the church of God and of his saints, and given over to Satan until he should repent.

Confiding, honoured father, in your zeal for the advancement and protection of the church of Christ, we have not hesitated to give you a full account of the whole matter as it was conducted by us, with the greatest fidelity and truth; and this, both that you may not be deceived by the lying impostures of this excommunicated man, should he chance to come over to you; and also, that we ourselves may not be traduced by him as calumniators, both to yourself and to the holy fathers your colleagues. And we not only all of us

most earnestly entreat the interposition of your judgment
and authority in this business; but we implore also your
helping hand, that (should there be any occasion for it) you
will undertake and actively defend our cause, or rather your
own and that of the infant church, before the queen's majesty
herself: which labour that you will not refuse to undertake
for Christ, we earnestly entreat you again and again, and,
what is more, implore you by the name of Christ himself,
whom we will constantly pray to guide you with his mighty
hand, and to direct by his Spirit your counsels in so great a
charge committed to you; and that by the gift of true repentance he may bring back our wandering sheep (who
deserves indeed the severest punishment in case of his non-
repentance) into the way of salvation. Farewell, reverend
sir, and love and protect both us and our brethren, and the
whole church. Guernsey, Dec. 13, 1575.

Your most obedient in Christ,

N. BERNIUS,

has written this to you in the name of the whole church.

LETTER CVII.

WILLIAM BARLOW TO JOSIAH SIMLER.

Dated at ETON, March 13, 1576.

MUCH health. How great a loss, my Simler, your church
has sustained by the death of the elder Bullinger[1], of most
happy memory, yea, and our church also, towards which I
have heard that he always entertained a truly paternal and
affectionate regard, and indeed all the churches of Christ
throughout Europe, we shall all of us know by experience
sooner than we wish. We must pray Almighty God, the
Lord of the harvest, that he may send faithful labourers into
his harvest; and that, in pity to his flock, he may set over

[1 Bullinger departed this life Sept. 17, 1575.]

with yours.   I send also in his name the sum of five angels
to master Froschover, to deliver to yourself or master
Gualter, as a slight present, for the use of your common
hall.   We have, by God's blessing, no news stirring among
us, except that some ships of war are at this very time
being sent to guard the sea, and, as they say, to repress
the insolence of the people of Flushing[3], as also the ferocity
and violence of others.   I request you will respectfully salute
all our friends in my name.   Farewell.   Waltham, Aug. 11,
1576.

Yours,

WILLIAM BARLOW.

LETTER CX.

RODOLPH GUALTER TO ARCHBISHOP GRINDAL.

Dated at ZURICH, Aug. 24, 1576.

I SUPPOSE, most reverend father in Christ, that the letter
which I wrote to your eminence in the month of March, by
Laurence Bodley, has long since been delivered to you.   Although nothing worthy of mention has taken place in Germany since that time, yet the Lutherans are still carrying on,
with great zeal and contention, their purpose, about which I
then wrote; with the view, namely, of oppressing us and our
churches.   And they would doubtless have made some progress by this time, had not the affairs of Poland[4] given some
trouble to the emperor, of whose favour and concurrence they

[3 Some Dutch privateers had lately (1576) pillaged several English
merchant ships, under the pretence that they were carrying provisions
to Dunkirk, &c.   See Lodge's Illustrations of Brit. Hist. II. 77.]

[4 The duke of Anjou, having quitted Poland to ascend the throne
of France, on the death of Charles IX, was deprived of his royal dignity in the former country, and the throne declared vacant, on July
15, 1575.   The emperor Maximilian in vain endeavoured to succeed;
for the crown was bestowed on Stephen Batori, prince of Transyl-
vania, on May 1, 1576.]

stand in need.   He has appointed a conference at Ratisbon,
and went thither in person about two months since; but he is
sitting there almost alone, and waiting for the other princes.
In the mean time some of them met together in Saxony, at
the palace of the elector Augustus, to whom went also the
elector of Bavaria to the astonishment of many ; as he has
hitherto been the most bitter enemy of evangelical doctrine.
Those, however, of the more judicious sort suspect that they
are forming some designs against the elector Palatine, which
cannot be brought to pass without the concurrence of the
Bavarian, since the princes of Bavaria and of the Palatinate
are of the same descent and origin[1].   The visit of the emperor to Lewis, the son of the elector Palatine[2], who is in
command at Hamburgh, and who has hitherto openly dis-
agreed with his father in the sacramentarian controversy, is
also an object of suspicion with many parties.   Some are
afraid lest he too should come to an understanding with the
enemy, with the view of succeeding his father in case of his
being dethroned or banished.   Certain it is, that Augustus[3] is
most hostile to us, and fresh examples of cruelty are every
day exhibited by him against those whom he discovers to be
of our sentiments.   James Andreæ[4], an ambitious and abusive
man, is supplying torches to this flame ; and since he has nothing to reply to our Heidelberg brethren and ourselves, is
endeavouring to overwhelm us by the authority and power of

[1 Lewis II. duke of Bavaria married Mathilda, daughter of the
emperor Rodolph I., by whom he had two sons, namely, Rodolph,
from whom were descended the counts Palatine of the Rhine, and
Lewis, the head of the house of Bavaria.]

[2 Frederic III., in the year 1560, removed from their pastoral
functions the Lutheran doctors, and filled their places with Calvinists,
and at the same time obliged his subjects to embrace the tenets, rites,
and institutions of the church of Geneva.   This order was abrogated
in 1576, by his son and successor Lewis, who restored Lutheranism to
its former credit and authority.   Mosheim, Cent. xvi. ii. Chap. 2.]

[3 Namely, the elector of Saxony. See first series, Letter CXXVI.
p. 315. note 1.]

[4 James Andreæ was a professor at Tubingen, and was employed
in composing a form of doctrine in which all the controversies that
divided the church should be terminated and decided.   This was
called the form of Concord, and was adopted as a new confession of
the Lutheran faith first by the Saxons, in consequence of the strict
order of the elector Augustus. See Soames's Mosheim, Vol. iii. p. 362.]

princes. What therefore I lately recommended for the defence of our common cause, seems not more useful than it is necessary; namely, that her most serene majesty should interpose her authority. For the elector Palatine has long been an object of their hatred, and they are aware that he is not reverenced and honoured even by all his own subjects as he ought to be. The Swiss possess no influence whatever with the princes. As to Geneva, they not only hate but execrate it. But they cannot thus despise or disregard the most serene queen of England, who possesses weight both on the ground of her royal majesty and of her great resources; and who, in fine, is in a position to afford valuable assistance to the whole of Germany against their common enemies the papists. She will therefore truly perform the part of a pious nursing mother of the church, if she will consider this business; nor will there be wanting reasons for drawing the king of Scotland into co-operation with her, the accession of whom may be of great advantage to the cause in hand. But I understand that the Scottish[5] churches are on the most friendly terms with us, and I think they would be wanting in no service which ought to be required from christian men. Certainly some persons[6] of piety and reputation among them have advised me to dedicate my [commentary on the] Galatians (of which, most reverend father, I send you a copy) to the king of Scotland. I have thought right again to treat upon these matters, that you may perceive that an opportunity is still afforded you of doing a service to the church at large; and this opportunity is more plausible, because I scarcely think the emperor will rashly alienate the affections of any parties from him at this time, when he has need of numerous friends and allies, unless he is inclined to give up all hopes of the kingdom of Poland[7], and expose his Hungary to danger likewise. And the peace with France will add no little importance to this cause; for

[5 See the letter of the Scotch church to Beza, in the Appendix, No. 5.]

[6 One of these persons was probably Buchanan. The next Letter in the series at Zurich is one from Gualter to him, begging him to present the book here mentioned to the king of Scotland. He alludes also to the harmony between the two churches, the Scots having subscribed to the Helvetic confession set forth in 1566. See below, Letter CXVIII.]

[7 See above, p. 273. note 4.]

although the opinions and hopes of all parties respecting it are not the same, it is certain, notwithstanding, that the counsels of the common enemy are much confounded by the promulgation of it. I pray your eminence, most reverend father, to read these things and bear them with patience. For the public duty which I owe to the church, and which I doubt not you have greatly at heart, induces me to write them. May the Lord Almighty preserve you, and bless your most godly endeavours! My friend Julius Santerentianus, who desires to be commended to your eminence, heartily unites in the same prayer. Farewell. Zurich, Aug. 24, 1576.

Your eminence's most devoted,
RODOLPH GUALTER.

LETTER CXI.

LEWIN[1] TO JOHN STURMIUS.

Dated at [LONDON], *Aug.* 25, [1576.]

WHEN the letters which you had written to the queen, the lord treasurer, and sir F. Walsingham, were first brought to me, as there was wanting a copy of your letter to the queen, and the matter on which you wrote was itself uncertain, I thought it better to suppress those letters, and to write to you upon the same subject, if it seemed good, more certainly and decidedly, shortly after. But when your other letter was brought to me on the day following, which you had written long before, and in which was inclosed the letter sent you by Lanscade; since I had also received instructions upon this subject, and had recommended you to forward any such letter that might be sent to you; I adopted a new plan, to carry all your letters to the lord treasurer, and make use of his advice, either to present your letters written to the queen and sir F. Walsingham, or to suppress them.

I can scarcely describe to you how much the lord treasurer was gratified with this mark of respect, from you in the first place, and then also from me: I shall only state, that

---

[1 Strype mentions a Dr William Lewin, who was judge of the court of faculties.]

he both read your letter, and admitted me into his private cabinet with the greatest courtesy. He recommended that your letter, and that also of Lanscade, should be delivered to sir F. Walsingham. But he did not advise the letter to be sent to the queen, both because the copy was wanting, and because the subject was still in uncertainty. And he recommended me to state this to sir F. Walsingham. I have therefore stated these things to sir F. Walsingham, and have given him your letter, and also that of Lanscade; besides also the letter to the queen, which however I do not think that he has presented. But that I might ascertain the fact, the lord treasurer advised me to meet them both in London on the day following.

When I was on my way back, and had almost reached the city, lo! I, who was before somewhat weak both in my eye-sight and the rest of my body, was seized on the journey by a tertian fever, under which I laboured for twelve days, so that I could neither wait upon the lord treasurer, nor upon sir F. Walsingham. But I hope that both of them have written to you by their merchants, as they promised me they would do.

While I was still labouring under the attack of fever, I sent your letter to the archbishop for his perusal; and at the same time requested him to advance your pecuniary matter[2] with our nobility as far as he could: respecting which also I had much conversation with the lord treasurer, and a few words also with sir F. Walsingham, in the queen's palace; for the time would not allow me to say much. But I would have you know how much you are indebted to the lord archbishop; for he has so managed your cause during my illness, and still continues to manage it, that I hope that you will certainly recover your money before many months.

But you must feel anxious to know by what means this can be effected. You must know then that our people have decided upon sending a new ambassador into France, a most discreet, brave, and noble personage[3]. The lord archbishop has been diligently urging him personally to undertake your cause. He has also requested the lord treasurer and sir F. Walsingham to recommend it to him; that it may be

[2 See below, Letter CXIII. note 1.]
[3 Sir Amias Paulet.]

treated, not as that of a stranger, but a citizen; not as that of a private individual, but of an English ambassador, and one too who is most learned, most godly, and who deserves well both of ourselves, and of the French who profess the [protestant] religion. If we can get the business carried on in the queen's name, we shall seem to have gained every thing. I doubt not but that he will so commend the case to [the duke] d'Alençon, as to tell him that it will gratify the queen if he will take care that you are paid as soon as possible. I am unable, nor is it permitted me, to give you every reason you have to hope that you will by these means be relieved from debt. I only tell you this, that the archbishop was exceedingly delighted at the thought of the happiness it would occasion you, when all the money should be paid to the last penny; which, my father and my master, most accomplished Sturmius, I pray Almighty God may very speedily be the case.

But you must know that no offices or exertions of mine shall be wanting, or indeed, have been wanting, to this object; on account of which, when I was in a weak state of health, I undertook a long journey, and fell into a fever in consequence. But I would have you know that I am now well again, and am diligently employed on this same business of yours.

I have not yet received your autumnal pension[1], as it is neither due nor payable by the treasury before Michaelmas. I have however made arrangements with Santrinus, and given him authority to pay it you at this Frankfort fair. You will therefore expect and demand from Bernus as much as he paid you before; for our friend Santrinus has promised to manage this. But I wish to know how many florins Bernus paid you, that I may ascertain whether I can transmit you the money in any way more conveniently through another merchant.

I have written this by starts and in a hurry, as you may guess from the writing itself. Do you take care that nothing which is written or recorded by the historians be wanting in your commentaries on Demosthenes and Cicero. Farewell, Aug. 25.

[1 Namely, the salary which Sturmius received in his character of agent to queen Elizabeth at Strasburgh. See above, Letter LXXXV. p. 211.]

See also that you thank the archbishop for having been so prompt and ready to relieve you from debt.

Yours, you know who,

from the subject of this letter,

[LEWIN.]

LETTER CXII.

JOHN RAINOLDS[2] TO RODOLPH GUALTER, JUNIOR.

Dated at Corpus Christi College, OXFORD, *Aug.* 13, [1576.]

In proportion to the infrequency of our intercourse, most accomplished Gualter, when you were resident among us, (not that I was wanting in inclination, but in the opportunity either of enjoying your friendship, or testifying my good will,) do I candidly acknowledge myself the more obliged to you, and exceedingly rejoice, that although separated by so great a distance, and wholly occupied by matters both of a public and a domestic nature, you nevertheless both retain in your mind, and cherish by your kindness, so grateful a remembrance of me. For if experience taught Aristotle that continued absence caused oblivion to cast a shade over friendship itself; that the flower as it were of our acquaintance (not the maturity of friendship), instead of withering away, should have grown up by length of absence, it would be ungrateful in me not to feel more gratifying in proportion as it has been unexpected. Your singular kindness in this respect has taught me, how great is the difference between a christian and a heathen friendship : the latter of which, according to Aristotle, oblivion obscures, by reason of long continued separation of *persons;* while the former, according to Gualter, is enlightened by christian love, by reason of the lasting union of *souls.* But, for my part, though I will never allow you to excel me in the love wherewith you love one

[2 John Rainolds became president of Corpus Christi College, and took a leading part in the Hampton Court conference in 1603. He was appointed one of the translators of the Bible, but died before the work was finished, in May 1607.]

who loves you in return; yet I must necessarily allow you the priority in this respect, that you have preceded me in the manifestation of your regard. I admire your poem[1], either because it is yours, or because it is what it is, or rather, for these reasons united. For, as far as I can judge, it is sprinkled over with splendid evidences both of talent in the composition of the verse, and of judgment in the management of the subject, and of pious regard towards a well-deserving bishop, and of affection to the church of England, whose pious defender, Elizabeth, you commend, while you wound that cruel executioner, Bonner;—scourge her bitter adversaries, the papists;—comfort her afflicted members, the Christians;—deplore her wretched condition as she is now in languishment;—and, lastly, implore Christ Jesus to favour her with divine compassion. Your father prevented you from honouring our university with your praises, by having preceded you in commending noble Oxford to the learned English, as "The home of Pallas, Phœbus and the Muses," far more, I am afraid, than she deserves: but we acknowledge his affection, and thank him for it.

I warmly congratulate you upon having the charge of a church committed to you, and also upon being united in marriage to a most excellent lady; for such I feel assured she is, from her being approved both by your father and yourself. I will not sing your epithalamium in return for your epicedium: but I both hope and wish that she may prove such a wife to you as Gregory of Nazianzum the son tells us that his mother was to Nazianzene his father; not only a helpmate, but as it were a guide, a mistress in godliness, both by her words and actions urging him on to the best pursuits. Master Caius, the very dear friend of us both, a young man of remarkable piety and learning, has left the university to feed a flock committed to his charge, about forty miles from this city. It happened, however, most opportunely, that on the evening of that very day in which the copy of your verses was sent me to be forwarded to him, he came to Oxford; but as he was obliged to go away early the next morning, he asked and obtained of me that I would both thank and salute you in his name: both which I now do. Our fel-

[1 This was a copy of verses, on the death of Parkhurst. They are still preserved at Zurich.]

lows too, whom you desired master president to salute, wish you every happiness in return. May the great and good God ever enlighten with his light, protect with his favour, and guide by his Spirit both yourself and your father, and all your friends, and the whole church of Zurich! Farewell. Dated from Corpus Christi College at Oxford, August 13th, 1576.

Yours in Christ Jesus,

JOHN RAINOLDS.

LETTER CXIII.

LEWIN TO JOHN STURMIUS.

Dated at [LONDON,] *Sept.* 8, [1576.]

I WROTE you word a few days since, most accomplished Sturmius, with what design and by what motives I was especially induced, after that Lanscade's letter had been sent to me by you, to carry to court, together with that letter, those others written to the queen and the lord treasurer, and [sir Francis] Walsingham; also, how gratifying they both were to both those noblemen, and for what reasons I thought that the third letter addressed to the queen had not been delivered to her.

I wrote at the same time, and that at some length, respecting your pecuniary and French[1] affairs; especially

[1 Sturmius, out of zeal for religion, and compassion to the state of the professors of it in France, about the year 1562, had not only lent considerable sums of money himself of his own, but took up more at interest of the merchants of that place [Strasburgh] for the supply of the prince of Condé and Coligny the admiral of France; at what time also the queen herself lent them men and money. Sturmius was now pressed with this debt: and sir Amias Paulet being now, in September, going in an ambassage towards France, the archbishop took this opportunity to intercede with the lord treasurer; shewing him "how he [the archbishop] was moved as well with the old years, as also with the singularity and excellency of the man, earnestly to desire his lordship to recommend his case unto sir Amias. That whereas some order had been proposed by the present prince of Condé for the satisfaction of the said Mr Sturmius, by assisting him in obtaining a certain quan-

about our primate, the archbishop of Canterbury, who is
indeed most anxious for your welfare and interests; and also
the method he devised both of relieving you from this debt,
and restoring you to your former tranquillity and ease,
whereby you may pass the remainder of your life with
the gentle muses.

From that time you must know that the lord archbishop
has used his utmost exertions in your behalf; that he has
pleaded your cause with prudence, diligence, and friendly
regard.   For besides having again and again commended
yourself and your affairs to sir Amias Paulet, a most noble-
minded and valiant man, to whom a new embassy to France
is entrusted, he also treated thenceforward separately, first
with the lord treasurer, and afterwards with sir Francis
Walsingham, that they might render this same Paulet for
many reasons more interested in yourself and your fortunes.
And the sum of this recommendation was, that those two
noblemen, who possess the greatest influence and authority
among us, should request and entreat Paulet to arrange your
French business with the duke d'Alençon and the prince of
Condé, either in the queen's name, or at least publickly
in that of our nobles; which they both of them, moved in
part by his authority, and partly too by the circumstances
of your case, positively promised to do.   And I have no
doubt myself, nor, my Sturmius, would I have you to doubt,
that they have already done as they were requested to do.

Paulet, having taken leave of the queen six days since,
is preparing for his journey to France, and will very shortly
set out.   He is a man of great talents and of a powerful and
lofty mind.   I perceive that you inquire respecting the earl
of Oxford, whether he also did not recommend your case to
Paulet.   But you must know that I diligently interested
myself with the earl, who replied, that he would not only
recommend his friend Sturmius to Paulet, but would also

tity of salt in Languedoc or Provence, in lieu of the said money, by sir
Amias's good means unto the duke of Alençon and the said prince,
that purpose might take effect, or some other order be devised for his
relief.   So as thereby he might take some comfort and pleasure of his
life, now in his old years; and with more quietness finish many good
works, which he [the archbishop] knew had been purposed and begun
by him."   Strype, Grindal, p. 322.]

request the earl of Leicester to recommend him in every possible way. He added also, that unless you are relieved from France, he will take care that assistance shall be obtained for you in England; lastly, that he had a most high opinion of you, and had made most honourable mention of you : which things afforded me the greatest pleasure when I heard them, and certainly ought to delight you on being informed of them. But do you, as an old man, both make much of our archbishop, who is also advanced in years, and who is so firm and stedfast in friendship; and do not disparage this young earl, who has so favourable an opinion of you : from both I dare hope every thing, while from the one I dare promise every thing.

But now, my Sturmius, you will perhaps expect me to state what I advise or recommend to yourself. First of all, you should write as soon as possible to sir Amias Paulet, knight, and who will be our ambassador in France before this letter reaches you. You may state what you have heard from me from England, especially respecting the good-will and interest on your behalf manifested by the lord archbishop; and you may, if you please, add that of the lord treasurer and sir Francis Walsingham. I hope also that the earls of Leicester and Oxford will commend you to Paulet, but this is not yet ascertained by me : I heard from the earl of Oxford that they would do so, but do not yet understand that they have done it.

Perhaps also it might be desirable, that if you have any faithful and trustworthy friend in France, you would send him to Paulet with your letter, that he may sometimes put him in mind of you, and write you word back from France, what is doing, and what is to be done on your part. But if you have not at this time such a friend in France, nor can procure one to go thither at his own expense, I dare not recommend you to send any one at yours. For it is not, perhaps, the part of a prudent man, who is already in debt, to involve himself yet more deeply. I hope that your letters, if you frequently send them to Paulet, as both giving an account of the affairs of Germany, and also full of your zeal and service, will prove sufficiently diligent remembrancers to him, who is naturally a worthy man, and is much beholden to the noblemen who have recommended you to him, and will certainly endeavour to shew himself grateful to them, and kind and liberal to yourself. This one thing must not be omitted, namely, that you inform Paulet, as soon as possible, of the amount that is owing to you, both in respect to the money you borrowed, and in respect to the interest which you paid the merchants on that account. I drew up from your letters a short statement of the whole debt you have incurred, and stated all the circumstances which might interest our nobles in your behalf; but the lord archbishop, with the greatest discretion, erased whatever might offend the French in case they should see it. One copy of this was delivered to the lord treasurer, another to sir F. Walsingham, and I doubt not but that Paulet has seen both. The lord archbishop retains the third, for the purpose of making other noblemen acquainted with your case; and that you may perceive yourself how the matter has been stated by me, and make any addition that may be requisite, I send you a fourth copy of this statement, and that just as it was interlined and corrected by the archbishop. I will omit nothing that I may think conducive to your interests; and if anything occurs to you, take care to let me know. There is one thing that I am thinking of, and that is, to induce one of Paulet's domestics, who has some respectable situation in his household, to interest himself in your affairs, and remind his master of you, when occasion arises; and lastly, to write me word when there is anything further to be done here.

My father and master, I will neglect no duty of a dear brother, since indeed you regard me in that light. My ability is but little, but I devote myself to you as far as I am able. Bernus will pay your autumnal pension at this Frankfort fair. Santrinus, an English merchant, whom I have made use of before, also promised to do this a fortnight since, respecting which I also wrote to you in my last letter. Farewell, Sept. 8.

Yours,

LEWIN.

The archbishop requested me to salute you in this letter in his name. I am still suffering from weakness in my eyes, which makes me use the handwriting of another. Once more farewell.

LETTER CXIV.

SIR FRANCIS WALSINGHAM TO JOHN STURMIUS.

Dated at the palace of HAMPTON COURT, *Oct.* 27, 1576.

MOST learned Sturmius, I have earnestly requested her majesty's envoy[1], who is now in France with the king, to interest himself as much as possible in the arrangement of the money matters between you and the friends of the true religion; in which he solemnly promised his credit and exertions, with this limitation, as far as his influence and power extended. Of whose word I am so far from entertaining any doubt, that I know and am fully assured, that all my own affairs, among which I place yours, will not be less attended to by him than his own: and I doubt not but that, if they will second his efforts in a manner suitable to their piety and religion, the matter will shortly be accomplished according to your wish and desire. With respect to what that worthy man, master Lanscade[2], wished to be mentioned to her majesty, the lord treasurer has her commands to send you an answer by master Lewin.

As to the means by which you should procure your letters to be forwarded to us, I have declared my mind and pleasure to master Ashby, which I know he will explain to you; lest hereafter any of you who shall entertain a desire of writing to us, whenever any occasion may arise, may find any difficulty in this respect. I earnestly entreat you, again and again, to write more frequently, according as you have leisure. Farewell and happily. Dated at the palace of Hampton Court, Oct. 27, 1576.

Your sincere friend,

FRANCIS WALSINGHAM.

[1 Sir Amias Paulet.]   [2 See Letter XCVII. p. 239.]

LETTER CXV.

SIR FRANCIS WALSINGHAM TO JOHN STURMIUS.

Dated at LONDON, *April 23*, 1577.

MOST learned Sturmius, I am obliged to reply to your many letters by a single one of mine: not but that I could wish, as it is right I should, to return you letter for letter; but I am prevented doing so by reason of my want of time, and the state of my health, which has now for some months past been very unfavourable. But I would have you assured that your letters were most gratifying, not only to myself and your other friends, who love you as they are wont to do, but also to her royal majesty, who ascribes as much to her friend Sturmius, as your virtue justly claims to itself by its own merits. This only thing is wanting in you, that you write more at length and more fully respecting the state of the times and the dispositions of men; and this the rather, in proportion as the times in which we live are abounding in dangers, and the dispositions of the men with whom we have to contend, are not without their infinite recesses and deep concealments: which nevertheless betray themselves I know not how, and are laid open for our good, in proportion as they are more diligently observed, and as we consider the new alliances which they are making every day. Your Germany has many sovereigns, whose friendship and alliance is courted by foreigners, who desire to gratify themselves rather than you: and to which party every one of them seems inclined, and what encouragement they afford either to the favourers of religion or the opposers of it, is neither without its use to know, nor will it be unwelcome for you to inform us. Send us word especially, what opinion you think we should entertain of the emperor, of the Palatine[1] of the Rhine, and Casimir: whether they will unitedly continue in that regard and good-will, which their pious and noble parent recommended to them on his death-bed, to the advancement

[1] Louis VI. and John Casimir were sons of the Elector Palatine Frederic III., who died Oct. 8, 1576.

of the gospel and of the general peace; or whether by their
dissensions and domestic quarrels they will occasion destruction both to themselves and their people.   There will not
perhaps be wanting those who will leave no stone unturned
to cast this torch into that illustrious house of the Palatines,
and set it on fire; and for this reason we must guard against
them with the greater diligence.   If you will write upon
these matters, and inform us whether any thing of the kind
is to be suspected, and by what ways and means it may be
guarded against, you will do a most welcome service both to
ourselves and to the whole christian world.   Farewell and
happily.   From my house at London, April 23, 1577.

Your most attached,

FRANCIS WALSINGHAM.

LETTER CXVI.

SIR FRANCIS WALSINGHAM TO JOHN STURMIUS.

Dated at LONDON, *July* 22, 1577.

I HAVE received your letter, most learned Sturmius, and
the book which you were pleased to dedicate to me; for both
which I owe and return no common acknowledgements to
your kindness.   The contents however of your letter, which
I thought would be for the interest of the queen's majesty
to be made known to her, I have laid before her majesty,
who received it graciously, as she does every thing else that
proceeds from her friend Sturmius, who is neither unwelcome
nor disagreeable to her.   But your letters will be, as they
are, the more acceptable, in proportion as they are more frequent, and as they inform us of those matters, which (as
those who are well and in health are touched with no
feeling of the sufferings which persons in ill health endure in
wretchedness and pain) do not any way move and affect us.
This is one evil attending prosperity, which, if not the only
one, is certainly a very grievous one, that it makes us forget,
or at least be very indifferent, not indeed of its own nature,
but through our corruption, to those evils and calamities by

which others are oppressed. If in these circumstances you would arouse us who are in a deep sleep and heedlessly secure, and by your more frequent letters would warn us of impending danger, you would shew most honourable zeal, and do us a most useful service. For I point out to you this disease of ours as one who is affected with it, and you, as a skilful and good physician, must apply the remedy: should you heal the disease, you will have the reputation of being a most excellent physician; and should your endeavours fail of success, it is still well, for you will have done your duty.

You write word that the Genevese are under some apprehension from the Spaniards: but if it is true what is related to us, and that frequently, our neighbours the Flemish and ourselves have more reason to be afraid of them; for it is reported, and that by persons of no small credit, that the Austrian[1] is thinking of recalling his Spaniards into Flanders, (and indeed has already done so,) and of raising up fresh disturbances against the prince of Orange and the better portion of the Flemish; that he promises himself great things from some of the leading men of those classes, which by his corruptions and flattering promises he has drawn over into his own schemes, that is, to the desolation of their country, and their own immediate ruin and destruction. This statement, I say, is what those parties bring over to us: you shall learn more hereafter; for time, the daughter of truth, will place every thing in its proper light. Meanwhile, take care of your health, and whatever you observe, write us word, and this as frequently as you can. You will thus do us great and valuable services. Farewell and happily.

Dated at London, July 22, 1577.

Your very loving,

FRANCIS WALSINGHAM.

[1 Don John of Austria.]

LETTER CXVII.

SIR PHILIP SIDNEY TO HUBERT LANGUET[2].

Dated at COURT, *Oct.* 1, 1577.

MY very dear Languet, of your three letters which, in that written on the 24th of August, you affirm that you have sent me, I have only received two. Those indeed were full of all kindness and real friendship; but this is nothing new. Do you fancy that you can by this means perform the promise that you so solemnly made about your paying me a visit? That would be indeed, master Hubert, a downright imposition. I am very glad that you are so near Spires, where you may be properly dealt with.

There was a nobleman here a short time since, of the name of de Tamars, with whom I formed an acquaintance, and this the more readily, because he very frequently in my presence made honourable mention of you. So likewise Aldegonde[3] and the prince himself, when I was staying with his highness, often said a great deal by which I perceived that you were very dear to him. But why do I tell you these things? Plainly to persuade you to visit him, if you can do so with safety, and to come from thence to us. You will there have a most excellent field for putting into practice, in the formation of this new commonwealth, those principles which you have so diligently studied during the whole course of your

[2 Hubert Languet had been minister of state to Augustus, elector of Saxony, from whose service he retired in consequence of the controversy between the Lutherans and Zuinglians about the eucharist, on his taking part with the latter. He afterwards accepted an invitation to Antwerp from the prince of Orange. He was the intimate friend of Melancthon, Thuanus, and Du Plessis, by the last of whom his character is thus described: " Is fuit quales multi videri volunt; is vixit qualiter optimi mori cupiunt." He died at Antwerp, Sept. 20, 1581.]

[3 Philip de Marnix, lord of Mont St Aldegonde, was the personal friend and adviser of William, prince of Orange, and in 1575 was one of the deputies sent by the States to desire the protection of queen Elizabeth. He was engaged in a Dutch version of the scriptures, when he died, in 1598. See Moreri, Bayle, Melchior Adam.]

life. And I hope indeed, that I shall come over thither, before many weeks have elapsed; for I have a great regard for that prince, and have perhaps in some way been of more service to him than he is aware of. The leaning of our minds is such at this present time, that (should the wars be continued in Flanders) I am in some hope that the prediction, which you formerly uttered respecting me at Vienna, will have a happy fulfilment. The marquis d'Havre[1] demands assistance, and I think, if occasion so require, he will obtain it[2]. The peace with France in some measure disturbs our queen; for she thinks she has not been properly treated. You know the reason. For my own part I consider these things as of little importance; for they will always have both a reason and a disposition to make a rupture, provided only they see any certain ground on which to rest.

I wrote to you a year ago about a certain Frobisher[3], who, in rivalry of Magellan, has explored that sea which he supposes to wash the north part of America. It is a marvellous history. After having made slow progress in the past year, so as only to pass in the autumn the Feroe isles and an island which he supposes to be Friesland[4], discovered by the Venetian Zeni[5], he touched at a certain island for the purpose of recruiting both himself and his crew. And there by chance a young man, one of the ship's company, picked up a piece of earth[6] which he saw glittering on the ground, and

[1 This was Charles Philip de Croy, a younger brother of the duke d'Arschot, who was at this time, 1577, commanding a part of the troops of the States at or near Antwerp.]

[2 The marquis d'Havre and Adolph Metherk were sent over by the States to borrow of queen Elizabeth a hundred thousand pounds sterling for eight months. Wright's Queen Elizabeth and her Times, II. 70. See also Camden, Elizabeth, p. 221.]

[3 Sir Martin Frobisher left Blackwall on his first voyage in June 1576, under the patronage of Ambrose Dudley, earl of Warwick, and arrived at Harwich on his return, Oct. 2. See Hakluyt, III. 29, 57.]

[4 "The 11th day (July) at a S.E. sun, we had sight of the land of Friesland bearing from us W.N.W. sixteen leagues, and rising like pinnacles of steeples, and all covered with snow. I found myself in 61 degrees of latitude." Hakluyt, as above. This is however now generally supposed to be Cape Farewell, in the south of Greenland.]

[5 Nicolas and Antony Zeni professed to discover this country in the 14th century, being driven thither from Ireland by a tempest.]

[6 "One brought a piece of black stone much like to a sea-coal in

shewed it to Frobisher; who, being engaged in other matters, and not believing that the precious metals were produced in a region so far to the north, considered it of no value. But he returned home at the beginning of winter. The young man kept the earth by him, as a memorial of his labour, (for he had no thought of any thing else,) till his return to London. And there, when one of the friends of the young man perceived it shining in an extraordinary manner, he made an assay, and found that it was the purest gold, and without any intermixture of other metal. Wherefore Frobisher[7] went back to the place this last spring, under orders to explore that island[8], and, should it answer his expectation, to proceed no farther. This he has done, and has now returned, bringing his ships, of which he had only three[9], and those of small size, full laden; and he is said (for they have not yet unloaded) to have brought two hundred tons of ore. He has given it as his decided opinion, that the island is so productive in metals, as to seem very far to surpass the country of Peru, at least as it now is. There are also six other islands[10] near to this, which seem very little inferior. It is therefore at this time under debate, by what colour, which by the weight seemed to be some kind of metal or mineral. This was a thing of no account in the judgment of the captain at first sight, and yet for novelty it was kept in respect of the place from whence it came. After his arrival in London, being demanded of sundry of his friends what thing he had brought them home out of that country, he had nothing left to present them withal, but a piece of this black stone. And it fortuned a gentlewoman, one of the adventurers' wives, to have a piece thereof, which by chance she threw and burned in the fire, so long, that at the length being taken forth, and quenched in a little vinegar, it glittered with a bright marcasite of gold. Whereupon the matter being called in some question, it was brought to certain gold-finers in London to make an assay thereof, who gave out that it held gold, and that very richly for the quantity." Hakluyt, as above.]

[7 Frobisher left Blackwall on his second voyage, on Whitsunday, May 26, 1577, and returned to England on the 28th of September.]

[8 This was an island bearing the name of Hall, whence the ore was taken up, which was brought into England this last year, 1576; the said Hall being present at the finding and taking up thereof, who was then master in the Gabriel with Capt. Frobisher. Hakluyt.]

[9 Namely, the Aide, of two hundred tons, the Gabriel, and the Michael, of about thirty tons each.]

[10 Viz. in the neighbourhood of Frobisher's straits.]

means these our hitherto successful labours can be still carried
on in safety against the attacks of other nations, among whom
the Spaniards and Danes seem especially to be considered;
the former, as claiming all the western parts by right from
the pope; the latter, as being more northerly and therefore
nearer; and relying on their possession of Iceland, they are
better provided with the means of undertaking this voyage.
They are also said to be sufficiently skilled in the art of
navigation. I wish, therefore, for the sake of our mutual
friendship, that you would send me your opinion on this subject, and at the same time describe the most convenient
method of working those ores. You promised that you
would send me the laws of Guttenberg[1]. I pray you to do
this as soon as possible. Some light may possibly be obtained
from them; for we understand this art little better than we
do the cultivation of vines. Remember therefore so to write,
as that you may answer to the great reputation you enjoy
among us; for, unless you forbid it, I will shew your letter
to the queen. The thing is truly of great importance, and
one which may probably, some time or other, be of use to
the professors of the true religion. I have written to you
three times on that important affair[2] of mine; so that I think
you are satisfied on that score.

I pray you to write to me with all diligence, and I shall
perhaps shake off my slothfulness. Send your letter to my
friend Freming. For de Taxis[3] has too much worked his swift
horses. I am truly sorry for that man's misfortune. My
friend Beale[4] is now, I believe, sweetly renewing in your
society the advantages of ancient friendship. I love him,

[1 Guttenberg was a town in Bohemia, in the neighbourhood of which
there were certain silver mines; and the laws here mentioned seem to
refer to the municipal code which regulated the working of them.]

[2 This appears to be some affair unknown to the biographers of
Sir Philip Sidney. Languet often refers to this *magnum negotium*,
but without giving a hint of its nature.]

[3 Languet says in a letter to Sir Philip Sidney, in 1575, "Consulo
ut scribas ad Joann. Baptistam de Taxis qui stationariorum equorum
procurationem habet in Belgio."]

[4 Robert Beale was clerk of the council, and often employed in
private missions to the protestant princes of Germany, an account of
which, written by himself to the lord treasurer, is given in Strype,
Ann. IV. 117.]

and yet I envy him.   Our friend Lubetius has been conferring with me about the money which the king of France owes to the free cities of Germany.   Here truly I perceive the council are much inclined to oblige the German cities. But, as you know, you Frenchmen have for a long time owed us the whole of Aquitaine and Normandy, but you would sooner make yourselves bankrupts, than discharge the debt ; and yet we esteem such debtors very little, and such bad farmers [of the revenue] far less.   I beg you will write me word as to what is the state of your affairs.   You very much wrong me, if you are not fully persuaded of my entire readiness to serve you by every means in my power.   And you must not charge upon me the saying, "out of sight, out of mind :" for I have never felt any diminution of that ardent affection with which I have always regarded you ; but it has rather increased from day to day, and it is when absent, that I have most of all felt the sweetness of your society.   But observe what Aristotle says of old men in his Rhetoric ; namely, that they are cold in love, and that we are deceiving our own spirits in cultivating friendship, as if they were nothing else but the smoke of youthful ardour.   But who, I pray, will now dare to accuse me of laziness, seeing that I have written so long a letter ?   See that you write me one yet longer in return ; for you will have a month at least to do it in.   Farewell, and commend me to the worthy Bain[5], our friend Lubetius, Clusius, the excellent Jordan, and my Andrew[6].   And so offer my services to Butrech[7], the best doctor among reisters[7], and the best reister among doctors, (as, if I mistake not, Cicero says of Scævola and Crassus[8],) as the services of one who loves them all, and desires to gratify

[5 Bain. This seems a familiar abbreviation of Banosius, often named by Languet in his letters.]

[6 The name of this person was Andreas Paulus. He is often mentioned by Languet.]

[7 Languet, in one of his letters, calls the same person "doctor equestris." He appears, from a "letter of news," MS. Cotton. Galba, c. 254, to have been in the suite of prince Casimir. *Reister* is an old word for a trooper. Daniel Rogers writing from Enchusen, July 26, 1577, to the earl of Leicester, speaks of Don John "making a levy of reisters." Wright's Elizabeth, II. 60.]

[8 An allusion to Cic. de Oratore, I. 39. *Juris peritorum eloquentissimus, eloquentium juris peritissimus.* See also ibid. 50.]

and be of use to every one of them. Again, my Hubert, farewell. From the queen's palace, Oct. 1, 1577.

Your most loving,

PHILP SIDNEY.

I wonder that I have not of a long time heard any thing of Wacker. Henry, baron of Lichtenstein, was here shortly after my return from Germany, to whom I did not shew so much courtesy as I ought to have done, having been at that time so much involved in business; and by reason of the absence of my father and uncles, who were then at Bath, I was not prepared to receive him as I could have wished. I pray you therefore, when an opportunity occurs, to make my excuse. He is certainly an excellent young man, and one whom I love from my heart; and whenever any of his friends shall come hither, I will endeavour to atone for my fault. My cousin Greville[1] dutifully salutes you.

LETTER CXVIII.

RODOLPH GUALTER TO GEORGE BUCHANAN.

Dated at ZURICH, about *Dec.* 22, 1577.

WHEN my homilies upon the epistle of St Paul to the Galatians, dedicated to the most serene king of Scotland, were published last year, I wrote to you, most excellent and honoured sir, on the 31st of August, and sent two copies of that book, one of which I requested you to present to the king's majesty in my name, and to keep the other for yourself as a mark of my affection and respect. But from that time I have received no intelligence either from England or Scotland, as to what has been done with the books. The London merchant, to whom our printer [Froschover] had entrusted the parcel, told him that it had been duly and safely forwarded to you. But of this I am rather inclined to doubt, partly from your so long silence, and partly from his covetousness, which I have discovered in many other instances, and which renders the man careless

[1 Fulke Greville, Lord Brooke.]

in the execution of such commissions as he perceives to be unattended with any advantage to himself. And the noble youth the lord George Keith, the son of the earl Marischal of Scotland, has increased my suspicion; for he also thinks that there has occurred something of the kind, knowing as he does your great facility and eagerness in cultivating the friendship of worthy men. When, therefore, he wrote to me in the month of August respecting the foul murder of his brother William[2], and requested my services in honouring his memory and his death, and moreover very kindly offered his assistance in taking charge of my letters; I thought that so desirable an opportunity was on no account to be neglected, and paid such a tribute to his brother's memory as I was able to do in the midst of the occupations and weighty affairs which call me away from the study of poetry, in which I formerly so much delighted; and at the same time I have sent this letter to be forwarded to him at Lausanne, that he may send it you from thence together with his own: and I entreat you, most learned Buchanan, to receive it in such sort as you are wont to receive the services of one by whom you are so greatly esteemed; and relieve me, I pray you, from my present anxiety, by letting me know whether my homilies have come to your hands, and how they have been received by the king's majesty. This I solemnly declare to you, that I have no other object in my lucubrations than to benefit the church: which object if I can in any measure attain unto, I shall not repent of any labour or inconvenience. Farewell, most excellent and much honoured sir. Zurich, on the day of the winter solstice, in the year of Christ's birth, 1577.

Your excellency's most attached,
RODOLPH GUALTER.

[2 William Keith, son of lord William Keith and brother of George, earl Marischal, was unfortunately killed in an excursion into the country, while prosecuting his studies at Geneva. Beza, Gualter, and other learned men honoured his memory with eulogies. M'Crie's Life of Melvill, 1819. Vol. I. p. 428.]

LETTER CXIX.

SIR PHILIP SIDNEY TO HUBERT LANGUET.

Dated at [COURT], *March* 1, 1578.

MY very dear Hubert! Robert Beale[1] and Rogers[2], and
your friend Butrech, arrived here together, with your most
wished for letters; so that I seemed to myself both to hear
and see you at the same time to my exceeding delight. You
sharply accuse me of slothfulness, and in the meantime fall
into the same fault, nay, a far greater, inasmuch as I am
always made better by your letters, while mine must of
necessity grate upon your ears to no purpose. And the use
of the pen, as you may perceive, has plainly fallen from me;
and my mind itself, if it was ever active in any thing, is now
beginning, by reason of my indolent ease, imperceptibly to
lose its strength, and to relax without any reluctance. For
to what purpose should our thoughts be directed to various
kinds of knowledge, unless room be afforded for putting it
into practice, so that public advantage may be the result,
which in a corrupt age we cannot hope for? Who would learn
music except for the sake of giving pleasure? or architecture
except with a view to building? But the mind itself, you
will say, that particle of the divine mind, is cultivated in
this manner. This indeed, if we allow it to be the case,
is a very great advantage: but let us see whether we are
not giving a beautiful, but false appearance to our splendid
errors. For while the mind is thus, as it were, drawn out
of itself, it cannot turn its powers inward for thorough self-
examination; to which employment no labour that men can
undertake, is any way to be compared. Do you not see
that I am cleverly playing the stoic? yea, and I shall be

[1 See above, p. 293, n. 6.]

[2 Namely, Daniel Rogers, the son of John Rogers, the proto-
martyr in queen Mary's reign. He is said by the writer of the Athenæ
Oxonienses to have been "the most accomplished gentleman of that
time, and a very good man, and excellently learned." He was sent to
the prince of Orange in the year 1575, when the queen had declined
to assist him and the Netherlands against the violence of Spain. See
Strype, Ann. III. i. 392, 394.]

a cynic too, unless you reclaim me. Wherefore, if you please, prepare yourself to attack me : I have now pointed out the field of battle, and I openly declare war against you.

But I wonder, my very dear Hubert, what has come into your mind, that, when I have not as yet done any thing worthy of me, you would have me bound in the chains of matrimony; and yet without pointing out any individual lady, but rather seeming to extol the state itself, which however you have not as yet sanctioned by your own example. Respecting her[3], of whom I readily acknowledge how unworthy I am, I have written you my reasons long since, briefly indeed, but yet as well as I was able. At this present time, indeed, I believe you have entertained some other notion; which I earnestly entreat you to acquaint me with, whatever it may be : for every thing that comes from you has great weight with me; and, to speak candidly, I am in some measure doubting whether some one, more suspicious than wise, has not whispered to you something unfavourable concerning me, which, though you did not give entire credit to it, you nevertheless prudently, and as a friend, thought right to suggest for my consideration. Should this have been the case, I entreat you to state the matter to me in plain terms, that I may be able to acquit myself before you, of whose good opinion I am most desirous : and should it only prove to have been a joke, or a piece of friendly advice, I pray you nevertheless to let me know; since every thing from you will always be no less acceptable to me, than the things that I hold most dear.

There is no news here, except that it is a novel and almost unheard of circumstance in government, that nothing novel has occurred. Frobisher's gold is now melted, and does not turn out so valuable as he at first boasted : however these islands at the sixty-second degree are not to be despised; but they keep this as a great secret, lest, as you know, the opportunity be forestalled. Nay more, they expect to be able to cross the sea at the same latitude; so incorrect is the description of the world as given by cosmographers : but if there should be open sea at such a temperature, you perceive it will be of great importance.

[3 Lady Penelope Devereux, of whom Sidney was an admirer, may probably be alluded to.]

I believe the queen will do what you wrote to me about for the sake of Prince Casimir; but I was loth at this present time to say much upon that subject, as I know that it is our disposition not to do any thing in a hurry. What else can I now write to you, when I am so very sleepy, except that I love you as my own heart, and that I desire nothing more earnestly than that I may sometime be able to prove it? My friend Greville salutes you. Humbly salute in my name the count and countess of Hanau, and write me word how they like the dogs I sent them. I have now written to Lubetius, Banosius, Andrew, Anselm, Merell. Am I then lazy? I pray you to salute Clusius, and tell master Salvart[1] that I am greatly indebted to him for the book he sent me translated into French. When it was put into my hands, I was exceedingly busy; but I will sometime shew myself deserving of his courtesy. Salute also master Glauburg, whom I will willingly oblige. Farewell, dearest Languet. March 1, 1578.

Yours,

PHILIP SIDNEY.

I will shew Beale every friendly office in my power, both for his own deservings, and especially for your recommendation of him.

LETTER CXX[2].

LAURENCE HUMPHREY TO [ABRAHAM MUSCULUS.]

Dated at OXFORD, March 3, 1578.

IMMANUEL. Your son has left us, and has staid some months in London; where however I have no doubt but that he has been attentive to his studies, and to the hearing of sermons. He was very dear to me both for the sake of your honoured and venerable father, and yours, and also for his own. For when I lived at Basle, I saw some translations of

[1 Salvart was in the suite of Prince Casimir.]

[2 The original of this Letter is preserved at Zofingen.]

master Musculus[3] at the house of Frobenius[4], and passed them through the press. If any thing remains yet unpublished, I pray you let it be brought to light; for he was a man of various reading, refined judgment, and unwearied industry. Nor can I forget with what courtesy he entertained me and some companions at Berne. I therefore cherish the remembrance of so great a man, and pray God to bless you and his posterity. But it somewhat distresses me that your son has left us so soon, and that I was not able to be of so much service to him as I wished. He had however a great desire to see the university of Cambridge, and other parts of England, with a view of returning with more learning, though not with more money. As to yourself, most learned sir, I pray and exhort you in the Lord to continue to follow your father's footsteps, and visit us Britons, although separated by so long a distance, with your letters; yea, and so profit us by the learned monuments of your literary works, that we may perceive that such a writer [as your father] has revived in his son. For we must take advantage of this singular blessing of peace, and all our exertions must be directed to the good of the church, as long as the present tranquillity of the times will permit. Go on as you have begun, and may the Lord Jesus long preserve you in health and happiness to the universal church and your country and ourselves!

Oxford, March 3, 1578.

Yours,

LAURENCE HUMPHREY.

[3 Wolfgang Musculus published translations of some of the works of Chrysostom, Basil, and other fathers; and also of the ecclesiastical history of Eusebius and other Church historians.]

[4 Jerome Frobenius was the son and successor of the eminent printer, John Frobenius, who died in 1527. He carried on the business with the same reputation that his father enjoyed, and printed, among other works, those of Basil, Chrysostom, Augustine, and Jerome.]

LETTER CXXI.

SIR PHILIP SIDNEY TO HUBERT LANGUET.

Dated at COURT, *March* 10, 1578.

My very dear Hubert! I wrote you by our friend Butrech what then came into my mind. I have now written to you by master Rogers, rather that I may not omit any opportunity of saluting you, than because any thing here offers itself worthy even of a thought. We have so failed in satisfying Butrech, that I believe, unless his kindness prevent it, we shall have a bad character in Germany. And yet, to speak candidly and confidentially, they did not appear to manage your affairs with much firmness, while the prince of Orange seemed to aim at one thing, and the illustrious Casimir at another. And from this the queen has taken occasion to defend her tardiness in executing her designs, against Leicester, Walsingham, and others, who had persuaded her to a more active course; which I much regret. My friend du Plessis will, I believe, shortly quit us, without being able to obtain what would have been most advantageous to a Christian government. For my own part, unless God powerfully counteract it, I seem to myself to see our cause withering away, and am now meditating with myself some Indian project. The queen is your friend, as I hope you will learn in a short time: meanwhile, I would have you love me affectionately, as you are wont, and commend me to all our common friends. From court, March 10, 1578.

Yours,

PHILIP SIDNEY.

I have received Swendius's[1] treatise from the count of Hanau; I have not yet had any from yourself. I pray you to love my friend Rogers more and more for my sake.

[1 Languet in one of his letters mentions a baron Swendius as a good soldier. He wrote a short treatise on the defence of Hungary against the Turks, which is probably the writing referred to in the text.]

LETTER CXXII.

LAURENCE HUMPHREY TO ABRAHAM MUSCULUS.

Dated at LONDON, *June* 5, 1578.

IMMANUEL. I have received your letter, most learned sir, and am glad if I have been of any service to your son Wolfgang, or in any way useful to you. Having been a stranger myself, I have learned to befriend strangers; and I have only to regret that my ability does not correspond with my inclination. Then too, there has at this time been suddenly imposed upon me the important office of being sent as a deputy into Germany, to a synod at Smalcald; where, as far as I understand, I have to confer with my brethren about Lutheranism, and that unhappy controversy respecting the Lord's supper, which has been carried on so long with so much heat and party spirit, that I do not see how it can be settled. I wish other deputies would come from Switzerland and Geneva, that we might assemble with calling upon God in prayer, and in a friendly and fraternal spirit. The queen's majesty is most anxious for this. God must be implored both by you and ourselves, to bring this important business to some happy issue. We are altogether impotent, and therefore pray that his strength may be made perfect in our weakness. I will see after your son on my return, and render him all the assistance in my power. We have as yet heard nothing certain respecting those two Englishmen. In haste, at London. May the Lord Jesus have compassion upon his church and yours, and preserve you with all your family! Farewell. June 5, 1578.

Yours wholly,

and one who was much attached to your father

Wolfgang Musculus,

LAURENCE HUMPHREY.

LETTER CXXIII.

GEORGE BUCHANAN TO RODOLPH GUALTER.

[Without place or date.]

HEALTH. Your letter, most excellent sir, written at
Zurich on the 31st of August, was delivered to me eight
months after, namely, on the first of May. Your present,
as it was a noble and honourable one, so was it willingly
and graciously accepted by the king: but the expectations
of yourself and other good men yonder concerning him
were exceedingly gratifying, not only to himself, but to us[1]
also, who have the charge of his education; for if the disposition which is now so delightfully budding forth in him
shall in due time be matured, and bring forth fruits worthy
of our expectation, he will indeed prove such a character as
both he himself and we also may attribute in great measure
to you: he, in that you encourage by your commendations
his yet infirm capacity, and by your exhortations, setting
before him as it were the rewards of success, you render
more easy the labours that are so irksome to boys of his
age; and to us, unless we would be most ungrateful, it cannot
but be most gratifying that such men as you should voluntarily take upon yourselves a part of the burden imposed
upon us. For it is not the mere voice of the teacher that
advances the studies of the learner; but whatever encourages
the wearied mind, and diminishes the irksomeness of application, and places the form of true virtue before the eyes, is
to be regarded also as performing the office of a master.
Besides which, these things are more readily listened to than
mere precepts; as they come not in the authoritative character
of a command, but allure by the bland invitations of honour
and renown. And these presents of yours, as coming from
places very far off, possess the additional advantage of distance,
and are free from any suspicion of flattery; while the services

[1 James VI. of Scotland had four principal masters, George
Buchanan, Peter Young, the abbots of Cambuskenneth and Dryburgh.
Melvill's Mem. p. 125.]

of immediate attendants are accepted, not with the feeling that they are brought forth from the garner of liberality, but as the mere discharge of a debt.

But enough of the king. I am very much gratified by your approbation of my poems: for if you are mistaken in your opinion, you are not deceived by the weakness of your judgment, but, actuated by kindness, are less clear-sighted as to their defects; while, if your approbation is well founded, I also have just ground for rejoicing, like Hector in Nævius, that I am praised by an individual who is himself so worthy of commendation. But there are many hindrances to prevent this rejoicing from being solid and without alloy. For such is the indolence of our age, that no one will willingly bestow much labour upon any pursuit from whence he can expect little or no reward for his pains. Those persons also neither are nor will be wanting, who do not, it may be, despise that most noble aphorism of a noble poet, in which he contends that virtue is its own reward; but who nevertheless reject all this kind of writing, as both useless, and designed only to please the ears.

[The remainder of this letter is imperfect.]

LETTER CXXIV.

SIR FRANCIS WALSINGHAM TO JOHN STURMIUS.

Dated at ANTWERP, *Sept. 5,* 1578.

GREETING. I do not now reply to your last letter, by reason of the more important engagements with which I am overwhelmed, and the sudden departure of the bearer of these presents. We were a few days since in some hopes of coming to an arrangement[2] respecting the Low Country affairs: but

[2 Lord Cobham and sir Francis Walsingham were sent to the Netherlands at the beginning of this year, 1578, to treat of a peace, in concert with Monsieur Pompon de Bellievre, and the count of Schwartz-enberg, the French and Imperial ministers there; but without success, since Don John, according to Camden, would by no means admit of the reformed religion, and the prince of Orange flatly refused to return into Holland. Sir Francis Walsingham in a letter to sir Christopher Hatton, dated Sept. 9, says: "My lord Cobham and I have cause to

that hope has fallen to the ground, through a letter which the duke of Austria (if we may believe him) has received from the catholic king, in which he states that the whole management and definitive arrangement of these Low Country affairs had been committed and entrusted to his imperial majesty, who took upon himself the settlement of that business; but at what time, and upon what terms, and with what success, we are still ignorant. There are other subjects upon which I would gladly write to you, but business and want of time do not allow me. I will defer them to another opportunity: do you continue to love me as you are wont. In haste. Antwerp, Sept. 5, 1578.

Yours heartily, as his own,

FRA. WALSINGHAM.

LETTER CXXV.

RICHARD HILLES TO RODOLPH GUALTER.

Dated at LONDON, *Jan.* 10, 1579.

MUCH health, I understood, my very honoured and beloved friend in Christ our Lord and Saviour, by your letter dated at Zurich on the seventh of last November, that you were in good health; and I pray our gracious God very long to preserve you to his glory and the edifying of his church. It afforded me indeed great comfort to learn from your aforesaid letter, that you have borne with such firmness and resignation the loss of your very dear sons and intimate friends; because "blessed are the dead which die in the Lord; even so, saith the Spirit, for they rest from their labours." For if you were to wear yourself out by constant grief, you could never expect any benefit or advantage therefrom: for it is most certain that they will never return into this world, and it is equally certain that you will go to them.

think ourselves most unfortunate, to be employed in a legation that is like to have so hard an issue." Wright's Q. Elizabeth's Life and Times, II. 93.]

The letter which I received inclosed in yours, for master Laurence Humphrey, I sent to him at Oxford, on the last day of December, by a trustworthy messenger, who brings letters from the university every week : so that there is no doubt but that he has most certainly given your letter aforesaid to master doctor Humphrey before this time.   But I pray you, that in case you should have any other letters directed to me, you would send them to Strasburgh, to master Theobald Behem, a merchant there, who can send them to me without any difficulty ; and that you will not forget to send the money for the postage at the same time ; for otherwise I fear that he will not send the letters so readily by the Spires post.

I have to thank you for having written me the news you had then heard about the duke d'Alençon, (who is, as I understand, the brother of the king of France); and I now send you word in return, that this same duke d'Alençon, at the end of last December, went away into France, together with all his troops, from a town of the Low Countries, called Bergen in German, and Mons in French.   But the Flemish themselves say, that it is in this way he means to defend that town against king Philip, as his grandfather did the city of Metz[1] against the emperor Charles the fifth.   I pray you, commend me to my old friend Julius Sancterentianus (who is employed in Froschover's printing office as a corrector of the press), and tell him that I received two months since his kind letter, dated at Zurich on the 24th of August, and also, a month after, the five books specified in the same letter.   One of these I have kept for myself, as he desired ; the others I have sent to Oxford by a trusty messenger, to master Herbert Westphaling, canon of Christ church.   Tell him too that, according to his desire, I will, God willing, repeat the service I have hitherto done him, in procuring his Oxford pension. I sent my letter, dated in August last, to the late autumnal fair at Frankfort, to master Christopher Froschover, of Zurich, respecting which I expect shortly the answer of Julius Sancterentianus.   And I hope that this was the letter which you

[1 Metz was besieged by the emperor Charles V. in 1552, and defended by the duke of Guise, who was nominated to take the command in that city by Henry II. of France, *father* of the duke d'Alençon. See Ranken's Hist. of France. Book VI. ch. 1.]

understand to have been the last written by me to your friend
Julius, as you mentioned at the beginning of your letter.

My wife, who is now-a-days a great invalid, (though
she is now, thank God, tolerably well,) especially salutes you.
I pray God of his goodness to preserve you in safety, together
with your wife and all your family. Farewell. London, Jan.
10. In the year of Christ's birth, 1578. English style.

Yours, according to my ability,

RICHARD HILLES.

LETTER CXXVI.

FRANCIS, EARL OF BEDFORD, TO [RODOLPH GUALTER.]

Dated at EXETER, Feb. 28, 1579.

YOUR letter, most excellent sir, wherein you recommended
John Rodolph Ulmer[1], gratified me exceedingly : and he also
is dear to me, not only by reason of my general good-will
and affection for his country, and especially for yourself and
his father; but I have also a wonderful regard for him by
reason of his manifold good qualities. For he is a youth of
honourable principles, such an one indeed as all good men will
both love and praise as he deserves; and, as I understand
from those who were acquainted with him at the university
of Oxford, he is not only devoted to learning, but likewise
entirely engaged in the pursuit of it, in which he has, by the
divine blessing, made such progress, that I have no doubt but
that his studies will ere long tend to the glory of God and
the benefit of his church.

I greatly rejoice that your country is flourishing and
prosperous both in religion and in all other respects; and
am glad, most learned sir and reverend father in Christ,
that you are not yet worn out in your holy zeal for godliness, and your endeavours to promote the glory of God.
And I heartily pray God to strengthen you more and more,

[1 See first series, Letter CXXXII. p. 326. Ulmer was the son of
John ab Ulmis, who came to England in king Edward's time, under
the patronage of the duke of Suffolk, and was made fellow of St John's
College, Oxford. He died in 1580, and his descendants took the name
of Ulmer.]

and enrich you with his gifts, and defend you with his protection. Most excellent sir, farewell. Exeter, Feb. 28, 1579.

Your most devoted in the Lord,

F. BEDFORD.

P.S. I thank you very much, most learned sir, for your singular kindness to me when I was with you in your country; and I earnestly entreat you to do the same in my name to the whole host of my Zurich Mæcenases.

LETTER CXXVII.

WILLIAM COLE TO [RODOLPH GUALTER.]

Dated at OXFORD, *Feb.* 28, 1579.

THERE has come to me, most learned sir, a young man of Zurich, Ulmer's son[2], who after some days, as he tells me, is about to return to you. I could not refuse giving him a letter to you, who deserved so well of me when I was an exile many years since; not that I have at this time any thing worth your reading, but lest you should suppose, from my not writing, that I am unmindful of the obligations I have received. I hear that your son[3], lately a scholar of Oxford, and a youth of excellent promise, has been removed by an untimely death: which event indeed we all of us, to whom he was familiarly known during his sojourn in this place, most deeply deplore, not only on your account, as having lost a son of so much expectation, but much more, as it is right we should do, because at this time the church of Christ cannot spare so much talent without great injury.

With respect to our English friends who were in exile with me at Zurich, I have nothing to write, except that out of so many scarcely five are now remaining. Master Horn, the most excellent bishop of Winchester, is in a very infirm state of health. Master Mullins[4] is archdeacon of London;

[2 See the preceding Letter.]

[3 See above, Letter CXII. p. 279.]

[4 John Mullins was fellow of Magdalene college, Oxford, and one of the exiles at Zurich in 1555. He was made successively archdeacon of London, canon residentiary of St Paul's, and rector of Bocking. Strype, Whitgift, I. 245.]

master Reniger[1] archdeacon of Winchester: master Humphrey and myself preside over two colleges at Oxford, he at Magdalene and I at Corpus Christi. All the others have departed this life. From this you see to how small a number they are reduced, who sometime lived with you as exiles; and you see too in what a state are the affairs of us who as yet survive them. But if you wish to know what is the state of religion throughout all England, it is precisely the same as it has been from the beginning of the reign of our most gracious queen Elizabeth. There is no change whatever. The queen of Scotland is with us, but not as an independent sovereign, nor is she at liberty to wander about at her pleasure. In Scotland they are most actively guarding and protecting the true religion, and every thing there is in a state of quiet and tranquillity. I hear that the duke of Parma[2] is preparing an army against the Low Countries. Casimir[3] has been honourably received by our queen, nor do I know whether any visitor has ever been more agreeable to her. The duke d'Alençon[4] is daily expected. He is in hopes, as I hear, of forming a matrimonial alliance here in England. I have thought fit to tell you these things at this time, especially as I have met with so opportune a messenger. Salute all my friends, and especially masters Lavater, Bullinger, Froschover, my Julius, &c. Farewell, my very dear sir, and return my affection for you. Oxford, Feb. 28, 1579.

Your most attached,

WILLIAM COLE.

[1 Michael Reniger was expelled Magdalene college, Oxford, by Bishop Gardiner, and became an exile. He was afterwards chaplain to queen Elizabeth, and prebendary of Winchester. Strype.]

[2 The duke of Parma was appointed governor of the Netherlands on the death of Don John of Austria in the autumn of 1578. Strype, Ann. II. ii. 159.]

[3 For an account of this reception see the first series, p. 330, and Strype, Ann. II. i. 160.]

[4 The duke d'Alençon, or d'Anjou, to which title he succeeded on the accession of his brother to the throne of France, arrived privately in England with one or two only in his company, and came to the queen unexpectedly at her court at Greenwich. He made a second visit in 1581. See Strype, II. ii. 317. Camden, Eliz. 233, 267.]

LETTER CXXVIII[5].

HUBERT LANGUET TO PETER HUBNER.

Dated at BADEN, *June* 4, 1579.

MUCH health. I am surprised that you have not written
to me respecting the studies of our young gentleman, master
Sidney ; for I very much expected from you some account of
them.   I suppose you remember what I told you, when conversing with you respecting his education ; namely, that it
is the especial desire of his illustrious father and brother,
that he should acquire a correct knowledge of the German
language : which I do not think will be difficult for him, if
only the quickness of his understanding and strength of his
memory are seconded by diligence and application ; and if
you frequently admonish him of his duty, and attentively
perform your part, not only in explaining to him such passages
in German as he may afterwards turn into Latin, but especially by conversing with him in German ; for his being accustomed to converse in German is of far more importance
to him than the study of German writers ; for whatever
German works contain any thing that may tend to the cultivation of his understanding, are almost all of them translated into languages with which he is acquainted.   And he
will never learn to speak German with fluency by the study
of the German writers, even though he should devote a whole
life to that object, unless he add thereunto the habit of conversation.   The commencement of such a habit will indeed be
disagreeable to him, but it will grow pleasant in time ; for
when he shall perceive that he has made any progress, he
will derive pleasure from that circumstance, and be stimulated
to greater alacrity in making farther advancement.   But
you must take care not to be wanting to him in this
matter ; for you are well aware that I particularly requested
it of you, and that you gave me your promise : and if you
find your admonitions not very agreeable to him, you must

[5 The original of this letter is preserved at Zofingen.]

not desist on that account, but persevere in your instruction. And if you do this, there is no reason to doubt but that he will at length feel thankful to you: for he will perceive that you are acting with a desire for his advantage; and as he is of a generous disposition, he will in no wise make an ill return for the benefit. Farewell. From Baden, June 4, 1579.

Your most attached,

HUBERT LANGUET.

LETTER CXXIX.

GEORGE BUCHANAN TO RODOLPH GUALTER.

Dated *July* 24, 1579.

I RECEIVED your former letter, together with the books, many months after you had sent them. The book I gave, as you desired me, to the king, who received it as he ought, that is, with a most favourable disposition towards you. He also sent in return such a message as occurred to him at the moment, and especially the following : "Whereas all my subjects are very greatly indebted to you, you have not only wished to make me also indebted to you, but absolutely bound to your service, inasmuch as you take your share of a most heavy burden, partly to lighten our labour, partly to cultivate our yet inexperienced mind, and prepare it to receive the seed of learning and to bring forth good fruit." And since the labours of each of us has respect to the cultivation of the understanding, our share in it may fitly be compared to the industry of the husbandman, and yours to that celestial influence which renders all labour productive, and by the due temperature of the seasons gives the corn its increase. But your last letter, dated at Zurich in December 1577, did not reach us until August 1579. I have now been absent from court more than six weeks, by reason of ill health ; but as soon as I return thither, I will endeavour, that the king shall steal a few moments from his occupations, to give you a testimony of his favourable regard towards you with his own hand : and should I not be able to accomplish this myself, I will take care that it shall be managed by my colleague, the pious and learned Peter Young[1], who will watch for a favourable opportunity of introducing the subject.   Meanwhile I send you my commentary upon government[2], written indeed in troublous times, but now at last published after a moderate interval, the tumult being assuaged, and the minds of men having become more accustomed to discourses of this kind.

My labour may possibly seem superfluous, and especially as the lucubrations of so many most learned men have already been set forth upon the same subject.   But when they had collected a few scattered, though very excellent, maxims upon this matter, I thought that I should not altogether lose my pains if I were to reduce them into method, and discuss the whole subject, not at random, but in an orderly and well-digested manner.   And if good and learned men shall think that I have not failed in my endeavours, I shall not regard the approbation of the many.

July 24, in the year of Christ's birth 1579.

[1 Mr Peter Young was one of king James's preceptors, and also his almoner.   Sir James Melvil says of him, that he was gentle, and loath to offend the king at any time, carrying himself warily, as a man who had mind of his own weal, by keeping of his majesty's favour.   Melvil's memoirs, p, 125.]

[2 This work was published in 1579, and entitled *De jure regni apud Scotos*.   It was answered by Adam Blackwood in a book entitled *Adversus Georg. Buchanani Dialogum de jure regnandi apud Scotos pro regibus apologia*.   Pictavii, 1581; and by W. Barclay in his book, *De regno et regali potestate*, Parisiis, 1600.   It was condemned, together with other books, by the university of Oxford in full convocation, July 21, 1683; which decree however was ordered by the House of Lords to be burnt "by the hangman," March 25, 1710, after the trial of Dr Sacheverel.]

LETTER CXXX.

RODOLPH GUALTER TO GEORGE BUCHANAN.

Dated *March* 8, 1580.

I was indeed surprised, most excellent and much honoured
sir, that I had for three whole years received no reply to
my letters to the most serene king and yourself. But I have
lately discovered that your letter met with the same fate as
my own; for that which you wrote on the 24th of July last
year, I received on the 6th of January. The longer however it was in coming, the greater pleasure it afforded me,
as announcing that my book had been so graciously received, and that this service of mine had been approved by
so learned as yourself, whose opinion I prefer to multitudes
of others. I regret however, that I am in the meantime
deprived of that pleasure which I should have derived from
your first letter. But as I have not seen it even unto
this day, it must either have been destroyed by the perfi-
diousness of the malevolent, or from some other cause. But
it is enough, as I said, that my service was not unacceptable
both to the most serene king and to yourself. And should
there be added the testimony of the royal favour towards
me written with his own hand, as you have so kindly promised,
I shall then think myself happy in this respect.

There arrived together with your letter your book,
De jure regni apud Scotos; which I have not only read
myself, but have lent to my colleagues and fellow-ministers
to read and examine; all of whom entertain the same opinion as myself, namely, that the book is written with as
much learning and authority as piety. And I wish that
all kings would be persuaded of what you so well and piously
state in it; for then would their subjects be more happy,
and they themselves would not only reign happily on earth,
but would also enjoy a participation of the heavenly kingdom
with the King of kings and Lord of lords, Jesus Christ. But
because few of them entertain these feelings, and the greater

part of them are corrupted by the blandishments of flatterers
and most abandoned characters; while they fancy themselves
kings, they become the slaves of the most vile affections and
vices; besides which they fleece the flock committed to their
trust, of which they ought to be the shepherds, and at last
ruin them together with themselves.   I therefore esteem the
most serene king of Scotland as fortunate and happy, in
having obtained, in so corrupt an age, such an instructor,
who is able to imbue his youthful mind with most wholesome
precepts, and implant in him the seeds of truly royal virtues.
And I hope that God, who has bestowed upon him this favour,
will also grant that he may obey these salutary rules of conduct, and live happy and prosperous with his people, and rule
them to the glory of his name.

Thus have I thought fit to reply to your letter, and at
the same time to recommend that if no more direct mode
of transmitting letters to us should occur, you should send
them to the most reverend Edwin Sandys, archbishop of
York, with whom I have kept up a friendship of many
years continuance, and who will take care that they shall be
forwarded to me by his agents in London.   Farewell, most
excellent sir. Zurich, March 8, in the year of the incarnation
of the eternal Son of God, 1580.

Your most loving,

RODOLPH GUALTER.

LETTER CXXXI.

HIEROME ZANCHIUS TO SIR FRANCIS WALSINGHAM.

Dated at NEUSTADT, Sept. 24, 1581.

GREETING. When that most excellent man, John Sturmius, left us yesterday, he desired me, most illustrious sir, to
write to you respecting his visit to us, the reason of it, and
also respecting his departure.   I said that I had not any
acquaintance, much less any familiar intercourse, with you :
he replied, that he knew for certain that my letter would be

agreeable to you, and that he hoped this my writing would prove as it were the beginning of a friendship between us; for that you were so exceedingly well-disposed towards the professors of learning and godliness, that I should never have to repent of this service. I have no occasion therefore, most honourable sir, to explain the reasons of my having thus ventured to write to you, as I have now briefly stated them. I only request that with your wonted discretion and kindness you will take in good part my simple style of writing, as that of an old man who has long since taken leave of all the ornaments of composition.

The good old man has suffered greatly by reason of his bold and open defence of the truth[1], which he has so stoutly defended, (as he is still determined to do,) that, being obliged in some measure to give way to the times, (for some even threatened him with imprisonment,) he quitted Strasburgh on the first of August, and came to us the following day; where he was most hospitably entertained by every one, and especially by our most illustrious prince, who presented him with a golden medal of himself, as a mark of respect; and he, on his part, wonderfully refreshed us all, and edified the whole city by his reverend presence, his weighty and most learned discourse, and, what is more, his decided evidences of piety, in hearing sermons and partaking of the sacrament of the Lord's supper.

He wrote during this time (for he was never unemployed) three books against the apostle of ubiquity[2]; but they have not yet seen the light. His cause was long agitated in the senate, and he was at length recalled by a letter from the magistrates, the public faith being pledged for his safety. Yesterday therefore, which was the 23rd Sept. 1581, all the expenses of his entertainment having been defrayed by the treasury of the most illustrious prince, he departed early in the morning for Strasburgh, well and hearty, and accom-

[1 Sturmius was at this time 74 years old. He died in 1589, in the eighty-third year of his age. He entertained Zuingle's opinions respecting the real presence; in consequence of which he was much persecuted by the Lutheran ministers of Strasburgh, and at last deprived of his rectorship of the university there, through the instrumentality of a divine named Pappus, with whom he had a long and tedious controversy. See Bayle, and Melchior Adam.]

[2 Namely, Brentius. See first series, p. 108. note 1.]

panied by some brethren, recommending to me repeatedly and most earnestly to write to you as he had desired.

You have then, most honourable sir, the fulfilment of Sturmius's injunction to me, that I should salute you, and acquaint you by my letter of his visit and his departure : which office I have undertaken the more readily, as I hoped that what Sturmius without any hesitation ventured to promise, would come to pass, namely, that my letter would not be displeasing to you, and that you would admit me among the number of your friends ; which that you may do, I earnestly entreat you. May the Lord Jesus Christ preserve the queen's most serene majesty, all the nobility, the church and state, yourself and all good men ; for by him, saith the apostle, do all things consist.

Your excellency's

H. ZANCHIUS.

Neustadt. Sept. 24, 1581.

LETTER CXXXII[3].

QUEEN ELIZABETH TO THE CONFEDERATE SWISS CANTONS.

Dated at OATLANDS, *Sept.* 1, 1583.

ELIZABETH, by the grace of God, of England, France and Ireland, queen &c., to the mighty and magnificent lords, the confederate lords of all Switzerland, health and prosperity.

On consideration of the proceedings which have lately taken place, and still are taking place, by the command and, as it is pretended, in the name of the duke of Savoy[5] my cousin ;

[3 The original of this letter is preserved at Schaffhausen.]

[4 In the year 1581, the duke of Savoy, by the pope and other popish setters on, and by his own ambition accompanying, laboured to obtain the city and dominion of Geneva, famous for its religion, and a great nurse of pious men, and harbourer of exiles for religion : and which had been taken, had it not been prevented by the seasonable aid of some of their neighbours the Helvetians. The council sent a letter to the bishops, and ordered a collection to be made in behalf of the Genevese. See Strype, Whitgift, 412, &c. See also Lauffer's Helvetische Geschichte, 10 Th. p. 286, 287.]

on consideration too of the causes of these disorders, and of the
result that may be expected from them; not to mention that
the most flourishing nations and fairest cities, which have
sprung from far more abject beginnings, are now lying overwhelmed and prostrate; it then came into my mind that it
would be a worthy service to inform you of the things necessary for you to be acquainted with, and in which you appear
to me to be especially interested. And of these there are two
things in particular: one of which relates to a good understanding among yourselves, and which should have very great
weight with you; the other, which requires you to aid and
assist in all their need those who are members of your body;
and the more especially, since whatever benefit you confer
upon them, will redound to yourselves. And I have no doubt
but that you duly weigh in your minds how profitable and
necessary these remedies, which I now state to you, will be
for your own liberty against every attack of your enemies.
The commendations of your wisdom are now celebrated in
the discourses and languages of almost all nations; to say
nothing of the distinguished praise of your valour, respecting
which no age will ever be silent; and on account of which
no one, however powerful he may be in every description of
troops, has at any time dared to form any plot against
your safety and commonwealth, except those who have
artfully insinuated themselves into the favour and friendship
of particular parties: if you give place, however, to men
of that kind, there is danger lest they should endeavour to
diffuse at length pestiferous poison through the whole body;
and this, while it will be advantageous to them, will be to
yourselves ruinous and destructive. They act rightly therefore, who reject artifices of this kind; for they will in this
way watch over their own safety, and will subdue their
enemies, even without any injury to themselves. For indeed
evil counsel is most dangerous to him who proposes it, and
deceitful artifices fall to pieces of their own accord; while as
the bond of peace is in the mean time daily becoming more
close, it can be weakened or dissolved by no stratagems
whatever.

Consider, I pray you, the state of France; look upon
Flanders; with what intestine wars France has for some
time been raging, and is almost reduced to desolation; while

Flanders is lying before our eyes prostrate and overthrown. Each has suffered a loss which they would never have experienced, if they had in the smallest degree studied peace and concord. But now they have mutually enfeebled each other, and neither of them dares trust the other; since confidence is not easily restored to reconciled friends, and they are continually open to the charge of suspicion.

But with respect to Geneva, I admit that it is not very powerful; it is nevertheless a member of your body, and therefore the greater injury it sustains, the more deeply wounded is the whole of your Switzerland. And although some of you, who entertain a different opinion, do not consider this, yet let them beware lest they some time experience the truth of it to their own cost. The friendly intercourse that has for some years past existed between yourselves and the city of Geneva, to the great advantage of both parties, you should be induced to confirm by mutual offices of kindness, as becomes neighbours: for if that still remain constant and uninterrupted, what mischief could happen to either party, which would not affect the other?

Add to this that Geneva is the market and key to your territory, by which your enemies may easily be hindered from making war upon yourselves. But when Geneva is taken, you will then have to consider for yourselves what security remains for you. Indeed, that very thing which is now in dispute between you and those who abuse the tender age of a good prince, supplied a reason to your ancestors to bind themselves in alliance with the people of Geneva under all circumstances whatever. Wherefore if they were right in what they did, you yourselves will easily perceive how you ought to act in the defence of this Genevese cause, both for your own advantage and with the approval of almost all nations.

I entreat therefore, and with all kindness request your wisdom again and again, to vouchsafe, after the manner and courage of the Swiss, to bestow your strenuous exertions and active endeavours with respect to this affair, which is one of common interest both to yourselves and the people of Geneva; and that you will be unanimous in defending this neighbouring city from all stratagems and attacks, as far as lies in your power. I beg moreover, that you will not think it beneath you to mitigate by your entreaties and intercession that ill-will, which this young prince has possibly conceived against your confederates, and to request his excellency to commit the matter to law, and prosecute it in a civil suit before competent judges; or rather let him know the whole state of the case, namely, how all things have been settled, and for what object; namely, that he will not have to deal with the Genevese only, but with the whole of confederate Switzerland; and that you are prepared to undergo any thing for them, who have hitherto offered and presented all their services and honours to his excellency; any thing, I say, that the pledged faith of your confederation shall seem to require. If you will do this, it will not only be to your perpetual honour and commendation among all nations, but you will also especially consult your own safety.   Farewell.

From my palace at Oatlands, Sept. 1, 1583.

Your confederation's very loving,

ELIZABETH R.

LETTER CXXXIII.

QUEEN ELIZABETH TO THE FOUR CITIES, &c.

Dated at OATLANDS, *Sept.* 1, 1583.

ELIZABETH, by the grace of God, of England, France, and Ireland, queen, defender of the faith, &c. To the mighty lords and most honourable consuls and senators of the four cities of Zurich, Berne, Basle, and Schaffhausen, our very dear friends.

Mighty lords, most honourable men, and very dear friends. To intercede with your piety on behalf of your allies, or to warn you of your danger now sufficiently foreseen and guarded against, would be an offence against our friendship, if we did it not out of entire affection for you: but as you will not be displeased that you are loved by us, and will plainly perceive that we are anxious for your common peace, we do not doubt but that our endeavours will be gratifying to you.

It is the affair and cause of the people of Geneva, that we commend to you; and which is neither alien from the communion of the same Christ and gospel that you profess, nor separate and estranged from the participation of your danger, inasmuch as they have the same enemies as yourselves; those namely, who, on account of the purity of the reformed religion which we profess, have conspired against the lives of all those who profess the gospel; and who indeed adopt various devices to overwhelm us separately, though they every where follow the same purpose and design. But since they are unable to attain their object by open violence, (for they would desire to cut us all off at one blow,) they lay their mines, and contrive secret artifices against us by severing us into parts, and mutually separating us from each other. And, in proportion as they are more active in this one object, namely, that they may divide us asunder, they render us more vigilant in cherishing and promoting concord among ourselves; and the sooner we perceive evil arising from the evil of our neighbours, the more active ought we to be in warding off from our neighbours an evil so near to ourselves, lest the contagion which by our fault has once begun to attack one member, may by an unavoidable fatality be extended over the whole body.

We have written thus briefly, that you may consider attentively, again and again, what ought immediately to be done under the present circumstances. And it is this; that you have a due concern for your allies; that you regard the danger which now seems to belong only to them, as your own in common: wherefore you must exert all your influence, all your assistance, all your endeavours for their relief; and agreeing among yourselves must at no time desist from their defence. This we have a right to request by reason of our friendship; and we shall never refuse you any thing, which you may think to appertain to the maintenance of your security. May your lordships live well and happily! Given from our palace at Oatlands, on the first of September, in the year of our Lord 1583, and of our reign the 25th.

Earnestly desiring your safety,

ELIZABETH R.

LETTER CXXXIV.

THE MINISTERS OF THE DUTCH CHURCH IN LONDON
TO THE LORD TREASURER.

Dated at LONDON, [about *April* 16, 1591.]

THE ministers and elders of the Dutch church in London
suppliantly set forth, that they have lately received letters
from Dantzic[1] from their brethren who fled from Flanders,
by which they understand that the church sojourning in those
parts is unable to hold their meetings and godly exercises
without difficulty and danger, by reason of some of the inhabitants who are hostile to religion, and who have not
hesitated from time to time to disturb the meetings of the
foreigners and accuse them of sedition. But since the aforesaid foreigners, who require the free and open exercise of
religion in their own language, are aware that a suitable
place either within or without the city will not readily be
granted them by the magistrates, unless the authority of
some person of influence, and especially of the king of Poland
who is the protector of that state, be exerted in their behalf;
they humbly request that her most serene majesty, in addition to her other benefits conferred upon that kingdom,
will, with her wonted benevolence towards all godly and oppressed strangers, graciously deign to procure from his majesty,
the king of Poland, some favour in this respect also to the
Flemish strangers. Whence they will not only be bound to
offer their constant prayers to God for the long life and
prosperous reign of her royal majesty, but also to shew their
gratitude by rendering to this kingdom and the united
provinces their faithful duty and service, in diligently giving
such information as they may obtain respecting the attempts
and designs of the Spaniards, or any other enemy.

Your most honoured lordship's devoted,

The ministers and elders of the Dutch church in London.

[1 See Loscheri Motus Relig.]

LETTER CXXXV.

QUEEN ELIZABETH TO THE KING OF POLAND.

Dated at GREENWICH, *April* 16, 159†.

ELIZABETH, by the grace of God, of England, France, and Ireland, queen, defender of the faith, &c. To the most serene prince and lord Sigismund, by the grace of God, king of Poland, grand duke of Lithuania, our very dear brother and cousin.

We do not doubt but that your serene highness, and all other princes of Christendom, well understand in what manner we have been induced to succour the states of Lower Germany, now almost entirely overwhelmed by the tyranny of the Spaniards; since we were previously unable by our frequent embassies and intercessions both with Spain and the governors of the Low Countries to obtain for them any equitable conditions of peace. And there are three motives which have especially induced us to do this: first, the cause of the more pure religion which they professed in common with ourselves; next, the ancient rights of commerce and alliance with a neighbouring nation; and lastly, the numerous and manifest tokens which shewed that the same enemies would turn their arms against us and other princes professing the same religion, that they might extend the bounds of a monarchy which they unjustly claim. It has thus come to pass that many inhabitants of those regions have been compelled to migrate into different provinces, and, among the rest, into some of the cities in Prussia, subject to your serene highness; in which many of them are now afraid, lest by reason of some difference in certain articles of religion, they may not be allowed the enjoyment of such immunity and free exercise of their religion as shall be suitable to their language and the former rites in which they have heretofore been instructed. And since we are informed that these Flemish, who are dwelling either in the city of Dantzic or in other sea-ports of Prussia, are not of that class of men who seek to overturn the lawful government and introduce anarchy, or who profess any heretical or impious error; we could not but, with our wonted affection towards the whole nation, commend them to your serene highness; entreating your serene highness, that, as it is plainly a royal act to deserve well of those who have been driven into exile from causes so honourable, your serene highness will exercise your authority in interceding with the magistrates of Dantzic, and others, if need be, that those parties who have migrated thither from Flanders may continue among them, without any difficulty or danger of this kind, the assemblies of the reformed religion, as they have been accustomed to do in their own country, and as they were for some time allowed in those cities; and that you will not suffer any injury to be done them, so long as they shall conduct themselves properly. For it cannot be either useful or honourable to your serene highness, nor to the cities themselves, to drive away strangers, and deny them the rights of hospitality, by reason of the evil disposition of certain individuals. Wherefore we earnestly request your serene highness to confer this benefit upon them for our sake, which we shall accept as a mark of the greatest kindness on the part of your serene highness, which we will repay in our turn to those who may be commended to us by your serene highness, whenever any opportunity shall present itself; and so we pray God for every happiness to your serene highness and your kingdom. From our court at Greenwich, April 16, 1591.

[ELIZABETH R.]

LETTER CXXXVI.

LORD STAFFORD TO WOLFGANG MEIER.

Dated at GREENWICH, *Aug.* 6, 1593.

MASTER Meier[1], I would willingly do what I can for you, and have done what I could; and the seniors of the

[1 Wolfgang Meier, of Basle, was born in 1577, and after a diligent pursuit of his studies at home, came to England, where he was received with great kindness, and in consideration of the merits of his

college have with great alacrity most willingly allowed you
fellow's commons. For your livery and books I have given
an order in the queen's name to the most learned and illustrious master doctor Nevill, to give you ten pounds sterling
a year, of which you will doubtless receive a portion every
quarter. As to a chamber, they will, if possible, provide one
for you, although it is a thing unheard of to allow to foreigners what is appropriated by the founders to our own countrymen. I therefore advise you, if they offer one, to receive it
most gratefully : if they are unable to provide one, you need
not much complain ; for this also is true, that if you have a
chamber, you must purchase a bed and other furniture, and
I think that it will not either be useful or necessary for you
to go to that expense for only one or two years; and it will
cost you less to hire a small lodging near the college, than
to spend your money upon those things which, when you wish
to return to your country, you will not be able to sell for
half their value. So farewell, and may God preserve you in
safety! Greenwich, Aug. 6, 1593. Your very loving,

E. STAFFORD.

LETTER CXXXVII.

THE STATE OF ZURICH TO QUEEN ELIZABETH.

Dated at ZURICH, *Aug.* 12, 1600.

To the most serene and mighty, the lady Elizabeth, of
England, France, Ireland, and the surrounding Islands, queen,
defender of the christian faith, our most benign mistress.
Greeting. The laudable and pious zeal, with which, most

grandfather Bucer, was supported in the university of Cambridge,
at the expense of queen Elizabeth. Having there distinguished himself in sound learning, he returned home through France, and even-
tually succeeded his father in his church at Basle. He became a
public lecturer, and afterwards ordinary professor of theology, A.D.
1611 ; and was sent to the synod of Dort in 1618. He died in 1653.
See Hoffman's Lexicon Universale.]

mighty queen, your most serene majesty has hitherto encouraged and favoured all foreigners studious of true godliness and of useful learning, and especially those who go over from our city to your majesty's famous universities, induces us, by reason of that most intimate connexion that exists between us in Christ, to present without hesitation this letter to your royal majesty, and afford you a fresh opportunity of manifesting the like regard. And we entreat your majesty to receive it with favour, as we confidently trust you will do.

Our beloved fellow-citizen Caspar Thoman[1], the bearer of this letter, has appeared before us, and, as he is inflamed with an ardent longing and desire of visiting your majesty's most flourishing universities of Oxford and Cambridge, and of pursuing his studies in some one of their colleges, if only he can obtain that favour from your kindness, he has humbly requested us to give him a recommendation to your most serene majesty, for the advancement of this laudable design, and which he himself doubts not will have very great weight with your majesty.

Having taken into consideration therefore his laudable petition, and having also ascertained that from the time when, first dedicated to the Muses, he began to attend our schools, he always reverently and dutifully conducted himself towards his teachers, lived well and soberly, and both at home and abroad, namely, at Geneva and Montpelier, diligently employed himself in the pursuit of useful learning and the liberal arts, by reason of which good qualities he was deservedly dear to all good men; we were unwilling to refuse compliance with his request.

Wherefore, O queen, we so entirely commend to your

[1 Caspar Thoman or Toman, one of the pastors or teachers of the schools at Zurich, (of which city his grandfather by the male line had borne the office of prætor,) having been recommended by the professors, teachers, and ministers of the church and school there, to live among, and receive an exhibition from, the Oxonians, A.D. 1599, did spend several years there, and occurs one of the first persons that was entered a student in the public library, when first opened for use. He was a learned man, and read a lecture in the university; but, his education having been mostly at Geneva, did with other strangers of the like breeding so corrupt the students with their Calvinistical doctrine, that it was many years before it could be rooted out. Wood's Athen. Oxon. Ed. 1691, Vol. I. 786.]

serene majesty this excellent young man, now journeying into England, that we cannot possibly commend him with greater care, zeal, and diligence; to the end that he may be enabled to pursue the praiseworthy course of his studies in your majesty's most illustrious universities, and (if it can be done with propriety) in one of their colleges, to the honour and advantage of our country, and of that church of which we are respectively members most intimately connected with each other.

Should our Thoman be graciously favoured by your most serene majesty with this indulgence, it will not only be most gratifying to us, but we will omit no opportunity of returning it.

We should have written more fully upon this subject, only that we should thereby have appeared to doubt the kindness and good-will of your most serene majesty towards us, of which you have hitherto afforded such illustrious manifestations.

It only remains therefore that we pray and shall continue to pray God, that upon your most serene majesty, the most honourable nursing mother of the orthodox church, and most pious defender of the true faith, he will bestow every good, defend you from every evil, and especially from the arts of antichrist, and continue to bless your godly counsels, to the advancement of the glory of his name, and the maintenance of the security of that church of which the most flourishing kingdom of England is as it were the true Sarepta of this our age.   Amen.

Written in our city, and confirmed by our usual seal. Aug. 12, in the year of the last long-suffering of God 1600.

The Provost and Council
of the State of Zurich.

LETTER CXXXVIII.

CASPAR THOMAN TO CASPAR WASER[1].

Dated at OXFORD, *Feb.* 1601.

PRAISE to God for evermore! In the year of the Saviour
1601. February. When I recall, my reverend patron, from
time to time, with a most agreeable remembrance of them,
the magnitude and extent of your favours, and acknowledge
my too limited ability to return your kindness; I easily perceive that for such great deservings on your part I am unable
to return any thanks, but that I do thank you in a very
small degree, while I am indebted to you in the greatest.
Since this is the case, I am under no slight apprehension lest
you should think that I have not only let slip the remembrance of these things, but that also every thought about
them has for ever escaped my memory; especially as so
many days and months have passed since you have received
any letter from me, by which I might at least testify my
grateful inclination, though without the power of shewing my
gratitude. But I hope that when you know the cause of my
long silence, you will hold me excused.

You must know, first of all, my reverend patron, that I
am in good health. I should be exceedingly glad to hear the
like account of yourself. I will shortly state the situation in
which my affairs are placed. When I arrived at Dieppe, I
inquired after a vessel, and having met with one, I put out
to sea, and reached Dover with a fair wind: from thence I
proceeded straight to London, and there delivered your letter
of recommendation to master Castoll[2], by whom I was courteously received. I then waited on the earl of Rutland[3], who
also read your letter, and promised me for your sake every

[1 Caspar Waser was a minister at Zurich, and professor of Hebrew
there in 1596. He married a daughter of Josiah Simler. In 1607 he
was made a canon of Zurich, and professor of Greek, and in 1611 was
appointed to the chair of theology. He died in 1625. Moreri.]

[2 John Castoll was the minister of the French reformed church in
London, "a discreet and learned man." Strype, Whitgift, II. 109.]

[3 Roger, fifth earl of Rutland, married the daughter of Sir Philip
Sidney. He died in 1612.]

assistance : he told me, however, that he did not think that
foreigners were admissible into our colleges, but he wrote to
the queen's physician to advance my business at court. On
the 7th of October I went to court, and meeting the physician as he was walking up and down before the palace, I
gave him the earl's letter. When he had read it, he told
me just as the earl had done, namely, that there were no
colleges in which foreigners could be admitted. When I
heard this, I lost all hope. I then waited upon Robert
Cecil[4], the principal secretary of England, (for every thing,
as you know, intended for the queen passes through his
hands,) with a petition that he would deign to present to the
queen's majesty the letter of the senate of Zurich. This he
promised to do, and I waited some days at court in the hope
of soon receiving an answer. But when this did not arrive,
I again called upon the secretary, an arrogant little fellow[5]
enough, to request him to intercede for me with the queen's
majesty, that I might the more speedily obtain an answer.
He at length told me to call again on the 15th of October,
when he would give me the queen's answer. When therefore I returned to him on the day appointed, he harshly
addressed me in this way, What do you want? I replied,
The convenience of pursuing my studies in some college by
the favour and liberality of the queen's majesty. He then
said, What claims of merit do you possess, that you presume to
make such a request? You do not know, he said, the constitution of this kingdom. The queen has read your letter;
she will not do any thing thereupon: this was his official
reply. Seeing myself disappointed of my hope, I took a
journey to London, to complain to master Castoll, who con-
doled with me on the harsh conduct of the secretary. Meanwhile master James Meadows[6], doctor in divinity, a man

[4 Sir Robert Cecil, the second son of lord Burghley, was lord
privy seal and secretary of state in 1596, and on the accession of
James I., he was created, 1603, Baron Cecil of Essingdon, in 1604
viscount Cranbourne, and in 1605 earl of Salisbury. He died in 1612
on his road from Bath; observing to Sir Walter Cope, "Ease and
pleasure quake to hear of death; but my life, full of cares and miseries,
desireth to be dissolved."]

[5 Sir Robert Cecil was somewhat deformed in his person.]

[6 James Meddows or Medowes D.D. in the university of Basle,
was a Cheshire man, born, and had formerly studied arts and divinity
at Heidelberg. He was in 1610 chaplain to Peregrine lord Willoughby,

illustrious both by nobility and learning, had heard that some persons from Zurich had lately arrived in London: he therefore sought us out with all diligence, and after having made a long search in all parts of the city, he found us out, and told us how exceedingly he was gratified by our coming. He gave Eppentianus and Werdmuller, who did not choose to remain in England any longer, money for their travelling expenses. I have not heard any thing from them since they returned to France. After their departure, doctor Meadows received me into his house, where I awaited the arrival of master Hungerford[1]. In the meantime, with the aid of doctor Meadows, I visited every thing in London that was worth seeing. Hungerford came to London on the 24th of October: as soon as I knew it, I waited upon him with doctor Meadows; but he no longer recognized me: as soon, however, as I told him who I was, he embraced me with both arms. I then related to him the reason of my coming, and what had occurred to me at court. When he was made acquainted with the facts, he was moved with compassion, and comforted me, and begged me not to be cast down, for that in conjunction with doctor Meadows he would provide for me in another way. On the 30th of October I was forced to borrow from master Castoll twelve French crowns for my necessary expenses. While master Hungerford and doctor Meadows were deliberating about me, I fell into a most severe illness, in which doctor Meadows and his wife bestowed much kindness upon me, just as though I had been their own son. Christophel Schweitzer also came to see me at great expense. When God had restored my former health, masters Hungerford, Meadows, and Castoll determined among themselves that I should go to Oxford; for that the letter from the church at Zurich would probably have some weight there. On the 13th of December I again had recourse to master Castoll in great distress, imploring his assistance in lending me four French crowns more. My

and afterwards to king James I. He translated from High Dutch into English a sermon preached before Frederick V. prince Elector Palatine and the princess Elizabeth, by Abraham Scultetus on Ps. 147. Lond. 1613. See Wood's Ath. Oxon. I. 809.]

[1 Anthony Hungerford, son of Anthony Hungerford of Downe Ampney in Gloucestershire, was a Roman Catholic till 1588. He took the degree of M.A. in 1594, was knighted in 1607, and died 1627. Wood, as above, p. 436.]

illness cost me more money than I wished, so that I have
now received from him sixteen crowns. I promised him,
and confirmed it with my own signature, that I would repay it
through you, my reverend patron, to Wolf at Frankfort. I
have also fully written to my mother about this matter, and
I earnestly request you, my reverend patron, to endeavour
that master Castoll may receive the money he lent me, at
the first opportunity; and that this may more easily be accomplished, I have been thinking about the exhibition of
Funckius, which is at the disposal of my cousin Henry
Thoman to bestow upon whomsoever he pleases. If I can
obtain that, master Castoll can be paid with less inconvenience.

On the 14th of December I left London for Oxford, being
supplied with letters of recommendation by masters Hungerford and Meadows. As soon as I arrived in Oxford, I delivered my private letter, and then the public one, to master
Thomas Thornton[2], who is now vice-chancellor; and who,
when he saw by whom the letter was written, expressed his
gratification at receiving a letter from the famous church of
Zurich, and moreover expressed his concern at not being able
to assemble the university at that time; for that they were
engaged in business of the greatest importance. I have been
awaiting the reply of the university, and am expecting it up
to this present day; for the vice-chancellor will give me an
answer this week. I cannot be admitted into any college, but
yet I think I shall obtain an honorary stipend[3]. But should I

[2 July 12, 1583. Thomas Thornton, vice-chancellor of this university, canon of Christ Church, Worcester and Hereford, of which last
place he was also chaunter, and about this time master of Ledbury
Hospital in Herefordshire, was actually created D.D. He died Apr. 15,
1629, aged 88, and was buried in the parish church of Ledbury, where
it is stated on his monument that he was born at Harrow on the Hill
in Middlesex, that he was *purioris Latini sermonis author primarius,*
that he was a benefactor to the poor people of Ledbury hospital, that
he was a common refuge for young poor scholars of great hopes and
parts, and tutor to sir Philip Sidney when he was at Christ Church.
To which Wood adds, that he was also tutor to the learned William
Camden, Clarencieux King of arms. See Wood's Athen. Ox. I. 754.]

[3 John Castoll writes to Waser, Feb. 11, 1600. "Since I wrote the
above letter to you, doctor Gentile, the professor of Civil Law at
Oxford, has informed me that the university has decreed, at a public
meeting, to master Thoman a yearly stipend of twenty pounds."]

not receive any liberal assistance from the university, I shall return to London; for there is a certain nobleman there who is very anxious for me to instruct his sons. I certainly experience the greatest kindness here from Dr Rainolds, the Phœnix of England. I pray you, if you think fit, to write to the following individuals, and thank them for their favours to me; masters Hungerford, Meadows, Castoll, Thomas Thornton, Rainolds, who is shortly about to publish his most learned works, and master Christophel Schweitzer.

It now remains for me to entreat that your dignity will at all times regard me with paternal love. I will take care that your dignity shall ever find me most grateful. Written in haste, at Oxford.

Your dignity's most devoted,

CASPAR THOMAN.

LETTER CXXXIX.

JOHN JOHNSTON[1] TO CASPAR WASER.

Dated at St Andrew's in SCOTLAND, *Aug.* 1, 1601.

GREETING. Your letter, my very learned and dear friend Waser, written on the 20th of last March, I received on the 20th of July; and I am the more obliged to you for it, as I had not sent you a letter at the fair preceding. The reason of this was a most severe attack of splenitis, owing to which my immediate death was expected by every one. And the Lord had given me this disposition, that I was willing to depart. But my most merciful God has decreed it otherwise, and after this very severe winter has afforded me a farther breathing time; but I cannot tell how long it may last. May the Lord grant that I may employ the remainder of this miserable life to the glory of his name!

Our country, by the divine blessing, is in the enjoyment

[1 John Johnston was a native of Aberdeenshire: he studied for some years at the most celebrated universities on the continent, where he gained the friendship of the chief learned men. After some residence in England he returned to his native country, well reputed as a scholar, a poet, and a divine. Melville never ceased till he procured him to be associated in the work of theological instruction in the university of St Andrew's, where he was appointed professor of divinity in 1593. He died in October, 1611.]

of perfect tranquillity. After a most severe winter, such as was never known before, there succeeded a milder summer, whence there has arisen a better hope for the autumn, and a reduction in the price of wheat. Her most serene majesty brought forth her little son Charles[2] on the 19th of last November. Prince Henry[3], who is flourishing, by God's blessing, both in mind and body, is educated with the greatest care at Stirling. His most serene majesty is now sojourning at Falkland in this neighbourhood. On the 12th of May last in the general assembly the solemn covenant[4] with God was renewed by the most serene king in person, and the congregation of the whole church, respecting the advancement of the pure worship of God, the extirpation of popery, the rendering obedience agreeably to the law of God according to the calling of each individual, that piety and justice may flourish together. And certainly from that time the law has been strictly enforced against offenders. A certain notorious papist, son of the laird of Bondson[5] near Montrose, was

[2 Prince Charles, afterwards king Charles I. was born at Dunfermline, Nov. 19, 1600.]

[3 Henry, the eldest son of James I. was at this time about six years old. He was a youth of excellent promise, and died Nov. 6, 1613, to the universal grief of the English nation.]

[4 The general assembly met at Burntisland in May 1601. The conduct of James I. on this occasion is thus noticed by the writers of the time: "The king, as I heard, made a comfortable confession of his sins and his faith, and promised most weightily and solemnly to abhor all papistry, idolatry, and superstition, and to live and die in the true religion wherein he was brought up, and which was preached and professed within his realm of Scotland presently; also to execute justice and to do all duties of a godly and a christian king, better than ever before." Autobiography and Diary of Mr James Melville, Wodrow Society's edit. p. 494. See also M[c] Crie's Life of A. Melville, Vol. II. p. 173, 4.]

[5 This name is incorrectly stated in the MS. It should have been written Bonytoun, of whom the following account is extracted from Calderwood's MS. Church History in the British Museum: "In the beginning of March [1601] mass was said in Edinburgh, in Andrew Naper's house, in Helene Sempill's chamber, at sundry times, by Mr Alexander Mackquhirrie. A little before this time, the young laird of Bonytoun and laird of Latoun, with their complices, brake up the old laird of Bonytoun's house in Angus, and took away all the evidences and other plenishing belonging to old Bonytoun, father to the said Bonytoun the younger; and within five or six days after resorted openly to Edinburgh, and were at the mass aforesaid. Bonytoun the

executed in the month of May for a most atrocious crime
committed against his parents. Blessed be God, and may he
give us grace both to will and to do well! John Erskine[1]
together with Edward Bruce of Kinloss, having discharged
a most honourable embassy to the English, shortly after
the decease of the earl of Essex[2] so much lamented by
all good men, and calamitous[3] to the whole island, on his
return appeared to renounce all cheerfulness. The rivalry of
secretary Robert Cecil[4] is said to have injured Essex much

younger and Latoun were apprehended, put in ward, presented to an
inquest, and accused criminally for the said theft allaverlie [only];
were convicted thereof, and consequently of treason, and the doom
given out upon them to be executed.—Upon Monday the 27th of April
the laird of Bonytoun was beheaded at the cross of Edinburgh, betwixt
six and seven in the morning, by a commission from the king directed
to the bailiffs of Edinburgh, timeously in the morning; for howbeit
great intercession was made by Huntley, Errol, Hume, and others,
yet the ministers were instant with the king to have a proof of his
sincerity. He died an obstinate papist, ever looking for pardon till the
last gasp. He pretended he suffered for the catholic Roman religion,
but it was no point of his dittay. Only the stealing of his father's evidences and writs was laid to his charge."

There is in the same MS. a monitory letter of John Davidson to
the assembly, in which, among other things, it is stated: " But Bonytoun is executed! A famous thief in the highest degree, for his vile
theft is punished! What is that to the cause of religion, whereof was
no question, as worthily might have been? Is there no papist, idolater,
nor wilful favourer and maintainer of papists in Scotland but Bonytoun? Speer [inquire] and see."]

[1 As soon as James heard of Essex's ill success, he appointed the
earl of Mar, and Bruce, abbot of Kinloss, to repair as his ambassadors
to the court of England. The former of these was the person by
whose means Essex had carried on his correspondence with the king.
They were commanded to solicit in the warmest manner for the earl's
life, but he had suffered before their arrival. Elizabeth, though no stranger
to the king's correspondence with Essex, was not willing it should be
known to the public; and in order to sooth James, and preserve the
union between the two courts, increased his subsidy. Robertson,
Scotland, III. 166. A somewhat different statement is given by Lingard, V. 593. See also Birch's Memoirs, II. 510.]

[2 The earl of Essex was beheaded in the Tower, Feb. 25, 1601.]

[3 Lingard says of the ambassadors, that "they found the adherents
of Essex plunged in the deepest despair, the people in a state of discontent, and Cecil possessing in reality the exercise of the sovereign
power."]

[4 The behaviour of sir Robert Cecil on Essex's trial is related

more than the crimes laid to his charge. Affairs are now quiet, but it is to be feared lest the mass of discontent at the death of Essex and other noblemen should break out into open violence. The lord Lewis Stuart[5], of royal blood, duke of Leven, embarked on the tenth of July on his way to France as ambassador with a noble and splendid retinue, to confirm the ancient and hitherto unviolated alliance between the two nations; and to congratulate the king of the French upon his kingdom being confirmed to him, upon his victories, and his late marriage. These are the ostensible grounds; the secret ones are not made known. Masters Melvin[6], Murray, Moniepennie[7], and your other friends are all well by God's blessing, and lovingly salute yourself and Howe. I most affectionately and dutifully salute all the pastors and professors, your most learned colleagues, whom I pray you to call upon individually, together with master Stuckius[8], my friend Simler, and Erne. Most devoted as I am to you and your honourable city, I pray for you every happiness from God. I request you dutifully to salute for me by letter master Benedict Erlach the father, and Wolfgang his son, my pupil, together with the whole family. Illness has prevented my writing. Continue to refresh us all by writing on the state of your affairs and those of the Genevese and the neighbouring churches. Farewell, all of you, most happily. St Andrew's in Scotland, Aug. 1, 1601.

Yours wholly,

JOHN JOHNSTON.

in Camden, Eliz. 617. The French ambassador, Boissise, describes in a letter of March 26, 1601, how Essex and Cecil contended for the first place in the favour of Elizabeth. Raumer, 16th cent. II. 174. An account of the two factions is given in Robertson, Hist. Scotland, III. 161.]

[5 In July 1601, Lodowick, duke of *Lennox*, was sent in an ambassage to France rather for confirming the old amity and friendship than for any business else. Spotswood, Hist. of church of Scotland, p. 465.]

[6 Andrew Melville is doubtless here intended.]

[7 David Moniepennie was dean of Faculty at St Andrew's, and one of the high commission named in 1610.]

[8 John William Stuckius was the author of a treatise on the festivals of the ancients, and their sacrifices. He also wrote a commentary upon Arrian. See Melchior Adam.]

LETTER CXL.

JOHN JOHNSTON TO CASPAR WASER.

Dated at ST ANDREW'S, in Scotland, *Feb.* 8, 1602.

GREETING. At the end of last July, most excellent Waser, I prepared a letter to you, which I thought I had sent in time to be forwarded to Frankfort by the September fair; but our friend Hart has since informed me that it was not sent thither in time, owing to the loitering of the bearers. I am, nevertheless, surprised that your usual practice of so lovingly writing to me and your old friends in this neighbourhood, and which has always given the greatest pleasure to us all, was interrupted at the late fair. We therefore all of us entreat you constantly to continue to refresh us with the most agreeable gales breathing from your snowy Alps as far as ourselves. Even the shortest letter from you will delight us exceedingly. As to myself, you may be assured that as long as I have life and health, I will send a letter to you every fair. At present, however, want of time will excuse a brevity which is also imposed upon me by my state of health, which has for some days been rather unfavourable, in consequence of the return of that disease of the spleen which had almost killed me last year, and which, as far as I can see, my brother, will by degrees carry me off, or rather lead me away; for I shall most willingly and readily follow the guidance of my most merciful God, who very lately, on the 20th of December, has sent before me your acquaintance, Thomas Cargill, the schoolmaster of Aberdeen, and that too at a time when he was in excellent health. And it will not perhaps be long before I follow him. Meanwhile the Lord renews my hope of a better life, and has also renewed my hope of a longer life in this world, by having given me another little son, Edward, on the 15th of January. And about the same time, namely, on the 18th of January, a third son, who is not yet named, was born to our most serene king. The princes Henry and Charles, with the princess Elizabeth, are by God's blessing alive and well.

We are, by God's blessing, in the enjoyment of peace

both in church and state. But the plague is threatening us very sadly. For it has begun to shew itself at Edinburgh, and Glasgow, and Crail, a town about six miles from hence. England is at this time very much refreshed by the defeat of the whole Spanish army[1] in Ireland, by the mercy of God, and the valour of lord Mountjoy. The Spanish had formed a conspiracy in Ireland with the earl of Tyrone, an Irish rebel, and had been meditating to bring the war into England from the opposite coast. But the Lord dissipated these designs. Certain intelligence of this has, within these few days, been sent to our most serene king, and thanksgiving was publicly made in the churches.

With respect to French, and Spanish, and Flemish news, you are better informed than we are. The blockade of Ostend is continued, as it were by miracle, through the whole of this winter, nor have the enemy much hope of reducing it; for the English chiefly, together with some Scots and French, under colonel sir Francis Vere[2], a most valiant knight, are holding it for the Flemish. All your friends here, to whom I communicate your letters, entreat you, as I also do, to continue to give us information as to your own affairs, and those of the Genevese. They bear you in their remembrance, and most affectionately salute you, namely, the Melvins, Moniepennie, Blake, Murray, and the rest.

I beg my dutiful and affectionate respects to masters Stuckius, Zuingle, Lavater, and your worthy colleagues, especially to my dear friends, masters Simler and Erne, to whom with yourself, your wife, and her father, I wish everlasting happiness.

St Andrew's, in Scotland, Feb. 8, 1602.

Yours wholly,

JOHN JOHNSTON.

[1 This army consisted of four thousand men, under the command of Don Juan D'Aguilar. They landed at Kinsale, Sept. 21, and were joined by the earl of Tyrone and others some days after. The united forces were defeated by lord Mountjoy, on the 21st of December, with the loss of twelve hundred men. Camden, 643; Lingard, 598.]

[2 An account of this siege is given by Camden, Eliz. 633, &c.]

LETTER CXLI.

***

THOMAS SAVILE[1] AND HENRY HAWKINS TO H. WOLFIUS.

[Without date or place.]

MOST excellent and much esteemed sir, and my very dear friend, it is very annoying to me, that my arrangements are so formed that a day or two is not left me for the inspection of your own and your father's labours: but what the pressure of time has deprived us of to our very great discomfort, your kindness, I hope, will sometime or other altogether replace and restore; and will at least favour us with the index of your father's lucubrations, by which we may be able in some measure to alleviate our extreme regret. That we may return the favour, we will diligently take care that the canon of Ptolemy shall be forwarded to you, and whatever else may be in our power. The book that you inquire after was published at Altorf with this title, " Gemini[2] εἰσαγωγὴ εἰς τὰ φαινόμενα." Farewell, most illustrious sir, and " go on, my friend, with prosperous foot, where virtue leads the way."

Your most devoted,

THOMAS SAVILE, ⎫ English
HENRY HAWKINS,⎭ gentlemen.

[1 Thomas Savile was a younger brother of sir Henry Savile. He was elected fellow of Merton, in the register of which college it is said of him : Fuit sidus lucidissimum, qui apud suos et exteros literarum et virtutis fama ac morum urbanitate percelebris, &c. Athén. Oxon.]

[2 The title of this work is Γεμίνου εἰσαγωγὴ εἰς τὰ φαινόμενα. Gemini probatissimi philosophi ac mathematici Elementa Astronomiæ, Græce ac Latine, interprete Edone Hilderico D. Altorfii, 1590. Geminus lived in the time of Sylla and Cicero.]

Lubecio nostro. Clusio. optimo Jordano. meoqz Andreæ.
et Benevenēio omnium ministerorum Doctoratissimo, et omnium doctori
ministratissimo (ut vero ni fallor de Scaevola et (Crasso) ita
mea officia defuncta utillius qui eos omnes amat, et cupit eis
singulis Gratificari et inservire/. Feron vale mi Huberte
Jn Aula Regia. 10° Octobres 1577.

Tui Amantissimus.
Philippus Sidneius.

F. Bedford

S. D. D. Occupationibus et facultatum meis, et quandam
corporis impotentia (vt interim taceam rei familiaris inopiam)
ne vna cum clariss: viris d. Buitlero, suisqz Richardo, iter istuc
mr facerem. Quam ego autem vobis iam absum, penuris æqui-
dem non dicam. Valde in cupio propriis vestrum contemplari vultibz.

Mihi Tuo Conrado

S. D: Vt tuas litteras a me rogatis Vir clariss: quid id rebar Fra-
glias dabro, pancis id cabo, confungiis vt er Philippi regem lißeraium
er virginã anglit ia est imis, conditionem indicat esse Reisgreplir2
angliam Sistami autmoris penuis constabat

Poli M.

APPENDIX.

I. HIEROME ZANCHIUS[1] TO QUEEN ELIZABETH.

Dated at HEIDELBERG, *Sept.* 10, 1571.

WE have been informed, most serene and most christian queen, to our exceeding grief, that the flame of discord respecting certain vestments, which we thought had been extinguished long since, has been stirred up afresh as though from hell, and rekindled, to the incredible offence of all godly persons, in your majesty's kingdom. And the occasion of this flame has originated from hence; forasmuch as your most serene majesty, at the persuasion of some individuals, excellent in other respects, and actuated by a zeal (though certainly not according to knowledge) for preserving uniformity in religion, has now more than ever formed the resolution, and decreed, willed, and commanded that all bishops and ministers of churches should be attired, during the performance of divine service, in the white linen garments that the mass-priests wear in the popish religion. And there is great reason to fear lest this fire be kindled, and send forth its flames far and wide; and that all the churches of that most flourishing and powerful kingdom be consumed, to the perpetual dishonour of your most serene majesty: for that the greater number of them are bishops, men distinguished both for learning and piety, who choose rather to give up their office and stations than to admit such vestments against their conscience, as being relics, or at least symbols, of idolatry and popish superstition, and to defile themselves therewith, and offend the weaker brethren by their example. But what else were this, than for the sake of those vestments to destroy the whole body of the church? For that doubtless is Satan's great object, by sowing the seeds of dissension among the bishops. This also was his aim in the early ages of the church, when he stirred up between the eastern and western churches the dispute respecting Easter[2], and other

[1 The original Latin of this letter, from which the present translation is made, is printed in the Epistolæ Zanchii, Lib. I. p. 423, Hanoviæ, 1609. A translation of it will also be found in *A Fresh Suit against Human Ceremonies*, 1633.]

[2 The Asiatic bishops commemorated Christ's death on the 14th of March, on whatever day of the week it happened, as being the day on which the Jews kept their passover. Hence it arose, for the most part, that the festival of Easter was held on other days of the week

ceremonies of the like kind. Wherefore it was not without reason that Irenæus, bishop of Lyons, in a letter[1] sent from France to Rome, sharply rebuked pope Victor, who, through a strange kind of zeal, but certainly not according to knowledge, desired to excommunicate all the Asiatic churches, because they would not celebrate Easter at the same time as they did at Rome. For this was nothing else than, through an unseasonable desire of retaining the same ceremonies in every church, to divide and tear in pieces the unity of the churches. As soon therefore as I heard that so great a destruction was impending over the church of Christ in that kingdom, I forthwith, from the duty which I owe as well to the church of Christ as to your serene majesty, and in fine to your whole realm, determined to write to you, and to endeavour to the best of my power to find out a remedy for so great an evil; some persons who fear Christ, and are friendly to your most serene majesty, exhorting me to undertake this office. But I had scarcely begun to turn it over in my mind, when, lo! our most illustrious prince commanded me to put it into execution; by which command indeed he has not only added spurs to me who was already going on of my own accord, but has also imposed upon me the necessity of writing. Your most serene majesty, therefore, will be the less surprised at this my boldness, since I am writing, not so much of my own inclination, and by the advice of my friends, as at the command of my most illustrious sovereign and your most serene majesty's great friend. But in the first place I have thought it most expedient for me to advise your majesty of what is your duty under existing circumstances; and then humbly to pray you, through Jesus Christ our Lord, resolutely to perform it. And I entreat your most serene majesty to take in good part this my writing: for it proceeds from christian love towards the church, and from the singular respect which I so abundantly entertain towards your most serene majesty. The Lord knoweth all things. And now to the subject.

than the first. For an account of the controversy, which began in the time of Anicetus, bishop of Rome, in the reign of Antoninus Pius, and was revived in the episcopate of Victor, towards the end of the second century, see Du Pin, I. 60. Mosheim, Cent. II. ii. ch. IX.]

[1 The substance of that letter is in Eusebius, Hist. Eccl. v. ch. 24.]

When the apostle, writing to Timothy[2], orders prayers to be made for kings, and for all that are in authority; and declares that the end of their being placed in authority is, that we may lead a quiet life in all, that is, in perfect, god-liness and honesty; he teaches with sufficient clearness what is the duty of godly kings and princes: namely, that they should take care and provide above all, that true religion and the true worship of God, if it has been banished, should be restored; and when restored, preserved in all its integrity; all things which in any wise savour of impiety being driven away: in the next place, that men should live honestly and holily, all kind of impurity and licentiousness being put to flight: lastly, that a public peace and holy friendship be cultivated among the people, all occasions of discord being removed as far as possible. That these are the three prin-cipal parts of the kingly office, and of that of every godly magistrate, is not only, as we have seen, openly taught by the apostle, but all men of learning, and who entertain proper notions of the duty of a magistrate, with one consent and one mouth confirm the same. And this being the case, I do not see how your most serene majesty can, with a good conscience, propose to the consciences of godly bishops the resumption of the habits in question, and other things of that kind which still savour of popish superstition, and which have once been banished from the churches; and so propose them, as by your command to compel the adoption of them. For first of all, this is repugnant to the chief and principal part of the kingly office. For if the magistrate is especially to provide that the worship of God may be maintained in all its integrity; and if on this account all things are to be removed, which can any wise violate this worship either of their own nature or incidentally; and therefore all things are, as far as possible, to be restored according to the rule of God's word, and the ancient and apostolic, and consequently purer and more simple, form of religion; in fine, if, as the apostle enjoins, we are to abstain, not only from all evil, but from all appearance of evil; how, I pray you, most serene and godly queen, can you introduce, by your royal mandate, into the church of God those things which are repugnant to the purity of apostolic worship; which savour of popish superstition; which neither

[2 See 1 Tim. ii. 2.]

tend to the edification of the godly, nor to order, or ornament,
except such as is meretricious; and which, lastly, can bring
no advantage to the church, but on the contrary may occasion
it much mischief? It is certain that by this law respecting
the habits all godly persons will be offended; the ungodly
will laugh in their sleeve, and hence hope for further con-
cessions; while the middle sort, that is, those who have but
lately turned from impiety to godliness, but are not yet
sufficiently established, will be in danger; and, if we may
speak from human judgment, will rather look back upon that
ancient superstition to which we are inclined by nature, than
fix their eyes firm and stedfast upon true religion: so that
this decree will not in the least advance godliness, while it
may probably tend very much to the advancement of ungodliness. For though these habits are not of themselves,
that is, of their own nature, evil or unclean, yet they cannot
be altogether free from impurity by reason of their having
been previously and so recently abused. It certainly cannot be denied, but that they may at least afford occasion to
much mischief and to the grossest superstitions. But we
are to avoid even the occasions of evil. To what end then
will you obtrude those things upon the church, from which
no benefit, but very great harm, must be expected? for this
is to tempt God.

Your most serene majesty should remember that it is not
written without a cause, that "whoever touches pitch shall
be defiled by it." Nor did the apostle command us without
reason to purge away the old leaven, because "a little leaven
leaveneth the whole lump." Nor were the Jews unadvisedly
rebuked by Hosea for having transplanted the shoots of
superstition from Israel into their garden, that is, into the
true church. It is most evident, most godly queen, that we
ought to have no business whatever with the papists in
matters of religion, except in such things as they have in
common with the apostles. Wherefore, I pray you, are
certain kings, although godly in other respects, rebuked in
scripture, for not having taken away the high places in
which Jehovah was wont to be worshipped before the building of the temple by their pious forefathers? Assuredly
because, after the building and appointment of the temple,
God would no longer permit any vestiges to remain of any

other place of worship. So also upon the manifestation of Christ's kingdom the Aaronic ceremonies and garments ought no longer to have any place. Wherefore the apostles very properly took care that they should be done away with after the ascension of Christ, so that not even any relics should remain. But if they piously removed them, the papists must impiously have restored them. And who is there so ignorant as not to know which it is best to follow, the godly simplicity of the apostles, or the ungodly pomp of the papists?

Your most gracious majesty may believe me, that the restoration of such popish vestments will be a far greater evil than may appear at the first glance, even to those who are most sharp-sighted. For I seem to see and hear the monks calling out from their pulpits, and confirming their people in this ungodly religion by your majesty's example, and saying, "What? why, the queen of England herself, most learned and prudent as she is, is beginning by degrees to return to the religion of the holy Roman church; for the most holy and consecrated vestments of the clergy are now resumed. It is to be hoped that she will also at length restore to their former position all the other doctrines, rites, and sacraments of the holy Roman church." This and similar language, most prudent queen, will the monks and Jesuits doubtless make use of from their pulpits; for they will let slip no occasion of establishing their superstitions. What else is it then, to re-introduce at this time these filthy vestments, and the other rubbish of the popish church into the church of Christ, than to afford an opportunity to the papists, and that a most excellent one, of confirming themselves and their people in their superstitions, and indeed to lend them, as it were, assistance towards this very object? But let us hear the prophet[1], who said to Jehoshaphat king of Judah, when he joined affinity with Ahab, "Shouldest thou help the ungodly, and love them that hate the Lord? therefore is wrath upon thee from before the Lord." And what else would this thing be, than to turn away the weak from the love of pure religion, and tacitly to recommend them to look back upon and return into Egypt? For a falling back unto ungodliness is easy to weak men, inasmuch as we are all of us by our very nature inclined to superstitions. So far therefore ought we to

[1 Jehu. See 2 Chron. xix. 2.]

be from affording any occasions of relapsing into ungodliness, that they should be altogether removed. What, I pray you, did God mean, when he forbade men " to plough with an ox and an ass together;" and provided that the same field should not be sown with divers seeds; and that men should not wear a garment of woollen and linen together[1]? It is odious and abominable to God, that the same field of the Lord should be tilled by ungodly and godly bishops at the same time; that in the same church the doctrine of popery be taught at the same time with the doctrine of the gospel; that, lastly, sacraments, ceremonies and rites, made up of apostolic and popish ones, be brought into use; and the church be clothed with them, as it were with a garment made of woollen and linen together. For what agreement hath light with darkness? Such a mingling together, that is, one so abominable and wicked, should also be detested by ourselves. And therefore the things which are not of God, but of those who have defiled the worship of God, are to be altogether cast off: and this is what the Lord himself commanded to be done, when he ordered that all the property of those persons who should persuade the people to go after strange gods, should be entirely destroyed, and their raiment and all their goods burned with fire, and that in the middle of the market-place; namely, to shew his abomination of such seducers, and that they might be accursed of the Lord[2]. And who does not know that these raiments are also included among the goods of the Roman deceiver? "And there shall cleave (he saith) nought of the cursed thing to thine hand, that the Lord may turn from the fierceness of his anger, and multiply thee, as he hath sworn unto thy fathers." What else then is the introducing of these garments, the ornaments of antichrist, into the church of Christ, but provoking the Lord to anger, and kindling his wrath against us? We may be well assured that no true friend of Christ will ever entertain the ornaments of antichrist in his own house, much less bear them in the church of Christ. For who would endure his enemy's coat of arms in his house, and especially in the most honourable place? And if God will have any thing to be destroyed and abolished, who are we, that we dare to set it up afresh?

[1 These prohibitions are recorded in Deut. xxii. 9—11.]
[2 See Deut. xiii. 12, &c.]

But God, after the death of Christ, would have all the Aaronic and Levitical vestments abolished: and in our time he has every where declared with sufficient clearness, that he would have all the ungodly and vain popish ceremonies, pomps, impostures, and trickeries chased away by the splendour of the gospel; inasmuch as they are of no avail towards the kindling of godliness, but tend very much to the extinguishing of it.

Nor indeed am I able to perceive what is the ultimate object proposed by these vestments, unless it be in fact (to come now to another head) to disgrace and dishonour the beautiful face, yea, the whole body of the church of England reformed according to the gospel: just as if a modest and honourable daughter of some king were to be clothed in the raiment wherewith some notorious and well-known harlot was wont to be attired, and, thus arrayed, compelled to go forth in public. But who would approve of this, or think such a thing to be endured? Wherefore, even if for no other reason, at least on this account, vestments of this kind ought not to be obtruded upon the church of Christ; because the Roman harlot has abused them, though they be not evil in their own nature, and still continues to abuse them to evil, and to conceal her harlotries, or rather to allure men to commit fornication. For all these pomps and popish ceremonies are nothing else but meretricious adornments, contrived for the purpose of alluring men to spiritual fornication. Is it not then a shameful thing to have them in the church of Christ? If the brasen serpent which had been ordained by God, and that too for the healing of the Israelites, was taken away by the godly king Hezekiah, because the Israelites abused it contrary to the word of God; and if Hezekiah was greatly commended for this act, namely, for having reduced that serpent to ashes, and commanding them to be cast into running water, that there might remain no vestige of it whatever; how much rather are these impure garments, which the apostles never used, but which are adopted by the Roman harlot in her idolatrous worship, and for the seduction of mankind, to be banished from the church of God! Nor indeed is it decent, that things which have been long made use of to the dishonour of God, even if they be in themselves indifferent, should be retained in the church to the peril even of the salvation of godly persons. Much less then should this kind of vestment, which is nothing else than an invention of man, or rather of Satan, devised for the seduction of the simple.

There is none of us who is ignorant of the commendation deserved by those states which provide by law against their citizens wearing strange apparel, and will not introduce them into the commonwealth, because they are the corrupters of good and pure morals, and therefore of the commonwealths themselves. How then can the counsel which is given to your majesty ever be commended; namely, that vestments unknown to the christian commonwealth in the time of the apostles and their immediate successors should be introduced into the church of Christ? For if a strange mode of apparel be not tolerated in well constituted states, how much less are idolatrous and gentile garments to be endured in the church, where God is to be worshipped in spirit and in truth, and where he requires but few ceremonies, and those of the most simple character? If too God has provided by law that the woman should not wear the garments of the man, nor, conversely, the man wear those of the woman, because both of these things are in themselves shameful and unseemly, and contrary to nature; why then must godly bishops and servants of Christ be attired, or rather degraded and deformed, in the habits of the ungodly mass-priests and bond-slaves of antichrist? Why should we not rather, as we are of a different religion, be distinguished from them also by external signs, such as the vestments are, at least in the performance of those duties which appertain to the worship of God? God certainly willed this, and required it of his people, that they should be distinguished from the profane gentiles even by a different kind of dress; and thus he declared by this public sign, that he would not let them have any thing in common with the gentiles. And why should not we also do the same? Are we not the people of God? Does not the justice of the same precept still remain? And if what is honest is so called from honour, what honour, I ask, would it be to the church of Christ to have their bishops in the ministry of the gospel and sacraments attired and masked in the disguise of popery, so as to be rather objects of ridicule to all, than of veneration to the people? And in what kind of honour will your most serene majesty be held by true churches and true believers, when you allow such fooleries to be re-introduced into your church? It is not therefore becoming, that godly bishops should be compelled to take up such masks. Nor indeed is the thing itself either worthy of honour and commendation, nor does it deserve the name of virtue. For suppose your most serene majesty were to issue a decree, that every Englishman should lay aside his ancient dress, most grave and decent as it is, and put on the Turkish robe, or array himself in a military dress, as they call it: who, I ask, would commend such a decree as a proper one? Much less then is it to be commended, that godly bishops be required, having laid aside or at least altered that ancient and becoming attire, which was used even by the apostles, namely, a common dress, but decent and becoming, to put on the ridiculous and execrable garments of the ungodly mass-priests.

And as it respects the third branch of the kingly office, nothing can be better devised, than a plan of this kind, to disturb the public peace. For all novelties, in religion especially, either, if evil, disturb the peace of themselves; or, if harmless, afford accidental occasion for men to contend with each other, the evil namely with the good. But as in things which are good in themselves (as, for instance, in the reformation of the churches according to the will of God) the disturbing of an ungodly peace, that is, of the peace of the world, is to be disregarded, (for Christ came not by his preaching to preserve such a peace, but rather to destroy it, and send a sword;) so assuredly, to disturb the peace of the churches, and to set the good and bad, or even the good only, at variance with each other, by insisting upon things indifferent, is a thing so evidently unjust, as to admit of no defence: wherefore on this ground it was that Irenæus rebuked Victor the Roman bishop, as has been above stated. For in such cases the churches must of necessity be split into factions, than which what can be more injurious? The instances which every where occur in ecclesiastical histories confirm openly and clearly enough what I say. How many and how great disturbances, I pray, were stirred up in the primitive church between those who, in addition to the gospel, urged also the observance even of circumcision and of the law, and those

who very properly rejected them? And what mischiefs
would this dispute have farther occasioned to the church of
Christ, unless the apostles had met the evil in time, by
assembling the synod at Jerusalem, and taking due cognizance
and consideration of the matter by the plain testimony of
the scriptures and by valid reasons? If your most serene
majesty, as it is your duty, desires both to be and to appear
apostolic, you must imitate the apostles in this matter: neither must you impose this yoke upon the necks of the disciples of Christ yourself, nor allow it to be imposed on them
by others. And if you perceive that the bishops disagree
among themselves upon this subject, you should call a synod,
and take care that the controversy be determined and judged
of by the scriptures; and then at length, whatever may have
been proved upon clear evidence and solid grounds, you
should set it forth for the observance of all parties, and order
it to be observed by act of parliament, and so remove all
contention from the church. For it is your most serene
majesty's especial duty to provide, that no change or innovation shall be made in religion, except according to the word
of God. By these means the true peace and concord and
unity of the churches will be preserved. But should the
contrary take place, what else will be the result than the
destruction of unity, and the disturbance of christian peace?

Nor do I think that I ought to pass over in silence, that
by this novelty not only will the public peace be disturbed in
that kingdom, but also elsewhere out of the kingdom will an
occasion be afforded to many persons of stirring up new contentions in the churches; and that not without great injury
to godliness, and hinderance of the course of the gospel. For
no one is ignorant, that almost all the churches which have
deserted the Roman pontiff for the sake of the gospel, not
only do not adopt such vestments, but even regard them with
abomination. Not however but that there are others, though
very few in comparison with the former, who still retain those
vestments that were made use of in popery, just as they
obstinately retain some other things; and that for this
reason, because at the first the reformers of those churches,
great men in other respects, and most faithful servants of
God, did not dare (nor indeed did they judge it expedient)
entirely to take away every thing that was papistical. But,

as is always the case, every one is in love with his own plans.
And I call a man's own, not so much what each has devised
of himself, as also what every one makes choice of, receives,
retains, adopts for himself, when it has been devised by others.
But when the examples of others are brought forward, they
become more and more confirmed in those things; and not
only confirmed, but also use all their endeavours, and by
their speeches and writings, yea, their hands and feet, they
leave no stone unturned so that they may bring every one
else into their way of thinking.   We easily perceive then
what will be the consequence, if your most serene majesty
should adopt that counsel, which is recommended to you by
I know not whom, about the adoption of the vestments and
other things pertaining to popery.   For some evil disposed
persons, stirred up by your majesty's example, will write and
disperse throughout all Germany little treatises upon these
things which they call indifferent; namely, that it is allowable to introduce them; yea, and that they must of necessity
be admitted, to the end that the papists may be less estranged
from us, and that we may thus come more nearly to an
agreement with each other.   As if the papists, even though
we were to allow all these things for the sake of peace, would
ever alter any doctrine, and banish from their churches, or
by any other means lay aside their false and impious dogmas,
their open and abominable superstitions and mad idolatries.
Then there will not be wanting those who will reply to such
books, should they be dispersed : so that from this flame,
kindled in England, will arise also a new conflagration in
Germany and France, on which the papists will sprinkle cold
water.   An excellent benefit in truth!   Who then does not
now perceive that this design has no other tendency than
the general unsettling of the churches ?   On the whole, that
golden saying of some learned man is most true and certain
and confirmed by long experience, "that matters of indifference, that is, the question respecting matters of indifference,
is the golden apple of discord."

And thus have I said enough with respect to the disturbance of the public peace.   But what shall I say of the consciences of individual believers ?   The dispute itself teaches
us, that they are disturbed beyond measure by the order
about wearing the linen surplice.   For their complaints are

so vehement, that their querulous lamentations and groans penetrate into and are heard even in Germany. And holy scripture informs us how grievous an offence it is and hateful to God, to disquiet the consciences of the godly; partly, when it commands us not to grieve the Holy Spirit, nor to offend the weak; and partly, when it denounces heavy punishments upon those who make no scruple of doing these things; and partly too, when it proposes the examples of the saints, and of Paul especially, who thus speaks: "If meat make my brother to offend, I will eat no flesh while the world standeth, lest I make my brother to offend." (1 Cor. viii. 13.) For in these words he affords by his example a general rule taken from the doctrine of Christ; namely, that nothing indifferent is to be admitted, much less enforced upon others, and still less commanded by act of parliament, if in admitting, enforcing, or commanding it the consciences of the faithful are offended. For a tender and God-fearing conscience is a most precious thing, and very acceptable to God. How then can we approve the design of setting forth by royal mandate a law respecting wearing the sacerdotal vestments in the ministry? For, to comprehend many things in few words, if vestments of this kind are to be proposed to the faithful, they must either be proposed as indifferent, or essential. If the latter, we act ungodlily, in making those things necessary, that Christ would have free: if the former, they must then be left free to the churches. For by commanding and enforcing them we make them essential instead of free, and thus fall into the same offence. Then again, they are either instituted of God by Moses; or delivered by Christ, to wit, God manifest in the flesh; or ordained by the Holy Spirit acting and speaking in the apostles; or else by men, either godly or ungodly. The ceremonies and Levitical vestments, which were instituted of God by Moses, were all of them by the will of God to cease upon the death of Christ; as is every where evident from the scriptures, especially from the epistles of Paul to the Colossians and Hebrews. For which reason they cannot be restored without a transgression of the divine will. It cannot be said that they were delivered by Christ, since there is not a word extant upon this subject; but rather, on the contrary, he plainly taught more than once, that the end of all the Mosaic ceremonies had arrived. I assert and affirm the same respecting the apostles. It remains therefore, that they must be allowed to have been ordained of men. If of godly men, they were either ordained by them to edification, or order, or decency. But now they neither tend to edification, that is, to the advancement of godliness, but rather on the contrary make for its overthrow, as we have before seen: neither do they tend to any good order, but rather to disorder; for by their means godly bishops are confounded with ungodly ones; whereas it is fitting that they should be distinguished from each other, even by their dress: nor lastly, do they add to the comeliness of the spouse of Christ; as has been proved by me a little before. They ought not therefore to be allowed by us. And as to what has been devised by men destitute of the Spirit of God, with that we have nothing to do. Lastly, the apostles did not use these vestments. For we have no authentic evidence that they did. But the church, as in doctrine, so also in ceremonies and vestments, is to be framed after the model of the apostolic church. To what end therefore are these vestments in the church? By whose authority can they be defended? What benefit or salutary use can accrue from them to the christian people? But it has been proved by us on the contrary, that godliness is weakened by them; the pure worship of God violated; popish superstition gradually restored; the godly offended; the ungodly confirmed in their ungodliness; the weak in faith thrown into peril of their salvation; occasions afforded of much mischief; monks and other popish preachers aided in confirming their people in superstition; God's wrath provoked against us; those things that God would have destroyed again set up amongst us; the whole face of the church defiled and disgraced; decent laws respecting the not wearing strange garments shamefully broken, and thus the whole church dishonoured. Besides this, the public peace of the church, yea, of many churches, is disturbed; bishops are brought into collision with each other; the consciences of the godly are burdened, and the feelings of excellent persons offended; the Holy Spirit in them is grieved, and lastly, the apple of discord is thrown, as it were, upon the table of the gods.

Since these things are so, most serene queen, not I only, but all my colleagues and all godly persons suppliantly entreat your most serene majesty, and implore you by Jesus Christ, who we are persuaded is loved by your serene majesty from your heart, not to carry into effect that design respecting which so much has been said, nor lend your ears to such advisers. For indeed, most pious queen, these counsels are neither for the benefit of your church and kingdom, nor are they consistent with the honour of your majesty: since they neither tend to the advancement of godliness, nor to the preservation of ecclesiastical propriety, nor the maintenance of public peace; but rather weaken most exceedingly all these excellent things, which your majesty ought most especially to maintain. Your majesty should rather consider, and should employ all your consideration, authority, and influence to this end, that you may have in the first place bishops truly pious, and well instructed in sacred learning, as by the blessing of God you already possess very many, and should encourage and attend to them. You should then take care that they diligently perform their duty; watch over the flock; teach sound doctrine; refute heresies; drive away the wolves; keep every one to his duty, and exhort, incite, and stimulate all persons to a life becoming a christian man. The elders in like manner and deacons are to be admonished that every one be diligent in his office, and should there be occasion, they must be compelled by the authority of your serene majesty; that neither the former by their slumbering or connivance allow the reins of licentiousness and carnal desires to be relaxed; nor the latter, from a too great regard for their own concerns, neglect the poor members of the church, and omit other duties pertaining to their office. For these three orders of men are the nerves of the church, upon which its safety or downfall depends. Moreover, your most serene majesty must use your endeavours, and that most diligently, that the universities, and good and pious professors in them, may be encouraged, cherished, liberally maintained and provided for. For these are as the mothers and nurses of the churches, in which and by whom those persons are disciplined, taught, educated, and adorned, who shall be called forth some time hence as being qualified to govern and direct the churches. Lastly, as those things which will not admit of correction by the word and by ecclesiastical discipline, must necessarily be cut off and removed by the sword of the magistrate, according to the word of God; provision must be made herein also by your most serene majesty, in case, for instance, of adulteries, blasphemies, and other capital offences of the like nature. For to this end is the sword committed to the magistrate by God, that ungodly deceivers, obscene profligates, and unquiet men, being restrained, the rest may be able to lead a quiet and peaceable life in all godliness and honesty. To this end, most serene queen, you must labour, to this end must your thoughts, your counsels, your strength and power, be directed; namely, to say all in one word, that we all, "denying ungodliness and worldly lusts, may live soberly, righteously, and godly in this present world." For this is the true and most beautiful garment of all, respecting which every one ought to be anxious; namely, that having put off the old man with his deeds, we may put on the new man, that is, our Lord Jesus Christ. Nor are there any other true ornaments that become christian bishops than those which the apostle has blended together, writing and speaking to Timothy and even to Titus, that "a bishop must be blameless, the husband of one wife; vigilant, sober, of good behaviour, given to hospitality, apt to teach; not given to wine, no striker, not greedy of filthy lucre; but patient, not a brawler, not covetous; one that ruleth well his own house, having his children in subjection with all gravity" [1 Tim. iii. 2—4]; "not self-willed, not soon angry, not given to wine, just, holy," &c. [Tit. i. 7.] For the garments and ornaments of the Aaronic priest were types of these true ornaments: they were the shadow, these the substance. Let them therefore be removed, and let these be introduced; and we shall then at last have not only the bishops, but the whole church, truly adorned.

I again suppliantly entreat your most serene majesty, that altogether laying aside all this consideration about external garments, you will apply your mind to the retaining, putting on, defending, these true and spiritual ornaments in the churches. And may your most serene majesty, as I said at the beginning, pardon with your wonted clemency my boldness in writing. May our Lord Jesus Christ long preserve your most serene majesty in safety and happiness to us and to the whole church!

Heidelberg, Sept. 10, 1571.

[H. ZANCHIUS.]

II. BISHOP HORN TO HENRY BULLINGER[1].

The Order of Administration of Common Prayer and the Sacraments in the Church of England in the time of Edward VI.

AT morning prayer the minister, habited in a white linen surplice, and standing where he may best be heard of the whole congregation, first of all reads some sentences of holy scripture, such as, "At what time soever a sinner doth repent him of his sin from the bottom of his heart," &c. Ezek. xviii. "Turn thy face away from our sins." Ps. li. "A sorrowful spirit is a sacrifice to God." Ps. li. "Rend your hearts, and not your garments." Joel ii.

He then moves the whole congregation to a public confession of their sins. The congregation confess their sins together. The minister repeats, instead of absolution, the promises of God respecting the remission of sins and the gift of the Spirit, to those namely, who truly and heartily repent of their sins. After this the minister and people repeat some of the psalms, so as that the whole psalter is read through once every month. When the psalms are ended, one chapter is read from the new Testament, and another from the old: which being finished, the morning service is concluded with prayers for Christ's universal church; for the king, the magistrates and people; and the Lord's prayer and the creed are repeated by the whole congregation. The like order is preserved in evening prayer.

On every Sunday, Wednesday, and Friday, the Litany is used, without any invocation of saints, or popish idolatry; and the whole congregation respond to each petition.

The order for the administration of the Lord's supper was as follows. First of all, the minister repeats the ten commandments, to each of which the people answer, "Lord, have mercy upon us, and incline our hearts to keep this law;"

[1 This document is here inserted, as illustrating the preceding correspondence. The original Latin is preserved, together with Bullinger's remarks upon it, in the archives of Zurich.]

and after the tenth they answer, " Lord, have mercy upon us, and write all these thy laws in our hearts, we beseech thee." After this, the minister prays for the universal church, for peace, for the king and people, to each of which prayers the people add their Amen.   The epistle and gospel are then read, after which the Nicene Creed is repeated by all the congregation.   There then follows a homily upon faith, or good works, or the law, or gospel; or the epistle is explained.   A collection is then made for the poor, and all persons are earnestly admonished not to come before the Lord with empty hands.   An exhortation follows that they should draw near, and so eat of that bread and drink of that cup.   All of them with one mouth make a general confession of their sins; after which the minister repeats some promises of scripture concerning the forgiveness of sins to those who truly acknowledge their sins and confess them to God.   There then follows the preface, " Lift up your hearts." _People :_ " We lift them up unto the Lord." _Priest :_ " Let us give thanks to the Lord." _People :_ " It is meet" [and right so to do²].   After the preface follows a prayer of the whole congregation, in which the minister and people openly confess before God that they do not come to the Lord's table trusting in their own righteousness.   Then are repeated the words of the Lord's supper, to which the people answer, Amen.   The distribution of the bread and cup then takes place, the minister saying to each individual to whom he breaks the bread, " Take and eat this in remembrance that Christ died for thee, and feed on him in thy heart by faith with thanksgiving.   Drink this in remembrance that Christ's blood was shed for thee, and be thankful to God."   There follows afterwards a general thanksgiving, and the hymn, " Glory be to God on high," which is repeated by all the people; after which the minister dismisses the people with the blessing of peace.

The bread which is used at the Lord's supper is of the usual kind, but the purest that may be gotten.

[² This sentence is defective in the original letter.]

The Ministration of Baptism.

If there are any infants to be baptized, they are brought on each Sunday, when the most people are come together to the morning or evening prayers. The minister reads an exhortation to the people, in which he teaches them what is the condition of those who are not born again in Christ, and what the sacrament of regeneration signifies. He adds with the church a prayer for the infants, rehearses the gospel from the tenth chapter of Mark, upon which he makes a brief exhortation, followed by a general giving of thanks. The godfathers and godmothers then approach, and demand the sacrament in the name of the infants. The minister examines them concerning their faith, and afterwards dips the infant in the water, saying, "I baptize thee in the name of the Father, and of the Son, and of the Holy Ghost." He then makes the sign of the cross upon the child's forehead; after which the Lord's prayer and a general thanksgiving is repeated by all. These infants are brought to the bishop to be confirmed, as soon as they are old enough to repeat and make answer to the catechism in their mother-tongue.

Then follows the ministration of baptism in private houses by women in time of necessity, which is only ministered by the woman baptizing the infant who is like to die, with calling upon the name of God, and baptizing in the name of the Father, Son, and Holy Ghost.

Matrimony.

The minister demands of the man, before the whole congregation, whether he be willing to take the woman to his wedded wife, and whether she be willing to take him for her husband. Their troth being given, the husband delivers unto his bride a ring by way of token. They afterwards receive the communion with the whole congregation.

In the Visitation of the Sick there are many godly prayers, together with the communion, should the sick person desire to receive it; in which is required a confession of sins, to which is added an absolution, which requires examination.

Whether should the office for the Churching of Women be retained?

III. BULLINGER'S REMARKS UPON THE PRECEDING.

THE most excellent master Horn presented the foregoing statements to me, Henry Bullinger, minister of the church at Zurich, requesting my opinion upon them. I replied in the following terms, and committed my answer to writing.

I do not approve of the linen surplice, as they call it, in the ministry of the gospel, inasmuch as these relics, copied from Judaism, savour of popery, and are introduced and established with injury to christian liberty. If it had seemed a thing of so great importance to the apostles, that the minister should be distinguished from the general body of Christians, why did they not retain the ephod, according to the Lord's institution? I wish, however, that the habit in which the minister performs divine service should be decent, according to the fashion of the country, and have nothing light or fantastic about it.

The lessons and prayers should be of moderate length, not too prolix and tedious; and should likewise be understood of all, and such as may edify the church. In the times of the apostles the greater part of the time was devoted to teaching. The ceremonies were very sober and concise. The sign of the cross indeed was usual among the early Christians, and they frequently marked it with the finger on their foreheads. When however we baptize infants in our churches, we do not sign them with the sign of the cross, partly because the practice is not derived from apostolic institution, and partly because the abuse of the cross is so implanted in all, as that it does not seem possible any longer to adopt that sign among the common people without superstition.

We altogether approve of catechizing[1], and use it in our churches; and we sometimes bring our children to church to receive confirmation. Respecting this, however, we have received no direction from the apostles.

We disapprove of baptism being administered in private houses by midwives or women in time of necessity, or in the prospect of death. Our reasons are elsewhere given in our

[1 See the Confession of Helvetia in the Corpus et Syntagma Confessionum, p. 55, Ed. Genev. 1654, and the Harmony of Protestant Confessions, p. 371. Ed. P. Hall, Lond. 1842.]

books[1]. We approve of the Visitation of the sick, but do not practise in our churches the private celebration of the Lord's supper for the sake of any one sick person. The reasons are explained in our books. So also we do not use the service for the purification of women after childbirth, which seems evidently to be derived from the [Jewish] law.

IV. THE STATE OF THE CHURCH OF ENGLAND AS DESCRIBED BY PERCEVAL WIBURN[2].

1. THE English clergy consist, partly of the popish priests, who still retain their former office, and partly of ministers lately ordered and admitted by some bishop there, at his pleasure; but a certain form of ordering ministers by the bishop is drawn up by public authority.

2. The different orders of the clergy are still retained, as formerly in the papacy; namely, two archbishops, one of whom is primate; after them are the bishops; then deans and archdeacons; and last of all, rectors, vicars, curates, &c.

3. Whoever desires to serve a church there must previously obtain licence in writing from the lord bishop or his deputy.

4. No pastor is at liberty to expound the scriptures to his people, without an express appointment to that office by the bishop.

5. Few persons there are called to the ministry of the word by reason of any talents bestowed upon them; great numbers offer themselves; whence it comes to pass that not very many are found qualified for this function.

6. No one is admitted to any ecclesiastical function, unless he acknowledge the queen to be the supreme head of the Church of England upon earth. There is no great difficulty raised about any other points of doctrine, provided the party is willing to obey the laws and statutes of the realm.

7. Ministers now protest and promise that they will observe and maintain the laws of their country, as being

[1 We teach that baptism should not be ministered in the church by women or midwives. For Paul secludeth women from ecclesiastical callings; but baptism belongeth to ecclesiastical offices. Later Confess. of Helvetia, ch. xx. Hall as above, p. 302.]

[2 From the archives of Zurich.]

good (as they are called) and wholesome, as well in matters external and political, as in the rites and ceremonies of the church, and all things which are there customary and in use; and this too they must attest by their manual subscription.

8.   It is provided by the laws that no one shall impugn the English liturgy either by word or writing ; and that no minister, by whatever name he may be called, may use in public any other mode or form either in the prayers or administration of the sacraments than what is there described.

9.   This book of prayers is filled with many absurdities (to say no worse of them) and silly superfluities, and seems entirely to be composed after the model and in the manner of the papists; the grosser superstitions, however, being taken away.

10.   The greater part of the Canon law is still in force there, and all ecclesiastical censures are principally taken from it.

11.   Excommunication there depends upon the decision of a single individual, to wit, the bishop, his chancellor, the archdeacon, commissary, official, or any judge of the ecclesiastical court; and is for the most part inflicted for mere trifles, such as pecuniary matters and other suits of that nature.

12.   The sentence of excommunication pronounced by the judge is forwarded to some pastor, who is required to read and pronounce it publicly in his church, before a full congregation.

13.   The party excommunicated, when the judge is so inclined, and often too against his will, is absolved in private, and without any trouble, for a sum of money.

14.   The marriage of priests was counted unlawful in the times of queen Mary, and was also forbidden by a public statute of the realm, which is also in force at this day ; although by permission of queen Elizabeth clergymen may have their wives, provided only they marry by the advice and assent of the bishop and two justices of peace, as they call them.

15.   The lords bishops are forbidden to have their wives with them in their palaces; as also are the deans, canons, presbyters, and other ministers of the church, within colleges, or the precincts of cathedral churches.

16. Many difficulties have to be encountered in respect to marriage and divorce, because the popish laws are retained there as heretofore.

17. In case of adultery even clergymen are not very severely punished; and it is compounded for by other parties with a sum of money, with the assent of the ecclesiastical judges, by whom the penalty is imposed. Some parties, clothed in a linen garment, acknowledge and deprecate their crime in the public congregation; and indeed the whole matter is altogether determined at the pleasure of the ecclesiastical judge.

18. The archbishop of Canterbury, the primate of all England, besides his episcopal court, has also his principal courts of arches and audience, as they call them, where ecclesiastical causes are determined. He has also the court of faculties, where, on the payment beforehand of a pretty large sum of money, licences are obtained for non-residence, plurality of benefices, dispensations for forbidden meats on the third, fifth, and sixth holiday, the vigils of the saints, Lent, and the ember days at the four seasons; for almost all these are seasons of abstinence from flesh: from hence, too, are obtained dispensations for solemnizing marriage at prohibited seasons; and that even boys, and others not in holy orders, may be capable of holding ecclesiastical preferment; with many other things of this kind.

19. Every bishop has his court for matters ecclesiastical, as has also every archdeacon, in which, as things are at present, there preside for the most part papists or despisers of all religion; and the other officers employed in these courts are of the same character: the consequence of which is, that religion itself is exposed to ridicule, the ministers of Christ are everywhere despised with impunity, loaded with abuse, and even sometimes beaten.

20. Besides the impropriations of benefices, there are also advowsons, by which, while the place is yet occupied, the next vacancies of the livings are gratuitously presented to others by the patrons, or else sold by them at a price agreed upon; for this too is permitted by the laws of the country. And the power of patronage still remains there, and institution, as it is called, and induction, as in the time of popery.

21. Many festivals are retained there, consecrated in the name of saints, with their vigils, as formerly; peram-

bulations on rogation-days; singing in parts in the churches,
and with organs; the tolling of bells at funerals and on the
vigils of saints; and especially on that of the feast of All
Saints, when it continues during the whole night.

22. By the queen's command, all persons, both men and
women, must reverently bow themselves in the churches at
the name of Jesus.

23. That space which we call the chancel, by which in
churches the laity are separated by the presbyter from the
clergy, still remains in England; and prayers are said in the
place accustomed in time of popery, unless the bishop should
order it otherwise.

24. Baptism is administered, in time of necessity, as
they call it, as is also the Lord's supper, to the sick in private houses; and the administration of private baptism is
allowed even to women.

25. In the administration of baptism the infants are
addressed respecting their renouncing the devil, the world,
and the flesh; as also respecting their confession of faith;
answer to all which things is made by the sponsors in their
name.

26. The party baptized is signed with the sign of the
cross, in token that hereafter he shall not be ashamed of the
cross of Christ.

27. The confirmation too of boys and girls is there in
use, and the purification of women after childbirth, which
they call the thanksgiving.

28. In the administration of the [Lord's] supper, for
the greater reverence of the sacrament, little round unleavened
cakes are re-introduced by the queen, which had heretofore
been removed by the public laws of the realm, for the taking
away superstition. Every one too is obliged to communicate
at the Lord's supper on his bended knees.

29. In every church throughout England, during
prayers, the minister must wear a linen garment, which we
call a surplice. And in the larger churches, at the administration of the Lord's supper, the chief minister must wear a
silk garment which they call a cope. And two other ministers, formerly called the deacon and subdeacon, must assist
him to read the epistle and gospel.

30. The queen's majesty, with the advice of the arch-

bishop of Canterbury, may order, change, and remove anything in that church at her pleasure.

31. In their external dress the ministers of the word
are at this time obliged to conform themselves to that of the
popish priests; the square cap is imposed upon all, together
with a gown as long and loose as conveniently may be, and
to some also is added a silk hood.

V. TO THE VERY EMINENT SERVANT OF CHRIST, MASTER THEODORE BEZA, THE MOST LEARNED AND VIGILANT PASTOR OF THE GENEVAN CHURCH[1].

HEALTH and peace from the Lord! We have lately,
most vigilant Christian pastor, read your letter sent to our
very dear brother John Knox, and it has indeed affected us
in various ways. For inasmuch as you state that your
churches are in the enjoyment of great peace and tranquillity,
this intelligence was very gratifying to us, as it ought to be.
But whereas you inform us that some persons are found in
the syncretism[2] of Augsburg, whom either ignorance or obstinacy may excite to raise disturbances among them, and for
whose sake there has even been appointed a conference of the
sovereigns, this is indeed painful and distressing news. But
as we understood from that same letter, that you and your
brethren earnestly request of us to signify our approbation
of your confession, and simple exposition of the orthodox
faith, and catholic doctrines of the pure Christian religion,
recently set forth in the month of March, with the unanimous
assent of the ministers of the church who are in Switzerland,
namely, those of Zurich, Berne, Schaffhausen, St Gall, the
Grisons, and their confederates Mulhausen and Bienne, to
which the ministers of the church of Geneva have joined
themselves; in this we acknowledge and declare the exceeding courtesy towards us, both of yourself and your brethren,
who express so much esteem for the Scots, a people serving
the Lord with the pure worship of religion in the farthest

[1 The original letter is preserved in the archives at Zurich.]

[2 Συγκρητισμὸς (σὺν and Κρῆτες): when opponents are reconciled
among themselves, and join their united forces against a third party.
See Plut. de Frat. Carit.]

corners of the earth, as to consider that their agreement will add much light and splendour to the christian religion which you have embraced in that treatise. Wherefore, that our diligence might not be wanting to so great courtesy, and so just a request, as soon as we received your letter, we all of us, from every town in the neighbourhood, assembled at St Andrew's, the most flourishing city as to divine and human learning in all Scotland; and there, as speedily as we could, when we had read over the book, we considered each chapter by itself, and left nothing unexplored, and diligently examined everything respecting God, the sacred laws and rites of the church. And it is impossible to express the exceeding delight we derived from that work, when we clearly perceived that in your little book was most faithfully, holily, piously, and indeed divinely explained, and that briefly, whatever we have been constantly teaching these eight years, and still, by the grace of God, continue to teach, in our churches, in the schools, and in the pulpit.

We are therefore altogether compelled, as well by our consciences, as from a sense of duty, to undertake its patronage, and not only to express our approval, but also our exceeding commendation, of every chapter and every sentence. For that little treatise rests altogether upon the holy scriptures, which we both profess, and are prepared to defend at the risk of our lives, or even to the shedding of blood. And we have all of us, as many as by reason of the shortness of the time allowed us were able to be present, both subscribed our names, and sealed this letter with the common seal of this university. But if you should think that it would be of use to your churches at any future time, we will send you by the first opportunity both the public subscription of this church, and the formulary of our confession of faith, confirmed in the assembly of the three estates of the realm[3]. This one thing, however, we can scarcely refrain from mentioning, with regard to what is written in the 24th chapter

[3 The confession of Scotland was first exhibited to, and allowed by, the three estates in parliament, at Edinburgh, in the year 1560; again ratified at the same place, and on the same authority, in 1567; and finally, subscribed by the king's majesty and his household at Holyrood House, the 28th day of January, 1581. Harmony of Protestant Confessions, Hall's edit. Lond. 1842. p. xxxix.]

of the aforesaid confession[1], concerning the "festival of our
Lord's nativity, circumcision, passion, resurrection, ascension,
and sending the Holy Ghost upon his disciples," that these
festivals at the present time obtain no place among us; for
we dare not religiously celebrate any other feast-day than
what the divine oracles have prescribed. Everything else,
as we have said, we teach, approve, and most willingly embrace. We have written you this letter as briefly as possible,
in consequence of the shortness of the time. But we earnestly
request you not to allow the friendly correspondence now
commenced between us to die away. If you will diligently
do this, we will endeavour to return you the like favour.
May the Lord Jesus prosper, as long as possible, the pious
exertions of yourself and brethren for the increase of the
church of Christ! Farewell. St Andrew's, Sept. 4, 1566.

Your most loving brethren in Christ,

> JOHN DOUGLAS, rector of the university of St Andrew's,
> and professor of St Mary's college.
>
> WILLIAM STRACHAN, dean of the faculty of arts there,
> and ordinary professor of law in the same college.
>
> JOHN RUTHERFORD, principal of St Salvator's college.
>
> WILLIAM RAMSAY, professor of humanity in the same
> college.
>
> DAVID GOULD, professor in the same.
>
> JOHN DUNCANSON, principal of St Leonard's college.
>
> JAMES WYLKIE, in the same.
>
> JOHN WYNRAM, superintendent[2] of Fife and St Andrew's.
>
> JOHN ERSKYNE, superintendent of Angus and Mearns.
>
> JOHN SPOTTISWOOD, superintendent of Lothian.
>
> JOHN KNOX, }
> JOHN CRAIG, } ministers of Edinburgh.
>
> JOHN ROW, minister of the town of Perth.
>
> ROBERT HAMILTON, minister of St Andrew's.

[1 See the latter Confession of Helvetia, ch. XXIV, and Hall, as
above, p. 382.]

[2 In July, 1560, the committee of parliament had appointed minis-
ters to most of the principal towns, and among the rest, Knox to
Edinburgh, Row to Perth, Fergusson to Dunfermline, Goodman to
St Andrew's, Christison to Dundee, and Heriot to Aberdeen. Five
persons were also nominated as superintendents, namely, John Cars-
well for Argyle and the isles; John Erskine of Dun, a layman, for
Angus and Mearns; John Spottiswood, parson of Midcalder, for
Lothian and Tweeddale; John Willock, for Glasgow and the west;
John Winram, prior of Portmoak, for Fife. See Wodrow Society's
Misc. Vol. I. p. 321.]

DAVID FERGUSON, minister of Dunfermline.
JOHN NORRIE, minister of [Lorn.]
GEORGE SCOT, minister of Kirkcaldy.
ANDREW FORRESTER[3], minister of Dysart.
WILLIAM CLERK, minister of Anstruther.
ALEXANDER SPENS, minister of Kilconquhar.
THOMAS JAMESON, minister of Largo.
JOHN SYMSON, minister of Scoonie.
THOMAS BIGGAR, minister of Kinhorne.
DAVID SPENS, minister of Monimail.
WILLIAM CHRISTISON, minister of the town of Dundee.
JOHN HEPBURN, minister of Brechin.
THOMAS ANDERSON, minister of Montrose.
NINIAN CLEMENT[4], minister of Aberbrothock.
ADAM HERIOT, minister of Aberdeen.
DAVID LYNDESAY, minister of Forfar.
JAMES MELVIL, minister of Fernie.
JAMES BALFOUR, minister of Guthrie.
ROBERT PONT, minister of Elgin.
DAVID LYNDESAY, minister of Leith.
PATRICK KINLOCHY, minister of Linlithgow.
JOHN DUNCAN[5], minister of Stirling.
R. WILSON, minister of Dalkeith.
JO. BURN, minister of Musselburgh.
ANDREW SYMPSON, minister of Dunbar.
JOHN BRAND, minister of Holyrood.
GEORGE SYLVIUS[6].

[3 Or, FORSTAR.]   [4 Or, CLEMETT.]   [5 Or, DUNCANSON.]
[6 Or, WOOD. There has been considerable difficulty in clearly ascertaining some of the names affixed to this letter, but the editor believes they are correctly given as now printed: this has been effected by the valuable assistance of Robert Pitcairn, Esq., F.S.A. Sc. who has made out, by examining contemporary authorities, several signatures which the copyist could not decypher.

INDEX.

EPISTOLÆ TIGURINÆ.

TABULA.

EPISTOLA I.

ANTONIUS COOKUS AD HENRICUM BULLINGERUM.

GRATISSIMAS attulit mihi literas tuas, Antistes eximie ac mihi merito plurimum observande, noster amicus, doctor Sandes, et frater in Christo dilectus; quibus non solum gratularis nobis Anglis, et nostro nomine lætaris, quod visitavit benignissimus Deus afflictionem nostram, et redemptionem fecerit populi sui, qui tuus affectus vere bono pioque pastore dignissimus est; verum etiam, ut nutrix quæ fovet alumnos suos, ita solicitus es ne qua mala bestia noceat, neve calamitas aliqua lætitiam hanc occeptam interrumpat. Valde tu quidem prudenter et amanter mones, eaque commemoras a quibus maxime metuendum sit. Utinam hæc mala prævideant ac sedulo præcaveant qui reginæ nunc a consiliis erunt! Spes tamen bona est, maxime si vera sint quæ scribuntur Antwerpia, papistarum animos in pedes concidisse, neque vim ullam paraturos, nisi nostrorum discordia præbeat occasionem. Illud jam deprecandum est, ne de matrimonio dissensio et factiones oriantur; quod si bonis auspiciis evaluerit, reliqua longe melius tutiusque procedent. De Philippo, quod petat, non miror, præsertim cum exempla nova sint: at si rebus suis bene consulat, amicitiam reginæ magis optaret quam conjugium; et illa neque si posset nunc opinor externo nuberet, neque si vellet sine summo periculo video quî possit. Sed hic humanis consiliis parum tribuo: verissima sunt enim quæ scribis, regnorum constitutionem in manu Dei sitam esse. Si regina tanti beneficii memor accepti Deo fidere voluerit; si Domino quotidie dicat, Arx mea, rupes, et refugium tu es; nec ipsi deerit Judithæ aut Deboræ spiritus, nec sapientia consiliariis, nec exercitui robur. Contra hostium consilia irrita, gladii retusi erunt, et equus cum sessore corruet. Id ita sit per Christum Jesum Dominum nostrum! Amen. Post biduum aut triduum ex Anglia literas alias exspectamus, et vos, si quid boni secusve fuerit, certiores fieri curabimus, quos ut dominos et fratres optime de nobis meritos perpetuo venerabimur et agnoscemus. Bene vale. Argentinæ, 8 Decem. 1558.

Tuæ præstantiæ devinctissimus,

ANTONIUS COOKUS.

EPISTOLA II.

JOHANNES HALLERUS AD HENRICUM BULLINGERUM.

EXTRICAVI me per Domini gratiam a legatione Lausannensi mihi nuper commissa: nihil enim mihi gravius contingere posset. Mittuntur alii, qui rectius omnia expedient quam ego potuissem præstare. Interea quid adhuc futurum sit ignoro. Exspectamus eventum. Angli nostri Arovienses per Leverum harum latorem hodie dimissionem a senatu nostro petiverunt, gratiis actis pro hospitio ipsis concesso. Dimissi itaque sunt cum bona gratia, et cum magna omnium piorum congratulatione. Timemus quidem ne nimis cito: sed dum cogitamus eorum præsentiam fore necessariam, non possumus improbare eorum consilium. Literæ interea ipsis dantur testimoniales quomodo se gesserint. Et quoniam me interprete apud senatum usi sunt, proposui etiam ex consilio D. Cos. Negelini ea quæ nuper ad me de literis ad reginam scribendis scripseras. Placuere ea senatui ita, ut literas ad reginam hisce ipsis dent deferendas. Non itaque necesse est ut vestri hac de re denuo ad nostros scribant, sed ut peculiares ipsi quoque ad reginam scribant: quod tu quoque apud tuos facile efficies. Alias nihil nunc habeo quod scribam. Festinant illi: itaque mihi quoque festinandum fuit. Salutant te nostri omnes, imprimis Musculus. Vale. Bernæ, 11 Januarii, 1559.

J. HALL. tuus.

INSCRIPTIO.
Clariss. viro D. Heinricho Bullingero,
Tigurinæ ecclesiæ pastori fidelissi-
mo, domino et compatri suo cariss.
et observandissimo.

EPISTOLA III.

RODOLPHUS GUALTERUS AD REGINAM ELIZABETHAM.

GRATIA et pax a Deo Patre per Jesum Christum. Gratulantur omnes pii regiæ tuæ majestati, Regina serenissima, quod ad regni paterni solium te evexerit Deus, qui solus regna conferre et transferre solet. At ego ipsi potius ecclesiæ Christi gratulandum esse censeo, cui Dominus hoc novissimo tempore, quo in extrema sua lucta antichristus omnes suas vires exerit, novum sidus oriri voluit; quando juxta prophetæ oraculum te illi nutricem dedit, quæ hactenus illius filia fidelis fuisti. Agnoscemus in hoc admirabilem Dei bonitatem, qui, cum minime speres, ecclesiam suam respicit, et a persecutionum laboribus recreat. Tuæ vero majestati precamur spiritum fortitudinis et sapientiæ, quo duce facere pergat, quod jampridem facere cœpit. Nota est enim omnibus piis præclara tua fides, qua evangelicæ veritatis lumen, regnantibus Heinricho patre et Edouardo fratre, piæ et sanctæ memoriæ principibus, amplexa es, et illud ipsum inter omnis generis pericula constanter retinere studuisti. Et nunc de ecclesia repurganda et religione instauranda majestatem tuam serio cogitare multi boni passim prædicant, et mihi facile fidem faciunt, quia te a pueris (sicut de Timotheo suo Paulus scribit) sacras literas novisse ex fide dignis testibus compertum habeo. Quapropter tuæ majestatis clementia et pietate fretus meas hasce dare non dubitavi, quibus et regno tuo gratularer, et mei animi sententiam de religione instauranda, liberius fortasse quam hominem ignotum deceat, exponerem. Id enim ecclesiæ ministris licere puto, apud eos imprimis quibus ecclesiam suam Deus commendatam esse voluit, quando reges illius nutritios, reginas vero ejusdem nutrices fore prædixit. At hic, Regina serenissima, duo mihi potissimum observanda videntur: primum, ut juxta Dei verbum omnis ecclesiæ et religionis reformatio instituatur; alterum, ne ulli ex consiliis locus detur, quorum omnes rationes eo tendunt, ut sanctissimum et omnium maxime necessarium opus aut omnino impediant, aut saltem differendum adhuc esse persuadeant. Quoad primum enim scimus non paucos esse, qui si papatum totum nec honeste defendi nec commode retineri posse vident, mox religionis formam ex papatu et evangelio infeliciter mixtam ecclesiis obtrudere conantur, a qua tandem facilis sit ad avitam superstitionem transitus. At cum ex Dei verbo ecclesiam nasci apostolus testetur, nosque in Christo regenerari et novas creaturas fieri oporteat; una cum veteri Adamo exuendum et deponendum erit quicquid Christi doctrinæ ex aliqua parte repugnat: nec ulla ecclesiæ reformatio Deo revera placere poterit, nisi quæ cum ipsius verbo per omnia conveniat: et hoc nomine scriptura Davidis, Hezekiæ, et Josiæ fidem prædicat, quod juxta leges divinitus præscriptas ecclesiam reformarint; aliorum vero ignaviam non obscure perstringit, qui cum religionis instauratores et assertores haberi vellent, excelsa tamen relinquebant, in quibus contra[1] Dei præceptum populus immolare insueverat. Nec ignorat majestas tua Christi dictum, qui novum illud evangelicæ doctrinæ assumentum veteribus superstitionum pannis convenire posse negat; idemque graviter monet ne fervidum et salutare evangelii sui mustum vetustis utribus committatur, nisi et hos perire et illud simul effundi velimus. Nos certe non paucis nostræ Germaniæ exemplis edocti scimus nunquam vel ecclesiarum paci vel religionis puritati consuli posse, quoad aliquæ superstitionum reliquiæ servantur. Nam ut illis infirmi plus æquo tribuunt, ita iisdem rudes offenduntur, et simul

[1 MS. *propter.*]

*1—2

inde veritatis hostes superstitionis aliquando reducendæ et instaurandæ
spem concipiunt.   Neque hic carnis rationes audire convenit, quæ etsi
manus aratro admovit, fere tamen a tergo respicere, et undiquaque cunc-
tandi occasiones captare consuevit.   Nam, apostolo teste, hic evangelicæ
prædicationis finis et scopus est, ut per fidei obedientiam verbo Dei sub-
jiciamur, qui solus rerum agendarum consilia saluberrima suggerit, et
idem suo Spiritu iis adest, ut exitum felicem sortiantur.   Exemplo nobis
est David, qui etsi regni sui principia satis turbulenta videret, et hostes
experiretur multos, quorum alii aperta vi, alii insidiosis machinationibus
illi perniciem struerent, omnibus tamen illis per Dei gratiam superior
factus, magna cum laude et incredibili successu rempublicam simul et
religionem instauravit.   Possem ejus generis multa exempla allegare, sed
minime opus est apud majestatem tuam, quæ non ita pridem simile quid
in sanctissimæ memoriæ rege Edouardo fratre vidit, qui, vixdum puerilem
ætatem egressus, ob singulare pietatis et religionis instaurandæ studium
omnibus regnis admirationi fuit, et antichristi tyrannidem in suo regno
fortiter evertit.   Quo exemplo testari voluit Deus, quod exiguas adeoque
nullas vires ad regnum suum defendendum antichristus habeat, ut primum
verbi divini lux tenebras discusserit, quibus ille sese occultare solet.
Quia tamen sic merebatur ingratitudo nostra, piissimum regem (ut Josiam
olim) in bona pace ad se transtulit justus Deus, ne horribilem religionis
dissipationem videret, quæ illi procul dubio ipsa morte acerbius visa
fuisset.   At idem nunc Anglici regni et communis ecclesiæ denuo misertus,
te suscitavit, ut quod frater rex sanctissimus pie et bene inchoaverat, tuæ
majestatis studio et zelo feliciter absolvatur.   Forti igitur animo, Regina
serenissima, exsequere quod te jamdudum animo concepisse nemo pius
dubitat; et de tua majestate veram doctrinæ et religionis assertionem
avide exspectantem ecclesiam felix exhilara, et omnem moram illicitam
puta quæ cum alicujus animæ periculo conjuncta est.   Optant hoc omnes
pii, et supplicibus votis Deum solicitant, qui et populi tui animos in
tuum obsequium flectet, et pro ipsius gloria laborantem adversus quævis
pericula proteget.   Paucis ista attingo, quia majestati tuæ nec judicium
nec fidos et prudentes consiliarios deesse satis scio.

   Atque imprudens (fateor) censeri possum, qui non requisitus ista
moneam.   At imprudentiæ crimen lubens subeo, dummodo officium
faciam, quod et publicum ecclesiæ ministerium exigit, et me Angliæ tuæ
ob privata beneficia debere fateor: in qua olim prope puer humanissime
exceptus sum, et ab eo tempore ex Anglis amicos habui non paucos, quos
non postremo loco observandos esse putavi: inter quos facile primas tenet
vir eruditione et fidei constantia eximius Johannes Parkhurstus, qui sinceram in Christum fidem, quam annis ab hinc retro viginti duobus, me
Oxonii agente, profiteri cœpit, in hunc usque diem constanter retinuit;
et eandem inter diuturni exilii graves molestias ita confirmavit, ut mihi

non semel admirationi fuerit, meque ejusmodi hospitem habere gauderem,
in quo vivum fidei ac doctrinæ christianæ exemplar coram spectare possem.
Quem si tua majestas favore aliquo singulari prosecuta fuerit, officium
faciet, cujus remuneratorem fidelissimum Christum Jesum est habitura;
et ipsum Parkhurstum non pœnitendum in vinea Domini operarium fore
polliceri ausim. Mitto majestati tuæ meas in Johannis apostoli catholicam
homilias, Edouardo regi sanctæ memoriæ dicatas, sed ab illo non lectas,
quod aliter videretur Deo Patri, qui ingratum mundum tanto tamque raro
ingenio diutius frui noluit. Tuam ergo majestatem rogo, ut vel ob jucun-
dissimam fratris memoriam illas excipere et suo favore tueri dignetur,
quoad occasio dabitur qua mei animi erga majestatem tuam studium
luculentius testari possim. Deus Pater misericordiæ majestatem tuam
suo Spiritu regat, suo favore protegat, et ecclesiæ suæ regnoque Angliæ
in multos annos salvam et incolumem conservet! Amen. Datæ Tiguro
primaria Helvetiorum urbe, anno salutis humanæ 1559.

Regiæ tuæ majestati deditissimus,

RODOLPHUS GUALTERUS,

Tigurinæ ecclesiæ quæ apud

D. Petrum est minister.

INSCRIPTIO.

*Serenissimæ Angliæ, Franciæ, et
Hiberniæ reginæ Elizabethæ,
dominæ suæ clementissimæ.*

EPISTOLA IV.

RODOLPHUS GUALTERUS AD D. FRANCISCUM RUSSELLUM.

GRATIA et pax a Deo Patre per Jesum Christum. Etsi meæ tenuitatis mihi probe sim conscius, illustrissime princeps, multis tamen
causis me moveri et impelli sentio, ut animi mei voluntatem, qua
erga regnum vestrum afficior, apud tuam clementiam exponam per
literas. Cum enim pii omnes Angliæ totis animis gratulentur, quod
reginam nacta sit, cujus pietas jam ante per totum orbem prædicabatur, et cujus zelo religionem veram, quæ annis aliquot misere col-
lapsa erat, instaurandam esse omnes sperent; ingratus merito videri
poteram, si solus ego in hac communi lætitia tacerem, qui ob multas
causas me Angliæ obstrictum esse fateor. Nam ut humanitatem, quam
in vestro illo regno olim incredibilem expertus sum, et privata beneficia omittam, publica ecclesiæ Christi causa hoc abs me summo jure
postulat, ut si nec consilio nec auctoritate vos in reparanda religione

juvare possum, saltem animi mei studium aliquo indicio prodam. Et
hæc mihi præcipua causa fuit, quæ ut ad regiam majestatem literas
darem suasit; et eadem ut tuæ etiam clementiæ scribam, potissimum
admonet. Simul vero animum mihi addit egregia tua virtus, quam
amici multi apud nos sæpe prædicarunt, et cujus non obscura signa
videre licuit, cum superiori anno per Tigurum in Italiam iter faciens
de omnibus iis, quæ ad ecclesiæ et religionis causam faciunt, adeo diligenter inquirebas, ut facile pateret hanc tibi præ omnibus aliis rebus
cumprimis cordi esse. Et sane jam tum gratulabar tibi tacitus, quod
Dei gratiam in te non inanem aut otiosam viderem : nunc tamen magis
et tibi et Angliæ gratulor, quod te a regia majestate in summum dignitatis locum subvectum esse intelligam, in quo et pietatem tuam publice testari, et de patria dulcissima optime mereri, et Deo officium cul-
tumque præstare potes, quo illi nullus alius acceptior esse solet. Cum
enim ille ecclesiam suam pupilla oculi sui (sicuti apud prophetam testatur) cariorem habeat, et eandem Filii sui unigeniti morte redemptam
voluerit; eandem certe omnibus commendatissimam esse vult, imprimis
tamen regibus et regum consiliariis, quos illius nutritios et tutores fore
per Isaiam prædixit, quæ mihi omnium maxima principum dignitas
esse videtur. Nam terris late patentibus dominari, per terras et maria
imperium extendere, et subditos legibus coercere possunt et impii et
Dei ignari homines, quales olim in omnibus prope regnis fuisse scimus.
At Filium Dei exosculari (ut divinus et regius psaltes ait), et illius
sponsam curare atque tueri, hoc demum insigne illud et incomparabile
principum decus est; quod nonnisi iis confertur, quos Deus ex peculiari
gratia ut gloriæ suæ vasa sint elegit, et qui Spiritu suo illuminati se
totos illi consecrarunt. Atqui talem te esse, illustrissime princeps, multi
boni testantur, et multi hactenus experti sunt. Ego autem Deum as-
siduis precibus rogo, ut talem te semper conservet, et tam tua quam
aliorum, qui modo rerum gerendarum curam vestræ fidei commissam
habetis, consilia ad sui nominis gloriam et ecclesiæ propagationem et
patriæ salutem dirigat; quem finem proculdubio assequi dabitur, si
sincero Domini timore (quem sapientiæ principium sapientissimus Sa-
lomon esse dixit) animis vestris [ea, quæ ad] ecclesiam et religionem
spectant, non aliunde quam ex sacræ scripturæ fontibus petenda esse
memineritis. Neque hic nos ullis periculis terreri convenit, quando
Dominus qui rerum agendarum consilia præscribit, idem consiliorum
eventus sua manu dirigit, ut licet interdum parum progredi videantur,
tandem tamen finem lætissimum attingant. Et ut omnia fallant, quando
ob mundi ingratitudinem sanctissima consilia Deus suo effectu privat,
attamen haud leve bonum est, si nos officio functos esse sciamus, sic ut
eorum sanguis, quos sua ipsorum malitia perdidit, a nobis exigi non
queat. Quod ista tam libere moneam, illustrissime princeps, non teme-

ritati, sed meo in Angliam studio, et tuæ clementiæ tribues, cujus consideratio mihi hæc scribendi fiduciam fecit. Dominum Johannem Parkhurstum tuæ clementiæ commendarem multis, nisi illum abs te amari et magni fieri scirem, id quod facile deprehendi, cum illum domi meæ tam amice et amanter inviseres. Et sane dignus est qui ametur, tum ob singularem pietatem, quam exilio testatus est, tum ob eruditionem sinceram et a contendendi studio alienissimam. Nec dubito magnum illius usum fore, si tuæ clementiæ auctoritas illum provehere dignetur. Dominus Jesus Christus clementiam tuam regat et tueatur ad ecclesiæ suæ et puræ religionis propagationem! Amen. Tiguri, 16 Januarii, anno salutis 1559.

INSCRIPTIO.

Illustriss. principi, D. Francisco Russello,
Comiti Bedfordiensi, privati sigilli
custodi et regiæ majestatis consiliario,
domino suo clementissimo.

EPISTOLA V.

RODOLPHUS GUALTERUS AD RICARDUM MASTERUM.

S. GRATULABAR mihi non parum annis superioribus, quando regnante Edvardo sexto sanctæ memoriæ tu prior scribendi officium, quod multis annis intermissum fuerat, repetere cœpisti. At nunc multo magis et tibi et mihi gratulor, vir doctissime et frater in Christo observande, quod ea tempora Angliæ vestræ per Dei clementiam reducta esse audimus, quando sub reginæ piissimæ tutela piis hominibus Deum vere colendi libertas restituetur, et amicorum literæ tuto hinc inde ferri et referri poterunt. Agnoscimus in his admirabilem Dei sapientiam et bonitatem, qui ecclesiæ suæ ærumnas lætis vicibus temperare solet, ne tentationum fluctibus toti obruamur. Faxit idem ille, ut spei fidelium, quam de Angliæ regno jam omnes conceperunt, satisfiat. Quod eo magis futurum puto, si quotquot illic in aliquo dignitatis gradu collocati estis, ecclesiæ et religionis curam ad vos cumprimis pertinere memineritis, nec illorum admiseritis consilia, qui cum papatum nec honeste defendi nec totum retineri posse vident, ad artes convertuntur quibus religionis formam mixtam, incertam, et dubiam fingunt, et eandem sub evangelicæ reformationis prætextu ecclesiis obtrudunt, ex qua deinde facillimus est ad papisticam superstitionem et idolomaniam transitus. Quod non eo scribo, quod tales apud vos esse sciam, sed quod ne tales sint metuo. Jam enim annis aliquot in Germania magno ecclesiarum

malo experti sumus, quantum ejusmodi homines valeant, eo quod illorum
consilia carnis judicio modestiæ plena, et [ad] alendam concordiam cumprimis idonea esse videantur; et credibile est, publicum illum humanæ salutis hostem apud vos quoque sua flabella inventurum, quorum opera
papatus semina retinere studeat; quibus scripturæ sanctæ et verbi divini
armis constanter resistendum fuerit, ne dum circa prima initia aliquam
mediocrem animorum offensionem declinare studemus, multa ad tempus
duntaxat duratura admittantur, quæ postea vix ullo studio et non
absque gravissimis contentionibus omnino tolli possint. Exempla hujus
mali Germanicæ ecclesiæ multa viderunt; quorum consideratione edocti,
suspecta habemus quæcumque cum sincera verbi doctrina aliqua ex
parte pugnant. Nec me alia ratione ut hæc moneam adduci credas,
quam quod Angliæ vestræ ob veterem consuetudinem, cujus vel sola
recordatio mihi etiam hodie jucundissima est, mirifice faveo. De rebus
nostris certiorem te reddet Parkhurstus noster, frater et hospes meus
dilectissimus, quem tibi commendatissimum esse velim. Sustinuit ille
jam toto quinquennio graves exilii molestias, inter quas tamen admirabilem fidei constantiam et patientiam incredibilem conjunxit. Nunc spe
læta plenus in patriam contendit, ut ecclesiæ renascentis causam pro
talento suo adjuvet. Nec dubito, quin bonam operam præstiturus sit,
cum scripturarum cognitionem habeat præclaram, et veritatis studiosissimus sit, et a contentionibus abhorreat, quarum studiosi vix aliquem in
ecclesia fructum faciunt. Optime ergo feceris, si tua auctoritate illum
juves et pro virili provehas. Mihi vero nihil jucundius fuerit, quam
si ex tuis literis intelligam nostræ amicitiæ memoriam penes te adhuc
salvam esse, quæ certe in animo meo nunquam intermori poterit. Vale,
vir præstantissime. Tiguri, 16 Januarii, 1559.

INSCRIPTIO.

Domino Richardo Mastero, medico
regio, amico veteri et fratri suo
dilecto.

EPISTOLA VI.

ANTONIUS COOKUS AD PETRUM MARTYREM.

Literas tuas, vir præstantissime, una cum literis D. Bullingeri reginæ
nostræ in manus ipse tradidi. Quarum lectione quantopere affecta sit,
testis est Cecilius, qui lacrymas ejus inter legendum obortas viderit.
Rogabat an lubens Angliam repetere velles: nam tale quiddam audivisse
videbatur. Ego de voluntate tua respondi me nihil dubitare, pro ardenti
amore studioque tuo in regem illum Edvardum, in ipsam, et totam Angliæ

rempublicam; sed eo tempore per literas a te nihil certi accepisse: optare
tamen ut ex academiis alteram tua præstantia curaret ornandam. Qua de
re scribet, uti spero, propediem, tum ad te ipsum, tum ad senatum Tigurinum. Nunc de papæ tyrannide in comitiis expellenda satagimus,
et de regia potestate revocanda ac restituenda religione vera. Ἀλλὰ λίαν
βραδέως σπεύδομεν. Neque desunt hoc tempore Sanaballæ et Tobiæ, qui
muros ac ædificationem impediant. Quo magis illud nobis cogitandum
est, "Indesinenter orate." Magnus est reginæ zelus, magnum nobilitatis
et populi studium; nimis tamen adhuc hæret opus. Non satis quorundam
animis insedit, Confide Deo et prudentiæ tuæ ne innitaris: nec illud,
ὁ δρασσόμενος τοὺς σοφοὺς ἐν τῇ πανουργίᾳ αὐτῶν. Sed exitus comitiorum
spem meam confirmabit, quantum ipse judicare possum. Saluta, quæso,
nomine meo multum D. Bullingerum et reliquos fratres. Da operam ut
valeas et itineri sufficias. Vale. Londini, 12 Februarii, 1559.

ANTONIUS COOKUS,

Omnino tuus.

INSCRIPTIO.
Eximio viro D. Petro Martyri
τῷ θεολόγῳ. *Tiguri.*

EPISTOLA VII.

RICARDUS HILLES AD HENRICUM BULLINGERUM.

S. P. LITERAS tuas 22 Decembris proxime elapsi, mi Domine colende,
ad me datas lubenti animo accepi. In hiis tamen quod non libenter
legeram accepi; hoc est, quod quidam tibi scripsere semel et iterum,
me dedignatum esse tuas accipere literas. Quippe nullius dedignor literas
legere unquam, tui quam maxime. Arrogantiæ esset enim (meo quidem
judicio) tam docti et gravis viri literas contemnere. Quamdiu tamen
regnabat hic Maria nostra, regina satis truculenta ac superstitiosa, adeo
mihi metuebam de bonis, de periclis, immo de vita etiam, ut vix qualibus
tu sis, scribere audebam ipse, vel scripta recipere ab eis. Proclivis est,
inquis, lapsus hominis, et in plurimis aberramus omnes. Mirum itaque
non est, si et ego impegerim, hominesque plusquam decebat et revereri
et timere cœperim, tum etiam quædam recipere, a quibus ante annos
plurimos abhorrerem plurimum. Illuc me pertraxit sanctorum etiam
Patrum quorundam lectio voluminum, in quibus ni fallor nonnulla sunt
dogmata, quæ omnium fere illorum consensu traduntur, etiam quæ tui
et similium doctrinæ minime sunt consentanea. De his autem plura
scribere non libet, quia si tu ad hæc mea scripta respondere velles,

rescribere non mihi vacat fere, nec placet. Ita mihi est molestum Latine scribere, et jam ferme obsoletum. Inter doctos enim viros nunc non versor, qui sua Latina eloquuntur lingua. Gratias tibi permagnas certe habeo, quod meæ memoriæ dignatus fueris reducere, quomodo noverim gratiam et misericordiam esse copiosissimam apud Dominum, qui redeuntes ad se non rejicit, sed benigne recipit. Quod igitur per me peccatum est hactenus confiteor Domino; Domino do gloriam, Domini imploro misericordiam ut consulis: nec dubito quin ipsam sim consequuturus. Videbo autem ut in posterum fidelis sim, et veram religionem (cujus maxima pars in confessione fidei exhibita invictissimo Imp. Carolo V. in comitiis Augustæ, anno 1530, continetur) totis, ut mones, promovebo viribus. D. Petro Martyri, Julioque ejus famulo, et tuæ conjugi honestissimæ, habeas me commendatum oro. Salutat te eosque omnes uxor mea ex animo, multamque vobis precatur salutem. Vale. Londini, ultima Februarii, 1559. Tuus,

RICARDUS HILLES, Anglus.

Quod ad religionem attinet, per mandatum regium catholicis (ut dicuntur) concionatoribus impositum est silentium, et evangelicis concessa est libertas satis ampla—coram regina ipsa ter in singulis hujus quadragesimæ hebdomadis prædicare, et sua ex sacris probare scripturis. Ad publica etiam comitia, sive ad commune regni hujus concilium, seu (ut nostri illud nominant) parliamentum, jam per sex fere hebdomadas convenitur. Nihil tamen adhuc certi de abolenda superstitione papistica, et puriori religione christiana restituenda publice actum est. Spes tamen magna est omnibus nostris prædicti parliamenti civibus fidelibus, aliisque viris piis, omnia sacra vel ad formam quæ fuit nuper regis Edvardi sexti temporis, vel quæ est in prædicta confessione Augustæ, per principes protestantes Germaniæ exhibita, reformata fore brevi.

INSCRIPTIO.

Doctissimo et integerrimo viro D. Heinricho Bullingero, amico mihi observando tradentur literæ. Tiguri in Helvetia.

EPISTOLA VIII.

EDMUNDUS GRINDALLUS AD CONRADUM HUBERTUM.

SALVE in Christo. Credo tibi satis notum esse Gulielmum Salkyns, famulum Ricardi Hilles, qui diu nobiscum Argentinæ vixit. Illi ego nuper scripta quædam Buceri tradidi, ut ad te perferrentur. Unum

erat disputatio ipsius publice habita, quum in doctorem apud nos erat
inauguratus : alterum fuit de tota controversia inter ipsum et Jungum,
quem tu solebas fungum appellare.   An hoc posterius etiam quædam
alia contineat, nescio.   Ita enim scriptum est, ut divinatore potius opus
sit quam lectore, nisi quod tibi fortassis, in hujus viri scriptis exerci-
tato, non adeo erit difficile omnia eruere et extricare.   Doctor Parkerus, qui hæc ad me misit, scripsit se alia quædam fragmenta habuisse;
sed quum ea nunc ex latebris eruisset, in quibus toto hoc tempore in-
cendiario delituissent, invenisse corrosa a soricibus et prorsus corrupta.
Quare si quam voluptatem ceperis ex istis, eam rursus statim amittes,
quod omni spe in posterum plura accipiendi destitueris.   Exemplar responsionis ad antididagma Latine versum a Martino Bremio dixisti te
habere; apud nos nihil amplius est Buceri, quod ego sciam.   In nundinis
vestris Argentinensibus non dubito quin Salkynus omnia fideliter tradet.

   De rebus nostris Anglicanis sic paucis accipe.   Invenimus ecclesiam
nostram miserrime laceratam ac tantum non oppressam.   Urgebamus quidem statim ab initio, ut iniretur publica reformatio.   Sed comitia regni
diu rem distulerunt, neque quicquam immutarunt, donec inter principes,
Philippum, Gallum, et nos de pace conclusum esset.   At jam tandem,
divino adspirante numine, in recessu comitiorum promulgatum est edictum,
ut papa cum sua jurisdictione prorsus exulet, et religio in eam formam
restituatur, quam habuimus tempore Edwardi Sexti.   Si qui episcopi aut
alii prælati de renuncianda episcopi Romani potestate juramentum susci-
pere noluerint, illi omni functione ecclesiastica priventur et deponantur.
Post festum S. Johannis Baptistæ proximum nemo missas faciat, nisi qui
gravissimam mulctam subire velit.   Itaque vulgo existimatur omnes fere
episcopos, multos etiam alios prælatos, episcopatibus et functionibus suis
renuntiaturos, ut quos jam pudeat post tantam tyrannidem et crudelitatem
sub papæ vexillis exercitam, et ipsi nuper juratam obedientiam, iterum ad
palinodiam adigi et manifesto perjurio obstrictos teneri.   Magna ministrorum bonorum penuria laboramus.   Multi enim, qui in hac persequutione
defecerunt, jam ex animo papistæ facti sunt; qui vero antea moderati (ut
ita dicam) papistæ fuerant, jam sunt obstinatissimi.   Sed nostrum est quod
possumus præstare, cunctum Deo committere.   Quod superest, oro ut nos
et ecclesiam nostram in precibus tuis Deo commendes, et D. D. Marpachium ac D. D. Sebaldum meo nomine diligenter salutes.   Vale in
Domino, vir humanissime ac frater in Christo carissime.   Londini, 23
Maii, 1559.

Tui in Domino studiosissimus,

EDMUNDUS GRINDALLUS,

Anglus.

   Dubito (ut sum satis obliviosus) egone an Lakinus in se susceperit

totam exhumati Buceri et Fagii historiam transmittere. Sed tamen, ne
tu voto tuo prorsus frustreris, omnino constitui ad Doct. Parkerum hujus
rei gratia scribere, qui mihi (ut spero) veram ejus rei descriptionem concin-
nari curabit ; quod si fecerit, curabo etiam ut transmittatur. Si Lakinus
idem faciat, qui nunc Londino abest, poteris ex utroque, quod maxime ad
rem fecerit, decerpere. Iterum vale. Non dubito quin literas istis in-
clusas primo quoque tempore pro tua humanitate tradendas curabis.

INSCRIPTIO.

Amico et fratri in Domino caris-
*   simo D. Conrado Huberto, verbi*
*   Dei apud Argentinenses minis-*
*   tro fidelissimo.*

EPISTOLA IX.

LAURENTIUS HUMFREDUS AD HENRICUM BULLINGERUM.

Quod a me antehac officium jure exigere potuit, id nunc ut præstem,
invitat occasio; quod tamen ut debui et ut vellem facere non patitur subi-
tus adventus et discessus tabellarii, ac temporis angustia. Brevitatem ergo
et in scribendo negligentiam pro tua paterna humanitate hoc tempore boni
consules. Venit ad me fasciculus literarum meis inclusus a D. Abelo, quem
per hunc Tigurinum et fidum hominem et tibi non ignotum ad pietatem
tuam mitto. Alterum illum quem petebas adhuc videre non contigit ;
diligenter tamen et mea causa et tua aliorumque imprimis quæsivi, et
adhuc percontari non desino. Respondetur aurigam cuidam apud insigne
hominis sylvestris spelunca tradidisse. Quid inde actum sit nescio. Si in
manus meas inciderint, quod tamen despero post hoc intervallum tam
longum, accuratius efficiam, ut ad te Deo volente perveniant. Atque
hæc est prima occasio, quæ me ad scribendum, vir integerrime, impulit.
Altera est Frenschami mei vel morbus vel mors : si vivat, ut pro tuo
more consolando, hortando, juvando, hominem erigas jacentem ; cujus consilium ille semper plurimi fecit, et ni fallor, jam semimortuus et animam
agens audiet : si mortuus sit, ea cura hominem complectaris mortuum,
quæ ei in sinu Abrahami vel Christi potius requiescenti convenit. Audire
et ego et D. Foxus cupimus, quo in statu res ejus sint, id est, obieritne an
superstes sit : ut vel vivo adsimus corpore, si opus sit, vel absentes precibus ;
sin minus, ut funus nostri amicissimi saltem pia lacrymula prosequamur.
Tertium quod volebam, nimirum ut tibi gratias agerem de tuis in me aliosque (cum Tiguri cum meis vixeram) beneficiis, in aliam opportunitatem
differam. Interim pietatem tuam et sanctos labores commendo Domino,

qui et nostram ecclesiam renascentem et vestram jam diu confirmatam suo sancto Spiritu dirigat, et ad omnia honesta, pia, sancta provehat. Amen. Junii 23.

Tibi deditissimus,

LAURENTIUS HUMFREDUS.

INSCRIPTIO.

Doctissimo et integerrimo viro,
Tigurinœ ecclesiœ antistiti,
Dom. Henrico Bullingero.
Tiguri.

EPISTOLA X.

EDMUNDUS GRINDALLUS AD CONR. HUBERTUM.

S. D. QUEMADMODUM ante præsens solebam tua humanitate satis familiariter uti, carissime in Christo frater, ita etiam nunc absens operam tuam in re, ut spero, tibi non admodum difficili implorare non dubitabo.   Opus enim mihi est amanuensi aliquo, qui mihi in gravioribus occupationibus et studiis, ad quæ quotidie vocor, ad manum sit. Nostris juvenibus, qui huic negotio apti esse possint, quia bonorum ministrorum maxima penuria laboramus, ad ecclesiæ ministeria uti cogimur.   Peto igitur a tua pietate, ut si quem ex vestris adolescentibus invenire poteris, qui hoc laboris non illibenter subire velit, et mihi hac in re æquis conditionibus inservire (quarum te arbitrum constituo), illum ad me mitti cures, ac Johannis Abeli vel Gulielmi Salkyns opera hac in re utaris.   In eo qui mittetur hæc requirerem, ut satis expedite Latine scriberet, und das die geschrift ziemlich gut wäre; præterea ut Græce, maxime vero ut Hebraice aliquantulum calleret, et a S. literarum studio non abhorreret.   Quæ quidem omnia in vestris adolescentibus plerumque reperiuntur.   Has vero conditiones ego vicissim offero.   Primum, itineris ad nos sumptus ego perferam, et de pecunia numeranda Johanni Abelo scripsi: optarem etiam, si fieri posset, ut in ipsius comitatu veniret.   Deinde utar eo non ad opera ulla laboriosa aut servilia, sed ad legendum, scribendum, et similia exercitia, nisi quod mensæ aliquando ministrare debeat, &c.   Præterea in singulos annos, præter victum et duo Anglico more vestimenta, viginti aureos Rhenenses, aut (quod perinde est) viginti coronatos Anglicos ex pacto pro stipendio dabo, præter illud, quod ex mea liberalitate, prout occasio tulerit, adjicietur.   Postremo, si aut propter valetudinem aut propter aliam justam causam (nimirum si Anglia illi non arriserit, aut

si a parentibus aut amicis avocatus fuerit), ego etiam pro reditu in
patriam sumptus illi suppeditabo. Quod si nostram linguam, quæ non
multum distat a Germanica, addiscere voluerit, non erit mihi difficile,
uti spero, de conditione satis honesta illi prospicere. Quod si conditiones non satis æquas videar offerre, facile patiar, ut tua prudentia
æquiores assignet. Eas ego, volente Domino, præstabo : tantum ut mihi
probum ac pium adolescentem compares, quem ita tractare conabor,
ut Angliam vidisse eum pœnitere non possit. Oro ut D. Doct. Marpachium meo nomine salutes, sine cujus ope atque auxilio hoc con-
fici non posse satis scio, sed spero illum pro sua humanitate hanc
petitionem satis æquis auribus accepturum. Neque enim vestris ecclesiis
inutilior erit, quisquis fuerit, si post collectam ex aliquot annorum
peregrinatione experientiam ad vos redierit.

Ecclesiæ nostræ status (ut ad eam rem veniam) fere idem est,
qui ante fuit, quum proxime ad te scriberem, nisi quod jam in dies
executioni mandantur, quæ antea de reformandis ecclesiis edictis ac
legibus constabilita fuerunt. Episcopi papistici pene omnes depositi
sunt, et si qui sunt reliqui, intra aliquot dies deponentur, quia nolunt
papæ obedientiam abjurare. Sed tamen satis leniter, ne dicam nimium,
cum illis agitur ; permittitur enim illis privatam vitam vivere, et ecclesiarum spolia (ut D. Bucerus loqui solebat) devorare. Pœnitet jam
illos (ut multi existimant) suæ constantiæ, postquam Galliarum regem
Henricum II. non sine manifesto divinæ vindictæ indicio e medio sublatum vident, in quo summa ipsorum spes collocata fuerat. Multi ex
nostris, qui in Germania exulabant, jam sunt episcopi designati. Hæc
fere habui de rebus nostris quæ scriberem. Buceri cremati historiam
propediem missurum me confido. Oro ut Lutheri opera Germanica
omnia, compacta a Christophoro vestro bibliopola, etiam mihi mittenda
cures. Abelus aut Salkynus pecuniam numerabit. Hæc una causa est,
cur Germanum amanuensem cuperem, quia vestram linguam prorsus
dediscere nollem. Quod si apud vos neminem inveneris, scribe, quæso,
ad amicos tuos Basilienses, ut vel inde mihi aliquem pares. Rescribe,
quæso, tribus verbis, quid horum efficere poteris. Cetera fusius expli-
canda Jo. Abelo aut Gulielmo Salkyns relinquo. Opto te in Domino
quam optime valere. Londini, 14 Julii, 1559.

Tuus totus in Domino,

EDMUNDUS GRINDALLUS, Anglus.

Amico et fratri in Christi carissimo
  D. Conrado Huberto, fidelissimo
    divini verbi ministro. Argentinæ.

EPISTOLA XI.

PETRUS MARTYR AMICO CUIDAM IN ANGLIA.

Te totum, mi N., in tuis literis vidi. Utrinque times. Nam si rejicias ministerium, videris occasionem rei bene gerendæ corrumpere: sin vero functionem oblatam susceperis, jure meritoque vereris, ne iis institutis assentiri videaris, quæ purum Dei cultum non tantum imminuunt et diluunt, sed etiam corrumpunt, et mirum in modum labefactant, etsi hominibus erga evangelium infirme animatis parum habere ponderis ac momenti videantur; nam ea omnia pro adiaphoris habent. At quis paulo rectius de religione institutus, videns te, Christi nuntium et strenuum evangelii buccinatorem, ad altare vestibus indutum coram imagine crucifixi precari, verba sacra recitare, distribuere sacramenta, non existimabit abs te quoque ritus istos non tantum ferri, sed etiam approbari? Unde tibi postea secus docenti fides minime habebitur. Qui enim aliter docet atque faciat, quæ destruit ædificat, et quæ ædificat vicissim evertit. Neque tali facto exemplum apostoli prætexi potest, qui Judaicas cæremonias aliquandiu integra conscientia retinuit: quoniam instituta Mosaica Dei auctoritate ac lege olim invecta fuerunt, non humano consilio reperta, neque damnata cultus gratia. At ista de quibus nunc agimus, et ab hominibus instituta sunt citra ullum divinum oraculum, et cultui, quem hodie quotquot pii sunt execrantur, splendide inservierunt. Utinam vidissent, qui hæc censuerunt conservanda, evangelium iis manentibus non satis esse firmum! Profecto si ex animo superstitiones odissemus, vel ipsa eorum vestigia omnibus modis curaremus extirpanda. Utinam hostium nostrorum perverso studio evasissemus aliquanto doctiores! Illi omnia sedulo evitant, quæcunque nostram religionem quocunque modo resipiunt, et data opera, quantum possunt, a simplici cultu Christi et apostolorum vetustissimo ritu discedunt. Cur nos vicissim non curamus ab illorum perniciosis institutis quam longissime abesse, atque simplicitatem apostolicam non tantum in doctrina, sed etiam in administratione sacramentorum æmulari? Non video qui hæc a vobis retenta possint recte adiaphora judicari. Certe spectatoribus quando referunt pestiferæ missæ expressam speciem, qua sibi ipsis impii homines admodum placebunt, missam quippe adeo rem sanctam fuisse dicent, ut ejus illustre simulacrum nec nobis quidem displicere potuerit; nam quamvis eam non retinemus, multis attamen et præclaris modis imitamur: quis ad hæc obstabit, quin ex adstantibus ii, quibus adhuc in præcordiis hæret papatus, imaginem crucifixi adorent? Facient porro, nec animi eorum motus prohiberi poterit. An dicent istorum consiliorum architecti non id suo, verum illorum vitio

fieri, qui male sunt imbuti, et superstitionum suarum nimium tenaces?
At se occasionem dare non poterunt inficiari : væ autem hominibus
per quos venerit scandalum! Neque suæ cogitationis ullum argumentum vel ex divinis literis vel ex ecclesiæ primitivæ institutis afferre
poterunt. Quod si studium tantummodo faciendi novi fœderis ad hæc
impellit; meminerimus pactum, inter nos et Deum sancitum olim, humanis fœderibus præstare, ac videndum quam attentissime, ne dum
civilia sectamur, cœlestium jactura fiat. Quare, mi N. carissime in
Christo frater, cum res hoc loco sint, duo tibi consulo : primum, ut
concionandi functionem retineas, nec desinas publice ac privatim veritatem dogmatum propugnare, atque ritus offensionis et scandali plenos
convellere; alterum, ut a ministerio sacramentorum tantisper abstineas,
donec istæ non ferendæ maculæ auferantur. Hac ratione rei bene gerendæ occasio non amittetur, neque tuo exemplo alios in superstitionibus confirmabis. Atque hoc non mei unius consilium est : sed idem
quoque reverendo atque viro clarissimo D. Bullingero videtur. De
quæstione autem priori me rescripsisse memini : fortassis literæ aut aberrarunt, aut sunt interceptæ. Atque nunc denuo respondissem; verum
ubi sint tuæ literæ ignoro, nec quæsitas reperire valui. Quod si ad eas
rescribi optas, non graveris quæ rogaveras iterum scribere. Salutes omnes amicos. Hic D. Bullingerus, uxor mea, et Julius cum sua et reliquis domesticis te salvere jubent. Ego vero tuæ uxori ac Giannæ
privatim salutem dico. Decimo quinto Julii. Anno 1559.

EPISTOLA XII.

CONRADUS HUBERTUS AD THOMAM BLAURERUM.

Salutem in Servatore Christo. Triduum jam præterfluxit, vir integerrime et mihi plurimum colende, ex quo literas ab amico mihi familiariter noto D. Edmundo Grindallo accepi. Is quum ob evangelii professionem cum aliquot aliis Anglis hic aliquandiu exulasset, mutata
facie religionis, propter pietatem illius eximiam eruditioni conjunctam
a regina revocatus in episcopum Londinensem nuper electus est. Quid
vero inter alia istis literis a me petat, Diethelmus filius dabit descrip-
tum, et meum amicorumque aliquot consilium simul aperiet. Tu qua
es pietate et prudentia, huic (si approbaveris) calculum etiam tuum addere, occasionemque promovendi filium mihi carissimum, meo quidem
judicio haud vulgarem, vix negligere voles; præsertim in hac tua libe-
rorum benedictione. Equidem, ut verum fatear, institutum vestrum de
abalienando quasi a studiis Diethelmo ad artem grammatisticam parum

mihi placuit, et nescio an fato impeditum hucusque fuerit, quemadmodum copiosius ipse referre tibi poterit.   Paucis unum hoc tibi de
me persuadeas velim, optime Blaurere, Hubertum tui tuorumque esse
amantissimum, vestrarum etiam utilitatum percupidum.   Brevior jam
esse cogor partim propter ingredientis iter festinationem, partim vero
propter negotia typographica, quibus tantum non obruor.   Quare si
quid aliud sit, quod tua scire referat, epistolam vivam eamque longe
gratissimam hic habes.   Vale in Christo cum omnibus tuis feliciter.
Argentorati, 7 Augusti. Anno 1559.

Tuus CONRAD. HUBERTUS.

EPISTOLA XIII.

THOMAS LEVERUS AD HENRICUM BULLINGERUM.

SALVE plurimum in Christo. Quoniam de multis majoribus negotiis
nostræ reipublicæ et ecclesiæ Anglicanæ aliorum literis plenius et
melius te doceri sciam, de minoribus paucis pro mea tenuitate nunc
scribam.   Inter redeundum a vobis versus Angliam, in itinere Argentorati vidi proclamationem, id est edictum literis editum auctoritate
reginæ Elisabethæ severe prohibentis omnem prædicationem et sacræ
scripturæ expositionem, aut ullam religionis immutationem per totam
Angliam, donec summum concilium, quod nos vocamus parlamentum,
postea convocandum, de religione concluderet.   Sic ut in Angliam redii,
juxta prædictam proclamationem vidi, imo videre nolui, missas et omnes papales nænias atque abominationes ubique legum auctoritate mu-
nitas, atque evangelium ubique nullum, nisi inter quosdam Londini, qui
aut coram regina in aula, solo quadragesimali tempore, pauculis con-
suetis diebus, admittebantur; aut in congregatione perseverante in latebris
per totum tempus persecutionis, et tunc erumpente non ultra apertas
privatas ædes, cessante persecutione per reginam Elisabetham, in privatis
ædibus apertis, sed in nullis publicis templis permittebantur.   Fuerat
enim in tempore persecutionis sub Maria latitans congregatio fidelium
Londini, inter quos semper prædicabatur evangelium cum sincera administratione sacramentorum; sed rigente persecutione sub Maria sese
sedulo occultabant, atque cessante persecutione sub Elisabetha perseve-
rabant in eadem congregatione etiam manifeste.   Sed quia legibus regni
damnata fuit illorum religio pia, magistratus, connivens ad frequentes
conventus in privatis ædibus, noluit tamen permittere ut illa publica
templa occuparent.   Ad istos igitur non in publicis templis, sed in
privatis ædibus, frequentes confluebant. Et quando inter illos celebrabatur

cœna Domini, non admittebantur extranei ulli, nisi qui a papismo et omnis infamiæ nota puri servabantur, aut qui, suam ipsorum defectionem et offensionem publicam ingenue agnoscentes, coram omnibus humiliter veniam et reconciliationem peterent. Sic sane ego sæpius interfui, et vidi plurimos cum lacrymis redeuntes, et plures similiter cum lacrymis recipientes tales ad communionem; ita ut nihil unquam potuerit esse suavius mutuis lacrymis illorum omnium sibi invicem condolentium peccata, et congratulantium reconciliationem atque societatem renovatam in Christo Jesu. Istis inflammati quidam concionatores e Germania in Angliam reversi, et intelligentes silentium mandatum usque ad tempus longum et incertum non convenire cum Paulino mandato et obtestatione prædicandi verbum Dei tempestive et intempestive, rogati statim in quibusdam templis publicis prædicabamus evangelium, ad quod avide confluebat frequens auditorium. Atque cum de conversione ad Christum per veram pœnitentiam serio agebatur, tum multæ multorum lacrymæ obortæ testabantur prædicationem evangelii valere ad veram pœnitentiam et salutarem resipiscentiam magis quam quicquid totus mundus excogitare aut probare possit. Nam dum ista inter privatos nulla publica auctoritate probante gerebantur, ecce eodem tempore apud præcellentes potentia, opibus, et muneribus publicis, summa auctoritate legum, edictorum et consuetudinum, celebrabantur missæ cum omni papali idololatrica superstitione. Et jam tandem auctoritate parlamenti papismus abrogatur, atque vera religio Christi restituitur: hic mundus immundus, ut in illo, sic in ista non nisi turpe lucrum et fœdam voluptatem sectatur. Convertuntur plurimi sic ab illo ad istam, ut nec illius fœces expurgare, nec istius puritatem amplecti, sed ad formam hujus seculi se fingere velint. Nam monumenta superstitionis, emolumenta lucri, libertatem, imo voluptatem carnis, magno cum scandalo et ignominia religionis quam profitentur, multi amant, habent, atque ostentant. Dabit tamen Deus tandem victoriam parvulis pusilli gregis Christi adversus potentes mundi tyrannos. Sanguinarii enim episcopi omnes hic apud nos deponuntur: docti, pii et prudentes ad visitandas omnes Angliæ regiones emittuntur. Zelosi prædicatores evangelii, qui primo contra edictum reginæ prædicabant, nunc in literis sigillo reginæ signatis habent liberam facultatem prædicandi per totam Angliam. Atque ego, qui diu in remotioribus partibus fui evangelizans inter imperitissimos, decrevi, Deo volente, cras e Londino revertere ad eosdem et similes, qui raro et nunquam audivere ullam evangelii Christi expositionem. Tales enim mihi videntur maxime desiderare et lubentissime excipere oblatam ædificationem et consolationem in evangelio Christi. De me ipso non est quod amplius scribam, nisi quod nunc promittere velim per literas, quod pro occasione et facultate, quam Deus suppeditabit, semper fideliter præstabo; me omnem operam daturum, ut intelligatis tu et vestrates,

qui Anglos exulantes religionis causa benigne fovistis, nos tantæ bene-
ficentiæ memores et non ingratos perpetuo perseveraturos. Commenda
nos omnium piorum precibus. Saluta mihi uxorem tuam, optimam
meam hospitem, cum liberis vestris, et totam familiam, quibus opto
plurimas Dei benedictiones in Christo. Saluta ministros ecclesiæ apud
vos, et seorsim præcipuas ejusdem columnas D. Bernardinum, D. Martyrem et D. Gualtherum. Dominus Jesus diu servet vos ad universæ
ecclesiæ suæ ædificationem in Christo. Amen. Londini 8 Augusti,
1559.

       Tuus tui semper studiosus fideliter in Christo,

TH. LEVERUS.

INSCRIPTIO.

Doctissimo simul et sapientissimo patri,
   D. Henrico Bullingero, pastori ec-
   clesiæ vigilantissimo in Helvetia.
Tiguri.

EPISTOLA XIV.

PETRUS MARTYR AMICO CUIDAM IN ANGLIA.

Quas literas ad me 27 Augusti dedisti, circa finem Octobris accepi :
quare si respondeo tardius, culpa in me non hæret, presertim cum tabel-
larios fidos Argentinam crebro non habeamus. Verum de tota ea re de
qua nunc rogas, me scio ad te aliis meis literis luculenter scripsisse.
Quare vel aberrarunt literæ, vel cum ista scriberes nondum acceperas.
Attamen ut operam et consilium meum hic non desideres, quæ antea
scripsi repeto. De impropriationibus nihil videtur esse laborandum : non
enim in tua manu est, unde aut quomodo regina velit aut episcopo
aut parochis victum seu stipendium persolvere. Quod si videantur illi
esurire, pro eis vos ipsi precari ac intercedere poteritis ; vel si abun-
datis, de vestro victu, si lautior fuerit, aliquid impertiri. De pileo
quoque rotundo vel habitu extra sacra gestando, non arbitramur esse
plus quam oporteat rixandum ; non enim ibi superstitio videtur pro-
prie locum habere. At de vestibus ut sacris in ministerio ipso adhi-
bendis, cum speciem missæ referant, et sunt meræ papatus reliquiæ,
Dominus Bullingerus censet non esse illis utendum, ne tuo exemplo res
quæ scandalo est confirmetur. Ego vero etsi usui ejusmodi ornamentorum semper sum adversatus, quia tamen videbam esse præsens periculum, ne concionandi munere abdicaretis, et spem fortassis aliquam
fore ut quemadmodum altaria et imagines ablatæ sunt, ita etiam illæ
species missæ auferantur, si tu et alii episcopatum adepti prorsus in id

*2—2

incumberetis; quod minus forte procederet, si loco tuo alter successerit, qui non tantum illas reliquias repelli non curaret, sed potius defenderet, foveret, ac tueretur: idcirco tardior eram ad suadendum ut potius episcopatum recusares, quam ut illarum vestium usum reciperes. Attamen quia scandala ejus generis vidi prorsus evitanda, propterea in sententiam ejus facile cessi. Altaribus vero ac imaginibus conservatis, ego ipse ultro, quemadmodum aliis literis scripsi, nequaquam ministrandum censeo.

Hæc sunt quæ possum de re præsenti scribere. Tu vero id videto ne adversus conscientiam quicquam facias. Ceterum vereor ne literæ sero veniant; quam tamen culpam ego præstare non debeo, cum facultatem nullam scribendi omiserim. Ad extremum ego id te scire velim, quæstiones hujus generis nobis quoque duras esse; ideo consilium non tam facile dari potest. Ego cum essem Oxonii vestibus illis albis in choro nunquam uti volui, quamvis essem canonicus: mei facti ratio mihi constabat. Quare tibi quoque consulo, ut in arena consilium capias. Novi exemplum meum non debere tibi justam esse confirmationem: quod vero me movit et adhuc movet, et te fortasse movere poterit, nempe id non faciendum, quod ea confirmet, quæ conscientia mea non probet. Breviter jussisti ut scriberem, scripsi breviter. Tu boni consule, pro me ores, salutes amicos. Tibi salutem dicit D. Bullingerus, uxor mea, Julius cum sua. Plurimum vale, suavissime frater et domine in Christo colendissime. Tiguri, 4 Novembris, 1559.

EPISTOLA XV.

JOHANNES CALVINUS AD GULIELMUM CECILIUM.

RETULIT mihi nuncius, cui meos in Isaiam commentarios serenissimæ reginæ offerendos dederam, quia mihi ob libellos quosdam hic editos offensa erat, officium meum ejus majestati non adeo fuisse gratum. Summam quoque mihi recitavit, clarissime vir, sermonis a te habiti, in quo mihi durior visus es, quam humanitas tua ferebat; præsertim quum jam tibi ex meis literis compertum esset, quantum mihi de tuo erga me amore promitterem. Etsi autem justæ causæ impediunt, quominus anxia disputatione me purgem, ne tamen silentio meo viderer malam conscientiam quodammodo fateri, paucis verbis ut res habeat duxi præstandum esse. Ante biennium Johannes Knoxus in privato colloquio quid de imperio muliebri sentirem me rogaverat. Respondi ingenue, quia a primo et genuino naturæ ordine deflecteret, mem randum esse inter homines desertione afflictos non minus quam servitutem; ceterum mulieres quasdam sic interdum fuisse donatas, ut singularis benedictio, quæ in illis fulgebat, palam faceret cœlestibus auspiciis fuisse excitatas, sive quod virorum ignaviam damnare vellet Deus talibus exemplis, sive ut gloriam suam melius illustraret. Huldam produxi et Deboram: adjunxi non frustra Deum per os Isaiæ promittere reginas fore ecclesiæ nutrices, qua prærogativa a privatis fœminis discerni minime obscurum est. Tandem hæc fuit clausula, quoniam et more et publico consensu et longo temporis usu receptum foret, ut hæreditario jure ad fœminas regna et principatus venirent, hanc quæstionem non videri mihi movendam; non solum quia res odiosa esset, sed quia meo judicio fas non esset imperia quæ peculiari Dei providentia ordinantur convellere. De libro nihil sum suspicatus, ac toto anno editum esse nescivi: admonitus a quibusdam satis ostendi, quam mihi non placeret ejusmodi paradoxa vulgaris; sed quia secus erat remedium, putavi malum, quod jam corrigi non poterat, sepeliendum esse potius quam exagitandum. Inquire etiam ex socero tuo, cum me per Bezam commonefecisset, quid responderim. Et adhuc vivebat Maria, ut non debeat suspecta esse assentatio. Quid libri contineant, nescio; me vero non aliter locutum esse Knoxus quoque ipse fatebitur. Ceterum etsi querimoniis piorum hominum movebar, quia tamen non fueram in tempore edoctus, ne majores exorirentur turbæ, vehementer contendere ausus non sum. Si quem offendit mea facilitas, merito mihi timendum fuisse arbitror, ne re in judicium adducta, ob inconsideratum unius hominis fastum, misera exulum turba non tantum ex hac urbe, sed etiam ex toto fere orbe profligaretur; præsertim quia jam aliter malum sanari non poterat, quam mitigatione adhibita. Ultra quidem immerito gravor, quo magis sum miratus, ne liber meus admitteretur, quasi prætextu quæsito aliena deliria in me conferri. Poterat regina, si non placebat, oblatum munus uno verbo repudiare; idque erat magis ingenuum, mihi certe longe fuisset gratius, quam præter ignominiam repulsæ falsis criminibus onerari. Ego tamen serenissimam reginam semper venerabor, et te quoque, clarissime vir, ob præstantissimum ingenium aliasque virtutes amare et colere non desinam, quamvis minus amicum expertus sim quam speraveram, et mutuam quoque in posterum benevolentiam non referas; quod tamen ominari nolo. Vale, amantissime vir, et mihi observande. Dominus tibi semper adsit, te gubernet, tueatur, et donis suis locupletet. Genevæ. Quia dubito an tibi redditæ sint literæ meæ priores, exemplar tibi mittendum putavi.

JOHANNES CALVINUS.

EPISTOLA XVI.

FRANCISCUS COMES BEDFORDIENSIS AD RODOLPHUM GUALTERUM.

SALUTEM in Christo. Literas tuas Januario ad me datas accepi: quibus hoc saltem Januario respondere malui, quam nunquam, ne non tardus modo in scribendo, sed omnino vel tui immemor vel officii hac in parte oblitus videar. Quod citius id factum non sit, in meliorem partem interpretaberis, si cogites nos longissimo intervallo locorum disjunctos esse, et non sæpe in fidos homines incidere, qui literas ad vos nostras perferant. Ut autem tandem aliquando rescribam, scias velim, literarum tuarum pietatem, consilii gravitatem, ecclesiæ nostræ singularem curam ac sinceram solicitudinem, et benevolentiæ erga me tuæ haud obscuram significationem valde placuisse; tibique applaudenti et hortanti gratias habeo. Utinam applaudentis laudes mererer, quas tribuis! hortantis consilium utinam tam sequi possem, quam cupio, tam præstare, quam teneo memoria! Utinam ea nostra esset felicitas, ut res nostras sic esse cerneremus, quemadmodum et ego opto et tu mones! longe tum melius ageretur nobiscum, tum præclarius. Sed non ignoras pro tua prudentia, rerum nascentium primordia difficiliora esse, nec consiliorum rationes subito sequi felicitatem successus, at sensim perfici; ac ut cetera omnia, sic religionem, cruda et infirma habere principia, habere auctus et progressus suos et maturitatem. Idque, spe bona fretus et misericordia Dei nostri clementissimi nixus, videor mihi vere posse polliceri, religionem hanc nostram, tyrannide temporis ceu turbine afflictam ac prostratam, divino beneficio nonnihil revirescentem magis ac magis radices acturam, et quæ nunc paulatim serpit et crescit, uberius et lætius florituram. Ego quoad possum in hoc versor pro virium mearum imbecillitate: contendunt eo et alii, ac imprimis huc collimat concionatorum quorundam pia sedulitas, nominatim vero Juellus episcopus nunc designatus, et Parkhurstus tuus; quibus ego, tum prædicatione tua tum commendatione virtutum ipsorum incensus, optime volo, ita uti debeo, et majoribus adeo fortunæ ornamentis dignos censeo. His aliisque fabris atque architectis opus est ad extruendam ecclesiam Dei. Opus est et opera vestra. Vobis ac piis precibus vestris commendamus nos et Angliam nostram. Orate ut hanc domum inchoatam in sanctum templum exædificet ad gloriam nominis sui et ad suorum consolationem. Is benedicat piis tuis laboribus. Vale, Gualtere, doctissime et humanissime vir. Salutabis mihi omnes in Domino fratres, quibus omnia fausta precor. Christus studia vestra fortunet, ut Satanæ regnum et mundi gloriam et antichristi potentiam indies magis ac magis

evertere studeatis et demoliri, quo Christi ecclesia apud vos et in omnibus locis salva et inconcussa conservetur.

Londini, 1560, Januar. 21.

Tuus ex animo,

F. BEDFORD.

INSCRIPTIO.

D. Rodolpho Gualthero, Tigu-
rinæ ecclesiæ, quæ ad D.
Petrum est, ministro digniss.
Tiguri.

EPISTOLA XVII.

PETRUS MARTYR AD THOMAM SAMPSONUM.

S. D.   Binas abs te literas, mi frater in Christo carissime, ac Domine
magna reverentia suspiciende, unas Octobri mense datas, alteras vero
Decembri, simul accepi, nempe 24 Januarii.   Vides igitur quam tarde
perferantur.   Ad tuas interrogationes jam antea bis respondi.   Sed si literæ
intercipiuntur, aut quam tardissime redduntur, non sum accusandus neg-
ligentiæ : quin potius literarum nostrarum dolenda est infelicitas, quam
nos damnandi quasi officium scribendi intermisimus.   Ceterum, missis
querimoniis, ad ipsas res de quibus interrogas venio.   Primum te hortor
ne oblatæ functioni te subducas, propter miram isthic ministrorum penu-
riam.   Unde si vos, qui estis veluti columnæ, detrectaveritis ecclesiastica
munera obire, et pastoribus destituentur ecclesiæ, et lupis et antichristis
locum cedetis.   Extra functionem permanentes non emendabitis quæ dis-
plicent, imo concessa vix retinebitis.   Quod si ad gubernacula ecclesiæ
sedeatis, spes est multa, etsi non omnia, posse corrigi.   Abstulerunt, inquis,
prædia : sed cogita vos non abalienasse.   Inconsultis vobis hæc facta sunt :
nullam ergo culpam hic præstare tenemini.   Parochis interea quid stipendii relinquitur ?   Ab episcopis pascendi erunt.   Hic fidendum est Deo,
qui aliquam viam patefaciet, et rationem eos alendi commonstrabit.
Pascit volucres cœli, lilia vestit in agris, nec quemquam deserit recte
in sua vocatione ambulantem.   Cavendum vero ne judicemini ab his qui
occasiones quærunt, spectare vos scilicet commoda et opes.   De pileo
quadro et vestitu externo episcopali non arbitror multum disputandum ;
cum superstitione vacet, et rationem civilem in isto regno præsertim habere possit.   De vestibus quas vocant sacras, fateor aliquid esse durius,
et quod me ipsum non nihil perturbet, ut mirer illas adeo mordicus re-

tineri. Optarim enim omnia quam simplicissime fieri. Cum tamen
cogito, si inter Saxonas et nostras ecclesias quoad dogmata pax obtinere
posset, propter hujusmodi vestes haudquaquam separationem futuram;
etsi enim illas minime probaremus, ferremus tamen nobis gratulando
quod eas abrogaverimus : vestibus ergo istis uti posses, vel in concione
habenda vel in cœna Domini administranda, tamen ut dicere et docere contra earum usum pergeres. Nunquam vero consulam, ut vel concionaturus
vel cœnam dominicam administraturus crucifixi imaginem super mensam habeas. De correctione papistarum quoad præterita, memineris
pro pace non semel intermissam, et in ecclesia factam quandoque ἀμνηστίαν,
hæreticosque receptos cum pristinis honoribus et gradibus, modo sanæ
religioni subscriberent. Id vobis providendum est, ut in posterum nihil
admittant, quod religioni modo receptæ adversetur. Illi vero qui vobis
per advocationes offeruntur promovendi a patronis, non debent a vobis
institui, nisi religioni quæ modo viget subscripserint : quod si non fece-
rint, puto vobis relinqui liberum ut eos repudietis. De pane infermen-
tato qui adhibetur cœnæ sacræ, tu ipse nosti omnes ecclesias nostras non
litigare, imo omnes passim uti. Quod vero scribis permultos offendi
vestitu illo episcopali et sacris vestibus, ut eas vocant, facile credo. At
vos ibi culpam effugietis, si vestris concionibus ostenderitis eas vobis
quoque displicere, atque omni studio conabimini ut aliquando tandem
abrogentur. De illis autem ambulationibus in hebdomada Rogationum,
quæ videntur ab ethnicorum Ambarvalibus defluxisse, quid recti consulere possim vix habeo. Id dico, superstitiones omnino vitandas. At si
in ambulationibus iis Deus tantummodo oretur, ut novos fructus benigne
suppeditet, et eorundem bonum usum largiatur, simulque gratiæ agantur
de alimentis præteriti anni, videbuntur fortassis evitatæ superstitiones.
Quamvis et contra hujusmodi ritum sit et magistratus et populus edo-
cendus, et pro viribus agendum ut explodantur seu reliquiæ Amorrhæorum.

Hæc habui, mi frater, in præsentia quæ scriberem. Deus aut hæc tibi
persuadeat, aut meliora suggerat. Hac de re tota cum D. Bullingero
contuli, qui et assentitur, et plurimam tibi salutem dicit. Mea quoque
una cum Julio et Anna tibi ac tuis omnibus salutem volunt ascribi.
Tiguri, Feb. 1560.

Tuus quantus quantus est,

PETRUS MARTYR.

EPISTOLA XVIII.

RICARDUS COXUS AD GEORGIUM CASSANDRUM.

Si omnia humanitatis tuæ officia erga me enumerare pergerem, frustra equidem laborarem, carissime in Christo Cassander. Interim in pectoris mei adyto reposita ea esse scias, utpote quorum nulla me unquam ceperit oblivio. Postquam visum fuit Domino nostro, de cujus providentia semper pendemus, nos in patriam revocare, cum primis ipse Wormatia discessi, et Coloniam veni, ibi Cassandrum Corneliumque salutaturus eisque valedicturus. Neutrum reperi. Illinc recta in Angliam. Ibi pacata omnia, (sit Deo gratia!) mortua Maria. Regnat Elizabetha, pietatis amatrix et fautrix: per hanc pulsa superstitio papistica, restauratum evangelium Christi, pulsi ministri papistici, restituti pastores Christi. Det Dominus ut evangelii Christi professionem vita evangelio digna exprimamus, ne scilicet posthac deterius nobis contingat. Non contentio est, sed neque integra inter nos consensio de imagine crucifixi in templis erigenda, quemadmodum hactenus usurpatum fuit. Alii existimant licere, modo absit cultus aut veneratio ipsi imagini exhibenda. Alii putant ita in universum omnes imagines prohibitas, ut nefas sit ullam omnino in templis perstare propter periculum ita inseparabiliter annexum. In hoc autem statu nunc sumus, ut nulla hodie in ecclesiis extare cernatur. Hac in re, quoniam judicio tuo plurimum semper detuli, te vehementer rogatum velim, ut animi tui sententiam paucis mihi explicare digneris. Quod scribam ad te hoc tempore nihil relatu dignum habeo, nisi quod Scoti nobis vicini sibi nonnihil a Gallis metuant, præsertim qui evangelium amplectuntur, quæ pars illorum bene magna est. Rogandus Dominus ut ab illorum partibus stare dignetur. Libenter cognoscerem ducem vestrum, pro ea qua illum prosequor veneratione, veram Christi religionem propagare invitis papistis omnibus. Vale in Christo, carissime Cassander, salutemque dicito fidissimo Achati tuo, dominisque meis dilectissimis Gerardo Mercatori, Johanni et Gualtero Gymnico et Ambrosio, Duisburgensibus. E civitate Londini in Anglia ex ædibus meis Holburnensibus. 4 Martii, 1560.

Tui studiosissimus,

RICARDUS COXUS,

Eliensis Episcopus.

INSCRIPTIO.

Eximiæ pietatis et eruditionis viro,
D. Georgio Cassandro, amico meo
longe carissimo, apud Coloniam
Agrippinam.

EPISTOLA XIX.

GEORGIUS CASSANDER AD RICARDUM COXUM.

Accepi abs te, reverende Domine, literas 4 Martii Londini scriptas, quibus quod tardius et brevius respondeo, in causa fuit vehemens morbus, qui me paulo post acceptas tuas literas invasit, unde vixdum convalescere cœpi. Evectum te ad dignitatem seu potius munus et officium episcopi libens intellexi, rogoque Deum ut suum tibi Spiritum impertiatur, cujus subsidio munus illud ad tuam salutem et gregis tibi crediti ædificationem impleas. Te autem in eo fastigio collocatum nostræ adhuc tenuitatis et humilitatis non immemorem fuisse habeo gratiam, ac munusculum illud duorum coronatorum, quod literis inclusum erat, pro symbolo pristinæ nostræ consuetudinis libenter accepi. Intelligo de imagine crucis seu crucifixi in templo collocanda non per omnia inter vos convenire: nec satis tamen intelligo, an de crucis tantum nuda figura, an de imagine Christi cruci quoque appendentis agatur. Vidimus hic figuram quandam typis expressam, quæ in medio crucem tantum continebat, testimoniis quibusdam scripturæ sacræ lingua Anglicana utrinque ascriptis, unde suspicor de crucis tantum figura quæri. Quod autem meam sententiam hic postulas, modestiam vestram agnosco: cur enim, cum tot uberrimis fontibus abundetis, tam exiguo et turbido fonticulo aquam potatis? Dicam tamen breviter quando ita vultis. Scit vestra excellentia, apud priscos Christianos quam frequenti in usu, et quanto in honore fuerit crucis character ut passim in ædibus sacris, profanis, publicis, privatis collocaretur et depingeretur, idque antequam consuetudo aliarum imaginum, vel Christi ipsius vel sanctorum, in templis constituendarum recepta esset; ut monumentis omnibus idololatriæ, quibus omnia contaminabantur, abolitis, in eorum locum crucis figura, quæ Christianismi tanquam sacrum quoddam symbolum erat, auspicio meliore succederet. Et quemadmodum in evangelicis et apostolicis literis crucis vocabulum mystice passionem, mortem, triumphum Christi et afflictiones sanctorum significat; ita figura quoque crucis passim constituta et in oculos incurrente, tanquam mystico quodam symbolo, hæc omnia designari et hominum animis infigi voluerunt: quare inter crucis figuram seu characterem, et reliquas imagines magnum discrimen posuerunt. Qua de re videre licet Carolum Magnum, L. II. c. xxviii. contra Synodum Græcorum: "In his enim simplicem et nudam esse significationem; in illa vero arcanam et mysticam repræsentationem." Quare non pro nudo signo, sed pro mysterio quodam habebatur, sic ut non tantum materia et coloribus in templis, ædibus, et parietibus exprimeretur, sed etiam manibus in fronte et pectore crebro deformaretur; cui rei antiquissimi scriptores ecclesiastici

Græci Latinique summa consensione testimonio sunt. Quæ observatio cum antiquissima sit per omnes ecclesias, nolim eam superstitionis argui : superstitionem vero populi, quæ optimis quibusque rebus et institutis agnosci solet, rescindi et caveri velim : quod in figura illa quam nos hic vidimus studio habuisse videmini. Sed boni consuletis, quæso, si, quid in ea desiderem, libere dixero. Primum enim in hoc signo crucis efformando optarim ad ipsius archetypi (hoc est veræ crucis, in quo Servator noster oblatus est) speciem et ideam respectus haberetur; quod in reliquis quoque imaginibus illustrium et sanctorum hominum si diligenter observaretur, minus esset incommodi; videlicet ut ad solam memoriam conservarentur et inspicerentur, quomodo hodieque in numismatis Romanorum principum et aliorum insignium virorum effigies servari videmus. Porro crucis figura quæ fuerit, tum ex vetustis aliquot imaginibus et statuis, quarum aliquot vidimus, tum perspicue ex antiquissimo scriptore Irenæo et recentiore Gregorio Turonense apparet; cui rei et ipsa quoque ratio suffragatur. Nam qui quæso fieri posset, ut humanum corpus jam morte quoque imminente ingravescens, et exporrectum dependens, non mole sua et pondere palmas affixas discerperet? Cui rei ita prospectum erat, ut in medio fere stantis et erecti stipitis tabella immitteretur, cui plantæ hominis eo supplicio affecti insistebant et claves affigebantur, ita ut non tam pendentis quam stantis hominis speciem repræsentaret. Verba Irenæi perspicua sunt. "Ipse," inquit, "habitus crucis fines et summitates habet quinque, duos in longitudine, et duos in latitudine, et unum in medio, ubi requiescit qui clavis affigitur[1]." Iis plane consentit Gregorius Turonensis : "Clavorum ergo," inquit, "dominicorum gratia, quod quatuor fuerint, hæc est ratio : duo sunt affixi in palmis et duo in plantis; et quæritur cur plantæ affixæ sint, quæ in cruce sancta dependere visæ sunt potius quam stare? Sed in stipite erecto foramen factum manifestum est. Pes quoque parvulæ tabulæ in hoc foramen insertus est. Super hanc vero tabulam tanquam stantis hominis sacræ affixæ sunt plantæ[2]." Hujusmodi crucis figuras non parvas vidi, tum in his locis antiquitus expressas, tum unam insignem in ultima Armenia depictam, quam Armenius quidam sacerdos in libro sacrarum precum suæ gentis lingua et characteribus descriptam circumferebat; in quibus omnibus figuris tabella hujusmodi ex descriptione Irenæi et Gregorii Turonensis manifeste imminebat. Quæ etsi minutiora quidam judicabunt, aliis tamen decori amantibus displicitura non puto.

Alterum est quod vobis exponendum propono, num convenientius esset, loco illorum testimoniorum scripturæ, quibus undique crucis illam figuram cinxistis et muniistis, ea testimonia adscribi, quæ crucis mysterium et arcanam significationem explicant; quæ et satis multæ et ad institutionem populi aptissimæ in scriptis novi testamenti extant, atque totum et re-

---

[1] Lib. ii. c. 42.   [2] Lib. i. de Glor. Mart. c. vi.

demptionis nostræ per Christum et regenerationis nostræ in Christo mysterium continent: cujusmodi sunt Coloss. cap. ii. : "Et vos, cum mortui
essetis in delictis et præputio carnis vestræ, convivificavit cum illo, donans
vobis omnia delicta, delens quod adversus nos erat chirographum decreti,
quod erat contrarium nobis, et ipsum tulit de medio affigens illud cruci,
et exspolians principatus et potestates traducit confidenter palam trium-
phans illos in semetipso." Et cap. i. : "Et ipse (scilicet Filius Dei) est
caput corporis ecclesiæ, qui est principium, primogenitus ex mortuis,
ut sit in omnibus ipse primatum tenens, quia in ipso complacuit omnem
plenitudinem inhabitare, et per eum reconciliare omnia in ipsum, paci-
ficans per sanguinem crucis ejus, sive quæ in terris, sive quæ in cœlis
sunt." Et Gal. vi. : "Mihi autem absit gloriari, nisi in cruce Domini
nostri Jesu Christi, per quam mihi mundus crucifixus est et ego mundo."
1 Cor. i. : "Ut non evacuetur crux Christi." Gal. ii. : "Ego enim per
legem legi mortuus sum, ut Deo vivam: cum Christo confixus sum
cruci." Et Matth. x. : "Qui non accipit crucem suam et sequitur me,
non est me dignus." Et cap. xvi. : "Si quis venire vult post me, ab-
neget semetipsum, et tollat crucem suam, et sequatur me." Hæc et
his similia testimonia populum de vero usu mysterii crucis edocerent:
sed hoc vos pro vestra prudentia melius. Ego imprudens, qui "sus
Minervam," nisi mihi non aliquo modo meam erga te observantiam
declarare nefas duxissem.

　　Tu (non dubito) qua modestia et humanitate ad nos scripsisti, eadem
hæc nostra rudia et inculta scripta suscipies.

Vale.

EPISTOLA XX.

PETRUS MARTYR AD THOMAM SAMPSONUM.

S. D. Ad eas literas quas me 6 Januarii scripsisti non antea respondi,
quoniam Kalendis Martiis eas accepi, neque Tiguri tabellariorum copiam
facilem habemus. Nunc id tibi persuadere debes, quæ tibi et tui similibus dolent, et mihi et fratribus vehementer dolere. Ut autem quæstionibus tuis denuo respondeam, non arbitror esse admodum operæ pretium, quia meas omnes existimo ad te pervenisse; quibus ut potui, non
fortassis quantum res exigebat, quantumve ipse desiderabas, respondi:
attamen ea dixi quæ tunc ad negotium facere videbantur. Quæ vos
timetis, nos a vobis non possumus nisi precibus avertere, quod sedulo,
mihi crede, facimus et faciemus. Denique, ut ad tuam postremam
questionem veniam, crucifixi habere signum in sacra mensa, dum cœna

Domini administratur, ego inter adiaphora non habeo, neque consulerem
cuiquam ut eo ritu sacramenta distribueret. Tu autem, qui es in ipso
certamine, consilia hinc non exspectes, valde quippe sumus a vobis procul; in ipsa arena consultetis. Vocatio non est temere abjicienda, nec
etiam cum veritatis injuria suscipienda. Summa est, imaginum cultus
nullo modo toleretur. Nec vel D. Bullingerus vel ego talia pro adiaphoris habemus; imo tanquam prohibita repudiamus. Tu vero nisi ad
hæc adigaris, quod offertur ministerium ne recuses. De scribendis literis
ad reginam ista de causa, sic accipe. Tantis nunc obruor occupationibus, ut etiam si maxime velim non possim. Etenim a duobus pro-
pemodum mensibus in schola solus doceo, causam vero non est quod
literis committam. Huc deinde accedit, quod meas literas non existimo
habituras multum ponderis. Scripsi jam bis publice ac privatim; nec
intelligere potui an ea quæ scripsi accepta fuerint. Præterea si, ut dicitur, consilium est vestratum, ut Augustanam confessionem amplectan-
tur, et fœdus protestantium ambiant, ipse cogitare potes quo loco meæ
ac mei similium literæ sint habendæ. Quod unum possum, non deero
precibus, ut regnum et ecclesia vestra una cum serenissima regina quam
felicissime vivant. Causam tamen egi ut volebas cum Domino Bernardino.
Is est valetudinarius, cum senio tum recurrentibus senum morbis : attamen scribendi provinciam non recusavit; imo se facturum pollicetur
cum poterit. De Bullingero non dubito quin sit scripturus; est enim
in hac causa quam optime animatus, quanquam lectis tuis literis nihil
adhuc mihi indicaverit, quod queam tibi significare. Sed sane vos estis
mirabiles homines. Publicis literis Helvetiorum nihil defertis, imo ne
quidem respondetis : quantum privatæ apud vos, obsecro, valebunt ?
Sed hæc apud te habeto, nec ad ea quicquam respondeas, ne literæ vel
aberrent vel intercipiantur. Vale. D. Bullingerus, omnes symmystæ,
mea uxor, Julius cum sua tibi salutem dicunt. Mihi natus est filius
2 Martii, et 10 obiit. Omnes tuos meo nomine salvere jubeas, et Martyrem tuum amare non desinas. 20 Mart. 1560.

Tuus quantus est,

PETRUS MARTYR.

EPISTOLA XXI.

NICOLAS GALLASIUS AD JOHANNEM CALVINUM.

EPISCOPUM adii, a quo perhumaniter sum exceptus. Literas tuas,
mi pater, ei obtuli, quas aperto et hilari vultu perlegit me præsente,
ac statim quid in iis contineretur paucis mihi retulit : gratias agens

tibi, quod tam familiariter ad eum scriberes, atque etiam de officio suo ipsum moneres. Accessit ad seniores qui mecum ad ædes venerant, quorum nonnullis parum gratus erat adventus meus; ipsosque admonuit ne ingrati essent Deo et vobis, quum plus obtinuissent quam ausi essent sperare; ut parerent adhortationibus meis, et omnia deinceps tractarent consilio meo; ut se mihi præberent humanos, totamque ecclesiam de officio erga me suo admonerent. Tum seorsim ad me conversus, se suaque omnia mihi obtulit, ut quoties vellem ad ipsum accederem familiariter. Petii ut ipsius auctoritate omnia in ecclesia nostra statuerentur, quo melius in officio continerentur nostri homines, et cum legerentur vestræ ad ipsos literæ, ipsi adesse vel potius præesse liberet. Respondit se omnem auctoritatem in hac re suam mihi resignare; si quid tamen prodesse possit, se libenter adfuturum. Addidit postea nonnihil de adlegendo collega Petro Alexandro, qui populo gratus erat, et colligere cœperat ecclesiam ante adventum meum; atque eo gratior quod nulla stipendia peteret, neque tenui nunc et inopi ecclesiæ oneri futurus esset: habet enim opimum sacerdotium Cantuariæ, cujus reditus absens hujus muneris prætextu facile perciperet. Dixi de hac re amplius deliberandum et communicandum esse, nihil vero me inconsulto ipso facturum. Londini, Prid. Cal. Jul. 1560.

EPISTOLA XXII.

EDMUNDUS GRINDALLUS AD CONRADUM HUBERTUM.

S. D. MITTO jam tandem, Conrade humanissime, promissam exhumati Buceri et Phagii historiam, quam a docto quodam viro, qui totius tragediæ spectator fuit, diligenter describendam curavi. Quod autem satis tarde promissam fidem exsolvo, multæ causæ fuerunt, quæ partim ex muneris mei occupationibus, quæ in ista evangelicæ doctrinæ restitutione, quam Domini benignitate per illustrissimæ reginæ nostræ ministerium dudum sumus assecuti, satis multæ et magnæ fuere, partim vero ex captata opportunitate restitutionis famæ (ut vocant) D. Buceri et Phagii per academiam Cantabrigiensem, publico et solenni decreto perficiendæ, ortæ sunt. Nolui enim ut patriæ nostræ (licet oppressum tum temporis tyrannide Romanensium) erga Buceri manes ingratitudinis atque immanitatis prius extaret testimonium, quam gratitudinis et pietatis. Habes igitur jam Bucerum non solum exhumatum, verum etiam restitutum et quodammodo redivivum. Mitto etiam auctarii vice quædam ipsius Buceri scripta, quæ hactenus inter reverendissimi D. Cantuarensis schedas delituerant, ab ipsomet mihi in hunc finem tradita. Salutes (quæso) meo nomine universum collegium, tum ministrorum, tum etiam Professorum apud vos; imprimis DD. Marpachium, Johan. Sturmium, D. Zanchum, DD. Andernachum et Sebaldum. Commendate Deo in precibus vestris ecclesias nostras, jam denuo in Christum caput suum coalescentes. Reipublicæ Argentinensi cum ego, tum ceteri omnes, exilii nostri tempore humanissime ibi hospitio suscepti, omnia fausta ac læta precamur; parati etiam omnem gratitudinem vicissim exhibere, si qua in re usui illi esse possimus. Salutabis etiam hospitem meum humanissimum D. Jacobum Heldelinum, pastorem Wasselheimensem, una cum sua conjuge honestissima.

Dominus vos omnes conservet et Spiritu suo regat. Amen.

Datæ Londini, 3 non. Octobris, anno M.D.LX.

Tui in Christo amantissimus,

EDMUNDUS GRINDALLUS,

Ep. Londinens.

Misi fere ipsa archetypa. Si in ordine aut orthographia quid peccatum fuerit, poteris in erratis corrigendis tuo judicio uti.

INSCRIPTIO.

Dem Ersamen wolgelerten Herren Conraden
Hubert diener der kirchen zu Strasburg
meinem insonders lieben und gutten
fründ zu handen. Straszburg.

EPISTOLA XXIII.

RODOLPHUS GUALTERUS AD D. FRANCISCUM RUSSELLUM.

GRATIA et pax a Deo Patre per Jesum Christum. Redditæ sunt mihi, illustrissime princeps, literæ, quas tua clementia Januarii 21 anni superioris ad me dedit. Fuerunt illæ mihi multis modis gratissimæ. Nam et animi tui vere pii et christiani specimen luculentum exhibebant, et de communi apud vos religionis statu ea prædicabant, quæ non poterant non jucundissima esse omnibus, qui et Angliæ privatim et toti per orbem ecclesiæ publice consultum volunt. Etsi vero ad tuas respondendi animus semper mihi promptus esset, distuli tamen in hunc usque diem, quod indignum putabam, si clementiam tuam; gravioribus negotiis occupatam, literis non usque adeo magni momenti interturbarem. Nunc vero scribendi occasionem mihi dedit Joannes Heinrichus Fabritius, qui has tibi reddet. Est is patricio genere natus, indolis bonæ et magnæ spei juvenis. Patrem habet summæ in nostra republica auctoritatis virum, et signiferum (uti vocant) supremum. Is cum filium primo domi meæ toto triennio educari

et institui curavisset, postea in Galliam ablegavit, ut illic studia bonarum
literarum continuaret.   Paulo post a rege Navarræ in aulam adoptatus
est, ubi inter pueros nobiles primum reginæ, deinde ipsi regi inservivit ;
et tandem evoluto eo tempore, quo ejus ordinis pueri servire solent, honorifice dimissus est.   Pater vero, quia filio propter ætatem minus adhuc
consultum arbitratur, si illum domi apud se retineat, Germanorum vero
principum aulas hominibus ebriosis et lascivis refertas esse novit, quorum
commercio optimi quoque juvenes potius corrumpi possunt, quam in melius
proficere, ex meo et imprimis D. Bullingeri consilio illum in Angliam
ablegare voluit, si forte vel apud tuam clementiam vel apud serenissimæ
reginæ majestatem, aut alium principem pium, locum inveniat.   Linguam
Latinam mediocriter tenet, in Gallica cum dicendo tum scribendo plus
profecit, quam homo Germanus facile sperare queat.   Aulicæ vitæ officia
obire didicit: ingenio autem et industria sic valet, ut illius servitium nec
ingratum nec inutile ei fore speremus, qui illum recipere dignabitur.   Tuæ
vero clementiæ potissimum illum voluimus commendare, quia de hac
nobis spes magna est, et eandem apud regiam majestatem et alios regni
proceres auctoritate plurimum valere scimus.   Et si id nobis per tuam
incredibilem humanitatem licet, etiam atque etiam rogamus, ut juvenem
optimum tibi commendatum habeas.   Ita enim et patri ejus, viro integerrimo, gratificaberis, et Tigurinam quoque rempublicam tibi beneficio
non vulgari obstringes, in qua ille (si vixerit) aliquem locum non postre-
mum est habiturus.   Deus Pater misericordiæ tuam clementiam suo
Spiritu regat, et in Filii sui Jesu Christi cognitione perpetuo servet atque
confirmet. Amen. Datæ Tiguri, 16 Martii, anno Christi incarnati M.D.LXI.

INSCRIPTIO.
Illustrissimo principi, Domino Francisco
Russello, Comiti Bedfordiensi.

EPISTOLA XXIV.

FRANCISCUS COMES BEDFORDIENSIS AD RODOLPHUM GUALTERUM.

S. P. D. Tanta fuit vestrum omnium tuaque imprimis et D. Bullingeri
erga me humanitas, quum isthic essem, ut non dedisse, sed accepisse
beneficium existimem, quoties vobis ulla in re gratificari possum.   Adolescentem per vos mihi commendatum promovi apud vice-camerarium
serenissimæ reginæ, virum et pium et in summa auctoritate.   Spero
itaque illi honeste prospectum.   Interim si quid illi acciderit, in quo
mea opera prodesse poterit, non deero: eandem tibi et toti ecclesiæ vestræ paratissimam semper fore, ut persuasissimum habeas cupio.

Quo in statu sint res nostræ, ex Julio plene ac minutim intelliges : quare non ero prolixior in præsentia. Tu interea bene ac feliciter vale cum piis omnibus, meque familiariter utere quoties occasio dabitur. Londini, die 16 Junii, 1561.

Tuæ pietati ac eruditioni addictissimus,

F. BEDFORD.

INSCRIPTIO.

Egregia pietate ac eruditione præstanti,
D. Rodolpho Gualthero.

EPISTOLA XXV.

RICARDUS MASTERUS AD RODOLPHUM GUALTERUM.

Statim post coronationem illustrissimæ nostræ reginæ literas tuas accepi, dulcissime Gualtere, per Parkhurstum nostrum in suo reditu ad nos a Tiguro traditas. Quibus non multo post respondi, sed Antwerpiam missæ: post unius anni spatium eas intercidisse intellexi, et una cum iis tabellarium in mari submersum. Quod mediusfidius non tam tuli graviter, quam vehementer timui ne me spretæ amicitiæ reum argueres, quod ad tuas non responderim post longum inter nos habitum silentium ; idque merito facere potuisses, nisi me tam justa excusationis ratio absolvisset. Hanc opinionem auxit Burcherus, confirmavit Julius, uterque a Tiguro ad nos sine literis. Sed noli, obsecro, mi Gualtere, tam sinistram de me opinionem concipere. Eo enim semper fui ingenio, ut in suspicionem neglectæ amicitiæ alicui venire admodum reformidem, ut etiam in contrariam reprehensionem longe malim incurrere. Nec quenquam puto esse, qui de me hac maxime in parte possit juste conqueri. Quid enim eam fastidirem quæ honesta aliqua ratione conciliatur? Sed eam potius amplector, veneror, et tantum non superstitiose colo, quam mihi cum tui similibus, id est, doctis et probis viris, studia literarum morumque integritas (quæ duo sunt amicitiæ arctissima vincula) pariunt, augent, servantque constantissime. Tuum me esse, teque et quæ a te proficiscuntur omnia esse gratissima mihi et carissima (ut digna sunt), obsecro ut existimes. Quod re ipsa experieris, si quavis in re tibi gratificari potero. Alius enim non sum ab eo qui eram, cum dulcissima consuetudine colloquioque gratissimo Oxonii agens fruerer, dum religio vera in herba esset.

Quod ad literas tuas pertinet, religiose tibi affirmo, easdem ipsas ostensas fuisse reginæ nostræ, ut quid inde caperet consilii in sincera religione stabilienda et mixta vitanda, aliorum docta malis, etiam atque

etiam videret; effecique ut optimatibus iis ostenderentur, quos sciebam
promptos ad id quod tu pie exhortabaris promovendum.   Sed quid factum
est, quando vivam epistolam Julium habeo, non opus erit exponere.   Non
dubito Deum Opt. Max. quod feliciter inceptum est, ad maturam frugem
perducturum; idque votis communibus comprecemur.   Vale, ac tibi persuade, qui plura fausta feliciaque tibi ominetur, qui denique magis ex
animo te amet ac diligat, quam Masterus esse neminem.   Iterum ac
millies vale.   Ex aula Grenevichia prope Londinum, 16 Junii.

Tuus ex animo velut frater,

RICHARDUS MASTERUS.

INSCRIPTIO.

Piissimo ac omni virtutis genere orna-
tissimo viro D. Rodolpho Gualtero,
divini verbi in ecclesia Tigurina con-
cionatori.   Hæ tradantur in Helvetia.

EPISTOLA XXVI.

PETRUS MARTYR ILLUSTRISSIMO PRINCIPI N. IN ANGLIAM.

PERMULTIS magnisque de causis, illustrissime princeps, tuæ celsitudini sum vehementer obstrictus.   Etenim erga me, satis vilem et obscurum homuncionem, quem tantum semel et vix quidem in Anglia videris,
ita es affectus, ut nunc Julium administrum meum humanitate atque
benevolentia singulari exceperis, illumque prosequutus fueris favore non
mediocri, sed maximo, in suo negotio exequendo.   Quamobrem tuæ
celsitudini gratias ingentes ago.   Præterea id huc accedit, quod ad me
literas dedisti: literas autem? imo laudes et præconia cum doctrinæ
tum virtutum mearum; quas licet in me non agnoscam, attamen judicio
tuo non potui non oblectari, quod id amoris et benevolentiæ tuæ in
me testimonium certissimum intellexerim, neque alia de causa me sentiam abs te amari, quam pietatis ac religionis ergo.   Mitto commemorare quam egregiam voluntatem ostendas mei reditus in Angliam, quam
etiam tibi cum piis et doctis viris affirmas esse communem.   Quanti
vero id est, quod majestati reginæ suggesseris vocationis meæ rationem
esse habendam, atque me apud illam in gratiam posueris!   Denique
pollicitus es omnia studia et commoda quibus me possis afficere, ac
dixisti causas et quidem præclarissimas hujuscemodi tui affectus, caritatem patriæ, et excellentem verbi Dei promovendi curam.   Talem principem quis non amet?   Porro mihi pietas, nedum humanitas defuerit,

si tantæ benevolentiæ totque beneficiorum oblivio animum meum unquam ceperit. Dabo itaque operam, et quidem maximopere, ut mihi nunquam excidant.

Quod autem superest de reditu meo in Angliam, etsi quod vehementer cuperem nequeo respondere, tu, illustrissime princeps, quæ tua clementia est, in bonam partem accipias quod rescribo. Primum, nolim putes a me quicquam vehementius expeti, quam Angliæ solidam firmamque in Domino salutem. Unde illius commodis et ædificationi, æque ac olim feci, optarim etiam nunc inservire, atque regno vestro et ecclesiæ tum gratificari cum prodesse. Verum in præsentia rationes meæ sic habent, ut civitati et ecclesiæ Tigurinæ sim addictus, et ideo non mei juris. Propterea tam magistratus quam symmystarum judicium et voluntatem hac de re quæsivi. Et sane in eis reperi singulare studium propensissimumque animum satisfaciendi vestro desiderio. Etenim cave putes illis quicquam aut gratius aut antiquius esse, quam ut veritas evangelica latissime propagetur. Verum altera ex parte, quæ sit constitutio, status, ætasve mea, non minus prudenter quam amanter expendunt, et satis verentur, ne jam gravis annis et quodammodo fractus laborem itineris ferre nequeam, quod satis longum est, varium, et non ubique facile. Vident præterea in diversis locis pericula non levia imminere. Deinde considerant me ad labores multo graviores quam hic feram evocari. Quamobrem facile fore conjiciunt, ut neque sibi neque vobis possim inservire : judicant itaque multo satius esse, ut hic maneam, quo docendo, scribendo, ac edendo quæ fuerim commentatus, ipsis, vobis, et aliis pro mea virili sim adjumento.

In hoc vero bipartito responso, primum caput mihi similitudinem veri habere videtur; nam ipse quoque metuo ne sim ferendo itinera et labores. At in altero vereor ipsos falli, qui arbitrentur me hic manendo et quiescendo posse tam multis prodesse ; meas quippe lucubrationes pluris faciunt quam mereantur. Ego vero, quem tenuitas, jejunitas, et exilitas meæ doctrinæ minime latet, solum prioris capitis ratione illis assentior ut maneam. Nam facile adducor ut credam, itinere ac laboribus me facile debilitandum ac labefactandum, ita ut inutilis prorsus reddar. Quamobrem tuam celsitudinem imprimis, deinde probos et doctos viros quæso, ut voluntatem accipiant, ubi rem ipsam, quam sibi optant impendi, ob meam imbecillitatem assequi non possunt. Durum quippe telum necessitas, contra quam luctari videtur nihil aliud esse quam Deum tentare. Sed illud interea te velim meminisse, illustrissime princeps, ubivis gentium me tuæ celsitudini semper fore deditissimum. Vicissim autem rogo, ut caritatem patriæ religionisque promovendæ studium non tantum retineas, verum indies cures etiam atque etiam in tuo christiano pectore augeri, quo pennæ olim evangelio Filii Dei præcisæ renascantur, et ita renascantur, ut celeri cursu omnes vestras provincias, urbes et vicos, uberrimo fructu pervadat. Hoc utique duplici studio si ut occepisti perpetuo inflammeris, et Deus Opt. Maxim. te probabit, et omnes cordati piique viri ut probum civem utilemque principem celebrabunt. Deus te per Christum incolumem ac felicem diu tueatur! Datum Tiguri, 22 Julii, 1561.

EPISTOLA XXVII.

RODOLPHUS GUALTERUS AD D. FRANCISCUM RUSSELLUM.

GRATAS fuisse clementiæ tuæ literas meas, quibus Johannem Heinry-chum Fabricium commendavi, vehementer gaudeo. Is certe tuæ cle-mentiæ studium erga se et egregiam erga nos omnes voluntatem mirifice prædicat: quo nomine dignus videtur, quem tua clementia amare et fovere pergat. Narravi patri ejus, viro apud nos summæ auctoritatis, quanto studio et favore illum complectaris; qui ut suo nomine tuæ clementiæ gratias quam maximas agerem præcepit. Curabimus omnes nos, sicubi dederit occasio, ne beneficium in ingratos contulisse videare. Angliam vestram tum in religione tum in aliis omnibus bene et feliciter habere, ex Julio nostro intelleximus. Rogamus autem Deum Patrem Domini nostri Jesu Christi, ut quod bene cœptum est suo favore ad finem optatum et sui nominis gloriam deducere pergat. Urget concilii Tridentini continuationem Romanus antichristus, et ex suis partibus habet reges et principes non contemnendos. Sed fortior omnibus istis est Christus Dominus, cui omnis potestas in cœlo et in terris data est. Videt is contra se conjurantium conatus, et ex alto deridet, sicuti David in Psalmis testatur. Plura non scribo, ne clementiam tuam pluribus et gravioribus negotiis occupatam diutius detineam. Deus Pater miseri-cordiæ illam suo Spiritu regat, et in Filii sui Jesu Christi cognitione perpetuo servet atque confirmet! Amen. Datæ Tiguri, 26 Augusti, 1561.

INSCRIPTIO.
Illustrissimo principi D. Francisco Russello, comiti Bedfordiensi.

EPISTOLA XXVIII.

RICARDUS MASTERUS AD RODOLPHUM GUALTERUM.

S. in Domino semper. PRIUSQUAM literas tuas acceperam, doctis-sime Gualtere, in Henrici Fabricii optimi juvenis favorem scriptas, quid

illi tui et tuorum causa in primo suo ad nos adpulsu obtulerim, quando
ego nunc non exponam, ille quum ad vos redierit palam referet;
tametsi, ut verum fatear, tunc non intellexeram te ullam majorem curam
illius recepisse, quam vel plebei cujusquam alterius Tigurini. Sed postquam per literas tuas perspexi quam esset tibi carus, rursus sedulo
hominem adivi, omnia sciscitans quæ in rem suam fore arbitrabar; in-
citansque illum quam potui alacriter, ut ei quid esset quo opus haberet,
et in quo illi gratificari poteram, id mihi exponeret, meque illi non
defuturum quovis modo, adeo ut vel proprias ædes, vel quæcunque
alia quæ eram præstando, haberet sibi paratissima. At ille profecto, ut
est juvenis apprime modestus, omnia recusans, nullius se indigere pro-
fitebatur. Tum postea expiscari cœpi, quid causæ esset quod cum domino
comite Bedfordiensi non degebat. Ille narrat D. comitem hanc ob
causam locasse illum cum D. Knowles, vice-camerario, homine vere pio
ac a secretiore concilio reginæ nostræ, ut melius sibi esset perspecta
aula Anglica, et ea præcipue nostræ regionis pars quam regina nostra
invisere decrevit eodem tempore, longa profectione suscepta, cum magna
nobilium caterva comitante, comite tamen ipso interim domi suæ rure
degente, ut sanitatis suæ melior ratio haberetur, quam æstate fervente
in tam longinqua profectione ob illam quam habet corporis polysarciam,
illam periclitari sinere. Statim post hanc profectionem finitam bonis avibus tuas literas acceperam, ex quibus occasionem arripiebam D. comitem
conveniendi de nostri Fabricii statu. Ille hæc eadem retulit quæ antea
Fabricius mihi, insuperque dedisse illi equum viginti coronatis emptum,
et viginti solidos nostratis monetæ ad illam profectionem perficiendam;
addidisseque se ut cum D. Knowles Fabricium locaret bonas rationes
habere, quando præcipue ob hanc causam illum huc appulisse relictis
Gallis sciverat, ut aulam et nostrorum populorum mores videret et urbes;
velleque se adventante hyeme illum recipere in suam familiam usque
ad principium veris, quo tempore, inquit, ad suos illum remittere decrevi,
quum nulla spes sit illum cum regina in loco aliquo honesto locandi.
Abelus tamen, quantum possum ex Fabricio colligere, scripsit ad suos
Tiguri absolute, nullis circumscriptis limitationibus, D. comitem illum
accepturum veluti in perpetuum famulitium; quum tum comes mihi con-
stituerat tempus illi Tigurum revertendi, ad principium veris, neque
decrevisse se illum detinere diutius apud se, quam donec hyems fini-
retur. Abelus Fabricium admodum anxium reddidit, ne pater ejus per
illas literas putaret, aliquid vitio verti posse Fabricio, quod comes diutius
illum non retineret quam ad principium veris. Sed, crede mihi, profecto
nulla in juvenem transferenda est culpa; sed in Abeli potius creduli-
tatem, qui D. comitis verba aliter quam ille protulit interpretatus est
vobis per literas. Fabricius, ut bonus et pius filius, nihil magis in humanis timens quam patris sui erga illum alioqui amantissimi indigna-

tionem, me rogavit ut nudam et simplicem veritatem tibi exponerem, id quod, Deum Opt. Max. testor, facio. Hæc ad Fabricium. Quantum ad me ipsum, optime Gualtere, facilius erit profecto tibi mente concipere quam mihi verbis exprimere, quantum me tibi devinctum putem, cum ob illas quas misisti perdoctas homilias, tum ob amicissimas tuas literas : pro utrisque, ut debeo, gratias ago maximas. Abelus a me tibi vicissim reddet, pro aliquo mei erga te amoris specimine, sesquiulnam nostratis panni, pro caligis conficiendis aptissimi, quem ut boni consulas etiam atque etiam oro. Fabricius quæ sunt apud nos nova de Scotis et Gallis melius quam ego scribet, scio. Faxit Deus ut omnes nos, quibus Christus nomen dedit, salutem in illo constanti fide amplectamur, et vitam vivamus illius professione dignam. Dominum Bullingerum, qui primus me Christo regenuit, papismumque relinquere fecit sua ope, rursus ex me saluta. Vale. Londini, 22 Februarii, 1562.

Tui observantissimus,

RICHARDUS MASTERUS.

INSCRIPTIO.

Eruditione et pietate præstantissimo viro
D. Rodolpho Gualtero, divini verbi
apud Tigurinos ministro eximio. Hæ
tradantur in Helvetia.

EPISTOLA XXIX.

FRANCISCUS COMES BEDFORDIENSIS AD HENRICUM BULLINGERUM ET RODOLPHUM GUALTERUM.

S. P. D. JOHANNEM Henricum, quem vestris mihi literis tantopere commendastis, cum vestra tum ejus causa lubenter vidi. Mansit circa septem menses cum vice-camerario serenissimæ reginæ, apud quem ego ad tempus locaram, ut nostram aulam et mores facilius cognosceret. Optassem equidem illum ad majora promotum, atque id efficere studui : sed doleo statum nostrarum rerum hujusmodi esse, ut hoc, his præsertim temporibus, magis optari quam sperari possit. Hæc autem cum plurimorum experientia satis et nimium vera esse animadverteret, ex aula discessit, suisque sumptibus Londini hucusque mansit. Hic se honeste gessit, summaque cum probitate atque modestia. Ceterum quod ejus rebus hic non melius consultum sit, potius temporum difficultati quam amicorum voluntati attribuendum.

Quod ad religionem regnique statum attinet, hic omnia Dei gratia quiete (ut antea) et pacate geruntur, semperque subinde meliora speramus. Idem quoque vobis et ecclesiis vestris ut perpetuo sit, Deum oro. Bene valete cum universa Dei ecclesia.

Londini, 16 die Martii, 1562.

Vestræ pietati addictissimus,

F. BEDFORD.

INSCRIPTIO.

Clarissimis viris D. Heinricho Bullingero, et D. Rodolpho Gualtero, fidelissimis ecclesiæ Tigurinæ ministris. Tiguri.

EPISTOLA XXX.

ROGERUS ASCHAMUS AD JOHANNEM STURMIUM.

S. P. Quid hoc est, mi Sturmi? Michaelis Toxites, tam communis amicus, tam optatus tabellarius, istinc huc sine tuis ad me? An Cokus, an Halesius, an quisquam Anglorum omnium aut tui studiosior aut tuarum literarum avidior quam ego sum? Ast videor audire te contra, Heu! mi Aschame! Tu mecum silentium scribendi expostules? qui ne γρῦ quidem literarum hoc triennium ad me. Verum, mechriste, dicis, mi optatissime Johann. St. Et tota hæc mea expostulatio non iracunda, non objurgatoria, sed insidiosa prorsus et a me, data opera, subornata est. Verebar enim, quod jure poteras, ne tu priores de taciturnitate expostulandi partes occupares. Sed valeant ista: jam vere et aperte scribam, mi Sturmi. Non voluntate mea, non oblivione tui, non neglectione officii factum est hoc tam longum scribendi intervallum. Non quia deerat mihi vel scribendi materies vel mittendi facultas, tamdiu nostræ conticuere literæ: sed cum justam causam a me audies, non iram tibi et stomachum contra me, sed dolorem et mœstitiam pro me, quem, scio, amas, commovebo. Hos quattuor proximos superiores annos ita continentibus febribus correptus sum, ut una vix me unquam reliquerit, quin eam altera statim sit consequuta. Atque sic rationes salutis meæ omnes istis nexis ac jugatis febribus sunt fractæ et convulsæ, ut jam corpus meum omne febris illa hectica occupaverit: cui medicorum filii allevamentum aliquando, remedium solidum nunquam pollicentur. Jam qui sunt veri amici mihi, et inter eos certissimus amicus meus Johannes Halesius, crebro occinunt mihi lugubre illud Thetidis ad filium apud

Homerum carmen, ἐπεί νύ τοι αἶσα μίνυνθά περ, οὔτι μάλα δήν. Et
quamquam legimus clarissimos viros ὠκυμορωτάτους fuisse, quid hoc
ad me, hominem non alti sed demissi animi? Istam consolandi rationem sive ποιητικὴν sive ἱστορικὴν prorsus ego repudio. Sed quando
refero me ad nostrum illum veræ integræque salutis præceptorem, qui
affirmat tantum adjici homini interno quantum adimitur externo, non
mœroribus me dedo, sed nova novæ quidem vitæ gaudia præcipio. At
de his rebus plus alias: cupio enim hoc tempore longum tecum instituere sermonem, cum revera minimum otii ad id efficiendum in præsenti mihi suppetat; sic me meumque tempus omne his ipsis diebus
serenissima regina ad scribendum tot literas distrahit.

Recentissimæ tuæ ad me literæ datæ sunt 15 Januarii 1560. Quarum literarum duo capita, alterum de negotio Scotico, alterum de
reginæ connubio, me commovebant ut eas ipsi reginæ legendas darem.
Illa in utroque singularem tuam erga ipsam observantiam et prudenter
animadvertit, et amabiliter agnovit atque prædicavit. De rebus tum temporis Scoticis tuum valde probavit judicium, et te de tua pro nobis et
nostris etiam nunc deamat solicitudine. Locum de connubio ter, probe
memini, perlegebat, suaviter quidem subinde ὑπομειδιῶσα, et pudice admodum et verecunde conticescens. De illius connubio, mi optatissime Johan.
St. certi quicquam nec ego quod scribam, nec quisquam alius (scio) apud
nos, quod statuat, habet. Non de nihilo, mi Sturmi, sed judicio olim
in primis ego meis illis prolixis ad te literis scripsi, illam in omni vitæ
suæ ratione Hippolytem, non Phædram, referre. Quem locum ipse tum
non ad corporis cultum, sed ad animi castitatem omnino referebam.
Natura enim sua, non cujusquam consilio, a nuptiis tam aliena et
abstinens existit. Cum sciam aliquid certi, primo quoque tempore
scribam ad te. Interea de rege Suecorum non habeo ullam quam tibi
spem faciam.

Cupio ut aliquando scribas ad D. Cecilium. Est enim et in religione integerrimus, et in republica prudentissimus, et utriusque sane
post Deum et principem columen firmissimum. Est etiam literarum et
literatorum hominum amantissimus, et in utraque lingua ipse quoque
pereruditus. De rebus nostris aves, scio, audire ex me. Neque ego
habeo quod potius scribendum putem quam de ipsa regina. Complectar
igitur breviter quam magnas ipsa atque præstantes res, ex quo gubernacula rerum suscepit, et prudenter molita est, et feliciter perfecit.
Primum officium suum Deo dicavit. Nam religionem, quam misere
fœdatam invenit, præclare perpurgavit; in qua re perficienda eam adhi-
buit commoderationem, ut ipsi papistæ non habeant dicere secum duriter
actum fuisse. Hanc pacem cum Deo constitutam secuta est pax cum
omnibus vicinis principibus; et tamen, cum ipsa ad summam rerum
accessit, regnum hoc gemino implicatum bello, Scotico et Gallico, in-

venit. Deinde Guisianis, mira spirantibus contra nos, tam fortiter atque
prudenter restitit in Scotia, ut jam inter utrumque regnum et inter
utramque principem tam secura pax, tam arcta amicitia intercedat, quam
inter duas vel quietissimas vicinias vel concordissimas sorores queat
intercedere. Postquam religio primum, deinde respublica, tam optatæ
tranquillitati fuerat restituta, animum appulit ad alia regni magis domestica ornamenta rite constituenda. Pecuniam depravatam universam,
et totam factam æneam, argenteam puram putam effecit, opus arduum
et regium, quod non Edvardus, non Henricus ipse vel aggredi unquam
ausus est. Armamentarium conquisitissimo apparatu sic instruxit, ut
nullus Europæus, scio, princeps par ostendere queat. Classem itidem
ab omni apparatu, sive rerum copiam sive hominum facultatem spectes,
ita ornavit atque munivit, ut opes opulenti alicujus regni in hanc unam
rem erogari videri queant.

Hæc publica et totius regni sunt. Ipsius magis propria sive studia
sive mores aspiciamus. Injuriæ privatæ facile obliviscens, justitiæ communis severe colens est. Sceleris gratiam nulli facit, impunitatis spem
nemini relinquit, licentiam omnium omnibus præcidit. Res et opes
subjectorum minime omnium principum appetit; suas ad privatam omnem voluptatem parce et frugaliter, ad publicum quenquam sive communis commoditatis usum, sive domesticæ magnificentiæ splendorem,
regifice et largiter attribui jubet. Quas vero laudes ex se habet, et
quæ sunt in illa ingenii et doctrinæ ornamenta, in aliis literis ad te
perscripsi : hoc nunc adjiciam, non esse in aula, in academiis, non
inter eos qui vel religioni vel reipublicæ præsident, apud nos quattuor
nostrates, qui melius intelligant Græcam linguam quam ipsa regina.
Cum legit Demosthenem vel Æschinem, admirationem mihi ipsa sæpenumero movet, cum video illam tam scienter intelligere, non dico verborum potestatem, sententiarum structuram, proprietatem linguæ, orationis
ornamenta, et totius sermonis numerosam ac concinnam comprehen-
sionem, sed illa etiam quæ majora sunt, oratoris sensum atque stomachum, totius causæ contentionem, populi et scita et studia, urbis
cujusque mores atque instituta, et quæ sunt hujus generis reliqua omnia.
In aliis linguis quid et quantum potest, omnes domestici, plurimi exteri,
testes existunt. Adfui ego quodam die, cum uno tempore tribus oratoribus, imperatoris, Gallico, et Suecico, triplici lingua, Italica uni, Gallica
alteri, Latina tertio, facile, non hæsitanter, expedite, non perturbate, ad
varias res tum illorum sermone, ut fit, jactatas respondebat. Ut ipse
videas quam polite illa scribit, mitto ad te his literis inclusam sche-
dulam in qua habes verbum, *quemadmodum*, propria reginæ manu con-
scriptum. Superius meum est, inferius reginæ. An jucundum tibi est
spectaculum et gratum munus, proximis literis tuis significa.

Et hæc de nostra nobilissima regina, et mea seorsum munificentis-

sima domina, et Johannis Sturmii etiam perstudiosa. Atque si contigerit
unquam tibi in Angliam venire, ex ipsius ore, credo, intelliges, Rogerum
Aschamum Johannis Sturmii apud tantam principem memorem amicum
fuisse. Hunc sermonem de hac præstantissima nostra regina et tu, credo,
legis, et ego certe scribo, cum summa utriusque nostrum voluptate. Si
nuberet, laudi ampliori locum non relinqueret : utinam tu, mi Sturmi,
omnem illam, quam ex optimis et sapiendi et dicendi fontibus hausisti,
sive διάγνωσιν ex Demosthene, sive eloquentiam ex Cicerone, ad hanc rem
persuadendam adhiberes ! Neque a te honestior causa suscipi, quam hæc
est, nec a me major facultas optari, quam in te est, altera ulla potest.
Ut ipsa delegat quem vult cupimus : ut alii quenquam ei designent,
non cupimus, et nostratem potius quam ullum exterum omnes nos expe-
timus. Nolui te hæc nescire, si fortasse tu aliquid aliquando de hac
re cogitare velis. Nam si ad tot illa ejus erga hoc regnum beneficia,
quæ a me paulo ante commemorata sunt, hoc unum addat, nulla gens
nobis beatior esse poterit. Καὶ τῇδε ταῦτα. De aliis rebus nostris alias ;
nunc venio ad te, mi Sturmi.

Gaudebam cum intellexi ex tuis ante annum literis ad Johannem
Halesium scriptis, Aristotelem tuum Rhetoricum esse absolutum ; et
mirifice mihi placuit illud quod addidisti, "In illis vos omnes, etiam
Morysinus et Checus." Cum intellexi ex sermone Toxitæ nostri, eos
libros omnes Werteros fratres secum in Thuringiam deportasse, minime
quidem gaudebam. Cavere debent illi fratres, ne non tam genere et
doctrina nobiles, quam hoc facinore nobilitati sint. Injuriam faciunt
tibi, ipsis literarum studiis, et multorum bonorum solicitæ exspectationi,
et nisi de me ipse scriberem, imprimis etiam mihi ; qui licet non
auctor, hortator tamen tibi fui, ut hos præclaros labores, luce et im-
mortalitate dignos, tenebris et sordida aliqua cistula indignissimos, sus-
ciperes. Si vero isti præstantes ingenii tui fructus per horum juvenum
sordes atque avaritiam putrescant et intereant, ego ipse profecto expe-
riar,—sed reprimam me, nec gravius aliquid in eos dicam, priusquam
de hoc illorum facto sententiam tuam intellexero. Itaque si me amas,
mi Sturmi, dum adhuc vivo, (nam, ut scripsi, hectica mea mihi ὠκυμο-
ρίαν minitatur,) ne permittas me fraudari suavisimo horum librorum
fructu. Primum et alterum librum habui ; sed primum, quem legendum commodabam Gualtero Haddono, supplicum libellorum magistro,
negligentia famulorum ejus amisi. His libris sæpe perlectitandis me ipse
delectavi. His superioribus nundinis reliquos omnes exspectabam. Effice,
quæso, ne diu frustretur hæc nostra exspectatio, quæ cum tua tanta laude,
cum studiosorum omnium tanta commoditate, conjuncta est.

Vehementer gaudeo te, quod scribis, ad Halesium scripsisse pro
Philippo contra Staphylum sycophantam. Ex scriptis illius colligo eum
esse non solum Gnathonem circumforaneum, sed Thrasonem etiam ali-

quem scilicet honorarium. Nam quam inepta sit ejus et insolens arro-
gantia, satis apparet ex subscriptione suarum literarum ad episcopum
Æystatensem, ubi ait, "T. D., &c. Fredericus Staphylus Cæsareæ majestatis consiliarius;" id quod populus scire curat scilicet, nec puto ego hanc
esse impressoris culpam, sed ipsius Staphyli projectam impudentiam :
nam hoc idem ipse de se in libello Ἀπολογητικῷ contra Philippum scribit.
Liber ad Æystatensem episcopum superiore anno ab eo scriptus est
Germanice, versus Latine, opinor, per fratrem Carmelitanum, impressus
Coloniæ, totus virulentus atque διαβολικός. Rogo te, non per Sicelides
musas, sed per ipsas sacras literas, ut librum tuum contra Staphylum
in lucem exire primo quoque tempore permittas.

Mirifica perfundebar lætitia, cum legi in literis tuis impressis ad
Cokum nostrum, te scripsisse de controversia cœnæ librum, ut ipse ais,
minime iracundum, tamen ut tu speras argumentosum. Facile fidem
tibi adhibeo, mi Sturmi. Novi enim naturam tuam ad quietem et pacem,
non ad iracundiam et contentionem, totam propositam. Novi etiam doctrinam tuam, qua facile soles et probare quod suscipis, et vincere ubi
pugnas, et ubi vires tuas exercendas jure esse censes. Gaudium mihi
grandius non contigit hos multos annos, quam cum Toxites noster mihi
narravit tua studia sacris literis mirifice esse addicta. Causa religionis
plurimum quidem amisit discessu Philippi et Martini Buceri, sed plus
profecto recuperabit accessu Johannis Sturmii ad illius propugnationem.
Precor a Deo Patre, et Domino nostro ac Deo nostro Jesu Christo, ut
cujus Spiritus accitu evocaris e latibulis Parnassi et Heliconis ad læ-
tissima pascua montis Sionis, montis pinguis, in illius Spiritus ductum
te totum ipse des. Et quanquam ipse tibi libenter concederem et hospitium Romæ et diversorium Athenis, ut ad utram velis urbem voluptatis causa et veteris necessitudinis atque familiaritatis recolendæ gratia
aliquando divertas; assiduam tamen habitationem tuam, et tabernaculum
non solum vitæ, sed studiorum tuorum omnium, in ipsa Hierusalem,
civitate magni Dei, optarem perpetuo collocari. Et credo ego multa
orationis et clariora lumina et grandiora fulmina posse abs te ostendi
in nostris illis, Davide, Esaia, Johanne et Paulo, quam in omnibus Pin-
daris, Platonibus, Demosthenibus atque Ciceronibus unquam emicuere.
Oro Deum, si fas sit hoc petere, ut eam mihi hujus vitæ usuram concedat, aliquando ut videam aculeos styli tui vel tua sponte exertos,
vel quovis alio elisu excussos, contra fucos pontificios qui cellas cela-
tiores et nidos omnes fere molliores in ipso templo Dei occupant.

Vereor, mi Sturmi, ne plus te hac præsenti mea prolixitate offen-
dam quam omni illa mea superiori ἀεισιγίᾳ καὶ ἐχεμυθίᾳ. Quanquam si
partiri vis hanc loquacem in varias literas, dici non potest quin multas
ad te jam scripserim. Sed ignosces meæ, uti spero, prolixitati; quam,
si offensam tibi ullam pariat, ulciscere (quæso) prolixioribus tuis.

Rogo te, mi Sturmi, quid sentias de Dionysio Halicarnassio? Credo
ego illum fuisse ipsum Dionysium qui docuit in ædibus Ciceronis, et
cujus frequens mentio est in epistolis Ciceronis. Cicero ejus probat eruditionem plurimum, mores non item. Cum discesseris ab illa una urbe,
et ab illa una Philippi et Alexandri ætate, non video quem Græcum
(non Plutarchum ipsum excipio) cum hoc Dionysio Halicarnassio possis
comparare. Cupio scire ex te, an hæc opinio mea judicio tuo sit aliqua,
an prorsus inanis. Libellus ejus ad Tuberonem de judicio suo de historia Thucydidis mirifice mihi placet. Uxor mea quia scit te a me
amari, ipsa etiam diligit tuam uxorem, et benevolentiæ suæ μνημόσυννον,
annulum aureum, in formam sagittæ redactum, ei mittit cum hac in-
scriptione, Donum fidelis amici. Toxites habet annulum. Ignosces literis;
non enim vacabat describere, ita festinabat Toxites noster. Vale in
Christo Jesu. Ex ædibus meis Londini, 11 Aprilis, 1562.

Tui studiosissimus,

R. ASCHAMUS.

INSCRIPTIO.
Ornatissimo viro, eruditissimo homini,
D. Johanni Sturmio, amico meo
carissimo. Argentinæ.

EPISTOLA XXXI.

EDMUNDUS GRINDALLUS AD CONRADUM HUBERTUM.

Salutem in Christo. Carissime domine Conrade, multum laudo
pietatem tuam erga Buceri manes, communis præceptoris nostri. Aliorum autem ingratitudinem non possum non accusare, qui vestræ urbis
apostolum ac patrem, qui eam in Christo genuit, tanquam pravorum
dogmatum auctorem aut hæreticum traducere conantur. Quid enim
aliud faciunt, quum ipsius scripta quo minus publicari possint impediunt? Miror magistratum vestrum istis novis oratoribus tantum permittere, ac non plus apud eos valere Buceri mortui memoriam quam
istorum clamores. Sed nolo esse in aliena republica curiosus. Sero
jam supponunt humeros Atlantes vestri cœlo Saxonico jam ubique ruenti.
Nuper vidi literas Brema missas, illius civitatis statum referentes. Post
ejectionem doctoris Alberti gravissima edicta contra Zuinglianos, seu
potius Albertinos, proposuerant, carceres, exilia, ac proscriptiones mini-

tantes. Clarissimum virum D. Danielem a Buren, quo minus consulatum, qui ad vices ejus ordine pervenerat, superiore Januario inire posset
effecerant, quod nostræ sententiæ faveret, alium ipsius loco substituentes.
Sed is summo civium consensu consulatum recuperavit, ac postea in-
quietos istos concionatores, seu potius coaxatores, ejecit. De prædestinatione vero mirum est eos tantas tragœdias excitare. Consulant saltem
Lutherum suum in Servo Arbitrio. Quid aliud docent Bucerus, Calvinus,
Martyr, quod Lutherus eo libello non docuit? Nisi forte ad aliquam
Lutheri, quem tantum non pro Deo habent, palinodiam confugere velint.
Optime quidem de ecclesiæ meritus est Lutherus, dignusque quem omnis
posteritas celebret : esset autem mihi celebrior, si non isti Chanaani
patris sui nuditatem, quam omnes pii obtectam cupiunt, perpetuo rete-
gerent. Tu vero, Conrade doctissime, perge in Buceri fama tuenda, ac
veritate propugnanda. Dominus non sinet hanc causam, quæ ipsius est,
perpetuo supprimi. Non dubito quin apud omnes pios multum efficiet
tua modestia ac constantia. Gratulor etiam tibi in hoc tam sancto
negotio collegam et adjutorem D. Johan. Sturmium, quem ut meis verbis
diligenter salutes oro. Ago gratias pro exemplaribus ; sed ea nondum
recipere potui : hærent fortassis alicubi in via. Accipies ab Abelo aut
Salkyno (si is istas deferat) duos nummos aureos nostrates, nova arte
ac quasi typographica excusos : eorum alterum D. Sturmio ex me dato,
alterum tibi serves. D. doctorem Sebaldum quæso etiam ut ex me
salutes, cui alterum etiam ejusdem monetæ misi, quem oro ut ipse illi
tradas. Dithelmus meus patris jussu brevi in Gallias est profecturus.
Opto te in Domino quam optime valere. Londini ex ædibus meis.
6 Junii, 1562.

Tuus in Christo,

EDMUNDUS GRINDALLUS,

Episc. Londinensis.

Tres illos nummos aureos, arte quam pretio spectabiliores, istis in-
clusi, ac una tabellam quandam, quam quidam ex nostris typographis
nuper emisit, de secundo funere Buceri.

INSCRIPTIO.

Amico et fratri in Domino carissimo
D. Conrado Huberto, Argentinensis
ecclesiæ ministro fidelissimo. Ar-
gentinæ.

EPISTOLA XXXII.

COMES BEDFORDIENSIS AD HENRICUM BULLINGERUM.

S. P. D. REDIT ad vos Jo. Henricus, quem mihi vestris literis commendastis. Is sane apud nos honestissime se gessit. Equidem optassem illius et vestra causa plura efficere, sed non semper optatis successus respondent. Quod ad me attinet, nunquam sane isthinc aliquis veniet mihi per vos commendatus, quin sit futurus longe gratissimus. Quare de meo erga vos animo et voluntate nunquam addubitetis. Tibi et ecclesiis vestris ut omnia prospera et felicia succedant, cupio et exopto. Nec plura in præsentia. Vale et salve cum universo piorum cœtu. Londini, 10 die Junii, 1562.

Tuæ pietati addictissimus,

F. BEDFORD.

INSCRIPTIO.

Clarissimo viro D. Henricho Bullin-
gero, fidelissimo ecclesiæ Tigurinæ
ministro. Tiguri.

EPISTOLA XXXIII.

COMES BEDFORDIENSIS AD RODOLPHUM GUALTERUM.

S. P. D. JOHANNES Henricus Fabricius, qui ad vos revertitur, hic tam honeste se gessit in suis actionibus apud omnes, ut singulare et egregium testimonium suæ probitatis reliquerit. Equidem illi non defui, ubi aliquid ejus causa efficere potui ; et plura etiam voluissem, si hiç tam faciles quam alibi promotiones essent. Rogo itaque ut meum animum, qui alioqui semper in te vestramque ecclesiam propensissimus fuit, eritque in posterum, æqui bonique consulatis. Quid aliud in præsentia scribam non habeo. Bene ac feliciter valeas cum universa ecclesia. Londini, 10 die Junii, 1562.

Tuus longe amantissimus,

F. BEDFORD.

INSCRIPTIO.

Singulari pietate ac eruditione
præstantiss. viro, D. Rod.
Gualtero.

EPISTOLA XXXIV.

ANTONIUS COOKUS AD HENRICUM BULLINGERUM.

Quod a me per literas et a D. Wrotho dudum petebas, clarissime
D. Bullingere, ut hic juvenis in aula reginæ nostræ locum aliquem
honestum haberet, id a nobis sedulo curatum est, si minus ex ejus animi
sententia, saltem ut res et nostra tempora tulerunt. Nunc quum illum
patriæ desiderium revocat, hæc ad te pauca scribere fuit consilium, ut
intelligas et persuasum habeas, nullam neque temporis diuturnitatem
neque locorum longinquitatem meum erga te studium, officium, observantiam imminuere, nedum expungere aut delere posse. D. Petrum
Martyrem, D. Bernardinum et D. Gualterum, quos honoris causa nomino,
quæso meis verbis plurimum salutes. Dominus noster Jesus Christus
vos gregi suo quam diutissime salvos et superstites esse velit. Londini, 14 Junii, 1562.

Tuæ pietatis studiosiss.,

ANTONIUS COOKUS.

INSCRIPTIO.
*Clarissimo doctissimoque viro, D.
Henrico Bullingero, Tigurinæ
ecclesiæ antistiti plurimum observando. Tiguri.*

EPISTOLA XXXV.

ANONYMUS QUIDAM AD PETRUM MARTYREM.

Dominationem tuam, pater in Christo colendiss. carissimeque[1]...inter-
pellandi occasionem aliam non habeo, quam ab inclusis literis dan...
mihi amicus quidam tuus, ut ad te fideliter transmitterem, commisit....
autem una coronatos aureos Gallicos triginta; quos ego tabellario huic
una cum literis inclusis, ut ad te perferat, concredidi. Cum primum
itaque literas has atque aureos, sive justum eorum pretium, receperis,
roganda est dominatio tua, ut utrumque nostrum tum amicum[2] tum
me per literas denuo certiores facere, utque meis quas ad amicum dabis
literas includere digneris. Pauca hæc pro præsenti occasione, ne plu-

[1 Epistola originalis defecta est.]   [2 MS. *omnium*.]

ribus pia studia tua interturbentur, sufficiant. Nostrates pii omnes paternitatem tuam supplices precantur, assiduo in orationibus tuis ecclesiarum
nostrarum ut memor esse velis, deprecans Dominum, ne irreligiosam circa
religionem tepiditatem Anglorum ad papismum, aut si quid pejus sit,
relabi patiatur. Tuam autem paternitatem Dominus ecclesiæ suæ incolumem servet et benedicat imperpetuum. Amen. Londini, 26 Junii,
1562.

Tuæ in Christo prosperitatis cupientissimus.

INSCRIPTIO.
Eximia doctrina ac pietate viro
D.D. Petro Martyri.
Tiguri.

EPISTOLA XXXVI.

MATTHÆUS PARKERUS AD MATTH. FLACIUM ILLYRICUM, JO. WIGANDUM ET MATTH. JUDICEM.

Perquam mihi grata est, religiosi viri, hæc pia humanitas vestra,
qua redditi mihi sunt nuper a vobis per fidum quendam nuntium com-
mentarii vestri, unde faciliorem mihi vestro nomine dedistis defensionem,
si qui posthac falso doctrinam, quam profitemini, calumniabuntur. Quam
quidem doctrinam et fidem vestram, quomodocunque ex parte cunctis
non placet; tamen aperte profiteor, ingenue vos sincereque fecisse, quod
tam plene, tam cumulate, tam sine omni fuco et ambiguitate mentem
et sententiam vestram indicastis. Quibus tamen opinionibus vestris diligenter consideratis, non possum non dolere, quod aliqua sit in præcipuis
religionis controversiis inter nos dissensio, utrosque præsertim instructos
una scripturæ regula, uno etiam ardore animi ductos, et restituendi
veritatem, et e finibus Christi ecclesiæ quam procul exterminandi omnem errorem et mendacium. O quanta hic occasio lapsus præbetur
bonis! quantum hic probris et maledictis ab hostibus vexatur ipsa
evangelii restitutio! Utinam quidem alter alteri, sedatis affectibus, patienter magis et attente auscultare vellet, et neuter ita faveret sententiæ,
ut faceret hanc publicam religionis causam materiem gloriæ, ambitionis,
dissensionis! Quod ad præcipuam illam causam attinet, ob quam venit
domesticus vester tabellarius, ad vos scilicet deferendi causa ejusmodi
veterum commentarios, quales obtinere a nobis speravistis; cognoscite,

quo diligentior fui, ut desiderio vestro hac ex parte plene satisfacerem, vel potius ut laborem, quem ad magnum universæ christianæ ecclesiæ commodum sumitis, juvarem ; eo infelicius mihi res ex animi mei sententia adhuc successit : et ubi reposueram maximam spem nanciscendi quod cuperem, ibi jam omni prorsus spe privor. Atqui posteaquam plurimos plurimis et locis et viris frustra misissem nuntios, tandem animabar[1] ad recuperandum D. Balei libros, quos, ut dicebatur, spes esset acquirendi, si periculum ipse facerem. Didici igitur tandem inquisitione facta, ad cujus manus post ejus fugam ex Hibernia hi pervenere ; quorum cum ingens acervus ad me perferebatur, reperi haud dubie nullos mea sententia vel dignos vetustate, vel argumenti ad vestrum institutum commodi ac utilis : quos tamen cum vidisset vester Nigerus, una cum meis et aliorum, complures multum juvare posse dicebat. Habet igitur hac conditione, ut intra annum transmittantur. Quod si sit apud vos nostræ nationis scriptorum tam locuples quasi instrumentum et apparatus, quam mentio fit in vestro catalogo, arbitror superesse vobis multo plures de nostris, quam sint rursus in toto Angliæ regno, quorum sit apud nos certa intelligentia atque cognitio : sive hoc sit, quod quidam nolunt gratificari vobis in hoc utili conatu, et ex privata quadam offensione non respiciunt publicum ecclesiæ bonum ; sive quod quidam hæc se possidere neminem conscium esse velint. Atque ita, ut canis in præsepi, nec ipsi fruuntur, nec ex his fructus ad alios redire sinunt. Regineæ porro majestatis bibliotheca non ea possidet, per quæ hoc munus quod exigitur præstare queat : id quod mihi retulit is, qui illius curator et custos præficitur. Atque ita se res habet, ut vestræ petitioni, sicuti vellem, non satisfaciam ; licet (priusquam experientia eram edoctus) certo credidi me vestram causam plus juvare potuisse. Certe academiæ et quæcunque fuerunt religiosorum ædificia prius diripiebantur, quam animadvertebatur, quantum incommodi rediturum esset ecclesiæ Christi ex hac librorum clandestina direptione et jactura. Papistæ autem nihil exhibebunt, penes quos (fertur) cum essent hujusmodi monumenta, quæ vel maximam doctrinæ suæ partem labefactarent, bonos quosdam auctores commisere igni, invidentes mundo horum inspectionem : id quod mihi constat de Vigilii libris, quibus sic abusi sunt.

Plura scripsissem de his rebus et de hoc tam molesto onere, attamen fructuoso, quod suscipitis in componenda hac historia, nisi quod partim morbo, partim aliis rebus sic impedior, ut his cogitationibus libere, quod cuperem, vacare non concedatur. Sunt qui in historia vestra auctorum, quorum vos nudam tantum commemorationem facitis, ipsa verba recitata esse desiderant : quod etsi in historia tam grandi sit laboriosum, et viris multæ lectionis usum non præbet ; tamen initiatis non-

[1 MS. *animarer.*]

*4

nihil lucis sit allaturum, et contra maledicos magni etiam futurum momenti. Sed huic deinceps prospicere sit vestræ prudentiæ cogitatio.

Mitto vobis viginti angelatos, significationem grati mei erga vos animi, quam boni consulatis rogo. Interim precor, ut adsit vobis Sanctus Dei Spiritus, perpetuus adjutor conatus vestri. In Christo valete. 18 Julii, Croidoni.

Edidit hanc epistolam ex originali in conspectu supellectilis suæ librariæ p. 6, an. 1736, cl. Jo. Christoph. Wolfius Hamburg. eique sequentia subjicit :

"Hactenus epistola, librarii, ut puto, manu scripta, cui mox ipsius Parkeri manus hæc subscripsit :

'Vestri studiosus,

MATTHÆUS PARKER.'

Ceterum mentio in his literis fit Commentariorum sibi transmissorum, qui deinde historiæ nomine appellantur : utramque vocem de Centuriis ecclesiasticis accipio, quas Flacium, Wigandum, et Judicem (quibus hæ literæ inscriptæ sunt) imprimis adornasse constat. Nec fallor fortasse, si dixero, commentarios illos ad Parkerum cum literis missos esse eo tempore, quo centuria iv., Elizabethæ Angliæ reginæ a. 1562. dedicata, eo mittebatur : hoc nempe tempore Parkerus primatem Angliæ agebat.

Quod vero ad monimenta veterum spectat, quæ Flacius cum sodalibus requisivit, ea puto ad adornandum vel perficiendum catalogum testium veritatis requisita fuisse. Jo. Strypius certe in vita et rebus gestis Parkeri Anglice editis, p. 31. Appendicis, adfert Flacii ad Parkerum epistolam, qua orat ut ad catalogum illum perficiendum opem sibi ferre velit. Compara Acta eruditorum Lipsiensium, a. 1712, p. 442."

EPISTOLA XXXVII.

H. ZANCHIUS AD EDMUNDUM GRINDALLUM.

S. Quod mihi gratularis, Domine observande, illam qualemcunque constantiam, qua me donavit Dominus in defendenda causa bona, agnosco pietatem tuam : quod vero munusculo me ornaveris, sentio amorem et animum erga me tuum esse haud vulgarem. Pro hoc ago et habeo gratias : pro illa rogo me tuis precibus apud Dominum juves. Quæ enim res plurimum in civitatibus, præsertim apud ineruditos, possunt, hæ contra me faciunt hoc tempore in hac causa, auctoritas et loquentia ministrorum. Ii enim, tum privatim tum publice, ineruditæ plebi contra me quidquid volunt calumniarum facile persuadent ; præsertim cum ego et exterus sim, et vulgarem linguam ignorem, et nullius sim auctoritatis apud hoc hominum genus. Hoc unum me cumprimis consolatur, quod veritas solita semper est vincere ; deinde quod senatus est justus, nec quidpiam aget præcipitanter aut tyrannice. Accedit tertium, quod Sturmius noster et visitatores ac reliqui omnes fere professores atque collegæ

capituli nostri causam, quia noverunt esse bonam, pro sua virili tuentur, et sese in ea defendenda mihi adjunxerunt. Nemo vestrum posset
imaginari, quantum ecclesiam et scholam hanc Satan annos jam duos
vexarit, turbarit, labefactarit: defuncti sunt fere omnes senes, et illi etiam
duo qui supersunt tolerari ab ista imperita juventute non possunt. Si
mihi liceret, scriberem res quidem verissimas, atque hic omnibus notis-
simas, sed quas nullo modo credere vel tu vel quispiam alius vestrum
posset. Ego ipse miror meam patientiam, sed multo magis patientiam
senatus. Dominus adsit suæ ecclesiæ! Satan, qui nonnunquam se trans-
figurat in angelum lucis, tandem quis sit agnoscatur et patefiat necesse
est. Vobis vero vestram pacem atque in pura doctrina consensionem
gratulor, et Dominum precor ut regnum Christi in isto regno conservet,
tueatur, atque amplificet: reginam proceresque regni protegat, servet.
Faxit autem Deus ut res succedant in Gallia ex voto atque ex sententia piorum. Video futurum ut totus orbis renovetur. Vale.

H. ZANCHIUS.

EPISTOLA XXXVIII.

RICARDUS HILLES AD HENRICUM BULLINGERUM.

Venerabilis et amantissime amice, accepisse quidem me literas tuas
vicesimo secundo præteriti mensis Junii Tiguri conscriptas, hæc te
certiorem faciant. Et tibi maximas habeo gratias, propterea quod non
solum ad me illas dare non graveris, verum etiam digneris mihi scribere,
cum quid nunc apud vos novi geratur, tum (quantum audis) qui[1] rerum
exitus dehinc esse possunt. De concilio vero Tridentino haud aliter sentiendum est, quam conjurationis sive conspirationis potius alicujùs in
protestantes esse indicium[2], quam synodi ullius causa fidelium catholi-
corum simpliciter in veritate convenientium, ut, qui[1] in ecclesia Christi
abusus irrepserint, pro viribus extirpent. Haud etiam parvo afficior
dolore, cum audiam vos, qui in Helvetia evangelium profitemini, neque
sana vestra doctrina nec bonis vivendi exemplis commilitones vestros
confederatos posse ad evangelii cultum attrahere; qui adhuc etiam rebus
vestris de religionis reformatione ita resistunt, ut nunc suspicare[3] ad inimicitias aut bellum rem brevi perventuram. Quantum autem ad statum
rerum Gallorum, et præcipue de iis quæ Parisiis et Rothomagi geruntur, certum est (uti affirmas) de iis posse nos tam cito hic certiores
fieri, quam qui Tiguri habitant. De rerum autem gestarum veritate,

[1 _Quæ_, MS.]   [2 _Indictum_, MS.]   [3 Fors. _suspicere._]

*4—2

quæ in superioribus Galliæ provinciis aguntur (ut quæ Aureliis et Lugduni), non nisi longo temporis intervallo certo intelligimus. Nos autem
Angli adhuc (Deo gratiæ!) quiete multaque in pace vitam degimus.
Nihilominus tamen de malis quæ nobis possunt fortassis imminere, regina modo cogitare videtur et dubitare, ne quid infortunii per negligentiam aut socordiam regno accedere possit : hoc est, ne externus aliquis
princeps (si forte tumultus, qui in Gallia etiamnum est, sedaretur) a
pontifice Romano aut aliquibus extraneis pontificiis sibi adhærentibus
excitaretur, ut aliquid inveniret, quo cum illa inimicitias exerceret, cum
revera occasionem capiat, quod suæ majestatis auctoritate in concilio
parliamenti, et regionis totius consensu, illius usurpatam potestatem,
continuationem superstitionum, abusuum, et idololatriæ quæ antea in ecclesiam catholicam irrepta sunt, explodit. Habet etenim regina magnum numerum tum militum tum navium jam nunc præparatum in
defensionem regni sui, si opus fuerit. Uxor mea una cum liberis (Deo
gratias!) bene valet, et tibi ob suæ[1] memoriam in literis tuis gratias
agit, teque una cum uxore tua ex animo salutat : quam quoque meo
nomine salutes rogo ; tum etiam Dominum Ludovicum Lavaterum. Vale
ac saluti tuæ consule. Londini, ultimo Julii, anno 1562.

Tuus,

RICARDUS HILLES.

INSCRIPTIO.

Doctissimo theologo, mihique amico ca-
rissimo, D. Heinricho Bullingero,
tradantur hœ literœ. Tiguri.

EPISTOLA XXXIX.

HERMANNUS FOLKERZHEIMERUS AD JOSIAM SIMLERUM.

CEDO, mi Josia, quid in mentem venit, ut mihi, homini curiosissimo
vestrarum rerum, postremis literis nihil magnopere scribendum duxeris ?
Quid ergo ?   Literulæ nostræ quid agant, quid amici valeant, qui floreat
hortus, animo quidem tum et cogitatione tantum, sed tamen in quin-
cuncem cœptus dirigi, nesciam ?   Sed mehercle mereris aliquam nihilominus (fateor) gratiam, quamvis epistola tua brevis, quamvis inauspicata
sit, quod hoc tamen melioribus avibus, salutem patris non prætermi-
seris.   Me Sarisberiensis episcopus amicissime cum rogasset ut se inviserem, civilibus autem discordiis ita viderem Galliam perturbatam, ut
jam plane jacerent optima doctrinarum studia, relicto Pictavio me Ros-

[1 Sic MS.]

chelam, Galliæ portum non incelebrem, contuli. Salinas Bruagenses alia-
que vicina loca per otium non sine periculo perlustravi : nactus autem
sic satis commodam tempestatem (nam quamvis ἐξ οὐρίας minime contigisset, non aspernabar δεύτερον πλοῦν) tertio Cal. Sextil. Roschela solvi.
Nihil erat molestius, quam quod comitem quicum loquerer non haberem : in mentem simul veniebant scopuli, tempestates, brevia, piratæ,
nauclerus improbus, atque adeo quid Arioni quondam contigisset. Sed
Deus exercituum, qui mari, ventis, tempestatibus imperat, qui in omni
anteacta vita fidissimus mihi semper fuisset comes, non verebar ne tum
desereret, quod se cumprimis navigantium curam gerere profiteatur.
Itaque invecti mare, quod Hispanicum vocant, ita constantem nocte
dieque cursum tenuimus, ut quamvis procellæ de more furerent, ancho-
ram tamen nisi semel non jaceremus.   Octo dierum spatio cum jactati
sic fuissemus, apparere nobis optatissima tandem terra cœpit, relictaque
ad dexteram Vecti insula appulimus Hamtonam.   Hic egi[2] Deo magnas
gratias, meque quod essem ex oceani jactatione debilior confirmavi.
Triduo post, celerem forte nactus equum, perveni Sarisberiam. Episcopus ubi me conspexit, nonnulla cum suorum qui circumsisterent
admiratione, festinantius accessit ingredientem, arctissimeque complexus,
O mi, inquit, Hermanne, salve : venis hospes quo ego longo tempore
majore cum lætitia salutavi neminem. Tum studiose, Martyr, Julius,
Bullingerus, Josias, Lavatherus, Zuinglius, ceterique communes nostri
amici quid agerent ? ecquid illis omnia pulchre ? percontatus. Respondi
me utique sic sperare ; certi quidem propterea nihil scire, quod in Gallia
commoratus tam dubiis temporibus, tam turbulentis, vestrarum rerum
factus essem neque literis nec fama certior. Sermo deinde reliquus in
commemoratione rerum Galliæ consumebatur. Dedit comites gnaros
linguæ Gallicæ duos ornatissimos juvenes, qui me quo vellem deducerent.
Spectavimus urbem, templa, rivulos qui summa amœnitate singuli pla-
teas omnes perfluunt. Me tamen, quamvis urbs ad episcopum tota per-
tineret, domestica magis delectabant. Ædes primum ea amplitudine et
magnificentia, ut reges ipsi, si quando in hæc loca veniant, iis excipi
recte et possint et soleant.   Hortus deinde spatiosissimus cultus industria singulari, ut in æquitate, descriptione, varietate nihil prætermissum
videatur. Decurrit per medium fluvius limpidissimus, qui cum per se
voluptati sit, oloribus tamen innatantibus, pisciumque copia, quos jam
cancellis ferreis includi curat, efficitur multo commendatior multoque
amœnior. Humanissime cum postridie me salutasset, conversus ad suos,
Cingantur, inquit, et frænentur equi, atque hunc hospitem in venationem
deducite. Assumptis atque[3] canibus, cum pervenissemus ubi feræ con-
suessent latitare, damas[4] deprehensas insectati sumus, quas ambas, antequam fatigarentur, canes incredibili pernicitate celeriter sunt assecuti,

[2 *Ego*, MS.]   [3 Sic. Qu. *itaque*.]   [4 Qu. *duas*.]

prehensasque facile prostraverunt. Vocibus autem quibus in venatione
Xenophon suos incitat, εὖγε, εὖγε, καλῶς, ὦ κύνες, καλῶς καλῶς, vix opus
erat, quod officium nostri canes etiam non excitati facerent. Quæris
venemurne sæpius? Equidem D. episcopum video non nimium hoc
delectationis genere delectari. Quid, inquit, obsecro, voluptatis inde
capitur, quod timidam feram, quæ resistit nemini, fugatur etiam stre-
pitu, crudelissimis canibus fugientem persequamur? Ego vero mentiar,
si me delectari negem. Sed si tamen sæpius idem faciam, vereor ne
non æque sit voluptati. Sed quamvis episcopus in venationem probe
nunquam, ego raro proficiscar, non tamen otiantur canes. Venatoribus
pueris ea est commendata cura, ne ferinæ desint, ut semper mensa
fidem faciat alacres fuisse canes, venantiumque studia non defuisse.

Sed quoniam nunc agere tecum juvat more nostro, more inquam con-
junctissimorum sodalium, dabo hanc mihi licentiam garriendi, et a minu-
tissimis etiam rebus (quamvis tu quidem nihil vel hujusmodi mereare,
qui tam præclare caves[1] ne mihi vel jocis vel seriis afferas unquam
tædium) non abstinebo. Age, optime Josia, vide brevissimo tempore
quam dispari in fortuna fuerim. Ego e Gallia solvens tacitus atque
abditus, versatus in maxima solitudine, nihil habui præter libellum, quo
mitigarem tædium: omnia squalida, tetra, horrida, ut movere nauseam
navis etiam subducta posset; "extructa mensa," ut ait Cicero, "non con-
chyliis aut piscibus, sed multa carne subrancida; idem coquus, idem atri-
ensis: pistor Pisoni nullus domi;" nobis ne foris quidem: illi "panis et
vinum a propola atque de cupa[2];" nobis miseris, cum lagunculas evacu-
assemus, a quo peteremus nullus propola, nulla cupa fuit, unde maximo
pretio vel minimum quisquam promeret; ut cum quinto statim die vinum defecisset, aquam aceto misceremus, quæ tum plerisque nostrum
sitibundis a vino differre non ita multum videbatur. Attigi fortunatam
insulam, perveni Sarisberiam. Dii immortales! quantam repente muta-
tionem sensi, quantam dari facultatem ex diuturno carcere libere respirandi! Deducor in amplissimam hominis fortunati domum, quicum
summus usus ac domestica (nosti) consuetudo fuerat. Hic me sic ex-
cipit, memor pristinæ familiaritatis, ut ne germanum quidem fratrem
amantius potuisset: innuit suis, qui a nostra sordida nautarum turba
permultum differebant, lectissimis e nobilitate juvenibus, ut afferatur
vinum. Adest pincerna statim aureum craterem ferens maximum. Jam
vero cum prandii tempus vel cœnæ venerit, quid ego tibi argenteum
supellectilem, quid copiam, quid magnificentiam prædicem? quæ tametsi
summa sunt, ipsum tamen, qui possidet, magnopere non delectant, ut
hospitum potius quam sua gratia comparentur. Sed quamvis cetera
non commemorem, facile tamen, qualia sint, suspicari potes, et judicare
quantum navis ab aula differat. Equidem facile patior, quibus usque

[1 *Canes*, MS.]   [2 Orat. in Pison. 67.]

adeo philosophari placet, ut cum Xenophonte sic existiment nusquam rei familiaris curam diligentius geri, quam in navibus, utque patres familias eorum industriam jubeant imitari, dummodo mihi sit integrum sentire quæ sentio. Decimo tertio Cal. Augusti sic satis magno cum equitatu rus profecti sumus, quod se mihi episcopus demonstraturum diceret quæ mirarer. Hic in mediis campis intuens equitatum, Cur non, inquam, Josias horum spectator est? aut Bullingerus, aut omnino quisquam Tigurinorum? Nam P. quidem Martyri satis omnia vestra nota sunt. Utinam vero, ait, adessent optimi viri! Sed quid eos nunc putas agere? Prandium fortasse sumpserint, inquit, jamque mihi Martyrem videor in sua cella curuli sedentem. Paulo longius cum processissemus, omnem situm opportunitatemque regionis perhumaniter demonstravit. Ibi, inquit, exporrecto brachio, fuit antiqua quondam Sarisberia, ibi aggeres etiam nunc quos vides, ibi munitio. Atque alio deinde loco, Hic castra Romanorum veterum, quorum sunt hæc vestigia, quæ videmus. Pervenimus eo denique, quo me maxime Juellus evocarat, quo loci quid viderim scribere dubitassem, nisi gravissimis testibus possem confirmare; propterea quod ea ratio persæpe mea fuerit, ut si quid esse verum deprehendissem, quod fidem tamen prima facie superaret, non commemorare maluerim quam (ne forte vanus haberer) prædicare. Vidi in latissimis campis a mari remotissimis, in solo cui cum petrarum nihil ac rupium natura commune quidquam videretur, vidi, inquam, ingenti saxa magnitudine, quorum prope singula[3], si ponderibus examines, elevarent vel domum tuam; saxa, quæ non congesta, non etiam collocata, sed ita sint erecta, ut bina[3] tertium sustineant. Hic tu mihi ingenii tui vires explica: divina, si potes, quibus ea viribus, aut potius (quid enim vires?) machinis ea comportata, quibus erecta, quibus in altum sublevata fuerint; tum quid sibi omnis illa molitio tandem velit. D. quidem episcopus se videre negat, quo pacto convocatis omnibus suis municipibus vel unicum loco moveat; arbitrari vero Romanos ibi quondam hæc sibi trophæa constituisse: quod ipse saxorum positus jugi quandam speciem præ se ferat.

Sed scire cupias, quibus ego me tandem studiis usque adeo conficiam, ut mihi tot remissionis genera quæram, toties recreem. Crede mihi, prope nullis quæ quidem seria sint. Ex quo tempore Lutetia sum profectus, Euclidi nostro, Archimedi, atque adeo Ptolemæo, multum per me fuit otii; nunquam gravissimos philosophos interpellavi. In jurisprudentia omnem laborem atque industriam, si qua fuit, consumpsimus. Interea cum nonnunquam tamen historias interponerem, diligenter quæ ad Arabiæ Felicis geographicam descriptionem pertinere possent annotavi; ut urbium fluviorumque situs, promontoriorum, sinuum, fontium. Ab Arriano vero, qui mare rubrum et sinum Persicum

[3 MS. *singuli, bini.*]

perlustravit, quod his Arabia contineatur, oræ maritimæ descriptio
peti poterat. Itaque hoc quidem tempore historiis maxime operam
damus, quarum summam nobis copiam Juelli bibliotheca præstat. Gallicæ res me vehementer commovent. Imploro Dei optimi maximi misericordiam, ut gravissimorum scelerum quæ commisimus memoria posita,
atque unico carissimoque Filio condonata, gloriæ suæ rationem habeat
suique nominis. Ipse noster dux et signifer velit esse; exercitum nostrum non muro, cancellis, fossa, sed, ut promissit, cohortibus angelorum
sepiat. Filii sui sceptrum aureum, quod fortissimæ manui commendavit, aliquando proferatur, illamque fictilem testaceamque turmam
confringat, atque ita dissipet, quo pulveres volitent illi quidem ut
merentur, nec locum, ubi consistant, reperire possint; sed ita tamen
ut nihil officiant laudi et gloriæ Christi sui, nullas offundant clarissimæ
luci tenebras. Meo nomine plurimum salutis uxori tuæ dicito, carissimo
meo patri atque optimo Petro Martyri, Julio, Bullingeris, Hallero,
Lavathero, Zuinglio, Pellicano, Gualthero, Wolphio, Funckio, Gesnero,
cui velim diceres me de Phocæ pelle scripsisse fratri, qui si minus diligenter ut νεόγαμος eam curet, me promittes diligentiorem fore. Vale,
suavissime mi Josia, vale. Idib. Sextil. an. MDLXII. Sarisberiæ.

EPISTOLA XL.

ROGERUS ASCHAMUS AD JOHANNEM STURMIUM.

S. P. In Christo Jesu. Cum nos inter nos eodem erga literas, religionem, rempublicam, et mutuam amicitiam, studio, judicio, animo,
atque sensu conjungimur, opto ego sæpe adeoque volo ut nostri itidem
aliquo certe nexu nonnulloque paris inter se quoque amoris alendi in-
citamento contineantur. Et propterea, cum uxor mea ante octo dies me
tertio jam patrem fecerit, filiolo meo in perpetuam meæ amicitiæ memoriam nomen imposui, Sturmius Aschamus. Precor a Deo, inque dies
singulos precaturus sum, ut is, perinde ut nominis, ita doctrinæ virtu-
tisque tuæ aliquam similitudinem referat. Hunc ergo tuum tibi, licet
non agnatione nec gente, ipsa tamen nominatione ac parentum voluntate
conjunctum, quomodo fieri potest, tuæ fidei trado, tuæ tutelæ commendo;
ut si quid humanitus mihi accidat, tu eum eadem humanitate, benevolentia καὶ στοργῇ complectare, qua me patrem ejus antea semper prosequi consuevisti. Περὶ μὲν γὰρ τῆς ἡμετέρας ὠκυμορίας satis fuse
lacrymis et nimis dolenter in prolixioribus illis meis literis, superiori
Aprili per Toxitem nostrum ad te missis, ipse scripsi. Solicitus sum et
avidus sciendi, an illæ literæ ad manus tuas pervenerint. Scripsi etiam

ad te per Henricum Knolles, oratorem hoc tempore serenissimæ nostræ reginæ ad Germaniæ principes. Ab eo (est enim tui perstudiosus) commodissime intelliges omnem rerum nostrarum in Anglia statum. Serenissima regina est et optime animata, et ab omni re commodissime parata, ad frangendam vim illam et tyrannidem Guisianam, ad propugnandum pro incolumitate impuberis regis, pro salute innocentis populi, sine omni vel injuria in illum regem, vel detrimento in illud regnum ullo modo intentando. Hac credo die nostri milites ingressi sunt in Normaniam, quod tu prius ex ipso rumore quam ex his meis literis intelliges. Utinam, mi Sturmi, tu scribere velles separatam historiam hujus Guisianæ conjurationis! Nec tamen sum nescius, ut ille noster in simili causa ait, quantis indies susceptarum gravium rerum oneribus premeris. At sum ipse quidem cupidus non minus tuæ gloriæ quam mei commodi. Materies præclara est, digna tua doctrina, facultate, studio erga puram religionem, amore erga illam gentem, animo in ipsam causam, et stomacho etiam contra illos tam impiæ tyrannidis immanisque crudelitatis auctores. Sæpissime legi, meminero semper illius præclari loci, quem tu tractas de recta ratione scribendæ historiæ, in quadam tua epistola ad Erasmum episcopum vestrum Argentoratensem. Cum ad illam facultatem, quam in te esse is locus arguit, respicio, nescio quomodo ceteros omnes facile contemno; et ut tu aliquando tale munus suscipias, a Deo optimo maximo precibus et votis exposco. Hoc meum desiderium multum lenivit sermo huc e Germania elatus, tibi a principibus Germaniæ provinciam esse datam persequendi stylo tuo τὰ παραλειπόμενα vestri Johannis Sleidani. Hoc ita esse ipse reginæ nostræ omni asseveratione affirmavi. An ita sit, quæso me certiorem facias. De Rhetore tuo Aristotelico, de libris, altero contra Staphylum, altero de cœna Domini, aveo scire, de reliquis item studiis ac rebus tuis. Halesius noster ruri est: hodie ad illum scripsi. Cocus quoque ruri est. Cecillus studio, ingenio, prudentia et constantia, cum magna et ejus laude et nostrorum utilitate, et exterorum (uti spero) salute, primum illum versum secundi libri Epistolarum Horatii præclare sustinet. Ipse nunquam (Deo sint gratiæ!) in majori gratia fui apud serenissimam reginam. Aliquid Græce aut Latine mecum quotidie legit. Mea uxor tuam ac te salutat. Vale in Christo. Londini, 21 Octobris, 1562.

Tui studiosissimus,

R. ASCHAMUS.

INSCRIPTIO.

Clarissimo viro D. Johanni Sturmio,
 Argentoratensis academiæ rectori,
 amico meo carissimo.

EPISTOLA XLI.

HERMANNUS FOLKERZHEIMERUS AD JOSIAM SIMLERUM.

Quæ de felici proventu surculorum, quos insevi, scribis, Josia caris-sime, quamvis per se grata sint, meque in hac tenui saltem scientia non-nihil atque arte posse gaudeam ; jucundiora tamen sunt, quod me ob eam causam tam amice ad nuptias cohorteris.   Equidem naturæ ipsius blanda invitatione inductus, consilioque utriusque parentis mei, nimis a tua sententia non abhorreo.   Sed perpetuæ de uxoribus et quotidianæ querelæ vestræ, quibus eas omnis injucunditatis in vita, molestiarum, tædii conciliatrices esse criminamini, vel optime sentientem commonere et ab instituto revocare possunt.   Itaque ut M. Titurio, qui cum se vacuus omni cura recreandi causa abjecisset in herbam, UTINAM HOC ESSET LABORARE, diceret ; ita mihi in mentem venit, cum navigo, vehor, equito, optare ut hoc esset rem domesticam gerere, et officio fungi boni patris-familias.   In patriam certe jam diu, sollicitatus tot meorum parentum et necessariorum literis, rediissem, nisi in me singularis episcopi Saris-buriensis amor me rogare coegisset, ut mihi diutius abesse permitterent. Eum vero fructum absentiæ meæ capio, ut cum domus nostra primariis viris frequentetur, graves eorum quotidie sermones audiam, non meher-cule de luminum servitutibus aut jure stillicidiorum, sed de munitione, vectigalibus, commeatu, mercibus invehendis aut exportandis, et quæ sunt ejusdem generis.   Sed quid ego tibi, mi Josia, de his plura ?   Certant inter se studio mei et amore duo amplissimi viri atque optimi, Sarisburi-ensis episcopus et Vigornensis.   Vigornensis perpulchrum equum et præstantem dono mihi nuper dedit, meque rogat amicissime ut ad se quam primum veniam.

De D. Petro Martyre propterea scribere nihil statui, quod ejus viri desiderio ita commovear, ut sine lacrymis illius memoriam sermonibus vel etiam literis prosequi mihi quidem difficillimum videatur.   O nonæ Februarii, quibus cum festinatione, lassis equis et ipsi defessi, Lundi-num ad comitia venimus, O ! quam tristes (inquam) nobis, quam lugubres extitistis, quæ tanti viri obitum vel abitum potius ac digressum, sed tamen longum, nunciastis !   Verum permulta sunt, quæ nos consolari possint ac dolorem nostrum luctumque minuant.   Ac inter cetera, si est gloriosa minimeque deploranda mors eorum hominum, qui aut scribenda, ut ille ait, egerint, aut facienda scripserint ; utique D. Martyris conten-tiones et studia, quibus utrumque consecutus est, non satis grato animo interpretamur, si, quasi ante tempus discesserit, pergamus adeo moleste illius mortem graviterque ferre.   Hæc et consimilia ab utroque nostrum cogitari facilius quam scribi possunt, quamvis a te quidem copiosius.

Ego, ut ante cognovisti meis literis, historia et antiquitatis cognitione
mirifice capior, ita tamen ut ea minime deseram, quæ me scis ab aliquot annis instituisse. Animi causa superioribus mensibus Fl. Arriani
περίπλουν τῆς ἐρυθρᾶς θαλάσσης καὶ Εὐξείνου πόντου quam potui maxime
propriis aptisque verbis in Latinam linguam transtuli ; et quod esset
obscurior[1], commentationibus, hoc est, locis ex annalium veterum libris
et geographorum scriptis, paulo clariorem reddidisse videor.   Mare rubrum præterea, Persicum, Barygazenum, Gangeticum, cum locis medi-
terraneis Arabia, Perside et India citeriore, descripsi ad Gangem fluvium.
Secutus in eo sum Ptolemæi dimensiones primum, deinde quæ a ceteris
geographis et historia sic traduntur, ut ad hanc diligentem certamque
rationem longitudinis ac latitudinis revocari possint. Bene vale, mi
dulcissime, et res Gallicas una mecum Deo nostro commendato.   Salutem
velim diceres uxori tuæ plurimam, Bullingeris item patri et filiis, Lavathero, Gesnero, Julio, Pellicano, Zuinglio, Hallero, Funckio, Gualthero, Guldebecko, Collinis, atque omnibus in universum qui me noverint.
Vale. Lundini, Idib. Martii anno 1563. Ignosce huic meæ festinationi,
te precor, mi Josia, et si videtur sal[1]. M. M.

> INSCRIPTIO.
> *Vitæ innocentia et literis præstanti*
> *viro D. Josiæ Simlero, amico*
> *suo cariss. Tiguri.*

EPISTOLA XLII.

EDMUNDUS GRINDALLUS AD JOHANNEM CALVINUM.

S. D. Multum tuæ pietati, clarissime D. Calvine, atque adeo universæ
ecclesiæ vestræ debemus, qui D. Gallasii viri doctissimi copiam tam
diu nobis fecistis : qui et ecclesiam suam, quam adveniens valde perturbatam invenit, D. Cognato successori suo pacatam ac bene institutam
reliquit, et mihi nostrisque ecclesiis consilio ac prudentia magnopere
profuit.   Equidem non libenter illum dimisissemus, nisi justiores discedendi causas haberet quam optamus. Cœlum nostrum, ipsius consti-
tutioni parum, ut videtur, conveniens, valetudinem ejus valde afflixit, et
conjuge carissima (ut de liberis interim taceam) orbavit : adeo ut quem
nunc reddimus valetudinarium, si alteram hyemem apud nos egisset,
verendum esset ne non omnino redderemus.   Valde igitur erat necessarium, ut ad pristinum aërem ad valetudinem recuperandam rediret.

[1 Sic.]

Nihil autem magis in votis habemus quam ut uterque vestrum in communi patria evangelium libere annunciare possitis. Hoc etsi isto rerum statu, partim propter quorundam cunctationem vel potius tarditatem, partim propter aliorum præproperam (ne quid gravius dicam) transactionem, minime sperandum esse videatur; tamen non dubitamus quin Deus ipse rationibus nobis incognitis, ut non gloriemur in hominibus, hoc totum negotium feliciter sit confecturus. Doleo ex animo te ista ætate, et tam tenui corpore, in podagricos dolores (nam ita mihi retulit Gallasius) incidisse. Non dubito autem quin studiorum ac laborum intemperantia quadam hoc malum tibi contraxeris. Posthac igitur remittendum est tibi aliquid de pristinis laboribus et lucubrationibus intempestivis, ne, dum tibi non parcis, morbum in immensum augeas, et ecclesiæ minus prosis. Intuere in Nazianzenum, qui dum de vitæ austeritate, quam juvenis utcunque sustinebat, ætate provectus nihil remittit, perpetuo fere decumbere est coactus, et ista ratione ecclesiæ minus utilis redditus. Quia tu cum Bullingero ex primis illis columnis pene soli superestis, vobis quam diutissime (si ita Domino visum fuerit) frui cupimus. Brentium studio prætereo, qui nunc suscepto pessimæ causæ patrocinio, non videtur nos amplius pro fratribus agnoscere. De regni et ecclesiæ nostræ statu optime referre potest D. Gallasius, qui istas defert: ut his de rebus scribere hoc tempore opus non sit. Salutes, quæso, meo nomine D. Bezam ac ceteros symmystas tuos; D. Antonium etiam professorem Hebraicum. D. Jesus pietatem tuam nobis et ecclesiæ suæ quam diutissime incolumem conservet. Londini, 19 Junii, 1563.

Deditiss. tibi in Domino,

EDMUNDUS GRINDALLUS,

Episcop. Londinens.

INSCRIPTIO.

Do. Johanni Calvino, ecclesiæ Gene-
  vensis pastori fidelissimo, ac
  fratri suo in Christo carissimo.
  Genevæ.

EPISTOLA XLIII.

H. ZANCHIUS AD EDMUNDUM GRINDALLUM.

TARDITATI meæ ignosces, observande Domine. Nuper enim redii ex finibus Italiæ, et prope infinitas reperi quibus respondendum sit literas.

Aves intelligere, quomodo compositum sit nostrum dissidium: dicam breviter. Propositum fuerat de principio dominis nostris, ut audio et video, ita in hac nostra controversia sese gerere, ut quoad ejus fieri posset, salva et sarta tectaque maneret utriusque partis dignitas: idque propter ministerium, tum concionatorum in ecclesia, tum nostrum in schola. Tametsi igitur per istud biennium, quo causa fuit apud dominos acta, optime ex perlectis actis, utriusque partis scriptis, et multarum ecclesiarum academiarumque de meis thesibus judiciis cognoverunt, actionem contra me ab adversariis institutam fuisse iniquam, et doctrinam meam, quæ accusata damnataque fuerat tum novitatis, tum hæreseos, neque novam neque hæreticam esse; noluerunt tamen vel pronunciare de causa, vel saltem ut disputatione decideretur permittere: sed accersitis quatuor theologis et aliquot jurisperitis, partim Tubinga, partim Biponte, partim Basilea, curarunt ut per istos dissidium componeretur. Isti, præsentibus etiam quatuor ex senatu, legerunt acta, et utriusque partis scripta: perspicue viderunt insignem et mihi et veritati factam fuisse injuriam: retulerunt ad senatum suum judicium de scriptis et actis. Hic D. Petrus Sturmius scholarcha palam dixit, Ubi igitur nunc tot et tantæ hæreses quæ Zanchio objiciebantur?

Egerunt deinde seorsum cum utraque parte pro concordia. Cum ventum est ad me, primum disertis verbis dixerunt compositores, partem adversam idem quod et nos de prædestinatione sanctorum sentire; probare enim doctrinam Augustini, Lutheri, Buceri: iis autem tribus post scripturas totam meam doctrinam copiosissime confirmaveram in meis lectionibus et confessionibus: tantum superesse aliquid controversiæ de cœna: etsi igitur legerint meam confessionem de cœna, se tamen cupere adhuc clarius ex me audire quid sentiam de præsentia corporis Christi in cœna: in mea enim confessione nihil de præsentia disputaveram, sed tria tantum præcipua capita explicaveram; primum, non sola symbola percipi, sed etiam rem ipsam, verum corpus Christi et verum ejus sanguinem, hoc est, Christum ipsum; alterum, utrumque manducari ac bibi non ore corporis sed spiritus, hoc est, fide; tertium, idque a fidelibus tantum. Hic respondi, me de hac quæstione non libenter disputare, quod ne unum quidem verbum apertum de præsentia corporis Christi in cœna in scripturis reperiam: sed tamen, ne putent me subterfugere et non audere explicare etiam de hac quæstione meam sententiam, dicturum me quod sentiam. Principio, me nullo modo posse admittere præsens esse corpus Christi in cœna corporibus nostris; illam enim rem dici alicui esse præsentem, quæ se aliquo modo ei, cui dicitur esse præsens, communicet, et ab ipso percipiatur: illam vero dici esse absentem, quæ nullo modo sese communicet, et percipiatur ab eo cui dicitur esse absens; sive ea res, quantum ad localem vel longinquitatem vel propinquitatem attinet, sit propinquior vel remotior. Deambulabat ibi Sulcerus, cum Jacobus An-

dreæ assidens mecum ageret de cœna. Exemplum igitur ab ipsis desump-
tum attuli in hæc verba: Vos, Domini compositores, dicimini esse et
vere estis mihi, hoc est, corpori meo præsentes, quia ipsi vos commu-
nicatis mihi et meis sensibus, et a me percipimini, dum ego meis oculis
vos video et auribus audio; et tam mihi præsens est D. Sulcerus qui
deambulat, quam vos reliqui qui assidetis: quanquam quod localem
distantiam et propinquitatem attinet, ille remotior sit a me quam vos,
et vos quam ille propinquiores. Qui vero foris sunt, extra hoc hypo-
caustum, (erant enim aliquot famuli Dominorum foris,) dicuntur abesse,
quia illos nec audio nec video, nec ullo corporis sensu percipio. Manifestum est autem, verum et substantiale corpus Christi non communicari corpori meo in cœna: nullis enim sensibus corporis id percipio,
cum nec oculis videam, nec auribus audiam, nec naribus olfaciam, nec
manibus tangam, nec palato gustem: non possum igitur ullo modo dare,
corpus Christi præsens corporibus nostris esse in cœna. Ceterum quin
idem corpus Christi verum et substantiale præsens sit menti meæ in
cœna, ubi maxime efficax est, inficiari non possum; cum extra controversiam sit, illud vere fidelium mentibus communicari, et ab ipsis vere
percipi: oculo enim fidelis mentis seu interioris hominis videtur, ejusdemque manu capitur et ore comeditur; atque ita comeditur, ut illius
virtutem et effecta salutaria in nobis ipsis sentiamus. Non possum igitur
simpliciter negare veram et substantialem, hoc est, veri et substantialis
corporis Christi in cœna præsentiam; sed in eum sensum, quem explicavi.

Hic Jacobus Andreæ cum admiratione, Profecto, inquit, vos idem
sentitis quod et nos. Audivisti, inquam ego, sententiam meam, D.D.
Si hæc est quoque vestra sententia, gaudeo mihi, gratulor vobis et
ecclesiæ. Nunc, inquit ille, video cur tot argumentis confutes (nempe
in mea confessione) id quod nos dicimus, "Corpus Christi ore etiam
corporis manducari," quia putatis nos ita sentire, corpus Christi ore
nostri corporis manducari, quasi corpus Christi nostrum os et corpus
attingat. Omnino, inquam, ita e vestris scriptis judicavi vos sentire.
Minime, minime, inquit ille, ita sentimus: sed nos ita loquimur propter
unionem sacramentalem. Tum ego, Si non aliter sentitis, non damno
istam locutionem; nam et ego admitto propter sacramentalem unionem
id attribui corpori Christi, quod est proprium panis; et contra pani id
quod proprium est corporis Christi. Sed de manducatione indignorum
quid sentis? inquit ille. Si nomine indignorum, respondi, intelligatis
homines plane impios, qui vera fide destituti sunt, non possum admittere ab illis corpus Christi manducari. Si vero homines fide quidem
præditos, sed ea imbecilliori, et solutioris vitæ quam Christianum deceat,
non refragor. Tales enim fuerunt illi Corinthii, quos Paulus dicebat,
quia indigne manducarant corpus Domini, a Domino judicari, hoc est,
castigari, ne cum hoc mundo damnarentur. Non potuit inter nos de

hoc articulo convenire. Sed ego non dubito, inquit ille, quin si diligentius hunc articulum examinaveris, sis in nostram sententiam ven-
turus. Satis, inquam ego, diligenter examinavi, et aliter quam sentiam
sentire non possum. Bene: satis est, inquit, de cœna dictum. Agimus
gratias Deo, quod in hoc etiam articulo de cœna non est magna dis-
crepantia inter vos; cum utrique fateamini veram et substantialem præsentiam. Ita discessum fuit.

Conceperunt deinde articulos quosdam de prædestinatione : hos
dederunt utrique parti inspiciendos. Sed mihi cum tanta festinatione
exhibuerunt legendos, ut nollent eos vel unam noctem apud me
pernoctare. Tandem ubi viderent me nolle illis subscribere, nisi prius
a me diligenter domi examinarentur, permiserunt ; sed hac lege, ut
neque describerem neque curarem describendos. Adjecerunt illis, ut
etiam de cœna aliquid statuerent saltem in genere, confessionem Augustanam et articulos concordiæ inter Lutherum et Bucerum. In articulis de prædestinatione nihil deprehendi aperte impium, et quod non
posset bona conscientia admitti; quemadmodum et postea D. Calvinus
tum ad me, tum ad pastorem nostrum scripsit. Tantum vidi, ita
eos artificiose fuisse compositos, ut tamen liquido appareret, compositores magis curasse ut articuli controversi obductis quibusdam tenebris
sepelirentur, quam ut veritas aperta luce explicaretur. Hæc fuit una,
præter alias causas, cur diu, hoc est, ad extremum fere restiterim, ne
subscriberem. Tandem cum viderem per me unum tantum stare, ne
sublato tanto dissidio, quod erat non inter unum aut alterum, sed inter omnes ministros una ex parte, et omnes professores ex altera parte,
pax et consensio fieret; et viderem me salva conscientia posse subscribere, præmissa præsertim protestatione; assensus sum. Cum igitur
ventum esset ad locum, ubi erant domini nostri et compositores, omnesque professores et aliquot alii, post actas gratias iis quibus debeban-
tur, dixi me subscripturum, sed præmissa prius hac protestatione, primum
me nolle ut hac mea subscriptione aliquod fiat præjudicium aliis ecclesiis, academiis, et veritati ; deinde nolle ut aliquid derogetur illi doctrinæ quam hic Argentinæ docui per octennium, et quæ continetur in
meis prælectionibus, disputationibus, confessionibus; postremo ut mihi
liceat, tam Augustanam confessionem, apologiam, et articulos concordiæ,
quam hos præsentes articulos, interpretari juxta regulam verbi Dei, doctrinam Augustini, Lutheri et Buceri. Deinde conditionaliter subscripsi in
hæc verba: " Hanc doctrinæ formulam ut piam agnosco, ita etiam recipio.
Ego H. Zanchius." Postridie, condonatis omnibus injuriis, datæ fuerunt dexteræ societatis et φιλαδελφίας. Ita compositum fuit dissidium,
ut nihil detractum sit de veritate doctrinæ.

Interim tamen non desunt qui improbent factum : sed isti non per-
pendunt, quid sit illud, "Christus non sibi placuit;" neque cogitant quanta

mala secum adferant dissidia. Cur propter pacem inter tot et ministros
et professores unius civitatis non debuissem Augustanæ confessioni et ejus
apologiæ subscribere, eo præsertim modo quo subscripsi, et admissa mea
a compositoribus explicatione, et deinde etiam protestatione? Offenduntur illis verbis apologiæ, "Corpus Christi adesse in cœna vere et substantialiter." At ego explicavi quo pacto admitti possint, et illud dici
præsens esse vere et substantialiter, quod vere et substantialiter partici-
patur: cum sol est supra nostrum hemisphærium, et suum verum et
substantiale corpus nobis visendum et per corpus calorem atque lucem
participandam communicat, an non dicimus, et quidem recte, solem nobis
esse præsentem vere et substantialiter? quemadmodum et contra, quum
progressus ad aliud hemisphærium, quia non amplius sese videndum et
participandum nobis communicat, dicimus abesse: quum tamen quoad
localem propinquitatem aut longinquitatem tam procul distet a nobis, cum
est supra nostrum, quam cum est supra aliud hemisphærium? Quid
igitur prohibet quin etiam dicamus, corpus Christi adesse vere et substantialiter illis quibus vere et substantialiter se communicat?

At, inquiunt, alii non ita intelligunt et interpretantur ut tu. Neque
ego subscripsi aliorum interpretationibus; sed tantum verbis Augustanæ
confessionis, idque juxta illum sensum quem ego pium esse agnosco, et
interpretatio mea fuit admissa. Aliter certe Calvinus judicat, cujus judicium longe pluris facio quam multorum aliorum, quia vere Spiritum Dei
habet; et magis spectat ecclesiarum ædificationem, quam nescio quam
gloriosam in nostris phrasibus, dictionibus, et syllabis pertinaciam. Is ad
pastorem nostrum scribit, sibi non probari, ut simpliciter recuset subscribere; et consulit ut subscribat, modo addantur et admittantur excep-
tiones: et ad me scribit, ut tester magistratui, me serio pacis studio
adductum subscripsisse, sed cum illis exceptionibus; et me idem etiam
nunc profiteri et confirmare. Si spes ulla fuisset vel impetrandæ disputa-
tionis, in qua palam triumphasset veritas, vel audiendæ definitivæ (ut
vocant) sententiæ de tota controversia, vel tollendi aliqua alia meliori
ratione dissidii, ego nunquam subscripsissem. Sed cum nihil horum possemus sperare, quid, obsecro, agendum nobis erat? Credo te, quæ tua est
pietas atque prudentia, non aliter quam nos fecimus facturum fuisse.
Quod si fallor, ignosce huic meo de tua pietate judicio: ignosce etiam,
rogo, non jam amplius brevitati, sed nimiæ meæ prolixitati: et vale meque
in numero amicorum tuorum conserva. Jubeo vero salvere meos quatuor compatres generosos, D. Wrottum, Coocum, Henr. Knollum, et D.
Hetonem; et cupio ut cum illis communices et aliis doctis hanc nostram
compositionem, et quid de ea et tu et illi sentiant, ad me candide scribas. Dominus Jesus suo vos Spiritu semper regat ac protegat!

[H. ZANCHIUS.]

EPISTOLA XLIV.

HERMANNUS FOLKERZHEIMERUS AD JOSIAM SIMLERUM.

Præter omnem exspectationem meam et (vereor) officium quoque tuum, Josia, factum fuit, quod literas a te Franckofordiensi mercatu proximo non acceperim. Ac mehercle permoleste tuli summæ nostræ necessitudinis tam dulcem atque adeo solum fructum periisse, quem, negata domestica consuetudine, scribendis tamen literis caperemus. Quamvis in Anglia me diutius apud se retinere primarii illi viri atque optimi vehementer cuperent, permotus tamen meorum literis ac desiderio, in patriam redire malui. Itaque cum jam equum, quem Vigorniensis dono mihi dederat, accepissem, ejusque educendi mihi esset literis Roberti magistri equitum facta copia, de navigatione cogitabam. Equum, cum mare refluxisset et navis in arena fluctibus destitueretur, trinis funibus ventre religatum in altum traximus, ut ita demissus in nave posset statui. In Belgicam recta navigare institueramus; sed passuum circiter quinque millium confecto spatio, Favonio in Galliam quamvis inviti rejecti sumus. Equitem nausea, equum fame confectum, cum nonnihil recreassem, lætus in Belgicam me statim contuli. Urbes celebriores occurrebant, Caletum, Gravelinga, Dunkerkum, Brugæ, Gandavum; tum in Brabantia Bruxellæ, Lovanium, Mechlinia, Antverpia; in Geldria denique, relicta ad sinistram Hollandia, Hochostratum, Nemagum, Arnum, Daventria. Groninga conveni Ulricum fratrem una cum uxore et filiolo; magna utrinque gratulatio. Octiduum apud eum commoratus Emdam discessi. Multa mihi in vita acciderunt, quæ afferrent plurimum voluptatis; sed, O dii immortales! quid cum illa meorum parentum, sororum, fratrum salutatione, quid illis complexibus conferri potest? Ulyssis tantum desiderium non jam sum vehementius admiratus, cui tanti essent domus, uxor, liberi, ut si fumum patriæ videre contigisset, immortalitatem posset contemnere. Deo Optimo Maximo nunquam debitas egero justasque gratias, quod ea tam cumulate præstitit, quæ frequenter soleo postulare.

Daniæ rex et Suetiæ bellum parant gravissimum. Dux Ericus Brunsvicensis magna contracta manu se ad regem Daniæ contulit. Dicitur pedestribus copiis et equitatu præstare Danus, classe Suedus. Semel atque iterum mari acerrime dimicatum fuit. Daniæ rex nihil existimatur in Suetia vel majoribus etiam copiis effecturus propter fluviorum et lacuum multitudinem, quibus ubique revulsis ac rescissis pontibus aditus intercludatur, ita ut hyems exspectanda sit necessario, quæ glacie sternat fluvios atque aditum patefaciat. Est apud vos Egbertus quidam Brassius, concionatoris optimi viri filius. Hunc si opera et

*5

consilio tuo juves in persequenda studiorum ratione, atque adolescentem pietatis ac literarum perstudiosum complectare, nihil alienum ab humanissimo Josia feceris. Una cum Froschovero constitueras ad nos et hinc in Angliam proficisci, quod ut faciatis, ego, frater, ceterique necessarii vehementer petimus atque obsecramus. Idque velim fieret dum ipse domi adhuc essem; nam in Italiam iter cogito. Vale, mi Josia, et uxorem tuam ἅμα τῇ γείτονι, Bullingeros, Gualterum, Zuinglium, Lavatherum, Johannem Frisium, Hallerum, Julium, Pellicanum, Guldebeccum, Collinos, Funckium, Wolfium, Bibliandrum et quos præterea nosti, communes amicos nostros pervehementer salutes officiose meo nomine. Embdæ, 12 Cal. Septembr. anno 1563. Defholdium præterea nostratem juvenem cum pædagogo saluta quæso.

INSCRIPTIO.
Literis et ingenio viro præstantissimo
D. Josiæ Simlero amico suo longe
certissimo. Tiguri.

EPISTOLA XLV.

EDMUNDUS GRINDALLUS AD CONRADUM HUBERTUM.

S. D. DITHELMUS BLAURERUS, qui tuo hortatu ac suasu ad me in Angliam venit, jam redit in patriam, revocatus a patre. Non potui igitur committere ut sine literis meis ad te rediret, qui tuis mihi fuit commendatus. Æquum est etiam ut, quemadmodum est promeritus, de pie atque honeste apud me acta vita testimonium illi feram. In multis ipsius opera mihi usui fuit: in multo pluribus vero futura fuisset, nisi me infinitæ occupationes, quæ cum hoc munere meo sunt conjunctæ, varie distraxissent. Ne autem sis nescius quibus conditionibus illum dimiserim, numeravi in discessu integrum stipendium, quod ad Michaelis proxime sequentis pro quarta anni parte solvendum erat, coronatos videlicet Gallicos quatuor, et pro sumptibus itineris quatuor libras nostrates, quæ conficiunt 13 coronatos Gallicos et paulo plus. Addidi etiam quædam munuscula. Hæc non aliam ob causam scribo, quam ut ipsam rei veritatem cognoscas. Numeravi etiam Abelo pro expensis Dithelmi, quum primum ad me venit ex Germania, ultra 14 coronatos, quod hyeme adversis ventis in litore Flandriæ diutius paulo hærere sunt coacti. Audio vestra dissidia jam esse composita: faxit Deus ut sit pax firma ac sincera, minimeque fucata. De vobis nihil dubito; timeo ne altera pars novas aliquando turbas excitet. Tibi vero, carissime D.

Conrade, ex animo gratulor istam pietatem erga communem præceptorem, D. Bucerum felicis memoriæ, cujus famam tam constanter hactenus es tutatus. Opto te in Domino quam optime valere. Ex suburb-
ano nostro Fulhamiensi ad ripam Thamesis, 23 Augusti, 1563.

Tuus in Christo,

EDM. GRINDALLUS,
Episc. Londinensis.

INSCRIPTIO.

Domino Conrado Huberto Argentinen-
sis ecclesiæ ministro fidelissimo et
fratri suo in Christo carissimo.
Argentinæ.

EPISTOLA XLVI.

H. ZANCHIUS AD EDMUNDUM GRINDALLUM.

S. Mitto ad te, reverende episcope et Domine, judicium de dissidio
ecclesiarum in cœna Domini meum, quod generoso Domino Knollo, compatri meo, certis de causis dicavi. Non composueram quidem illud eo
animo ut invulgaretur, quemadmodum tu ipse potes tum ex brevitate
tum ex stylo conjicere: sed quoniam amici, inter quos Sturmius, ita
probarunt, ut me coëgerint invulgare, malui morem gerendo amicis
videri imperitus, quam reluctando in ecclesias ipsas esse ingratus. Tu
igitur exemplum hoc accipies, ut testimonium observantiæ erga te meæ.
Mittam brevi, ut spero, meliora et copiosiora. Dominus sicut antea vos,
ita hoc anno nos, hoc est, ecclesiam meam Clavennensem, visitavit pestilentia. Meam dixi, ut intelligas me non amplius profiteri Argentinæ,
sed ministrum agere Clavennæ, quæ est in foribus Italiæ, ac propterea
Clavenna appellatur, quod ostii ex Italia in Germaniam, et vicissim e
Germania in Italiam, sit clavis. Cur vero discesserim tandem Argentina, intelliges ex libro quem brevi ad vos etiam mittam. Tu nosti cur
bonus Martyr piæ memoriæ non potuerit amplius esse Argentinæ; ac
proinde ad Tigurinos concesserit. Ego præter illam ἀνθρωποδουλείαν
habui alias etiam graves causas. Qua de causa ego discessi, de eadem
etiam Gallicana ecclesia, quæ Argentinæ erat, fuit dissipata: non amplius sunt contenti illi boni domini, ut si quis velit apud se vel profiteri vel ministrum agere, Augustanæ confessioni subscribat; sed volunt
etiam ut in omnibus et per omnia, et quoad Augustanæ confessionis
intelligentiam, et quoad scripturarum interpretationem, cum suis con-

cionatoribus sine ulla disceptatione consentiat. Auctorem nosti : Dominus misereatur illius urbis! Nihil non feci ut meam retinerem stationem, hac tantum de causa, ut veterem illius ecclesiæ doctrinam, quam novi esse Christianam, in schola saltem retinerem. Sed quid agas, cum Dominus vult aliquem populum propter suas iniquitates punire? Negotium illud mei affinis Laurentii Limacii tibi commendo. Vale, optime pater et amice singularis. Mense Augusto, 1564. Ex montibus Claven.

H. ZANCHIUS.

EPISTOLA XLVII.

H. ZANCHIUS AD HENRICUM KNOLLUM.

S. Meum de dissidio ecclesiarum in cœna Domini judicium, quod tibi, observandissime compater, in eum finem dicavi, ut publicum sit idemque perpetuum grati mei erga te animi testimonium, dederam optimo et diligentissimo, adde et doctissimo omnium typographo, Johanni Oporino, pulchris typis excudendum. Sed quia, ut video, non potuit a censoribus facultatem hunc libellum imprimendi (causam tu ipse cogita) impetrare, eum dedit typographo Mylhusiano. At is, sive oscitantia, sive imperitia, plenum erratis in lucem misit : id quod vehementer mihi displicuit. Quare coactus fui, quotquot habui exemplaria, manu emendare. Emendatum igitur exemplum unum ad te mitto, et rogo ut boni consulas has paucas chartulas : misissem plura exemplaria ad reliquos amicos, si qui voluissent ferre nactus fuissem. Cetera, valemus omnes Dei beneficio : et tua profilia jam ablactata garrit, discurrit, simiam agit. De discessu meo Argentina credo te ab aliis jam pridem intellexisse ; sed causam fortassis minime. Ea fuit, ut uno verbo dicam, propter quam bonus quoque piæ memoriæ Petrus Martyr longe ante me Tigurum discesserat ; indigna scilicet Christiano ac multo magis theologo ἀνθρωποδουλεία. Cum igitur vidissem mihi non amplius licere libere docere, neque eam tueri doctrinam, quam ante me viri doctissimi Bucerus, Capito, Martyr, Calvinus, e fonte S. literarum haustam, in ea schola auditoribus multos annos propinaverant ; imo quam ego etiam annos novem ibidem in lectionibus tradideram, et publicis disputationibus defenderam ; renuntiavi priori conditioni, et novam, nimirum Clavennensis ecclesiæ ministerium, amplexus sum. Dominus vero mirabiliter meam afflixit ecclesiam, imo totum oppidum, pestilentia, qua duas fere partes abstulit, una tantum relicta, ut etiam est apud Zachariam. Sed hæc pestis non tantum hic, sed alibi quoque multis in locis, tam in Germania, ut Basileæ, quam in Gallia, ut Lugduni, grassatur. Domi-

nus nostri omnium misereatur! Italia vacua est ab hoc malo: sed caritate annonæ laborat. Tua commater multam tibi salutem dicit. Ego
vero salvere jubeo amicos, atque imprimis generosos Dom. Wrottum et
Cookum, deinde etiam Hetonum, compatres meos. Vale.

EPISTOLA XLVIII.

RICARDUS MASTERUS AD RODOLPHUM GUALTERUM.

Ex quo ad te proxime scripseram, piissime vir, tres epistolas a te
accepi amoris tui erga me plenissimas; quibus quod citius non responderim, neque negotia, quibus eram implicatus, neque oblivionem tui aut
aliud quidpiam causari volo, præter pestem, quæ tam diu sæviebat
apud nos, ut aula regia a Londino longo tum loci tum temporis intervallo abfuerat: quo tandem cum rediverimus Deo favente incolumes,
has ad te mittere decrevi. Homilias tuas in prophetas minores accepi
per manus Johannis Abeli concivis nostri amici mihi traditas, quas ab
omnibus doctis et piis ita amplecti[1] intelligo, ut hodie in tota Europa
vix unus aut alter habeatur, in sacris interpretandis, qui te illorum judicio aut æquet aut superet; avideque exspectant reliquas, quas promisisti in divum Johannem. Narravi præterea iis qui apud nos præ-
stant maxime, quanto amore nos prosequaris nostrumque reipublicæ
statum, dum tam anxie egisse te scribis, nostri et veræ religionis causa,
cum iis qui de fœdere inter vos et Gallos sanciendo tam sedulo sate-
gerunt. Guisiana factio in Galliis quotidie magis magisque infirmatur,
adeo ut nuper parum abfuit, quin cardinalis ille Lotheringius una
cum nepote suo duce Guisio interfecti fuissent, aggrediente illos in via
publica Parisiis Momorentio, Parisianorum præfecto (mariscallum vocant)
senioreque filio Annæ ducis Momorentii, summi Galliæ equitum magistri
(constabularium vocant), in quo tumultu ceciderunt quinque ex armatis
satellitibus cardinalis Lotheringii, isto et nepote suo vix se recipientibus in
mercatoris cujusdam domum, velut in asylum pro tempore. Legati reginæ
nostræ et regis Hispaniarum in principio hujus veris conveniunt in Flan-
dria, pro commercio inter nostros mercatores et suos resarciendo, ut antea
est consuetum, Antwerpiæ; quod duobus tribusve annis, cum utriusque
nostro magno malo, discordia inter mercatores utrinque orta, interruptum
fuit: alias, quantum ad politiam pertinet, omnia apud nos sunt pacata
et tranquilla. In Scotia monasteria prosternuntur, monachatusque et
idololatria abolentur; regina solummodo ex familia Guisiana (filia enim
sororis ducis interfecti est) adhuc retinente missam suam. Comes noster

[1 Sic MS.]

Bedfordiensis ab aula abest, abfuitque per sesquianni spatium : præfectus enim factus est urbis Barwicensis in confinio Scotiæ, nosque ab illis disterminantis : illi tamen absenti significavi quod memor esses illius, teque illi per meas literas commendavi.   Vale. Dominus Deus te tueatur et regat ad nominis sui gloriam, et ut diu vivas laboresque in vinea sua. Londini, 4 Martii, 1565.

Tuus ex animo totus,
RICHARDUS MASTER.

INSCRIPTIO.

Piissimo viro Domino Rodolpho Gual-
tero, verbi Dei apud Tigurinos in
Helvetia ministro dignissimo, hæ
tradantur literæ.

EPISTOLA XLIX.

JOHANNES PARKHURSTUS AD JOHANNEM WOLFIUM.

Non est, mi Wolfi, quod [in] re tantilla tantas agas gratias.   Quæso boni consulas tenue munusculum, mei erga te amoris qualecunque mnemosynon.   Accepi literas abs te ante biennium : et quia tum temporis infinitis oppressus eram negotiis, tibi seorsim non respondi; sed uno epistolio tibi et Lavatero vel Simlero satisfacere sum coactus.   De rebus nostris et Scoticis ad alios scripsi : tu ex illis discito.   Non possum singulis singula exponere.   19 Maii horreum meum longum pedes 215 corruit, nullo læso homine, nulla bestia.   Maximis impensis fere reædificavi.   Bene vale.   Saluta uxorem tuam meo meæque nomine, ceterosque amicos omnes.   Raptim. Ludhamiæ, 19 August. 1565.

Tuus,
JOHANNES PARKHURSTUS,
Nordovicensis.

INSCRIPTIO.

Doctissimo viro D. Johanni Wolfio.
Tiguri.

EPISTOLA L.

MILO COVERDALUS ET ALII AD GULIELMUM FARELLUM ET ALIOS.

Et molesti pietati vestræ videri possimus, honorandi domini et fratres, qui per amicos et literas sæpe interpellamus, et officii erga ecclesiam pa-

rum memores, qui gravioribus rebus districtos nugarum commemoratione
obstrepamus. At enim temporum nostrorum infelix conditio et nova tempestas cogunt nos ad vos confugere; ut et vos statum rerum nostrarum,
deinde et opinionem nostram plenius cognoscatis, et nos sententiam vestram plenius intelligamus. Res nostræ non in melius commutatæ, sed,
proh dolor! in deterius prolapsæ sunt. Hæc enim acta et transacta sunt,
ut loco panis vulgaris placentula azyma habeatur; ut communio geni-
bus flexis a plebecula sumatur; ut foris pileum quadrum, collipendium,
toga longa et lanea gestentur; in ministerio autem sacro vestis alba et
capa retineantur. Qui his parere nolunt, hi fortunis, dignitatibus, omni-
que munere ecclesiastico spoliantur: fratres scilicet a fratribus et episcopis,
quorum domus jam quorundam concionatorum carcer est; qui jam in
viscera sua sæviunt; qui jam hæc onera non modo corporibus suis, sed
aliorum etiam humeris imponunt; eo denique tempore, quando omnium
doctorum judicio sublata et abrogata esse oportuerunt. En! habetis
formam et imaginem qualemcunque nostræ ecclesiæ.

Nunc quid nobis videatur, accipite. In hac quæstione sic statuendum censemus, religionem Judaicam, Turcicam, Christianam, papisticam
sua quædam propria sacramenta et signa habere; et doctrinæ cujusquam
externam professionem, testem, et tesseram esse debere; et exemplum
nobis non e cisternis aut lacunis hostium, sed e fontibus scripturarum
et ecclesiarum Dei petendum; ut a quorum religione toto pectore ab-
horremus, cum his nulla rituum similitudine conjungamur: quod in
sabbato et paschate Judæorum, in jejuniis Manichæorum, in trina
mersione hæreticorum, majores nostros diligenter observasse legimus.
Neque vero prorsus ἀδιάφορα putamus, cum accedit coactio, cum etiam
superstitionis macula inusta est: nec quicquam auctoritate principis
obtrudendum, sine legitima in christiana synodo disceptatione: nec
convenientia in ceremoniis ubique necessario exigenda, maxime si cum
adversariis fidei communis sit: nec in Christi ecclesia vel Aaronico
sacerdotio vel Pharisaicæ ambitioni locum esse, ut hodie in templo
christiano sacræ vestes usurpentur, aut in communi usu habitus non
communis, sed distinctus et singularis, præscribatur. Sed cum Celestino
judicamus, discernendum esse clerum a plebe doctrina, non veste, con-
versatione, non habitu, mentis puritate, non cultu; ne studere novitati
incipiamus, ne traditum a patribus ordinem calcemus, ne simpliciorum
animis et oculis imponamus, ne locum supervacuis superstitionibus
faciamus.

Præterea, quotquot ista ex ecclesiis nostræ fidei commissis ejecimus, sine
grandi scandalo et nefario scelere revocare non possumus. Cum etiam
aditus ad alia iniquitatis mysteria aperiatur, et caritas piorum offendatur, et cristæ animique impiorum erigantur, ædificatio autem nulla
quæratur; cum non liceat juxta D. Pauli regulam in rebus indifferen-

tibus unumquemque in suo sensu acquiescere; sed quod certis quibusdam hominibus libitum est, id licitum existimetur : consultius ecclesiæ
existimavimus in libertate cum accessione bonorum stare, quam cum
offensione multorum et doctrinæ purioris titubatione a suscepta sententia et recepta consuetudine discedere. Hæc nostra opinio est, hæc
etiam eximii viri. Nunc vos, clarissimi et carissimi domini et fratres, per
arctissimam in Christo communionem rogamus, ut nobis fluctuantibus
cynosuram ostendatis; ut vel errantibus viam meliorem commonstretis,
vel dubitantes in sancto proposito confirmetis.

Difficilis, fatemur, et scrupulosa consultatio; cederene tempori an
discedere, relliquias Amorrhæorum admittere an stationem deserere, oporteat. Utrumque durum, utrumque grave, utrumque nobis et ecclesiæ
incommodum. Utrum sit melius, vos pro sapientia vestra, quia nos
ancipites inter sacrum et saxum hæremus, edisserite. Rogamus item vos
et alios symmystas aliquem tractatum de natura rerum indifferentium, de
ceremoniis, de vestitu sacerdotali primo quoque tempore emittere : unde
ecclesia nostra et Saxonicæ erudiantur, et principum zelus ad omnia
antichristianismi insignia demolienda accendatur. Ad extremum rogamus, ut literis episcopos nostros admoneatis, ne propter vestem Jose-
phum persequantur, nec tantulam ob causam tali schismate ecclesiam
lacerent; sed ut, etiam in dissimilitudine rituum, animorum suavissimam
conspirationem et φιλαδελφίαν tueantur. Absit enim ut nos de illis
aliter quam amicos, aliter quam fratres decet, sentiamus. Summa
est : hæc tria petimus, responsionem vestram ad quæstiones hic a nobis
propositas, et libellum aliquem ad omnes ecclesias generatim; literas
ad episcopos privatim, et (si placet) ad vobis notos R. M. consiliarios :
ut tota hæc controversia christiana pacificatione, non crudeli separatione,
dirimatur. Literas hasce cum fratribus omnibus communicate, ut quid
ore duorum aut trium testium Dominus loquatur, accipiamus. D. Jesus
ecclesiam suam puram et inviolatam ad diem usque justi judicii sui conservet. Julii, 1566.

Vobis deditissimi,

MILO COVERDALUS,
Quondam Exoniensis.

LAUR. HUMFREDUS.

TH. SAMPSON.

INSCRIPTIO.

D. G. Farello, P. Vireto, Th. Bezæ et
reliquis symmystis Genevæ et per
Sabaudiam, patribus ac dominis
in Christo observandissimis.

EPISTOLA LI.

GULIELMUS TURNERUS AD HENRICUM BULLINGERUM.

S. D. QUEMADMODUM de Christo Filio Dei, cum hic in terris inter
mortales degeret, magna fuit inter Judæos opinionum varietas; ita ex occasione responsionis tuæ ad fratres nostros, quam Latine et Anglice, te
inconsulto, superintendentes nostri, ut putamus, in lucem ediderunt, multæ
de te, ejus jurato et fideli discipulo et ministro, inter eos qui repurga-
tiorem religionem apud nos profitentur, opiniones nuper exortæ sunt,
et de te varii varie sentiunt. Faxit Deus, ut tu nullam justam de te
sinistre suspicandi ansam volens nostratibus porrexisti, ita ut omnes
responsionem tuam eo animo interpretentur quo eam scripsisti. Utcunque alii de te sentiunt, hoc mihi persuasissimum habeo, si humano
more in errorem aliquem imprudens incidisses, modo amice et humaniter
esses admonitus, te errorem tuum haud gravatim velle agnoscere, et ejus
occasionem velle libenter confiteri. Sed quo te melius et plenius defendere possis ab iis quæ tibi impinguntur, consueto tuo et omnibus
notissimo candore fretus, pergam nostrorum hominum de te opiniones
breviter referre.

Non desunt qui putant Samaritanos nostros utroque genu claudi-
cantes (nam tales multo plures habemus quam sinceros evangelicos)
multa tibi secus atque veritas habet suggessisse; atque adeo tibi
auctores aut saltem suasores fuisse, ut omnia tua tela in nostros
misellos concionatores torqueres, primariorum nostrorum ministrorum
et aliorum vitiis dissimulatis, qui ob asini prospectum tot doctos et
pios pastores dignitatibus omnibus exutos in carceres conjecerunt, et
gregem Christi lupis, Papistis, Lutheranis, Sadducæis, et Herodianis
inermes exposuerunt. Sunt nonnulli qui audacter affirmant, in responsione
tua multa esse, quæ non solum cum tuis ipsius antea editis libris, sed
cum scriptis omnium evangelicorum pastorum, manifeste pugnent. Reperiuntur etiam quidam e nostris qui de te, in tota Europa doctissimo et
de universa doctrina christiana optime sentiente, idem sentiunt, quod de
Philippo Melancthone præceptore suo Saxonici concionatores senserunt;
qui, cum Carolus quintus interimisticas et adiaphoristicas impietates
omnibus reformatis in Germania ecclesiis obtrudere tentaret, cum magna[1]
libertatis christianæ et veritatis jactura non vulgari (ut ipsi scriptis editis

---

[1 MS. *magno*. Forsan post *christianæ* excidit *detrimento* aut simile quid.]

testantur) ad interimistas et adiaphoristas defecit, posteaque omni metu deposito ad meliorem mentem rediit.

Qui de te etiam præclarissime sentiunt ita te propugnant. Dicunt te nihil minus cogitasse quam ut responsio tua Latine et Anglice excusa in vulgus spargeretur; illam non definiendi animo aut dogmata statuendi, sed exercitii literarii causa, ad fratres nostros doctissimos viros esse missam. Sed quum extra omnem controversiam sit, per illam jam evulgatam multos non malos viros graviter esse offensos, consilium esse judico, tam ad scandala tollenda quam ad veritatem, quam in tot libris editis fortiter, pie et diligenter tutatus esses, asserendam, et a falsitatis suspicione vindicandam, ut libello aliquo excuso ingenue et clare, omni metu excusso, testificeris, num sentias principes aut prælatos ecclesiasticos, quos tu vocas primarios ministros, vestes quasdam præscriptas et similes ceremonias, sive a paganis mutuo sumptas, sive a levitica lege translatas, aut a papa inventas sive approbatas, et ad idololatriam fovendam destinatas et usitatas, citra libertatis christianæ offensionem et manifestam ecclesiæ injuriam, pastoribus ecclesiarum sub pœna deprivationis et carceris invitis posse obtrudere.

Hæc ideo ad te audacius scripsi, qui animum in te meum exploratiorem habeas, dum nominis tui famam salvam et integram esse velim, et doctrinam tuam ab omni erroris suspicione liberam. 23 Julii, 1566. Vale.

Tuus,

GULIELMUS TURNERUS,

Medicus, a divinarum literarum
lectione non abhorrens.

INSCRIPTIO.

Eruditione et pietate clarissimo viro
D. Henrico Bullingero, amico
suo non vulgari.

EPISTOLA LII.

JOHANNES PARKHURSTUS AD JOHANNEM WOLFIUM.

PRO doctissimis tuis et Martyris commentariis in duos libros Regum ago gratias, propediem relaturus. Bene feceris, si conciones tuas in Deuteronomium, Judices, Ruth, &c. divulgaveris: memini enim in musæo tuo quasdam legisse quæ mihi valde placebant: placebunt et aliis, si hoc placeat tibi. Hæc paucula non sine molestia scripsi, utpote qui vix e

morbis convaluerim. Tu brevitatem boni consule. Cetera tibi Gualtherus.
Dominus servet Tigurinos omnes. Raptim. Ludhamiæ, 21 Aug. 1566.

Tuus,

JOHANNES PARKHURSTUS.

INSCRIPTIO.

D. Johanni Wolfio.

EPISTOLA LIII.

THEODORUS BEZA AD HENRICUM BULLINGERUM.

MISSA huc sunt, mi Pater, exemplaria literarum utriusque principis
Landgravii, quæ spem faciunt fore ut Erfurdiensia illa comitia non pro-
cedant; quod utinam eveniat! Quod autem addunt et nos satis sciebamus, cautum esse nimirum Augustæ de peregrinis ecclesiis non damnandis,
quoniam video ab illis astute factum, qui sic effici posse putarunt, ut
non interveniremus (id enim in primis norunt consiliis suis efficere), id,
inquam, non multum me exhilarat. Obsecro enim, si damnabitur nostrarum ecclesiarum doctrina, idque sub Zuinglianismi et Calvinismi
nominibus, et sive per nostrum sive per illustrissimi principis latus
confodiatur veritas, nonne eodem res recidit? Sed age exspectemus quod
dabit Dominus, qui utinam efficiat, ut ipsum pro nobis excubare hic
quoque sentiamus!

De rebus nostris nihil prorsus habeo novi quod scribam. In Gallia
videtur ecclesiarum pax a rerum Flandricarum exitu pendere; quod plane
miserum est. Nam certe illam agendi rationem probare nullo modo
possum; et quamvis laeta videantur initia, tamen tristissimum et funes-
tissimum exitum videor mihi jam prospicere, nisi Dominus imprudentiæ
quoque illorum benedicat. Quod ad te scriptum fuit de quibusdam ex
magistratu cæsis et urbe occupata, commentitium est, si vera sunt quæ
abhinc biduum accepimus literis 12mo hujus mensis scriptis, nempe nulli
prorsus, ne sacrifico quidem adhuc factam injuriam, nullum idolum a
nostris eversum; interesse tantum innumerabilem turbam concionibus
quæ extra urbes sub dio habeantur, et incredibilem esse audiendi verbi
sitim. Commendemus igitur hæc quoque Domini providentiæ.

Jam venio ad Anglicanum negotium, quod ut nobis tristissimum
fuit audire, ita libenter optassem fieri posse, ut ista maxima molestia
careres: sed quid agas? Miseri fratres consolationem, consilium, preces
ab iis ecclesiis petunt, quarum olim caritate sunt recreati, et nunc

quoque se recreandos sperant.   Morosuli sunt nonnulli, fateor; sed in
tantis miseriis difficile est modum tenere, et quum scopus illorum sit
optimus, condonandam arbitror hanc importunitatem.   Ex iis quæ sigil-
latim ex hoc nostro fratre audies, quorum etiam exemplar hic apud
me reliquit, cognosces, neque unquam illinc ejectum fuisse papatum, sed
ad regiam majestatem potius translatum; neque nunc aliud captari, quam
ut sensim restituantur quæ utcunque fuerant instaurata.   Putavi aliquando de pileis tantum et nescio quibus externis agi; sed postea longe
aliam esse controversiam intellexi, et nunc palam video, non sine incredibili animi dolore, qui utinam mihi uni proprius et peculiaris esset!
Primum, quum externa vocatio, præeunte justo doctrinæ et morum examine, non ab uno aliquo, sed a fratrum saltem cœtu facta, sit ecclesiastici ministerii velut basis et fundamentum, quid turpius, quid immo-
deratius ista episcoporum licentia, ut non vocatos sed ultro accedentes
pro arbitrio immatriculent; mox nullo assignato loco tamquam idoneos
vel ad inserviendum (ut vocant) vel ad docendum approbent; ac tandem, quum vacant ista ministeria, pro libitu hos vel illos, tradita certo
pretio scheda et accepto duabus de rebus jurejurando, (una regiam
majestatem pro supremo post Christum Anglicanæ ecclesiæ capite agni-
turos; altera leges regni et inprimis præclarum illum reformationis librum
ritusque omnes ita secuturos, ut nihil prorsus improbent,) quibus libuit
ecclesiis assignent?   Si de disciplina ecclesiastica quæritur, quænam tandem illic est, ubi, non aliter quam sub papatu, loco presbyterii legitime
delecti suos decanos, cancellarios, archidiaconos habent, qui pro arbitrio
et ut in foro civili fieri solet, ex jure tamen canonico, excommunica-
tionem pronuncient etiam ob pecuniarias et ejus generis lites; quam sententiam postea, ut judex suo apparitori, sic dominus episcopus vel ejus
officialis ministro legendam in ecclesia transmittat, tantisper scilicet
valituram, donec cum judice transegerint?   Eadem enim est plerumque
absolutionis quæ excommunicationis ratio.   Quantulum autem absunt a
lege cœlibatus, qui uxores sine expressa reginæ venia et D. episcopi et
duorum quorundam justitiariorum pacis assensu ducere, ductas autem
vel in collegiis vel intra cathedralium ecclesiarum septa, ut impuras
nimirum sive ut vitetur offendiculum, alere prohibentur?   Quid quod
papistis non tantum beneficiorum reditus, sed etiam ipsa ecclesiastica munera relicta sunt, præstito tantum reformationis servandæ jurejurando, adeo ut plerisque et indoctis et veræ religionis in corde infen-
sissimis hostibus pii fratres plerumque subsint, eorumque jurisdictionem
subire teneantur?   Quid quod publice veneunt in metropolitani curia
dispensationes nonresidentiæ, pluralitatis beneficiorum, ciborum delectus,
matrimonii extra constituta tempora celebrandi, beneficii etiam in pueritia
obtinendi, ceteraque id genus, quibus ne ipsa quidem Roma turpius et
indignius quicquam habet?   Quid quod baptismus ipsis mulierculis in

casu (quem vocant) necessitatis permittitur? Et quasi ista cum aliis quibusdam nihilo melioribus non sufficerent, ecce! jam pauculi illi puri
evangelii doctores alii quidem exauctorantur, alii vero etiam in carceres
detruduntur, nisi illa omnia se inviolabiliter approbaturos jurent, ut
neque verbo neque scriptis contradicere liceat, ac tandem etiam
pileis quadratis, collipendiis, superpelliciis, casulis et ceteris id genus
sacerdotes Baalis referant. Neque hic est miseriarum finis, sed illud
quoque expresse cautum est, ut quidquid regiæ majestati, adhibito vel
solo Cantuariensi, in ecclesia ritus instituere, mutare, tollere libuerit,
firmum statim et ratum habeatur.

Hic est igitur Anglicanarum ecclesiarum status, valde, ut mihi videtur, miserabilis, atque adeo plane intolerabilis. Pauculi autem illi duplex
consilium a nobis flagitant : unum, qua tandem ratione regina et episcopi possint officii admoneri? alterum, quid ipsis interea bona conscientia liceat? Quod ad prius illud attinet, videtur quidem hoc malum
soli jam Deo medicabile; sed tamen experiendum aliquid arbitror potius,
quam patiendum ut tantum ædificium silentio corruat. Duplicem autem viam hic invenio; unam quidem nobis asperiorem, illis vero multo
(ut mihi quidem videtur) commodiorem; alteram vero leniorem, sed non
ita compendiosam. Vestra una ecclesia est, mi pater, cujus auctoritate
tum regina, tum episcopi illi permoveri posse videantur : illa quidem,
ut secum expendat quatenus et quo sensu dicantur reginæ nutrices ecclesiæ; isti vero, ut sicut olim Augustus de reddenda republica cogi-
tavit, ita ipsi ecclesiam a majoribus suis oppressam tandem restituant.
Nam quod ad hanc ecclesiam attinet, velim scias ita esse illi reginæ
exosam, ut propterea ne levissimo quidem verbo sibi gratum esse mearum annotationum munus significarit. Causa hujus odii duplex est: una,
quod nimium severi et rigidi habeamur, quod iis maxime displicet, qui
reprehendi metuunt; altera, quod olim, inscientibus tamen nobis, vivente
adhuc Maria, editi sint duo libelli Anglicano sermone, unus adversus
fœminarum imperium a D. Cnoxo, alter de jure magistratus a Godo-
manno scriptus. Uterque, quum quod continerent intellexissemus, nobis
quoque displicuit, ac proinde prohibitus est venire. Sed illa nihilominus
conceptam opinionem fovet. Itaque si dignam hanc causam statuis esse
quæ a nobis suscipiatur, hæc commodissima et fratribus utilissima ratio
esse videretur, ut magistratus vestri si non autoritate, saltem permissu
vel conniventia, deligeretur ex vestro cœtu, qui in Angliam hanc ipsam
ob causam proficiscens omnibus istis malis coram remedium apud reginam et episcopos quæreret. Heroicum sane esset hoc factum, vestra
civitate dignum et Deo longe, arbitror, gratissimum, etiamsi non succederet prorsus ex animi sententia. Via per Galliam plana est penitus et
brevis, quum hinc usque in Dieppensem Normanniæ portum, unde
secundo vento decem horis in Angliam trajiciunt, undecim diebus facil-

lime posset perveniri. Salutarentur et confirmarentur per vias Gallicæ
ecclesiæ plurimæ. Inviseretur Amiralius cum Andeloto fratre, uterque
in ipso itinere occurrens. Nec difficile esset fratrem unum et alterum
ex doctioribus et cordatioribus legationis comites, si opus fuerit, impetrare, qui suam operam vestro legato adjungerent. Si et nos aliquid
hic posse judicaveris, id est ecclesiæ literas, nulla erit in nobis mora.
Nosti hunc fuisse veteris ecclesiæ morem, ut etiam non vocati accurre-
rent tamen ad incendia extinguenda, et multos exorientes tumultus hac
ratione in plurimis provinciis fuisse compositos. Nec dubito, quin pia
et caritatis plena hæc legatio sit reginæ et piis episcopis valde placi-
tura, quos audio studiose idoneam occasionem captare, una cum magni
sigilli custode, viro sincero et religioso. Favent etiam multi e nobilitate; multi ex reliquis ordinibus suspirant. Omnes istos probabile est,
si externis quoque ecclesiis salutem suam tantæ curæ esse viderint, animum sumpturos, ut apud regiam majestatem fortius instent, donec illam
flexerint. Tempus quoque valde opportunum est, quum illic instent
comitia, in quibus certum est fore ut de his omnibus rebus agatur.
Dicam etiam aliquid amplius bona cum tua venia, mi pater. Si non
displicebit vobis hoc consilium, unus D. Gualtherus ad hoc curandum,
administrandum, conficiendum negotium ita videtur modis omnibus ap-
positus, ut pœne, si ipsum delegeritis, ipsa velut Dei voce illuc ad recreandos miserrimos fratres, denique ad servandum illud regnum, missus
videatur.

Hæc una via est promptissima, quantum ego quidem judico, nec
ita magni sumtus aut laboris. Sin vero hoc non placet, saltem literas
graviter et copiose scribendas tum ad regiam majestatem, tum ad episcopos arbitror, ut sui muneris et officii commonefiant, quum præsertim
illos videas literis tuis contra voluntatem tuam ad augendum hoc malum
abuti. Scripseram ego de hoc argumento ad Londinensem episcopum,
quarum literarum exemplum tibi, si opus erit, frater hic noster suppeditabit. Audieram enim jam tum aliquid rerum istarum, ac proinde
malui episcopos a quibus fovetur hoc malum urgere, quam fratribus
quicquam consilii dare, quum præsertim hoc a vobis factum non dubi-
tarem. Vestras autem literas, si vobis ita videbitur, vel signis nostris
appositis comprobabimus, vel aliis ejusdem prorsus argumenti confirma-
bimus: adeo non dubitamus, quin sitis quod rectum et æquum est
scripturi.

Venio ad alterum hujus consultationis caput: possintne fratres interea his legibus bona conscientia in ministerio perseverare ? Quominus
vero illos ad perseverandum exhorter, neque illæ omnes corruptelæ neque
leges de pileis et vestibus faciunt, quum e contrario vel ob hoc ipsum
oporteat sedulos ipsos esse in ejusmodi omnibus paulatim ex animis
hominum evellendis et verbi divini gladio amputandis. Sed multa hic

me movent in contrariam partem, quamvis tristissimum sit in tanta
desolatione, quanta jam illic est, miseras oviculas lupis mox ingressuris
relinquere. Aliud enim est quædam tolerare quæ mutare non possis,
aliud jam sublata resumere certo cum plurimorum offendiculo. Scis
autem Petrum a Paulo non aliam ob causam coram reprehensum, quam
quod unis infirmis sic consuleret, ut alios interea subverteret; nec mihi
videtur hoc de quo nunc agimus dissimile. Imo existimo minus etiam
multo habere istos legislatores quod prætexant, quam Petrum, non idcirco tantum quia traditiones humanas iniquum est cum divinis institutis comparare, sed multo magis quia nullus erat qui receptis ritibus
offenderetur; puta quod communis panis in cœna adhiberetur, quod fran-
geretur panis, non autem placentula ori ingereretur, quod nulla esset
genuflexio nec crucis consignatio, quod ad Jesu nomen non assurgeretur,
quod denique ministri quamvis communi, decenti tamen pileo et veste
uterentur. Fictitium ergo est offendiculum, cui remedium quæritur;
quum contra innumerabilium conscientia ista mutatione offendatur, quorum tamen adeo ratio nulla habetur, ut etiam propterea bonis suis
pastoribus priventur. Quid ergo hic agant pastores? Deinde quum ex
illis quæ adeo urgentur, neglectis iis quæ præcipua sunt, multa sint
quæ propter adjunctam opinionem cultus animis multorum adhuc insi-
dentem potius abominanda sint, quam inter res medias numeranda, quæque adeo sint ad veteres superstitiones sine dubio populum revocatura;
an hæc rursus in usum revocare ministri ipsi bona conscientia poterunt?
Sed aliud est multo etiam his omnibus gravius. Quum teneantur ministri
quoscunque episcopo vel ejus officiali libuerit excommunicare et rursus
pro absolutis habere; quum ex aliorum nutu omnia cogantur administrare in suis ecclesiis, et, quod omnium gravissimum est, non alia lege
ad ministerium docendi admittantur, quam si jurent se toti illi reformationi, id est intolerabilibus illis corruptelis, nec scriptis nec verbo
repugnaturos; adeoque se, quicquid reginæ et Cantuariensi placuerit
mutare, tollere, addere, pro firmo et rato habituros,—quis hanc conditionem bona conscientia subierit? Quid igitur? Certe non deserunt
ecclesias, qui vel ejiciuntur, vel, quod sese et greges suas perdere jube-
antur, parere nolunt.

Valde tamen optaverim, mi pater, hæc ceteraque omnia prius isthic
expendi et sententiam vestram nobis significari, quam quicquam hac
de re ad illos scribamus, quoniam utrinque periculosi sint abyssi. Si
quid tamen medii consilii hic inveniri potest, est fortasse hujusmodi, ut
qui jam sunt ejecti in proximis comitiis audientiam petant; qua impe-
trata quam humillime ostendant, se rebelles non esse, verum propter
conscientiam ad tempus cedere maluisse, quam turbas excitare; et deinde
quæ mala hinc consecuta sint, reverenter et placide ostendant. Si res
bene cesserit, laudabunt Dominum: sin minus, excutiant pulverem pedum

suorum. Nam, ut dixi, qua conscientia possent illo jurejurando se
obligare, nos quidem non videmus. Qui vero adhuc manent in ministerio, illis suaserim, ut adhibita protestatione modesta coram episcopo,
et plebe diligenter præmonita, ne ista ad superstitionem rapiant, in
ministerio perseverent tantisper dum res in comitiis decidatur. Si decisio
tolerabilis erit, pergant in officio quamdiu licebit; sin pergant episcopi
male agere vel male agentibus assentiri, tum ego suaderem, ut fortiter
corripiant correptione dignos, et potius sese ad crucem comparent, quam
vel contra officium faciant, vel ministerium deserant.

Hæc habui de his rebus longe molestissimis. Utinam mihi quidem
liceret privato meo ministerio sic defungi, ut alius quivis ista curaret!
Nec enim ignoro, qua jam pridem suspicione laborem apud eos qui me
parum norunt. Sed tuebor me conscientiæ testimonio, et fratres Deo
favente pergam, si non consilio, quod utinam nunquam quisquam requireret, saltem precibus juvare. Sollicitus responsum tuum exspecto. Bene
vale, mi pater. Dominus Jesus te, si ullo unquam tempore, multis ecclesiis
necessarium servet, et tibi magis et magis benedicat. Fratres omnes
et collegas velim ut et meo et totius nostri cœtus nomine diligenter
salutes. Iterum vale. Genevæ, 3 Septembris. (1566.)

Tuus,

BEZA.

Ecce! hoc momento literas accipimus Lugduno, quæ significant de
acceptis per cursores literis Antwerpia datis 23 et 27 Augusti, tumul-
tum a puerulis adversus sacrificulum quendam exortum eo usque effer-
buisse, ut omnia idola eversa illic sint et missa profligata, neminem
tamen illo unico sacrificulo excepto cæsum. Ita jam tenetur urbs a
nostris, si modo nostri sunt, occupata. Hæc sunt, nisi falsus sim vates,
tantorum malorum initia, quanta nondum vidimus. Misereatur suorum
Dominus!

EPISTOLA LIV.

HENRICUS BULLINGERUS AD MILONEM COVERDALUM.

S. D. CREDAS sane, reverende mi in Christo Domine et frater
carissime, literas illas nostras non in hoc a nobis esse scriptas, ut vul-
garentur, neque ut iis incendium apud vos in re vestiaria exortum
augeremus, sed, si fieri potuisset, extingueremus: id quod ex ipsis
cuilibet patere, modo citra affectum candide legantur, arbitramur. Rem
vestiariam tractavimus solam; de aliis, de quibus nunc quæri et con-

tendi inter vos intelligimus, nullam disputationem instituimus. At huc
unice spectavimus, ut illis quibus videbatur melius esse ecclesias Christi
deserere, quam vestibus illis uti, persuaderemus consultius fore si vestibus illis uterentur, simul et cum ecclesiis suæ fidei creditis manerent,
etc. Sed ne hoc quidem fratribus temere obtrudere voluimus, sed tantum exponere quid nobis ea in re videatur fructuosius, ipsis interim
liberum relinquentes sequi quod videatur optimum. Ceterum quando
nunc intelligimus, literas nostras eo rapi a quibusdam, quasi omnes con-
troversos inter vos articulos, (quos tamen quales fuerint, tunc cum literas
nostras scriberemus ignorabamus,) scribimus ad viros aliquot pios atque
prudentes, quorum auctoritatem in hac causa valituram speramus, rogantes in hoc sint toti, ne nostris ulli abutantur publicatis literis, neve
in comitiis ipsarum prætextu sordes, ut ais, stabiliantur; sed fideliter
potius laborent, sua ecclesiis libertas integra maneat, fidelesque ministri
non vexentur, et eeclesia Anglicana ab iis repurgetur, quæ a veræ religionis puritate sunt aliena. Orabimus interim Dominum ut ipse res
moderetur, et hasce turbas feliciter sopiat, dispulsisque contentionibus
tranquillitatem ecclesiis reddat. Gratia Domini Jesu sit tecum! Salutat
te D. Gualtherus. Ora tu pro nobis Dominum. Datæ Tiguri, 10 Septembris, Anno Domini 1566.

HEINRYCHUS BULLINGERUS senior,
tuus ex animo totus.

INSCRIPTIO.

Reverendo viro D. Miloni Coverdalo
Anglo, domino meo colendissimo et
fratri carissimo.

EPISTOLA LV.

HENRICUS BULLINGERUS ET RODOLPHUS GUALTERUS AD D. FRANCISCUM RUSSELLUM.

Cum anno superiori intellexissemus apud vos, illustrissime princeps,
contentionem aliquam de habitu ministrorum exortam esse, vehementer
timebamus, ne ea ulterius progressa aliquid majoris mali daret ecclesiæ:
et ideo a viris piis et cordatis requisiti, consilium dedimus quod tunc
nobis tutum et pium videbatur. Monuimus enim ecclesiarum ministros,
ne ob rem non adeo magni momenti ab ecclesiis discederent, et eas
lupis et superstitiosis seductoribus vexandas relinquerent. At non fefellit

nos gravioris periculi metus, quem nos tunc concepisse diximus. Audimus enim jam non de solo vestitu apud vos contendi, sed insuper multa alia obtrudi piis ministris, quæ merum papatum redolent, imo in antichristi schola primum fabricata sunt, et proinde salva pietate recipi aut dissimulari non possunt. Dolorem autem nobis non levem parit, quod epistolam, quam privatim ad amicos pauculos ea de re dedimus, typis excusam esse fertur, et quod multi nostrum de re illa vestiaria judicium ad alia usque extendunt, quæ in controversia esse tunc nesciebamus, et quæ a nobis nunquam probari poterunt. Et sane justissimi doloris causa est, nostri nominis auctoritate pios fratres gravari, quibus consilium et consolationem afferre potius quam molestiam exhibere studuimus. Magis tamen urimur scandali consideratione, quod inde exortum esse non dubitamus. Auget præterea tristitiam nostram infelix ecclesiæ Anglicanæ conditio, quam cum semper amaverimus, non possumus non totis animis commoveri, quod quæ ex sanguinariis fidei purioris hostibus vixdum liberata nonnihil florere cœperat, nunc intestinis dissidiis labefactatur. Et quia de tua virtute, illustrissime princeps, nobis satis constat, et non pauca exstant tuæ pietatis argumenta, ad tuam excellentiam literas dandas esse putavimus, de qua pii quamplurimi spem non mediocrem conceperunt. Rogamus autem, ut apud serenissimam reginam, et in comitiis (quæ brevi futura audimus) apud regni proceres, causam ecclesiæ pro more tueri pergat, neque suum patrocinium piis fratribus deneget; qui etsi aliqua in re peccarunt, veniam tamen merentur, quando illos ferventi pietatis zelo commotos fuisse constat, et hoc unum quærere, ut ecclesiam ab omnibus papisticis sordibus repurgatam habeant. Neque illi modo nobis digni videntur, quos pii principes propugnent; sed tota hæc causa ejusmodi est, ut qui in illa agenda studium et industriam adhibent, eo facto demum testentur, se principum nomine dignissimos esse. Dignatus est illustres viros eo honore Dominus, ut ecclesiæ ejus nutritii dicantur; quæ sane laus omnem hujus mundi gloriam atque dignitatem longe superat. Erunt autem fideles nutritii, si ecclesiam non modo ex hostium manibus eripiant, verbi prædicationem instaurent, et sacramentorum usum legitimum restituant; verum etiam caveant, ne quæ Christo adduci debet sponsa incontaminata, ullo superstitionum fuco defœdetur, aut ullis ritibus a simplicitate christiana alienis fidem suam suspectam reddat. Et notum est illud Hoseæ, qui ecclesiam Israeliticam monebat, ut scortationes suas non ab uberibus modo, verum etiam a facie removeret.

Quare etiam atque etiam excellentiam tuam rogamus, ut, quod hactenus fecit, nunc imprimis facere pergat, et sua auctoritate apud serenissimam reginam et regni proceres efficere studeat, ne cum magna totius orbis admiratione instituta ecclesiæ Anglicanæ reformatio novis sordibus et postliminio reductis infelicis papatus relqiuiis deformetur. Nam si id fiat, non modo inconstantiæ nota multis in regno vestro florentissimo inuretur, verum etiam infirmi offendentur, et vicinis Scotiæ, Galliæ, et Flandriæ ecclesiis, sub cruce adhuc laborantibus, scandalum præbebitur, cujus pœnæ in auctores ejus proculdubio redundabunt. Imo ex vobis exemplum sument vicini veritatis evangelicæ hostes, ut ipsi quoque in suis locis liberiorem veri Dei cultum novis tyrannicæ superstitionis legibus circumscribant. Liberius hæc dicimus, illustrissime princeps, non quod de tua pietate quicquam dubitemus; sed id partim tua humanitate incredibili freti facimus, partim rei necessitate adducti. Tuæ excellentiæ et multis aliis de hac causa cogitandi materiam et occasionem ampliorem præbere cupimus. Precamur autem Deum Optimum Maximum, ut ecclesiæ suæ misertus pacem veram illi restituat, et tuam excellentiam tuique similes principes suo Spiritu regat, suo favore protegat, et potenti brachio servet ad sui nominis gloriam et ecclesiæ suæ conservationem. Amen. Tiguri, 11 Septembris, Anno 1566.

Tuæ excellentiæ deditissimi,

HEINRICHUS BULLINGERUS senior,

et ROD. GUALTHERUS.

INSCRIPTIO.
Illustrissimo principi D. Francisco Russello, comiti Bedfordiensi, etc.

EPISTOLA LVI.

RODOLPHUS GUALTERUS AD JOHANNEM PARKHURSTUM.

CUM primum apud vos, reverendi in Christo patres, controversiam de ministrorum vestitu exortam esse audiremus, vehementer ea res nos terruit, quia timebamus, ne ea longius progressa majus aliquod malum daret; et ideo, quantum in nobis fuit, studuimus aliquos placare, ne ob rem non adeo magni momenti tumultuarentur. Et certe non fefellit nos animi præsagium, si quidem vera sunt quæ audimus; nimirum præter vestes illas multa alia obtrudi ecclesiis, et ministros ab ecclesiis ejici, quod decretis quorundam subscribere nolunt, qui vel reginæ nomine abutuntur, vel sua indulgentia illam in ejusmodi rebus audaciorem reddunt, ut quidvis ex suo arbitrio statuat. Dolorem etiam nostrum auget, quod epistolam nostram, qua unum et alterum mitigare studuimus, excusam esse videmus, et nostri nominis auctoritate pios fratres gravari, nosque apud multos in suspicionem venire, quasi sordes papisticas probemus. Suasimus quidem ministris, ne propter pileum et superpellicium ecclesias deserant, sed quoad salva pietate possint, gregem Domini pascant. Interim eorum sive superstitionem sive ineptias nunquam probavimus, qui piis ministris talia obtrudunt, et ex papæ schola, seu culina potius, sordes corradunt, quibus et pastoribus bonis negotium faciant et scandalum dent infirmis. Imprimis vero durum nobis videtur, episcopos executionis istius ministros se præbere, ut per ipsos ejiciantur, qui parere nolunt. Utinam illi expenderent, quod Dominus voluerit, quando de œconomo perfido loquitur, qui dum familiam ejus pascere debebat, cum ebriosis comessatur et ludit, conservos autem cædit! Quam procul enim ab hujus moribus absint non video, qui superstitiosorum aulicorum figmenta tam facile probant, et ministros pios tam inhumaniter tractant. Neque mihi unquam in mentem venire potuisset aliquem inter episcopos inveniri, qui se hujus temeritatis ministrum præbere, aut saltem ignava dissimulatione illam confirmare, voluisset. Putabamus enim hoc omne a quibusdam provenire, qui serenissimæ reginæ auctoritate abutuntur; episcopos autem sperabamus ministrorum causam defensuros, et rationes quæsituros esse quibus malo huic remedium afferretur.

Sunt, fateor, quidam ex fratribus istis morosuli, sed tamen causa illorum non mala, multo minus impia est: imo optandum foret, ut illorum sententia vinceret. Quod quia nunc nobis impossibile visum fuit, monuimus, ut rebus præsentibus se accommodarent, et spem haberent in Domino, qui aliquando daturus esset occasionem, qua omnia in melius restituerentur. Quia autem, mi pater, inter ceteros tuam pietatem imprimis prædicari audio, ut et D. Pilkintoni nostri, qui hactenus neminem ejicere volueritis; tu mihi pro veteris amicitiæ jure admonendus videbaris, ut in ea pietate constanter pergas, et memineris sat peccatorum unumquemque nostrum in semetipso habere, ut minime opus sit alienis communicare. Est Christus ecclesiæ suæ sponsus et vindex acerrimus, et fidelissimis servis factam injuriam non sinet inultam. Huic olim ratio nostræ functionis reddenda erit, non reginæ, non papæ, aut illis, qui pontificiam tyranidem sibi in ecclesia vindicant. Hæc extempore quidem, non autem sine fraterni amoris solicitudine scripta, tu pro tua suavitate boni consule. De rebus nostris plura scripsi in literis, quas ex nundinis accipies. Tiguri, 11 Septembris, 1566.

N.B. Epistolam hanc scripsi ex relatione Percivalli Viburni, Angli.

[ROD. GUALTERUS.]

EPISTOLA LVII.

RODOLPHUS GUALTERUS AD THEODORUM BEZAM.

Jam pridem veriti sumus, observande in Christo frater, contentiones
ob rem vestiariam in Anglia exortas longius progressuras esse. Videbamus enim aliquos in re minoris momenti morosiores esse, quam quæ
tum erat illic rerum conditio ferre posset : et ideo a viris bonis et piis,
qui ecclesiarum vastitatem timebant requisiti, consilium dedimus, quod
tunc necessarium et utile, neque a pietate alienum videbatur, et quod
illos jam ante a D. Petro Martyre piæ memoriæ viro accepisse sciebamus.
Quia enim de solo habitu ministrorum lis erat, quos regina a laicis
distingui voluit, et in edicto regio conscientiis infirmorum diserte cave-
batur, ne quis in illo vel ministerii vel sacramentorum dignitatem sitam
existimaret, simulque non obscura spes fieret, illa pro temporis mutatione mutari et corrigi posse ; non potuimus illorum sententiæ accedere,
qui propter pileum et togam ecclesias relinquendas esse censebant. Nam
non ignorabamus in illorum locum successuros vel aperte papistas, vel
Lutheranos, qui majores sordes inferrent, et simul doctrinam quoque
corrumperent. Monuimus ergo, ut sancta et pia modestia rebus præsentibus se accommodarent, populum vero inter docendum diligenter admonerent, ne quis inde aliquam arriperet superstitiosi cultus aut veritatis
abnegatæ suspicionem ; ut denique occasionem prudenter captarent, qua
regina et regni proceres sui in hac re officii commode admonerentur.
Nec dubitamus ea ratione turbis illis primum gliscentibus occurri potuisse,
cum mitius multo agerent consiliarii, quam nunc, quum longiori contentione multorum animi exacerbati sunt, ut pauculis istis non contenti
ea obtrudere conentur, quæ salva pietate admitti non possunt. Sed
quo res devenerit, vides, mi frater, et nos non sine dolore videmus.
Quia tamen scimus, fratres nostros pio zelo fecisse quicquid fecerunt,
illos non accusamus, sed commiseratione dignos judicamus ; et utinam
eosdem consilio atque auxilio nostro possemus sublevare !

Equidem quod tibi remedium videtur in hac rerum necessitate præsen-
tissimum, ut vel ego ipse vel alius ex nostris in Angliam profectus causam
hanc coram agat, mihi minime molestum aut grave videretur ; imo jucundum et volupe esset eadem opera et Gallicas ecclesias invisere, quas in
Domino amo et exosculor, et in Anglia amicos veteres videre, rebusque
ecclesiæ afflictissimis opem ferre : neque me ullius laboris aut periculi pigere
posset in causa tam bona, tam sancta, tamque necessaria. Sed sat
scio hoc nos a nostris nunquam impetraturos esse, ut non vocati eo
proficiscamur. Neque videre possum, quæ istius profectionis, seu lega-

tionis, utilitas sperari possit. Nam regina, quæ potestate sua hucusque
in multis pro suo arbitrio licenter nimis abusa est, et suorum consiliis
atque admonitionibus moneri non potuit, multo minus ab homine externo admoneri vellet. Et periculum est, ne suspicione gravarentur pii
fratres, quasi ab ipsis, illa inconsulta, vocatus essem, ut mea opera
novos tumultus excitare, aut jam excitatos augere possint. Videmus
præterea quorundam animos ita commotos esse, ut nisi illis per omnia
assentirem, mihi cum illis rixandum esset, propter quos potissimum ego
tantum laborem atque periculum subiissem. Accedunt his multæ aliæ
rationes, quibus monemur, ne quid hujus a nobis tentetur. Et speramus nos ex nundinis Francfordianis literas accepturos esse, quæ nos de
tota hac causa plenius instituant, et fortassis consilii quoque melioris
materiam præbeant. Interea, ne cui occasioni desimus, literis agere
visum est apud utramque partem, id est, apud eos, qui ex parte utraque
nobis noti et hucusque nostro consilio usi sunt. Monemus autem episcopos, ne in alicujus hominum gratiam aliquid faciant, quod cum veritate pugnet, et cum scandalo conjunctum sit: imprimis, ne quid durius
statuant in symmystas, verbi Dei administros; et ut de tollendis potius
quam reducendis papisticis sordibus cogitent. Testamur item nobis non
parum dolere, imo injuriam nobis fieri non levem, si nostra epistola
abutantur ad eorum defensionem, quæ neque probavimus unquam, neque probaturi sumus, nisi mentem nobis meliorem Deus eripiat, de
cujus bonitate meliora speramus. Et in quibusdam spes adhuc bona
est. Constat enim, neque Parkhurstum meum, qui Nordovicensem episcopatum tenet, neque Pilkintonum, qui Dunelmensis antistes est,
aliquem ministrorum adhuc ejecisse, nec etiam in posterum ejecturos esse.
Veniet itaque res in deliberationem ampliorem, et spero aliquos in viam
redituros esse, qui fortassis jam nunc vident, quantum mali ipsorum
indulgentia dederit. Deinde quia illic auctoritate plurimum valet illustris
vir, Bedfordi comes, qui nunc Varvici cum imperio est, ad illum quoque scripsimus, ut causam hanc suscipiat et in regni comitiis constanter
tueatur; quod illum facturum non diffidimus. Nam non pauca egregiæ
pietatis specimina dedit, et ecclesiarum nostrarum observator est et præco
diligentissimus. Et hoc quidem in præsenti sufficere putamus, quia cum
aliis regni proceribus nulla nobis familiaritas intercedit: ad reginam vero
scribere supervacaneum foret, cum quo animo illa erga nos sit affecta
ignoremus; neque nobis multa possimus polliceri de ea, quæ nullis
nostrorum literis unquam responderit. Nolumus etiam apud illam eos
in suspicionem venire, de quorum voluntate nobis spes bona est, et
quos nostri studiosissimos esse non ignoramus.

Quoad vero alterum tuæ epistolæ caput idem plane tecum sentimus,
non ita consulendum esse infirmis, ut multorum aliorum fides evertatur.
Neque eos probamus, qui humanas leges divinis æquant aut temere miscent.

Detestatione etiam dignas dicimus eas constitutiones, quas in ipsa antichristi schola fabricatas esse constat; et ipsi quidem centies moriendum potius nobis esse sentimus, quam illas vel subscriptione vel ignava et turpi dissimulatione confirmare. At si de solo ministrorum habitu ageretur, et omnes edicti regii super hac re facti verbis insisterent, quibus diserte negatur, neque eandem cum verbo Dei auctoritatem istis legibus tribuendam esse, neque alicujus conscientiam iisdem debere obstringi; non videmus, cur ob vestes solas ecclesiæ deseri, et lupinis dilaniandæ relinqui debeant. Sed difficile nobis est de causa non plene cognita pronuntiare, et quæ inter illos agitur, quos maxima animorum contentione inter se commissos esse constat. Imprimis autem nobis probatur, quod postremo de ministris, qui suum locum adhuc obtinent, scribis, ut officium faciant cum pia et modesta protestatione, et comitiorum decretum exspectent; et si quid statuatur a veritate et religionis puritate alienum, quidvis potius ferant, quam impiis aliorum decretis subscribant aut consentiant.

Hæc, mi frater observande, non tam meo quam D. Bullingeri patris mei colendi nomine, ad tuas literas modo respondere potuimus. Et quamvis periculum sit primis evidens, speramus tamen in Domino, qui in illo etiam regno reliquias suas servabit, ex quibus olim ecclesiam puriorem et sanctiorem instauret. Quæ de Antwerpia scribis, nos quoque admodum solicitos habent. Faxit Deus, ut omnia cedant ad sui nominis gloriam et ecclesiæ ædificationem. Salutem tibi plurimam precantur symmystæ omnes, et inter hos præcipue D. Bullingerus, qui literis in Angliam scribendis occupatus, mihi tuis respondendi munus injunxit. Salutabis nostro nomine fratres, qui in vestra ecclesia ministrant, quorum labores utinam Deus benedicat! Vale. Tiguri, 11 Sept. 1566.

[ROD. GUALTERUS.]

EPISTOLA LVIII.

GEORGIUS WITHERUS ET JOHANNES BARTHELOTTUS AD BULLINGERUM ET GUALTERUM.

Reverendi in Christo patres, quoniam vobis visum est epistolam episcoporum Londinensis et Wintoniensis coram nobis perlegere, qua sese apud vos ita purgare conantur, ut et veritatem obtenebrare, et causam pro qua contendimus levissimam maximeque frivolam facere studere videantur; nos necessarium duximus ad singula ejus capita hoc scripto respondere, ut vobis, qui humanissime omnem vestram operam polliciti estis, magis pateat et elucescat veritas. Sed si in capitibus recensendis

aliquid vel omittamus vel aberremus, dabitis veniam ; tum quod non
alibi hæc quam apud vos agimus, tum quod memoria parum valemus
singula consequi.

Epistola.—Dicunt perpaucos tantum exauctoratos, et ut pios, neminem tamen doctum præter unum Sampsonem.

Responsio.—Respondemus multos eorum ita doctos, ut ab episcopo
Londinensi digni reputati sint qui apud crucem Paulinam coram celeberrimis et doctissimis totius Angliæ concionibus prædicarent; utpote
Leverus, Peneus, Gressopus, Crowleus, Goughus, Philpotus, Wiburnus.
Reliqui aut in academiis gradibus insigniti, aut tempore persecutionis
probati, post in ministerium cooptati, summa cum laude ecclesiis præ-
fuerunt. Et quanquam eorum nonnulli Latinam linguam non callebant,
tamen ope et adjumento librorum quorundam Calvini, Musculi et aliorum, qui in Anglicum sermonem translati sunt, scripturas optime interpretari potuerunt.

Epistola.—Dicunt unam, solamque illam propositionem quam reci-
tant, esse controversam ; nempe de re vestiaria.

Responsio.—Vicesimo sexto die Martii, anno 1566, convocati omnes
Londinenses ministri comparuerunt coram archiepiscopo Cantuariensi,
episcopo Londinensi, decano Westmonasteriensi et nonnullis canonistis :
ibique sunt rogati an acquiescere velint in progressibus regiis de rebus
religionis, statutis et statuendis; nec erat de vestibus solis mentio. Qui
recusarunt, sunt exauctorati. Archiepiscopus etiam cum concedat licentiam prædicandi alicui, alligat eum his verbis : *Proviso semper quod in
concionibus tuis non suadebis populo ut alterationem, innovationem quam-
cunque in religione instituant, præter aut contra eam quam regia majestas fecit vel factura sit.* Si unquam ullis de re vestiaria propositio
sit proposita sola, aut ulla disputatio habita, quemadmodum in libello
ab episcopis edito in defensionem vestium patet, sic illi defenderunt ut
tam sacramenta quam ministri ex his pristinam avitamque dignitatem
æstimationemque jam pene amissam recuperarent; ut patet ex examina-
tione, figura prima, sectione prima.

Epistola.—Negant mulieres baptizare. Negant item sibi probari fidei
ab infante extortionem et crucis obsignationem.

Responsio.—Quam vere hæc negant, apparet ex formula baptismi
quam tradidimus vobis, et etiam patet ex monitis episcoporum articulo
16, ubi ipsi jubent ne infans baptizetur alio quam quo præscriptum est
modo. Insuper fratres multos tulerunt episcopi commissarii carceribus
puniri, tractarique minus pie et christiane, qui recusarunt patrinos et
matrimos suis eligere infantibus.

Epistola.—Negant archiepiscopi esse curiam facultatum.

Responsio.—Omnia inde exeunt sub nomine archiepiscopi, regia suprema
auctoritate mediante. Et quamvis hanc curiam facultatum episcopi

vocant in quodam loco epistolæ curiam fiscalem; nullo potest modo sic vocari, nisi forte concedas illam esse fiscalem curiam, ex qua etiam singuli episcopi concedunt licentiam matrimonii solemnizandi in loco quocunque, ac temporibus prohibitis; quæ tempora quoque manent eo modo apud nos, quomodo in papismo erant.

Præterea, si hæc curia non erat fiscalis, cum eam Romani pontificis legatus de latere (qui solebat tempore vigentis apud nos primatus moram trahere in Anglia) tenebat; neutiquam et nunc potest appellari fiscalis. Ratio est, quia cum primatus translatus est ad regem Henricum octavum piæ memoriæ, et omnia quæ de jure canonico ad pontificem Romanum tanquam ecclesiæ monarcham pertinebat, ei data sunt, tunc ille, rex et papa, constituit alterum archiepiscopum, quippe Cantuariensem, sibi legatum, ea tamen lege ut censum annuum penderet illi, quoniam et solebat legatus de latere Romano papæ. Et hic archiepiscopus Cantuariensis eam curiam habet ratione eadem, et modo simili.

Epistola.—Dicunt non probari sibi cantum tremulum puerorum, et organa musica.

Responsio.—Tamen omnes fovent in ecclesiis suis, et imprimis suis nummis curavit organa in ecclesia sua metropoli archiepiscopus Cantuariensis fabricari.

Epistola.—Multa dicunt de synodo, ubi ministri sunt triplo (ut aiunt) plures quam ipsi sunt, quibus liberum est cognoscere et statuere de quibuslibet.

Responsio.—Cognoscunt et statuunt, sed ita, ut nihil firmum ratumque habeatur nisi assentiente regina et archiepiscopo. Unde fiebat ut multa ad maximam ecclesiæ utilitatem, a penultima synodo conclusa, supprimerentur, neque in lucem exierunt. Causa vero nostra erat synodo proposita postremis comitiis a quodam doctissimo viro spectante ad Nordowicensem episcopum; sed episcopus quidam interpellabat hominem, dicens, Quid hæc ad vos? Nos cœpimus hanc rem, nosque ad exitum perducemus. Respondit ille, Nos reginam hujus rei auctorem existimavimus, at nunc vos esse perspicimus: et ita non sunt passi hanc causam agi. Præterea superinducendi quas velint per universas regni ecclesias ceremonias reginæ et archiepiscopo potestas ex acto parliamenti data est.

Hæc, patres reverendissimi et domini in Christo plurimum observandi, freti solita vestra bonitate et pietate, cujus in ecclesiam Angliæ nos fecistis testes, scripsimus, et quod veritatem causæ vos latere nolumus, et ut potius vos scripta quam verba unde eam petatis habeatis. Nihil enim, nisi quod verissimum esse cognoscimus ac luce meridiana clarius, consentientes subscriptioni talionis scripsimus. Patent enim omnia quæ prius egimus, ex episcoporum monitis, ex quibusdam injunctionibus regiis, ex baptismatis utriusque formula, quæ omnia prius in Latinum sermonem conversa vobis tradidimus. Prima ecclesiæ apud nos initia, ejus progressus variasque commutationes, controversiæ nostræ ortum, ecclesiam vero ministerio carentem, in epistola ad illustrissimum Heidelbergensem principem destinata perspicue descripta vobis intueri licet. Nunc, patres, illud petimus, et in Christo contendimus etiam atque etiam, (quod vos ultro benignissime polliciti estis,) ut Londinensis, Wintoniensis ac Cantuariensis episcoporum animos exacerbatos molliatis, et si non amplius aliquid potestis, saltum hoc tantum exoretis : ut et in fratres nostros adhuc in Anglia remanentes mitiores esse velint, et fæces ex suis ecclesiis removentes, si non adjuvare at saltem tolerare, et ipsorum factis connivere velint : utque vos reverendis Nordovicensi, Wigorniensi et Dunelmensi episcopis, in vestris epistolis pollicitis, justas suæ pietatis laudes persolvatis ; atque illis, simul et fratribus ministris studentibus repurgationi ecclesiarum, animos pergendi in proposito addatis. Hæc si pro vestra summa benignitate (ut confidimus) impetraverimus, non modo non fatigabimus alias ecclesias novis precibus, sed et nos omnesque vere pii omnia vobis ob pacem et concordiam vestra opera ecclesiæ partam debebimus, et Deus Optimus Maximus vobis per Dominum nostrum Jesum Christum æternam coronam tribuet. Amen.

Vestræ dignitatis studiosissimi,

GEORGIUS WITHERUS,

JOANNES BARTHELOTTUS, *Angli.*

INSCRIPTIO.

Reverendis in Christo patribus, ac dominis suis longe colendissimis, domino Henr. Bullingero et D. Rodolpho Gualtero, ecclesiæ christianæ Tiguri ministris fidissimis, etc.

EPISTOLA LIX.

HENRICUS BULLINGERUS AD THEODORUM BEZAM.

Hoc autem apud te libere fateor, ea quæ a D. Sampsone scribuntur semper mihi esse suspecta. Vir alioqui est non malus, sed valde irrequietus. Dum apud nos Tiguri vixit, et dum rediit in Angliam, nunquam D. Petro Martyri beatæ memoriæ molestus esse desiit. Sæpe ille a me questus est, Nunquam Sampson literas scribit quas non sarciet querelis, nunquam homini huic satisfit, semper ille quæstiones et actiones habet imp... issimas.   Quoties ille, cum adhuc hic esset, inciperet sua mihi proponere, ego amicis verbis illum a me dimittebam, ut cujus ingenium scrupulosum et inquietum mihi est notissimum.   Habet Anglia hujusmodi ingenia plurima quæ quiescere non possunt, quibus nunquam fit satis, qui nunquam non habent quod conquerantur.   Ego certi natura ab hujusmodi abhorreo.

[H. BULLINGERUS.]

EPISTOLA LX.

THEODORUS BEZA AD HENRICUM BULLINGERUM.

...In Anglia vero quid potest boni sperari rebus ita manentibus? Putavi de re vestiaria laborari: aliquos superesse nævos, in quibus tardi fortassis essent episcopi, aut, ut ubique usu venire solet, non impetrarent quod maxime volunt.   Verum si ita se res habet ut audio (et sane confingi ista vix possunt), quæ talis unquam Babylon exstitit?   Quanquam autem solus Deus his malis alioqui insanabilibus mederi potest, tamen quum hi fratres isthuc ad vos ire per se decrevissent, nolui ab hoc consilio illos deterrere: etsi enim sunt vobis haud sane jucunda allaturi, tamen spero fore ut vos non pigeat de rebus istis plenius quam unquam antea certiores esse factos, et ipsi tum consilium tum consolationis aliquid a vobis reportantes, aliquatenus saltem miseriarum et dolorum suorum onere leventur.   Rogo te igitur, mi pater, nec te solum, sed etiam reliquos fratres et dominos mihi plurimum observandos, ut quamvis tristissima narrantes tamen libenter audiatis, et consilii ac consolationis egentes commiseremini; quod etiam sponte facturos vos minime dubito pro vestra singulari φιλαδελφία.   Ego quidem hanc rationem tenui, ut suspenso in rebus quoque, ut mihi videtur, manifestissimis judicio de fratribus absentibus, (quorum etiam non sum constitutus judex,) ipsos ad animi lenitatem, et patientia potius quam ullis accusatoriis querelis lenienda hæc mala hortarer: qua in re mihi sum visus illos mansuetudinis spiritu præditos comperire.   Ad hæc ubi vestra etiam auctoritas, quam, sicuti debent, plurimi faciunt, accesserit, revertentur animo pacatiore, et Dominus procul dubio tandem remedium inveniet.

Genevæ, 29 Julii, 1567.

Tuus,

BEZA.

EPISTOLA LXI.

HENRICUS BULLINGERUS ET RODOLPHUS GUALTERUS AD THEODORUM BEZAM.

D. THEODORO Bezæ Bullingerus et Gualterus S. D. Excepimus quanta potuimus humanitate hos per te, carissime frater, commendatos nobis Anglos. Proposuerunt illi nobis scripta quædam, quæ tamen antea videramus, petentes nostrum, ut qui plurimum apud Angliæ episcopos possemus, consilium et auxilium. Respondimus id dudum præstitisse nos quod potuimus, ampliora nos non posse; sed et ipsos ita pro se respondere episcopos, ut videatur causa ipsorum non esse passiva. Recitavimus itaque illis epistolam nostram ad episcopos hoc de negotio scriptam, et responsionem episcoporum vicissim nobis datam. Illi vero causabantur illam non esse bona fide ab episcopis conscriptam; rem enim longe aliter habere. Nos qui omnem fidem episcopis, viris alioqui piis et integerrimis, omnino derogare non debuimus, cum his tam andabatarum more pugnare contendereque noluimus, ideoque causam hanc in medio reliquimus. Quid pluribus opus? Videtur mox ab initio peccatum ab his rigore nimio, et progressu increvisse, incaluisseque (ut fit) contendendo rixas, et animos utrinque exacerbatos, ut jam utrinque peccetur, et ægre ulla huic malo medela inveniatur. Certo ex horum sermonibus apparet animos eorum infensissimos esse episcopis, ut qui de ipsis nihil fere referant quod non sit atro sale conditum, odiumque redoleat Vatinianum. Orandus est itaque Dominus, ut ipse cordium moderator huic causæ miseræ medeatur. Vehementer nobis probaretur, si istis quoque probari posset, quod tu inter alia scribis, videri tibi patientia potius quam ullis accusatoriis querelis hoc malum esse leniendum. Et nos quidem episcopis ut non possumus præcipere, ita suam causam agentibus et se suaque probabiliter apud nos defendentibus, adversarii esse, et cum his ipsorum accusatoribus conjungi, adeoque et huic controversiæ immisceri, plane noluimus. Interim commiseratione pia polliciti sumus his nostris fratribus, scripturos nos ad episcopos et intercessuros apud illos pro eis: id quod, Deo volente, bona fide ad futuras Francofordienses nundinas præstabimus. Neque aliud in præsenti possumus. Ostenderunt illi nobis præterea supplicationem paratam et illustrissimo principi Palatino electori offerendam. A quo ipsorum consilio eos non deterruimus, si forte Dominus vel hac ratione turbas illas infelices componere velit. Hæc sunt quæ cum illis egimus, tametsi apud nos statueramus porro nihil prorsus cum quoquam hac in contentione amplius vel verbis vel scriptis agere velle; ut et nunc nobis firmiter

proposuimus: verum si qui alii huc venturi sunt, fac sciant se frustra
huc venire.

Rem feceris nobis longe gratissimam, si diligenter scripseris de rebus Gallicis, de quibus et regina maxime mirifici sparguntur rumores.
Nos hæremus in his dubiis, ideoque oramus Dominum ut evertat impiorum arguta ac truculenta consilia, et ecclesias non tam servet a malo
quam vera fide vitæque emendatione sibi conciliet. Alioqui enim gravia
nobis impendere non abs re metuimus. Zancho inscriptas per te literas
propediem curabo fideliter. Baldvinus, de quo tu scribis, Lutetiæ in
lectione publica, quod ad me scribit Lutetia studiosus quidam, me re-
prehendit propter traditiones humanas, citans locum ex Apocalypsi mea
ex cap. 2. Affinxit quoque reprehensioni suæ putidum mendacium,
quod ea de re mecum contulerit, nec tunc habuisse me quod fere respon-
derem: cum ille semel me duntaxat et quidem obiter salutarit, nulla
de re unquam mecum contulerit. Sed non procedent amplius hi homines,
quod ait apostolus, nam damnatio illorum evidens erit omnibus. Bene
vale. Salutat te D. Gualterus. Salutant et fratres reliqui omnes. Saluta tu quoque fratres nostros qui apud te sunt.

Tiguri, 3 Augusti, 1567.

H. BULLINGERUS senior,
GUALTERI
Et suo nomine.

EPISTOLA LXII.

GEORGIUS WITHERUS AD PRINCIPEM PALATINUM ELECTOREM.

Non nostra culpa ad te oratum mittimus, princeps amplissime; sed
cogit vis, impellit pietas, flagitat patria, denique Anglicana ecclesia
jam jacens, et mox (si aliquo modo ei subventum non sit) peri-
tura, nos quasi præcipites agit. Ac si non in ecclesiam pietas et in
omnes pios amor singularis, quæ te ceteris omnibus principibus prælu-
cere faciunt, satis nobis innotescerent, nunquam ad tuum præsidium
confugere fuissemus ausi. Nunc vero cum ea nos non latent (quomodo
enim latere possint, quæ omnibus manifesta sunt?) non est mirum si
nobis facile persuasum sit te eundem miseris laturum opem, qui spem
dedisti. Quare, princeps optime, si nos domibus ignobiles et tibi ignoti,
variis calamitatibus pressi, ecclesiæ nunc laboranti a te subsidium petimus, non est a nobis impudenter factum; et quamvis audacius fortasse
facere videbimur, tantum tamen nobis concedas questus, quantum pio
dolori concedendum esse putaveris. Sathan enim quoniam aperto Marte

nihil officere valuit, ex insidiis ecclesiam Anglicanam adoritur : et quoniam integrum papismum restituere non valet, ad Lutheranismum, sed
sensim et gradatim, nos reducere conatur.   In quo cum multa tristia
sunt, tum nihil magis est dolendum, quam quod jam non per papistas
suos, non per homines sanguine sanctorum saginatos, non per perditis-
simos, sed per nos nobis, per eos qui aliquando optimi habebantur optimis viris periculum inferre conatur ; et quos vi, ferro, face delere non
potuit, hos nostrorum auctoritate, evangelicorum sententiis et religione
opprimere se posse sperat.

Sed ut causam nostram planius et melius perspicias et intelligas,
prima exordia et ipsa veluti cunabula ecclesiæ apud nos nascentis, et
primo exorientis, deinde ipsius progressus et varias temporum commutationes, tibi demonstrare necesse est ; ut inde scias et quam procul a perfectione semper fuimus, et tamen ab ea libertate, in quam
beneficio Christi semel perveneramus, recessimus.   Anglia auspiciis
Henrici ejus nominis octavi Romanum antichristum totius regni finibus
expulit, sed ita ut ipsius auctoritas non tam suppressa quam ad
regem translata videretur.   Missa reliquiæque papisticæ spurcitiæ pristinum locum gradumque retinuerunt.   Post ejectum pontificem monasteria ubique diruuntur.   Monachi, fratres, nonnæ, nomen et vestem deponere et mutare coguntur ; postea peregrinationes vetitæ sunt, imagines
vero apud quas tam horrenda committebatur idololatria, sublatæ et
confractæ sunt ; deinde sub ipso fine ipsius regni biblia vernacula lingua impressa omnibus permissa sunt, et in omnibus templis dominicam
orationem, symbolum fidei, decem Dei præcepta, et epistolam et evangelium diei Anglico sermone recitare sacerdotes jussi sunt.   Atque hæc
sub regno Henrici initia jacta sunt, cui defuncto Edwardus piæ memoriæ
princeps in regno successit ; qui convocatis totius regni nobilissimis et
doctissimis viris ex ipsorum consilio ecclesiam reformare cœpit.   Sta-
tuas et simulacra omnia omnibus in locis dirui et confringi jussit.
Deinde missam precesque peregrina lingua ubique abolevit.   Populo
calicis pariter ac panis in communicanda cœna accipiendi potestatem
dedit.   Formulam publicarum precum Anglice conscriptarum edidit ; quæ
ab Latinis (nisi quod spurcissima quæque abolebantur) fere nihil differebant.   Administratio sacramentorum Lutheranismum prorsus sapit.
Ministris venia uxores ducendi data, eorum filii lege ad hoc lata legi-
timati sunt. Altaria, organa, theatricæ papistarum vestès, et hujus generis
alia sub nomine ornamentorum templi et ministrorum retenta sunt. Postea
pius iste rex, animadvertens adhuc quam procul ab meta abesset, denuo
rem suscepit, novam precum formulam edidit, superstitionis monumenta
omnia quæ prius reliquerat (excepto superpellicio et genuflexione in
cœna dominica, mulierum baptismate ac fidei ab infante extortione)
sustulit et prohibuit.   Quæ vero reliquit ita libera erant, ut nemo qui

est reluctatus ad ea adigeretur. Rex vero vere Dominum timens, his progressibus non adhuc contentus, extremam huic operi erat admoturus manum : comitiis totius regni publicis diem indixit : omnes optima spe et exspectatione pleni erant : at interea rex optimus immatura morte ereptus est. Successit soror Maria regni (utinam et pietatis!) hæres. Omnia tum repente commutata, papatus in integrum restitutus est.

Sed quid notissima commemoro? accedam ad ea quæ fortasse tibi incognita sunt. Quamvis primo ecclesia videbatur funditus eversa, et pii ubique terrarum dispersi, tamen haud contemnenda piorum manus sese collegit Londini, communi consensu ministros elegit, diaconos constituit, atque inter medios hostes, Argo oculatiores et Nerone crudeliores, ecclesia Dei denuo renovatur omnibus suis numeris (ut uno verbo dicam) absoluta et perfectissima. Et quamvis sæpe hostium incursu dissipata sit, maximusque numerus ignibus crudelibus absumptus esset, tamen quotidie crescit et indies augetur. Interim Maria moritur. Elizabetha soror omnibus præ gaudio gestientibus regnare cœpit. Tum reginæ mandato qui carcere et vinculis religionis causa detenti erant, libertate donati sunt; qui exilio solum verterant, in patriam reversi sunt. Ecclesia vero quæ in mediis permanserat flammis, edicto nescio quo sublata est. Quod difficile factu non fuit, cum omnes exspectarent, ut non minus pura reginæ auctoritate et regni legibus restitueretur. Senatus summus totius regni est convocatus, papatus denuo ejectus, et secunda precum formula, quam moriens Edouardus reliquit, ecclesiæ est restituta. Ceremoniæ vero, quæ prima reformatione Edouardi (quemadmodum prius dictum est) relictæ in ecclesia sunt, sub eodem nomine restituuntur. Reginæ præterea et archiepiscopo superinducendi quas velint ceremonias potestas data est, qui statim postea et panem communem prius ad celebrandam cœnam constitutum aboleverunt, et novioris renovationis causa placentulam rotundam, ad formam ejus qua papistæ utebantur, constituerunt. Ad prolationem autem nominis Jesu omnes pileos exuere et genua flectere jusserunt. Tum papisticis expulsis episcopis novi erant subrogandi, et plerique ex eorum numero qui exules erant. Hi primo ceremoniis resistere cœperunt ; postea vero, quum aliter spes nulla esset episcopandi, cesserunt et susceperunt, quemadmodum aliquis illorum palam fassus est, contra conscientiam suam. Interim fratres, quos adhuc reluctari videbant, consolabantur, pollicentes iis administrandi ecclesias suas facultatem liberam, quod et per aliquot annos præstiterunt. Qua libertate nacta, purgabant illi sedulo ecclesias suas omnibus nævis et spurcitiis papisticis. Quorum exemplo commoti alii, qui ab initio cesserant, similiter ecclesias reformare incipiunt. Quorum ut numerum et auctoritatem crescere apud plebem viderent episcopi, putabant de gloria sua actum esse, si non inferiores ministros ad ea suscipienda quibus ipsi utebantur adigerent. Rem itaque reginæ mandato suscipiunt. Sampsonem, virum doctissimum et maximæ apud

ecclesiam auctoritatis, exauctorant. Hujus rei metu sperant facile reliquos fore deterritos. Sed cum præter opinionem omnes viderent ad
resistendum magis paratos, denuo rem aggrediuntur, et convocatis omnibus ecclesiæ Londinensis ministris rogant, ut polliceantur se parituros
omnibus reginæ decretis jam tum in religione factis et fiendis. Quod
cum negarent se salva conscientia facere posse, prout tum res sese habebant, uno eodemque die plures triginta exauctorati sunt. Sed cum hæc
non succedere, sed omnium odia et præsertim piorum in sese concitasse
viderent, alia via rem aggressi sunt. Prohibent ne quisquam in sua par-
ochia scripturas interpretetur, sine speciali episcopi venia sigillo ipsius
signata. Revocant præterea omnes ante certum diem concessas licen-
tias : nemini vero denuo concedunt, nisi qui prius iis quæ ipsi volunt
consenserit. Si quis sine ipsorum venia interpretari scripturas ausus
fuerit, rapitur in judicium, contemptus nimirum reus. Quod si tum non
ipsis consenserit, carcere vel exilio multant.

Vides igitur, princeps optime, miserandam ecclesiæ Anglicanæ faciem,
vides quam deformis jacet. Cum enim tres sunt præcipuæ ecclesiæ partes,
doctrina salubris, pura sacramentorum administratio, et ministerium rite
institutum, quæ pars etiam continet disciplinam nervosam : doctrinam ecclesiæ nostræ non attingam, quæ quamvis in plurimis sana est, in nonnullis
tamen claudicat. Sacramenta quomodo deformata humanis inventis sunt,
ex publica precum formula, ex regiis injunctionibus et ex episcoporum monitis (quæ advertisamenta vocant) facile patebit. Ministerium vero prorsus
nullum, nulla disciplina. Non enim ministri Christi, sed servi hominum
dicendi sunt, quibus nihil ad præscriptum verbi, sed omnia ad reginæ et
episcoporum nutum sunt facienda. Quid quod plerique sunt papistarum
sacrificuli, missæ consecrati, reliquorum maxima multitudo homines im-
peritissimi, ex sententia plebis creati, non ad verbi ministerium, sed ad
officium diei sive festi perlegendum, quæ puer fere quivis non incom-
mode facere posset ? Quid [quod] qui ecclesiis præsunt, studii vel famula-
tus causa ab ipsis abesse possunt ? Quid quod innumera multitudo eorum
sit, qui nullam habent ecclesiam neque consistendi locum ? Quid quod
verbum prædicare episcoporum privilegium est, qui tamen raro huic
negotio vacant ? Quid denique quod excommunicationis gladius, ministris præreptus, jurisperitis traditur ? Qualem putas eam esse ecclesiam,
princeps illustrissime, in qua nec sacramenta pure administrata, nec ministerium nisi hujusmodi audivisti ullum ? Quare si quid gratia vel
auctoritate apud serenissimam reginam nostram vales, id in tam pia causa
ad medendum tantis ecclesiæ malis, ad papismi memoriam omnem ad
æternum damnandam, experiare quæsumus et rogamus : sed ita ut si
non possis (quod optamus) pleniorem ecclesiæ totius reformationem obtinere, tamen (quod te consecuturum speramus) his qui antichristi reliquias detestantur libertatem (id est, ne contra conscientias suas velut

has usurpent nec ministerium deserant cogantur[1]) exores impetresque. Et
si nobis et ecclesiæ nostræ, quod nos certo nobis persuademus, consultum esse cupis, princeps optime, summopere cavendum est ut ab regina omnem culpam in episcopos amoveas, qui apud ipsam monitorum
officium, prout decet parque est, satis libere non faciunt. Quod enim
tam apud nos quam apud exteros sese non probare, sed regina impel-
lente facere dicunt, id libris publice ad hoc editis et ipsi jubent, et bono
pioque consilio et cum totius ecclesiæ commodo a regina factum esse
scribunt. Unde non est mirum, si ipsa illorum blanditiis et assenta-
tionibus decepta in nos tamquam in rebelles et contumaces severi aliquid statuat. Sed quod et scimus te per te satis ad nobis opitulandum
proclivem, et ab gravissimis tuæ reipublicæ negotiis diutius a nobis im-
pediri par non est, non longius evagabitur oratio nostra, cui hic finem
imponimus.

EPISTOLA LXIII.

[RICARDUS HILLES] AD HENRICUM BULLINGERUM.

SALUTEM precor tibi, vir colendissime carissimeque amice, plurimam.
Magnum librum, Esaiam tuum, tuis videlicet expositum homiliis, una
cum literis tuis mihi gratissimis 25 Februarii proxime præteriti datis,
a domino Johanne Abelo (qui te etiam salvere jubet plurimum) ante
quatuor menses accepi. Quo me volumine dono dedisti, sicuti fiet volente Deo, ut hoc muneris a te habeam in perpetuæ amicitiæ symbolum.
Danielem etiam cum epitome, homiliis tuis LXVI exposito, mihi a
prædicto domino Johanne Abelo fratre carissimo comparavi. Utrique
mihi quam maxime complacent libri; speroque homilias illas voluminis
utriusque non parum utilitatis allaturas fidelibus et diligentibus lecto-
ribus. Quantum ad hoc attinet, quod cupias de rebus Brabanticis certo
edoceri, et me rogas, ne hic te negligam, quantum quidem mihi licuerit
per otium et negotium; certiorem te nunc facio, carissime domine, me
jam de iisdem rebus, quantum certi ipsemet novi, vel per amicos scire
potui, literis commisisse, et quasi historiolam perbrevem inde scripsisse.
Quam quidem si Latine transferri procurare possim (sicuti pædagogus
quidam mihi amicus promisit se facturum), mittam ad te, vel saltem
Francofordiæ pro te, ad nundinas proximas quadragesimales, si tamdiu
mihi Deus concesserit vivere. Gaudeo certe tuas illas duas natu minimas

[1 Omnia sic MS.]

filias nubiles ita rem domesticam tam prudenter et egregie tibi administrare, ut commode poteris vivere viduus.   Fertur hic pro certo, ducem
de Alva, qui cum regiis Hispaniæ copiis jam nunc Lovanæ aut Gandavo
venit, atque ibi in inferiore Germania et Antverpiæ copias illas collocavit,
nomine regiæ illius majestatis, velle omnibus illius patriæ civitatibus, quæ
prædicationem protestantium proxime elapso anno admiserunt, seu libere
permiserunt, libertates et privilegia adimere, et inferiorem Germaniam
in justam monarchiam redigere.   Domini voluntas fiat, absque cujus per-
missione nihil faciet.   Precemur ex animo ut nobis pacem dare dignetur
in diebus nostris : quæ adhuc perseverat integra per Dei gratiam hic in
regno Angliæ ; præterquam quod adhuc aliqui ex concionatoribus nostris
(quamvis non ex doctissimis), scrupulositate magna detentis, seu inani
quadam gloria, vel vulgi aliquibus applausibus devictis, deturbant quandoque eam, propterea quod repugnant seu contradicunt reginæ et regni
totius ordinationi de lineis vestibus utendis vel gestandis, dum psalmi in
ecclesia canuntur, lectiones sacræ leguntur, et sacramenta administrantur.
Ego autem sentio cum beato Hieronymo (libro primo adversus Pelagianos),
non esse "inimicitias contra Deum, si episcopus, presbyter et diaconus, et
reliquus ordo ecclesiasticus in administratione sacrificiorum candida veste
processerint." " Porro religio alterum habitum habet in ministerio, alterum
in usu et vita communi : vestibus autem lineis utebantur Ægyptii sacerdotes" (qui etiam, ut optime nosti, tempore Hieronymi christiani fuerunt)
"non solum intrinsecus, sed et extrinsecus." (In commentario in Ezechielem,
lib. XIII. cap. 44).   Et vere Christi discipuli, quantum in illis est, pacem
colebunt[1] cum omnibus hominibus ; neque offendiculo erunt incredulis
neque ecclesiis Dei.   Orandus est Dominus, ut unanimes nos faciat habi-
tare in Dei domo, quæ est ecclesia, et ut omnes contentiones supervacaneas
et malå tollat omnia offendicula.   Dominus servet te. Londini, 23 Au-
gustii, anno 1567.

Tuus ex animo, etc.

[RICARDUS HILLES.]

INSCRIPTIO.

Doctissimo viro domino Henrico
*   Bullingero, amico mihi caris-*
*   simo dentur literæ. Tiguri.*

[1 Sic MS.]

EPISTOLA LXIV.

HENRICUS BULLINGERUS ET RODOLPHUS GUALTERUS AD ED-
MUNDUM GRINDALLUM, EDWINUM SANDUM, ET JOHANNEM
PARKHURSTUM.

REVERENDI viri, domini colendissimi, et fratres in Domino carissimi.
Dominus Jesus benedicat vobis, et servet vos ab omni malo!

Quo vehementius favemus vobis, reverendi domini et fratres carissimi, eo dolemus gravius dissidere vos a fratribus aliquot, viris doctis,
in Anglia gradu suo dejectis.   Atque ideo dilectioni nostræ dabitis sin-
ceræ, quod frequentius eadem de re aures vestras obtundimus.   Vidimus
et accepimus vestram in hac causa excusationem: interim Angli exules
ad nos veniunt, qui affirmant Londinensis ecclesiæ doctores, nec non aliarum in Anglia ecclesiarum, in Mariana persecutione probatos homines,
quorum fide et diligentia ecclesiæ Anglicanæ in sævissimis istis tempestatibus conservatæ sint, nunc pelli; nec pelli tantum, sed gravi etiam persecutione premi, adeoque et in tetros retrudi carceres.   Addunt plures esse in
Hibernia ecclesiarum ministros, qui non aliter sentiant aut faciant quam illi
ipsi qui in Anglia sustinent persecutionem; illos autem episcopi sui beneficio et apud regiam majestatem interventu agere in summa tranquillitate.
Unde isti colligunt, si episcopi qui in Anglia sunt apud regiam majestatem
etiam intercederent, fore ut et ipsi tranquille sibi commissas possint retinere et gubernare ecclesias: et, quod hac in causa præcipuum est, episcopos non diffiteri meliorem habere causam afflictos et dejectos: nam
agnoscere eos ecclesiam rectius constitui et constitutam gubernari sine illis
ceremoniis ritibusve et institutis, quam cum illis; adeo ut si ipsismet
offeratur optio, malint ipsi sibi ecclesiam deligere sine illis, quam illis
oneratam sibi dari.   Id quod inde quoque colliquescat manifestissime,
quod in regni comitiis non semel episcopi petierint a regia majestate ut tol-
lantur illa, et purgatior ornatiorque aut minus saltem onerata fiat ecclesia.

Quæ cum ita sint, reverendi domini et fratres carissimi, incitabit vos
ipsos haud dubie vestra pietas ad consultandum quomodo fieri possit commode et mature, ut fratribus istis afflictis consulatur, et ne ita gravi persecutione premantur; quin potius regiæ majestatis clementia in regno toleren-
tur, donaque in ipsis utilia ecclesiæ per abdicationem non extinguantur.
Non est autem quod multis rationibus aut exemplis vos alioqui peritissimos
omnis pietatis et æquitatis urgeamus: tantum hoc oramus per Dominum,
ut si apud regiam majestatem afflictis afflictionem vel imminuere vel prorsus
adimere potestis, pro christiana caritate illis omnem vestram fidelem im-
pendatis operam; et nostram hanc admonitionem fraternam boni con-

sulatis, solitoque amore nos vestri amantissimos prosequi pergatis. Valete,
honorandi domini. Tiguri, 26 Augusti, 1567.

BULLINGERUS ET GUALTERUS.

INSCRIPTIO.

Londinen. Wigornien. et Norvicen.
episcopis in Anglia.

EPISTOLA LXV.

CHRISTOPHORUS MONTIUS AD HENRICUM BULLINGERUM.

Vicesima septima Septembris D. Funckius hinc mane abiit; in vespera
ejusdem diei allatae sunt ad me literae ex Anglia a Rev. episcopo Londinensi ad magnitudinem tuam transmittendae, quas nolui sine meis ad magnitudinem tuam ablegare. Puto episcopum parricidium reginae Scotiae ad
dominationem tuam scribere, et meritissimam ejusdem poenam; nempe quod
capta sit, tum quod se regno abdicare coacta sit, confessa sua ope et consilio
maritum sublatum esse; moechum quoque sceleratissimum aufugisse in quandam arcem maritimam in rupe sitam: laudabile est hujus ignobilis gentis
in vindicandis sceleribus exemplum et studium, quod docta Italia cupidinis
impetu et furore excusasset. Mirabilis apud Belgas laniena vobis ignorata
esse non potest: nescio si ii, quibus jus gladii a Domino commissum est,
in tanta innoxii sanguinis profusione otiosi spectatores et dissimulatores
excusati sint. Si bellum gerere contra Turcas omnibus seculis et ab omnibus pontificibus, cardinalibus, monachis, clericis, scholasticis scriptoribus
permissum et comprobatum est, quia in veram religionem arma inferant,
et in eo bello mortuis gloria et immortalis honos attributus sit; an sedi-
tiosus et perduellis habendus sit, qui necessaria et justa arma induat pro
focis et aris tuendis, ad injustam vim repellendam, ad veram religionem
conservandam et ad posteros transmittendam? Quid si legitimus rex in
tyrannum degeneret? an is Dei minister dici possit? Pax colenda, obedientia praestanda, simul quoque naturalia jura, leges et consuetudines
regnorum, dominiorum, et ditionum servandae sunt, et imprimis Deo quae
Dei sunt danda. Praeclara constitutio est imperatorum Theodosii et Valen-
tiniani, digna vox majestate regnantis, legibus alligatum se principem profiteri; adeo de auctoritate juris nostra pendet auctoritas. Nec principes ideo
soluti sunt legibus, ut omnia pro libidine eis liceant; sed, auctore Aristotele,
tanta virtutis exuperantia ceteris praestare debet, ut universorum virtus
cum hoc non sit comparabilis, et qui ipsa justitia et aequitate tam ceteris praestet, quam sol elementis informibus et rudibus. In talem nulla
prorsus legislatio est, quippe qui ipse lex viva et animata sit. Laude

digni sunt Helvetii, qui ex impotenti dominatu et tyrannide se in libertatem asseruerunt. Non velim classicum cani contra legitimos et juste
imperantes principes, sed contra Vejoves, qui ex libidine, avaritia, cru-
delitate, fastu, quoquo se verterunt, omnia corrumpunt, commiscent,
conturbant, contaminant omnia solo nutu circumagentes et quatientes,
dignissimi qui censoribus Helvetiis et Scotis in ordinem cogantur. Ut
genero tuo R. G. ex me salutem dicas rogo. Equidem vobis omnia
mea officia defero. Argentinæ, 11 Octobr. 1567.

Quem nosti,

[CHRISTOPH. MONTIUS.]

INSCRIPTIO.

Reverendo et doctissimo domino Henrico
Bullingero, meo faventi Domino.
Turici.

EPISTOLA LXVI.

EDMUNDUS GRINDALLUS AD THEODORUM BEZAM, ETC.

SAL. in Christo. D. Joannes Cognatus, Gallicæ ecclesiæ, quæ apud
nos est, minister fidelissimus, et frater meus in Domino carissimus, hodie
mihi ostendit literas suas quas ad vos in causa ecclesiæ Londino-Belgicæ
conscripsit, atque una cum istis mittit. In illis literis origo et summa
omnium controversiarum dictæ ecclesiæ simplicissime et verissime expli-
cantur. Oro igitur, carissimi fratres, ut illis literis fidem habeatis, et
vestro consilio non solum Londino-Belgicam, sed et alias ejus linguæ
ecclesias, juvetis et ad pacis unitatisque studium amplectendum serio
cohortemini. Non dubito quin vestræ exhortationes atque admonitiones
plurimum apud illos efficient. Scripsissem hac de re, atque adeo de
nostrarum ecclesiarum statu, paulo copiosius, nisi me oculorum dolores,
qui tertianæ febri successerunt, impedivissent. Sed dabit Dominus, uti
spero, posthac meliorem opportunitatem. Dominus vos conservet et
ministerio vestro benedicat, carissimi fratres! Londini, 17 Aprilis,
1568.

Vester in Christo,

EDMUNDUS GRINDALLUS,
Episcopus Londinensis.

INSCRIPTIO.

Carissimis in Christo fratribus D. Theo-
doro Bezæ ceterisque ministris Gene-
vensis ecclesiæ.

EPISTOLA LXVII.

CHRISTOPHORUS MONTIUS AD HENRICUM BULLINGERUM.

Binas nuper ex te accepi literas, alteras scriptas 13 Decembris, alteras 16, quas ad me pertulit D. Antonius Franciscus; cui tum ob eruditionem, tum ob pietatem libenter gratificatus fuissem, si qua ratione potuissem. Literas quæstoris vestri filio ejus inscriptas, quandoquidem citius mittere non potui, dedi D. Antonio perferendas, qui cras hinc Heidelbergam iter ingredietur.   Ex Gallia nihil certi ad dominationem tuam adscribere possum : tam enim omnia istinc ad nos incerta adferuntur, ut paucis admodum narratis fidere audeamus.   Hoc unum indicium rerum Hugenottorum nondum desperatarum habemus, quod regii alioqui vani et inflatissimi novitatum suarum amplificatores tacent, et moderatiores facti sunt. Credo Italos probe et pro merito exceptos non temere in Galliam decursuros[1].   Hispanorum crudelitas et impia tyrannis Turcarum armis ultricibus retaliabitur.

Scripsit ad me episcopus Londinensis 10 Octobris, quas literas ad vicesimam Decembris tandem accepi.   Cum enim destituti modo simus commoditate Belgica in transferendis literis, et mare Germanicum modo clausum sit, facilitate et transmittendi et accipiendi invicem orbati sumus. Episcopus in suis literis voluit ut dominationem tuam suis verbis salutarem.   Equidem quæ illinc accepi, tibi ut fautori et cupido rerum Anglicarum communicanda judicavi. Norfolciæ Dux, qui hactenus obedienter et pacifice in Anglia, prout nobilem virum decuit, se gessit, is tumidis et ambitiosis promissis inflatus, infelicissimas nuptias contrahere in animum induxit cum Medea parricida et sanguisuga, et hac deliberatione inflammatus se ab aula subduxit in avita prædia.   Hac ejus præsumptione comperta, per caduceatorem in aulam citatus fuit, qua vocatione neglecta in paternis agris substitit.   Regina, his principiis obstandum pro sua prudentia intelligens, præfectum stipatorum regiorum cum una centuria misit ad eum adducendum ; quod is intelligens ultro ad aulam iter ingressus est, in quo itinere substitit mandato reginæ, neque ei copia facta est accedendi ad aulam.   Post tridui moram Londinum in arcem abductus est, ubi asservatur.   Duo alii comites jussi sunt se intra suas domus continere, qui ut ejus consilii conscii suspicionibus gravati sunt.   Duce capto et aliis in ordinem redactis totum regnum quietum et tranquillum est.   Nisi illa serpens sublata fuerit, suis gentilitiis artibus et dolis plurimam perniciem parturiet, ut illa quæ ardentem facem sibi gignere visa est.   Hæc serenissima regina hactenus sine ullius sanguinis effusione pacifice regnum administravit ; qua felicitate ut porro fruatur Deus det et concedat.

[¹ MS. *decursores*.]

Nuper legatus quidam a rege Hispaniæ ad serenissimam Angliæ reginam missus est, qui regis nomine petiit commeatum pro tribus legionibus vel regimentis Belgarum peditum in Hispaniam transfretandorum, ut eorum opera rex utatur contra rebelles Mauros. Reginam ex tempore respondisse fertur, tantorum militum secundum Angliæ litora navigare multitudinem periculosum posse esse; nam cum venti mutabiles et instabiles sint, et navigantibus multa evenire possint secus quam putarent, si hic miles, necessitate aliqua oborta, in Angliæ portus appellere cogatur, tantorum militum adventum sine maleficio fieri non posse, adeoque opus fore ut regina litora et portus suos præsidiario milite armet et muniat: quod si rex hos sumptus ferre velit, et obsides dare quod non in alium usum Germanici militis opera uti quam contra Mauros velit, se regi gratificaturam. Sed considerandum est hæreticis non esse fidem, et si [violandum est] jusjurandum, regni causa violandum. Julius Papa dictitare solebat, mercatores fide obstringi, non principes.

Ex Saxonia nihil audimus. Auraicus adhucdum apud Saxonem moratur. Elector ipse adfuturus nuptiis filiæ suæ dicitur, quæ adducetur Heidelbergam, ubi nuptiæ peragentur ad quintum diem Februarii. De militibus in Galliam adducendis nihildum apud nos constat: exiguæ copiæ penetrare non possunt: magnæ maximi constabunt, et pietatis ergo sumptus facere et discrimina subire Sampsonis opus est. Ego mea officia dominationi tuæ defero. Argentinæ, 7 Cal. Jan. Anno 69. Instantis anni ut feliciores successus divina clementia consequamur comprecandum est. Rogo ut Anglicos titulos in literarum inscriptionibus omittas. *Qui sapit, in tacito gaudeat ille sinu.*

C. M.

INSCRIPTIO.

Clarissimo D. Bullingero,
patrono colendissimo.
Zeuric.

EPISTOLA LXVIII.

REGINA ELIZABETHA AD JOHANNEM STURMIUM.

Elizabetha Dei gratia Angliæ, Franciæ et Hiberniæ Regina, Fidei Defensor, &c. Johanni Sturmio amico nobis sincere dilecto salutem. Accepimus literas tuas decimo nono Martii ad nos scriptas, ab illis quibus tu eas perferendas dedisti ad nos allatas. Ac ipsis quidem hominibus eam quam literæ tuæ expetiverunt, et fidem præbuimus, et quæ illi in mandatis habebant accurate omnia intelleximus. Ex quibus pristinam tuam erga nos voluntatem, et de statu nostro curam ac solicitudinem multis rerum notis jam olim nobis perspectam recognoscentes, nec multum sane mirabamur pro veteri tua in nos observantia, et multum tamen gaudebamus, atque etiam magnas nunc gratias agimus.

De rebus vero per illos ad nos relatis sic statuendum esse duximus : ut quoniam quidem fidelem nostrum servitorem Henricum Killigrew istuc nuper cum mandatis misimus, cui una cum doctore Montio, homine nobis fideli, tibi familiariter cognito, fidem in rebus nostris haberi volumus, ea omnia illis libere patefacias, et cum utrisque aut illorum altero integre communices. Nos vero de tali vestro inter vos colloquio ab illis certiores factæ, de rerum summa quod et causa et nobis dignum erit Deo approbante statuemus. Bene valeas. Dat. ex regia nostra Westmonasterii. Calend. Maii, Anno Dom. 1569, regni vero nostri undecimo.

ELIZABETH. R.

INSCRIPTIO.

Spectabili et erudito viro Johanni
Sturmio, amico nostro caris-
simo.

EPISTOLA LXIX.

JOHANNES STURMIUS AD REGINAM ELIZABETHAM.

Qui sacra biblia sermone convertit Hispanico, unus est, serenissima Regina, ex eorum numero, qui improborum hominum calumniis circumventi eas sedes retinere non possunt, in quibus quasi collocati a Deo videntur. Invidit serpens ille omnium bonorum hostis hunc virum et opus istud Angliæ, imo ecclesiæ Christi invidit; et coactus fuit optimus vir insidiis inimicorum ex Anglia discedere. Sed neque studium suum erga religionem, neque benevolentiam suam erga Angliæ regnum, neque observantiam erga majestatem deposuit; et superavit diaboli vim, opusque perfecit, quod libenter auspiciis majestatis vestræ divulgasset, si id ferre posse Hispanos arbitraretur, et si dignum putasset vestræ majestatis patrocinio; non quod ipse dignus non sit optimorum et potentissimorum propter virtutem et doctrinam propugnatione, sed quia de se nimis judicat humiliter. Optat tamen probari majestati vestræ opus hoc suamque operam, et a me postulavit commendari utrumque, ut si ipse in Angliam non veniat, habeant tamen biblia locum in quo[1] diu multumque cum ipso auctore jactati queant quiescere. Commendo igitur majestati vestræ et virum et labores ejus contra malevolorum calumnias. Sed hi suas magnas

[¹ Quibus, MS.]

pœnas dederunt; quorum vitæ exitus, qualis vitæ eorum cursus fuerat, magnis argumentis comprobavit. Verum ita ego pro auctore intercedo, ut pro me etiam deprecer, quod in hac tanta mole rerum gerendarum, præsertim his orbis terrarum tumultibus, molestus sim : cogitans tamen et sperans, ut Deo, sic magnis hominibus et principibus imperiorum atque regnorum non ingratas esse humilium hominum preces atque supplicationes. Deum oro ut majestatem vestram sanam, salvam, felicem et prosperam conservet. Argentorati, 8 Id. Septembris, 1569.

Serenissimæ majestatis vestræ
fidelis famulus et servus,

JOH. STURMIUS.

INSCRIPTIO.

Serenissimæ principi et dominæ
Elizabethæ, Angliæ, Franciæ
et Hiberniæ Reginæ, dominæ
suæ clementissimæ.

EPISTOLA LXX.

JOHANNES STURMIUS AD GULIELMUM CECILIUM.

SCRIPSI serenissimæ reginæ de bibliis Hispanicis, atque ea majestati ejus commendavi. Sed opus hic habeo etiam patrocinio auctoritatis tuæ, ut si hæc mea deprecatio aliquid dubitationis habeat, adsis nobis ; ut ne plus valeat Hispanorum pontificiorum calumnia, quam evangelicorum qui in illis partibus sunt desideria. Fideliter, ut audio, translata sunt, et vir ipse qui vertit ita mihi probatur, ut de illius fide et innocentia vel jurare non dubitem. Judicio certe acutulo et erudito est præditus. Petimus solum ut istius majestas patiatur istic in officinis librariorum prostare, si quæ forte istuc exemplaria deportentur. Majora ausi estis et audetis facere; et istud etiam pietatis est officium, dare hospitium Spiritui sancto.

De rebus Gallicis hic nos nihil audimus, usque adeo omnia sunt occupata itinera. De vobis tamen magna exspectatio, et item de conventu Neuburgensi nostrorum principum. Cæsaris legati commissarii jam multas hebdomadas in hac urbe nostra frustra exspectant legatos electoris Saxonici, et electoris Brandeburgii, ignari quid sibi velit hæc mora. Vale, vir clarissime. Argentorati, octava Septembris, 1569.

Tuæ dignitatis observantissimus,

JOH. STURMIUS.

EPISTOLA LXXI.

JOHANNES PARKHURSTUS AD JOHANNEM WOLFIUM.

SALVUS sis in Christo, humanissime Wolfi. 1 Julii literas tuas una
cum doctissimis tuis Commentariis in Nehemiam accepi : pro quibus ingentes ago gratias, relaturus cum primum alterum Abelum nactus fuero.
Omnes tuum Nehemiam plurimi faciunt et certatim emunt. Bene feceris,
si Estheram item tuis lucubrationibus illustraveris. Memini me in tuo
musæo semel vidisse homilias tuas in Deut. Jos. et lib. Judicum, quæ
mihi adeo placebant, ut curaverim aliquot mihi exscribendas. Quæso,
mi Wolfi, ne sinas eas diutius cum blattis et tineis rixari ; sed quamprimum in publicum prodeant ad gloriam Dei, ad utilitatem multorum,
et ad non vulgarem tui ipsius laudem. Quæcunque habui nova, ex literis
D. Bullingeri et Gualteri discere potes. Saluta meo nomine optimam
tuam uxorem et carissimum fratrem tuum Gasparem Wolfium, medi-
cum (ut audio) insignem et novum calendariorum concinnatorem; quem,
cum Gualterum et me ad cœnam humaniter invitaveris, mensæ adsi-
dentem vidi, et adhuc ejus vultum mihi videre videor. Saluta præterea
optimos viros Simlerum, Vonlichium, Hallerum, Lavaterum, Wickium,
Zuinglium, Froschoverum, Julium, et omnes alios, quos in Domino diligo.
Dominus servet Tigurum et Tigurinos omnes. Amen. Vale. Raptim.
Nordovici, 16 Januarii, 1571.

Tuus ex animo,

JO. PARKHURSTUS.

INSCRIPTIO.
Domino Johan. Wolfio.
Tiguri.

EPISTOLA LXXII.

HENRICUS BULLINGERUS AD EDMUNDUM GRINDALLUM
ET ALIOS.

REVERENDISSIMI in Christo patres, domini honorandi et fratres carissimi. Multum me pietati vestræ debere fateor, qui cum tanto invicem
intervallo simus disjuncti, (vos quidem trans mare habitetis in Anglia, ego

vero non procul ab Alpibus vivam in Helvetia,) nihilominus pietas vestra
frequentibus literis amicitiam fraternitatemque nostram olim contractam
tam studiose colat, conservet, atque magis et magis in diem augendo
provehat. Unde merito me gratum pietati vestræ obsequiosumque modis
omnibus exhibere debeo. Cumque submissa superioribus diebus bulla Pii
V. episcopi Romani, quam antea non videram, neque de ea quicquam audieram, occasionem mihi suppeditastis agendi aut conandi saltem aliquid
pro gloria Christi Redemptoris nostri unici, et pro salute ejus, quæ apud
vos est in Anglia, ecclesiæ contra antichristum Romanum; en! pietati
vestræ refutationem hanc meam bullæ oppositam dedico, et exactissimis
vestris judiciis subjicio, ut pro pietatis vestræ beneplacito stetque cadatque
tota. Oro autem ut hunc meum conatum, animumque causæ bonæ vestræ-
que pietati devotissimum, benigne accipiatis. Alioqui fateor libere facultates
meas admodum esse exiguas, vestram vero eruditionem amplissimam, ut me
hanc causam longe felicius potuissetis, si quidem ita libuisset, pertractare.
At cum intellexerim hoc meo labore qualicunque me pietati vestræ gratifi-
caturum, nolui illa in me desideraret quicquam. Faxit Christus Dominus,
ut uberrimo cum fructu multorum disseram. Salutare quæso dignemini
reverendos meos dominos et fratres carissimos, D. Robertum Hornum,
Wintoniensem episcopum; D. Edwinum Sandum, Londoniensem episcopum; D. Johannem Parkhurstum, Nordovicensem episcopum; D. Jacobum
Pilckintonum, Dunelmensem episcopum; D. item Joan. Almerum, Sam-
sonem, Humfredum, Leverum, Foxum, et reliquos exilii quondam vestri
in Helvetia et per Germaniam socios, quorum omnium precibus me commendo. Sed et omnes ministri et fratres, qui hic sunt, vobis omnibus
omnia felicia in Christo Jesu Domino nostro precantur. Dominus Jesus
benedicat ministerio pietatis vestræ, et servet ab omni malo. Tiguri, mense
Febr. anno salutis nostræ 1571.

INSCRIPTIO.

Ad reverendissimos piisimosque et vigilantis-
simos inclyti regni Angliæ episcopos, D.
Edmundum Gryndallum, archiepiscopum
Eboracensem, D. Richardum Coxum, episco-
pum Eliensem, et D. Joannem Juellum, epi-
scopum Sarisberiensem, dominos meos hono-
randos et fratres in Christo carissimos.

EPISTOLA LXXIII.

RICARDUS HILLES AD HENRICUM BULLINGERUM.

SALUTEM plurimam in Domino. Sicuti filius meus Barnabas Hilles per literas suas ad fratrem in Christo dilectum, Julium Sancterentianum, 26 die Novembris proxime elapsi datas, illum certiorem fecit, domine et amice colendissime; egomet tuas literas, 27 Augusti proxime elapsi scriptas, hic Londini accepi per eruditum et pium juvenem Henricum Butlerum: quem post unam atque alteram hebdomadam, postquam prædictas literas acceperim, ad Dunstanum quendam Feltonum, domini Johannis Butleri defuncti filium, una cum fidelibus comitibus equitare curavi, ad vicum quendam Anglicum Chilton nuncupatum, in comitatu Suffolciæ. Unde a prædicto Henrico literas accepi scriptas ex ædibus amitæ suæ, viduæ, matronæ valde piæ. Ego etiam ex animo quam diligentissime curabo omnia illa negotia quæ tu per tuas prædictas literas exequi cupiebas. Literas autem quasdam, quas filio meo Barnabæ prædicto Francfordiæ tradidit D. Christophorus Froschoverus, per fidelem nuncium ad prædictum Henricum Butlerum 26 die Novembris transmisi. Accepit etiam filius meus Barnabas Hilles, a prædicto D. Froschovero, una cum prædictis literis quatuor libros Germanicos, quos, quibus inscripti erant, fideliter reddi curavit: habemusque tibi, ego et uxor mea, ingentes gratias, quod illorum librorum duos nobis dono miseras.

Doleo equidem, quod non adhuc, cum prædictas tuas literas scripseras ad me, a morbo tuo plene convaluisti. Spero tamen quod ante hunc diem multo melius te habeas, quod faxit Deus. Nullas nuper accepi literas ab episcopis nostratibus sive dominis hic in Anglia commorantibus, ad te transferendas. Si tamen posthac in illum finem literas ullas accepero, summa diligentia ad te transmitti curabo. Dominus Edmundus Grindallus, qui nunc (ut audivisti) archiepiscopus est Eboracensis, circa Eboracum sive in civitate ipsa Eboraco, ut audio, continuo manet. Brevi autem arbitror huc Londinum veniet, sicuti ceteri fere episcopi omnes venient; quia nunc, mandante regia majestate, indictum est celebre concilium totius Angliæ, quod apud nos parliamentum vulgo dicitur: apud vos autem comitia imperialia Latine, si bene memini, dicuntur, et Germanice Reichstag. Dominus Edvinus Sandus, episcopus qui nuper fuit Wigorniensis, jam noster est episcopus Londinensis; mihi vero non admodum notus, præterquam ex facie: veluti fere ceteri omnes episcopi sunt mihi fere ignoti, præterquam doctissimus et humanissimus, imo potius divinus episcopus, dominus Juellus Sarisburiensis. Vereor namque (quanquam nunquam sum expertus ipsemet) ne eorum aliqui (ut scripsit eruditissimus Hieronymus de episcopis aliquibus sui temporis), velut in aliqua sublimi specula constituti, vix dignentur mortales videre et alloqui conservos suos. Dominus Coccius episcopus Eliensis, amicus tuus, qui ante annum duxit viduam juvenem domini Doctoris Turneri medici, vivit adhuc et per gratiam Dei bene valet. Sed prædecessor ejus dominus Thirlbeius[1], qui regnante hic Maria regina episcopus fuit Eliensis, et apud reverendissimum Matthæum Parkerum, archiepiscopum Cantuarensem, (sed in ædibus ejus detentus), propter papisticæ doctrinæ protestationem vitam agebat, nuper ante sex aut septem menses obiit Lambethi in palatio dicti archiepiscopi Cantuarensis. Nonnulli vero ceterorum episcoporum sive prælatorum, qui libertate restricti erant propter obstinatiam[2] suam, vivunt adhuc: sed nullum fere perpessi sunt cruciatum, præterquam fortassis animi aliquam mœstitiam propter desideratam libertatem et refrænatam licentiam maledicendi et malefaciendi. De hiis omnibus Nicolaus Hethus, qui sub Maria regina archiepiscopus fuit Eboracensis, minus sævus vir fuit, atque ideo forsitan majorem invenit gratiam apud serenissimam nostram reginam Elizabetham: nullam enim aliam habet carcerem, præterquam in rure suas proprias ædes, satis commodas et salubri in loco sitas.

Hic apud nos per Dei gratiam in ecclesia et republica omnia sunt pacata. Dominus hoc nobis diu concedat. Audio etiam regem Galliæ pacem illam, quam mihi scripsisti fuisse confectam, prudenter colere; gaudeoque multum ac Deo habeo gratias maximas, quod in conclusione illius pacis saluti fidelium satis cautum erat, utpote scripsisti et jam videmus. Doleo tamen admodum sectam illam Arianorum pestiferam multis in locis extra Helvetiam repullulare. Verumtamen quum venerit Dominus Jesus ad judicium, num inveniet fidem in terra? Julium Sancterentianum prædictum meo et uxoris meæ nomine salutare digneris precor. Adhuc inter serenissimam nostram reginam et ducem de Alva non adeo bene conventum est de relaxatione personarum et bonorum sive mercium utriusque arrestatorum vel detentorum per biennium. Attamen quamvis concordiæ jam non sit res, est autem spes aliqua. Sed de futuro brevi commercio, quale per nonnullos, imo complures, annos continuatum est inter reges Angliæ et archiduces Austriæ et Burgundiæ, nec superest, quantum ego video aut conjicere possum, ulla res aut etiam spes. Tertio hujus mensis die obiit etiam alius quidam papista, vel (ut ipse sibi videbatur) catholicus magnus, cognomine Boxallus, qui prædictæ reginæ Mariæ secretarius fuit præcipuus; vir multum continens (ut præ se ferebat) et humanus; qui etiam per aliquot annos in ædibus reverendissimi archiepiscopi Cantuarensis vixit, libertatem eundi quo voluerit desiderans. Dominus Jesus te tuosque conservet in æternum! Londini, 8° die Martii, anno salutis nostræ 1570, secundum supputationem ecclesiæ Anglicanæ.

Tuus ex animo,

RICARDUS HILLES.

[1 *Thurlstonus*, MS.]   [2 Sic MS.]

EPISTOLA LXXIV.

JOHANNES DAIUS AD HENRICUM BULLINGERUM.

SALUTEM tibi, reverende in Christo pater, exopto. Postquam finem libri tui imprimendi fecerim, quod secundum exemplar mihi a reverendo in Christo patre doctore Coxo traditum, et ab eo prius summa diligentia emendatum, et vere et fideliter confectum esse confido; idem, fidelissime pastor, voluit ut sex vel plures ex iisdem libris tibi mittendos (si commode fieri posset) curarem: quod ut facerem opportunum inveni tempus. Præterea propter operam tuam in illo libro conficiendo positam (maximum voluntatis tuæ in Angliam, tanto intervallo a te disjunctam, indicium) ipsi reverendi patres suis proximis ad te literis dignissimas acturi sunt gratias. Te interea et universam suam ecclesiam ita Dominus gloriæ suo sanctissimo consoletur Spiritu, ut ejus veritas promoveatur, et antichristi regnum confundatur et prorsus evertatur. Faxitque Christus Dominus ut plures ex omni terrarum orbe in hanc curam, summo reipublicæ christianæ commodo, tota mente incumbant omnemque adhibeant operam. Meum quæso in hoc opere laborem qualemcunque æqui bonique consulas. Vale, vigilantissime pastor. Londini, mense [Augusti, 1571.]

Tui observantissimus,

JOHANNES DAIUS.

INSCRIPTIO.

Reverendo in Christo patri D.
Henrycho Bullingero seniori.
Tiguri.

EPISTOLA LXXV.

H. ZANCHIUS AD JOHANNEM JUELLUM.

EST verum, doctissime Præsul Juelle, me, licet te semper, jam inde ab eo tempore quo eramus Argentinæ, propter tuam singularem tum pietatem tum virtutem observaverim, nunquam tamen ad te scripsisse, et, ut debebam, istam tibi dignitatem, ad quam tua te virtus evexit, gratulatum fuisse. Fateor totum hoc esse verum. Sed si quis inde vellet inferre, me igitur parum erga te fuisse et esse affectum, negarem sequelam, et dicerem ab hoc tali homine paralogismum admitti, qui "non causa ut causa" dicitur. Aliæ enim sunt causæ cur hoc officium a me fuerit,

non dicam, neglectum sed omissum ; quas si vellem recensere et explicare,
longior foret excusatio mea, quam ut ferre posset patientia tua.　Unam
tamen non possum silentio præterire.　Ea est quod post vestrum in
Angliam patriam vestram carissimam reditum ego mirum in modum
fui et *terris jactatus et alto*, cum maxima rerum mearum jactura, partim
ab hostibus veritatis Argentinæ, partim ab inimicis disciplinæ, quibuscum conjungebant copias suas Servetiani Clavennæ, supra fidem vexatus.
In iis autem tam magnis tempestatibus, quis omnium et singulorum
meminisse posset amicorum?　Primis vero gratulandi vel de aliqua re
scribendi occasionibus neglectis, res est omnino supervacanea et intempes-
tiva illis de rebus aliquid porro scribere.　Mihi autem nullum scribendi
ad te argumentum deinceps datum fuit, tua virtute et dignitate dignum,
nisi in præsentia.　Non defuit quidem mihi causa aliqua necessaria, sed
mea privata, quæ ad te quoque ut scriberem me non tam commone-
faciebat, quam quasi compellebat : verum, ut ingenue fatear, non id apud
te ausus fui quod apud quosdam alios, quippe quibus, licet maximis
viris, familiarius tamen, Argentinæ cum essem, usus sum quam te.　Tu
enim discesseras cum Martyre Tigurum, nos manseramus Argentinæ.
Inde factum fuit, ut amicitia et familiaritas inter me et reliquos nobiles
ac doctos viros magis ac magis creverit, non autem inter nos potuerit
tam facile coalescere.　En causam unam cur nullas antehac a me acceperis literas.　Nunc non potui ulla ratione prætermittere, quin ad te
scriberem.　Res enim gravis et te dignissima offertur, quæ me ad scribendum cogit.

　　Cum D. Montius ex Anglia mense Junio rediisset, indicavit mihi
præter alios denuo excitatum esse dissidium in istis ecclesiis, de nescio
quibus vestibus, quibus velit serenissima regina indui episcopos et ministros, cum verbum aut sacramenta administrant : esse autem non paucos
vestri ordinis homines, qui malint et officium resignare, et loco etiam
cedere, quam tales admittere vestes.　Hinc vero maximam ecclesiarum
istarum metuendam esse ruinam.　Se itaque rogare me ut tum ad serenissimam reginam scriberem, eamque sui monerem officii, tum etiam ad
illos episcopos, qui mihi noti sunt, et quibuscum aliqua intercedit familiaritas ; ac te cum primis nominabat : te enim propter virtutem et propter
auctoritatem ex virtute comparatam plurimum posse.　Excusavi quidem
me, et meas extenuavi vires : sed nulla valuit excusatio.　Fui itaque
tandem, post multorum amicorum persuasiones, etiam ab illustrissimo
principe meo id facere officii jussus.　Quare coactus scripsi primum ad
serenissimam reginam literas, ut confido, non malas, quibus hortor et
supplico, ut ne talia audiat consilia, quæ certe cum officio boni principis
pugnant.　Nihil magis est in votis, quam ut serenissima ipsius majestas
non tam meum quam omnium meorum collegarum virorumque piorum,
quam illustrissimi ipsius principis nostri, consilium audiat.　Quod ut

faciat, non tam ipsam quam Deum rogamus. Verum quoniam quid factura sit ignoramus, et fieri poterit ut in sua persistat sententia; interim vero si ipsi etiam episcopi nolint ulla ratione mutare sententiam, periclitabitur ecclesia; idcirco judicarunt fratres scribendum quoque esse ad aliquot præcipuos et prudentiores episcopos, et rogandos ut reliquis sint auctores, ne, si regina amoveri nullo modo possit a sententia, ipsi propterea suas deserere malint stationes quam edicto regio obtemperare : non enim videri cur liceat pastori suum deserere gregem, quoties ei licet libere docere, et sacramenta ex verbo Dei administrare, tametsi aliquid agere cogatur, quod usquequaque non probetur, modo non sit ex tali rerum genere, quæ per se et sua natura malæ sint. Si enim talia mandentur, dicendum esse cum apostolis, Obedire oportet Deo magis quam hominibus : et interim in sua pergendum esse vocatione, suumque sibi curandum esse gregem. Si vero res sua natura adiaphoræ lege mandatoque regio præcipiantur, quando alterutrum necesse sit, ut aut cedatur loco aut tali mandato obtemperetur, obtemperandum potius esse, sed cum legitima protestatione, et docendum esse populum, cur et qua lege tali sit a se obtemperatum mandato, quam exspectandum dum pastor exauctoretur, et gregem alteri cedere cogatur. Esse vero hanc sententiam ita certam et perspicuam, tum in sacris literis, tum apud patres et in historiis ecclesiasticis, ut supervacaneum omnino sit ullam adferre probationem apud illos, qui vel mediocriter in scripturis sint exercitati. Nunquam enim propter res sua natura adiaphoras deserenda est vocatio legitima et necessaria.

Hæc tibi, doctissime Juelle, nota esse non dubitamus. Rogamus itaque te, ut tuam interponas auctoritatem, et pro tua eruditione atque prudentia ita cum aliis reverendissimis et colendissimis fratribus episcopis agas, ut in sua quisque se contineat vocatione atque statione. Nam certe nihil aliud molitur Satan, quam ut quo jure quave injuria veris episcopis a suo grege avulsis, tota ecclesia dissipetur. Est igitur resistendum, ne ille sui fiat impii et sceleratissimi voti compos. Dominus et te et reliquos omnes pios ac sanctos episcopos ecclesiæ suæ servet, suo regat Spiritu, et vestra opera promoveat regnum suum! Vicissim ut pro nobis, atque imprimis pro nostro illustrissimo principe, Dominum rogetis, etiam atque etiam oramus. Ego vero speciatim me tibi, piissime et doctissime præsul, commendo. Commendo item Rudolphum Gualterum, et Rudolphum Zuinglium, Zuinglii illius magni nepotem, utrumque studiosum et pium adolescentem. De statu rerum nostrarum ab ipsis poteris intelligere.

. Heidelbergæ, 2 Sept. 1571.

H. ZANCHIUS,
Suo et collegarum nomine.

EPISTOLA LXXVI.

RODOLPHUS ZUINGLIUS AD EDVINUM SANDUM.

CUM dignissimus nostri collegii præfectus, D. Mag. Shepherd, ad vos iter facere constituisset, non committendum putavi, reverende in Christo pater, quin aliquid ad amplitudinem tuam literarum darem, quibus amplitudini tuæ pro singulari in me meosque benevolentia summaque liberalitate gratias agerem, eidemque tuæ amplitudini statum mearum rerum significarem, idque paucis. Neque enim te gravioribus curis et negotiis occupatum multum tædii atque temporis in legendis hisce meis consumere par est; neque hoc meæ sortis, vel potius tenuitatis, ratio postulat ut pluribus verbis amplitudinem tuam suspensam detineam. Quare ut paucis rem absolvam, tibi, Rev. D. episcope, gratias quas possum habeo maximas pro singulari tua in me benevolentia et favore, imprimisque pro piis tuis curis atque laboribus, quos in promovendis meis studiis adhibuisti, quibusque effecisti, ut non solum in florentissima Cantabrigiensi academia locum haberem, verum etiam in collegium celeberrimum inter studiosos honestos reciperer procurasti; pro quo singulari tuo in me studio gratias tuæ amplitudini quas possum habeo maximas, vicissimque quod mei officii est polliceor me non ingratum aut immemorem tantorum beneficiorum futurum, tantamque tuam in nos liberalitatem semper nostris hominibus et imprimis parentibus nostris prædicaturum; talemque me semper erga amplitudinem tuam exhibiturum, qualem pium juvenem et a piis ortum parentibus decet.

Interim vero de statu rerum mearum hæc amplitudini tuæ nota et cognita esse velim, me in collegio, in quod ab amplitudine tua constitutus sum, locum nactum esse satis idoneum atque commodum ad studia mea persequenda. Prospexit enim mihi D. præfectus pro singulari suo in me amore, non tam de habitatione satis commoda, victuque utcunque sufficiente, quam de tutore fidelissimo, cujus consilio et opera liberrime utor, tam in expediendis meis studiis, quam aliis rebus necessariis procurandis; adeo ut mihi parum ad persequenda mea studia defuturum putem. Gaudeo autem non tam mea quam studiorum meorum causa, mihi occasionem et facultatem oblatam esse audiendi clarissimum illum et doctissimum virum D. Antonium Cevalerium, cui vix Germania nostra in Hebraicæ linguæ cognitione parem habet, qui cum eo comparandus sit, excepto Immanuele Tremellio, quem Heidelbergæ Palatinatûs doctissime profitentem audivi, ex cujus quoque lectionibus non parum, ut opinor, profeci; neque minus ex hujus lectionibus profecturum puto, Domino mihi suam gratiam dante. Tuæ autem amplitudini, quicquid ex his atque aliorum lectionibus utilitatis capio, acceptum fero, utpote cujus singulari liberalitate effectum prospectumque est, ut mihi non solum in celeberrima Cantabrigiensi academia vivendi locus relictus, verum etiam commoditas facultasque oblata sit optimos quosque audiendi professores, quorum opera adjutus me non exiguos in studiis progressus facturum spero. Interim vero, ne prolixius quam par est progrediar, amplitudini tuæ me commendo, eamque rogatam volo ut me suæ tutelæ et patrocinio commendatum habeat semper, atque hæc pauca boni consulat, tanquam tenuem meæ erga amplitudinem tuam observantiæ significationem. Deus Opt. Max. amplitudinem tuam quam diutissime salvam et incolumem servet, et ecclesiæ suæ superstitem esse dignetur!

Cantabrigiæ, 26 Januarii, 1572.

Tuæ amplitudinis observantissimus,

RODOLPHUS ZUINGLIUS,

Tigurinus.

INSCRIPTIO.

Reverendo in Christo patri et domino
D. Edvino Sando, episcopo Lon-
dinensi dignissimo, D. suo summa
reverentia colendo. Londini.

EPISTOLA LXXVII.

HENRICUS BUTLERUS AD EDVINUM SANDUM.

Cum primum, reverendissime Domine, tuæ humanitatis liberalitate atque benevolentia musis fui restitutus, nihil prius faciendum putavi, quam inquirere, cui ad te literas grati animi indicia continentes darem. Percontanti vero diu obtulit suam in scriptis perferendis operam observandissimus Dominus Shepherd, Johannis collegii præfectus. Quem tam opportune nactum nequaquam absque memoris tuorum in me beneficiorum voluntatis significatione dimittendum censui. Ac licet pro tuis amplissimis in me officiis, nullis non laudibus dignissimis, gratias agendi rationem instituere in animo habuerim ; tamen ob eorum magnitudinem omnem non solum orationis vim, sed gratias etiam universas, excellunt atque vincunt. Nam si reliquis et familiarium[1] et consanguineorum tua conferantur bene-

[1 *Familiariis*, MS.]

merita, tanquam lucifer suo splendore, omnia illorum antecellent eaque obscurabunt : cum praesertim corpori tantum, idque maximis adducti precibus, alimenta isti praebuerint ; a te vero non corpus solummodo, servitute oppressum, pristinae libertati sit restitutum, sed et animae maerore prope emortuae medicina sit allata ultro saluberrima. Quo enim pharmaco afflictus perturbatione animus citius salute donari potest, quam praestanti et morum integritate et pietatis studio viro, D. magistro Allin, tutoris vice tam uti humaniter? Quapropter, domine ac patrone omni observantia dignissime, cum hisce tuis cumulatissimis in me officiis dignas nequaquam agere gratias, multo minus referre queam; ut animi gratitudine[2], quam inviolatam semper et integram reservare constitui, contentum te reddere digneris etiam atque etiam peto ; promittens insuper eam me, quam mihi tuo adjumento ac divina etiam providentia obtigisse video, Spartam non modo nunquam deserturum, sed nullis non diligentiae[3] et virtutis floribus exornaturum. Hisce tuam committo humanitatem bonitati divinae, optans ex animo Nestoream tibi tuisque omnibus aetatem.

Datae in collegio Christi 27 Januarii.

HENRICUS BUTLERUS,

Tigurinus, Anglogena,

tuae dignitatis observantissimus.

INSCRIPTIO.

Clarissimo praestantissimoque viro D.
episcopo Londinensi, domino ac
patrono suo omni honore et obser-
vantia reverendissimo. London.

EPISTOLA LXXVIII.

RICARDUS COXUS AD HENRICUM BULLINGERUM.

LITERAE tuae 20 Aug. 1571 scriptae mihi fuerunt traditae mense Januario proxime elapso per tres illos adolescentes, quorum in ipsis literis mentionem feceras, dilectissime in Christo frater. Equidem superiori aestate mittebantur ad te literae nostrae cum aliquot libris tuo nomine impressis contra bullatas illas papae nugas. Imo liber tuus, absolutissime et verissime dictatus, atque emendatissime scriptus, non potuit nobis et piis omnibus non esse gratissimus. Ob quod munus merito fatemur, nos

[2 MS. *gratitudinem.*]   [3 MS. *diligentia.*]

tibi plurimum devinciri: imo ipsa regina librum tuum legit, non sine
gratulatione.   Spero te longe antehac et literas et libros et exigua munuscula a nobis accepisse[1]: unde abunde intelliges, quid egerimus in libro
tuo edendo.   Jam ad literas, quas misisti.   Quod ad adolescentes vestros
attinet, bono sis animo; nam quibus commendati sunt, amico animo et
pietatis affectu illis sedulo prospicient.   Et hoc quidem merentur et D.
Zuinglii, et D. Bullingeri, et Rodolphi Gualteri zelus, studium, et infiniti
labores in propaganda religione sincera et subdolis falsæ religionis machinis
evertendis.   Tui vero filii, quoniam eum inprimis Eboracensi, Sarisburgensi
et mihi commisisti, curam suscipiemus, ut tu omnino sis sine cura: quanquam Sarisburgensis (quod sine gemitu narrare nequeo, erat enim ecclesiæ
Anglicæ thesaurus) diœcesin suam visitando animam exhalavit, et ad cœlum
hinc emigravit, suo quidem commodo, at nostro incommodo maximo et in-
tolerabili.   Neque vero interim vel Gualteri filium vel Butlerum, quem mihi
etiam atque etiam commendas, negligemus.   Ut autem voto tuo satisfiat,
duo vestri in academia Cantabrigiensi, sed in diversis collegiis sedes habent,
et cœtu numeroso versantur et docto.

   Res nostræ ingenti Dei beneficio, ne dicam miraculo, satis commodo
loco sunt.   Nuper apud nos dux Norfolcensis clam cum papistis atque
adeo cum papa ipso conspiravit in perniciem serenissimæ nostræ reginæ
atque regni, imo in subversionem sacrosancti Dei evangelii.   Sed suis semper adest benignus Dominus.   Diu non sine suspicione mali inclusus fuit
in carcere.   Tandem prodita est ipsius perdita nequitia.   Productus est in
judicium et, jure condemnatus, morti adjudicatur.   Erupit tandem papistarum conspirantium fœtida sentina.   Benedictus Dominus Deus, qui
tempestive tanta scelera produxit in lucem!   Jam (uti speramus) pacata
sunt omnia, nisi quod non cessat Satan circumire et rugire, quærens quem
devoret.   Hic mutuis nos juvemus precibus.

   D. Gualterus superiori (opinor) anno literas dedit ad fratrem nostrum
Parkhurstum, Nordovicensem episcopum: quæ quia nonnihil turbarum
excitarent in hominibus suæ sententiæ, qui innovationes semper moliuntur,
neque ordinationibus in ecclesia nostra constitutis subdi volunt, putavi
monendum esse fratrem nostrum D. Gualterum, ut cautior sit, ne suis
scriptis contentiones vel ignarus vel invitus fovere videatur.   Si acerbior
adpareat oratio mea, cogitet a quo animo sit profecta, certe a benevolo
ejusque amantissimo.   Dominus Jesus ecclesiæ suæ te diutissime servet
incolumem!   Ex Insula Eliensi in Anglia, duodecimo Februarii, 1571.

   Pene præterieram libellum, quem ad me misisti de auctoritate scripturæ
et ecclesiæ.   Vere aureus est libellus, et dignus qui piorum omnium manibus teratur.   Papistæ tamen obgannire non cessant.   Multa (inquiunt)
sunt dogmata, quæ patrum ecclesiæque consensu nituntur, non autem
scripturæ, cujusmodi sunt ista.

[1 Manu Bullingeri: "Nihil allatum est, nihil accepi, nec quicquam hujus vidi."]

Multa creditu necessaria, quæ non sunt in scripturis :

Perpetua virginitas Mariæ.

Pater est ingenitus.

Filius est consubstantialis.

Spiritus a Patre Filioque procedit.

Infantes sunt baptizandi.

Baptizatus ab hæreticis in forma ecclesiæ est vere baptizatus.

Deus est tres personæ.

Apostoli fuerunt baptizati.

Utimur suffocato et sanguine.

Christus descendit ad inferna.

Aqua miscenda est vino in calice.

Martyrium supplet locum baptismi.

Orationes, oblationes et eleemosynæ prosunt defunctis.

Nemo admittitur ad eucharistiam priusquam baptizetur.

Tuus in Christo frater,

RICARDUS COX,

Eliensis Episcopus.

INSCRIPTIO.

*Viro eximia doctrina et pietate prædito,
et fratri meo carissimo D. Henrico
Bullingero, ecclesiæ Tigurinæ pastori dignissimo.*

EPISTOLA LXXIX.

RICARDUS HILLES AD HENRICUM BULLINGERUM.

S. P. LITERAS tuas, amice colendissime, 23 die Augusti proxime elapsi ad me datas, ante menses duos accepi per nepotem tuum Rodolphum Zuinglium, qui jam ut audio [Cantabrigiæ] studet. Rodolphus Gualterus [Cantabrigiæ] sectatur studia : fuerunt ambo hic Londini 15 die Decembris proxime præteriti, non longe postquam Nordovico ab Embdena in Frisia Orientali sita appulerunt in Anglia. Literas vero tuas, de quibus mentionem facis, ad reverendissimos quosdam nostrates episcopos ipsi tradi curaverunt : videlicet, prius domino Johanni Parkhursto suas reddiderunt Nordovico, et Londinensi episcopo suas deinde, postea autem reliquas omnes reddi curarunt iis quibus tu ipse inscripsisti episcopis. Utrum autem Rodolphus tuus episcopum accesserit Eliensem necne, eique tuas literas præsentaverit, equidem ignoro. Porro decimo sexto die Decembris prædicti, Rodolphus tuus et Rodolphus Gualterus valorem undecim florenorum et undecim batzionum Germanicæ monetæ pro floreno ad quindecim batziones computatorum a me hic Londini ad usus necessarios acceperunt mutuo, in proximis nundinis

Frankfordiensibus per amicum tuum D. Christoferum Froschoverum reddendum. Filius etiam meus Gerson Hilles, qui una cum illis a Franc-
forto Embdonam usque venit, valorem triginta florenorum et * batzionum
Germanicæ monetæ illis mutuo dedit. Quam quidem summam in prædictis nundinis quadragesimalibus filio meo Barnabæ Hilles, vel famulo meo
Roberto Mascallo, per eundem dominum Froschoverum reddendum pro-
miserunt; de qua etiam solutione (sicuti quoque de solutione prædictorum
illorum undecim florenorum et undecim batzionum) minime dubito. Attamen certe, quemadmodum in proximis, quas a me in mense Octobri accepisti, literis intelligere poteris (sicuti nuper ex literis domini Rodulphi
Gualteri, Tiguri, 16 ejusdem mensis ad me datis intelligo), tuæ pietati
scripsi, magis fore in rem vestram, tuam dico et D. Gualteri, si prius
pecunias vestras quas cupitis hic in Anglia duobus juvenibus prædictis
solutas esse, Frankforti numerari procurare velitis, ut postea possum hic
illis valorem earundem persolvere.

Libellum illum pulcherrimum de auctoritate scripturæ et ecclesiæ,
quem mihi misisti, accepi, habeoque pro eo humanitati tuæ gratias.
Salutem meo nomine D. Rodolpho Gualtero seniori precare quæso: habeoque illi gratias (dicas), quod mihi de signo quod in sole fuit apud
vos penultima Septembris visum scripsit: potest autem fieri, sicuti ipse
existimabat, ut tandem secuturum sit mundo infelici et pœnitere nescio
vindictæ divinæ exemplum non vulgare. Doleo quidem dominum Rodolphum Gualterum proxima æstate febri acuta et ardenti correptum
fuisse, quæ eum ita afflixit, ut de vita dubitare inciperet. Sed gaudeo
sic illius misertum Deum, ut valetudini et ecclesiæ simul restituit, ita
ut cum sancto propheta Davide post infirmitatem poterit recte dicere,
Vivam et non moriar, narrabo opera Domini. Nec certe dubito quominus ille, quicquid pecuniarum jam nunc in prædictum suum filium
Rodolphum contuli, summam videlicet prædictam florenorum undecim et
totidem batzionum, bona fide mihi ad proxime futuras nundinas Frank-
fordienses reddi curabit. Rogo autem te, domine Bullingere, per Dominum, ne indignius feras quod tuæ caritati et D. Gualtero ita conjunctim
literas meas ad vos nunc scribo; ac non divisim ad vestrum alterutrum.
Est enim mihi nunc dierum (cujus certe mei multum pudet) permolestum
Latine literas dare, ut quas valde lente scribo; ita ut tot literas jam hodie
vix duabus horis possum scribere, quot olim in juventute mea semihora
expedire potui. Benedictus autem Dominus Deus meus in omnibus et in
omni tempore—omni tempore et semper, sive in prosperis, sive in adversis!
Amen.

Æquum quidem foret, si aliquid saltem paternarum opum cederet justis
hæredibus Johannis Butleri. Sed quum ipsemet vendidit hic omne suum
patrimonium, et juxta legem atque commune jus regni Angliæ idem emp-
tori nostrati et hæredibus suis concessit et affirmavit, sive (ut nostri juris-

consulti seu legisperiti barbare loqui solent) assuravit et seisinam, id est legitimam possessionem, dedit, nulla restat spes, quod dicti domini Butleri hæredes (maxime autem qui ex muliere non Angla extra regnum Angliæ nati sunt) patrimonium illud venditum, aut ejusdem aliquam partem, jure Anglico recuperare (ut nostri jurisconsulti loquuntur) vel repossidere poterint, quantum ego saltem intelligere vel discere possim. Patientiam ergo oportet Henricum Butlerum habere, et in ista causa spem contra spem non habere.

Posteaquam tibi proxime scripsi in mense Augusto, nullas accepi literas ad te, neque ad D. Rodolphum Gualterum, a reverendis dominis episcopis, neque ab ullis aliis (quod memini) viris doctis. Si autem nunc ad te volunt scribere per meum prædictum famulum Robertum, qui hoc mense Februario hinc Hamburgum versus, Deo volente, navigio profecturus sit, spero meum filium Barnabam literas illas Hamburgo Frankfurtum optime posse perferre pro te ad D. Froschoverum prædictum.

Puto te audivisse ducem Norfolciæ nostratem nuper de crimine læsæ majestatis accusatum fuisse; 16 autem die Januarii publice a proceribus regni Angliæ, juxta consuetudinem ejusdem regni in cognoscendis hujusmodi criminibus, morti adjudicatus est. Inter cetera crimina, quæ (ut audio) perpetratus est, hoc erat unum de pluribus : quod uni duorum comitum, qui ante biennium in boreali Angliæ parte rebellis fuit, et contra reginam nostram serenissimam arma gessit, magnam pecuniarum summam misit. Brevi, ut fertur, decollabitur hic Londini, prout meritus est. Det illi Deus gratiam, ut eum pœniteat ex animo suæ ingratitudinis et iniquitatis multæ, quam contra Deum Opt. Max. atque contra regiam majestatem commisit ! Nuper hic duo viri morte plectebantur propter sua impia facinora, qui inter alia etiam in necem D. Wilhelmi Cecilii, baronis de Burghley, præcipui secretarii regiæ majestatis, conspirarunt : prout unus illorum ad furcas confessus est. Deus per providentiam suam rem omnem in lucem protulit, antequam facinus illud nefandum opere fuit impletum. Vale, Deusque Optimus Maximus te ad gloriam suam promovendam atque ad ecclesiæ suæ ædificationem quam diutissime conservet ! Londini, 18 Februarii, anno 1571.

Tuus quem nosti,

HILLES, *Mercator.*

INSCRIPTIO.

Doctissimo viro D. Henrico Bullin-
  gero amico suo colendissimo red-
  dentur hæ. Tiguri.

EPISTOLA LXXX.

JOHANNES PARKHURSTUS AD JOHANNEM WOLFIUM.

SALVE, mi Wolfi. Gaudeo te in explicando Esdra pergere. Si tuas conciones et commentarios in Hesteræ librum edideris, rem facies tuis studiis dignam et piis studiosisque utilem. Quod serenissimæ nostræ reginæ dedicare velis, ego valde probo. Nolo te in epistola nuncupatoria nimis esse prolixum. Non possum non improbare tam pertinax Horni et Juelli silentium. Nam vel illi ingrati fuerunt, si ad te non rescripserint; vel tabellarii perfidi, si literas tibi tradendas non curarint. De filio tuo alias. Nunc non vacat plura scribere, ita variis occupationibus distineor. Saluta meo nomine uxorem tuam, fratrem Casparem et amicos omnes. Raptim Ludhamiæ. Mea vos omnes. Martii 10, 1572.

Tuus,

JOHANNES PARKHURSTUS,

Nordovicensis.

INSCRIPTIO.

D. Johanni Wolfio.
Tiguri.

EPISTOLA LXXXI.

MALLIETUS AD HENRICUM BULLINGERUM JUNIOREM.

CUM ante quatriduum D. Rudolphus affinis tuus, D. Gualteri filius, literas mihi Cantabrigia a D. Petro Chevalerio Genevensi cognato meo, illic Hebraicæ linguæ professore, attulisset una cum D. Zuinglii filio, qui jam per aliquot dies ægrotus Londini in hospitio decubuit; ex eoque tabellarium, qui ad te has commode perferre posset, sciscitatus essem, meque meas ad te dari posse certiorem fecisset; nolui datam occasionem prætermittere, ne ei ingratus viderer a quo tot et tanta accepi beneficia: cum præsertim ex quo e Germania in Gallias, inde in Angliam migrassem, nulla scribendi ad te sese obtulisset occasio. Mihi enim tam carus cum sis, vestraque patria tam dulcis, non possum quin dies et noctes recordatione tui sæpissime transigam, et maximo ardeam desiderio (si mihi in patriam redeundum sit, aut iter in Italiam suscipiendum) invisendi vos iterum, dummodo meis votis Deus favere velit. Dominus Carolus Liffortius Biturigibus doctor juris creatus est ante tres menses : ejus enim rei gratia Lutetiam venerat, ubi una per menses septem viximus ; inde se Aureliæ et Biturigibus contulerat, ego vero ab ejus a me discessu in Angliam : ubi comitis de Lennox fratrem, interfecti Scotorum regis et hujus patrui, curam docendi et administrandi ei suscepi, non sane sine magno meo labore et studiorum meorum impedimento. Verum magnatum hujus regni et precibus et pollicitationibus adductus, id onus ad aliquod tempus detrectare non potui, cum mihi hinc discedendi quotiescunque libuerit libertas relicta sit. Agit juvenis ille decimum sextum jamprimum annum, qui magnam de se spem in posterum pollicetur. Solus enim jure hæreditario coronæ Scotorum post mortem hujus regis nepotis sui sine liberis legitimis succedit, et regno et imperio præfici debet. Sic matre ejus sanguini regio Anglico post mortem hujus reginæ nullus propinquior, cui pariter filius, quem unigenitum habet, fit hæres ; quamvis conventus fiat omnium statuum, quod lingua vulgari parlamentum dicitur, ut certus hæres regni communi omnium suffragio designetur, ne posthac, si forte fortuna regina obiret, ullus tumultus oriatur. Quid sit futurum nescio. Aliquid certi potero rescribere post peractum parlamentum, si Deus faveat. Audio tamen inter cetera de capite reginæ Scotorum agi. Dux Norfolk condemnatus adhuc in turri jacet. Legati reginæ in Galliam triduo abhinc sunt profecturi, ad pacem inter utrumque regnum stabiliendam. Rex Galliæ ob eam rem ducem de Momorancio huc missurus est, qui hic etiam magno cum apparatu exspectatur. Quæ scribam plura in præsentia non habeo : tantum te oratum velim, ut pro benignitate et clementia tua ad me de tua tuorumque bona valetudine scribere non dedigneris, quæque istic fiant certiorem facere. Audio enim Genevenses in numerum confæderatorum Helvetiorum ascribi, quos vulgo Cantonos vocant ; an verum sit, adhuc ignoro. Ad dominum Urbanum Lowenberger rescripsissem, itemque ad D. Schneberger, si ubi degant rescirem ; eosque me ut excusatum habeant, orabis, meoque nomine plurimum salutabis. Vale. Datum 26 Maii, 1572. Londini ex hospitio Graiorum, vulgo *Grais inne.*

Dominam meam uxorem tuam salutabis pariter plurimum meo nomine totamque familiam. Parentem, quem honoris causa nomino, nolim oblivisci, quem animi integritate, morum probitate, doctrina atque eruditione nulli postponendum scio. Sic salutem meam imperties D. Gualtero, D. Simlero, D. Lavatero, dominæ Veritati atque Dorotheæ sororibus carissimis, uxori

D. Simleri, ceterisque omnibus quos mihi bene cupere scis. Vale etiam atque etiam.

Tuus in æternum,

MALLIETUS.

INSCRIPTIO.

Domino Henrico Bullingero, domino
  suo colendissimo.
Domino Bullingero juniori, prope
  ædem Petri. Tiguri.

EPISTOLA LXXXII.

RODOLPHUS GUALTERUS AD PATREM SUUM RODOLPHUM GUALTERUM.

S. Si quid in præsentibus omissum fuerit, observande pater, non mihi sed animo mœsto et perturbato attribuas velim. Accidit enim nobis casus tristis admodum, quem etsi mihi grave sit tibi indicare, tamen necesse est ut id faciam, cum præcipue vestrum intersit rem cognoscere. Facile autem te cum D. Bullingero propter summam constantiam animi hunc casum laturum puto, quo Rodolphus Zuinglius consobrinus meus suavissimus a Deo optimo maximo ex mortali vita et hujus seculi miseriis ad cœlestem vitam evocatus est. Quod quia prolixius significandum est quam ego possim tam brevi tempore ad te perscribere, cum et filius Hillæi Hamburgum properet, et funeris Zuinglii curandi onus in nos jam impendeat, paucula tantum de ipso scribam, ad nundinas proximas omnia ordine ad D. Bullingerum perscripturus. Cantabrigiæ cum essemus ad 12 Maii diem, Londinum cupiebat proficisci Henricus Butlerus ob negotia quædam: ei sese adjungere voluit Zuinglius noster, si forte posset Londini pecunias ab episcopis aut aliunde ab Hillæo accipere, quia præcipue tum pecunia laborabat. Habebam ego in animo Cantabrigiæ manere, partim quod non magna haberem negotia, partim quod si quæ essent mihi agenda, per literas possem expedire. Tandem me quoque in sententiam suam pertraxerunt, ut facile iter mihi nec incommodum nec admodum commodum ingrederer. Causa quoque præcipua erat, ut comitia generalia reginæ serenissimæ principum et episcoporum viseremus. Profecti itaque fuimus 12 Maii, vehementissimo flante vento, ut non eundum sed obnitendum esset contra ventum, ut toto illo die vix 12 milliaria Anglica, quæ 2 nostratia conficiunt, perficeremus. Erat tum (more isto Anglico) dies jejunii, ut nihil in hospitiis præter salsos pisces et alia

similis farinæ possemus nancisci. Crastino die, qui fuit 13, confecimus 32
Anglica milliaria, et Londinum pervenimus, quod 44 milliaribus tantum
Cantabrigia distat. Erat vehementissimus æstus. In itinere nunquam conquestus fuit, nisi cum abessemus 8 circiter milliaribus Londino; et tamen
strenue pergebat, ut circiter horam 8 in hospitium optatum pervenerimus.
Eo die nihil fere comedit, ut nec tribus sequentibus. Cum itaque 17 Maii
apud Eliensem episcopum pranderemus, post prandium statim decubuit,
et per 8 dies fere ægrotavit, de calore interno conquestus, qui tamen
nec in urina nec in pulsibus poterat deprehendi. Aderant medici D.
Turnerus et D. Pennius, Anglorum judicio totius fere Angliæ peritissimus; qui nihil potuerunt deprehendere, ex quo qualisnam esset morbus
possent judicare. Suspicati sunt aliquantulum melancholicos humores in
venas diaphragmatis influxisse, qui sitim excitent et calorem augeant.
Tandem accessit morbus et dolor lateris sinistri, quem emplastris, etc.
sustulerunt. Itaque intra 9 vel 10 diem convalescebat. Sed statim
sequenti die ad pristinum dolorem relapsus est, videlicet calorem in-
extinguibilem, qui nec tribus venæ sectionibus nec ullis potationibus
refrigerantibus potuit restingui. Accedebant strepitus supra cubiculum
nullius plane animalis: videbantur potius trunci seu homines ingentes
procumbere; quæ statim mihi de aliis similibus cogitanti spem omnem
exemerunt. Tandem cum nulla spes esset melioris valetudinis, cupiebat
ex diversorio publico eum transferre in ædes proprias D. Eliensis cum
uxore sua matre Turneri. Eo quia non poterat proficisci nec pedes nec
eques, nec ulla ratione uti cogitabamus propter imbecillitatem, retinuimus
in diversorio ad 4 usque Junii, quo die, suadente Turnero et Pennio,
et summopere flagitante episcopo Eliense, in ædes ipsius lectica portatus
est. Sed mihi jam pridem imaginem mortis in vultu videbar conspicere:
itaque, faustissima precatus a Deo optimo maximo, in ædibus episcopi
eum ad summum, si posset, dormire cohortati sumus, non dissimulantes
interim (quod mihi quoque velim fieri) periculum, et medicos fere de-
sperasse, cohortati ut in Deo fiduciam collocaret. Butlerus, quia præ-
cedentibus quoque noctibus mecum vigilaverat, cœpit prima vigilia, quæ
mihi indicta erat, dormire: cum vero viderem eum angustos spiritus
ducere, veritus ne imparatus suffocaretur, advocavi ministrum episcopi,
qui ipsum cohortatus et cum illo precatus jussit bene in Deum sperare.
Media circiter nocte, cum solus adessem ipsi, cœpit bis adeo longum
ducere anhelitum et oculos invertere, ut animam videretur agere: itaque
alte in aures inclamans ut animam Deo committeret, repetii verba,
singultu crebros impediente sonos. Aspersi aquam rosaceam et acetum
rosaceum ori et labiis, ut ad sese rediret, quod factum est; et libro precum accepto, cum ipso alta voce cœpi Deum invocare, et rursus appellato
ministro cum Butlero singulis momentis ultimum exspectabamus spiritum.
Interea tam cordate, tam ardenter Deum invocabat, ut nobis esset ad-

mirationi. Quinquies videbatur animam agere, quinquies refocillavimus
jam expirantem. Hora circiter tertia matutina nos non amplius nosse in-
inceperat, et aliquantillum delirare : tandem a quarta ad quintam, arden-
tissimis precibus ad Deum fusis, cœpit tranquillius agere, et ante 6 circiter
dimidiam horam neque audivit nos, neque vidit, neque sensit : in solo
spiritu videbamus adhuc vivere ipsum, qui tamen angustius cœpit meare,
et ad sextam horam omnino deficere ; et tandem signo summæ constantiæ
ad cœlum erectis palmis dato, nobis ipsi acclamantibus verbis Christi,
" DEUS, suscipe animam meam," et precationem Dominicam in aurem occi-
nentibus, expiravit, et vitam hanc mortalem cum immortali et inenarrabili
gaudio cœlestis vitæ commutavit.

De aliis accidentibus scribam proximis nundinis ad Bullingerum, quomodo ubiquitarios insectatus fuerit, etc. quia jam non vacat, partim
quod infirmior sum, cum quatuor vel quinque noctibus continuis vix
somnum ceperim, partim etiam quod intra duas horas curatio funeris
instet. Sepelietur in templo D. Andreæ Londini e regione ædium episcopi Eliensis in vico dicto *Howbrun.* Sunt omnia satis sumptuosa.
Accepi dum ipse ægrotaret ab episcopo Dunelmensi (qui ad parlamentum
morbo impeditus non venit) 12 angelottos inter nos ambos ex æquo
dividendos : dederat ipsi angelottum unum et mihi quoque episcopus
Vintoniensis, Parkhurstus unum, quæ omnia proximis nundinis supputabo.
Debentur pharmacopolis angelotti quinque, non multo minus, si modo sufficiant, propter clysteres, decocta, medicamenta, epithemata, et alia ejus
generis innumera insumpta. Supellectilem omnem, quamprimum Cantabrigiam reversus fuero, ad me recipiam, et catalogum ad vos transmittam :
commodum enim arbitror ut cum meis rebus ex Anglia iterum vehantur,
si mihi Deus ad vos concesserit reditum, quod spero : sed fiat voluntas
ejus. In sepultura si non sufficiant ejus pecuniæ, addam de meis, et
omnia significabo proxime : simul ad tuas respondebo literas, quas hic
accepi cum quatuor libellis quos transmisi et tradidi. Juellus mortuus est,
ut jam scis proculdubio. Plura si scriberem, et funus et literas has
negligerem : itaque his eris contentus, et D. Bullingerum de omnibus facies
certiorem. Vale, mi pater, et me invitum fere hic versantem amore paterno
prosequere, ut aliquid habeam consolationis : vale rursus. Datæ Londini
5 Junii, quo die Zuinglius obiit, 1572. Revertemur intra triduum
Cantabrigiam.

Tui observantissimus filius,

RODOLPHUS GUALTERUS.

INSCRIPTIO.

Erudito et pio viro D. Rodolpho Gual-
tero, ecclesiæ Tigurinæ ministro
fidelissimo, patri suo plurimum
observando.

EPISTOLA LXXXIII.

CHRISTOPHORUS MONTIUS AD HENRICUM BULLINGERUM.

LITERÆ tuæ scriptæ 22 Junii ad me allatæ sunt, vir clarissime, opera filii Lavateri, adolescentis bona spe et exspectatione decorati. Jam varia incertis et levibus auctoribus hic vulgantur de belligeris actionibus, et multo feliciora quidem quam ut ea credere ausim. Classem Lusitanam opulentis mercibus oneratam Geusii ceperunt, tribus tantum navibus inter pugnandum elapsis: multæ civitates Belgicæ, fastu, insolentia, libidine fœda, et prædandi et expilandi inexplebili avaritia Hispanorum pressæ, Hispanos intra mœnia recipere pernegant; quare ut rebelles regi ab Albano declaratæ sunt. Una Flessinga, oppidulum parvum, Hispanos aliquot nobiles captos in mari suspendio occidit. Nisi Galliæ rex, Angliæ regina, et Germaniæ principes hanc telam exorsam perficiant, horribilis laniena et concisio miseros manet. Albanus Bruxellis pro more præsidet et mandata edicit, et quatuor peditum legiones recenset in Luccenbergensi et Treverensi agro. Duo loca delectuum ab Auraicis disturbata sunt. Ipse dux induratus magna pervicacia bellum molitur, capitaneis et ductoribus, Bulwilero, Fronsbergio, Schaumbergio, Eberstenio comitibus, et aliis plerisque impia arma molientibus. Otto comes ab Eberstein ante dies octo per Rhenum descendere voluit in inferiorem Germaniam nave armis onerata; verum infra Wormatiam coactus est appellere in littus, ubi ab electoris Palatini sclopetariis interceptus et in Alsheym abductus est. Principum protestantium conventus brevi habebitur Naumburgi in Saxonia. Princeps Auraicus egressus ex arce Dillenburg 23 Junii dicitur in inferiorem Germaniam, comitatus sexcentis equitibus et mille sclopetariis, ad loca delectibus et lustrationibus militum destinata. In Anglia modo omnia quieta sunt, et omnium ordinum regni modo comitia habentur, quorum decreto et censura Norfolciæ dux secundo die Junii decapitatus est: de reliquorum conjuratorum fortuna nihildum accepi.

Has quaternas literas ex Anglia ad me in præsentes nostras nundinas Hamburgo allatas, domino T. et clarissimo tuo genero D. Rodolpho G. inscriptas, vobis una cum obsequiorum meorum addictione transmitto. Argentina, 8 Julii, anno 1572.

CHRISTOPHORUS MONTIUS.

INSCRIPTIO.

Reverendo et doctissimo viro D. Henrico
Bullingero, pastori ecclesiæ Tigurinæ,
patrono colendissimo.

EPISTOLA LXXXIV.

RODOLPHUS GUALTERUS F. AD JOSIAM SIMLERUM.

S. Neque negligentia, neque offensione aliqua, aut oblivione tui, observande affinis, factum est ut rarius ad te scriberem; sed quod ipse mihi displicens et Francofurti et Emdæ in hospitio publico vix ad amicos scribere potuerim. Accedebat, quod literas illas scribebam æquo animo laturus sive perderem sive traderem; ignoto enim tabellario tradebamus. Quod autem ne salutem quidem tibi in literis ascripserim, id imprudentiæ meæ tribuas velim, qui, etsi raro tui et omnium vestrum obliviscar, tum temporis tamen mihi excideras. Quod siquidem non malo animo factum est, mihi condonabis. An enim arbitraris me cuiquam plus placere cupere quam tibi? Quæ opinio etsi firma mihi inhæreret, tamen juvenibus, præsertim minus circumspectis, non ubique præsens est animus ubi oportebat. Sed cesso me excusare apud te, qui jam ignovisti, quod testantur literæ tuæ, alioquin ad me nullæ scribendæ. Vellem autem, ut hoc tempore levius aliquid tibi significarem potius, quam tristissimum hoc mihi peræque atque tibi. Nam 5to Junii superioris mensis mortuus est pie admodum et fideliter R. Zuinglius, consobrinus meus, quem nobis hoc tempore ereptum doleo, quo omnia fere ruunt in pejus. Sepultus fuit honorifice, præsentibus episcopis Eliense et Londinense, quorum hic publice habuit funebrem concionem. Sed nolo de his ad te scribere pluribus; quandoquidem, si quid desideras, id a clari viri D. Bullingeri literis potes petere, ad quem fuse omnia perscripsi. Supervacaneum ergo esset te onerare inutilibus scriptionibus, et me singulis fere momentis dolorem refricare.

Etsi autem ego me in manu Domini esse sciam, nec sine ejus voluntate quisquam mori possit, aliquantulum tamen me terruit, præsertim cum videam et sentiam hanc regionem nostræ valetudini adversari. Testatur mors Zuinglii, testatur Butlerus eodem fere morbo quoque sublatus; testatur denique corpus meum, quod etsi (Deo sit laus!) sit firmæ adhuc valetudinis, tamen minus vegetum, imo singulis fere diebus decrescit, et ego plane macresco. Suasit D. Turnerus, qui Zuinglii medicus fuit, ut in aliam regionem me conferam: sed quia, si quid sinistrius accidat, pater adeo in me invehitur, malo hic finem vitæ reportare, vel ejus venia aliquando discedere. Nihil posthac ab illo petam: si quid studiis meis prodesse potest, viderit ipse; dummodo ego non cessem ubique locorum graviter incumbere libris et officio fungi, puto me erga Deum esse excusatum. Nuper με ἐς κόρακας abire et alium quærere jubebat, cui famularer: et si quid leviusculum in literis meis omissum aut prætermissum est, puta aliquarum literarum quas miserit redditionem, (nam silentio meo testor ea quæ volebat esse transacta,) statim clamat, fulminat, num eum adeo futilem et vecordem esse existimem, ut de rebus necessariis non commonefaciam. Sed cesso questibus te quoque obtundere. Interea ames tu me, et, etsi vivo patre, te quoque mihi patrem præstes; consilio juves et foveas. Ego faxo, ut neque observantiam neque officium neglectum requiras aut desideres. Nova nulla sunt, aut tibi ex aliorum literis nota. Literas tuas episcopo Londinensi ipse tradidi, ut et Parkhursto Nordovicensi. Juellus incommodum et patriæ et nobis pridem mortuus est. Plura non scribo, sed his brevibus contentus ignosces mihi aliis literis scribendis plus æquo occupato. Salutem dic omnibus amicis, præsertim sorori uxori tuæ, quam pro auctoritate tua ad mei amorem mutuum magis et magis excitabis. Vale in Christo, affinis observande. Datæ Cantabrigiæ, 29 Julii, anno 1572.

Tui observantissimus affinis,

RODOLPHUS GUALTERUS.

Nuper Oxonii fui deambulandi gratia profectus: allocutus sum Humfredum, qui tibi jussit salutem renuntiari, si quando scriberem. Statui ego, Deo favente, brevi, hac academia relicta, in illam commigrare.

INSCRIPTIO.

Eximiæ eruditionis et pietatis viro D. Josiæ
    Simlero, in schola Tigurina theologiæ
    professori doctissimo, domino et affini
    suo plurimum colendo.

EPISTOLA LXXXV.

GULIELMUS CECILIUS AD JOHANNEM STURMIUM.

TRADITÆ sunt mihi literæ tuæ, ornatissime Sturmi, et quæ ad me privatim conscriptæ sunt, et quæ datæ sunt ad majestatem reginæ nostræ: quibus certiores nos facis de obitu D. Montii, hominis propter illius summam in procurandis hujus regni negotiis, et multorum annorum usu testificatam, diligentiam et fidem et suæ majestati et nobis omnibus commendatissimi. Cujus tamen desiderio non magis afficimur, quam ista significatione benevolentiæ atque officii tui, quasi æqua quadam compensatione, levamur. Quæ sane propter opinionem religionis, sapientiæ,

integritatis tuæ peropportune accidit, his præsertim temporibus, in quibus,
ad exploranda hominum consilia et facta, propter recentes Galliarum
calamitates et totius fere Europæ turbulentos motus, magna tum prudentia tum fide opus est. Quare sua majestas istam officii tui tam
diligenter et propense oblatam observantiam ita uti par est amplectitur,
teque perlibenter in Montii locum surrogatum eodem stipendio donabit.
Quod etsi pro tua sive humanitate sive facultate parum sit, tamen arbitramur te id potius ipsius majestatis amplitudine et voluntate quam
magnitudine sua metiri velle, teque totum, si quid hac in parte defuerit,
in illius benevolentia beneficentiaque positurum esse. Hoc ego ad te
stipendium ex voluntate reginæ, literasque a majestate sua misissem, si
aut nuncium istum satis idoneum existimassem, aut quicquam huic itineri,
quod illi propter novas has et locorum et temporum et rerum asperitates
videtur fore impeditissimum, præter has literas, testes voluntatis majestatis
suæ, et meæ etiam privatim erga te benevolentiæ, credere voluissem.
Quocirca nihil interea a nobis amplius exspectabis, qui in istorum incen-
diorum tam vicinorum flamma a nostris finibus prohibenda occupatissimi
sumus. Quorum quum furor divina bonitate restinctus vel sedatus fuerit,
tum tu ipse commodius et literarum tuarum ad nos transmittendarum,
et stipendii hujus ad te transferendi, rationem reperies. Vale. Dat. Wood-
stoci, 15 Sept. 1572.

Tui benevolentissimus,

GULIELMUS CECILIUS BARO BURGHLEIENSIS.

INSCRIPTIO.

Ornatissimo amico meo D. *Johanni*
Sturmio.

EPISTOLA LXXXVI.

RODOLPHUS GUALTERUS F. AD JOSIAM SIMLERUM.

S. Ex iis, quas pater ad me 28 Augusti dedit, intellexi te adversa
valetudine premi, ideoque ad me nullas literas te dedisse puto. Doluit
mihi et semper dolebit, quod te, observande affinis, tua ista podagra nunquam liberari audio; præsertim cum rariores eam ob causam a te accipiam
literas. Ego quidem, etsi a te nunquam ne verbum quidem acciperem,
tamen puto mei officii esse et observantiæ te de meis rebus certiorem
facere. Et quod ad studiorum meorum statum pertinet, sunt in pristino

statu. Versor adhuc Cantabrigiæ, brevi Oxoniam profecturus: exspecto enim in singulos dies literas commendatitias a Parkhursto ad D. Humphredum, quas ubi accepero quamprimum hinc migrabo. Jam pridem tædebat mansionis, cum omnia hic videam strepere litibus. Boni et pii verbi Dei ministri in carcerem detruduntur, quod adversus otiosos ventres concionentur. Alii alio modo vexantur, partim verbis partim factis, prout occasio sese istis tyrannis offert: et ita ἄλλον μειλιχίοις, ἄλλον στερεοῖς ἐπέεσσι Νείκεον. Ego tamen ea ad me nihil pertinere puto, utcumque animum discrucient, quod molesta gravius sit videre quam audire. Domum aliquando reversus plenius narrabo ut hic res gerantur. Interea a te peto, ut me tibi habeas commendatum, et ut studia mea bene se habeant, quantum in te est, cures. Ego vicissim pro virili operam dabo, ne tam mihi professores quam ego ipsis defuisse videar. Saluta omnes amicos rogo. Vale in Christo, affinis observande, quem precor ut te diu incolumem conservet.

Datæ Cantabrigiæ, 4 Februarii, 1573.

Tui observantissimus,

RODOLPHUS GUALTERUS F.

INSCRIPTIO.

Erudito et pio viro D. Josiæ Simlero,
S. theologiæ in schola Tigurina
professori, doctissimo domino et
affini suo observando.

EPISTOLA LXXXVII.

LUCAS CLAYSONUS AD RODOLPHUM GUALTERUM F.

TAMETSI bene sero ex Chestertonensi navigatione domum reversus eram, committere tamen non potui, mi Gualtere, quin pro nostra familiaritate ac consuetudine in sinistro oculo, culi mundi[1], contracta salutem saltem tibi scriberem; et quoniam te scio certiorem fieri velle, quis fuerit controversiæ inter nos et subulcum nostrum eventus, id quoque paucis significabo. Ego fide Punica meorum sociorum usus, eo fui redactus, ut nondum productis testibus arbitrorum judicio collegii causam committerem. Itaque decretum est, ut ego cum altero socio exacto restituamur, et statuta collegii depravata corrigantur restaurenturque. Quod quidem si ea qua spero fide agetur, neque sumtus neque laboris me pœnitet. Sin minus, ad rastros mihi haud dubie res rediit, et quærenda melior conditio est, quo in genere

[¹ Sic MS.]

*9

tua mihi fortassis erit opus industria. Plura ut scribam tempus non patitur. Jam enim *nox humida cœlo Præcipitat, suadentque cadentia sidera somnos.* Vale, et de statu rerum tuarum fac nos certiores. Ego vicissim nullum scribendi officium prætermittam. Raptim. Jacobus te salutat millies, Gallice *millefois.* Nono cal. Julii, 1573.

Tui studiosissimus,

LUCAS CLAYSONE.

INSCRIPTIO.
Summæ spei adolescenti Rodolpho
  Gualtero, amico suo singulari.
  Oxoniam.

EPISTOLA LXXXVIII.

RODOLPHUS GUALTERUS AD COMITEM BEDFORDIENSEM.

S.   VEREOR equidem, illustrissime princeps, ne tuæ clementiæ molestæ essent literæ nostræ, quibus modo hunc modo illum commendamus, nisi jampridem perspectam haberemus tuam humanitatem, et pium in bonis promovendis studium.

Ea etiam est interdum hominum nobis amicissimorum conditio, ut hoc officium illis negare non possimus, quod et per se pium est, et illis aliquam utilitatem afferre potest. Id vero imprimis intelligi velim de eo, qui has tibi literas reddet. Est is generosi et amplissimi viri, baronis ab Alto Saxo, filius, bonæ indolis et maximæ spei adolescens, qui cum aliquamdiu Heidelbergæ vixisset, inde ad illustrissimum principem Megaloburgensem profectus est. Nunc autem ex patris voluntate in Angliam venit, ut locum aliquem apud reginam serenissimam inveniat suis natalibus dignum. Audio illum ab illustrissimo principe palatino electore reginæ commendatum esse, cujus commendationem tanti ponderis fore non dubito, ut nostra hæc prorsus supervacanea videri possit. Quia tamen pater adolescentis eum nostris etiam amicis commendari volebat, non potuimus ejus petitioni deesse. Est enim ille vir piissimus, Dei cultor eximius, et in provehendo Christi regno non minus constans quam diligens. Etenim paucis abhinc annis e sua ditione, quæ papistis undique cingitur, omnes cultus illicitos ejecit, puriorem verbi doctrinam reduxit, et verum sacramentorum usum cum disciplina morum christianis hominibus digna instituit. Conflavit sibi eo facto multorum odia, et aliquamdiu adversarios habuit potentes, qui nihil non adversus illum conati sunt. At servavit illum Deus Opt. Max. ut nunc in ejus terris Christus prædicetur, quas prius papistica superstitio totas occuparat. Habet is filios complures, quos in principum christianorum

aulis educari et institui cupit, ut generis sui, quod apud nos antiquissimum
et illustre est, dignitatem tueri possint, et simul ea addiscant, quorum cognitio et ipsis ornamento sit, et communi patriæ aliquod emolumentum
ferat.   Decet quoque christianos principes optimi et piissimi herois vota
juvare; quod tuam clementiam eo libentius facturam puto, quod ipse jampridem senseris, qui labores et quæ pericula illis subeunda sint, qui Christum Jesum vera fide amplexi, ejusdem gloriam provehere student.   Facies
ergo, illustrissime princeps, quod sæpe jam fecisti, et adolescentem genero-
sissimum juvabis, ut sua familia et genere dignam conditionem vel apud
reginam serenissimam vel apud alium principem illustrem obtineat.   Quod
si tua clementia effecerit, opus faciet Deo gratissimum, et heroem piissimum
sibi perpetuo devinciet, seque ipsam nostris hominibus novo hoc benefi-
centiæ exemplo ut plurimum commendabit.   Deus Opt. Max. tuam clementiam benigne servet, ac suo Spiritu regat ad sui nominis gloriam!
Amen.   Tiguri, 17 Julii, anno 1573.

INSCRIPTIO.

Illustrissimo principi et domino, D.
     Francisco Russello comiti Bed-
     fordiensi.

Testimonium baronis de Alto Saxo.

Universis Christi fidelibus, ad quos præsentes literæ testimoniales pervenerint, Laurentius Humfredus, illustrissimi comitis Leicestriensis vice-
cancellarius sive commissarius in alma academia Oxoniensi, salutem in
Auctore salutis.   Cum ante paucos menses ad istam academiam accesserit
nobilis ac illustris vir dominus Joannes Philippus ab Alto Saxo liber baro
in Sax. et Forsteck, etc., in Helvetia, etc., et per quatuor menses cum
doctissimis viris in ista academia familiariter conversatus, quamplurima
ediderit sua rari ac singularis ingenii specimina, ut non solum ob illustrem
familiam, sed propter eruditionem et eximias ejus ingenii dotes vere nobilis
haberi possit: visum est universitati nostræ, in testificationem sui in eum
non solum amoris sed potius judicii, decimo octavo die mensis Maii anno
Domini mill^{mo} quingen^{mo} septuag^{mo} quarto eundem titulo magistri in artibus insignire et decorare, ut deinceps nostræ in eum benevolentiæ non
obliviscatur, et nos ejus notitiæ recordatione perpetuo fruamur.   Et quia
jam tandem desiderio teneatur invisendi patriam, nos eum caritate prosequentes, eundem sine testimonio nostro non dimittendum duximus.   Hæc
igitur omnia et singula vobis bona fide significamus per præsentes, sigillo
officii cancellariatus Oxon. in testimonium omnium et singulorum præmissorum communitas.   Dat. 30 die mensis Julii, anno Domini mill^{mo}
quingen^{mo} septuag^{mo} quarto.

EPISTOLA LXXXIX.

GULIELMUS BURGHLEIUS AD JOHANNEM STURMIUM.

Accepi tuas literas, Sturmi, quas ad regiam majestatem et ad me simul dedisti huic familiari Phil. Sidnei, qui has vicissim tibi a me reddet. Quibus non est in hoc tempore quod respondeam pluribus. Quod meum consilium secutus ad ipsius majestatem scripseris, valde probo; id enim ei gratum fore sciebam, sicuti sane fuit. Verum unum est quod te deinceps admonitum velim, ut cum denuo scribes ad suam majestatem, curam adhibeas cum in scribendis tum in perlegendis tuis literis paulo magis accuratiorem. Erat enim in utroque genere ea incuria, ut nec facile ab ea legi possent, nec propter verborum defectum satis intelligi. Quod ego tribuebam festinationi tuæ, et fortasse etiam occupationibus quæ te aliquæ premebant, quominus tuas literas licuit perlegere. Sed miror eas in rebus Germanicis tam breves fuisse. Quod Philippum Sidneium tanta humanitate accipis, habeo tibi multam gratiam, quam scio honoratissimos parentes ejus tibi reddituros multo cumulatiorem. Bene vale, Sturmi, et si quid erit quod nostri intererit, fac nos ut commode poteris certiores. Londini, 18 Julii, 1573.

Tuæ dignitatis semper amantissimus,

GUL. BURGHLEIUS.

INSCRIPTIO.

Spectabili et illustri viro Johanni
Sturmio, serenissimæ reginæ
Angliæ procuratori in Ger-
mania.

EPISTOLA XC.

RODOLPHUS GUALTERUS F. AD JOSIAM SIMLERUM.

S. Literas tuas, observande affinis, reddidit mihi D. Wilhelmus Barlo, quo jamdudum Heidelbergæ usus fueram familiariter. Ex iis intellexi te merito commotum fuisse ob quorundam sciolorum, qui hic sunt, calumnias, quibus, licet imperitissimis, nihil nisi comtum et politum omnibusque numeris absolutissimum probari potest. Verum quandoquidem omnibus istis satisfieri non potest, nobis existimandum erit, nos officio nostro probe defunctos, si optimis quibusque conatus nostros et desiderium in republica literaria promovenda probemus. Inter Oxonienses, ad quos mense Junio me contuli, pauciores sunt ex ipsorum numero, partim quia integriores sunt, partim quia hic papistarum omnia plena, paucique sese puriori religioni addicunt; unde neque libros nostrorum inspiciunt, qua ratione ejusmodi calumniandi in specie fiducia et ansa ipsis praeripitur.

Sed de his nimis multa apud te praesertim, affinis doctissime, quem scio et hic et ubique terrarum bonis omnibus esse carissimum. Paucis post diebus aliae tuae mihi redduntur, in quibus me negligentiae accusas, quod neque pannum emerim, neque aliquid literarum ad te dederim. De posteriori facile me negligentiae accusari scio, praesertim cum innocens sim. At jam te accepisse meas a Chevalerio arbitror, cui adversa tempestas obfuit, quominus citius ad vos perveniret. Quoad prius, parum equidem, cum primo in Angliam venissem, apud Hillaeum efficere potui, qui cum hoc dicterium semper in ore habeat, pecunias mercatoribus idem esse quod rustico aratrum, nihil nisi praesente pecunia facit. Cum vero in posterioribus ad me literis nullum ejus rei mentionem faceres, putavi te mutato consilio pannum non amplius magnopere desiderare. D. Gulielmus Barlo tamen, cum hac denuo transiret, totum istud onus in se recepit, et Londini se cum notis mercatoribus ea de re acturum pollicitus est. Si mihi Londinum proficiscendi occasio fuisset, libenter hac in parte omne officium tibi praestitissem. Sed Barloo rem procurante, arbitror meo consilio non admodum opus esse.

Quod ad res meas, in collegio Magdalenensi (cujus praeses Humfredus est) Oxonii dego satis commode. Nam et hic doctorum virorum est copia, et me ipsis propter singularem erga me amorem plurimum debere fateor. Inter omnes tamen elucet singularis D. Humfredi et Coli benevolentia, quibus a D. Parkhursto fui commendatus. Et quia haec academia prae Cantabrigiensi arrisit, ut hic commodius degerem et in majori honore, gradum magisterii petii, qui 6 Julii ab universitatis senatu unanimi consensu mihi fuit delatus; ad cujus gradus confirmationem proxima hebdomada lectiones publicas habebo tam in morali quam in naturali philosophia. Deus fortunet inceptum meum, et dirigat omnes meos conatus ad sui nominis gloriam! Cupio autem nunc hic diutius versari, quam statueram, partim propter gradum, partim propter summam commoditatem. D. Parkhurstus enim me ita Humfredo commendavit, ut omnes sumtus mihi conferat, ab ipso recepturus; unde sine ulla patris expensa hic posthac vivere possem, quod hactenus ob sumtuum incertudinem fieri non potuit. Rogo autem te, observande affinis, ut semper, quod studiis meis commodum sit, suadeas et consulas, ne citius quam par sit domum revocer. Nam si citius opinione domum revocarer, fortasse pater ea in re obedientiam meam desideraret. Sed scio, tam patri quam tibi et omnibus ista curæ esse, ut me de illis anxium esse minime sit opus.   Plura igitur hoc præsertim tempore non scribam, rogaboque te ut his contentus me, quod facis, ames.   Deus Opt. Max. te cum uxore et liberis diu incolumem conservet!   Vale.   Datæ Oxonii ex collegio Magdalenæ.   Julii 20, 1573.

Tui observantissimus affinis,

RODOLPHUS GUALTERUS F.

INSCRIPTIO.

Eximiæ eruditionis et pietatis viro
D. Josiæ Simlero, sacræ theologiæ
in schola Tigurina professori, doc-
tissimo domino et affini suo re-
verenter colendo.

———————

Testimonium Rodolphi Gualteri junioris.

Universis Christi fidelibus, ad quos præsentes literæ pervenerint, Laurentius Humfredus, illustrissimi comitis Leicestriæ vice-cancellarius sive commissarius in alma academia Oxoniensi, salutem in Domino sempiternam. Quia nihil magis juri et æquitati convenit quam veritati testimonium perhibere, ob cujus defectum innocentum plerumque status per calumniatorum injurias falsis probris convellitur et labefactatur, hinc est quod nos, petitione dilecti nobis in Christo Rodolphi Gualteri Tigurini moti, ad universitatis vestræ notitiam deducimus, vosque certiores fieri volumus per præsentes, quod præfatus Rodolphus Gualterus nostræ academiæ alumnus exstitit per duos annos integros elapsos, et in collegio Magdalenensi operam literis dedit non minus feliciter quam diligenter, se interea laudabiliter gerens. Inde, meritis suis id exigentibus, 12mo die Octobris, anno Domini 1573, in celeberrimis comitiis nostris inauguratus est artium magister: juvenis ob morum candorem amabilis, ob conditionem spectabilis, ut ornatissimi et singularis patris Dni. Rod. Gualteri Tigurini professoris non solum nomen, sed virtutis specimen facile referat et repræsentet. Et quia jam tandem desiderio tenetur invisendi patrem et patriam, nos eum caritate prosequentes, eundem sine testimonio nostro non dimittendum duximus. Hæc igitur omnia et singula vobis bona fide significamus per præsentes, sigillo officii cancellariatus Oxon. in testimonium omnium et singulorum præmissorum communitas. Dat. 30 die mensis Julii, A.D. 1574.

EPISTOLA XCI.

JOHANNES WOLLEYUS AD JOHANNEM STURMIUM.

Ut ad te hoc tempore scriberem, ornatissime Sturmi, Leicestriensis comitis patroni mei singularis voluntas fecit : qui cum ipse ad te aliis de rebus scriberet, voluit etiam me meis literis ad tuam amicitiam et familiaritatem aditum patefacere. Quod feci quidem cupidissime.

Nam cum Aschami tui in ejus apud regiam majestatem munere subeundo successor sim, ejus etiam amicitiarum et necessitudinum, tuæ præsertim, hæres esse pervelim. Recipe me igitur in Aschami locum, cujus quanquam facultate in optimis disciplinis sim inferior, at in te amando et colendo conabor esse superior. Voluit illustrissimus comes ut ad te (quanquam nunc ocreati et in procinctu simus) de re non magna, sed quæ magnas apud nos tragedias excitat, hoc tempore scriberem.

Magna apud nos jam diu (quod te ignorare non arbitror) quæstio exstitit, debeantne ministri et verbi prædicatores certo vestitus generi, præsertim quo missatores sacrifici in papatu usi sunt, publica auctoritate alligari : quæ apud nos contentio ita est agitata, ut multi evangelii prædicationem potius relinquere voluerint, et quotidie etiam relinquunt, quam ut eo genere vestitus utantur astringi. Hæc certe res apud nos magnas turbas excitavit, et tractando adhuc lis crevit.

Optat igitur vehementer nobilissimus comes, aliquam a te iniri rationem, qua doctissimorum Germaniæ theologorum, Bezæ præsertim, Gualteri, et aliorum magni nominis censuris hac de re ad universitates nostras conscriptis hæc jam gliscens contentio sopiri possit. Qua de re ad te alias plura : nunc reginæ ab hoc loco demigratio festinationis plena vix hæc quidem me scribere permisit. Tu harum literarum festinationi (quæ jussu comitis scriptæ sunt) ignosces, et me inter tui amantissimos numerabis. Quod a te iterum atque iterum vehementer peto. Vale, ornatissime vir. Dat. Orpintoni, qui Cantii provinciæ pagus est. Die mensis Julii 24, A.D. 1573.

Tui observantissimus,

JOHANNES WOLLEYUS.

INSCRIPTIO.

Ornatissimo viro Johanni Sturmio,
  Angliæ reginæ in Germania
  agenti.

EPISTOLA XCII.

GULIELMUS COLUS AD RODOLPHUM GUALTERUM.

Benevolentia, quam apud vos præ ceteris omnibus Tiguri expertus sum, mihi e memoria excidere nunquam potest, ornatissime vir. Propterea sic tibi persuadeas volo, me animo et voluntate semper fore Tigurinum, tametsi corpore longe remotissimum. Et si omnes eo nomine, quod Tigurini sunt, mihi commendatissimi esse debeant, multo magis tuus filius est summo amore prosequendus. Nam, præterquam quod Tigurinus est, patris eum pietas et amicitia mihi, doctrina piis omnibus facit commendatiorem. Quoties enim opera tua piis ob oculos obversantur legenda, toties illis tanti patris filius commendatur. Anno jam elapso, cum tuus filius nostris comitiis interesset, non potui non præstare tibi officium qualecunque. Nam statim conspecto tuo filio, nescio quomodo mihi in mentem venit, quicquid in nos Anglos jam ante multos annos beneficiorum contuleris. Quocirca jam plane video inveterascere nunquam posse apud me tanta beneficia: ita recens et grata erat eorum recordatio. Scripsit ad me episcopus Nordovicensis, dominus mihi multis nominibus colendissimus. Ex illius literis intellexi, quam carus sit illi tuus filius, ita ut te absente in Helvetia, audeam affirmare, Nordovicensem dominum non minus tuo filio affuturum in omnibus, quam si tu præsens illi prospiceres ipse. Paucis ergo sic accipe, Gualterum tuum fore mihi semper intimum, me nunquam illius commodis defuturum. Novarum rerum fere nihil apud nos. Audio in Hollandia civitatem quandam nomine Harlem post longam obsidionem, tandem etiam vehementer Hispanis repugnantibus, intromisisse subsidiarios milites ex Anglia et Scotia, atque ea ratione bene Harlemensibus prospectum esse de rebus ad victum necessariis. Atque hoc factum est ante aliquot dies non sine aliqua strage utriusque partis. Parant aliquot nobiles nostrates expeditionem magnam in Hiberniam, et jam sunt in itinere omnes. Magna est animorum conjunctio inter nos et Scotos, et nostra ope hac æstate usi protestantes illius regionis in suam potestatem redegerunt arcem munitissimam Edenburgensem. Regina illorum est apud nos cum quodam comite, cujus fideli custodiæ committitur, ita ut egredi, nisi eo concedente, et sine satis justo satellitio non possit. De rebus Gallicis nihil habeo quod scribam. De Rupellanis omnia adhuc sunt incerta. Quæso, mi domine, velis reverendum illum patrem D. Bullingerum cum reliquis

symmystis et piis plurimum salutare meo nomine. Te Christus servet.
26 Julii, 1573.

Tuus tibi deditissimus,

GULIELMUS COLUS.

INSCRIPTIO.

Doctissimo viro, D. Rodolpho Gual-
tero, ecclesiæ Tigurinæ ministro
dentur hæ literæ. Tiguri.

EPISTOLA XCIII.

GULIELMUS BARLOUS AD JOSIAM SIMLERUM.

S. P. MITTO ad te, præstantissime Simlere, pannum, sicut petiisti;
sed hoc ego a te vicissim peto, ut in primis tuis ad me literis mihi rescribas,
quomodo tibi et pannus et pretium placeat. Usus quidem sum in hac re
illorum ope, quorum peritia aliqua saltem debebat esse; qui satis splendide pollicentur, sed, quia omnis fides e terra periit, te etiam atque etiam
rogo, ut adhibito aliquo, qui in hac re judicio valet, tute ad me rescribas
quid sentias, antequam denariolum pecuniæ mittas, quod facies absque
omni meo aut incommodo aut molestia. Mercator, qui Deo favente his
autumnalibus nundinis pannum D. Froschovero tradet, pecuniam ante
proximas vernales non accipiet; tunc demum vel huic vel alicui alii hoc
dabo negotii, ut ista pecunia mihi quædam Francofurti coemat: interim
quid tibi videatur de panno, certiorem, si placet, facies. Novi nihil habemus, nisi quod coloniæ ducuntur ex Anglia in Hiberniam, ut istam partem
insulæ occupent, quæ Scotiæ est vicinior. Iis præficitur comes Essexiæ;
magni sunt apparatus. Status civilis apud nos adhuc, Dei beneficio, est
tranquillus; ecclesiæ vero nostræ omnia plena turbarum et rixarum.
Quamprimum aliquid otii nactus fuero (quod sane mihi ab eo tempore,
quo in Angliam jam veni, quod fuit sub initium Junii, vix contigit) aliqua
saltem expiscabor, quæ hospiti D. Wiccio meo mittam: interim illi a me
salutem dices. Saluta obsecro officiose meo nomine reverendos in Christo
patres D. Bullingerum seniorem, et D. Gualterum, etiam atque etiam D.
Lavaterum, D. Stuccium, D. Bullingerum juniorem, D. Lemannum, D.
Jac. Frisium. Conveni filium D. Gualteri affinem tuum (qui literas tuas
mihi tradidit datas 5 calend. Maii) Oxoniæ; obtuli illi meam opellam,
si ulla in re illi grata esse poterit, quemadmodum ex officio debeo. Ille

jam tandem nactus est locum in collegio Magdalenensi studiis non incommodum. Londini, postridie calend. Augusti, anno, etc. 1573.

Tuus,

GULIELMUS BARLOW.

Saluta etiam quæso nostrum Julium meo nomine, dicasque ei me
nuper alloquutum esse illius nomine episcopum Londinensem, et literas
illius omnes fideliter curasse.

Mitto ad te his literis inclusam particulam panni tui, quam integro
aptare poteris, ne commutetur in itinere. Pretium panni septem libræ sunt
Anglicanæ atque quatuor solidi Anglicani: unaquæque libra Anglicana
facit batsiones octaginta.

INSCRIPTIO.
Doctissimo optimoque viro D. Josiæ
Simlero. Tiguri.

EPISTOLA XCIV.

RODOLPHUS GUALTERUS AD DOMINUM RICARDUM COXUM.

S.   GRATUM tibi, pater in Christo reverende, tuisque collegis fuisse
meum officium, quo meum erga vos et ecclesias Anglicanas studium
mearum in priorem ad Corinthios homiliarum dedicatione publice testatus sum, magna cum voluptate ex tuis et aliorum, tum etiam filii mei
literis intellexi, qui tuam erga se liberalitatem mihi diligenter prædicat;
pro qua, ut etiam pro mnemosyno (ut tu scribis) ad me misso, gratias
tuæ amplitudini ago, non quales illa meretur aut quales ego vellem, sed
quas possum: simulque Deum Opt. Max. precor, ut aliqua mihi detur
occasio qua demonstrare possim, me beneficiorum vestrorum, quæ in me
et filium contulistis, non esse immemorem. Manebit hic in vernum usque
tempus apud vos, et ita fieri necesse est, quoniam meæ literæ, quibus
de mea voluntate ad illum scribo, vix ante Novembrem ex nundinis
ad illum perferri possunt: quo tempore navigatio minus commoda, nec
etiam satis tuta est. Ineunte autem vere, si nihil incidat quod ejus
institutum remoretur, in Daniam trajiciet, ubi eum commendavi amico
singulari, D. Erasmo Læto, Hafniensis academiæ theologo, qui nuper
Venetiis hac transiens, suam mihi operam in illo excipiendo et Ros-
tochium transmittendo pollicitus est, ut inde, lustratis etiam Saxoniæ
scholis, Vitemberga nimirum et Lipsia, tandem (si ita Domino visum

fuerit) domum ad me redeat. Interea, quod hactenus fecistis, ut porro
faciatis rogo, et ipsum studiaque ejus habeatis commendata, ne tempus
male perdat, aut moribus malis corrumpatur.

Ut vero ad literas tuas redeam, in quibus tu mearum quoque mentionem
facis, quibus ego meæ epistolæ ad D. Parkhurstum Nordovicensem de
vestris controversiis scriptæ rationem reddidi : vehementer mihi dolet, me
per vestra certamina quasi in theatrum protrahi, dum utrinque meæ literæ
typis vulgantur. Inique certe et inhumaniter ab adversariis vestris factum
fuit, quod quas ego ad veterem amicum pro nostræ amicitiæ et familiaritatis jure liberius scripseram, publicaverunt. Debebat illis sufficere, quod
nostra credulitate abusi, admonitionem illam acriorem nobis extorserant.
Quod vero alteram epistolam, quam eadem de re ad te dedi, D. Vuitgiftus
libro suo, quo adversariis vestris respondit, inseruit, facilius ferre poteram,
siquidem hoc causæ necessitas requirebat : molestum tamen mihi est, quod
illos ex ea novam queritandi, vel etiam calumniandi occasionem arripere
audio, quasi quod prius bene dixerim, nunc in vestram gratiam recantarem.
Solatur me tamen mens bene sibi conscia, et spero cordatiores quosque
intellecturos, me a levitatis crimine esse alienissimum. Videbunt enim me
non absque causa apud hominem amicissimum conquestum fuisse de iis,
quæ, si ita fierent sicuti ad aures nostras pervenerant, acriorem quoque
correptionem merebantur. At cum nobis fucum factum fuisse audiam, cur
non me excusem ? Nolim certe aliorum levitate et petulantia a viris bonis
et amicis alienari : sed quantum ex tuis literis conjicere possum, jam illi
telam novam exorsi sunt, quo minus miror me ab illis in arenam protrahi.
Petis tu, ut ad articulos novem respondeam, quorum assertione illi vobis
negotium faciunt. At si hi soli apud vos controvertuntur, meo judicio vix
digni sunt quibus confutandis aliquis divinus occupetur ; cum præter
novitatis studium nihil spirent, et utinam nulla invidiæ aut cæcæ æmula-
tionis amaritudine essent aspersi !

I. Volunt e medio tolli archiepiscoporum et episcoporum aliorumque
officiariorum nomina. At ego illos velim modestius agere, neque in mu-
tanda reipublicæ aut ecclesiæ forma sibi ipsis pietatem majorem vindicare
quam ipsis data sit. Non inficior sane in omnibus regnis multa esse, quæ
ad veterem et apostolicæ simplicitatis regulam melius institui possint. At
quum ea est nostri seculi calamitas, ut ne illi quidem principes, qui evangelio Christi portas suas aperuerunt, omnia mutari et corrigi sinant, multæ
etiam remoræ aliunde accedunt; satius mihi esse videtur, ferre patienter regnorum hujus seculi incommoda, dummodo nobis doctrinæ puritas et con-
scientiarum libertas salva maneat, quam de externa ecclesiæ administratione
litigando summam rerum in periculum adducere. Et miror illos tantopere
ab episcoporum vocabulo abhorrere, quod apostolorum temporibus usurpatum, et postea quoque semper in ecclesiis servatum fuisse non ignorant.
Sed et archiepiscopos olim fuisse scimus, quos alio nomine patriarchas dixe-

runt. Quod si posteris temporibus ambitione et tyrannide peccatum est, ut tituli isti non absque causa piis exosi facti sint, non video tamen quid obstat quominus sublato abusu episcopi sint et dicantur, qui certo ecclesiarum numero præfecti ea curent, quæ ad religionis et doctrinæ puritatem conservandam pertinent. Non possum tamen hoc loco dissimulare, inveniri passim extra Angliam vestram viros pios et probos, imo nobiles quoque, qui in episcoporum vestrorum moribus et pompa multa reprehendunt. Et qui nuper ex Anglia venerunt (ut ex amicorum literis intelleximus) conquesti sunt multa illic inhumanius designari in pios et doctos verbi ministros, qui aliquando non absque eximio fructu Christum prædicarunt, nunc autem propter causas non adeo usque graves, et tantum non indicta causa, vel saltem non legitime cognita, in carceres detrusi sint, episcopis ad id conniventibus, imo etiam consentientibus. Quod an vere de vobis dicatur nescio: meliora certe nobis de vobis omnibus pollicemur. At si quid hujus fiat, rogatos denuo vos velim, ut cogitetis quantopere vobis cavendum sit, ne contra Petri præceptum in cleros vobis dominium usurpetis, aut ex eorum numero sitis, qui conservos suos inhumaniter cædunt. Condonabis mihi, pater reverende, hanc dicendi libertatem, cujus mihi non alia causa est, quam quod vos amo, imo colo et observo, vestrique nominis honori simul et ecclesiis Anglicis optime consultum cupio. Vos quoque spero nihil eorum detrectaturos esse, quæ ad meliorem ecclesiæ statum facere videbuntur. Et si plerosque vestrum recte novi, puto malle vos onus istud, quod magno cum labore et tanta cum multorum invidia sustinetis, deponere, si liceret, quam reformationi meliori obstare. Quod si vero serenissima regina et regni proceres ecclesiæ formam, quæ nunc est, mutari nolunt, velim ego alteros illos fratres nostros eandem patienter ferre, neque vobis molestiam exhibere: vicissim autem vos cum episcopali dignitate modestiam et humilitatem conjungere, neque eos fastidire qui in eadem vobiscum Christi vinea laborant.

II. Electionem ministrorum verbi ad plebem revocari debere contendunt, et non ab episcopis fieri. At ego hic quoque prudentia et animi moderatione opus esse existimo, ne dum jus summum urgemus, multi de injuria sibi a nobis facta conquerendi occasionem habeant. Fateor equidem apostolorum tempore doctores publico totius ecclesiæ consensu, et non sine jejuniis et precibus, electos fuisse, ut in Matthiæ electione, Pauli item et Barnabæ ordinatione ad gentes apparet. Quem morem adhuc D. Augustini seculo in usu fuisse, ejus epistola testatur, qua Evodii successoris sui electionem describit. Verumtamen tunc quoque potiores partes eorum fuisse constat, qui vel apostolici nominis dignitate vel officii ratione et honorum prærogativa aliis præstabant. Et notum est Pauli factum, qui Titum ideo in Creta reliquit, ut oppidatim presbyteros atque doctores constitueret. Jubet idem ille, ut omnia decenter et ordinate fiant; quod quomodo absque certa officiorum ecclesiasticorum distinctione fieri possit, non video. Ceterum turbatus est posteris temporibus universus ecclesiæ ordo sub antichristi tyrannide, quam regum et principum superstitio confirmavit. Cum enim hi, in fide Christi minus recte instituti, peccata sua externis sacris et conductitiis aliorum precibus expiari posse putarent, mox sacrificulorum, monachorum atque monialium collegia instituere, eademque annuorum redituum et decimarum proventibus ditare cœperunt. Qua occasione factum est, ut una cum decimis aliisque parochiarum (uti vocant) reditibus, jus electionis (quod illi patronatus dixerunt) ad collegiorum præfectos, episcopos et abbates, denique ad mulieres quoque abbatissas, sit devolutum ; ut jam de aliis nihil dicam, qui illud aliis rationibus obtinuerunt. Apud nos certe (ut hoc exempli loco adducam), qui ex singulari Dei misericordia jam annis totis quinquaginta evangelii prædicatione libera fruimur, in multis parochiis ministrorum electio penes episcopum Constantiensem et abbates papisticos est, qui ex veterum regum donatione in agro Tigurino decimas et reditus habent maximos. Quos si suo jure et possessione longi temporis præscriptione jam confirmata spoliare velimus, Deum immortalem! quas turbas daremus! quantum periculi nostris accerseremus ecclesiis! Consultius quoque nobis esse videtur, ut illi suo jure cum decimis fruantur, nobis vero pacem et libertatem religionis concedant, seque ab amplissimo senatu nostro eo usque astringi sinant, ne quem ministrum ecclesiis præficiant, quam qui in nostra ecclesia educatus et legitimo examine probatus sit. Addo et hoc, nullam in urbe et agro Tigurino ecclesiam esse, quæ jus ministros eligendi retinuerit, præterquam eam quæ ad D. Petrum est, cujus me ministrum Deus esse voluit, et a qua ante annos 31, unanimi totius plebis consensu, cum annum ætatis vigesimum tertium nondum implevissem, electus sum. Et miraculo simile est, sub immani papatus tyrannide, cum partim Constantiensis episcopus et summi templi canonici, partim inferioris collegii abbatissa aliique abbates, omnibus ecclesiis dominarentur, et decimas circumquaquam omnes ad se pertraxissent, huic tamen ecclesiæ suam libertatem salvam mansisse : in quo singularem Dei curam agnosco, qua me non semel vehementer confirmatum esse sensi. Interim nemo est qui hoc exemplo sibi similem libertatem turbulenter vindicat; neque ego aliarum ecclesiarum ministros ut illegitime ordinatos pro me contemno, quod illis electionis ratio diversa obtigerit, quæ ad apostolicorum temporum consuetudinem non tam prope accedit. Cur enim illis fraudi sit temporis prioris iniquitas, quæ res eo adduxit unde non absque tumultu et publico periculo restitui possunt? Ferenda potius esse putamus, quæ pie et absque salutis æternæ jactura ferri possunt, mutari autem absque turba et periculo non possunt. Quod si vestri quoque diligentius observent, æmulationi minus locum dabunt, et pace optata brevi (ut spero) fruemini.

III. Quod præscriptis precibus neminem alligari debere dicunt, nescio quo sensu dicant. Si hoc volunt, ne vim precum verbis conceptis aut

certis formulis precandi superstitiose alligemus, idem ego quoque sentio :
nam hoc exorcistarum est et magorum.   At si certas precum publicarum
formas in ecclesia damnant, ego illos cum ratione insanire dixero, et nimium
rerum novandarum studio excæcatos, lividis oculis omnia notare, ut calumniandi occasionem inveniant.   Illas enim omnibus seculis in usu fuisse,
nemo negare potest : et ut retineantur plusquam necesse est, quoniam
plerique vel ita inepti, vel etiam animis perplexi sunt in periculis et tenta-
tionibus, ut preces vix animo, nedum verbis, concipere possint.   Quæ causa
est quod Spiritus sanctus multas servorum Dei preces conscribi et in sacrarum literarum codicem referri voluit.   Et ipse Christus certam precandi
formulam nobis tradidit, quod ante illum Johannes quoque Baptistes fecerat.
Nec tamen hoc obstat, quominus singuli privatim pro ipsis et afflictionum
suarum ratione preces suas instituant, et verbis utantur quæ Spiritus suggerit ; ministri item sub finem concionum suarum preces subjiciant ei argumento, quod tractarunt, convenientes : quod tamen ita fieri velim, ne eas
negligant et prætermittant, quæ singulis ecclesiis quasi propriæ et longo
usu jam confirmatæ sunt.

IV.   Sacramenta absque Dei verbo administrari debere, nemo sanus
dixerit ; quoniam nisi verbum accedat ad elementum, non erit sacramentum,
ut Augustinus olim monuit.   Et cœnam dominicam, quæ publica totius
ecclesiæ actio est in memoriam et prædicationem mortis Christi instituta,
non puto recte administrari posse, nisi concio sacra præcedat, qua de
Christi beneficio et suo insuper officio singuli admoneantur.   Baptismi
tamen alia ratio est, quoniam per hunc infantes quoque in ecclesiæ societatem recipiuntur, quos doctrinæ nondum capaces esse constat, licet Dei
fœdere comprehendantur, et regni cœlorum hæredes sint.   Possunt ergo
tunc sufficere lectiones et preces, quibus de suo officio admoneantur, qui
baptismi testes adsunt, et Dei gratia impetretur.   Interim nequaquam improbo earum ecclesiarum morem, in quibus certus in septimana dies baptismo constitutus est, et concio sacra habetur, qua finita, quotquot ea septimana nati sunt infantes ex ordine baptizantur.   Et in nostro agro fere
infantes tingi solent iis diebus, quibus conciones statæ fiunt.   At quia hoc
non omnibus in locis opportunum sive commodum est, ego nolim cuiquam
temere negotium facessere, quominus ecclesiæ singulæ sua libertate absque
scandalo fruantur.

V.   Volunt præterea ut solus pater filium suum in baptismo suscipiat,
et non alii susceptores adhibeantur : in quo rursus inutile et curiosum
novitatis studium produnt.   Quæ enim religio obstat, quominus alii a
parentibus infantum rogati, hoc officium ipsis præstent, quod olim, cum
persecutiones adhuc passim ferverent, non minus necessarium quam utile
erat ; et quod hodie amicitiæ conciliandæ servit, denique jam adultis sæpe
prodest, dum ab illis liberius admonentur et corripiuntur, qui fidem suam
pro illis ecclesiæ obstrinxerunt ?

VI. Quod de ministrorum æqualitate adjiciunt, recensione non opus habet, cum de eo supra dictum sit. Damnamus ipsi quoque primatum cum ambitione et dominandi studio conjunctum : at inter ministros ecclesiæ ordinem certum apostolus quoque esse docuit, dum alios apostolos, alios prophetas, alios pastores et doctores constitutos esse dicit : et idem, ut donorum et facultatum, ita ministeriorum quoque discrimina esse facit. Et miror istos homines non ad proprii corporis fabricam et membrorum suorum dispositionem respicere, quæ illos admonere poterat quid hic sit sentiendum : qua similitudine apostolus in hoc argumento utitur. Interim tamen meminerint ii quibus sublimior gradus contigit, se tunc demum supra alios recte eminere, si (ut Christus monuit) omnibus serviant.

VII. Quoad confirmationem, non puto vos ludum illum theatricum probare quem papistæ inter sacramenta retulerunt. Quod si qui in catechismo recte instituti sunt, cum publico testimonio et manuum impositione (qua Christum quoque in pueris usum fuisse scimus) ad cœnam dominicam admittantur, non video cur de eo aliquis cum quoquam pugnare debeat.

VIII. Conciones funebres apud nos in usu non sunt ; et quoniam homines ad superstitiones natura proclives sunt, et quidem eas imprimis, quæ defunctorum salutem juvare creduntur, præstat illis vel omnino abstinere, vel ita illas instituere ut omnes intelligant, quicquid illic fit, propter vivos qui auditores adsunt, non propter mortuos fieri, de quorum salute, siquidem in fide et nominis Dei invocatione per Christum decesserint, tam certo persuasi esse debemus, ut nemini de illa dubitandi occasio præbeatur. Ex concionibus ejusmodi, quas olim a piis patribus religiose institutas fuisse scimus, posteris temporibus in papatu quæstuosissime illud ignis purgatorii, missarum, et exequiarum aucupium enatum est. Et quid hodie fieri soleat in quibusdam ecclesiis reformatis, ubi illæ adhuc retinentur, satis notum est. Nec enim desunt qui, ut nobilioribus familiis gratificentur, vel etiam dona aut munera pretiosiora recipiant, conciones fere totas in defunctorum laudibus consumunt, fictis plerumque, aut saltem admodum suspectis, et proinde scandali plenis. Verumtamen si aliqui illis absque superstitionis et quæstus privati periculo cum auditorum ædificatione uti possunt, nolim ego illorum libertati aliquid derogare. Ne tamen quod verissimum est dissimulem, res ista periculi plena mihi esse videtur, partim propter vulgi ad superstitionem animos proclives, partim propter innatam plerisque quæstus cupiditatem, quam ego quam rarissimis occasionibus provocandam esse censeo ; ne dum ministri αἰσχροκερδεῖς fiunt, doctrinam omnem una cum religione suspectam reddant. Et movit me, quod ut Deus olim nulla pro defunctis sacra instituit, ita sacerdotes a funeribus removit, ne his occupati polluerentur.

IX. Quæ lectiones apud vos in usu sint, nescio. Audio tamen sub initium reformationis per serenissimam reginam restitutæ illas ministrorum inopia fuisse institutas : et scimus olim quoque omnes sacræ scripturæ libros populo christiano ex ordine prælectos fuisse. Nec video quid hoc incommodi ferat, si qui lectionibus ejusmodi delectentur, modo non negligatur concionandi munus, in quo episcopos et omnes ecclesiarum ministros frequentes esse convenit: ut Dei verbum non obiter modo recitatum, sed rite sectum, ut Paulus monet, omnium institutioni, consolationi, et ædificationi accommodetur.

Hæc breviter annotare libuit in adversariorum vestrorum articulos: non quod vos meis animadversionibus opus habere existimem, sed quia tu, pater in Christo reverende, meum de his judicium requiris. Quod si quid per ignorantiam minus dextre dictum mihi excidit, de eo admoneri cupio. Utinam vero omnes qui christianum nomen profitentur, pacem studerent, et regnum Dei conjunctis studiis propagare satagerent, aliique aliorum onera patienter ferrent! Viderent utique, nunquam sibi tantum otii fore, ut, de alienis negotiis curiosi, contentiones de rebus vel non necessariis vel etiam noxiis cum publico scandalo susciperent. Enimvero vehementer metuo fore aliquando, ut qui nunc Christi ministros iniquius tractant, et purioris doctrinæ patronos episcopos ferre nolunt, utrinque lupos sentiant, qui ipsos novis certaminibus exerceant, et ecclesias horrendum in modum dissipent. Ita enim ministrorum dissensiones et ecclesiæ suæ distractiones Deus ulciscitur. Nicolai Sanderi librum de monarchia non vidi: si videam, et dignum putem cui respondeatur, faciam quod dederit Dominus; quem rogo ut te, pater in Christo reverende, cum collegis et omnibus apud vos Christi opus sedulo agentibus, servet, et studiis vestris sanctissimis benedicat. Amen. Tiguri, 26 Augusti, anni 1573.

Tuæ amplitudinis observantissimus,

RODOLPHUS GUALTERUS.

EPISTOLA XCV.

ROBERTUS COOCHEUS AD RODOLPHUM GUALTERUM.

Coactus sum, conscientia urgente, sensa mentis, idque in re gravissima et singulari mysterio aperire. De cœna Christi ultima instituitur oratio. In qua hodie et jam inde fere a Pauli ætate erratur: siquidem ipse cœnam proposuit Corinthiis vescendam, nos micam panis cœnæ ludibrium. Illi cibi potionisque varietatem atque copiam adhibuerunt, sic ut saturi discederent: nos famelici domum revertimur. Ut mensam nimium lautam, ita nimis tenuem et jejunam Paulus carpit. Modus optimus est. Neque majores nostri, qui ante natum Christum vixerunt, ea inedia, quæ νηστεία potius est quam δεῖπνον aut ἄριστον usi sunt; siquidem agnum edebant. Non est credibile, Christum velle curare tam sedulo Hierosolymis cœnam in triclinio parari, et tot convivas invitare, nihilque apponere præter minutissimam partem panis et vini tres guttulas. Tuum est, qui tot egregia opuscula in lucem aspectumque hominum protulisti, ut erroris et religionis labes abstergas aut penitus tollas. Quod præclare fecisti explanans epistolas illas, quibus Paulus affatus est Corinthios; in quibus pontificum arrogantiam, fulminaque pontificiorum, et inusitatam Calvinianorum ἀποσυναγωγίαν καὶ ἀφορισμὸν castigasti.

Ut in cœnæ mensæque modo ac ratione tua sententia vel stem vel cadam, ita de die quo Christus cum suis cœnam capiebat a Beza et aliis plurimum dissentio. Nam illi cœnam assignant 14° diei, ego 13°, in qua vetus Pascha non erat immolandum ex lege. Ergo novum Pascha instituit Christus in suæ mortis recordationem, nec aliud illa nocte cum suis edit. De istis rebus scripsi aliquot paginas, quas excudi vellem, sed tuam antea sententiam interponi summe cuperem. Neque hic in Anglia absque pontificum licentia quicquam imprimitur. Quare rogo te, si fieri possit, ut rescribas certioremque facias quid mihi potissimum faciendum censeas. Vale. Ex aula reginali, 5 Idus Augusti, 1573.

Tui amantissimus,

ROBERTUS COOCHEUS.

INSCRIPTIO.
Ornatissimo literis et pietate viro
D. D. Rodolpho Gualtero, Ti-
gurino, tradantur hœ.

EPISTOLA XCVI.

RODOLPHUS GUALTERUS AD EDWINUM SANDU

REDDITÆ sunt mihi, pater in Christo reverende, lite
mihi multis nominibus gratissimæ fuerunt: cum quod
essent, tum quod meas lucubrationes in Pauli ad C
tibi probari significarunt, cujus judicio ego semper
et aliorum symmystarum tuorum; qui cum se ide
tentur, aliorum sententias ego non multum moror,
scio, quam quod omnia illorum statuta atque co
quas utinam ego quidem probare possem! quod s
si illas cum scriptura per omnia convenire scirem.

[ZURICH LETTERS, II.]

sch
atq
comi
Prud
et stu

sub plausibili disciplinæ ecclesiasticæ titulo nescio quam εὐταξίαν, sine qua ecclesias consistere posse negant.   Sed ego vehementer metuo ne aristocratiam nobis pariant, quæ brevi in oligarchiam degeneret, et novi papatus sit initium.   Nam de solo presbyterio passim instituendo laborant: in quod adoptantur quidem ex communi cœtu viri boni et pii, sed ita ut decernendi potestas fere penes solos ministros sit, quorum sententia valeat et rata sit oportet, licet numero suffragiorum vincantur. Nuper Heidelbergæ sancitum est, ut nemo ad cœnam admittatur, qui non prius se pastori suo stiterit: neque illis sufficit Pauli regula monentis ut unusquisquam seipsum probet.   Non consenserunt in hoc decretum seniores ecclesiæ: nihilominus tamen illud totius presbyterii, imo totius ecclesiæ, nomine omnibus obtruditur.   Quid denique obstabit quominus summa rerum ad unum aliquem deveniat, qui reliquos pecunia et auctoritate vincit, et a cujus favore reliqui pendent? Sed et novæ tyrannidis specimen illic editum est non ita pridem, quod merito ter-rere debet omnes, qui ecclesiarum libertati consultum volunt.   Est illic Helvetius quidam, collegii Sandionysiani præfectus, quo neminem illic hactenus (absit invidia dicto) innocentius et sanctius vixisse omnes tes-tantur.   Verumtamen huic per sui presbyterii præconem Olevianus, qui pastorem illic agit, omnium seniorum nomine denunciavit, ne ad cœnam Domini accedat: causa additur, quod non absque animi sui of-fensione ipsum possit admittere.   Tulit is rem, ut par erat, indigne: quærit quid tanto supplicio dignum admiserit.   At illi nil respondent, nisi quod in sententia persistunt.   Offert ille supplices libellos illus-trissimo principi electori, ut is illos apertius loqui, et culpam, si quam admiserit, eloqui cogat.   At ne in hunc quidem usque diem aliquid ex illis extorqueri potuit.   Hæc est jam illic εὐταξία, hæc disciplina. Quare video nobis serio vigilandum esse, ne ex Romanæ Hydræ vix domitæ vulneribus nova capita pullulent.   Sed plura de his alias, &c.

[Desunt cetera.]

EPISTOLA XCVII.

JOHANNES STURMIUS AD REGINAM ELIZABETHAM.

Serenissima Regina, clementissima Domina : Christophorus Lant-dius toto imperio Germaniæ nobilissimus vir est, atque gratus e acceptus prope omnibus principibus, in consiliis palatinorum um annos quadraginta amplius diligenter et assidue exercitatus. s est præterea et pius vir, et puræ religionis cupidissimus simul iosissimus.

Is a me non excitatus, sed sua sponte motus atque affectus erga majestatem vestram, cupit unus esse in numero stipendiariorum vestræ majestatis. Princeps Suffolciana viri hujus novit virtutes atque honestatem; hospitalitatem etiam atque modestiam moderationemque cumprimis. Quoniam ego maxime illum appositum esse scio negotiis atque servitiis majestatis vestræ, non vereor ipsum et commendare et laudare. Ejus opera atque auctoritate, quæ in imperio et publice et privatim tractantur, facile possumus recognoscere; aditum etiam habere ad omnes principes.

Si ultro non peteret stipendium a majestate vestra, tamen ego illum conciliandum atque comparandum putarem: petit autem, quemadmodum majestas vestra iis literis intelliget, quas ad me hac de re scripsit. Ego quodcunque majestas vestra de hoc nobili et germano homine statuit, Deum precor ut felix faustumque sit majestati vestræ et regno Angliæ. Dat. Arg. 16 Nov. 1573.

Serenissimæ majestatis vestræ

Perpetuus et fidelis

Famulus et servus,

JOHAN. STURMIUS.

EPISTOLA XCVIII.

HENRICUS BULLINGERUS AD EDWINUM SANDUM.

S. Pro epistola illa tua, præterito anno Londini scripta, Augusti 15, et omni humanitate amoreque et studio erga me tuo singulari referta, gratias tibi domino meo honorando et fratri carissimo quas possum omnino maximas ago. Nec est quod de meo pari in te amore et studio addubites. Pergamus autem sic in Domino amare mutuum, quando constat caritate fraterna singularique fratrum conjunctione delectari Deum singulariter, ecclesiæque Dei nihil esse utilius, nihil necessarium magis. Cernimus enim hodie dissociatione ac discordia docentium nihil magis disturbare[1] ecclesias Dei. Hodie enim Lutheranorum quorundam morosorum insolentium et pertinacium dissociatio, qua avulsi a nobis dogmata quædam sua parum solida tuentur et omnibus obtrudere conantur, facit ut multæ per Germaniam ecclesiæ quid sequantur ignorent, interim et cursus evangelii apud multos impediatur, et dissidia foveantur augeanturque, suaviter interim in sinum ridentibus communibus nostris adversariis. Utinam non cogamur videre aliquando odiosa

[1 MS. *disturbari*.]

hæc certamina multos secum abstrahere in ruinam! Unde non vulgariter animo meo dolet, quod ex tuis intelligo literis, in Anglia quoque
gliscere hujusmodi certamina. Astu Sathanæ hæc proculdubio fiunt,
qui cum videt exterorum minis, vi, et persequutionibus ecclesias se non
posse subvertere, ad alias se artes convertit, et domesticis odiis et fratrum mutuis vulneribus ecclesiæ perniciem molitur. Dominus dejiciat
Sathanam sub pedes sanctorum, et componat perniciosa illa certamina
sancta pace et concordia.

Quos tu tamen mihi describis juvenes, oratores novos, qui totam
ecclesiæ vestræ faciem immutare, et novam ei formam inducere sata-
gunt, projectis etiam bonis ecclesiasticis omnibus, mihi quidem imitari
videntur Romanos illos tribunos seditiosos, qui agrariis legibus publica
largiebantur, ut sibi privatim opes et honores compararent; hoc est,
ut nobis ejectis ipsi succedant, etc. Sed et ecclesiam illi erigere conantur, quam nunquam eo quo volunt extollent, neque si erexerint
eandem conservare poterunt. Capita extractionis illorum a te delineata
vidi: de quibus quid sentiendum sit dudum est significatum. Propositionem primam, civilem magistratum nullum habere jus in res ec-
clesiasticas; item secundam, ecclesiam nullam admittere gubernationem
quam presbyterorum vel presbyterii; duas, inquam, has communes habent
cum papistis, qui et ipsi magistratum a gubernatione ecclesiæ deturbant,
et se ipsos solos substituunt. Quorum opinionem confutavi in refuta-
tione bullæ pontificis Romani, et in defensione mea reginæ Angliæ et
inclyti regni, etc., quam ante biennium ad vos misi. Utinam vero nulla
sit in presbyterii hujus auctoribus libido dominandi! Imo maximopere
cavendum arbitror, ne summa potestas sit apud hoc presbyterium, multo
minus ut sit peculiaris magistratus. Forte presbyterium hoc in una et
altera ecclesia locum habet, in omnibus non habet: de quo multa dici
possent. Sed et tempus multa revelabit, quæ nunc sunt occulta.

De nominibus et auctoritate episcoporum, de electione item ministrorum, Gualterus noster fuse scripsit ad reverendum dominum Eliensem,
D. Coxum. Ab eo requiras, si libet, licet.

Bonorum ecclesiasticorum abusum sentimus esse tollendum, ne serviant idolis et superstitioni. Potest autem eorum usus esse bonus, si
applicentur scholis, ministerio, ædificiis ecclesiæ, et sustentationi paupe-
rum: de quo disserui in decadibus nostris, sub finem prope operis.
Ecclesia non potest plane carere facultatibus. Eæ si non fuerint in
promptu, certe a fidelibus colligendæ sunt. Quæ ergo vesania paratas
abjicere, aut aliis cedere quibus non debentur, et novas de novo cum
fidelium magno incommodo colligere! Non video quo homines illi respi-
ciant. Metuo ne aliud quærant quam videri velint, etc. Si autem nemo
in suo grege concionari debet nisi solus pastor, quid fiet si hic ægrotet,
aut per alia negotia concionari non possit? An interea cœtibus eccle-

siasticis carebit ecclesia? Scio Chrysostomum durius excepisse Epiphanium, quod in aliena ecclesia sibi imperium usurpasset: sed longe alia est ea ratio. Apud nos evangelium tam late propagatum non fuisset, si pastores tantum in suis prædicassent ecclesiis.

Nolim sane ego quoque invitis parentibus papistarum infantes baptizari. Qui vero oblatos ecclesiæ rejiciunt, similes videntur esse apostolis, qui prohibebant infantulos offerri Christo Domino; quos ille acerbius increpavit.

De judicialibus Mosis legibus disserui in meis decadibus, Dec. III. Sermone 7 et 8. Videntur sane homines illi rerum novarum supra modum esse cupidi. Cuperem homines illos longius quam ad suas affectiones respicere. Dominus concedat ipsis spiritum pacis et quietis!

Pannus huc nullus est allatus. Dixit quidem Froschoverus noster, se aliquid audivisse de panno, sed nullum sibi fuisse datum; nec ullus huc a quoquam est missus. Nihilominus humanitati tuæ gratias ago maximas pro illa liberali tua beneficentia. Forte hæsit alicubi in itinere. Ego vero te rogo, ne posthac ullos propter me ejusmodi sumptus facias. Vidi literas a novatoribus illis scriptas, in quibus narratur episcopos doctis mittere munera, ut eos in suas attrahant partes. Mox quoque illi dicerent nos esse Balaamos. Scio sane bonos viros ab amicis suis honoraria et amica accipere posse munera. Verum scis quid Paulum moverit, quominus stipendium debitum sibi noluerit accipere. *Omnia*, inquit, *mihi licent, at non omnia conducunt.* Malo homines ad maledicendum calumniandumque expeditos ne modicam quidem nobis nostroque ministerio detrahendi habere occasionem. Hæc mea qualiacunque boni consulas rogo, et me tui amantissimum vicissim amare pergas oro. Dominus benedicat tibi, et servet te ab omni malo! Tiguri, 10 Martii, 1574. Obsecro reverendum dominum D. Hornum, episcopum Vintoniensem, meo nomine salutare digneris, eique et uxori ejus felicia imprecari omnia, et excusare quod peculiariter ei nunc non scribam. Scribam alias cum plus habuero otii.

Reverentiæ tuæ deditissimus,

H. BULLINGERUS.

EPISTOLA XCIX.

HENRICUS BULLINGERUS AD EDMUNDUM GRINDALLUM.

S.   REVERENDE et summa mihi observantia colende domine : Literas tuas ultima Julii superioris anni a te datas mense Octobri accepi.   Quo autem plus me oblectarunt, cupide diu exspectatæ, eo gravius contristarunt quod ex iis intelligerem, certamina apud vos restaurari a quibusdam turbulentis hominibus, et quidem junioribus, qui totam ecclesiæ faciem, non sine magnis laboribus ab optimis viris comparatam, expungere, et novam ad ipsorum placitum compositam inducere conantur.   Habentur ubique terrarum hujusmodi male feriati homines, qui cum in effectum producere non possunt quod instituunt, conatibus interim illis suis perturbant et vexant multos bonos, simpliciores offendunt, papistas in spem erigunt, sed et cursum evangelii vehementer impediunt.   Conquestus est hac ipsa de re anno superiore reverendus dominus Eliensis et apud Gualterum nostrum, et apud me reverendus D. Londoniensis.   Idcirco respondit ille ad quæstiones ejus aliquot, sicuti et ego paucula quædam nunc ad proposita hujus respondi.   Vexamur et per Germaniam ab hujusmodi ingeniis. Nec video hac in re consilium salubrius, quam si ad Dominum conversi sedulo precemur, ut turbulenta et ad novationes prompta hujusmodi ingenia gratia sua coerceat, et ecclesias in pace conservet : deinde, ut amicis collationibus vel colloquiis reducantur in viam; qui vero pertinaces insolentesque non sustinent reduci, ita suis depingantur coloribus, quo minus auctoritatem habeant apud cordatos, et ita noceant minus.   Sed non est quod ego vos in hac re instituam, cum ex diutino usu, et felici hactenus ecclesiarum gubernatione, quæ hic facienda aut omittenda sint, dudum didiceritis.

Sunt in Germania, qui se Lutheranos esse gloriantur, at revera rixatores, conviciatores, ac calumniatores sunt impudentissimi.   Hi non desinunt oppugnare ecclesias nostras, nos, et nostram doctrinam de cœna Domini, quam prægravant odiose apud ipsos Zuingliano nomine.   Et nunc de novo evulgarunt in nos et Heidelbergenses libros, quos si dissimulavissemus, videri jure poteramus proditores et doctrinæ sanæ ac sanctarum nostrarum ecclesiarum.   Partiti itaque sumus laborem vel molestiam respondendi, dilectus meus gener D. Josias Simlerus, theologiæ in nostra schola professor, et ego ; ut ille Latine et paulo copiosius adversariorum argumentis responderet, ego Germanice et breviter et populariter pro captu vulgi. Utriusque libri exempla mitto, et rogo ut benigne a me tui amantissimo accipias, et per occasionem legas.   Scis ardore et studio vincendi et altercandi Brentium (cum quo, dum viveret, multa et longa mihi fuit disputatio,

id quod libelli editi testantur) immiscuisse negotio cœnæ multos fidei
articulos, de quibus jam discipuli ejus altercari, eosque obscurare et in
dubium vertere pleraque non desinunt: ut, de una persona et duabus Christi
naturis, de omnipotentia et omnipræsentia (ut aiunt) humanitatis Christi,
de ascensione ad cœlos et cœlo, etc.   Coacti ergo sumus ad ea respondere
capita.   At tuum aliorumque virorum piorum erit de his nostris respon-
sionibus judicare.   Dominum oro ut multo cum fructu ecclesiæ de his
disseruerimus.   Respondimus potissimum ad res, non ad personas, absti-
nentes a conviciis, ne illis redderemur similes.   Alioquin in nostris ecclesiis
pacata sunt per Dei gratiam omnia.   Vident adversarii potiorem partem
populi passim nostræ (quæ Christi est) doctrinæ et ecclesiæ se adjungere;
furiunt ergo, etc.   Dominus coerceat eos!   Ceterum a sociis et vicinis
papæ adhærentibus indesinenter vexamur, instinctu pontificis, cui vehementer dolet doctrinam Christi in vicinia Italiæ prædicari, et hanc plus
quam velit serpere.   Studet ergo nos inter nos ipsos committere bello.
Dominus servet nos a malo!

Qui ex Italia veniunt dicunt Venetos incertos esse de pace cum Turcarum principe facta, ideoque classem misisse in Cretam, et armari de
novo naves et militem conscribi.   Legatum interim habent apud Turcam,
qui ultimo nunciavit se non omnino desperare; prodesse vero reipublicæ
Venetæ, si nihilominus rebus suis consulant, ne imparati, siquidem spes
pacis diffluat, opprimantur.   Præterea certum est nullum unquam Turcarum principem terra marique instructiorem fuisse quam hunc Selymum,
ac certum esse quod verno hoc tempore omnes copias sit producturus in
Hispanum et socios.   Ideo Melitenses ex tota Germania Meliten vel Mal-
tam festinanter contendunt.   Ita se instruunt in Apulia, Calabria et
Sicilia, etc.   Quid futurum sit, novit Dominus, quem ex animo oro ut
nostri misereatur.   Sed et in Germania sub Moguntia et supra Coloniam
conscribitur equestris et pedestris exercitus, qui sub ducibus Christophoro Palatino et Ludovico Nassovio dicitur ducendus in Lotharingiam,
alii arbitrantur in Belgium, sunt qui dicunt in Galliam.   Id tamen incertum est adhuc.

Dux Andium per Germaniam transivit in Poloniam.   In itinere ubique ei exprobratum D. Admiralii et fidelium parricidium.   A Polonis
exceptus est magnifice.   Præter hæc nihil præterea ea de re habemus.
Et nunc rumor increbrescit, regem Galliæ petiturum a suis fœderatis Helvetiis duas legiones.   Nihil tamen hic certi adfirmavero.   Rogo excellentiam tuam ut hæc digneris habere communia, si ita placet, cum D.
Pilkintono Dunelmensi, et me excusare quod privatim singulares ad
ipsum literas non scribo.   Cupio illum salvere et valere in Domino.   Certe
nisi scirem summam inter vos esse conjunctionem, utcunque plurimis oppressus sim negotiis, aliquid ad ipsum dedissem literarum.   Habet is etiam
his adjectum exemplum responsionis D. Josiæ Simleri de præsentia, etc.

Duo enim exempla jussi Froschoverum nostrum ad te mittere, ut alterum des Dunelmensi. Germanicum exemplum solum tibi misi, nullum Dunelmensi, quod sciam ipsum Germanica scripta legere non posse.

Sub finem literarum tuarum mentionem facis mnemosyni mittendi. Ego vero rogo ne ullos propter me sumptus facias. Quæ hactenus in te contuli et confero, sponte confero, non propter ulla munera. Interim non ingrata sunt fratrum amicorumque mnemosyna, amicitiæ mutuæ testimonia, sicuti ego hactenus apud te deposui labores nostros, in testimonium quod plane tuus sum, et in omnibus quibus possum tibi inservire gratificarique cupio, et quod sincere te diligo. Satis mihi est mutua tua amicitia, et si aliquando per otium scripseris, quod soles. Scio item amicos missis muneribus invicem contendere, et ejusmodi recipi posse a bonis: verum vidi literas novatorum vestrorum, quibus significant episcopos Angliæ doctis munera mittere, ut eos in suas partes reflectant. Hi videlicet pro sua virulentia possent et nos et ministerium nostrum infamare. Unde cum apostolo dico, *Omnia mihi licent, sed non omnia conducunt.* Potuisset ipse stipendium accipere, sed non accepit propter adversarios. Nihilominus gratias tibi pro illa beneficentia ago quam possum maximas. Sed et pro carmine mihi misso, de liberata per reginam Angliæ serenissimam a civili bello Scotia, ago humanitati tuæ gratias. Perplacuit illud. Dominum oro ut reginam confirmet atque conservet. Tibi quoque benedicat et omnibus tuis, et servet a malo. Tiguri, 10 Martii, anno Domini 1574. Julium nostrum tibi commendo.

Reverentiæ tuæ addictissimus,

HENR. BULLINGERUS.

EPISTOLA C.

RODOLPHUS GUALTERUS AD RICARDUM COXUM.

Quas 12 Junii mensis ad me literas dedisti, pater in Christo reverende, ego sub initium Octobris demum per nostros ex Francofordianis nundinis reversos accepi. Video autem te de illis prioribus tunc solicitum fuisse, quas vere ineunte miseras, una cum articulis quos adversarii vestri propugnant. At spero te nunc omni ista solicitudine liberatum esse per meas literas, quas Augusto mense scripsi, et quibus meum de illis articulis judicium, pro gratia mihi a Domino concessa, exposui. Mirarer ego istorum hominum importunitatem, nisi scirem hoc esse ecclesiæ statum, quod aut

hostes habet apertos, qui veritatis doctrinam vi et armis opprimere conantur, aut falsorum fratrum insidiis petitur, aut quæstionibus supervacaneis
sive inutilibus exercetur per eos, qui cum de summa doctrinæ recte sentiant, propter externam cæremoniam sive ritus turbas movent non neces-
sarias. Passi estis vos jampridem sævissimorum hostium vim, qui multorum innoxio martyrum sanguine rabiem suam apud nos satiare conati
sunt : et eodem tempore falsorum quoque fratrum insidiæ detectæ sunt :
quæ omnia cum vos per Dei gratiam egregia virtute et animi constantia
superaveritis, spero hic quoque Angliæ vestræ miserturum Deum, ut
tandem pace optata frui, et ad ecclesiæ ædificationem vestras operas unanimi consensu conferre possitis. Quod ut magno studio faciamus omnes,
quos Dominus suæ ecclesiæ ministros esse voluit, plusquam necessarium
mihi esse videtur. Etenim satis constat Romanum antichristum omnes
suas vires atque studia ad hoc conferre, ut Tridentini concilii executio
tandem suum effectum habeat. Non dissimulant hoc vicini vestri, qui
etsi per antiqua nostræ gentis fœdera et publicæ pacis conditiones, quibus
cavetur ne quis propter religionis diversitatem alteri molestus sit, im-
pediantur, multa tamen movent, ex quibus facile apparet illos occasionem
tumultuandi quærere.

De Hispaniæ et Galliæ regibus nihil pacificum sperari potest : quando
hic quidem neque Galliæ suæ ruinis, neque tot infandis fortissimorum
virorum cædibus movetur, ut pacem inter suos stabilem faciat : ille
vero florentissimam sibique prius quæstuosissimam Belgici provinciam
bello intestino potius eversam videre vult, quam illic Christo et evangelio ejus locum darę. Sed et Germaniæ episcopi, nescio quibus promissis confirmati, non parum ferociunt ; et qui inter principes papisticos
hactenus moderatius agebant, nunc ipsi quoque hostiliter fremere, et in
Christi cultores, quos in suis terris dispersos habent, severius animad-
vertere incipiunt. Omnibus autem istis optatissimum accidit, quod ad
Polonici regni solium evectus est Galli regis frater, qui a pueris sanctorum sanguini assuevit. Neque mihi illius causam Romanus pontifex
tanto studio acturus fuisse videtur, nisi ejus opera in vexandis Germaniæ
vicinæ ecclesiis uti vellet ; quo facilius hæ aliis etiam in locis debellari
possint. Quæ pericula cum in verbis nostris versentur, nos illis excitari
convenit, ut conjunctis animis Christi causam agamus, neque foveamus
turbarum auctores, quos vel ambitiosa emulatio vel etiam inscitia fascinat,
ut quæ ad communis ecclesiæ conservationem faciunt videre non possint.
Volunt illi antiquum illud presbyterium (ut tu scribis), quod in primitiva
ecclesia fuit, revocare : sed utinam de revocanda fidei simplicitate et
morum integritate, quæ olim floruit, cogitarent, neque rempublicam inva-
derent, cujus vetera jura atque formam non mutat Christus ! Senatu pro-
prio olim opus habuit ecclesia, quando sub ethnicis principibus fuit, qui
christianam religionem et huic connexam morum disciplinam non modo

negligebant, verum etiam persequebantur. Quid vero istud ad eos, quibus
Deus (sicuti per Esaiam pollicitus est) reges dedit nutritios et reginas
nutrices, qui denique magistratus habent erga religionem bene affectos, qui
morum disciplinam majori cum auctoritate et proinde fructu quoque ube-
riore instituere atque tueri possunt, quam si illi in singulis ecclesiis decem
presbyteria coustituant? At principes (inquiunt illi) non semper faciunt
officium. Fateor: num vero illis propterea licet novum magistratum instituere? Non faciebat officium Saul: at non ideo senatum novum
elegit Samuel: imo ne David quidem, qui quamvis se a Deo in regem
unctum esse sciret, noluit tamen aliquid movere in republica, sed exspec-
tavit tempus illud, quo Deo placuit tyrannum e medio tollere, et regni
faciem mutare. Hoc ipsum de omnibus prophetis dici potest, quos sub
malis aut saltem negligentissimis regibus nihil hujus unquam tentavisse
legimus.

Vehementer metuo ne sub presbyterio oligarchiæ affectatio lateat, quæ
tandem in monarchiam, imo in apertam tyrannidem, degeneret. Neque hoc frustra metuo. Novi enim (ut unum e multis attingam) urbem
non obscuram, in qua post introductam illam disciplinæ formam intra
triennii spatium tyrannidis exempla sunt edita, quorum Romanenses pu-
deret. Etenim virum optimum et spectatæ pietatis anno superiori per sui
presbyterii ministrum publicum monuerunt, ne ad cœnam Domini ac-
cederet, eo quod ipsum sine gravi suo scandalo admittere non possint.
Admiratus ille edictum hoc inexspectatum convenit Areopagitas illos, et
"quidnam admisisset?" quæsivit. Tum illi tergiversari et moras nectere,
causasque ex causis texere cœperunt. At ille bene sibi conscius ab ejus
loci principe per supplices libellos postulavit, ut sua auctoritate illos
cogeret rem edicere. Sed ne princeps quidem hoc a tantis disciplinæ
ecclesiasticæ vindicibus impetrare potuit. Et cum tandem undique ur-
gerentur, ad mendacia conversi, principi suaserunt illum sua sponte a
cœnæ usu abstinuisse, nunc vero suæ voluntariæ emansionis causas ab
ipsis velle extorquere. Facta sunt alia hujus generis multa, quæ commemorare longum foret. Cum vero hæc specimina edant, qui nondum
in plenam hujus novi regni possessionem pervenerunt, quid illos facturos
putabimus, si merum imperium obtineant? Vidit ista olim nostræ gentis
apostolus Zuinglius, qui, cum Œcolampadius bono et sancto zelo excom-
municationem in ecclesiam reducere vellet, vehementer sese opposuit.
Œcolampadius vero, cum ejus admonitionibus non pareret, et Basileæ quod
volebat obtinuisset, non multo post telam vix inchoatam relinquere coactus
fuit, et re ipsa didicit se rem tentasse quæ plus incommodi quam commodi
ferat. Non ergo possum eos improbare, qui sese istorum consiliis oppo-
nunt, qui hodie causam hanc magna cum animorum contentione agunt.
Ne tamen hi habeant plausibilem calumniandi occasionem, necesse fuerit
disciplinam morum vere christianam ex summi magistratus auctoritate

instituere, qua et ecclesiarum ministri, si dissolutius vivant, et nobilium licentia nimia et vulgi mores corrupti coerceantur.   Nam si id fiat, non habebunt illi quod queritentur, nisi apertam imperii assectationem profiteri velint.

Quoad me, mihi quidem molestum fuit me in arenam 'protrahi apud eos, quos ut amicos intimos et ut dominos mihi observandos semper amavi et colui.   At quia serenissimæ reginæ edicto hanc quidvis vulgandi licentiam repressam esse audio, non multum me movet porro istorum temeritas.   Quin video mihi aliunde graviora certamina exoritura esse, nisi Deus hoc scandalum removerit.   Sunt enim in Germania et alio quodam in loco, qui, nisi quam ipsi fabricarunt disciplinæ formulam, ubique locorum recipiatur, Christi regnum consistere posse negent.   Contineo me adhuc, ne ipse pugnam cœpisse dicar.   Sin illi classicum cecinerint, veritati[1] doctrinæ et ecclesiarum libertati deesse non potero, et spero non defuturos qui mecum hanc causam tueantur.

Hæc, pater in Christo reverende, modo tuæ amplitudini respondere libuit, quem rogo ut omnia boni consulas.   Filium Octobri mense per literas monui, ut te frequentius invisat, aut suis literis salutet.   Nescio tamen an adhuc illic sit, vel num in Daniam (sicuti nundinis autumnalibus jusseram) hoc vere jam trajecerit.   Quod si adhuc in Anglia moratur, scio illum tibi et aliis amicis atque dominis mihi perpetuo honorandis commendatissimum fore.   Volo tamen illum ante hiemem futuram ad me domum reverti, nisi conditio aliqua ei obtingat quæ ipsum detineat; de qua re ad veterem amicum D. Parkhurstum Nordovicensem scripsi.   Sed oblitus eram scribere ubiquarios theologos magis quam unquam alias jam insanire, adeoque se ipsos effreni maledicentia et conviciandi libidine superare.   Nec enim iis contenti quæ olim Lutherus adversus præceptores nostros immodestius scripsit, modo nos omnes Arianos et Mahomete deteriores esse clamant.   Quis illos spiritus agat scio; sed ad quem finem tendant, nolo nunc dicere.   Faxit Deus, ut mea opinione fallar.   Hunc ipsum ex animo precor, ut te, pater reverende, servet et tuis tuorumque collegarum laboribus benedicat.   Amen. Tiguri, 16 Martii, anno Christi nati 1574.

Tuæ amplitudinis observantissimus,

RODOLPHUS GUALTERUS.

INSCRIPTIO.

D. Ricardo Coxo, episcopo Eliensi
      in Anglia.

[[1] MS. *veritatis.*]

EPISTOLA CI.

ANTONIUS CORRANUS AD HENRICUM BULLINGERUM.

EGO ex eorum numero sum, vir eruditissime, qui tuis scriptis adjuti puriorem christianæ doctrinæ cognitionem acceperunt. Contigit enim mihi ante viginti annos, divini numinis providentia, idonea occasio evolvendi tuos libros, etiam ab ipsis inquisitoribus Hispanicis subministratos : unde quia uberrimos fructus me percepisse sentio, tibi gratias agere, quando referre nequeo, ex debito gratitudinis officio cogor. Cujas sim, et ubi terrarum agam, filius Rodolphi Gualteri, qui has perfert, verbis exponet. Ei etiam dedi libellum quendam, quem hisce diebus in lucem emittere optabam ; sed negligentia typographi, Latini sermonis ignari, uti sunt plerique omnes qui hic agunt, accidit ut tam multa obreperint errata, ut sane me pudeat lucubratiunculam hanc, alioquin nimis jejunam, tam negligenter excusam viris doctis obtrudere. Sed quia animus non est in hoc scripto ostentare quantum in me sit eruditionis (est enim parum aut nihil), sed quid sentiam de christiana pietate, ad diluendas quorundam calumnias, ecclesiis evangelicis ostendere ; idcirco optarem ut alius aliquis typographus dialogum hunc typis exprimeret, et exemplaria ad summum trecenta, quæ hic depravatissime excusa sunt, supprimerentur. Articuli religionis, quos in calce libelli posui, ex vestra confessione descripti sunt, ad confutandam illorum malignitatem, qui ob privatum odium, quo me prosequuntur, hos eosdem articulos manu scriptos, et ad meam ostendendam innocentiam oblatos, summa cum impudentia damnarunt, existimantes fœtum fuisse meum. Specimen hujus malignitatis perspicies in folio quodam hic Latino et Anglicano sermone excuso cum censuris cujusdam Aristarchi: ut ex unguibus, uti dici solet, possis dignoscere leonem. Folium tibi tradet ipse junior Gualterus, multoque plura narrabit de quorundam præpostera erga me agendi ratione. Interea, pastor vigilantissime, precor te, ut me habeas in eorum numero, quos tuis laboribus et vigiliis ad Christi cognitionem adduxisti; et si quid est quod tibi minus arrideat in hoc libello, pro tuo arbitrio insigni prudentia corrigas, et correctum typis tradi jubeas. Quod si feceris, majorem in modum me meumque obsequium tibi perpetuo devincies. Vale. Londino, nonis Julii, anno D. 1574.

Tui amantissimus et observantissimus,

ANTONIUS CORRANUS.

INSCRIPTIO.

Eruditissimo viro D. Henrico Bullin-
  gero, ecclesiæ Tigurinæ pastori
  vigilantissimo, D. ac patri meo
  unice colendo. Tiguri.

EPISTOLA CII.

GULIELMUS COLUS AD RODOLPHUM GUALTERUM.

Filius tuus, ut video, doctissime vir, accinxit se ad reditum, Simleri literis de voluntate tua certissime persuasus. Quamvis erat mihi multis nominibus longe carissimus, non solum tuis, sed etiam episcopi Nordovicensis literis non semel commendatus; tamen, ut ingenue fatear, ita vixit apud nos hoc tantillo tempore, ut jure suo, licet uterque vestrum non fuisset mihi notus, nec scripsisset quicquam, debeat jam discedens cum aliquo amoris mei indicio ad suos proficisci. Atque doleo eum hinc tam cito avocari, cum per temporis brevitatem omnino mihi non licuerit illum ornare ut volebam. Nam quia spes erat eum apud nos victurum diutius, fateor me pro suo merito eum non tractasse. Et tamen quoties ad me venit, non potuit mihi non esse hospes gratissimus. Illo enim praesente, in mentem mihi statim venit immensa beneficiorum multitudo, quibus nos Anglos Tiguri cumulastis exules. Si scire vis, quid de filio tuo ipse censeam, hoc habeo quod de illo affirmare audeam, esse juvenem probum moribus, religione pium, in bonis literis progressus fecisse non mediocres. Et si ipse hoc tacerem, nostra testaretur academia verum esse quod scribo. Nam tametsi natione est Helvetius, erit tamen etiam Tiguri, longissimo loci intervallo remotus a nobis, in artibus magister Oxoniensis, uno omnium consensu ad hunc apud nos dignitatis gradum evectus.

Dedit mihi Ds. Humphredus D. Simleri librum, ab illo editum adversus Brentianos. Est quod gratias tibi habeam propterea immortales, quia eum ad me miseris; illi, quia ecclesiam tueatur et defendat; utrique vestrum, quia non patiamini hostem pro libidine grassari in ovile. Deus vos servet incolumes, et vitam largiatur longissimam ad communem piorum omnium utilitatem! Salutes, quaeso, reverendum illum senem D. Bullingerum, duos praeterea mihi multis de causis omni observantia honorandos, Lavaterum, Simlerum, et Froschoverum typographum, et illius correctorem, familiariter mihi notum Argentinae apud Petrum Martyrem, meum Julium plurima salute impertiaris. Si qua ratione putas me tibi posse vel tuorum cuipiam usui esse hic in Britannia, invenies me ad quidvis esse paratissimum. Oxonii in collegio Corporis Christi pridie calendas Augusti, 1574.

Tuus, quoad vixero,

GULIELMUS COLUS.

INSCRIPTIO.

Doctissimo viro domino Rodolpho Gualtero, fidelissimo ecclesiae Tigurinae pastori, amico suo reverendo hae literae dentur. Tiguri.

EPISTOLA CIII.

REGINA ELIZABETHA AD JOHANNEM STURMIUM.

ELIZABETH R.

ELIZABETHA Dei gratia Angliæ, Franciæ et Hiberniæ Regina, etc.
Johanni Sturmio salutem.

Literas tuas, datas Northemio tertio Augusti, decimo octavo ejusdem
mensis die accepimus. Ex quibus intelleximus quantum res nostræ tibi
sint curæ, et quantum optes pacem quietemque inter christianos principes,
et eorum regna constabiliri.   Neque sane possumus non vehementer
probare eorum studia, qui legationibus, aut aliis quibuscunque bonis
rationibus[1], ut coeant et sopiantur in vicinis quibusque, præsertim quæ
Christum profitentur, regionibus discordiæ. Est enim hoc nobile vicini
principis et christiani officium. Quia tam paucas abs te literas accepimus, putamus non omnes ad nos fuisse perlatas.   Et ad cetera
mandavimus Thomæ Smitho, secretario nostro, ut particulatim tibi sententiam nostram rescribat.

Bene vale. E civitate nostra Thermarum 23 Augusti, 1574, regni
autem nostri decimo sexto.

T. SMITH.

EPISTOLA CIV.

RODOLPHUS GUALTERUS AD RICARDUM COXUM.

S. SPERO, pater in Christo reverende, fideliter tibi redditas esse postre-
mas meas literas, quas mense Martio dedi. Ego tuas, quas mense Februario
scripsisti, per nostros ex nundinis vernalibus redeuntes accepi. Non puto
autem prolixiori et operosa recensione mihi opus esse, cum quid de turbulentis istis rerum novatoribus sentiam in meis illis literis exposuerim,
adeoque tuas prævenerim quibus tu de illis non absque causa quereris. Et
sane ut in mea sententia persistam, exempla quæ in Germania similes
novatores quotidie nova edunt, me vehementer confirmant. Video enim
illis hominibus nihil ambitiosius, nihil insolentius, nihil ineptius fingi
posse. Nam quum quotidie multa de ipsis fiant iniquissime, non tamen
eos pudet zelum Dei prætexere iis, quæ contra Dei verbum impie et mali-
tiose in Christi servos designant. Et quantum conjicere possim, jam
illorum pudet multos, qui prius illis ad hujus disciplinæ fabricam consilia
et arma sua ministrarunt. Et quis spiritus vestros illos agat, ex eo colligi

[1 Sic MS. Deest verbum.]

potest, quod tanto studio in hoc sunt, ut bene de ecclesia meritos ex
bonorum ecclesiasticorum possessione et administratione dejiciant, neque
interea vident quid futurum sit si hoc assequantur; ut nimirum illa in
aliorum manus deveniant, ex quibus postea nunquam extorqueri poterunt
necessaria doctrinæ subsidia.   Malunt quidem illa prorsus ab ecclesiis
alienari, quam ea in illorum potestate videre quos semel cœperunt odisse.
Sed est hoc proprium hominibus, ut præsentem felicitatem ferre non possint, et sibi ipsis sponte malum atque molestias accersant. Verumtamen
vestrum fuerit cum importunis illis animi mansuetudine et prudentia
contendere, ne quid gravioris periculi tandem ex hisce contentionibus
exoriatur; neve qui hostili adhuc sunt erga puriorem religionem animo,
occasionem inveniant id perficiendi quod diu quæsiverunt, etc.

[Cetera desunt.]

INSCRIPTIO.

Ex literis ad D. Coxum, Elien-
sem episcopum, datis 26 Aug.
1574.

EPISTOLA CV.

GULIELMUS BARLOUS AD JOSIAM SIMLERUM.

S. P. LITERÆ tuæ datæ 10 Martii, 1574, quæ primæ post acceptum
pannum ad manus meas pervenere, ejusque me fecerunt certiorem, quinto
demum kalendas Septembris, 1574, ad me sunt delatæ; in quibus mentio
etiam fit aliarum literarum mense Decembri scriptarum, quæ (quamvis
alius December jam præterierit) a me nondum sunt visæ: tu conjicito
cetera, quam fideles ac certi nostri sint tabellarii. Imo, ut ingenue dicam
quod sentiam, usque ad illum 28 Augusti diem non nihil dubitabam,
utrum accepisses pannum cum literis necne.   Longioris moræ causa erat
non minima, præter longinquitatem itineris (veniunt enim per Hamburgam),
quod non ita crebro fuerim Londini, neque Oxonii, sed in occidentali parte
Angliæ, ubi tandem istæ tuæ literæ mihi traditæ fuerunt: tribus septi-
manis, postquam accepissem has literas, profectus sum Oxonii Rodolphi
nostri Gualteri conveniendi causa, ut cum illo de toto hoc negotio agerem;
sed is jam tum præter opinionem meam, ac meo magno dolore, navem con-
scenderat una cum præstantissimo et clarissimo juvene D. Philippo, barone
ab Hohensaxen; quem officii causa in Anglia, si Deus voluisset, libentissime
salutassem. Vides ergo, mi Simlere, quam non fit mea negligentia, quod
hucusque tuis literis non responderim: neque alicui hoc negotii dederim,
ut pecunias meo nomine a D. Froschovero peteret. Scio etiam, ni valde
fallor, me disertis verbis ad te scripsisse, ne ullo modo pecuniam mitteres,

priusquam me fecisses certiorem, quid tibi de panno videretur, placeret necne ; ac tunc demum me curaturum, ut aliquem haberem Francofurti, qui
pecuniam hanc acciperet, eademque mihi quædam ibi coemeret : quod
satis erat ad te levandum omni illa cura et anxietate, qua te in ultimis
tuis literis datis 28 Augusti solicitum esse video. Ideoque hæc tibi
tam verbose exposui, ut curam tibi istam argentariam ex animo penitus
excutiam. Nam et proximas tuas literas non nihil pertimesco, ne et illæ
de hac re aliquid querelarum adferant : sed quamprimum hæ ad manus
tuas devenerint (quod quam celerrime cupio) tibi abunde satisfactum fore
plane confido.

Casus ille quem scribis Witebergensium me mire afficit ; quid sperem,
quidve metuam, incertum facit : equidem lugubrem fateor, ac etiam
florentissimæ academiæ quasi funus et exitium minitari. Hoc sane mihi
cum universo studiosorum grege condolendum puto : e contra tamen,
cum Witeberga urbs illa sit, quæ quondam veritatis assertores habuerit
fortissimos, quique magis Deum quam homines sunt reveriti ; eam in hac
re adhuc antiquum obtinere, hoc inquam ego illi cum omnibus piis congratulari debeo, atque Deum Opt. Maximum precari, ut viros hosce in
omni doctrinarum genere præstantissimos ad finem usque constantes reddat,
dona sua in illis augeat coronetque.

Statum nostræ ecclesiæ tibi diligentissime perscribam, Deo volente,
cum mihi ipsimet fuerit cognitus ; quod verissime adhuc non fit : quædam etenim sunt mysteria, quæ nondum valeo assequi. Londini profitentur duo theologi valde celebres, Gallus alter, alter Hispanus. Gallo
nomen est Villerius, homo imprimis doctus et pius : Hispano nomen
est Corranus ; doctus et facundus, sed an pietate sit cum Villerio con-
ferendus, homines quidam non mali multum ambigunt. Auctoritates
nonnullorum optime de ecclesia meritorum non nihil extenuare solet ;
Castalionem ubique admiratur, de cujus translatione bibliorum hæc ejus
est sententia : eum pessime quidem egisse interpretem, quod nihil minus
quam verbum verbo reddiderit ; sin autem de paraphrasi loquaris, inquit,
tunc omnes alios multis parasangis excellit Castalio. Scio etiam illum
a quodam mihi optime noto studiose quæsivisse, haberet necne dialogos
quosdam de Trinitate, Basileæ impressos, anonymi cujusdam, eorum
tamen auctor, inquit, putatur fuisse Castalio ; illos se valde cupere. Ego
illius lectioni unicæ interfui, in qua invectus est in nostri seculi homines,
quorum aliqui volebant dici Lutherani, alii Calviniani, etc. : sed neque
Calvinus pro nobis mortuus est, neque Lutherus ; sed nos salvati sumus,
inquit, sanguine occisi Agni pro peccatis mundi : cum in textu sit, ab
initio mundi. Ne tamen videar culicem percolare ac fortasse camelum
deglutire, hic finem faciam, quanquam sane camelo culicem esse metuo.
Utinam mansisset Compostellæ !

Dicas (quæso) Julio nostro, mihi admodum dolere quod illius votis

nequeam satisfacere; me non posse adhuc expiscari, quinam fuerint
D. Juelli exequitores, aut quomodo res suas reliquerit; neque mihi
homini ignoto facile dari accessum ad comitem Bedfordiæ, ut causam
illius apud eum agere possim: quamvis tamen literas, quas Julius
mihi perferendas dedit, secretario illius tradiderim, qui mihi pollicitus
est se illas summopere domino suo commendaturum.   Te obnixe oro,
ut meo nomine officiose salutes reverendissimos patres dominum Bullingerum, D. Gualterum, hospitem meum humanissimum D. Wickium,
D. Lavaterum, D. Stuccium, D. Henricum Bullingerum juniorem,
D. Lemannum, D. Hallerum, D. Jacobum Frisium, D. Gualterum juniorem, Julium, reliquosque omnes. Libellos quosdam in Anglia impressos, non tamen ita magni momenti, statueram tibi mittere optimoque
viro D. Lavatero aliisque per manus Gualteri nostri: illumque plane
onerassem mandatis, si illius discessus (quod ob mea negotia in occidentali parte Angliæ fieri non potuit) mihi cognitus fuisset.   Novarum
rerum nihil habemus, si novum non sit lupum auribus tenere, aut anguem
sinu alere, quæ apud nos desiere esse nova: nam adhuc apud nos detine-
tur regina aquilonis, pestis Britanniæ, princeps tenebrarum sub forma lupæ.
Quod ad pecuniam attinet, scripsi D. Froscovero.   Sed longior sum quam
vellem, et vereor ne etiam tibi sim molestus; quod tamen nullo modo credam, si tu mihi epistolam longiorem remiseris: literæ etenim tuæ mihi
gratæ admodum sunt et jucundæ.   Maneo ut plurimum apud affinem
mihi carissimum, D. Guil. Deium, præpositum collegii regii Etonensis,
prope Windesoram, viginti milliaribus Londino; ubi sæpiuscule de vobis,
tam ecclesiis vestris, quam rebus publicis magna cum delectatione sermones
cædimus: hoc tamen nos accuratius facturos puta, si tu fortiter in instituto
tuo perrexeris, neque hinc illinc coadjutores nescio quos aut vicarium præ-
stolatus fueris.   Hujus operis exspectati prodromon ad me misit Julius
noster, quem quidem perlegere mihi nondum licuit propter quædam
negotia atque molestias, quæ mihi acciderunt de morte alterius mei affinis,
filii archiepiscopi Cantuariensis: is etiam unam ex meis sororibus in uxorem duxerat; qui nuper obiit.   Saluta obsecro meo nomine omnes tuos.
Etiam atque etiam vale. 25 Januarii, 1575.

Tuus totus,

GULIELM. BARLOUS.

Si aliquando per otium cures ad me mitti exemplar unum pugnæ Sem-
pachi commissæ, nonnihil coloribus illustratum, præsertim signa mili-
taria, mihi rem valde gratam facies. Iterum vale.

INSCRIPTIO.

Doctissimo optimoque viro D. Josiæ Simlero,
  theologiæ in schola Tigurina professori
  celeberrimo, domino et amico suo plu-
  rimum colendo.

EPISTOLA CVI.

NICOLAUS BERNIUS AD ROBERTUM HORNUM.

Ut nobis nihil unquam fuit optatius nihilque jucundius, reverende, quam te de ecclesiarum nostrarum statu ac felicibus initiis certiorem faciendi, tibique de nostro imprimis erga te officio vel potius observantia testificandi occasionem offerri; ita sane nihil gravius molestiusque fuit, quam nunc id nobis argumenti obtrudi, quo apud te patrem nostrum conqueri potius quam de prospero in Christi opere successu congratulari cogimur; minime quidem id facturi, nisi in eo negotio, quod ad tuum munus quoque spectat, opera potissimum tua atque auctoritate nobis opus esset; venia tamen digni, quod non ita jucundum nuntium coacti afferamus, de quo ut nobis pro christiana caritate pluribus tecum agere liceat rogamus, ut cum eo, de cujus sincero in ecclesiam Christi zelo non dubitamus.

Surrexit inter nostras incolas Elias quidam Bonamy, vir ἄτακτος, nec impietate et pertinacia minus nobilis, quam opibus et amicis potens. In cujus generationem patris capitali odio Christi ecclesiam igne ferroque ad extremum usque vitæ articulum ubique quondam persequentis iniquitatem justo suo judicio Deus visitare videtur. Is ante quinquennium in ecclesiæ cœtum adscitus data fide Dei verbo ac ejus ecclesiæ, ut Christi membrum verum decet, pro nostra consuetudine obsecuturum sancte suo pastori pollicetur, priorique triennio non alienum se ab religione animum habere simulavit: posteriori vero biennio, quod mœstum tristeque nobis fuit, detecta sua hypocrisi ita prædicationem Dei verbi neglexit, ut non nisi coactus et quam rarissime ad illud audiendum accingeret; et, quod longe gravius, a sancta Domini cœna non sine magna infirmorum offensione totos hos tres annos abhorruit, suoque exemplo a sacramentis multos abalienavit, qui tandem ab ecclesia defecissent, nisi Deus sua clementia eorum misertus in viam salutis, pastoris usus vigilantia, reduxisset. Minister interim probe suo defunctus munere hominem privatim sæpiusque amice præmonet, et aberrantem omnibus modis in viam revocare studet; sed frustra,—tanta est hominis istius pertinacia: nec desistit tamen, sed iterum coram uno et altero ecclesiæ senioribus christiane et moderate ipsum officii commonefacit, atque ut coram presbyterio sistat nonnihil ad Dei gloriam et animæ salutem auditurus, obnixe efflagitat: sed quanto moderatius cum eo agitur, tanto contumacior efficitur; nec pluris ecclesiastici senatus auctoritatem æstimat, quam Dei et sacramentorum majestatem fecit. In ecclesiæ synedrium dicteria prætereo, et hominis hujus in ministros Christi et ecclesiæ seniores sannas omitto. Itaque cum ejus pervicacia nullis humanis et

divinis legibus coerceri posse videretur, de hac re fratres suos pios et eru-
ditos Christi servos consulit, quando ita negotium postulare putabat; tum
ut huic tanto malo remedium opportunum afferatur, tum ut nihil nisi cum
fructu et ædificatione in ecclesia statuatur.   Hi rem tanti ponderis ad
synodum referendam censent, in qua uno Dei verbo de negotio judicetur.
Ideoque omnes hujus insulæ verbi Dei administri cum suarum ecclesiarum
quibusdam senioribus et nonnullis piis magistratibus in colloquium con-
vocantur, quod Eliam nostrum adesse jubet, qui acta et accusationes in se
factas audiat, et si quam vel justificandi, vel defendendi, vel excusandi
rationem habeat, libere respondeat.   Is postquam nonnulla callide de-
torquere atque declinare conatus esset, ecclesiam hic collectam nescire se,
et nullum hic presbyterium agnoscere dissimulat : tandem vero publicis
actis atque sine ulla exceptione testibus convictus, tanquam sibi male conscius, culpam, scandalum et rebellionem suam confitetur, seque ecclesiastici
cœtus judicio sine cujusquam suspicione sponte submittit. Itaque ne omnem
ei resipiscentiæ spem præclusisse videremur, post institutam debitam de-
lictorum et scandali cognitionem, unanimi omnium consensu atque sententiis statutum est, ipsum non modo coram synodo errorem suum cum
precibus ad Deum confessurum ; sed etiam, ut publico scandalo medeatur,
publice coram omni ecclesia, die dominico 27 Novembris, rebellionem suam
in ecclesiam agniturum ; idque alterius ecclesiæ ministro concionante
facturum, a quo tum suo pastori, tum ecclesiæ reconciliaretur.   Ille audita
ecclesiæ censura tergiversari cœpit, publicamque scelerum suorum confessionem facturum se plane negat.   Sed hæ sunt Satanæ artes tibi plusquam satis cognitæ, ut ejusmodi scandalis vulneratis infirmorum conscientiis Domini ædificium vel impediat vel dirimat.   Tandem vero precibus,
vel ex Dei verbi admonitionibus, vel potius tremendi ejus judicii minis
atque excommunicationis virga veluti quodam fulmine territus, ecclesiæ
censuræ acquiescit, ac coram nostro cœtu supplex a Deo veniam postulans
delictum atque contumaciam agnoscit ; idemque in ecclesia publice facturum die sibi præscripto pollicetur.

Hactenus omnia satis feliciter, vir reverende ; sed mirum et luctuosum
est, hominem toties Dei verbo victum, toties a ministris, amicis, adeoque
ab ipsa ecclesia commonefactum, serio non resipuisse : die siquidem præscripto, quo veræ resipiscentiæ fractique animi testimonium palam præbere, culpamque suam ad Dei gloriam, ecclesiæ ædificationem, suamque
salutem publice confiteri sancte juraverat, et divini judicii et ecclesiasticæ
auctoritatis, denique fidei promissæ immemor, nescio quo impulsore nisi
Sathano, perfidiose nos potius lunam e cœlo dentibus apprehensuros,
quam publicam a se flagitiorum suorum confessionem extorsuros, nec
sine regiæ majestatis tuæque potestatis comminationibus respondet : nec
ullis rationibus, (tanta est hominis istius cordis durities,) ut mutato per-
tinaci carnis seu potius diaboli consilio obsequium Deo et ecclesiæ præ-

staret, adduci poterit.   Quapropter delato ad synodum iterum convocatam
omni negotio, cui interfuit accersitus contumax iste, cujus cor induratum
ad resipiscentiam cum flecti nullo modo posset, propter ejus perfidiam,
contumaciam, et inpœnitentiam ecclesiæ visum est in Jesu Christi verbique
ipsius auctoritate eum tanquam putridum membrum ex ecclesiæ Dei ac
sanctorum communione publice die cœnæ proximæ in omnibus ecclesiis
nostris excommunicandum, atque Sathanæ, donec resipiscat, tradendum.

Rem istam tibi pluribus, observande pater, sicut a nobis gesta est,
summa fide ac veritate, zelo tuo ad amplificandam et tuendam ecclesiam
Christi confisi, significare non sumus veriti; tum ne excisi istius men-
dacibus imposturis, si forte ad te ierit, decipiaris; tum vero, ne nos
ipsi ut calumniatores ab illo apud te sanctosque patres collegas tuos
traducamur.   Qua in re non modo judicium tuum atque auctoritatem
interponi obnixe omnes flagitamus, sed manum etiam adjutricem implo-
ramus, ut (si quando opus sit) apud regiam ipsam majestatem, nostram,
imo tuam ac ecclesiæ nascentis causam suscipias et fortiter tuearis:
quam operam ut Christo præstare non recuses, vehementer etiam atque
etiam rogamus, atque adeo per ipsius Christi nomen obtestamur, quem
assidue precabimur, ut potente sua manu te custodiat, tuaque consilia in
tanto tibi commisso munere suo Spiritu dirigat; nostramque aberrantem
ovem (gravissima alioqui multa dignissimum, nisi resipuerit) veræ pœni-
tentiæ dono in viam salutis reducat.   Bene vale, reverende vir, et nos
fratresque nostros cum tota ecclesia et ama et tuere.   Gerenesii, Idibus
Decemb. 1575.

Tuus in Christo obsequentissimus,

N. BERNIUS,
hæc ad te ecclesiæ totius nomine scripsit.

INSCRIPTIO.

Reverendo in Christo patri ac domino
Wintoniensi episcopo Gerenesien-
sis ecclesiæ nomine Nicolaus Bern-
ius verbi Dei minister gratiam et
salutem a Domino.

EPISTOLA CVII.

GULIELMUS BARLOUS AD JOSIAM SIMLERUM.

S. P.   QUANTAM jacturam, mi Simlere, morte Bullingeri senioris feli-
cissimæ memoriæ fecerit ecclesia vestra, imo etiam nostra, in quam
animo vere paterno atque amanti semper fuisse intelleximus, atque adeo

omnes totius Europæ ecclesiæ Christi, citius quam velimus omnes expe-
riemur. Deus Optimus Maximus, messis Dominus, in suam messem fidos
ut mittat operarios orandus ; utque gregis sui misertus, fideles ei atque zelo
Dei, qui est secundum scientiam, flagrantes pastores præficiat, ac summi
pastoris Jesu Christi adventum acceleret. Superioribus nundinis autumnalibus 1575, scripsi dominum meum episcopum Wintoniensem ad te
aliosque dedisse literas; quas tamen incuria eorum, quibus hoc negotium commiserat, omissas et mercatori non traditas fuisse comperi : idem
ne his nundinis accidat, in me provinciam accepi. Tertio itaque non. Feb.
antequam Londinum ad parlamentum proficiscebatur, hominem compel-
lavi (quod ut facerem mihi sæpius injunxerat), ne ad Tigurinos scribere
intermitteret : ille vero, Imo, inquit, hoc tibi negotii mando, ut mercatori, qui tuas literas defert, scribas, ut meas etiam Londini a me petat,
quæ mittentur una cum tuis : tuæ enim, aiebat, et quæ ad te scribuntur,
sunt meis longe feliciores; quas etenim Tiguro novissime accepi, biennio antea scriptæ fuerunt; et quas ipsemet scripsi, an adhuc traditæ
sint plurimum dubito. Hanc provinciam, inquam ego, in me libenter
accipio, neque scribam alicui ut tuas a te petat; sed egomet ero, Deo
volente, Londini, antequam proficiscantur ad nundinas, atque tuas ipse
a te postulabo, ne in me tuæ intermissionis culpam aliquam derives; hoc-
que me ad te jam scripsisse illi, cum ad eum venero, significabo.

Mitto ad te his literis inclusum exemplar duarum epistolarum, in
quibus facile est videre (ut in palæstra nobili decertatum) quales quan-
tasque vires habeat, in nebulone aliquo improbo coercendo, inermis illa
quam tantopere jactitant nonnullorum disciplina : ex quibus etiam intelligas, omnes episcopos nostros non ita esse (ut quidam calumniantur) otio
et ventri deditos, et omnem deposuisse humanitatem, quin ex iis sint, qui
res fratrum diligenter curent; neque illorum invisam potestatem adeo
exosam esse, quin ad eam tandem (quasi claudus ad equum) ultro con-
fugiant. Gerenesia, ubi hæc gesta sunt, insula est in mare Britannico,
regibus Angliæ subdita, Wintoniensis diœceseos. Anglus quidam, Laurentius Bodleus, amicus meus summus, mihi indicavit se circa hoc tempus
Tigurum venturum : si is ad vos venerit, rogo ut illum comiter (hoc est,
vestro more) excipiatis : est homo parvæ staturæ, sed eruditionis et probitatis eximiæ, et vestræ ecclesiæ amantissimus. Ante duas menses obiit
doctrina atque pietate (apud nostros) nemini secundus, D. Pilkingtonus,
Dunelmensis episcopus. Archiepiscopum Cantuariensem habemus (Dei
beneficio) multis nominibus præstantissimum, D. Grindallum : faxit Deus,
ut illum diu habeamus : quis eum in Eboracensi archiepiscopatu suc-
cedet, nondum innotescit; plerique tamen arbitrantur Londinensem ; atque
vel in Londinensi, si is in Eboracum proficiscatur, vel Dunelmensi epi-
scopatu affinem meum D. Gul. Deium successurum, quidam non infimæ
sortis opinantur. Ego illum, sicut jusseras, tuo nomine salutavi, quod

illi gratum admodum fuit, meque rogavit, ut te denuo vosque omnes illius
nomine resalutarem . . . insuper orare, ut se quoque in numerum amicorum vestr. . . . . flagitabat.   Saluta . . renter meo nomine reverendissimum in Christo patrem D. Gualterum, D. Lavaterum, hospitem
meum D. Wiccium, D. Stuccium, D. Lemannum, D. Bullingerum, D.
Jac. Frisium, D. Froscoverum, etiam atque etiam Gualterum juniorem
ac Julium nostrum.   Vale.   Collegio Etonense, 5 non. Martii, anno, etc.
1576.

Tuus,

GULIELMUS BARLOW.

Triduo postquam hæc scripsissem, mi Simlere, præcedente nocte, qua
præterita summo mane profecturus eram Londinum, ea inquam ipsa nocte
febre correptus fui vehementer, sed his tribus novissimis diebus multum
remisit, adeo ut sperem Dominum eam hoc tempore avertisse.   Vale.

Collegio Etonense, 13 Martii.

INSCRIPTIO.

Ornatissimo viro D. Josiæ Simlero,
theologiæ in schola Tigurina pro-
fessori celeberrimo, domino et amico
suo plurimum colendo.

EPISTOLA CVIII.

H. ZANCHIUS AD EDMUNDUM GRINDALLUM.

S.   OBSERVANTIA qua te, reverendissime domine, semper sum pro-
secutus propter tuam singularem pietatem, humanitatem, virtutem, facit
ut non possum non gratulari tibi istam novam amplissimamque, de qua
ad me scripsit communis amicus Knolles, dignitatem.   Quid enim majus
exspectari amplius in isto regno tibi poterat ?   Gratulor itaque ex animo,
quoniam istæ divinæ benedictiones testimonia sunt, tum constantis in
Deum pietatis tuæ, tum immutabilis erga te benevolentiæ Dei.   Sed
non minus gratulor eandem rem toti isti regno, quod scilicet talem
jam nactum sit a Deo primatem, cujus cura et diligentia magis ac magis
in vera religione ac pietate promoveri possit.   Neque enim dubito quin
ista supremæ post regiam majestatem dignitatis accessio futura sit tibi
perpetuus stimulus, quo ad faciendum officium diligentius quam unquam
acriter exciteris.   Precor Deum sua etiam in te dona augeat, firmaque
et diuturna valetudine donare te velit, ad salutarem suæ ecclesiæ gubernationem.   Vivo adhuc, et quidem bona valetudine, Dei beneficio, pro mea
ætate, qui sexagesimum primum ago annum, cum uxore, liberis quin-

que, et qui brevi, ut spero, prodibit in lucem. Sunt autem et hæ magnæ Dei benedictiones, pro quibus ingentes illi ago gratias. Restat ut tum donis sui Spiritus eos repleat, tum quæ ad vitam hanc honeste transigendam necessaria sunt illis suppeditet; quod ut faxit toto pectore illum rogo per Jesum Christum; ac tibi etiam, amplissime archiepiscope, aliisque amicis ac bonis viris commendo. Dominus Jesus te diu nobis ad ecclesiæ salutem conservet incolumem! Exspectamus quotidie nostrum Casimirum.

Heidelbergæ, 22 Julii, 1576.

Tuæ amplitudinis, etc.

H. ZANCHIUS.

EPISTOLA CIX.

GULIELMUS BARLOUS AD JOSIAM SIMLERUM.

S. P. UTINAM, mi Simlere, si detur optio, interstitio tantum maris distaremus! sæpius sane et animo magis alacri Tigurum quam Londinum inviserem. Helvetiam tamen quamvis oculis contemplari non licet, mente saltem recolere, atque animo etiam totam, tuis jam adjutus laboribus, peragrare potero. Bullingeri vitam, quamvis avide, difficulter tamen et voluptate amaritudine atque præsagio nescio quo (utinam nunquam sciamus!) mixta futurorum eventuum perlego: solidum tamen fundamentum Dei cum suo signaculo perpetuo et ubique gentium (etiam inter Suevos et Saxones) manet: *Novit Dominus qui sunt sui*, etc. Quæ apud nos aguntur, ex hisce literis episcopi Wintoniensis domini mei ad D. Gualterum accipies, quas tuis etiam adjunxi: cujus etiam nomine mitto summam quinque angelottorum D. Froscovero, ut tibi aut D. Gualtero munusculum hoc in usum communis vestri hypocausti tradat. Novi apud nos (Dei beneficio) nihil habemus; nisi quod hoc ipso tempore mittuntur aliquot naves bellicæ, quæ mare custodiant, et (uti aiunt) Flussingensium audaciam et aliorum etiam ferociam atque rapinas reprimant. Nostros omnes rogo ut meo nomine reverenter salutes. Vale. Walthamiæ, 11 Augusti, anno, etc. 1576.

Tuus,

GULIELMUS BARLOW.

INSCRIPTIO.

Ornatissimo viro D. Josiæ Simlero,
theologiæ in schola Tigurina profes-
sori, D. et amico suo plurimum
colendo.

EPISTOLA CX.

RODOLPHUS GUALTERUS AD EDMUNDUM GRINDALLUM.

S.   Quas Martio mense ad tuam amplitudinem, reverendissime in
Christo pater, literas dedi per Laurentium Bodlæum, jampridem tibi
redditas esse puto.   Ab eo tempore etsi nihil scriptu dignum in Germania actum sit, adhuc tamen magno studio et contentione causam suam,
de qua tum scripsi, Lutherani agunt: ut nimirum nos et ecclesias nostras opprimant.   Et haud dubie jam aliquid effecissent, nisi res Polonicæ
imperatori negotium facerent, cujus favore et consensu illis opus est.
Indixit is comitia Ratisponam, et ante menses duos illuc ipse venit: sed
solus fere illic sedens principes alios exspectat.   Interea in Saxonia quidam horum convenerunt apud Augustum electorem, ad quos Bavarus
quoque profectus est: quod multi mirantur, cum hactenus evangelicæ
doctrinæ hostis fuerit acerrimus.   Qui vero cordatiores sunt, adversus
palatinum electorem illos aliquid moliri suspicantur, quod sine Bavari
consensione perfici non possit, cum eadem principum Bavariæ et palatinorum stirps atque origo sit.   Multis etiam suspecta est imperatoris
excursio ad Ludovicum, electoris palatini filium, qui Ambergæ est cum
imperio, et hactenus a patre in causa sacramentaria aperte dissensit.
Metuunt ergo nonnulli ne hic quoque cum adversariis consilia sua communicet, ut ipse patri dejecto aut expulso succedat.   Certum est Augustum
nobis infensissimum esse, et nova indies ab eo eduntur crudelitatis exempla in eos, quos nobiscum sentire intelligit.   Faces huic incendio suggerit Jacobus Andreæ, homo ambitiosus et maledicus, qui cum non habeat
quod Heidelbergensibus fratribus et nobis respondeat, principum auctoritate et potentia nos opprimere studet.   Quod igitur nuper monui, adhuc
ad communis causæ defensionem non tam utile quam necessarium esse
videtur; ut nimirum serenissima regina vestra suam auctoritatem inter-
ponat.   Etenim palatinus elector jampridem illis invisus est, et hunc
ne a suis quidem omnibus, ut par erat, coli atque observari norunt.
Helvetiorum nulla est apud principes auctoritas.   Genevam non oderunt
modo, verum etiam execrantur.   At serenissimam Angliæ reginam non
ita contemnere aut negligere possunt, quæ et regiæ majestatis nomine
commendatur, et opibus valet; eo denique loco est, ut Germaniæ toti
adversus communes hostes, papistas, utilem operam præstare possit.
Faciet ergo revera piæ nutricis ecclesiæ officium, si causam hanc sibi
curæ esse sinat; nec deerunt rationes quibus Scotiæ regem in societatem
trahat, cujus accessio causæ huic plurimum commodare poterit.   Audio

autem Scotiæ ecclesias nobis conjunctissimas esse, et puto has nulli officio defuturas quod ab hominibus christianis requiri debet. Ex illis certe quidam pii et insignes viri mihi suasores fuerunt, ut Galatas meos (quorum exemplum ad te, pater reverendissime, mitto) Scotorum regi nuncuparem. De his vero rursus scribi volui, ut videas adhuc vobis occasionem offerri, quo communi ecclesiæ officium præstetis : et illa quidem eo plausibilior offertur, quod vix puto imperatorem aliquorum animos temere abs se alienaturum esse hoc tempore, quo amicis et sociis plurimis opus habet, nisi omni spe regni Polonici excidere, et de Ungaria quoque sua periclitari velit. Neque parum momenti ad hanc causam conferet pax Gallica. Nam etsi de hac non eadem sit omnium sententia atque spes, certum tamen est ejus promulgatione consilia communium hostium vehementer esse perturbata. Hæc ut amplitudo tua, pater reverendissime, patienter legat et ferat oro. Ut enim ista scribam me publica cura movet, quam ecclesiæ debeo, et quam tibi cumprimis cordi esse non dubito. Deus Optimus Maximus te servet, et studiis tuis sanctissimis benedicat. Idem ex animo precatur Julius noster Santerentianus, qui se tuæ amplitudini commendatissimum esse cupit. Vale. Tiguri, 24 Augusti, anno nati Christi 1576.

Tuæ amplitudinis observantissimus,

RODOLPHUS GUALTERUS.

INSCRIPTIO.

Reverendissimo in Christo patri et do-
mino Edmundo Gryndallo, archiepi-
scopo Cantuarensi, et totius Angliæ
primati, domino suo cum omni reve-
rentia observando.

EPISTOLA CXI.

LUINUS AD JOHANNEM STURMIUM.

Cum primum mihi traderentur literæ tuæ, quas ad reginam et dominum thesaurarium D. Walsinghamum dederas, deessetque exemplum literarum tuarum ad reginam, et res ipsæ incertæ essent de quibus scriberes ; putavi consultius esse illas literas supprimere, teque iisdem de rebus paulo post, si videretur, certius et constantius scribere.

Cum autem postridie ad me perlatæ essent aliæ literæ tuæ, abs te quidem multo ante perscriptæ, in quibus Lanscadii ad te missa epistola implicata esset; quoniam hac de re et admonitus ipse essem, teque eam ut mitteres, si qua ad te mitteretur, admonuissem; en! cepi novum consilium, omnia scripta tua ad dominum thesaurarium ut perferrem, eoque auctore uterer literarum tuarum ad reginam et ad D. Walsinghamum scriptarum aut tradendarum, si vellet, aut supprimendarum, si nollet.

Quantum hoc officium, tuum imprimis, deinde etiam meum, domino thesaurario placuerit, perscribere ad te vix possum: hoc unum scribo, summa humanitate et literas tuas perlegisse, et me ad intimum conclave suum admisisse. Huic visum est ut domino Walsinghamo et literæ tuæ ad eum perscriptæ traderentur, et epistola etiam Lanscadii. Sed reginæ epistolam tradendam esse non suasit, et quia exemplum defuit, et quia res in incerto loco positæ erant. Idque ut D. Walsinghamo significarem, admonuit. Domino Walsinghamo igitur et hæc ipse declaravi, et literas tuas tradidi ac epistolam etiam Lanscadii; quin et literas etiam ad reginam, quas tamen tradidisse non arbitror. Id autem ut scirem, monuit me D. thesaurarius, ut utrique postridie in urbe Londinensi obviam facerem.

Ego cum in reditu essem, ac jam prope urbem attingerem, ecce, qui antea et oculis imprimis et reliquo corpore paulo infirmior essem, in itinere tertiana febri correptus sum. Hac ego duodecim dies laborans, dominum thesaurarium aut D. Walsinghamum adire non potui. Utrumque autem spero ad te per suos mercatores scripsisse; id ipsum enim se velle declarabant.

Febricitans vero literas tuas ad D. archiepiscopum legendas misi: simulque rogavi ut causam tuam pecuniariam quantum posset apud proceres nostros promoveret; de qua ego et multa cum D. thesaurario, et pauca etiam cum D. Walsinghamo in curia reginali: multa enim tempus non sinebat. Tu autem vide, quantum domino archiepiscopo debeas: is enim, me etiamnum laborante, ita egit et adhuc agit causam tuam, ut sperem certe te pecuniam tuam ante multos menses recuperaturum.

Qua ratione vero id fieri possit, cupis profecto intelligere. Sic ergo habeto; novam legationem in Galliam a nostris decretam esse, hominis prudentissimi, fortissimi, generosissimi. Cum eo diligentissime egit D. archiepiscopus, ut causam tuam ipse suscipiat. Petit etiam a D. thesaurario et D. Walsinghamo, ut huic eam commendent: tractandam illam, non ut hominis peregrini, sed ut civis nostri; non ut privati, sed ut legati Anglicani, ejusdemque doctissimi, religiosissimi, de nobis, Gallisque qui religionem profitentur, optime meriti. Si possimus assequi ut reginæ etiam nomine eam agat, omnia videmur obtinuisse. Non dubito quin ita commendaturus sit Alanconio, ut dicat gratum id acceptumque reginæ fore, si efficiat Alanconius ut tibi quamprimum solvatur. Non possum nec licet omnia scribere, quibus in spem adducaris te isto modo ære alieno liberatum iri. Hoc unum scribo, gestivisse gaudio D. archiepiscopum cum cogitaret, quanta id te lætitia perfusurum esset, cum tibi omnis pecunia ad

denarium solveretur: quod ut quamprimum fiat, mi pater mique præceptor, ornatissime Sturmi, Deum Optimum Maximum precor.

Scito autem nullum in me officium aut studium hanc ad rem defuturum: nec defuisse sane, cujus gratia, cum essem infirmus, longum iter
suscepi, ex eoque in febrem incidi: sed et jam convaluisse me intelligas
velim, et in eandem rem tuam diligenter incumbere.

Autumnalem pensionem tuam nondum recepi, cum ante festum Michaelis nec debeatur, nec a quæstoribus solvatur. Ego autem cum Santrino
egi, eoque nomine cautionem dedi, ut tibi his Francofordianis nundinis
solvatur. Tu ergo a Berno tantundem et exspecta et pete, quantum tibi
antea solvit: hoc enim mihi Santrinus noster effecturum se recepit.
Ego autem scire cupio quot florenos Bernus numerarit, ut intelligam an
ulla ratione commodius per alium mercatorem pecuniam ad te transferre
possim.

Hæc raptim et festinanter, ut ex ipsa scriptione poteris conjicere. Tu
vide, ne quid in commentariis tuis ad Demosthenem et Ciceronem desit,
quod ab historicis scribatur aut geratur. Vale, vicesimo quinto Augusti.

Vide etiam ut D. archiepiscopo gratias agas, quod tam promptus et
paratus sit ad te ex ære alieno redimendum.

Tuus quem nosti

Ex ipso argumento,

[LUINUS.]

EPISTOLA CXII.

JOHANNES RAINOLDUS AD RODOLPHUM GUALTERUM F.

Quo mihi minor tecum familiaritas intercessit, ornatissime Gualtere,
cum apud nos ageres; non quod voluntas, sed occasio, vel tuæ necessitudinis fruendæ vel meæ benevolentiæ testificandæ mihi deesset; eo me
tibi magis esse devinctum et ingenue fateor et impense lætor, qui tanto
terrarum intervallo disjunctus, curis qua publicis, qua domesticis, districtus,
tamen ita gratam mei memoriam cum animo retineas, tum colas beneficio.
Nam si rerum usus docuit Aristotelem, diuturnam absentiam efficere
videri, ut ipsam amicitiam inobscuret oblivio; notitiæ nostræ quasi florem,
non amicitiæ maturitatem, absentia diuturna non exaruisse, sed excre-
visse, quanto mihi minus fuit exspectandum, tanto nisi gratius videatur,
ingratus sim. Me quidem in eo tua singularis docuit humanitas, quantum sit discrimen inter christianam et ethnicam amicitiam: quarum
alteram apud Aristotelem propter diuturnam disjunctionem corporum
obscurat oblivio; alteram autem apud Gualterum propter sempiternam

conjunctionem animorum caritas illustrat. Ego vero etiamsi nunquam concedam, ut in amore sis superior, quo redamantem amas; tamen in eo priores tibi partes deferam necesse est, quod amantis animi testificatione me prævenisti. Poema tuum amo, vel quod tuum, vel quod tale, vel quod utrumque potius. Est enim insignibus, si quid ego judico, notis aspersum et ingenii in versibus limandis, et judicii in rebus persequendis, et pietatis in episcopum bene meritum, et caritatis in ecclesiam Anglicanam : cujus piam vindicem Elisabetham laudas; immanem carnificem Bonnerum saucias; infestos adversarios papistas exagitas; afflicta membra, christianos, consolaris; miserabilem statum languescentis deploras; denique Christum Jesum, ut divina misericordia propitius sit, obsecras. Academiam nostram ne laudibus ornares, impedivit pater tuus, qui prior antevertit, Oxonium nobile doctis Anglis, *Palladis et Phœbi Pieridumque domum*, prædicando, multo magis vereor quam meretur : sed amorem agnoscimus et gratiam habemus. Ecclesiæ tibi curam esse commendatam, et fœminam præstantissimam (sic enim mihi persuadeo, quia patri tuo tibique probatam) matrimonio conjunctam, vehementer gratulor. Non canam carmen ἐπιθαλάμιον, ut tuum remunerer ἐπικήδειον. Veruntamen eam futuram talem conjugem et spero et opto, qualem scribit Gregorius Nazianzenus filius fuisse suam matrem Nazianzeno patri; non adjutricem modo, sed etiam quasi ducem, magistram pietatis, verbis et factis ad optima commoventem. D. Caius utriusque nostrum amantissimus, insigni pietate et doctrina juvenis, academiam reliquit, ut ecclesiam quandam ad quadragesimum ab urbe nostra lapidem, ipsius curæ commissam, pasceret. Peropportune vero contingit, ut eo ipso die, quo tuorum versuum exemplar mihi traditum est ad eum transmittendum, Oxonium vesperi veniret. Ceterum cum esset illinc postridie mane discedendum, a me contendit et impetravit, ut suis tibi verbis et gratias agerem et salutem dicerem. Utrumque facio. Collegæque quoque nostri, quos a D. Præside salutari voluisti, tibi vicissim omnia felicissima precantur. Deus Optimus Maximus te et patrem tuum vestrosque omnes ac universam ecclesiam Tigurinam suo semper illustret lumine, favore protegat, Spiritu moderetur. Vale. Dat. e collegio Corporis Christi, Oxonii, Idib. Augusti, 1576.

Tuus in Christo Jesu,
JOHANNES RAINOLDUS.

INSCRIPTIO.

Ornatissimo juveni et mihi carissimo
    in Christo fratri D. Rodolpho
        Gualtero filio. Tiguri.
    Tradantur Froschovero Francofurti
        ad Mœnum.

EPISTOLA CXIII.

LUINUS AD JOHANNEM STURMIUM.

Scripsi ad te superioribus hisce proximis diebus, ornatissime Sturmi, quo consilio et quibus potissimum rationibus adducerer, ut postquam abs te Lanscadii mihi literæ traditæ fuerunt, cum his illas etiam alteras ad reginam et D. thesaurarium et D. Walsinghamum perscriptas ad aulam regalem perferrem; quam gratæ etiam utræque utrisque illis heroibus fuerunt, et quibus de causis existimarim tertias illas ad reginam datas traditas non fuisse.

Scripsi eodem tempore, ac id quidem fusius, de re tua pecuniaria ac Gallicana; de primate nostro imprimis et archiepiscopo Cantuarensi, tui sane tuæque salutis ac fortunarum omnium studiosissimo, quam ille rationem investigavit et te ex ære hoc alieno redimendi, et pristinæ tuæ tranquillitatis atque otii, quo reliquum tempus ætatis cum mansuetioribus musis transigas, recuperandi.

Ex eo tempore scito dominum nostrum archipræsulem rebus tuis summam operam navasse; causam tuam egisse prudenter, diligenter, peramanter. Nam præterquam quod Pauleto nostro, homini generosissimo ac fortissimo, cui nova in Galliam decreta legatio est, te resque tuas iterum atque iterum commendaret; egit etiam ab eo tempore separatim, primum cum domino thesaurario, deinde cum D. Walsinghamo, ut eundem te fortunasque tuas pluribus nominibus eidem huic Pauleto cariores redderent. Summa autem fuit hujusce commendationis, ut duo illi magnates, qui auctoritate et gratia apud nos plurimum possunt, Pauletum et rogarent et orarent, ut causam illam tuam Gallicanam vel reginæ, vel publico saltem procerum nostrorum nomine tractet cum duce Alanconio et Condiano principe; id quod utrique, cum illius auctoritate, tum tua nonnihil conditione permoti, facturos se prolixe pollicebantur. Ego fecisse jam quod rogati sunt nec dubito, nec te, mi Sturmi, volo dubitare.

Pauletus, salutata jam nudius sextus regina, iter in Galliam adornat et propediem proficiscitur, vir summi ingenii et animi invicti atque excelsi. Quærere te video de D. comite Oxoniano, annon is etiam Pauleto causam tuam commendarit. Tu vero scito, me diligenter etiam cum D. comite egisse; respondisse illum, non modo se Sturmium suum Pauleto commendaturum, sed petiturum etiam a Leicestrense comite, ut ipse omnibus modis commendet: addidisse præterea, nisi e Gallia subleveris, facturum se ut ex Anglia auxilia tibi inveniantur: denique multa et præclare de te sensisse, et locutum esse honorifice, quæ me cum audirem summa lætitia afficiebant; ad te cum perscribuntur, debent profecto exhilarare. Tu vero senex, et

ætate provectum archipræsulem nostrum, adeo firmum et constantem
in amicitia, plurimi facito, et adolescentem comitem de te optime sentientem noli contemnere : de utroque omnia sperare, de altero omnia
audeo polliceri.

Nunc autem te ipsum quid horter, aut suadeam, exspectas fortasse, mi
Sturmi. Primum certe illud, ut ad Amiamum Pauletum, equitem auratum,
antequam hæ tibi literæ traduntur, legatum nostrum in Gallia futurum,
quamprimum scribas : agnoscas quæ a me ex Anglia acceperis, præsertim de
domini archiepiscopi erga te voluntate et studio ; si placet, etiam D. the-
saurarii et D. Walsinghami licet adjungere. Spero etiam Leicestrianum
et Oxonianum comites te Pauleto commendaturos : sed id mihi adhuc
exploratum non est : facturos ab Oxoniano audivi ; fecisse autem nondum
intelligo.

Præterea illud etiam fortasse optandum esset, ut si quem habeas in
Gallia fidelem et constantem amicum, hunc ad Pauletum cum literis tuis
alleges ; qui eum aliquando admoneat tui ; qui quid agatur, quidque abs
te agendum sit, e Gallia rescribat. Talem autem virum si jam in Gallia
non habeas, nec habiturus sis, qui suis sumptibus proficiscatur, non audeo
suadere ut quenquam mittas tuis. Non est enim fortasse hominis pru-
dentis, cum ære alieno implicatus sit, se magis magisque involvere.
Spero literas tuas, si frequentes eas ad Pauletum dederis, cum rerum
Germanicarum nuncias, tum studii etiam tui officiique plenas, satis illas
diligentes Pauleto admonitores futuras : qui et ipse sua natura vir bonus
est, et multum debet proceribus qui te illi commendarunt, et laborabit
certe ut gratum se illis, tibi beneficum et liberalem ostendat. Unum
illud omittendum non est, ut quantum tibi debeatur, tum propter pecuniam illam quam mutuo dedisti, tum propter usuras quas negotiatoribus
eo nomine solvisti, ad Pauletum quamprimum perscribas : ego ex literis
tuis totius debiti contracti brevem historiolam confeci ; adhibui omnes
περιστάσεις quæ proceres nostros ad causam tuam possent adjungere ;
quæ vero Gallos offendere, si forte viderent, eas D. archiepiscopus
summa prudentia delevit : hujus exemplar unum D. thesaurario traditum est, alterum D. Walsinghamo ; utrumque autem vidisse Pauletum
non dubito. Tertium D. archiepiscopus apud se retinet, quo alios proceres in re tua possit instruere : ac ut ipse intelligas quomodo res a me
descripta est, et addas si quid addendum sit ; hujus historiolæ exemplum
quartum ad te misi, idque ita ut a D. archiepiscopo interpolatum atque
emendatum est. Nihil prætermittam quod ad rem tuam pertinere arbi-
trabor : tu si quid tibi in mentem venerit, fac ut sciam. Unum illud
cogito, cum famulo aliquo Pauleti, honestioris apud eum loci, agere, ut
rebus tuis faveat ; ut dominum, quando opus est, tui memorem faciat ;
denique, si quid isthic amplius agendum est, ad me perscribat.

Mi pater, mique præceptor, nullum officium prætermittam φίλου κασιγνήτον, quandoquidem hujusmodi me esse judicas: exigua nostra facultas est, sed ad ea quæ possum, me tibi dedo. Bernus his Francfordianis nundinis autumnalem tibi pensionem solvet. Santrinus, mercator Anglus, quo antea usus sum, id etiam nunc se facturum esse ante quatuordecim dies promisit, qua de re superioribus etiam ad te literis scripsi. Vale, octavo Septembris.

Tuus,

LUINUS.

D. archiepiscopus me monuit ut hisce literis te illius nomine salutarem. Ego infirmitate oculorum adhuc laboro, quæ facit ut alterius chirographo utar. Iterum vale.

EPISTOLA CXIV.

FRANCISCUS WALSINGHAMUS AD JOHANNEM STURMIUM.

Doctissime Sturmi, cum legato majestatis suæ, qui nunc agit in Galliis apud regem, egi vehementer, ut negotium tuum pecuniarium, quod tibi cum illis intercedit qui a partibus veræ religionis stant, sibi esset quam commendatissimum; in quo mihi sancte pollicitus est suam fidem et operam cum hac exceptione, quantum valeret, quantumque posset. De cujus fide tantum abest ne dubitem, ut sciam planeque mihi persuadeam, non minori sibi curæ omnes res meas esse, in quibus tuas pono, quam suas; neque dubito quin si ejus virtuti illi pro sua pietate et religione respondebunt, propediem confectum ibit negotium pro voto et voluntate tua. De eo autem quod attinet, quod bonus ille vir D. Landeshafus suæ majestati commendatum voluit, in mandatis habet D. thesaurarius ab eadem, ut per D. Luinum tibi respondeat.

De ratione autem qua literas vestras ad nos curetis transmittendas, patefeci D. Ashbeyo mentem et voluntatem meam, quam ille tibi explicabit, scio, ne postmodum in eo quis vestrum laboret, quem ad nos scribendi, quavis data occasione, studium capiet. Quod ut pro tuo otio quam facias sæpius, te vehementer etiam atque etiam rogo. Bene et feliciter valeas.

Dat. e regia de Hampton Court, 27 Oct. 1576.

Tui amicissimus,

FRA. WALSINGHAM.

INSCRIPTIO.
Doctissimo viro et amico suo carissimo
D. Johanni Sturmio, Argentorati.

EPISTOLA CXV.

FRANCISCUS WALSINGHAMUS AD JOHANNEM STURMIUM.

Doctissime Sturmi, unis meis literis cogor tuis pluribus respondere: non quod non velim pro tuis singulis, uti par est, meas singulas dare; sed quia temporis usura, qua fruor exigua, et valetudine, quæ mihi jam aliquot menses adversa fuit, excludor. Sic autem velim existimes gratissimas quidem fuisse tuas literas, non mihi solum ceterisque tuis, qui te ut solent diligunt, sed etiam regiæ majestati, quæ suo Sturmio tantum tribuit, quantum tua virtus suis meritis sibi jure vindicat. Unum autem hoc in te desideratur, ut pro temporum ratione et hominum moribus pluribus verbis et plenius scribas; eoque magis, quo sunt tempora nostra, in quibus vivimus, satis plena periculorum, et hominum ingenia, quibuscum conflictamur, non sine suis infinitis recessibus et profundis latebris. Quæ tamen nescio quomodo produnt sese, nostroque bono patefaciunt, quo observantur diligentius, et necessitudines quas indies novas faciunt animadvertimus. Habet Germania vestra plurimos principes, quorum amicitiam et conjunctionem exteri ambiunt, sibi magis quam vestris rem gratam facere cupientes: in quam quisque eorum partem propendet, quam de se spem præbet vel religionem faventibus vel a religione abhorrentibus, nec est inutile scire, nec erit ingratum ad nos perscribere. Imprimis autem, quid de Cæsare statuendum et existimandum judicas, quid de palatino Rheni, et Casimiro, velintne conjunctis animis in amore et benevolentia conquiescere, quam pius et nobilis parens moriens eis commendavit, ad propagationem evangelii et pacis publicæ, an suis dissensionibus et domesticis dissidiis tum sibi tum suis ruinam parere. Non deerunt forte qui nullum non movebunt lapidem, ut ignem hunc injiciant in præclaram illam palatinorum domum, eumque accendant; eoque diligentius illis cavendum erit. Hisce de rebus si scripseris, et si quid tale suspicandum sit, et quibus modis ac viis præcaveri poterit monueris, gratissima officia tum nobis, tum orbi christiano universo feceris. Bene et feliciter valeas. Ex ædibus meis Londini, 23 Apr. 1577.

Tui studiosissimus,

FRA. WALSINGHAM.

INSCRIPTIO.

Ornatissimo viro D. doctori Sturmio,
amico suo carissimo.

EPISTOLA CXVI.

FRANCISCUS WALSINGHAMUS AD JOHANNEM STURMIUM.

DOCTISSIME Sturmi, accepi literas tuas et librum quem meo nomini dicatum voluisti; pro quibus non vulgares humanitati tuæ et ago et habeo gratias. Quæ autem in iis tuis literis continebantur, et regineæ majestatis interesse putabam, ut ei nota ac comperta essent, ea ad majestatem suam retuli, quæ tam bonam in partem interpretatur, ac cetera omnia quæ a Sturmio suo, homine neque ingrato neque injucundo, proficiscuntur. Erunt autem tuæ literæ, ut sunt, eo gratiores, quo sunt frequentiores, et de rebus iis nos admonent, quæ (tanquam qui corpore valent et recte se habent, nullo sensu tanguntur eorum quæ male sani misere et cum dolore patiuntur) nihil nos movent et afficiunt. Unum hoc malum est, si non solum, at certe multum grave, rerum ad voluntatem nostram fluentium, quod oblivisci nos faciant aut saltem parum memores, non quidem natura sua sed nostro vitio, calamitatum et rerum malarum quibus alii premuntur. Hic si tu nos alte dormientes et improvide securos expergefeceris, et crebrioribus tuis literis admonueris nos imminentis periculi, honestissima studia et rectissima officia feceris. Hunc enim tibi morbum nostrum ut ægrotus indico; tu ut peritus et bonus medicus medicinam admoveto: si morbum sanaveris, non carebis fama honoratissimi medici; sin minus opera tua successerit, recte habet, liberasti fidem. Scribis metuere sibi Genevenses ab Hispanis: at si vera sunt quæ ad nos perferuntur, et crebro, magis metuendum est vicinis nostris Belgis et nobis ab illis; fertur enim, idque non per dubiæ fidei auctores, cogitare Austriacum, atque jam fecisse, de Hispanis suis in Belgium revocandis, parareque novas turbas contra Auriacum et meliores Belgas; magna sibi pollicitum de primoribus nonnullis ex ordinibus, quos suis corruptelis et blandis pollicitationibus in sua consilia, id est in patriæ suæ incendium et suam ipsorum præsentissimam ruinam et internecionem, pellexit. Hæc, inquam, adferunt ii ad nos: tu plura deinceps intelliges; referet enim omnia ut sunt filia veritatis tempus. Tu interea fac ut valetudinem tuam cures, et quæ observaveris ad nos perscribas, et quo poteris crebrius. Ita magna et optima officia apud nos deposueris. Bene et feliciter valeas.

Dat. Londini, 22 Julii, 1577.

Tui amantissimus,

FRA. WALSINGHAM.

INSCRIPTIO.

Doctissimo viro, D. Johanni Sturmio,
    amico meo carissimo. Argen-
    torati.

*12

EPISTOLA CXVII.

PHILIPPUS SIDNEIUS AD HUBERTUM LANGUETUM.

Mi carissime Languete! Ex ternis tuis quas literis 24 Augusti scriptis ad me misisse affirmas, binas tantum accepi, eas quidem omnis humanitatis veræque amicitiæ plenas; sed quid hoc novum est? Itane putas exsolvi posse promissum, quod sancte fecisti de nobis invisendis? Hoc esset plane, domine Huberte, verba dare. Gaudeo sane te non longe abesse Spira, ubi jure tecum agi potest.

Nuper hic fuit nobilis vir nomine de Tamars, quocum notitiam contraxi, et eo quidem libentius, quia sæpenumero honorificam tui mentionem me præsente fecerit. Sic et Aldegundus sæpe, ipseque princeps, cum apud illius celsitudinem diverterem, multa dixit, quibus intelligerem te summopere illi esse carum. Quorsum hæc? Plane ut tibi persuadeam, ut illum, modo tuto possis, invisas; inde ad nos venias. Habebis ibi pulcherrimum campum exercendi ea in hac nova republica formanda, quæ per totum vitæ tempus tam sedulo didicisti. Et sane spero me, antequam multæ septimanæ elabantur, eo venturum: amo enim principem illum, et forsan aliquo modo magis ei inservivi, quam ipse noverit. Ita sane nostri animi hoc tempore inclinantur, ut (si bella ex Belgio continuentur) in aliquam spem adducar, vaticinium illud tuum, quod mihi de ipso aliquando Viennæ dixisti, felicem eventum habiturum. Marchio Hauræus auxilium flagitat, credoque, si ita res postulaverit, exoraturum fore. Pax Gallica aliquo modo nostram reginam perturbat; putat enim secum male agi. Causam nosti. Ego quidem hæc parvi momenti judico; semper enim et causam et animum habebunt hæc rumpendi, modo aliquid certi fundamenti, quo niti possint, videant.

Scripsi tibi ante annum de Furbissero quodam, qui æmulus Magellani fretum, quod septentrionalem Americæ partem alluere existimatur, investigavit. Mira est historia. Is cum præterito anno tardius procederet, ita ut autumno Bauataos tantum insulamque, quam Frislandiam Zeno Veneto inventam esse judicat, præternavigaret, appulit insulam quandam, ut se suosque aliquo modo reficeret: ibique forte fortuna juvenis quidam ex sociis ipsius particulam terræ, quam resplendentem vidit, sustulit, monstravitque Furbissero. Ipse cum alia curaret, nec crederet in regione adeo septentrionali pretiosa metalla gigni, parvi ea pendit. Sed hieme jam incipiente rediit. Juvenis terram illam ut laboris sui signum, (nec enim alia conjectaverat,) secum retinuit donec Londinum rediret. Ibi primum quidam ex amicis juvenis cum animadverteret miro modo relucentem, experimentum fecit, invenitque esse aurum purissimum,

nulloque alio metallo mixto : adeo ut Furbisserus vere proxime elapso
eo remeaverit, jussus insulam illam perlustrare, nec ulterius progredi, si ea
exspectationi responderet ; quod et fecit, jamque reversus est, naves, quas
tres tantum easque parvas habuit, onustas referens ; diciturque (namque
adhuc non exportarunt) bis centum tonnas mineralis terræ tulisse : certum
judicium tulit, insulam adeo metalliferam esse, ut Peruinas regiones,
saltem ut nunc sunt, longe superare videatur.   Sunt et sex aliæ insulæ
huic vicinæ, quæ videntur parum ei cedere.   Hoc igitur tempore consilium
initur, quomodo hi nostri hactenus sane fructuosi labores integri possint
conservari contra injurias aliarum nationum, inter quas Hispani et Dani
videntur præcipue considerandi ; illi, quia Papaniano jure occidentalia
omnia sibi vendicant, hi quo septentrionaliores eo propiores, et Islandia[1]
freti aptius ad hoc iter accommodati.   Necnon dicuntur navigandi arte
satis valere.   De hac igitur re tuum judicium pro amore nostro mihi
mittas velim, simulque commodam viam describas illas mineras exercendi.
Promisisti te Gutebergica jura mihi missurum fuisse.   Hoc ut quam primum facias oro.   Ex illis forsan aliquid lucis erui potest.   Nos enim hanc
artem paulo melius scimus quam vindemiam.   Itaque scribere memineris,
ut famæ, quæ de te hic maxima est, respondeas : literas enim, nisi prohi-
beas, reginæ monstrabo.   Res est profecto magni momenti, et quæ veram
religionem profitentibus aliquando forsan conducet.   Scripsi tibi ter de illo
nostro magno negotio : quare puto tibi ea de re satisfactum.

Oro ut diligenter ad me scribas, et pigritiam forsan excutiam.   Literas
Fremingo nostro mittas.   Taxius enim veloces suos equos nimium exercuit.
Doleo sane casum illius viri.   Belus noster tecum jam, ut credo, veteres
amicitiæ fructus suaviter in memoriam vocat.   Amo illum, et tamen in-
video.   Lubetius noster mecum egit de pecunia quam rex Galliæ debet
liberis Germaniæ civitatibus.   Hic profecto video consiliarios libenter velle
civitatibus Germanicis gratificari.   Sed, ut nosti, vous autres francois nous
deves il y a long temp toute L'Aquitaine et la Normandie, mais vous feres
plus tost banquerouttes que les paier, et pourtant nous estimons peu tels
debiteurs et moins si mauvais fermiers.   Peto a te, ut mihi scribas, quo in
statu res tuæ sint.   Nisi persuasum habeas me, in quacunque re valeam,
semper fore paratissimum tibi inservire, scelestum me judicas.   Nec mihi
absentem animum objicias : nunquam enim aliquid remisi ex illo vehementi
amore, quo te semper prosequutus sum ; sed potius indies auxi, dulcedi-
nemque tuæ consuetudinis absens vel maxime sensi.   Sed tu vide, quid
Aristoteles in Rhetoricis de senibus habeat : esse nimirum in amore frigi-
dos, et nos irridere nostris spiritubus in amicitia colenda, quasi nihil aliud
essent quam juvenilis ardoris fumi.   Sed, Deus bone ! quis jam audet me
pigritiæ nomine accusare, cum ita longas literas scribam ?   Vide ut mihi
longiores rescribas ; habebis enim mensis unius ad minimum usuram.   Vale,

[1 Omnia sic MS.]

et me optimo Bano commendes, Lubetio nostro, Clusio, optimo Jordano, meoque Andreæ.   Et Beuterichio, omnium reisterorum doctoratissimo et omnium doctorum reisteratissimo, (ut Cicero, ni fallor, de Scævola et Crasso,) ita mea officia deferas ut illius, qui eos omnes amat, et cupit eis singulis gratificari et inservire.   Iterum vale, mi Huberte.

In aula regia, 1 Octobris, 1577.

Tui amantissimus,

PHILIPPUS SIDNEIUS.

Miror quod nihil de Wackero jam diu intellexerim.   Fuit hic ilico post reditum meum ex Germania Henricus, baro a Lichtenstein, cui sane talem humanitatem non exhibui quam debui; ita fui plane implicitus negotiis, e t præ absentia parentis et avunculorum, qui tunc temporis in Balneis erant, non bene instructus ad eum ut volui accipiendum.   Oro ut, cum tibi idoneum tempus fuerit, me excuses.   Est sane præclarus juvenis, et quem ego ex corde amo ; et quandocunque aliquis ex ejus amicis huc venerit, conabor hanc culpam compensare.   Consanguineus meus Grivellus te officiose salutat.

INSCRIPTIO.

. . . . mo viro domino Langueto,
domino meo carissimo.   Fran-
cofurti ad Mænum.

EPISTOLA CXVIII.

RODOLPHUS GUALTERUS AD GEORGIUM BUCHANANUM.

CUM anno superiori meæ in D. Pauli ad Galatas epistolam homiliæ, serenissimo Scotorum regi dicatæ, in publicum prodirent, pridie kal. Sept. ad te, vir præstantissime et domine mihi plurimum observande, literas dedi : et duo misi ejus libri exempla, quorum unum ut regiæ majestati meo nomine offerres, alterum in mei amoris atque observantiæ testimonium tibi retineres rogabam.   Ab eo autem tempore nihil vel ex Anglia vel ex Scotia vestra literarum accepi, quibus docerer, quid de libris illis sit factum.   Affirmavit quidem nostro typographo Londinensis mercator, cui ille fasciculum curandum dederat, hunc certo et [tuto illuc transmissum fuisse.   At mihi ejus fidem suspectam facit, partim tam diuturnum silentium, partim illius avaritia, quæ mihi plurimis aliis argumentis perspecta est, et hominem in iis curandis negligentem facit, quæ nullo cum lucro conjuncta esse videt.   Et auxit mihi suspicionem hanc generosus juvenis D. Georgius Keith, comitis Marescalli Scotiæ filius, qui et ipse tale quid factum existimat, cum te sciat in amicitiis bonorum amplectendis facilem et cumprimis officiosum esse. Itaque cum Augusto mense de indigna fratris sui Gulielmi cæde ad me literas daret, et meum in ejus memoria ac morte celebranda officium requireret, atque insuper operam suam in meis curandis pro sua humanitate mihi offerret; ego occasionem tam optatam minime negligendam putavi, et fratris manibus officium præstiti quale potui inter occupationes et curas graves, quæ me a poetico studio, quo olim delectabar, avocant; et simul has literas ad illum Lausannam perferendas dedi, ut inde eas cum suis ad te mittat, quas ut ea fronte accipias oro, mi doctissime Buchanane, qua hominis tui nominis studiosissimi officia accipere soles; et me quæso hac cura libera, ut num mei Galatæ ad tuas manus pervenerint, et ut a regia majestate accepti sint, intelligam. Hoc tibi sancte affirmo, me non aliud meis lucubrationibus quærere, quam ut ecclesiæ prosim: quod si assequar aliqua ex parte, me nullius laboris aut molestiæ piget. Vale, vir præstantissime et mihi cum reverentia observande. Tiguri in die solstitii brumalis, anno nati Christi 1577.

Tuæ præstantiæ observantissimus,
RODOLPHUS GUALTERUS.

INSCRIPTIO.

Præstantissimo viro D. Georgio Bu-
chanano, serenissimi Scotorum
regis præceptori fidelissimo, do-
mino suo plurimum observando.

EPISTOLA CXIX.

PHILIPPUS SIDNEIUS AD HUBERTUM LANGUETUM.

Mi carissime Huberte! Simul et Robertus Belus et Rogerius et Buterichius tuus cum tuis optatissimis literis venere, ita ut eodem tempore mihi et audire te et videre summa mea cum voluptate viderer. Tu me pigritiæ nomine acriter accusas, et interea in eandem culpam impingis, imo ideo majorem, quia tuis ego fio melior, meæ tibi inaniter obstrepant necesse est. Et stili usus, ut videre est, plane mihi excidit; et ipse animus, si forsan unquam aliqua in re valuit, incipit jam pro ignavo nostro otio vires suas et sine sensu amittere et non illibenter remittere. Quem enim ad finem sunt nobis nostræ cogitationes ad variam cognitionem excitandæ, nisi locus illius exercendæ detur, ut inde publica utilitas redundet, quod

in corrupto seculo sperare non licet? Quis musicam nisi ad delectationem,
architecturam nisi ad ædes fabricandas discit? Sed ipsa mens, inquies,
divinæ mentis particula, ita excolitur. Summum certe, si hoc fatemur,
fructus; sed videamus an non nostris splendidis erroribus pulchram, sed
fucatam speciem induamus. Dum enim mens ita quasi sibi extrahitur, non
potest aciem suam in se penitus intuendam convertere, cui operæ nulla
quam homines navare possunt comparari potest. Nonne vides me eleganter
stoicum agere? imo et cynicus ero, nisi tu me revoces. Quare, si velis,
para te in me: campum jam monstravi, et aperte tibi denuncio bellum.

Sed miror, quid tibi in mentem venerit, mi carissime Languete, quod
cum adhuc nihil me dignum egerim, velles me matrimonii vinculis obstringi; nec tamen aliquam denotas, sed potius ipsum statum, quem
tamen tu tuo exemplo hactenus non confirmasti, extollere videris. De
illa, qua quam indignus sim facile agnosco, jamdudum meas rationes
breviter sane, sed ut poteram, tibi scripsi. Hoc quidem tempore credo
te aliquid aliud sensisse, quod quicquid fuerit, ut ad me scribas vehementer oro: magni enim sunt ponderis apud me omnia, quæ a te pro-
veniunt; et, ut ingenue fatear, aliquo modo dubito, ne aliquis suspicionibus
magis quam sapientia validus aliquid sinistri de me tibi insusurraverit,
quod tibi quamvis non fuerit persuasum, voluisti tamen caute et amice
mihi considerandum præbere. Quod si ita fuerit, oro ut mihi rem ipsam
manifesto scribas, ut me tibi, cui cupio esse probatissimus, purgare possim:
sin tantum jocus aut amicum consilium fuerit, id quoque ut significes oro,
cum omnia tua mihi, non minus quam quæ sunt carissima, semper grata
veniant.

Novi hic nihil est, nisi quod novum in monarchia est et fere inau-
ditum, quum nihil eveniat novum. Aurum nostrum Furbisserum jam
liquefactum non ita magnas opes producit, ut primo ostentaverat: tamen
non contemnendæ insulæ sunt ad sexagesimum secundum gradum, sed
hoc inter maxime secreta tenent, ne ut scis præripiatur occasio. Imo
et eodem gradu sperant se posse fretum transire: adeo sunt nugæ ille
magnus mundus a cosmographis descriptus; si vero fretum tali tempe-
raturæ cadat, vides fore magni momenti. Credo reginam id in gratiam
principis Casimiri facturam, de quo mihi scripsisti; sed nolui hoc tempore
multa de ea re tractare, cum sciam nostrum ingenium esse nihil celeriter
perficere. Quid aliud jam plane dormituriens tibi scribam, nisi te a me
ut cor meum amari, meque nulli rei magis intentum esse, quam ut possim
hoc aliquando tibi demonstrare? Grivellus meus te salutat. Saluta
humiliter meo nomine Comitem et Comitissam Hannaviensem, et scribe
mihi, quomodo canes, quos misi, ipsis arrideant. Scripsi ad Lubetium
hoc tempore, Banesium, Andream Anselmum, Merellum: egone piger?
Oro ut Clusium salutes, et Domino Salvarto significes, me multum illi
debere ob libellum, quem mihi in Gallicam linguam traductum misit: ego

cum mihi traderetur, fui occupatissimus, sed aliquando hanc illius humanitatem merebor. Domino Glauburgo quoque plurimam salutem dicas, cui
ego libenter gratificabor. Vale, carissime Languete. Kalendis Martii,
1578.

Tuus,

PHILIPPUS SIDNEIUS.

Ego Belo omnia amica, quæ potero, officia præstabo, tum ob sua
merita, tum præcipue ob tuam commendationem.

EPISTOLA CXX.

LAURENTIUS HUMFREDUS AD [ABRAHAMUM MUSCULUM].

IMMANUEL. Discessit a nobis tuus filius, et ad aliquot menses hæsit
Londini, ubi tamen et literis operam dedisse et conciones audivisse non
dubito. Mihi et patris tui honorandi senis nomine et tua et sua ipsius
causa fuit carissimus. Basileæ enim cum vixi, aliquot versiones D.
Musculi apud Frobenium inspexi, et prælo præfui. Si quid latet, rogo ut
in lucem prodeat: fuit enim variæ lectionis, limati judicii, et indefessæ
diligentiæ. Nec oblivisci possum quanta humanitate me et aliquot comites
Bernæ exceperit. Itaque colo memoriam tanti viri, et rogo Deum ut
tibi ejusque posteritati benedicat. Nonnihil vero animum meum angit,
quod nos filius tuus tam cito reliquerit, et quod non licuerit illi prodesse
ita uti volebam. Sed enim ardebat quodam studio videndi academiam
Cantabrigiensem et alia loca Angliæ, quo doctior redeat, non nummatior.
Te vero, doctissime vir, rogo et hortor in Domino, ut pergas sequi patris
vestigia, et nos Britannos, quantumvis longo intervallo disjunctos, literis
invisere, imo et eruditis librorum monumentis juvare, ut in filio talem
scriptorem revixisse intelligamus. Fruendum est enim hoc singulari beneficio pacis, et omnes labores ad utilitatem ecclesiæ conferendi, dum licet
per hanc temporum serenitatem. Perge ut cœpisti, et D. Jesus te diu
ecclesiæ catholicæ et patriæ et nobis valentem et florentem custodiat.
Oxon. Mar. 3, anno 1578.

Tuus,

LAUR. HUMFREDUS.

EPISTOLA CXXI.

PHILIPPUS SIDNEIUS AD HUBERTUM LANGUETUM.

Mi carissime Huberte! Scripsi tibi per Beuterichium nostrum, quid tum mihi in animum veniret. Hoc tempore D. Rogerio hæc ad te dedi, potius ut nullam intermittam occasionem te salutandi, quam ut ulla hic offeratur occasio vel cogitatione digna. Ita male satisfecimus Beuterichio ut credam, nisi quo minus fiat ipsius obstet humanitas, male nos in Germania audituros. Et tamen, ut ingenue et tibi soli dicam, non ita constanter visi [sunt] vestras res tractare, cum aliud princeps Aurangius, aliud illustrissimus Casimirus viderentur appetere. Unde regina arripuit occasionem defendendi tarditatem suam in exequendis consiliis contra Leycestrensem, Walsinghamum et alios, qui eam vehementius ad agendum persuaserant, quod maxime doleo. Plessius noster brevi, credo, hinc discedet, qui nec ea potuit obtinere, quæ sane Christianæ reipublicæ fuissent salutaria. Ego profecto, nisi Deus potenter resistat, videor mihi causam nostram arentem videre, et aliquid jam Indicum mecum meditor. Regina tibi favet, ut spero te brevi intellecturum: interea me, ut soles, vehementer ames velim; meque omnibus nostris communibus amicis commendes. Ex aula regia 10 Martii, 1578.

Tuus,

PHILIPPUS SIDNEIUS.

Swendianum scriptum accepi a Comite Hannaviense; a te nullum hactenus habui. Meum D. Rogerium oro ut in meam gratiam adhuc magis ames.

EPISTOLA CXXII.

LAURENTIUS HUMFREDUS AD ABRAHAMUM MUSCULUM.

Immanuel. Accepi tuas literas, doctissime vir: si quid feci gratum filio Wolphgango, aut quod esse possit a re tua, gaudeo. Peregrinus ipse, didici peregrinis succurrere. Hoc solum molestum est, quod voluntati facultates non respondeant. Deinde hoc tempore impositum mihi subito grave est onus cujusdam legationis in Germaniam ad synodum Smalcaldensem, ubi cum fratribus conferendum de Lutheranismo, quantum intelligo, et de illa infausta cœnæ dominicæ controversia, quæ cum tamdiu tanto æstu et studio partium tractata fuerit, quomodo dirimi possit non video. Utinam alii legati ex Helvetia et Geneva adessent, ut possemus, invocato Dei nomine, et amice ac fraterne convenire! Regia majestas in id incumbit. Deus et a vobis et a nobis orandus, ut tantum negotium ad aliquem felicem exitum perducat. Miselli sumus: itaque precamur, ut in infirmitate nostra ipsius virtus perficiatur. Reversus curabo filium et adjuvabo pro viribus: hactenus de illis duobus Anglis nihil certi cognovimus. Hæc raptim Londini. D. Jesus suæ ecclesiæ et vestræ misereatur, te conservet cum tua familia! Amen. Anno 1578, Junii 5°.

Tuus totus et patri tuo Wolphgango Musculo

plurimum devinctus,

LAUR. HUMFREDUS.

INSCRIPTIO.
Doctissimo viro, et fratri in Christo observando, D. Abrahamo Musculo, ecclesiæ Bernensis ministro dignissimo. Bernæ.

EPISTOLA CXXIII.

GEORGIUS BUCHANANUS AD RODOLPHUM GUALTERUM.

S. Tuæ literæ, vir præstantissime, Tiguri scriptæ prid. kal. Sept., octavo demum post mense, hoc est, ad kalendas Maias, sunt mihi perlatæ. Ac a rege quidem tuum munus, ut erat amplum et honorificum, ita libenter et benevole est acceptum: spes vero de eo tuæ, et aliorum qui isthuc sunt bonorum, non modo ipsi, sed nobis quoque, qui ei instituendo sumus præfecti, longe gratissimæ acciderunt: nam si indoles quæ in eo nunc jucunde efflorescit, cum tempore maturuerit, et exspectatione nostra dignos fructus ediderit, erit profecto quod et ille et nos plurimum tibi debeamus: ille, quod ingenium adhuc infirmum laudibus vestris sustentetis, et adhortationibus vestris labores pueris molestos, velut ostentatis victoriæ præmiis, allevetis: nobis, quod oneris impositi tales viri in partem ultro subeatis, non potest non esse jucundissimum, nisi nos ingratissimi esse velimus. Neque enim sola vox præceptoris studia discentium promovet; sed quæcunque etiam animum jacentem exsuscitant, et laborum tædia minuunt, et virtutis veræ speciem ob oculos proponunt, etiam præceptorum vice funguntur. Accedit ad hæc, quæ dixi mollius ad aures quam præcepta accidant: ut quæ non velut pro imperio jubeant, sed honoris et gloriæ blandissimis invitamentis illiciant. Habent etiam illa vestra munera, quæ ex locis magno intervallo dissitis adveniunt, longinquitatis gratiam, et adulandi suspicione carent: at domesticorum plerumque officia non ex horreo liberalitatis depromi, sed tanquam æs alienum exsolvi existimantes accipiunt. Sed hactenus de rege. Poemata mea quod probes, est mihi pergratum: nam sive in eo erras, non judicii infirmitate falleris, sed benevolentia adductus minus errata perspicis; sive jure id facis, ego quoque jure gaudeo (ut apud Nævium Hector) a laudato viro laudari: sed ne id mihi solidum sincerumque sit gaudium, multa impediunt. Ætatis enim nostræ ea est ignavia, ut nemo in eo libenter magnum studio collocet laborem, unde aut minimum aut nullum speret operæ pretium. Nec desunt nec deerunt, qui non clari poetæ clarissimam sententiam, qua virtutem sui esse præmium contendit, contemnant; sed ut totum hoc scribendi genus, ut inutile et ad unam aurium voluptatem comparatum, abjiciant. Me vero hominem mediocri ingenio præditum, *vervecum in patria crassoque sub aere natum*, quæ potuerunt ullæ satis * * * * *.

EPISTOLA CXXIV.

FRANCISCUS WALSINGHAMUS AD JOHANNEM STURMIUM.

S. P. LITERIS tuis quas postremo accepi, nihil in præsens respondeo propter occupationes meas graviores quibus premor, et subitam discessionem latoris præsentium. Superioribus hisce diebus in aliqua spe eramus de rebus Belgicis componendis; sed illa spes concidit propter literas quas accepit Austriacus, si ejus fidei credimus, a catholico rege, quibus significat universum istud negotium Belgicum componendum et definiendum demandatum esse et concreditum majestati imperatoriæ, quæ in se suscepit res eorum componere; sed quo tempore aut quibus conditionibus, aut quam feliciter, ignoramus. Alia sunt quæ libens ad te perscriberem, sed negotium et temporis brevitas non sinunt: referam in aliud tempus, et me ut soles diliges. Raptim. Antwerpiæ, 5 Sept. 1578.

Tuus ex animo ut suus,

FRA. WALSINGHAM.

INSCRIPTIO.

Ornatissimo viro et amico suo carissimo D. Johanni Sturmio, Argentorati.

EPISTOLA CXXV.

RICARDUS HILLES AD RODOLPHUM GUALTERUM.

S. P.   Ex literis tuis septimo Novembris proxime præteriti Tiguri datis, domine colendissime et in Christo Domino Servatore nostro carissime, intellexi te bene valere, et Deum Optimum Maximum precor, ut te quam diutissime in ejus gloriam et ecclesiæ suæ ædificationem conservet. Tuæ dictæ literæ profecto magnum mihi attulerunt consolationem, quod tuorum filiorum carissimorum et necessariorum amicorum obitum ita bono et constanti animo tuleris, quia *beati mortui qui in Domino moriuntur: modo enim, dicit Spiritus, requiescunt a laboribus suis.* Si enim te-ipsum diuturno mœrore conficeres, nil lucri aut commodi inde unquam exspectare poteris.   Certissimum est enim, eos in hunc mundum non redituros: æque etiam certum est, te prius ad illos abiturum.

Literas, quas in tuis accepi pro D. Laurentio Humfredo, ultimo die mensis Decembris Oxonium misi, per tabellionem quendam fidum, qui singulis hebdomadis literas ab academia Oxoniensi defert; ita ut nullum sit dubium, quin literas tuas prædictas domino doctori Humfredo ante hunc diem certissime dederit.   Precor autem te, ut si quas alias literas mihi inscriptas Argentinam mittas, D. Theobaldo Behem, mercatori Argentoratensi, qui eas mihi quam commodissime mittere poterit, ut non dedigneris una cum illis literis pecuniam pro vectura earundem mittere: vereor enim alias, ne non ipsas literas tam libenter per postam Spieren-sem mandare velit.

Habeo tibi gratias, quod ea nova, quæ tunc temporis audivisti de Alansonio principe (qui est frater regis Galliæ, sicut ego intelligo), mihi scribere dignatus fueris; et ego vicissim nunc tibi rescribo, eundem principem Alansonium in fine mensis prædicti Decembris de oppido Belgico (quod Bergen Germanice et Mons Gallice vocatur) in Galliam cum omni-bus suis militibus abiisse.   Aiunt autem ipsi Belgici, quod eo modo illud oppidum contra regem Philippum animo habet defendere, sicut avus ejus urbem Mætensem contra Cæsarem Carolum quintum tutatus est. Amico meo veteri Julio Sancterentiano (in officina Froschoviana pro correctore ad typographiam suam servienti) habeas me commendatum precor; dicasque illi precor, me jamdudum literas suas benevolas 24 Augusti Tiguri datas ante duas menses accepisse; præterea etiam ante mensem unam quinque illos libros in iisdem suis literis specificatos: quo-rum unum, sicuti cupiebat, mihi ipse servavi, reliquos autem domino Herberto Westphalingo, præbendario Oxoniensi, Oxonium per fidum ta-bellionem misi.   Item quod secundum ejus desiderium, quod hactenus

præstiti officium in procuranda sua annuitate Oxoniensi, idem nunc etiam
officium, Deo volente, ei impendam ad proxime præteritas nundinas.
Francofordienses autumnales literas meas, die mensis Augusti proxime
præteriti datas, ad dominum Christoferum Froschoverum, Tigurinum,
misi, de quibus Julii Sancterentiani responsum brevi exspecto. Spero item
eas ipsas fuisse literas meas, quas tu postremo a me scriptas ad Julium
tuum intelligis, quemadmodum in initio tuarum literarum scripsisti.

Uxor mea, quæ nunc dierum subinde valde valetudinaria est, (quamvis jam, Deo gratias, utcunque valet,) quamplurimum te resalutat.
Deum precor ut is pro sua bonitate te una cum uxore tuisque omnibus
incolumem servet. Vale. Londini, 10 Januarii, anno nati Christi 1578,
stilo Anglicano.

Tuus pro posse,

RICHARDUS HILLES.

INSCRIPTIO.

Doctissimo viro domino Rodolpho
  Gualtero amico mihi caris-
  simo.

EPISTOLA CXXVI.

FRANCISCUS COMES BEDFORDIENSIS AD RODOLPHUM GUAL-
TERUM.

LITERÆ tuæ, gravissime vir, quibus Johannem Rodolphum Ulmerum
commendasti, mihi admodum gratæ fuere: et ipse quoque mihi carus
est, non solum propter studium et voluntatem communiter in patriam,
præcipue vero in te et in patrem ejus; sed etiam propter multiplices
illius virtutes illum mirifice diligo. Est enim adolescens honestis
moribus, talis nimirum, quem merito probi omnes et ament et commendent, et (quod ex iis intelligo, qui secum in Academia Oxoniensi
versabantur) bonis literis non solum deditus, sed etiam summopere in-
tentus, in quibus ita (Dei numine aspirante) profecit, ut non dubito
illius studia in Dei gloriam et ecclesiæ ejus emolumentum brevi evasura.
Patriam vestram tum in religione tum in aliis omnibus bene et feliciter
habere vehementer gaudeo; et te, doctissime vir et pater in Christo vene-
rande, in sancto pietatis studio et gloriæ Dei promovendæ cursu non
defatigari lætor. Ac Deum ex animo precor, ut te magis ac magis con-

firmet, suisque donis locupletet, ac præsidio tueatur. Vale, gravissime
vir. Exoniæ, prid. Cal. Mart. 1579.

Tui in Domino studiosissimus,

F. BEDFORD.

Postscriptum. Gratias ingentes tibi ago, doctissime vir, pro humanitate tua in me singulari, cum essem vobiscum in patria vestra: atque
ut idem meo nomine faceres toti Mæcenaticæ cohorti Tigurinæ precibus
a te contendo.

EPISTOLA CXXVII.

GULIELMUS COLUS AD [RODOLPHUM GUALTERUM].

Venit ad me, doctissime vir, juvenis quidam Tigurinus, Ulmeri filius,
ut narrat, post dies aliquot hinc ad vos reversurus. Huic meas literas
ad te denegare non potui, virum de me exule ante multos annos optime
meritum, non quod quicquam habeam hoc tempore dignum quod tibi
legendum offeratur, sed ne non scribendo beneficii accepti immemorem me
esse judices. Filium tuum audio, alumnum non ita pridem Oxoniensem,
summæ spei juvenem, præmatura morte esse sublatum: quod sane vehementer dolemus omnes, quibus erat, dum hic ageret, familiariter notus,
non solum tua ipsius causa, quod filium tantæ exspectationis amiseris,
sed multo magis, ut par est, quia sine magno damno ecclesia Christi
carere tanto ingenio non possit. De nostris vero Anglis, qui Tiguri
mecum exularunt, nihil est quod scribam, præterquam quod ex multis
vix quinque jam esse reliquos. D. Hornus Vintoniensis episcopus dignissimus valetudine utitur valde infirma. D. Mullins est archidiaconus Londinensis: D. Renigerus archidiaconus Wintoniensis. D. Humfredus
et ego præficimur duobus collegiis Oxonii, ille Magdalenensi, ego Somato-
christiano. Ceteri omnes emigrarunt ex hac vita. Ex his vides ad
magnam paucitatem eos esse redactos, qui vobiscum aliquando vixerunt
exules; et vides, quo in statu res nostræ sint, qui adhuc sumus superstites.
Quænam vero sit conditio religionis per universam Angliam, si scire
cupias, eadem est prorsus, quæ fuit ab initio regni Elizabethæ serenissimæ
reginæ nostræ: nulla est immutatio. Regina Scotiæ apud nos est, sed
non est sui juris, nec licet illi evagari quo voluerit. In Scotia religionem
veram acerrime tuentur et defendunt, atque omnia sunt illic quieta et
tranquilla. Audio a principe Parmensi parari exercitum in Belgas.
Casimirus honorifice acceptus est a regina nostra, nec scio an quis un-

quam fuerit illi hospes gratior. Dux Alanconius exspectatur in dies
singulos; sperat, ut audio, se nuptias adepturum hic in Anglia. Hæc
tibi impertienda existimavi hoc tempore, nuntium præsertim tam opportunum nactus. Salutabis amicos meos omnes, nominatim vero D.
Lavaterum, D. Bullingerum, Froschoverum, meum Julium, etc. Vale,
carissime vir, et amantem redama. Oxonii, pridie calendas Martias,
1579.

Tui studiosissimus,

GULIELMUS COLUS.

EPISTOLA CXXVIII.

HUBERTUS LANGUETUS AD PETRUM HUBNERUM.

S. P. D. MIROR te de studiis generosi nostri domini Sidnæi nihil ad
me scribere: nam ut de iis aliquid scriberes, maxime a te exspectabam.
Credo te esse memorem eorum quæ tibi dixi, cum de ejus institutione
tecum agerem: nempe illustrissimum ejus parentem ac fratrem maxime
cupere, ut veram cognitionem linguæ Germanicæ assequatur; quod puto
non fore ipsi difficile, modo ingenii ipsius celeritas ac memoriæ felicitas
a diligentia et industria non destituantur, et tu eum sui officii sæpius
admoneas, et quæ sunt tui diligenter facias, non solum explicando ei
Germanica, quæ in linguam Latinam postea convertat, sed præcipue
loquendo cum eo Germanice, cum ipsius sermonis Germanici usus sit
ei magis necessarius quam lectio scriptorum Germanicorum: nam quæcunque Germanica scripta aliquid continent, quo ipsius ingenium excoli
possit, sunt fere omnia conversa in linguas ipsi notas. Ut autem expedite loquatur Germanice, nunquam lectione scriptorum Germanicorum
assequetur, etiamsi totam vitam ei rei impenderet, nisi usum sermonis
ad eam adjecerit. Erunt quidem ipsi insuavia ejus rei initia, sed dul-
cescent tempore; nam ubi sentiet se profecisse, capiet ex ea re voluptatem,
et ad reliqua persequenda reddetur alacrior. Tu vero vide ne in ea re
ipsi desis: nam non ignoras me id a te præcipue petivisse, teque mihi
promisisse; et si videas tuas admonitiones non esse ipsi admodum gratas,
ne tamen propterea desistas, sed tuum institutum urge. Quod si feceris,
non est quod dubites quin tibi tandem sit gratiam habiturus: intelliget
enim te hæc agentem cupere ipsi consulere; et cum sit animo generoso,

pro beneficio nequaquam malam gratiam referet. Bene vale. Ex Thermis, 4 die Junii, 1579.

Tui studiosissimus,

HUBERTUS LANGUETUS.

INSCRIPTIO.

Optimo ac doctissimo viro, domino
  Petro Hubnero amico suo caris-
  simo. Argentorati.

EPISTOLA CXXIX.

GEORGIUS BUCHANANUS AD RODOLPHUM GUALTERUM.

TUAS priores literas una cum libris accepi, non paucis postquam a te missæ fuerant mensibus. Librum, ut voluisti, dedi regi, quem ille quo debuit, hoc est propensissimo in te, animo accepit. Rescripsit etiam pro tempore quæ visa sunt: illud videlicet imprimis, "Cum cives omnes mei tibi plurimum debeant, me non solum tibi obæratum, sed prope nexum esse volueris, ut qui in partem oneris gravissimi succedas, et nostrum laborem partim leves, partim animum adhuc rudem velut subigis, et ad semen doctrinæ accipiendum frugemque bonam proferendum paras." Et cum utriusque nostrum labor ad ingenii spectet cultum, nostræ partes agricolarum industriæ, tuæ vero cœlesti illi vi, quæ labores omnes fæcundat, et salubri temperie dat segeti incrementum, posse comparari videntur. Posteriores vero tuæ literæ, Tiguri bruma datæ anno 1577, ad nos demum perlatæ fuerunt ad Augustum anni 1579. Ego jam quadragesimum et eo amplius diem ob adversam valetudinem ab aula absum; sed cum primum eo rediero, dabo operam, ut rex ipse tantulum suis occupationibus suffuretur, ut ipse sui animi ad te testimonium sua manu det: sin minus id ipse præstare potero, curabo ut per collegam meum, virum pium et eruditum Petrum Junium (qui molles aditus et tempora observabit), id conficiatur. Interim ad te mitto commentarium nostrum de regno, scriptum quidem temporibus turbulentis, sed nunc demum emissum, spatio modico interjecto, mitescente tumultu, et auribus hominum ejuscemodi sermonibus assuefactis.

Potest fortasse noster labor supervacaneus videri, tot præsertim hominum doctissimorum jampridem ea de re lucubrationibus evulgatis. Sed cum illi sparsa quædam sed præclara in hoc genere præcepta collegissent, mihi sum visus operam omnino non lusurus, si in methodum ea redigerem, et non temere, sed via et ratione, de re tota disquirerem.   In hoc genere si operæ quid pretium viri probi et docti me fecisse existiment, multitudinis approbationem nihil moror.

9 kal. Aug. anno Christi nati 1579.

<hr />

EPISTOLA CXXX.

<hr />

RODOLPHUS GUALTERUS AD GEORGIUM BUCHANANUM.

Mirabar equidem, vir præstantissime et domine mihi plurimum observande, me de meis ad serenissimum regem et te toto triennio nullum responsum accipere.   At nuper intellexi et tuarum literarum eandem sortem fuisse: nam quas tu ad 9 kal. Aug. anni proxime elapsi dedisti, ego ultimo id. Jan. accepi.   Quæ quo tardiores ad me venerunt, eo plus voluptatis attulere, quod et librum meum propensissimo animo acceptum esse, et meum hoc officium tibi viro doctissimo, cujus judicium innumeris aliis præfero, probari nuntiarent.   Doleo tamen me interea caruisse eo gaudio, quod ex primis tuis literis percipere potueram.   Sed cum eas in hanc usque diem non viderim, aut hominum malevolorum perfidia aut alia aliqua causa interciderint oportet.   Sed sufficit, ut dixi, me serenissimo regi et tibi rem non ingratam fecisse.   Quod si accedat regiæ erga me voluntatis indicium ejus manu scriptum, quod tua humanitas pollicetur, tunc me hac parte beatum prædicabo.

Literis tuis conjunctus erat libellus tuus, " de jure regni apud Scotos," quem non ipse modo legi, sed symmystis et collegis meis legendum et examinandum præbui: quorum omnium idem est de illo judicium quod meum ; librum videlicet [non] tam docte et graviter, quam pie scriptum. Et utinam quod in eo bene et pie dicis, omnibus regibus persuaderi posset ! ita enim beatiores essent qui illis subjecti sunt populi, et ipsi non in terris modo beati regnarent, verum etiam cum Rege regum et Domino dominantium Jesu Christo regni cœlestis consortio fruerentur.   At quia pauci ita sentiunt, plerique autem adulatorum et perditissimorum lenociniis corrumpuntur ; dum se reges esse putant, turpissimorum affectuum et scelerum mancipia fiunt: et insuper suæ fidei commissum populum, cujus ποιμένες esse debebant, deglubunt, et tandem una secum perdunt.   Felicem ergo et beatum prædico serenissimum Scotiæ vestræ regem, cui hoc tam corrupto seculo talis institutor obtigit, qui animum juvenilem præceptis saluberrimis imbuere, et virtutum vere regiarum semina in illo plantare potest.   Et spero Deum, qui hac gratia illum complexus est, daturum etiam, ut præceptis salutaribus obediat, et cum populo suo felix et beatus vivat, et regnet ad sui nominis gloriam.

Hæc ad literas tuas respondere libuit, simulque monere ut si tibi nulla literas ad nos transmittendi via compendiosior offeratur, eas ad reverendissimum Eboracensem dominum Edvinum Sandium mittas, cum quo mihi aliquot annorum amicitia intercessit, qui eas per Londinenses suos ad nos perferri curabit. Vale, vir præstantissime. Tiguri, 8 Id. Mart. anno nati in carne æterni Filii Dei 1580.

Tui amantissimus,

RODOLPHUS GUALTERUS.

EPISTOLA CXXXI.

H. ZANCHIUS AD D. FRANCISCUM WALSINGHAMUM.

S. HERI cum a nobis discederet vir clarissimus D. Johannes Sturmius, jussit me ad te, vir magnifice, scribere de suo ad nos adventu, de causa adventus, deque etiam discessu. Dixi mihi nullam tecum intercedere amicitiam, nedum familiaritatem: respondit, se certo scire meas tibi futuras gratas, atque hanc meam scriptionem sperare se futuram aliquod amicitiæ nostræ initium; te enim summopere erga literarum et pietatis professores affectum esse, ut me hujusce officii pœnitere non possit. Quod ergo ad te, magnifice domine, hasce literas dare ausus fuerim, non est cur causas explicem, cum jam breviter illas indicarim. Tantum rogo ut meam simplicem scribendi rationem, tanquam senis, qui studio ornate dicendi jam valedixit, pro tua prudentia atque humanitate boni consulas.

Multa passus est bonus senex propter liberam et apertam veritatis defensionem, quam ita constanter defendit, et defendendi animus illi est, ut coactus aliquid tempori dare (quidam enim minati ei sunt carcerem), calendis Augusti Argentina discedens, ad nos altero die pervenerit, ubi ab omnibus amicissime exceptus, atque inprimis ab illustrissimo principe, qui aurea etiam sui imagine illum honoris causa donavit; et ipse vicissim omnes sua veneranda præsentia, gravissimis et eruditis colloquiis, et, quod plus est, sua constanti pietatis testificatione, audiendis concionibus, participando sacræ cœnæ sacramento, mirifice recreavit, totamque urbem ædificavit.

Scripsit per hoc tempus (nunquam enim otiosus fuit) tres libros contra ubiquitatis apostolum, sed nondum in lucem prodierunt. Causa diu agitata in senatu, tandem per literas quindecimvirûm revocatus fuit, data

*13

fide publica securitatis. Heri igitur, quæ fuit 23 Sept. 1581, persolutis omnibus ex fisco illustrissimi principis, qui in hospitio facti fuerant, sumtibus, summo mane, aliquot comitatus fratribus, Argentinam versus discessit, sanus atque hilaris, summa diligentia mandatam mihi ad te scriptionem non semel atque iterum commendans.

Habes, magnifice vir, executionem mandati Sturmiani ad me, de te salutando, et per literas meas de ipsius adventu ad nos et discessu commonefaciendo : quod officium eo libentius feci, quod speravi id fore, quod Sturmius sine ulla dubitatione ausus est polliceri, nimirum futuras literas meas tibi haud ingratas, teque recepturum me in numerum amicorum tuorum : quod ut facias, non vulgariter rogo. Servet serenissimæ reginæ majestatem, omnes proceres, ecclesiam et regnum, te cum omnibus bonis Dominus Jesus Christus ! per illum enim omnia consistere ait apostolus.

Neustadio, 24 Sept. 81.

T. M.

H. ZANCHIUS.

EPISTOLA CXXXII.

REGINA ELIZABETHA AD DOMINOS CONFŒDERATOS HELVETIÆ.

Elizabetha Dei gratia regina Angliæ, Franciæ et Hiberniæ, etc. potentibus et magnificis dominis, dominis confœderatis inclytæ Helvetiæ salutem et εὐπραξίαν.

Cogitanti mihi de rebus, quæ nuper mandato et, quemadmodum prætenditur, nomine ducis Sabaudiæ cognati mei peragebantur, et etiam nunc peraguntur, adversus urbem Genevensem ; cogitanti quinetiam de causis istiusmodi turbarum, et quem finem tandem sortiri possent, ut omittam florentissimas gentes et pulcherrimas urbes, quæ e primordiis longe abjectioribus promanarunt, nunc dirutas et prostratas jacere ; tunc in mentem venit me operæ pretium facturam, si de iis quas vos scire, et quarum vestræ interesse mihi videatur, vos certiorem facerem. Earum autem duæ potissimum sunt ; una quæ ad concordiam spectat et apud vos maximum pondus habeat, altera quæ postulat ut qui vestri corporis membra sunt, eos omni necessitate sublevetis et adjuvetis ; præsertim cum quicquid in ipsos beneficii conferetis, in vos redundabit. Non mihi dubium est autem, quin ista remedia, quæ a me vobis recensentur, ipsi satis animis perpendatis, nempe quam frugifera et necessaria sint vestræ libertati contra omnem vim hostium futura. Vestræ quandoque sapientiæ laudes jam pene omnium gentium sermonibus atque linguis celebrantur, ut nihil dicam

de eximia fortitudinis laude, de qua nulla unquam ætas conticescet: ob
quam nemo unquam, quocunque genere copiarum abundarit, vestræ saluti
et reipublicæ insidias struere est ausus, nisi qui callide in aliquorum
animos et familiaritatem influxissent: cujus farinæ hominibus si locum
detis, periculum est ne pestiferum venenum tandem in totum corpus
diffundere conentur, idque cum commodo suo, tum vestro exitio et in-
ternecione. Recte igitur faciunt qui ejusmodi calliditates amoliuntur:
ita enim saluti suæ vigilabunt, hostes autem etiam sine dispendio suo
domabunt. Consilium siquidem malum consultori pessimum est, et artes
Sinoniæ sponte collabuntur; vinculo interim pacis sese arctius quotidie
constringente, cum nullis insidiis labefactari aut dissolvi possit.

Considerate, obsecro, Galliæ statum, intuemini Belgium: ex quibus
Gallia jam aliquot annis intestinis bellis ardet, et pene ad vastitatem
redigitur; Belgium autem dum[1] projectum et dirutum ante oculos jacet:
defloruit utrumque, quod ipsis nunquam usu venisset, si vel tantillum
paci et concordiæ studuissent. Nunc autem alter alterum enervavit,
nec est qui alteri fidere ausit: amicis quandoque reconciliatis non facile
fides adhibetur, illique perpetuo suspicionis nomine insimulant.

Ceterum quod ad Genevam attinet, fateor eam adeo potentem non
esse: tamen est vestri corporis membrum, quod intelligo, ac proinde
quanto majoribus damnis afficitur, tanto acrius vulneratur Helvetia vestra.
De quo etsi aliqui vestrum, qui alia opinione induti sunt, non cogitent,
videant tamen illi, ne tandem aliquo detrimento suo experiantur quid sit.
Quod annis ante aliquot vobis cum urbe Genevense familiaritas intercessit,
cum bonis communibus, adduceremini equidem mutuis inter vos officiis,
id quod vicinos decet, confirmata est[2]; siquidem ea adhuc constans est et
manet, quidnam mali acciderit alterutri, quo non alteruter afficeretur?

His accedit quod Geneva emporium est, et transitus vestræ terræ,
quo vestri hostes facile de vobis bellum inferendo retardantur. Capta
igitur Geneva, ipsi jam cogitabitis quid vobis salutis restat. Sane illud
ipsum, de quo nunc inter vos et istos, qui boni principis tenera ætate
abutuntur, contenditur, causam præbuit, ut cum Genevensibus sese
societate obstrinxerint vestri majores omnem in eventum. Quare si
præclare ab illis factum est, ipsi facile animadvertitis, quo vestrum
ipsius[2] commodo et laude apud omnes pene gentes in defensione negotii
istius Genevensis præstituri sitis.

Oro igitur et clementer etiam atque etiam peto a vestra sapientia, ne
dedignemini more et fortitudine Helvetica huic negotio, quod vobis cum
Genevensibus commune est, strenue intendere et vestram operam navare:
unanimes urbem hanc vobis vicinam ab omnibus insidiis et irruptionibus,
quantum quidem in vobis est situm, tueri. Oro quinetiam non dedignemini malevolentiam, quam forte juvenis hic princeps contra vestros

[¹ Fors. *diu.*]   [² Omnia sic.]

*13—2

confœderatos concepit, precibus et intercessione mitigare, orareque excellentiam ipsius, ut negotium juri commendet, et legitimis coram judicibus illud civiliter prosequatur; vel porro omne cognoscat, nempe quomodo res omnes comparatæ sint, et ad quem finem spectant; nempe non cum Genevensibus tantum, sed tota cum Helvetia confœderata ipsi rem esse, vosque paratos esse quidvis pro istis, qui hactenus omnia sua officia et honores excellentiæ ipsius obtulerunt et detulerunt, perferre, quidquid, inquam, fides data vestræ societatis videbitur postulare.   Quod si feceritis, cum apud omnes gentes vobis perpetuo honori et laudi erit, tum vero atque imprimis vestræ saluti consuletis.   Valete.

Ex regia mea Ottlandia.   Kal. Septembrib. 1583.

Vestræ confœderationis amantissima,

ELIZABETHA R.

INSCRIPTIO.

Potentibus et magnificis dominis,
D. confœderatis inclytæ Helvetiæ,
amicis nostris carissimis.

EPISTOLA CXXXIII.

REGINA ELIZABETHA AD QUATUOR CIVITATES IN HELVETIA EVANGELIO CHRISTI REFORMATAS.

Elizabetha Dei gratia Angliæ, Franciæ et Hiberniæ regina, fidei defensor, etc. magnificis dominis et amplissimis coss. et senatoribus IV. civitatum, Tiguri, Bernæ, Basileæ atque Schaphusiæ, amicis nostris carissimis.

MAGNIFICI domini, amplissimi viri et amici carissimi.   Apud P. V. pro sociis vestris intercedere, vel periculi vestri jam satis prævisi et præcauti vos admonere, esset in amicitiam nostram peccare, si non ex summo erga vos amore faceremus: sed cum et amari a nobis non inique feretis, et nos solicitam esse de communi vestra pace plane cernetis, quin quod gratum vobis futurum sit nostrum studium non dubitamus.

Res est et causa Genevensium, quam vobis commendamus; neque aliena a consortio ejusdem Christi et evangelii, quod profitemini, nec secreta et disjuncta a communione periculi vestri, utpote quæ eosdem habeat hostes, quos et vos; eos nimirum, qui propter eam, quam profitemur, religionis reformatæ sinceritatem, in vitas omnium evangelium profitentium conjurarunt; qui quidem ad nos separatim opprimendos

variis artibus utuntur, idem tamen institutum et propositum ubique sequentes. Quod autem designant animis, quoniam apertis viribus assequi
nequeunt, (vellent enim uno ictu nos universos pessundare,) distributim
nos in partes secando, et a nobis invicem disjungendo, cuniculos agunt,
fraudem nobis clam machinantes. Qui quo magis in hoc elaborant uno,
ut nos videlicet in partes distrahant, eo nos reddunt ad concordiam
inter nos alendam colendamque vigilantiores; et quo citius malum ex
vicino malo percipimus, eo studiosiores esse debemus ad vicinum malum
a vicinis nostris propulsandum, ne quæ nostra culpa semel grassari
cœpit in unum membrum contagio, inevitabili fato per totum corpus
diffundatur. Hæc nos parcius, ut vos ex re præsenti attentius, quid sit
mature agendum, etiam atque etiam cogitetis. Id autem est, ut sociorum vestrorum curam habeatis; ipsorum, ut jam videtur proprium, vos
vestrum commune periculum faciatis; quoad eos levandos omnem opem,
omne auxilium, omne studium afferatis; et concordes inter vos ab eorum
defensione nullo unquam tempore desistatis. Istud merito nos pro nostra
amicitia rogamus, vobis nihil unquam denegatura, quod ad salutem vestram ornandam pertinere arbitrabimini. Bene et feliciter P. V. valeant.
Datæ e regia nostra Othlandiæ, primo die mensis Septembris, anno Domini
1583, regni vero nostri vigesimo quinto.

Incolumitatis vestræ studiosissima,

ELIZABETHA R.

INSCRIPTIO.

Magnificis dominis et amplissimis
coss. ac senatoribus civitatum IV.
Tiguri, Bernæ, Basileæ atque
Schaffusiæ, amicis nostris caris-
simis.

EPISTOLA CXXXIV.

MINISTRI ECCLESIÆ LONDINO-GERMANICÆ AD DOMINUM
THESAURARIUM.

Honoratissimo domino thesaurario S. R. M.

SUPPLICES indicant ministri et seniores ecclesiæ Londino-Germanicæ,
se nuper Dantisco a fratribus e Belgio profugis literas accepisse, ex quibus
intelligunt, ecclesiam ibidem peregrinantem non sine difficultate et periculo

conventus suos et pietatis exercitia agere posse propter quosdam religioni
infestos indigenas, qui peregrinos cœtus aliquoties turbare et seditionis
accusare non dubitarint.   Quoniam autem dicti peregrini, qui liberum et
apertum in vernaculo sermone religionis exercitium requirunt, non facile
sibi locum idoneum intra vel extra urbem a magistratu concessum iri
sentiunt, nisi superioris alicujus, præsertim vero regis Poloniæ illius
civitatis protectoris, intercesserit auctoritas ; demisse rogant, ut ad alia in
illud regnum collata beneficia serenissima regia majestas, pro sua erga pios
omnes et afflictos peregrinos benevolentia, apud ipsam Poloniæ regiam majestatem Belgicis quoque peregrinis eam ad rem aliquid favoris conciliare
clementer velit.   Unde non solum obstringentur, ut pro regiæ majestatis
diutina vita et prospera gubernatione preces assiduas apud Deum fundant ;
sed etiam, ut se gratos præbentes fidelem huic regno unitisque provinciis
operam et officium præstent in iis, quæ de Hispanorum aut aliorum
hostium conatibus et consiliis intellexerint, sedulo perscribendis.

Honoratissimæ vestræ dominationis addicti

MINISTRI ET SENIORES

Ecclesiæ Londino-Germanicæ.

EPISTOLA CXXXV.

REGINA ELIZABETHA AD REGEM POLONIÆ.

Elizabetha Dei gratia Angliæ, Franciæ et Hiberniæ regina, fidei
defensor, etc. serenissimo principi ac domino Sigismundo D. G. regi
Poloniæ, magno duci Lithuaniæ, fratri et consanguineo nostro carissimo.

NON dubitamus, quin serenitas vestra et ceteri omnes christiani orbis
principes bene intelligant, qualiter pertractatæ fuerimus ad subveniendum
statibus inferioris Germaniæ jam pene ab Hispanorum tyrannide oppressis,
cum antea crebris nostris et in Hispaniam et ad Belgii gubernatores legationibus et intercessionibus nullas æquas pacis conditiones poteramus illis
procurare.   Tria autem sunt, quæ nos maxime ad id faciendum permo-
verunt : primum, causa purioris religionis, quam ipsi nobiscum profite-
bantur ; deinde, vetera cum vicina gente jura commerciorum et con-
fœderationum ; ac demum, multa et aperta indicia, quæ declararunt
quasi subjugatos in nos et alios principes eandem religionem profitentes
eosdem hostes arma sua conversuros, ut monarchiæ, quam injuste affectant,

limites possint extendere. Sic evenit, ut multi earum regionum incolæ
in diversas provincias coacti sunt commigrare, et inter alias, in nonnullas
Prussiæ civitates, quæ serenitati vestræ sunt subjectæ: in quibus multi
nunc verentur, ne propter aliquam in quibusdam articulis religionis dis-
crepantiam non sint tali immunitate ac religionis exercitio fruituri, quæ
convenire possit ipsorum linguis ac prioribus ritibus, et quibus instituti
hactenus fuerunt. Cum autem certiores facti simus, non esse illos Belgas,
qui vel in civitate Gedanensi vel in aliis maritimis Prussiæ urbibus inhabitant, ex eo hominum genere, qui quærunt legitimum magistratum subvertere et anarchiam introducere, vel aliquem hæreticum vel impium errorem
profiteantur: non potuimus, quin pro nostra erga totam nationem affec-
tione eos serenitati vestræ commendaremus; rogantes serenitatem vestram,
ut cum regium plane sit bene mereri de iis, qui propter ejuscemodi honestas
causas exules sint, serenitas vestra velit pro sua auctoritate intercedere cum
magistratibus Dantiscanis et aliis, si opus fuerit, ut qui isthuc ex Belgio
commigrarunt, apud eos possint absque ulla difficultate aut periculo ejuscemodi cœtus reformatæ religionis continuare, prout in patria consueverunt,
atque iis aliquamdiu in illis urbibus fuit indultum; neque patiatur ullam
injuriam iis inferri, quamdiu se honeste ibidem gesserint. Nam propter
nonnullam malevolentiam peregrinos exigere et jura hospitalitatis ipsis
denegare, neque serenitati vestræ neque ipsis urbibus poterit esse vel utile
vel honorificum. Proinde subnixe a serenitate vestra petimus, ut illud
beneficium in eos velit nostra de causa conferre, quod nos pro summa benevolentia a vestra serenitate acceptabimus, et erga eos, qui a serenitate
vestra nobis commendabuntur, vicissim rependemus, ubi occasio aliqua se
obtulerit: sicque serenitati vestræ ac suo regno precamur a Deo Opt. Max.
omnia felicissima. Ex regia nostra Grenowici, 16 Aprilis, 1591.

EPISTOLA CXXXVI.

COMES STAFFORDIÆ AD [WOLFGANGUM] MEYERUM.

Domine Meyere, libenter facerem quid pro te possem, et procuravi quid
potui, et collegii seniores cum magna animi alacritate libentissime con-
cesserunt ut victum in collegio inter socios habeas. Pro vestitu et libris
ordinem dedi nomine reginæ eruditissimo et clarissimo domino doctori
Nevillo, ut decem tibi det per annum libras nostras, quas sine dubio reci-
pies singulis tribus mensibus divisim. Pro cubiculo, si possunt, hoc quoque

pro te facient, quamvis non sit res audita extraneis concedere quod patriotibus est per fundatores addictum. Consulo ergo tibi, ut si dant accipias gratissime; si non possunt, non multum queras[1]; nam hoc quoque verum est, quod si cubiculum habes, oportet ut emas lectum et supellectile, et pro anno vel biennio sumptus illos facere credo neque tibi utile esse nec necessarium; et minus constabit tibi parvum cubiculum prope collegium locare quam nummos tuos consumere in iis rebus quas non vendes pro dimidio, cum reditum in patriam cogere velis. Sic vale, et Deus te incolumem conservet! Grenvigiæ, 6 Aug. 1593.

Tui amantissimus,

E. STAFFORD.

EPISTOLA CXXXVII.

CIVITAS TIGURINA AD REGINAM ELIZABETHAM.

Serenissimæ ac potentissimæ reginæ D. Elizabethæ, Angliæ, Franciæ, Hiberniæ et circumjacentium insularum reginæ, fidei christianæ defensatrici, dominæ nostræ clementissimæ.

S. LAUDABILE et pium studium, quo serenissima tua majestas, regina potentissima, cum omnes veræ pietatis atque optimarum artium studiosos peregrinos, tum vero atque imprimis eos qui ex nostra urbe ad celeberrimas tuæ majestatis academias proficiscuntur, hactenus complexa est atque fovit, facit ut pro conjunctione illa arctissima, quæ nobis est in Christo, nulli dubitemus hasce ad regiam tuam majestatem literas dare, eique studii ejusdem declarandi novam occasionem præbere. Quod ut ipsa in optimam partem accipiat rogamus, hancque ita facturam certo confidimus.

Comparuit coram nobis dilectus civis noster Caspar Tomannus, harum literarum exhibitor, nobisque humiliter supplicavit, quandoquidem ingenti florentissimas academias tuæ majestatis, Oxoniensem nempe et Cantabrigiensem, adeundi, inque harum collegio aliquo sua studia continuandi æstu ac desiderio flagret, si modo gratiam obtinere per tuam clementiam possit, ut nos ad laudabile istud propositum promovendum ipsi commendationem ad serenissimam tuam majestatem clementer concederemus, quam quidem pondus habituram maximum ipse non dubitet.

Igitur ejus petitionem honestissimam agnoscentes, et simul attendentes eum ab eo tempore, quo primum musis dicatus scholas adire cœpit, præceptores suos pie et perofficiose semper coluisse, bene et modeste

[1 Sic.]

vixisse, inque optimarum literarum et liberalissimarum artium studiis, cum domi tum foris, Genevæ nimirum et Monspelii operam sedulam posuisse, ob quas virtutes merito bonis omnibus carissimus fuit; noluimus non ejus petitioni satisfacere.

Quare istum ac talem juvenem, jam in Angliam proficiscentem, serenissimæ tuæ majestati, regina, sic commendamus, de meliore (quod aiunt) nota, ut majore cura, studio, ac diligentia non possimus; quo laudabilem cursum suorum studiorum in nobilissimis academiis tuæ majestatis, inque earum collegio aliquo, si ulla honesta ratione fieri potest, possit continuare, ad patriæ nostræ ecclesiæque, in qua utrinque membra simus conjunctissima, honorem atque utilitatem.

Isthoc beneficio si Tomannus noster a serenissima tua majestate clementissime affectus fuerit, erit id non solum nobis gratissimum, sed ejus etiam compensandi occasionem nullam prætermittemus.

Scriberemus in hanc sententiam pluribus, ni videremur voluntati et benevolentiæ serenissimæ tuæ majestatis erga nos nostrosque, cujus hactenus illustria documenta dedit, diffidere.

Quod ergo reliquum est, Deum rogamus et rogabimus, ut serenissimam tuam majestatem, ecclesiæ orthodoxæ nutritiam laudatissimam et fidei veræ defensatricem fortissimam, omni bono cumulare, ab omni malo et præsertim antichristi technis defendere, ac piis vestris consiliis benedicere pergat, ad nominis sui gloriam propagandam, et ecclesiæ, cujus florentissimum Angliæ regnum ceu hujus nostri seculi vera Sarepta est, salutem tuendam. Amen.

Scriptum in urbe nostra, et sigillo solito communitum. Pridie Idus Sextilis, anno ultimæ Dei patientiæ 1600.

Consul et Senatus
Civitatis Tigurinæ.

EPISTOLA CXXXVIII.

CASPARUS THOMANNUS AD CASPARUM WASERUM.

Laus Deo semper! Anno Salvatoris 1601, Februarii.

Cum magnitudinem cumulumque beneficiorum tuorum, reverende domine Mæcenas, jucunda subinde recordatione repetam, et meam in referenda gratia nimis angustam facultatem agnoscam; facile quidem percipio gratias me pro tantis meritis nullas posse, agere vero perexiguas, et tamen debere longe maximas. His ita sese habentibus, non levis est

mihi incussus timor, ne putes harum rerum non solum commemorationem
omnem mihi excidisse, sed universam etiam earundem vel cogitationem
quidem perpetuo e memoria mea effugisse; cum tot præsertim dies men-
sesque præterierunt, ex quo nihil literarum a me accepisti, quibus vel
beneficam saltem meam voluntatem, cum res non suppeteret, ostenderem.
Sed spero cognita silentii diuturni causa te me excusatum habiturum.

Primo scias, reverende domine Mæcenas, prosperam corporis valetudinem; idem si de te intelligerem, maxima afficerer lætitia.   Quo in
statu res versentur meæ, breviter dicam.   Dieppam cum veneram, navem
quærebam; ea inventa portu solvi, et secundo vento in Dover appuli:
inde recta Londinum profectus ibi tradidi literas commendatitias D.
Castollo, a quo fui humaniter acceptus.   Postea adibam comitem Rut-
landiæ, qui epistolam tuam quoque perlegit, et mihi omnem operam tui
causa spopondit; tamen se non putare dixit peregrinis locum in collegiis
dari, sed scripsit medico regio, ut negotium meum in aula promoveat.
Septimo Octobris ad aulam me contuli, et medico ante palatium deambu-
lante invento, illi comitis literas dedi: medicus iis perlectis idem dixerat
quod comes, nulla nimirum collegia esse peregrinorum capacia.   His verbis auditis omnem amittebam spem.   Deinde Robertum Cecilium, Angliæ
secretarium primarium, (per ejus enim manus, ut nosti, cuncta reginæ
offeruntur,) supplex accessi ut senatus Tigurini literas regiæ majestati
tradere dignetur.   Ille hoc facturum promisit: commorabar aliquot dies
in aula, spe fretus mox accipiendi responsum.   Cum vero id non fieret,
denuo secretarium, homunculum sane arrogantem, rogans conveni pro me
intercedat apud regiam majestatem, quo citius responsum adipiscerer:
tandem dixit ut redeam 15 Octobris, tunc se mihi reginæ responsum
allaturum.   Cum itaque die constituto ad illum redieram, duriter me
allocutus est in hunc modum: Quid petis?   Ego respondi, Commoditatem beneficio et liberalitate regiæ majestatis in collegio quodam studia
continuandi.   At ipse rursus, Quid meritus, ut hæc petere audeas?   Tu
nescis, inquit, constitutiones hujus regni.   Regina legit tuas literas; nihil
propterea vult facere: hæc sunt ipsius formalia verba.   Spe me videns
frustratum, Londinum iter feci, D. Castollo conquestus, qui condoluit secretarii inhumanitatem.   Interea D. Jacobus Meddusius, theologiæ doctor,
vir nobilitate et eruditione præstantissimus, audiebat Tigurinos quosdam
nuper Londinum advolasse; summa igitur diligentia de nobis inquirebat.
Diu hinc inde in urbe cursitando, nos invenit; sibi gratum nostrum
adventum dixit.   Eppentiano et Werdmullero diutius in Anglia manere
nolentibus viaticum dedit.   Ego ab eo tempore, quo in Galliam rena-
vigarunt, nihil ab illis accepi.   Post illorum abitum me doctor Meddusius in domum suam recepit, ubi exspectabam D. Hungerfordi adventum.   Interim omnia visu digna, ope D. Meddusii, Londini videbam.
24 Octobris Hungerford Londinum venit: cum id cognovissem, una

cum D. Meddusio illum adivi : ille vero me non amplius noverat ; sed
cum illi dixissem cujus[1] sim, me ambabus ulnis amplexus est. Tum
narrabam illi cur huc venerim, et quod mihi in aula acciderit.   Ille
hisce intellectis, misericordia commotus, me consolatus est, et ne animum
abjicerem oravit ; se velle enim cum D. Meddusio mihi de alia prospicere
commoditate.   30 Octob. a D. Castollo ad vitæ necessaria 12 coronatos
Gallicos mutuo petere coactus fui.   Cum mei causa D. Hungerford et
doctor Meddusius deliberarent, incidi in morbum gravissimum, in quo
D. Meddusius et uxor ejus plura in me beneficia collocarunt, perinde
si illorum proprius fuissem filius : Christophel Schweitzer me etiam
magno cum sumptu visitavit.   Deus cum mihi pristinam sanitatem
restituisset, D. Hungerford, D. Meddusius, D. Castollus constituerunt
inter se ut Oxoniam proficiscerer ; forsan ibi ecclesiæ Tigurinæ literas
aliquod ponderis habituras : 13 Decembris ad D. Castollum cum
maximo animi dolore confugi iterum, implorans ejus auxilium ut mihi
adhuc 4 coronatos Gallicos mutuo daret. Ægritudo mea mihi plus
quam malebam nummum absumpsit, ita ut nunc 16 coronatos ab illo
acceperim.   Illi pollicitus sum proprioque chirographo confirmavi, me
illi per te, reverende Mæcenas, apud Wolfium Francofurti restituturum.
Hac de re etiam fuse scripsi matri meæ.   Te rogo etiam atque etiam,
reverende domine Mæcenas, enitaris ut D. Castollus pecuniam mihi
accommodatam prima commoditate recipiat : quo autem id facilius fieri
possit, cogitavi de Funckii stipendio, quod penes est cognatum Henricum
Thomannum dare cui velit ; id si accipere queam, minore cum molestia
D. Castollo satisfieri posset.   Londino, 14 Decembris, Oxoniam abibam,
munitus literis commendatitiis a D. Hungerfordo et D. Meddusio. Quamprimum Oxoniam perveni, particulares literas, post vero publicas, D.
Thomæ Thorentono nunc vice-cancellario tradidi ; qui cum viderat a
quo literas esse scriptas, lætari dixerat quod a celeberrima ecclesia Tigurina literas accipiat, et insuper se dolere aiebat quod non tum uni-
versitatem convocare possit ; nam illam gravissimis negotiis occupatam
esse.   Responsum academiæ exspectavi, et ad hunc usque diem exspecto ;
hac tamen septimana mihi vice-cancellarius respondebit.   In collegium
aliquod ascisci non potero : tamen accepturum stipendium honorificum
puto.   Si vero nihil omnino liberalitatis ab academia accepero, Londinum
proficiscar : ibi enim nobilis est, qui libentissime vellet ut filios instru-
erem suos.   Summam hic certe humanitatem experior a D. Rainoldo,
Angliæ Phœnice : quæso, si libuerit, scribe ad illos sequentes viros, et
illis gratias agas pro suis in me beneficiis ; D. Hungerford, D. Meddusio,
D. Castollo, D. Thomæ Thorentono, D. Rainoldo, brevi eruditissima
opera in lucem emissuro, D. Christophel Scwheitzer.

[1 Qu. *cujas.*]

Restat nunc ut tuæ dignitati supplicem me semper paterno amore prosequi velit. Videbo ego ut tua dignitas me subinde gratissimum reperiat.

Datum Oxonii festinanter.

Tuæ dignitatis studiosissimus,

CASPARUS THOMANNUS.

INSCRIPTIO.

Reverendo, summa eruditione in-
signi viro D. Casparo Wasero,
linguæ sanctæ professori, pa-
trono et Mæcenati colendo. Ti-
gurum.

(Scribit Joh. Castollus, 11 Feb. 1600: "Ab eo tempore quo superiores ad te scripsi literas affirmavit doctor Gentilis, qui jus civile Oxonii profitetur, publicis comitiis academicos viginti librarum stipendium domino Thomanno annuatim decrevisse.")

EPISTOLA CXXXIX.

JOHANNES JOHNSTONUS AD CASPARUM WASERUM.

S. D. LITERAS tuas, Vasere doctissime et amicissime, scriptas ad diem 20 Martii superioris, accepi ego ad diem 20 Julii; pro quibus eo majores tibi gratias debeo, quod antegressis nundinis nihil literarum abs me datum fuerit. In causa fuit gravissimuś morbus meus ex vitio lienis, ex quo objecta mihi præsentissima mortis species fuit omnium judicio. Et Dominus mihi hanc mentem indiderat, ut libens mori cupiverim. Verum secus visum est benignissimo Deo meo, qui dedit post acrem hiemem respirandi adhuc tempus, haud scio quam diu duraturum. Det Dominus ut quod reliquum est miselli ævi, transmittam ad gloriam nominis ipsius!

Patria nostra fruitur Dei beneficio summa tranquillitate. Post asperrimam hiemem, qualem nemo patrum vidit unquam, successit mitior æstus, unde melior spes autumni et imminuta pretia frumenti. Serenissima regina enixa est filiolum Carolum 19 Nov. superioris. Princeps Henricus, animo et corpore vegetus per Dei gratiam, educatur summa diligentia Sterlini. Serenissimus rex hoc tempore agit in vicina Falcolandia. Ad 12 Maii superioris in generali synodo renovatum est solemne fœdus a serenissimo rege præsente, et cœtu ecclesiæ totius cum Deo, de sincero Dei cultu pro··

movendo, de exstirpando papismo, de præstanda obedientia ex Dei præscripto, secundum uniuscujusque vocationem, ut pietas cum justitia floreat. Et certe ex eo tempore jus severiter exercitum est in facinorosos. Insignis quidam pontificius, Comarchi Bondsonii prope montem Rosarum filius, ob pudendum flagitium contra parentes patratum capite luit mense Maio. Benedictus est Deus, detque gratiam porro bene velle et agere! Johannes Areskinus cum Edouardo Brussio Kinlossio honorificentissima legatione apud Anglos defunctus paulo post exitum comitis Essexii, omnibus bonis lacrymabilem adeoque toti insulæ luctuosam, reversusque læta omnia visus est renunciare. Essexio æmulatio Roberti Cecilii secretarii plusquam objecta crimina nocuisse dicitur. Nunc res tranquillæ sunt, sed verendum ne maxima invidiæ moles et doloris ex Essexii morte et aliorum nobilium erumpat denique in nervum. Dominus Ludovicus Stuartus, regii sanguinis, dux Levinus, cum insigni et magnifico comitatu legationis nomine in Galliam iturus solvit ad 10 Julii, confirmaturus inter gentes antiquum et inviolatum hactenus fœdus, gratulaturus regi Francorum de regno ei confirmato, de victoriis, de novo conjugio. Hæc in vulgo : arcana non divulgantur.

D. Melvinus, Moravius, Monipenius, et amici tui recte valent Dei beneficio, teque cum Hovæo amanter resalutant. Salutem amantissime et officiosissime adscribo omnibus D. D. pastoribus et professoribus, collegis tuis doctissimis, quos quæso nominatim adeas singulos, cum D. Stuckio, Simlero meo et Ernio. Ego vobis ac inclytæ urbi vestræ addictissimus precor vobis omne bonum a Deo. D. Benedictum Erlachium patrem, ac Wolfgangum filium discipulum meum, rogo ut per literas officiose salutes a me cum tota familia. Valetudo laborem scribendi impediebat. Perge porro scribendo de rebus vestris et Genevensium et vicinarum ecclesiarum nos omnes reficere. Valete omnes felicissime. Andreapoli in Scotia. Kal. Aug. 1601.

Totus vester,

JOH. JOHNSTONUS.

INSCRIPTIO.

Reverendo et doctissimo viro D. Casparo Vuasero, sacræ linguæ et literarum professori ordinario in inclyta Tigurinorum schola, amicissimo meo. Tigurum.

EPISTOLA CXL.

JOHANNES JOHNSTONUS AD CASPARUM WASERUM.

S. D. Superiore Julio exeunte, clarissime Vuasere, literas ad te paravi, quas tempore visus sum dare Francofurtum perferendas ad nundinas Septembris; sed postea monuit me Hartius noster in tempore non fuisse eo delatas, perferentium cessatione. Miror tamen morem tibi solennem proximis nundinis fuisse intermissum, quo me pro amore tuo et veteres hic amicos salutare solitus es, quod nobis omnibus multo fuit jucundissimum. Itaque petimus omnes, ut constanter pergas nos recreare optatissima aura ex candidissimis vestris Alpibus ad nos usque spirante. Vel brevissimæ abs te literæ nos prolixe exhilarabunt. De me tibi persuasum esto, quamdiu vita est et valetudo, cum nundinis hoc iter literarum me perrecturum. Nunc autem brevitatem excusabit temporis angustia, quam et imperat mihi valetudo, per hosce aliquot dies minus commoda, recrudescente lienis morbo, qui me superiore anno pene confecerat, et si quid ego video, mi frater, trahet paulatim, imo ducet potius: sequar enim lubens volensque clementissimi Dei mei ductum, qui nuperrime 20 Decembris Thomam Cargillum, ludimagistrum Aberdonensem, valentissimum illum quidem, tibi notum, ante me præmisit. Et fortasse non erit diu cum ego sequar. Interea spem melioris vitæ renovat, et diuturnioris etiam inter mortales renovavit mihi Dominus, dato mihi altero filiolo Edovardo, ad diem 15 Januarii. Iisdem quoque diebus, nempe 18 Januarii, natus serenissimo nostro regi tertius est filius, cui nomen nondum impositum. Vivunt præterea et vigent, Dei gratia, Henricus princeps et Carolus cum Elizabetha filia.

Pace fruimur tranquilla, Dei beneficio, in ecclesia et republica. Verum pestis tristia nobis minitatur. Scintillare enim cœpit Edinburgi, et Glascuæ, et Caralliæ, urbe sexto lapide hinc distante. Anglia plurimum recreata est his diebus, profligato omni milite Hispano ex Hibernia, Dei benignitate et virtute baronis de Montjoy. In Hibernia Hispanus conspiraverat cum comite Tyronensi Hiberno rebelle, atque inde ex vicino loco bellum trahere adversus Angliam cogitaverat. Sed hæc consilia dissipavit Dominus. Hujus rei nuncius certus ad serenissimum regem nostrum his diebus missus est, et gratiæ Deo publice in templis dictæ. De rebus Gallicis et Hispanicis et Belgicis certiora ad vos perferuntur. Obsidio Ostendensis ad miraculum usque continuatur tota hac hieme; nec magna spes est hosti de expugnanda: tenent enim pro Belgis sub præfecto Fr. Weer, equite fortissimo, Angli plurimum, et Scoti cum Gallis. De rebus vestris et Genevensium ut nos pergas certiores reddere rogamus ego et

omnes tui hic amici, quibus copiam facio literarum tuarum. Illi tui
memores et studiosissimi te resalutant, D. Melvini, Monypenius, Blakius,
Muravius, ceterique. Salutem officiose et amanter dico D. Stuckio,
Zuinglio, Lavatero et collegisticis optimis, imprimis D. D. Simlero et
Ernio nostri amantissimis, quos tecum cum conjuge et socero æternum
valere jubeo. Andreapoli in Scotia, ad diem 8 Feb. 1602.

Totus tuus,

JOH. JOHNSTONUS.

INSCRIPTIO.

Clarissimo viro D. Casparo Wasero,
linguæ sanctæ et scientiæ professori
in illustri Tig. schola, amico et
fratri conjunctissimo. Tigurum.

EPISTOLA CXLI.

THOMAS SAVILIUS ET HENRICUS HAWKINS AD HENRICUM WOLFIUM.

CLARISSIME vir, domine atque amice observantissime : Valde mihi
molestum est res ac rationes meas ita esse constitutas, ut paternis tuisque laboribus inspiciendis dies unus atque alter non supersit: sed quod
nobis magno nostro incommodo angustiæ temporis eripuerunt, id totum
tua, ut spero, aliquando humanitas reponet ac restituet, communicabit-
que nobis indicem saltem paternarum vigiliarum, quo ingens nostrum
desiderium aliqua ex parte lenire possimus. Nos quidem ut vices repen-
damus, canonem Ptolemæi diligenter tibi perferendum curabimus, ac si
qua alia in nostra potestate sita fuerint. Liber autem quem quæris
Altorfii editus est hoc nomine, Gemini εἰσαγωγὴ εἰς τὰ φαινόμενα. Vale,
vir clarissime, atque *I, bone, qua tua te virtus ducit, i pede fausto.*
Dominationis tuæ clementissimæ

Studiosissimi,

THOMAS SAVILIUS,
HENRICUS HAWKINS,

Angli barones.

INSCRIPTIO.

Clarissimo viro Henrico Wolfio,
      &c.

THE

FOURTH ANNUAL REPORT

[FOR THE YEAR 1844.]

OF

The Parker Society,

For the Publication of the Works of the Fathers and Early
Writers of the Reformed English Church.

INSTITUTED A.D. MDCCCXL.

PROCEEDINGS

AT THE FOURTH ANNUAL MEETING OF

The Parker Society,

HELD AT

THE FREEMASONS' TAVERN,

GREAT QUEEN STREET, LINCOLN'S INN FIELDS, LONDON,

ON THURSDAY, THE 29th OF MAY, 1845.

SIR WALTER R. FARQUHAR, Bart, in the Chair,

THE RIGHT HONOURABLE LORD ASHLEY, M.P., THE PRESIDENT, HAVING BEEN
UNAVOIDABLY DETAINED BY A PARLIAMENTARY COMMITTEE.

COLLECTS suitable to the occasion were read by the Rev. M. M. PRESTON,
Vicar of Cheshunt.

The Report of the Council was read, whereupon

The following Resolutions were moved, seconded, and agreed to.

RESOLVED,

That the Report of the Council which has been read, be approved, and that
it be received and adopted, and printed for the use of the Members; and also,
that the thanks of the Society be given to the President and Council for their
valuable services during the past year.

The Secretary for General Business then read the Report of the Auditors,
and the Account of Receipts and Expenditure of the past year.—(See page 10).

Resolved,

That the statement of the Cash account be received, and that the same be printed, and that the thanks of the Society be given to the Auditors for their services during the past year.

Resolved,

That the following persons be the Council and Officers for the year ensuing, with power to fill up vacancies :—

THE RIGHT HONOURABLE LORD ASHLEY, M.P.,
was elected President.

SIR WALTER R. FARQUHAR, BART.,
was elected Honorary Treasurer.

GEORGE STOKES, Esq.,
was elected Honorary Librarian.

THE REV. R. G. BAKER,

REV. C. BENSON, Canon of Worcester.

REV. E. BICKERSTETH,

JOHN BRIDGES. Esq.,

JOHN BRUCE, Esq.,

REV. GUY BRYAN,

REV. RICHARD BURGESS,

REV. T. TOWNSON CHURTON, Fellow of Brasenose College, Oxford.

HON. WILLIAM COWPER,

REV. W. H. COX, Vice-Principal of St Mary Hall, Oxford,

REV. J. W. CUNNINGHAM,

REV. THOMAS DALE, Canon Residentiary of St. Paul's,

THE VENERABLE ARCHDEACON DEALTRY,

REV. JOHN HARDING,

REV. EDWARD HOARE,

REV. T. H. HORNE, Canon of St. Paul's,

JOSEPH HOARE, Esq.,

HONOURABLE ARTHUR KINNAIRD,

REV. DR. MORTIMER, Head Master of the City of London School,

HON. AND REV. B. W. NOEL,

HENRY POWNALL, Esq.,

REV. JOSIAH PRATT,

REV. M. M. PRESTON,

REV. DANIEL WILSON,

With the REV. JAMES SCHOLEFIELD, Regius Professor of Greek in the
University of Cambridge,
Were elected as the COUNCIL; with power to fill up all vacancies occurring
during the year; and

> THE HON. ARTHUR KINNAIRD,
> HENRY POWNALL, Esq.,
> REV. R. E. HANKINSON, and
> FRANCIS LOWE, Esq., were elected Auditors.

RESOLVED,

That the thanks of this Meeting be given to the Local Correspondents and
other friends of the Society, who have assisted the objects of the Institution
during the past year.

RESOLVED,

That the thanks of the Society be recorded, acknowledging the important
service to its proceedings afforded by the kind consent of Sir James Graham,
Bart. Her Majesty's Principal Secretary of State for the Home Department,
for a regular examination of the State Paper Office, with permission for the
Society to print such documents as may be found there, calculated to promote
the objects of this Institution. And that the Council be empowered to make
the arrangements in the publication of these documents which may be requisite
to carry into effect the intentions and wishes of Her Majesty's Government with
regard to such papers, by printing a certain number of copies for sale to the
public, in addition to the regular publication for members, and in such form as
the Council may deem to be expedient.

RESOLVED,

That the best thanks of the Meeting are due to the Right Honourable Lord
ASHLEY for his constant attention to the interests of the Institution, and to
Sir WALTER R. FARQUHAR, Bart. the Treasurer, for his kind services, and for
his presiding on the present occasion, in the absence of the President who has
been detained from the Meeting by his Parliamentary duties.

THE

FOURTH ANNUAL REPORT

OF

The Parker Society,

INSTITUTED A.D. 1840,

FOR THE PUBLICATION OF

THE WORKS OF THE FATHERS AND EARLY WRITERS OF THE REFORMED ENGLISH CHURCH.

PRESENTED TO THE GENERAL MEETING, MAY THE 29TH, 1845.

" He (*Archbishop Parker*) was a great collector of ancient and modern writings, and took especial care of the safe preservation of them for all succeeding times ; as foreseeing undoubtedly what use might be made of them by posterity : that, by having recourse to such originals and precedents, the true knowledge of things might the better appear."
" As he was a great patron and promoter of good learning, so he took care of giving encouragement to printing—a great instrument of the increase thereof."
Strype's Life of Archbishop Parker.

The Council of the Parker Society have much pleasure in being able to present a complete Report of the proceedings of the past year, to the General Meeting of the Members : the whole of the books for the year 1844 having been delivered, and the accounts for the year being closed. Thus the business of the Society has been brought into as advanced a state as is practicable.

The particulars of the Cash Account will be printed in the larger edition of this Report, to be delivered to the Subscribers with the first volume published for the year 1845. The Receipts were £7033 15s. 1d. and the expenditure £7018 2s. 8d. leaving a balance of £15 12s. 5d. to be carried forward to the account for 1845. The Cash Statement also contains further particulars relative to the reprints of 1841, and the account for the year 1843.

The number of Subscribers still continues to be fully Seven Thousand

Without any especial effort on the part of the Council, the new Subscriptions appear sufficient to fill the places of those discontinued from deaths or other causes. As some subscriptions remain unpaid from neglect or accidental oversight, the Council propose to pursue the plan found satisfactory last year, of requiring £1 5s. for all sets not paid for before the 1st of June, and to allot them so far as they extend, according to priority of application. This course seems to be required in justice to those who have paid at the proper time; and it enables the Council to proceed in printing the books, without the delay which would be occasioned by waiting until the decision of every member, in answer to the notice sent according to the second law of the Society, could be ascertained. They are glad to state that the Subscriptions for 1845 have been paid up much more promptly than in former years.

A list of all the Books printed by the Society is added to this Report. Those supplied for the subscription of the last year were—The Two Liturgies and Documents of the Reign of King Edward VI.; Sermons of Bishop Latimer; a volume of the Writings of Bishop Coverdale: and the Prayers and other Pieces of Thomas Becon.

It was estimated that the letter-press of the publications for 1844, would be equal to 181 sheets of demy octavo, to be bound in five volumes. But as the work progressed, each of the books exceeded the extent anticipated, and the Council deemed it advisable to make some changes in the arrangement, enlarging the books to a quantity of letter-press equal to 196 demy sheets, and delivering them in four volumes; leaving the Remains of Latimer to form a volume for 1845, and thus closing the transactions of 1844 earlier than otherwise would have been practicable.

The Council apprehend that the course thus pursued has been in every respect desirable, since the funds of the year enabled them to give the additional matter recommended by the Editors, and to return an increased quantity of letter-press. They consider, however, from past experience, that it will be desirable hereafter to notice the books intended to be printed, only in general terms. The proceedings always must be influenced by unavoidable contingencies, being liable to delay from the illness of Editors and other hindrances; but the four years' proceedings now closed have shown the Members the average return for their subscriptions, and it is hoped will also have satisfied them as to the probable stability of the Institution.

In reference to the Books for 1845, the Council will only state, that those most advanced, and which they expect to return for the present year, are, another volume of Letters from the Archives of Zurich; a volume of the Remains of Bishop Latimer, including some letters never before printed; a large volume of Bishop Jewel's works, containing the controversy with Cole and Harding; and a volume of Selections from the Devotional Poetry of the Reign of Queen Elizabeth. The first two are so nearly completed that it is expected they will be ready in the month of July; the printing of the other two has been commenced, but the volume of Jewel cannot be ready till after Christmas.

Many other Works are in preparation: among which may be mentioned, the completion of the Works of Archbishop Cranmer and of Bishop Jewel; the Liturgy and Forms of Prayer of the Reign of Queen Elizabeth; a further portion of Bishop Coverdale; Letters from Zurich, written by the English Reformers during the Reigns of King Henry VIII. King Edward VI. and Queen Mary; the Writings of Bradford; those of Archbishop Whitgift; and the work of Calfhill, in answer to Martial's Treatise on the Cross. The precise years and order of publication cannot be stated.

The Report of last year explained, that the additional letters found at Zurich included many written in the Reign of Queen Elizabeth, the dates of which supply several chasms in the volume previously printed; but it was not in the power of the Council to prevent the disadvantages of this separation. Some of the Members have recommended, that these letters should be re-printed in one volume, under a regular chronological arrangement, for those only who wish to obtain such a volume, the Latin originals being omitted. The circumstances are peculiar, and the Council propose to consider the question maturely before they decide upon it.

A distribution of books to Public Libraries destitute of funds for subscribing, from the surplus volumes of former years, and the copies of the volume of Liturgies and Documents of the Reign of King Edward VI. has been made to an amount exceeding the donations to the Society. The Council have to thank the Rev. M. S. Wall, of Madeira, for a further donation of Ten Pounds, to be applied toward this important object in the present year.

The Council can again state, that the business details have continued to improve by the experience acquired. These arrangements would be still further facilitated if the Members would always send fresh directions in cases of permanent change of residence. The trouble resulting from books, when once sent out, being returned, owing to removals or other causes, is considerable. The Council trust that the enquiries of Members have been promptly answered; but delays are sometimes unavoidable under the pressure of the very extensive correspondence of the Society.

It is desirable to remind the Members that the maintenance and efficiency of the Society materially depend upon its objects being extensively made known, so as to procure new Members every year, and thus to replace the subscriptions discontinued from death or other causes. The advantage of having each volume a separate publication, and of not requiring any engagement as to the continuance of subscriptions, or the purchase of preceding volumes, is now apparent. A charitable or eleemosynary contribution is not asked. All that is required is the payment in advance of One Pound, for which the return of four valuable books on an average is guaranteed. The value and acceptableness of these works to the Clergy, and Students in general, have induced many to subscribe, in order that they may present the books to others, when they do not wish to retain the volumes themselves.

The communications received from the Members during the past year manifest increased satisfaction with the proceedings: this encourages the future operations. As the objects and proceedings of the Parker Society have become more fully known, they have been generally appreciated and approved. The Council can also express their belief that the books of future years will be found still more valuable than those that have already appeared. They have to express their thanks for kind aid by the loan of books and otherwise, from many of the possessors of highly-valuable collections of works of the sixteenth century, which will be specifically acknowledged by the Editors of the publications thus assisted. Here may be mentioned the kind permission from the Right Hon. Sir James Graham, Bart. Her Majesty's Principal Secretary of State for the Home Department, allowing a full examination of the State Paper Office, in furtherance of the operations of the Institution, on the application of the President. This examination is now in progress, and its results, when ascertained, will be fully and fairly communicated to the members and to the public.

Thus the Council trust that the expectations held out in the early announcements are likely to be realised, and that "Students generally, those who have the care of public libraries, all who are interested in the best specimens of the English Literature of the Reformation, and readers of every class," have found, and will find, "the Parker Society well deserving of support."

The object which this Institution seeks to promote is indeed most important. It is to make known those works by which the Fathers of the Reformed English Church sought to diffuse scriptural truth. Their principles were clearly set forth in their writings, and their descendants are now called upon to manifest the same principles, with firmness and decision. One efficient means is the reprinting and circulating of their works; and while engaged in this effort, the Council would request all to unite in the aspiration with which the venerable martyred primate, Archbishop Cranmer, penned and sent forth one of the most important of these volumes:—

"Almighty God, the Father of light and truth, banish all such darkness and error out of His Church, with the authors and teachers thereof; or else convert their hearts unto Him, and give this light of faith to every man, that he may trust to have remission of his sins, and be delivered from eternal death and hell, by the merit only of the death and blood of Christ; and that by his own faith every man may apply the same unto himself, and not take it at the appointment of popish priests, by the merit of sacrifices and oblations!"—*Archbishop Cranmer's Answer to Gardiner. Parker Society Edition*, p. 348.

LAWS OF THE PARKER SOCIETY.

I.—That the Society shall be called THE PARKER SOCIETY, and that its objects shall be—first, the reprinting, without abridgment, alteration, or omission, of the best Works of the Fathers and early Writers of the Reformed English Church, published in the period between the accession of King Edward VI. and the death of Queen Elizabeth; secondly, the printing of such remains of other Writers of the Sixteenth Century as may appear desirable (including, under both classes, some of the early English Translations of the Foreign Reformers); and thirdly, the printing of some manuscripts of the same authors, hitherto unpublished.

II.—That the Society shall consist of such a number of members, being subscribers of at least One Pound each annually, as the Council may determine; the subscription to be considered due on the First day of January in each year, in advance, and to be paid on or before such a day as the Council may fix; sufficient notice being given of the day appointed.

III.—That the Management of the Society shall be vested in a President, a Treasurer, and Honorary Librarian, and a Council of twenty-four other subscribers, being members of the Established Church, and of whom not less than sixteen shall be Clergymen. The Council and Officers to be elected annually by the subscribers, at a General Meeting to be held in the month of May; and no persons shall then be proposed who are not already members of the Council, or Officers, unless their names shall have been transmitted to the Secretaries on or before the 15th of April in the current year, by nominations in writing, signed by at least five subscribers. And that there be two Secretaries appointed by the Council; also, that the Council have power to fill all vacancies during the year.

IV.—That the accounts of the receipt and expenditure of the Society shall be examined every year, previously to the General Meeting, by four Auditors, two of them selected from the Council, and two appointed by the preceding General Meeting.

V.—That the funds shall be expended in payment of the expenses incurred in producing the works published by the Society, so that every member not in arrear of his or her annual subscription shall receive a copy of every work published by the Society during the year, for each sum of One Pound subscribed, without any charge for the same; and that the number of copies printed in each year, shall be limited to the quantity required for the number actually subscribed for.

VI.—That every member of the Society who shall intimate to the Council a desire to withdraw, or who shall not pay the subscription by the time appointed, shall cease to be a member of the Society; and no member shall at any time incur any liability beyond the annual subscription.

VII.—That, after the commencement of the proceedings, no rule shall be made or altered excepting at a General Meeting, and after notice of the same has been communicated to the members by circulars, or by advertisement in two London daily newspapers, at least fourteen days before the General Meeting.

VIII.—Donations and Legacies will be thankfully received; the amount of which shall be expended by the Council in supplying copies of the publications to clerical, or other public libraries, destitute of funds to purchase the same, and for such other purposes, connected with the objects of the Society, as the Council may determine.

REPORT OF THE AUDITORS.

The Auditors having examined the further Cash Account of the Parker Society for the year 1843, shewing the amount received and expended since the last Audit, find that the balance due to the Treasurer on the 24th July, 1844, of £511 12s. 3d. has been wholly liquidated, and that a balance in favor of the Society, of £2 11s. 9d. remains to be carried forward to the account for the year 1845.

The Auditors have also examined the Cash Account for the year 1844, exhibiting the whole receipt and expenditure for that year, and find the same to be correct, according to the annexed abstract, and that there is a balance of £15 12s. 5d. in favor of the Society, which has been carried forward to the account for the year 1845.

HENRY POWNALL,
FRANCIS LOWE, } *Auditors.*

Abstract of the further Receipts and Expenditure of the Parker Society, on Account of the year 1843.

RECEIVED.

	£	s.	d.
Further amount received for the Reprints of 1841	210	0	0
Further amount received for the Books of 1842	20	0	0
Further amount received for the Subscriptions of 1843	280	4	0
Subscriptions for future years received in 1843	4	0	0
	£514	4	0

PAID.

	£	s.	d.
Balance due to the Treasurer, July 24th, 1844, as per last Account	511	12	3
Balance remaining to be carried forward to 1845	2	11	9
	£514	4	0

ABSTRACT OF THE CASH ACCOUNT OF THE PARKER SOCIETY,
FOR THE YEAR 1844.

RECEIVED.	£	s.	d.
Amount Received for the Subscriptions of Members for the Year 1844, to the present time (2nd April, 1845.)	6894	0	0
Amount Received for Separate Copies of the Liturgies of King Edward VI.	23	12	7
Amount Received for Subscriptions for future years	11	0	0
Dividend on Stock	73	11	3
From Exchequer Bill Account for 1844, being Balance of Premium and Interest	31	11	3
Total	£7033	15	1

PAID.	£	s.	d
Paid for Printing and Paper of the books for 1844	3995	17	0
For Binding and Delivery	1562	14	1
For Volumes purchased to complete sets	10	1	3
For Editorial Expenses	471	9	8
For Insurance from Fire	5	12	6
For Books purchased for Library, Copy for Printing and use of Editors, and for Transcripts	139	6	0
For Printing Plans, Reports and Circulars, and for Advertisements	124	8	8
For Rent of Office, Salary of Secretary, and Wages of Clerks and Porters	477	5	6
For Furniture and Fittings	63	10	5
For Stationery and Account Books	17	18	0
For incidentals, including postage, carriage, coals, and various petty expenses	149	19	7
Balance carried to 1845	15	12	5
Total	£7033	15	1

HENRY POWNALL,
FRANCIS LOWE. } *Auditors.*

THE FOLLOWING NAMES, WITH OTHERS, IN THE WHOLE

SEVEN THOUSAND,

ARE IN THE LIST OF SUBSCRIBERS TO

The Parker Society.

HER MOST GRACIOUS MAJESTY ADELAIDE, QUEEN DOWAGER.
HIS ROYAL HIGHNESS THE PRINCE ALBERT.
HIS MAJESTY THE KING OF PRUSSIA.
HER ROYAL HIGHNESS THE DUCHESS OF KENT.

HIS Grace the Duke of Devonshire.—His Grace the Duke of Manchester.—His Grace the Duke of Sutherland.—His Grace the Duke of Roxburghe.

The Most Honourable the Marquesses of Bute, Cholmondeley, Conyngham, Downshire, Northampton, Ormonde, and Salisbury.

The Right Honourable the Earls of Cavan, Chichester, Clancarty, De Grey, Essex, Galloway, Howe, Jermyn, Nelson, Rosse, and Spencer.

The Right Honourable and Rev. Lord Wriothesley Russell.

The Right Honourable Lord Viscounts Adare, Alford, Arbuthnott, Campden, De Vesci, Fordwich, Hill, and Lorton.

The Right Honourable the Lords Ashley (President), and Lindsay.

The Right Honourable and Very Reverend Lord Edward Chichester—The Right Honourable Lord Henry Cholmondeley—The Right Honourable and Reverend Lords Charles Thynne, John Thynne, Arthur Hervey, and George A. Hill.

The Right Honourable and Right Reverend the Lord Bishop of London.—The Right Reverend the Lords Bishops of Durham, Winchester, Chester, Chichester, Hereford, Lichfield, Lincoln, Llandaff, Peterborough, Ripon, Rochester, Worcester, and of Sodor and Man.

The Right Honourable and Right Reverend the Lords Bishops of Clogher, and of Meath.—The Honourable and Right Reverend the Lord Bishop of Killaloe and Clonfert.—The Right Reverend the Lords Bishops of Down and Connor, of Ossory and Ferns, and of Cashel and Waterford.

The Right Reverend the Lords Bishops of Calcutta, Bombay, Colombo, Toronto, Guiana, Australia, and of Tasmania.

The Right Reverend the Bishops of Ohio, New Jersey, South Carolina, Virginia, Maryland, Georgia, and of Delaware.

The Right Honourable the Lords Bolton, Calthorpe, Farnham, Littleton, Rayleigh, Teignmouth, and the late Right Honourable and Reverend Lord Aston.

Her Grace the Duchess of Argyle.—Right Honourable the Countess of Annesley. Right Honourable Viscountess Valentia.—Right Honourable Lady Ward, &c

The Right Honourable the Lord Chief Justice of Ireland.—The Right Honourable Lord Justice Clerk, Scotland.—The Honourable Mr. Justice Jackson. The Chevalier Bunsen.—The Right Honourable Henry Goulburn, Chancellor of the Exchequer, M.P. for the University of Cambridge.—The Right Honourable W. E. Gladstone, M.P., Master of the Mint, &c.

The Honourable and Very Reverend the Deans of Norwich, Windsor and Wolverhampton, and Manchester.—The Very Reverend the Deans of Chester, Durham, Gloucester, Peterborough, Salisbury, Westminster and Winchester. —The Deans and Chapters of Lichfield, Worcester, &c.

The Right Honourable and Very Reverend the Dean of Raphoe.—The Honourable and Very Reverend the Dean of Clogher.—The Very Reverend the Deans of Cloyne, Connor, Cork, Derry, Cashel, Emly, St. Patrick, Ossory, Kildare, Kilmacduagh, and Limerick.

The Honourable and Worshipful T. W. Law, Chancellor of Bath and Wells. —The Worshipful H. Raikes, Chancellor of Chester; E. T. M. Phillips, Chancellor of Gloucester; F. R. Sandys, Chancellor of Ossory; Marsham Argles, Chancellor of Peterborough.

The Venerable Archdeacons Bather, Berners, Bevan, Browne, Buckle, Davys, Dealtry, Hare, Hodson, Hoare, Law, Lyall, Mac Donald, Philpot, Shirley, Spooner, C. Thorp, and J. R. Wilberforce.

The Venerable Archdeacons Beresford, Creery, Digby, Mant, Monsell, Oldfield, Power, Stuart, Verschoyle and St. George.

Reverend Dr. Symons, Warden of Wadham Coll. Oxford, and Vice Chancellor of the University.—Reverend Dr. Phelps, Master of Sidney Sussex Coll. Cambridge, and Vice Chancellor of the University.—Reverend Dr. Graham, Master of Christ Coll. Cambridge.—Reverend Dr. Archdall, Master of Emmanuel Coll. Cambridge.—Reverend Dr. Tatham, Master of St. John's Coll. Cambridge.—Reverend Dr. Plumtre, Master of University Coll. Oxford.— Reverend Dr. Fox, Provost of Queen's Coll., Oxford.—Reverend Dr. Cotton, Provost of Worcester Coll. Oxford.—Reverend Dr. Jeune, Master of Pembroke Coll. Oxford.—Reverend Dr Thackeray, Provost of King's Coll. Cambridge.—Reverend Dr. Ainslie, Master of Pembroke Hall, Cambridge.— Reverend Dr. French, Master of Jesus Coll. Cambridge.—Joshua King, Esq. D.C L. President of Queen's Coll. Cambridge.—Reverend Dr. Procter, Master of Catherine Hall, Cambridge.—Reverend Dr. Webb, Master of Clare Hall, Cambridge.—Reverend Dr. Hampden, Principal of St. Mary's Hall, and Regius Professor of Divinity, Oxford.—Reverend Dr. Cramer, Principal of New Inn Hall, Oxford.—Reverend E. Cardwell, Principal of St. Alban's Hall, Oxford.

The Reverend Dr. Sadleir, Provost of Trinity Coll. Dublin.—The Venerable Archdeacon Thorp, Warden of the University of Durham.—The Very Reverend Dr. Lee, Principal of the University of Edinburgh.—Reverend J. Wheeler, President of the University of Vermont, U.S.—Rev. R. P. Buddicom, Principal of St. Bees College.—Reverend Dr. Williamson, Head Master of Westminster School.—Reverend Dr. Tait, Head Master of Rugby School, &c. &c.

LIBRARIES.—The Royal Library, Berlin.—Balliol Coll. Oxford.—Gonville and Caius, Pembroke, and Queen's Coll. Cambridge.—Wadham, and Worcester Coll. Oxford.—Trinity Coll. Dublin.—University of Edinburgh.—King's Coll. London.—Advocates' Library, and Library of the Writers to the Signet, Edinburgh.—St. Bees Coll.—Cathedrals of Chester and Cashel.—The London Institution.—The London Library.—The Chetham Library, Manchester; and many other Collegiate, Public, and School Libraries, &c. &c.

THE COUNCIL AND OFFICERS FOR 1844-5.

President.
THE RIGHT HONOURABLE LORD ASHLEY, M.P.
Treasurer.
SIR WALTER R. FARQUHAR, BART.
Council.

REV. R. G. BAKER.—REV. C. BENSON, Canon of Worcester.—REV. E. BICKERSTETH.—JOHN BRIDGES, ESQ.—JOHN BRUCE, ESQ.—REV. GUY BRYAN.—REV. RICHARD BURGESS.—REV. T. TOWNSON CHURTON, Fellow of Brasenose College, Oxford.—HON. WILLIAM COWPER.—REV. W. H. COX, Vice Principal St. Mary Hall, Oxford.—REV. J. W. CUNNINGHAM.—REV. THOMAS DALE, Canon Residentiary of St Paul's.—VEN. DR. DEALTRY, Archdeacon of Surrey.—REV. JOHN HARDING.—REV. EDWARD HOARE.—REV. T. H. HORNE, Canon of St. Paul's.—JOSEPH HOARE, ESQ.—HON. ARTHUR KINNAIRD.—REV. DR. MORTIMER, Head Master of the City of London School.—HON. and REV. B. W. NOEL,—HENRY POWNALL, ESQ.—REV. JOSIAH PRATT.—REV. M. M. PRESTON.—REV. DANIEL WILSON.

Honorary Librarian.
GEORGE STOKES, ESQ. Cheltenham.
Editorial Secretary.
REV. JAMES SCHOLEFIELD, Regius Professor of Greek in the University of Cambridge.
Secretary for General Business.
WILLIAM THOMAS, ESQ. at the Office of the Parker Society, 33, Southampton St. Strand, London.
Auditors.
HON. A. KINNAIRD, REV. R. E. HANKINSON, H. POWNALL, ESQ., & F. LOWE, ESQ.
Bankers.
MESSRS. HERRIES, FARQUHAR, AND CO., No. 16, St James's Street.

REGULATIONS FOR DELIVERY OF THE BOOKS PUBLISHED BY THE SOCIETY.

I. They will be delivered, free of expense, at the Office, or within three miles of the General Post Office, London.

II. They will be sent to any place in England beyond the distance of three miles from the General Post Office, by any conveyance a Member may point out. In this case the parcels will be booked at the expense of the Society, but the carriage must be paid by the Members to whom they are sent

III. They will be delivered, free of expense, at any place in London which a Member, resident in the country, may name.

IV. They may remain at the Office of the Society until the Members apply for them, but, in that case, the Society will not be responsible for any damage which may happen from fire, or other accident.

V. They will be sent to any of the Correspondents, or Agents of the Society, each Member paying the Correspondent or Agent a share of the carriage of the parcel in which the books were included. Arrangements are made for the delivery on this plan, in many of the cities and large towns where a sufficient number of members reside; *and it will be esteemed a favour if gentlemen who are willing to further the objects of the Parker Society, by taking charge of the books for the Members in their respective neighbourhoods, will write to the Office on the subject.*

VI. They will be delivered in Edinburgh and Dublin as in London, and forwarded from thence to Members in other parts of Scotland and Ireland, in the same manner as is mentioned above with respect to England.

𝔄 𝔏𝔦𝔰𝔱 𝔬𝔣 𝔱𝔥𝔢 𝔚𝔬𝔯𝔨𝔰

ALREADY PUBLISHED BY THE PARKER SOCIETY.

For the Year 1841.

The Works of Bishop Ridley.
The Sermons and other Pieces of Archbishop Sandys.
The Works of Bishop Pilkington.
The Works of Roger Hutchinson.

For the Year 1842.

The Examinations and Writings of Archdeacon Philpot.
Christian Prayers and Meditations.
Letters of Bishop Jewell, and others, translated from the Originals in the Archives of Zurich, (1st Series).
The Writings of Archbishop Grindal.
Early Writings of the Rev. T. Becon, Chaplain to Archbishop Cranmer, and Prebendary of Canterbury.

For the Year 1843.

Fulke's Defence of the English Translation of the Bible.
Early Writings of Bishop Hooper.
Writings of Archbishop Cranmer on the Lord's Supper.
The Catechism aud other Pieces of Becon.

For the Year 1844.

The Liturgies, Primer and Catechism of the Reign of Edward VI.
Writings of Bishop Coverdale.
Sermons of Bishop Latimer.
The Flower of Godly Prayers, and other Pieces of Becon.

NOW PRINTING FOR 1845, OR SUBSEQUENT YEARS.

Second Series of Letters from the Archives of Zurich.
Remains of Bishop Latimer.
Writings of Bishop Jewell.
Devotional Poetry of the Reign of Queen Elizabeth.
Writings of Bishop Coverdale.
Remaining Works of Archbishop Cranmer.

𝔏ist of 𝔚orks

ALREADY PUBLISHED AND UNDER CONSIDERATION BY THE

PARKER SOCIETY.

In Royal Octavo. — Becon—Cranmer—Jewel—Whitgift—Parker—Bullinger's Decades—Alley—Whitaker.

In Demy Octavo.—Ridley—Pilkington—Philpot—Fulke—Nowell—Coverdale —Curtis—Bale—Tindal—Frith—Barns—Sandys—Hutchinson—Grindal— Hooper—Latimer—Bradford—Cooper—Fox—Taverner, and some others; Royal Authors, Documents of the Reign of Edward VI.—Documents relative to the Reign of Queen Mary—Documents of the Reign of Queen Elizabeth—Zurich Letters, (three series)—Letters and Documents from Archbishop Parker's MSS. in C.C.C.C.—Occasional Services of Queen Elizabeth's Reign—The Homilies—Some volumes of Sermons preached before King Edward VI. and Queen Elizabeth, at St. Paul's Cross, in the Universities, and on various occasions—Several volumes of Tracts and small Pieces—Various Letters and Documents—Reformatio Legum Ecclesiasticarum—Queen Elizabeth's Prayer Book—Devotional Poetry of the Sixteenth Century—Christian Meditations and Prayers, and some other Devotional Manuals.

It is calculated that the Works above stated may be included in about 18 or 20 volumes royal octavo, and 50 volumes demy, and that the whole may be completed in sixteen years from the commencement. A few pieces of peculiar interest may probably be printed as fac similes, and these will be in the size of the originals. The list, however, is not to be considered as definitively settled. It is not possible to state the order in which the volumes will appear, but each will be complete in itself. The whole series (fully equal to a hundred volumes of demy octavo), when completed, will have cost the original subscribers only about sixteen pounds, paid in as many years, and in proportion for parts of the series.

All correspondence respecting subscriptions, or the delivery of the Books, is to be addressed to

WILLIAM THOMAS, ESQ., *Secretary for General Business,*

AT THE OFFICE OF THE PARKER SOCIETY, 33, SOUTHAMPTON STREET, STRAND, LONDON.

Printed at the Milton Press,
corner of Charing Cross Hospital, Strand.